Poor Law Records
of
Mid Sussex

1601-1835

POOR LAW RECORDS
of
MID SUSSEX

1601-1835

EDITED BY

NORMA PILBEAM and IAN NELSON

SUSSEX RECORD SOCIETY
VOLUME 83

Issued to members of the Society for the year 1999

Published 2001 by
Sussex Record Society,
Barbican House,
High Street,
Lewes,
East Sussex, BN7 lYE

ISBN 085445 050 5

Printed by Hobbs the Printers Ltd., Totton, Hampshire.

SUSSEX RECORD SOCIETY

VOLUMES ISSUED BY THE SOCIETY

Vol. 1 Marriage Licences at Lewes, 1586-1642
* Vol. 2 Sussex Fines, 1190-1248
Vol. 3 Post Mortem Inquisitions, 1558-1583
* Vol. 4 Ecclesiastical Returns for East Sussex, 1603; Sussex Poll Book, 1705; Sussex MSS in the Harleian MSS; Bishop Praty's Register, 1438-1445.
* Vol. 5 West Sussex Protestation Returns, 1641-1642
Vol. 6 Marriage Licences at Lewes, 1670-1732
* Vol. 7 Sussex Fines, 1249-1307
* Vol. 8 Bishop Rede's Register, 1397-1415 (Pt.1)
* Vol. 9 Marriage Licences at Chichester 1575-1730
* Vol. 10 Subsidy Rolls, 1296, 1327 and 1332
* Vol. 11 Bishop Rede's Register, 1397-1415 (Pt. I)
* Vol. 12 Marriage Licences at Chichester (peculiars), 1579-1730
* Vol. 13 Cuckfield Parish Register, 1598-1699
Vol. 14 Post Mortem Inquisitions, 1485-1649
Vol. 15 Bolney Parish Register, 1541-1812
Vol. 16 Star Chamber Proceedings, 1500-1558
Vol. 17 Ardingly Parish Register, 1558-1812
Vol. 18 Angmering Parish Register, 1562-1687
Vol. 19 Sussex Manors and Advowsons, etc., 1509-1833, A-L
Vol. 20 Sussex Manors and Advowsons, etc., 1509-1833, M-Z
Vol. 21 Horsham Parish Register, 1541-1635
Vol. 22 Cowfold Parish Register, 1558-1812
Vol. 23 Sussex Fines, 1308-1509
Vol. 24 East Grinstead Parish Register, 1558-1661
Vol. 25 Marriage Licences at Lewes, 1771-1837, A-L
Vol. 26 Marriage Licences at Lewes, 1772-1837, M-Z
Vol. 27 Preston Manor Court Rolls, 1562-1702
Vol. 28 Sussex Apprentices and Masters, 1710-1752
Vol. 29 Abstracts of Documents relating to the Dobell family, 16th-18th cents.
Vol. 30 Glynde Parish Register, 1558-1812
Vol. 31 Thirteen Custumals of the Sussex Manors of the Bishop of Chichester, c.1256-1374
Vol. 32 Sussex Marriage Licences at Chichester, 1731-1774
Vol. 33 Sussex Inquisitions (from Bodleian Library), 1541-1616
Vol. 34 The Book of John Rowe, Steward to Lord Bergavenny, 1622
Vol. 35 Marriage Licences at Chichester, 1775-1800, with Index covering Licences, 1731-1800
Vol. 36 Sussex Chantry Records, 1535-1652
Vol. 37 Hastings Rape Records, 1387-1474
Vol. 38 Chartulary of Lewes Priory (Pt. I), 11th-l4th cents.
Vol. 39 The Buckhurst Terrier, 1597-1598
Vol. 40 Chartulary of Lewes Priory (Pt. II), I2th-l4th cents.
Vol. 41 Transcripts of Sussex Wills up to 1560, Vol.1 Albourne - Chichester
Vol. 42 Transcripts of Sussex Wills up to 1560, Vol.2 Chiddingly - Horsham
Vol. 43 Transcripts of Sussex Wills up to 1560, Vol.3 Horsted Keynes - Pyecombe
Vol. 44 Records of the Barony and Honour of the Rape of Lewes, 1265-1466

Vol. 45 Transcripts of Sussex Wills up to 1560, Vol.4 Racton - Yapton
Vol. 46 Chichester Cathedral Chartulary, 13th-16th cents.
Vol. 47 Survey of Robertsbridge Manor, 1567-1570
* Vol. 48 The Town Book of Lewes, 1542-1701
Vol. 49 Churchwardens' Presentments, (Pt. I), Archdeaconry of Chichester, 1621-1628, 1664-1670
Vol. 50 Churchwardens' Presentments, (Pt. II), Archdeaconry of Lewes, 1674-1677
Vol. 51 Record of Deputations of Gamekeepers, 1781-1928
Vol. 52 Chapter Acts, Chichester, 1472-1544 (The White Act Book)
Vol. 53 The Manor of Etchingham cum Salehurst, 1597-1865
Vol. 54 Quarter Sessions Order Book, 1642-1649
Vol. 55 Ministers' Accounts of the Manor of Petworth, 1347-1353
Vol. 56 Lay Subsidy Rolls, 1524-1525
Vol. 57 Custumals of Sussex Manors of the Archbishop of Canterbury, 1285-1330
Vol. 58 Chapter Acts, Chichester, 1545-1642
Vol. 59 Chartulary of Boxgrove Priory, 12th-14th cents.
Vol. 60 Custumals of the Manors of Laughton, Willingdon and Goring, 1292-1338
Vol. 61 A Catalogue of Sussex Estate and Tithe Award Maps (Pt. I), 1606-1884
* Vol. 62 Minutes of the Common Council of the City of Chichester, 1783-1826
Vol. 63 The Book of Bartholomew Bolney, 15th cent.
Vol. 64 Rye Shipping Records, 1566-1590
* Vol. 65 Cellarers' Rolls of Battle Abbey, 1275-1513
Vol. 66 A Catalogue of Sussex Maps, (Pt. II) 1597-1958
Vol. 67 Estate Surveys of the Fitzalan Earls of Arundel, 14th cent.
Vol. 68 The Journal of Giles Moore of Horsted Keynes, 1655-1679
Vol. 69 The Town Book of Lewes, 1702-1837
* Vol. 70 The Town Book of Lewes, 1837-1901
* Vol. 71 Accounts of the Roberts Family of Boarzell, 1568-1582
* Vol. 72 Printed Maps of Sussex, 1575-1900
* Vol. 73 Correspondence of the Dukes of Richmond and Newcastle, 1724-1750
Vol. 74 Sussex Coroners' Inquests, 1485-1558
* Vol. 75 The Religious Census of Sussex, 1851
* Vol. 76 The Fuller Letters, 1728-1755
* Vol. 77 East Sussex Land Tax, 1785
* Vol. 78 Chichester Diocesan Surveys, 1686 and 1724
* Vol. 79 Saint Richard of Chichester
* Vol. 80 The Ashdown Forest Dispute, 1876-1882
* Vol. 81 Sussex Schools in the 18th century
* Vol. 82 West Sussex Land Tax, 1785
* Vol. 83 Mid Sussex Poor Law Records, 1601-1835

Volumes marked with an asterisk can be obtained from the Hon. Secretary, Sussex Record Society, Barbican House, Lewes, East Sussex, BN7 1YE.

Volumes 1-68 are available on microfiche from Messrs. Chadwyck-Healey Ltd., The Quorum, Barnwell Road, Cambridge, CB5 8SW.

CONTENTS

Page

Introduction 1
- The legislative framework 2
- Paupers in a rural economy 7
- The Poor Laws in action in Sussex 11
- The sources in use 14
- The parochial system in crisis 25
- Conclusions 27

Editorial Practice 31
Notes and references 35
Bibliography 36
Acknowledgements 38

Mid Sussex Poor Law records
- Albourne 41
- Ardingly 43
- Balcombe 49
- Bolney 52
- Clayton 69
- Cowfold 71
- Crawley 99
- Cuckfield 101
- Ditchling 141
- East Grinstead 146
- Henfield 226
- Horsted Keynes 249
- Hurstpierpoint 252
- Ifield 271
- Keymer 274
- Lindfield 277
- Shermanbury 305
- Slaugham 308
- Twineham 313
- West Hoathly 316
- Wivelsfield 332
- Woodmancote 337
- Worth 339

Appendix: Additional Poor Law documents 378

Index of Personal Names 389
Index of Place Names 435

ILLUSTRATIONS AND TABLES

Page

Frontispiece The parishes of mid Sussex

Budgen's map of mid Sussex, 1724 8

Settlement examination of John Geere, 1823 15

Settlement certificate of John and Elizabeth Hayls, 1727 .. 16

Removal order of Elizabeth Falkiner, 1789 18

Affiliation order of John King, 1820 21

Apprenticeship indenture of William Devall, 1712 23

TABLES

Table 1: Available mid Sussex Poor law records 28
Table 2: Mid Sussex landownership, 1785 30

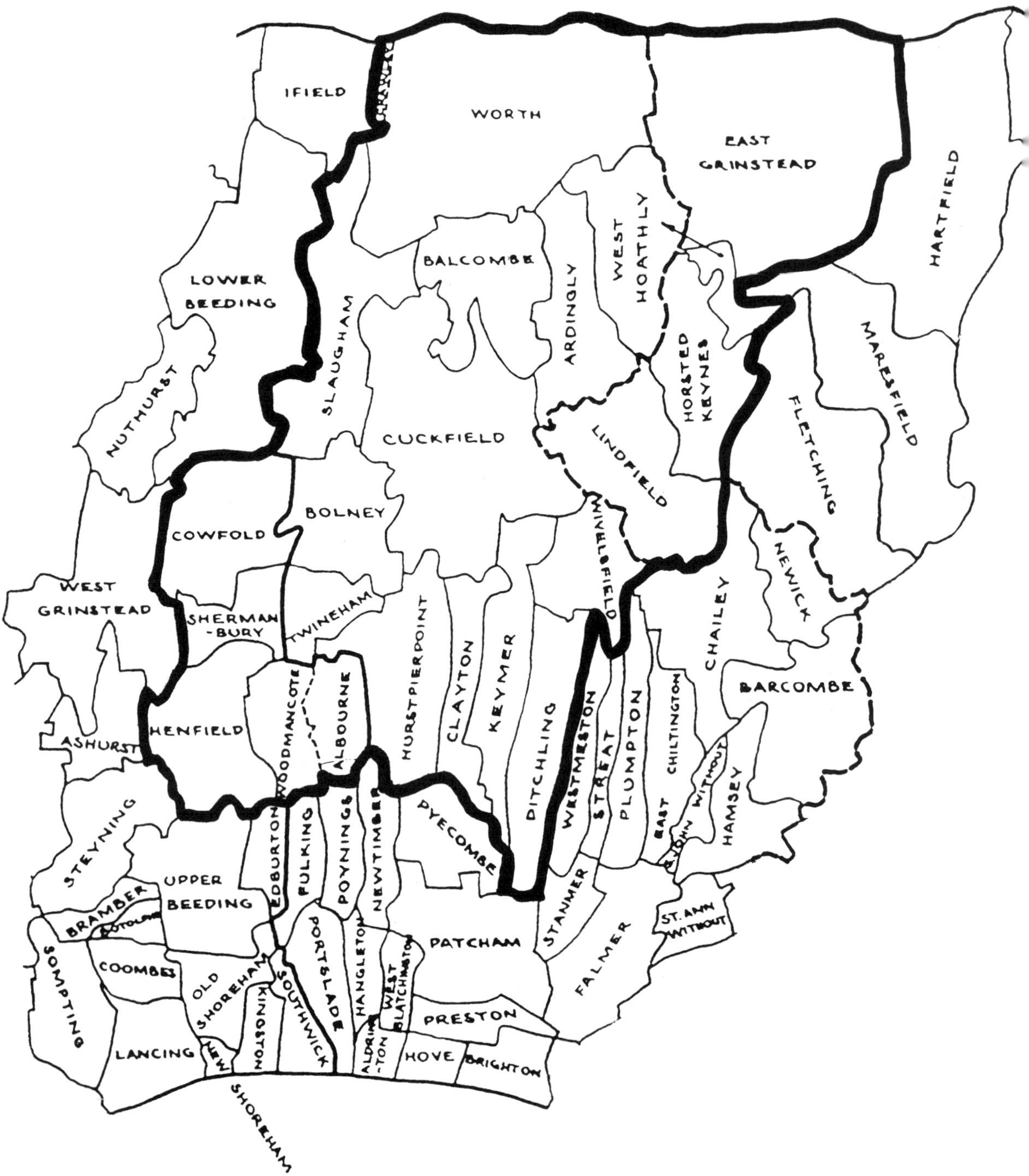

Fig. 1. The 23 mid Sussex parishes whose records make up this volume.

MID SUSSEX POOR LAW RECORDS
1601-1835

INTRODUCTION

The purpose of this volume is to provide details of individuals who were the objects of Poor Law administration in Mid Sussex during the period when the parishes were directly responsible for poor relief. In strict terms of national legislation this period covers the 234 years indicated in the title. Moreover, the Act of Settlement itself did not appear on the statute books until 1662. However it should be emphasised that practice sometimes predated law, with parishes dealing with problems at a local level before they were empowered to do so by central government. In addition, even after the establishment of the Unions under the provisions of the Poor Law Amendment Act of 1834, a number of parish documents continued to be issued. The perceived need for legislation and the specific relevant acts of parliament are reviewed in the next section of this introduction.

The individual names are recorded in over 5000 documents in the collections of parish records deposited mainly at West Sussex Record Office (WSRO), with a few at East Sussex Record Office (ESRO). The papers are in no sense complete, as some of the parishes have no extant records at all, others very few, and even the best are unlikely to represent the full extent of activities in this field. It has proved possible, however, to supplement them considerably by making use of the Sussex Quarter Sessions records (ESRO).

The entries should be of use to several different groups of researchers. Those interested in tracing family or surname connections will turn first to the index of names. Parish history data will be directly available from the alphabetical order (with the exceptions referred to later in this introduction). The documents should be set in context, and the scope of the Settlement activities is dealt with briefly in the following pages, set against both the concerns of society in general about the effects of pauperism and the specific rural situation in Mid Sussex; but it should be remembered that the topic is a complex one, and further reading is suggested in the bibliography.

Unlike some earlier Society publications, devoted to particular papers, this volume records a range of documents, covering all stages of official attempts to control and manage the problems which pauperism raised in local communities. In other words we have evidence of how the system worked as a whole in a particular area. The types of documents listed include Settlement Examinations and Certificates, and Removal Orders; Bastardy Examinations, and Maintenance Orders, Bonds and Warrants; Apprenticeship Bonds and Indentures; and all relevant entries in Quarter Sessions Order Books, cross-referenced with the parish papers wherever possible. Apart from official documents, there is evidence from other papers of the strenuous efforts made by parish officers, including many letters written between parishes relating to individual cases. As a sample of these, all the letters deposited by one parish are published in an appendix. On the other hand, this volume does not include the Poor Rates levied, the names of Overseers or their accounts (except where they relate specifically to removal costs), or the names of those receiving doles within the parish, either in the poorhouse or as out-relief, or documents relating to the relief of Militiamen's families. All of these latter represent the methods employed to alleviate established poverty, rather than those adopted to try and prevent or minimise its effect on communities in the first place.

The parishes investigated are indicated on the map (Fig. 1). They are listed in alphabetical order: Albourne, Ardingly, Balcombe, Bolney, Clayton, Cowfold, Crawley, Cuckfield, Ditchling, East Grinstead, Henfield, Horsted Keynes, Hurstpierpoint, Ifield, Keymer, Lindfield, Shermanbury, Slaugham, Twineham, West Hoathly, Wivelsfield, Woodmancote and Worth. A brief profile of each parish may help readers unfamiliar with the area. These Mid Sussex parishes have been chosen as a reasonably compact group, although with significant individual variations. The use of such a clearly delineated area enables us to provide a more complete picture, as the full range of records is not available for every parish.

As already stated, Mid Sussex should not be viewed in isolation. Its management of the problems of poverty must be seen against a national background. For this reason the next section of this introduction provides a brief summary of the successive pieces of legislation enacted by central government, and the perceived need for them. This will be followed by focussing on the variations in agricultural employment and their effect on the control of poverty. A review of the numbers of Mid Sussex documents available will enable us to assess the value of the archive, and lead naturally to a discussion about the significance of the different classes of documents themselves. Finally, within the introduction, it may be helpful to provide an outline of the developing circumstances which led to the eventual removal of poor relief from the control of the parish.

THE LEGISLATIVE FRAMEWORK

The developing perception that early modern society should support its weaker members may have derived from economic, social or political pressures, or a confused combination of these factors. Church-stocks of potentially productive animals and goods, charitable doles and almshouses began to be a significant factor in helping the poor in the twelfth century. Having declined in activity, they were ripe for revival during the social upheavals of the 1530s and 1540s. Later in the sixteenth century it was becoming clear that by themselves they were not sufficient to cope with the problems of pauperism.

Economically, the balance between an increasing population and frequent poor harvests and the resultant rising prices was often difficult to maintain. The contemporary view in the late seventeenth century was that 'the kingdom became then much more populous than in former times, and with it the poor greatly increased'.[1] Apart from those paupers (children, the elderly and infirm) who were unable to work, there were significant numbers in the 1530s who could not support their families in spite of 'all their will and labour to get their living with their hands'.[2] However, perhaps because of increasing expectations in living standards, perhaps because the rise in population outstripped the available resources, the expansion of poor relief continued unabated, even in periods of relative surplus, indicating that economic pressures were not the only elements involved. There were, of course, varying levels of poverty. Crises of sudden dearth, with the resultant high prices for staple foods, or accident or serious illness, could be superimposed on a background level of deprivation, but such events would be recorded simply in terms of numbers. This would not give any indication of the depth of poverty being suffered. In the seventeenth century it seems likely that the total number of poor increased, while those at the extremes of deprivation were fewer.[3] If we add to these factors the risk of life cycle poverty, when a significant proportion of the population could need relief at some period during their working life, particularly towards the end, it is not surprising that the genuine cases were treated sympathetically by their neighbours, who could so easily suffer a similar fate.

One further area of discussion relates to the family. Although the nuclear family has remained the basic element in the structure of society for hundreds of years, the level of immediate care for elderly members of the family decreased with new households being established on marriage, especially with a significant level of migration. This left those older members increasingly in potential need of communal support. In addition, attitudes in general were changing, with elements of humanism influencing central policy. As has been mentioned above, before 1500 assistance came from a number of sources: religious houses - monasteries, fraternities, guilds; local parish help - 'stocks' of materials to provide work, almshouses, church collections and the traditional charity obligations of the rich, including provisions made in wills. Nevertheless, by the later years of the sixteenth century the perceived virtue gained by helping the needy was beginning to be eroded in respectable society by a more condemnatory view of pauperism.

Certainly, personal charity appeared to be diminished in extent, an attitude reinforced by laws against begging introduced during this period (see below). For example, some wills demanded that beggars should be denied access to funeral feasts.[4]

Politically, there was great concern that idleness, dirt, disease, vagrancy and indiscipline represented potential risks to the stability of society. In Tudor times homeless monks dispossessed by the dissolution of the monasteries, labourers from the old feudal houses, beggars, itinerant players, bearwards and so on - the 'masterless men' - had become vagrants, infesting the roads and making travel hazardous for others. Central government required that control should be an essential part of poor relief. The simplest way of defending virtue and order was by defining vice and disorder, giving rise to the perception that the poor were outside society.[5] Enforceable laws were required. Even the humanist approach to poverty sought to link support with moral reform. For example, in 1516 Sir Thomas More, in the same work that recommended the freest toleration in other matters, felt that, alongside helping those really unable to help themselves, idleness should be forbidden.[6] One hundred and eighty years later there were complaints that the poor expected the parish to provide for '[them] who in plenty and cheap times will either work little or live without saving'.[7] 'There was a growing tendency for the authorities to define criminal and disorderly behaviour as the prerogative of the poor'.[8]

Although some legislation to deal with bastardy was enacted as early as 1235, and with vagrancy in 1388, the dissolution of the monasteries in the 1530s and 1540s, and the consequent loss of a large institutional charitable framework, had a considerable impact on the development of civil poor relief. Once it became apparent that the parish would be the unit to administer poor relief and deal with its attendant problems, legislation proliferated. Between 1531 (22 Hen VIII c.12 which distinguished between beggars able to work and those incapable) and the Poor Law Amendment Act of 1834 there were no less than 51 Acts of Parliament which related to Poor Law.[9] Of these, some were merely prolongations of previous Acts, others related to activities outside the remit of this volume, such as workhouses. The remainder focussed specifically on the problems of vagrancy, bastardy, poor apprentices, settlement and removal.

In 1536 Thomas Cromwell introduced legislation (27 Hen VIII c.25) to provide, on a parish basis, work for vagabonds and arrangements to put poor children out to service, with the impotent poor being supported by weekly collections instead of indiscriminate alms; punishments for begging were included. The main concern of the Council throughout was public order, for example in 1547 1 Ed VI c.3 enacted that someone wandering without employment should be branded with the letter V and compelled to work for two years as a slave to his captor; a further offence was punished by enslavement for life and branding with the letter S. Several further Acts were passed during the rest of the sixteenth century, some of which lapsed because of the impracticality of enforcement. For example in 1576 (18 Eliz I c.3) provision was made for houses of correction and work stocks with the aim of compulsory employment, but this tended to increase the numbers subject to the law without dealing with the causes. They culminated in the Vagrancy (which still allowed the whipping of vagabonds and their return home) and Relief of the Poor Acts of 1598 (39 Eliz I c.3 & c.6). All the earlier legislation was consolidated in the great act of 1601 (43 Eliz I c.2) and made permanent in 1640 (16 Car I c.4). This made the parish officers, the churchwardens and the overseers of the poor, responsible for the levying and collection of a poor rate, and for the distribution of relief to paupers in what workhouses and almshouses existed as well as doles to those still living in their own homes. Justices of the Peace acted only to supervise and hear appeals. The most serious aspect was that of the gangs of unemployed ruffians, one of which infested Horsted Keynes in 1633.[10] Their numbers increased during the Civil War years, reinforcing the view that legislation was necessary. These enactments required reports to the Privy Council of the numbers of vagrants punished and poor children bound as apprentices. The theory was that if fit idlers were dealt with, poverty would be eradicated. On the other hand, it was generally accepted that the truly poor had a right to relief in extreme need. So the debate centred around entitlement and how to define it. One solution was in the notion that everyone had a 'home' parish - where they were born, where they had lived and worked for a significant period, or where they came after marriage. This idea was formalised in the Act of Settlement of 1662 (14 Car II c.12), which, with later amendments, led to the need for the documents which are the subject of this volume. The preamble to the Act set out the reasons why it was deemed to be necessary:....'by reason of some defects in the law, poor people are not restrained from going from one parish to another, and therefore do endeavour to settle themselves in those parishes where there is the best stock, the largest commons or wastes to build cottages, and the most woods for them to burn and destroy; and when they have consumed it, then to another parish; and at last become rogues and vagabonds; to the great discouragement of parishes to provide stock, when it is liable to be devoured by strangers'. In fact the Act of Settlement allowed for some strictly controlled mobility, while the 1697 amendments (8 & 9 W III c.30) actually permitted the licensing of chapmen and encouraged migration to areas of labour shortage (but also required a badge to be worn if in receipt of relief as a hoped-for deterrent - it failed). The earlier emphasis on deterrents such as whipping was being relaxed and modified into concern about cost.[11]

Where there was no doubt that an individual pauper was a bona fide inhabitant of a parish, the officers might give weekly or monthly doles to enable him or her to continue to live at home. Alternatively, an Act of 1723 (9 Geo I c.7) authorised the purchase or renting of workhouses, and the employment of suitable persons as governors. Among the recipients of parish relief were those genuinely unable to work, particularly evident in rural parishes heavily dependent on seasonal activities. Other beneficiaries were widows with children, the elderly and infirm, and even problem families. The last were tolerated because their behaviour contrasted so sharply with the accepted standards.[12]

This toleration went beyond the strict problems of pauperism into those of petty crime. There is evidence that several acts of theft would often be ignored before official action was taken against the transgressor, in part perhaps because it required an individual to initiate proceedings and give evidence, but also because there was a feeling that the law was too draconian. Even if and when cases reached court, both charges and punishments were frequently reduced in severity, indicating a degree of local sympathy which ran counter to the full rigour of the law.[13]

On the other hand, non-settled inhabitants, vagrants or bastard bearers were sometimes the recipients of harsh treatment. The forcible removal of elderly sick people, such as the ejection of men thought likely to die shortly, risking leaving a widow and children dependent on the parish, occurred on occasions, but was perhaps more widespread after the period we are concerned with, as in 1847 (9 & 10 Vic c.66) it had to be stipulated that widows could not be removed.[14] Similarly pregnant single women were often bundled out without ceremony, occasionally in anticipation of the legal process, even during actual labour. On the other hand one has to bear in mind the pressures imposed on parish officers by their Poor Rate payers.

In cases where there was a possibility that someone else could be held to account, either an individual or another parish, the local officers used the full panoply of the law in attempts to reduce the burden on the Poor Rate. In order to provide a proper legal basis for these acts of expulsion a flourishing bureaucracy developed, with the appropriate forms being issued and revised as the years went by. Sometimes local initiative produced results, as in Wivelsfield in 1688 where the parish officers sold a coppice inherited by a pauper child to pay for his upkeep.

Pauper migration declined from about 1650 onwards, without any excessive influence from the application of the settlement laws, because of the increased provision of work opportunities locally, and because of the slow-down in population growth. When the latter increased again a century or so later the problem returned with renewed vigour, and the evidence of the scope of settlement disputes and decisions shows in the numbers of documents still available.

The paupers of this country existed under the control of this system until the Poor Law Amendment Act of 1834 withdrew management from the parishes and placed it in the hands of the Guardians of the Unions.

PAUPERISM IN A RURAL ECONOMY

Clearly, the extent of pauperism in a given area is a factor of the relationship between available employment and fluctuations in population levels. In a rural location such as Mid Sussex those elements will be different from those pertaining in large towns.

During the period of the documents, at least until the arrival of the turnpikes and the need for secondary services connected with them, these parishes were largely dependent on agriculture for their economic well-being. Even in such a small area the type of farming varied considerably, owing to the nature of the terrain, the soils changing in character from South to North (Fig. 2).[15] The Southern borders of Clayton, Ditchling, Hurstpierpoint and Keymer suffer from the stubborn Gault Clay at the scarp foot of the South Downs. This is succeeded by a narrow band of Lower Greensand in these parishes, together with Albourne and Woodmancote. This type of soil is much less in evidence here than further West in the county. Then comes the tenacious clay of the Low Weald areas of Bolney, Cowfold, Cuckfield, Henfield, Lindfield, Shermanbury, Twineham and Wivelsfield. This finally merges into the highly diversified country of narrow valleys and sweeping hills which constitutes the High Weald, with alternating clay, shale, sand and sandstone. Ardingly, Balcombe, Crawley, East Grinstead, Horsted Keynes, Ifield, Slaugham, West Hoathly and Worth lie wholly or partly in this area. Of course it must be remembered that the geological pattern does not change precisely at the parish boundary; several of the 'long' parishes, extending from the Downs to the Weald, will exhibit more than one type of soil.

As a result, farming varied throughout the region. Mixed sheep/grain and sheepwalks on the Downs gave way to mixed arable and livestock in the scarp foot zone. Mixed farming, cattle fattening and dairying were the main activities of the Low Weald wood pasture. While High Weald wood pasture farmers also carried on mixed farming and cattle fattening, they found the soils suitable for hops and orchards as well. Finally, the heath areas of the High Weald provided common grazing and coney warrens.[16]

The significance of this range of agricultural activities for us lies in the different levels of labour requirements. Arable farming used large numbers of labourers on a seasonal basis, at haymaking and corn harvesting for example; stock rearing and

Fig. 2. Mid Sussex from Richard Budgen's county map, 1724.

dairying needed fewer men, but their work was more continuous throughout the year. Poor harvests affected all, but smallholders on infertile sandy wastes would suffer more in times of dearth. Even dual employment would not always provide sufficient for economic survival. All of these factors, together with changes in agrarian structure and improvements in farming methods, increased the number of men vulnerable to unemployment in their own parish.

One aspect which has a bearing on poor relief in general and settlement control in particular relates to the social distribution of landownership, the settlement pattern and the retention of commons. The variations in these lead to the development of contrasting rural communities. One controversial model to describe this is that of 'open' and 'close' parishes.[17] There are indications that such contrasts existed to some extent before the nineteenth century.

'Close' parishes had small populations with low density and slow increase. Land was owned and managed by one or few resident gentry who controlled labour requirements and housing needs on large farms. The atmosphere was one of deference, including 'compulsory' attendance at the parish church. Because of the tight management, poor rates were usually very low.

The 'open' parishes were those with large, high density, rapidly increasing populations with many smallholders, peasant families, small farms, rural industries, and poor but plentiful housing. There was a greater leaning towards religious nonconformity and radical independence. By and large, poor rates, paid by the land occupiers and not the proprietors, were high, since regular continuous employment for superfluous agricultural labourers was much less certain.

During the period under review, neither type of parish exhibited the same sense of 'vertical community' that might have been seen in earlier centuries. It has been suggested that there were three main communities: the landholders, the richer farmers, and their families; the servants in husbandry, normally resident for only one year at a time; and the poor, often rootless and mobile.[18] In the area covered, because of the mixed nature of several of the parishes, the evidence for the usefulness of this model, while tending to illustrate parts of the thesis, is by no means overwhelming. However, as will be seen in the next section, dealing with the poor laws in action, a collation of the parish papers and the court records indicates that, with respect to settlement activity, mid-Sussex consisted largely of 'open' parishes.

Analysis of the land tax returns, based on the annual rental values of the properties for a specific year, gives an indication of the variation in land ownership in our parishes (Table 2). An arbitrary figure of £50 per annum has been chosen to indicate a dividing line between large and small landowners. A known Downland 'close' parish, Falmer, is included for comparison. It will be seen that in only three of our parishes, Albourne, Hurstpierpoint and Twineham, do the larger holdings comprise more than 70 percent of the total; in Hurst, despite the undoubted influence of the large Danny estate, a significant number of owners were required to achieve this figure. The remaining parishes show a more even distribution of landownership, and it was in these areas that less strictly controlled labour movement allowed squatting to occur, with the subsequent possibility of temporary or longer term unemployment. It should be remembered that it was the tenants who paid the tax, and it was these individuals who often undertook the various parish offices, including that of overseer of the poor, no doubt influenced to some extent by the attitudes of their landlords.

Once out of work such men became a potential liability to the payers of the Poor Rate, and every effort was made by these same parish officers to keep such a burden to a minimum. Those who had come from elsewhere seeking work, but not finding it, became subject to the settlement laws, and hence figure in the documents listed here.

THE POOR LAWS IN ACTION IN SUSSEX

As has been stated already, the numbers of documents which have been preserved vary enormously from one parish to another. Even the best record-keepers, or their successors, have left gaps, often for long periods, while for some parishes there are no extant papers at all. Statistics of the surviving documents - in both parish and Quarter Sessions collections are set out in Table 1. This means that any attempt at statistical analysis must be suspect. However, some figures may help to give a broad idea of the extent of the activity in this area of social control.

Obviously, one important factor to take into account is the population of the individual parish. Choosing a particular date at which to compare the populations cannot be entirely without critical comment. Before the institution of 10-yearly national censuses, the recording of parish populations was undertaken either for taxation purposes, such as the Hearth or Poll Taxes of the latter part of the seventeenth century, or by the ecclesiastical authorities to determine the extent of religious nonconformity, as with the Compton Census of 1676 or Bishop Bowers' survey of 1724. Any of these falls within the period of the settlement documents listed in this book, but they suffer from several limitations. The Hearth Tax did not apply strictly to the parish, but to some other administrative unit such as the tithing or the constabulary; even when exempt classes were listed, inaccuracies of interpretation have occurred.[19] The Compton Census returns were gathered by the parish priest, and some show suspiciously round numbers, while Bowers refers to families, not individuals, leaving the problem of deciding on an acceptable multiplier. Where available, each of these returns will be indicated in the separate parish entries.

For the purposes of this introduction the first census in 1801 falls within one of the periods of greatest activity in determining settlement, and has been used here as a simple benchmark. One would expect the smaller villages to have fewer cases of settlement to deal with, and this is perhaps implicit in the small number of documents which have been deposited from all of the following nine parishes, the figures in brackets indicating their 1801 census totals:

> Albourne (253), Balcombe (451), Clayton (337), Crawley (210), Keymer (465), Shermanbury (274), Twineham (238), Wivelsfield (442), Woodmancote (231).

However Ditchling (706), Horsted Keynes (591) and Slaugham (560) have no deposited Settlement records, while Ifield (637) only has documentation relating to 1 apprenticeship; our main source for these four parishes is the Quarter Sessions records, with 89, 52, 96 and 46 entries respectively. Ditchling cannot be classified as a small parish; indeed calculations from the parish registers indicate that its 1801 total may have been smaller than previously. Other evidence, in particular the reports to the Poor Law Commissioners in 1834, shows that Slaugham clearly had a pauper problem of considerable dimensions.[20] Worth, the immediate neighbour of Ardingly, Horsted Keynes and Ifield, while having nearly two and a half to three times as many inhabitants as any one of these parishes, has deposited 470 documents covering all the aspects of settlement management outlined earlier. Indeed, each of these five parishes figures frequently in the settlement records of other authorities. The clear conclusion must be that any documents relating to them which did exist have not been deposited in the county archives or have been lost completely.

The remaining ten parishes give some indications of assiduous attention to the various problems of settlement and pauper control, of reasonable contemporary recording, and of careful storage of documents prior to transfer to the Record Offices. Even here there is evidence of many discontinuities: periods when no apparent activity took place, followed by a sudden return to previous levels. It is difficult to imagine that this is a true reflection of what actually occurred; it is much more probable that many documents have been lost. Nevertheless it is the papers from these parishes which enable a picture to be drawn of the imperative imposed on the parish officers to control the pauper problem as efficiently as possible.

During the seventeenth, and, more consistently, the eighteenth and early nineteenth centuries, these larger parishes (although Bolney had a population in 1801 of less than 500) recorded in over 3000 documents to which we still have access, details of the administration of the Poor Laws in the areas under their supervision until the implementation of the Poor Law Amendment Act of 1834.

In order to fill some of the gaps in parish records, and to confirm other documents, it was decided to extract all relevant information from the Quarter Sessions Order Books (or from the Minute Book for the single gap in the Order Books sequence); and these have been listed under the relevant parishes. This part of the investigation provided an unexpectedly large quantity of data. It had been assumed previously that this appeals procedure would elicit only a small proportion of the total. In the event this proportion turned out to be approximately three quarters, and suggests that parish officers during the period under discussion were even more litigious than had been predicted. As a result, it has become possible to draw some tentative general conclusions about the whole area, and to put the information contained in the parish papers into a much fuller context. In particular, it suggests that all the parishes in the area fall into the category of 'open' rather than 'close', with a remarkable consistency in the pattern of settlement activity.

The ratios of Quarter Sessions removal orders to the parish population figures fall between 5% and 13% - for 17 of the 22 between 7% and 12% - with a combined figure for the whole area of almost 9%. We can assume that the parish records of three parishes (East Grinstead, Lindfield and Worth) are so extensive that they probably represent something approaching a complete archive. The ratios calculated can be tested by comparing the Quarter Sessions and parish figures for these parishes: 73% for East Grinstead, 84% for Lindfield and Worth. If 80% is applied to the total Quarter Sessions records, it gives a total for the area of 2390. For researchers in individual parishes (where the parish papers may range from the reasonably representative to the merely fragmentary) this formula can provide a crude indication of the likely number of settlement and removal transactions,. As far as is known, this collation exercise has not been carried out previously on this scalc.

One further point should be made regarding the Quarter Sessions records. A variety of terms was used to indicate any action taken in individual cases, and it may be helpful to list the phrases:

Recorded or Recorded and Confirmed: used either when any dispute between the parishes had been resolved amicably, or when the court imposed a final decision.
Quashed or Discharged: when an attempt to have an individual removed from a parish was not allowed.
Respited, Lodged or Adjourned: decision delayed pending further information; this sometimes resulted in removal to a third parish, not mentioned in the original documents.

In a significant number of cases, families were broken up and removed to different parishes, or one or both parents sent elsewhere while all or some of the children were 'allowed' to remain.

THE SOURCES IN USE

These came under three main headings: Settlement, Removal and Vagrancy; Bastardy; and Apprenticeship.

Settlement Examinations and Settlement Certificates:

Until 1795 these were conducted before one or more JPs on new arrivals and on those likely to become a burden on the rates; after 1795 such persons had to be actually chargeable. Under the 1662 Act the parish officers had to initiate proceedings within forty days, otherwise settled residence could be claimed. The inevitable disputes between parishes were calmed to some extent in 1685 by 1 Jac II c.17 that allowed the forty days to be calculated from the date of written notice to a parish officer, and in 1691 by 3 W & M c.11 which required the notice to be read in church, immediately after divine service, and then registered in the book kept for poor accounts. Although the cost of the examination, and that of any subsequent removal[21] may have weighed upon the overseers, the thought of the potential continuing drain on parish resources provided a stimulus to action. The person being examined under oath was required to give his or her age, place of birth, subsequent history of apprenticeship or hired service, place and date of marriage, together with any evidence of rental of a £10 tenement, payment to the poor rate or election to parish office. In 1697 (8 & (W III c.30) a new arrival could bring a certificate from his home parish accepting liability. The granting of such a certificate was left to the discretion of, and its cost fell on, the issuing parish. This must account, at least in part, for the absence of many such papers from our records. Any document which supported a claim to settlement would be carefully retained by the individual, while the overseers would be equally concerned to keep anything which showed evidence of settlement elsewhere (Figs. 3 & 4). The normal surviving parish archive consists of certificates acknowledging settlement outside the parish; but a few parishes have preserved a handful of certificates recording settlement within their own parish.

These certificates were a natural development from the earlier bonds, but there was no absolute requirement to issue certificates. Some parishes never gave certificates, while others only provided them when asked, following a migration by an individual. Such migration was normally over fairly short distances, and in Mid Sussex largely rural-rural. For example, of 140 bonds and certificates which have survived for Worth, 109 were granted from parishes within 10 miles, and only 15 from more than 15 miles away.[22] The motives were almost always economic, following the well understood 'push-pull' model, relating either to changes in the environment or to changes in the motives of the individual - either lack of employment or poor accommodation driving individuals from their home parish,

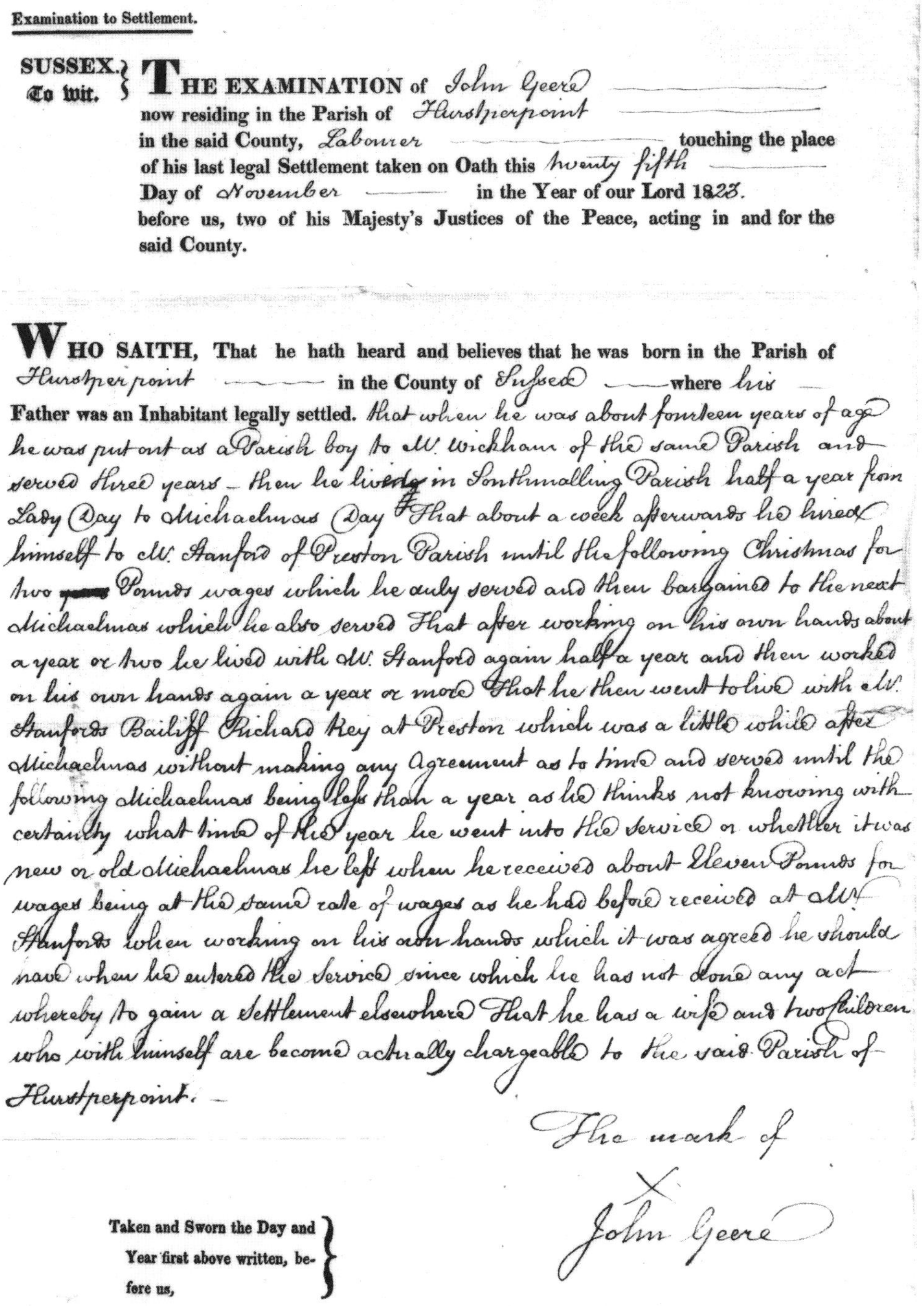

Examination to Settlement.

SUSSEX. To wit. } **THE EXAMINATION** of John Geere
now residing in the Parish of Hurstpierpoint
in the said County, Labourer touching the place
of his last legal Settlement taken on Oath this twenty fifth
Day of November in the Year of our Lord 1823.
before us, two of his Majesty's Justices of the Peace, acting in and for the said County.

WHO SAITH, That he hath heard and believes that he was born in the Parish of Hurstpierpoint in the County of Sussex where his Father was an Inhabitant legally settled. That when he was about fourteen years of age he was put out as a Parish boy to Mr Wickham of the same Parish and served three years – then he lived in Southmalling Parish half a year from Lady Day to Michaelmas Day That about a week afterwards he hired himself to Mr Stanford of Preston Parish until the following Christmas for two Pounds wages which he duly served and then bargained to the next Michaelmas which he also served That after working on his own hands about a year or two he lived with Mr Stanford again half a year and then worked on his own hands again a year or more That he then went to live with Mr Stanfords Bailiff Richard Key at Preston which was a little while after Michaelmas without making any agreement as to time and served until the following Michaelmas being less than a year as he thinks not knowing with certainty what time of the year he went into the service or whether it was new or old Michaelmas he left when he received about Eleven Pounds for wages being at the same rate of wages as he had before received at Mr Stanfords when working on his own hands which it was agreed he should have when he entered the service since which he has not done any act whereby to gain a Settlement elsewhere That he has a wife and two children who with himself are become actually chargeable to the said Parish of Hurstpierpoint.

The mark of
X
John Geere

Taken and Sworn the Day and Year first above written, before us,

Fig. 3. Settlement examination of John Geere of Hurstpierpoint, 1823. (WSRO Par 400/32/4/5)

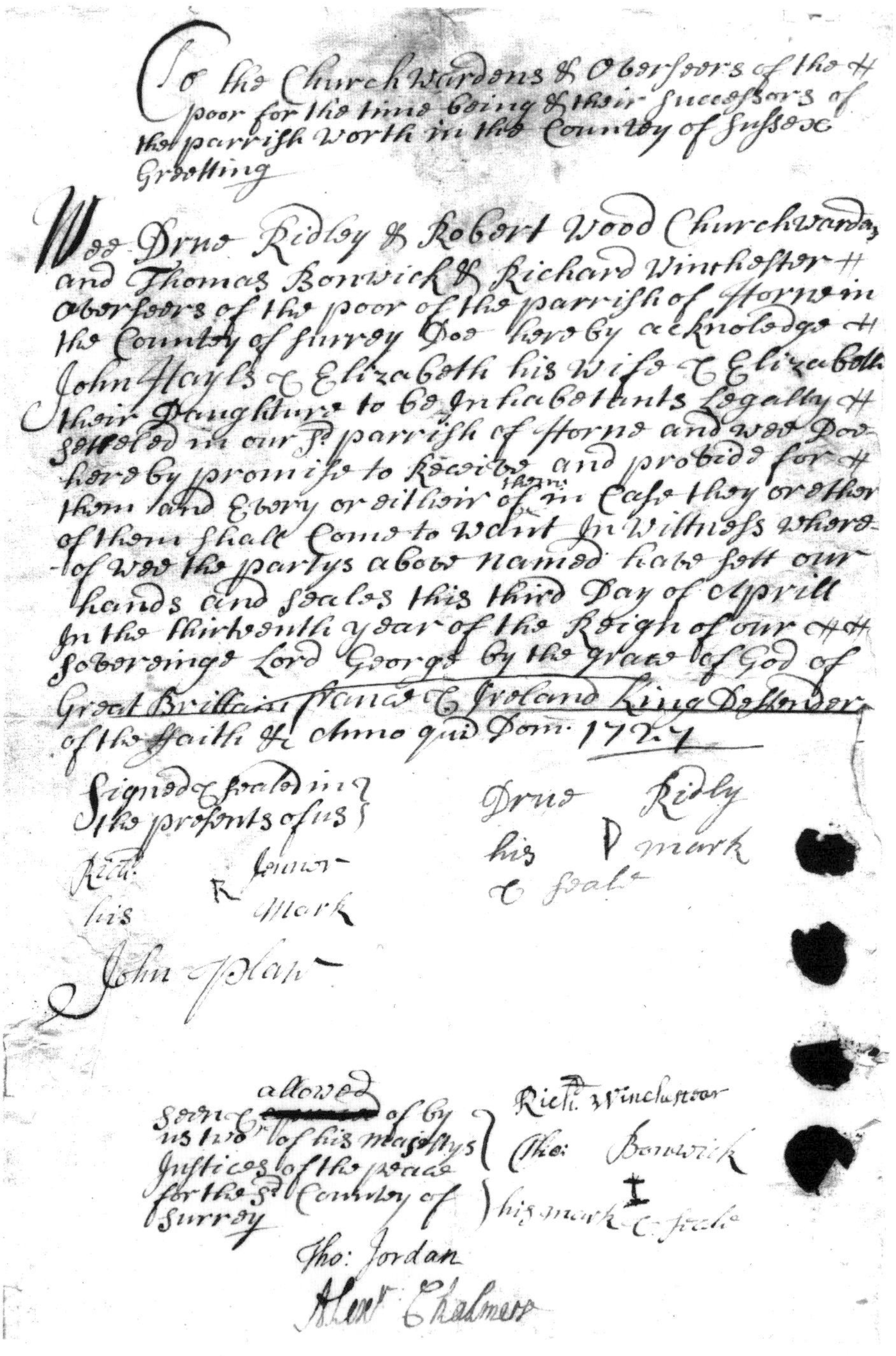
To the Churchwardens & Oberseers of the poor for the time being & their successors of the parrish Worth in the County of Sussex Greeting

Wee Drue Ridley & Robert Wood Churchwardens and Thomas Benwick & Richard Winchester Oberseers of the poor of the parrish of Horne in the County of Surrey Doe hereby acknoledge John Hayls & Elizabeth his wife & Elizabeth their Daughter to be Inhabitants Legally settled in our sd parrish of Horne and wee Doe hereby promise to receive and probide for them and Every or either of them in Case they or either of them shall Come to want In Wittness whereof wee the partys above named have sett our hands and seales this third Day of Aprill In the thirteenth year of the Reign of our Soveraigne Lord George by the grace of God of Great Brittain France & Ireland King Defender of the Faith &c Anno que Dom 1727

Signed & sealed in the presents of us
Richd his R Jenner Mark
John Plaw

Drue Ridley his D mark & seal

Richd Winchester
Tho: Benwick his mark & seale

allowed of by us two of his majestys Justices of the peace for the sd County of Surrey
Tho: Jordan
Alext Chalmers

Fig. 4. Settlement certificate of John and Elizabeth Hayls of Horne, Surrey, given to the overseers of Worth, 1727. (WSRO Par 516/32/1/36) or higher wages, greater opportunities for developing a special trade and better housing making another area more attractive.

Although in the High Weald parishes dual employment was not uncommon, it is to be expected that the largest number of settlement examinations in a rural area would involve agricultural workers. Even in a market town parish like East Grinstead 56 percent of those whose occupations were recorded in examination documents were directly connected with agriculture. Other occupations were mentioned, but it is reasonable to assume that for almost all the others their trade depended on the farming going on in the rural parts of the parish. In the East Grinstead lists there is only one individual whose occupation is difficult to relate to the land: a peruke maker. Apart from the yeomen, farmers, husbandmen and labourers, trades included wheelwrights and blacksmiths, butchers and poultrymen, cordwainers and shoemakers, brickmakers and masons, flaxdressers, weavers and tailors, innholders and coopers. The statement that 'The Settlement Laws hardly incommoded the artisan'[23] is not borne out in Mid-Sussex.

Removal Orders:

If the magistrates were satisfied that another parish was the legal place of settlement, and that an immigrant might become chargeable on the parish of residence (later, had actually become a charge), an order would be made to remove the pauper from the parish. In instances where the home parish was at some distance, the order could include details of intermediate parishes through which the individual should be conveyed (Fig. 5).

Also found in deposited records are documents relating to later confirmations of orders, suspensions of orders (perhaps on grounds of ill health), or appeals against orders. Such papers are often evidence of hearings at Quarter Sessions. It is here that we have examples of the strenuous efforts of the overseers to defend their parish ratepayers from avoidable expense, of the 'callous shuttlecocking' of people from place to place.[24]

A decision was made to include Quarter Sessions record in an attempt to correlate fully the extant parish documents with the records of the courts. This has proved that such an exercise is possible only to a limited extent. Many of the removal orders listed in this volume do not appear in the Quarter Sessions Order Books.[25] An explanation of this may be that the majority of the orders were uncontested. Conversely, many of the orders issued and appeals heard by the Court have no parish papers to confirm particular actions, probably merely a result of document loss. Thus, the inclusion of all official records, from both parishes and courts, will extend the value of the volume.

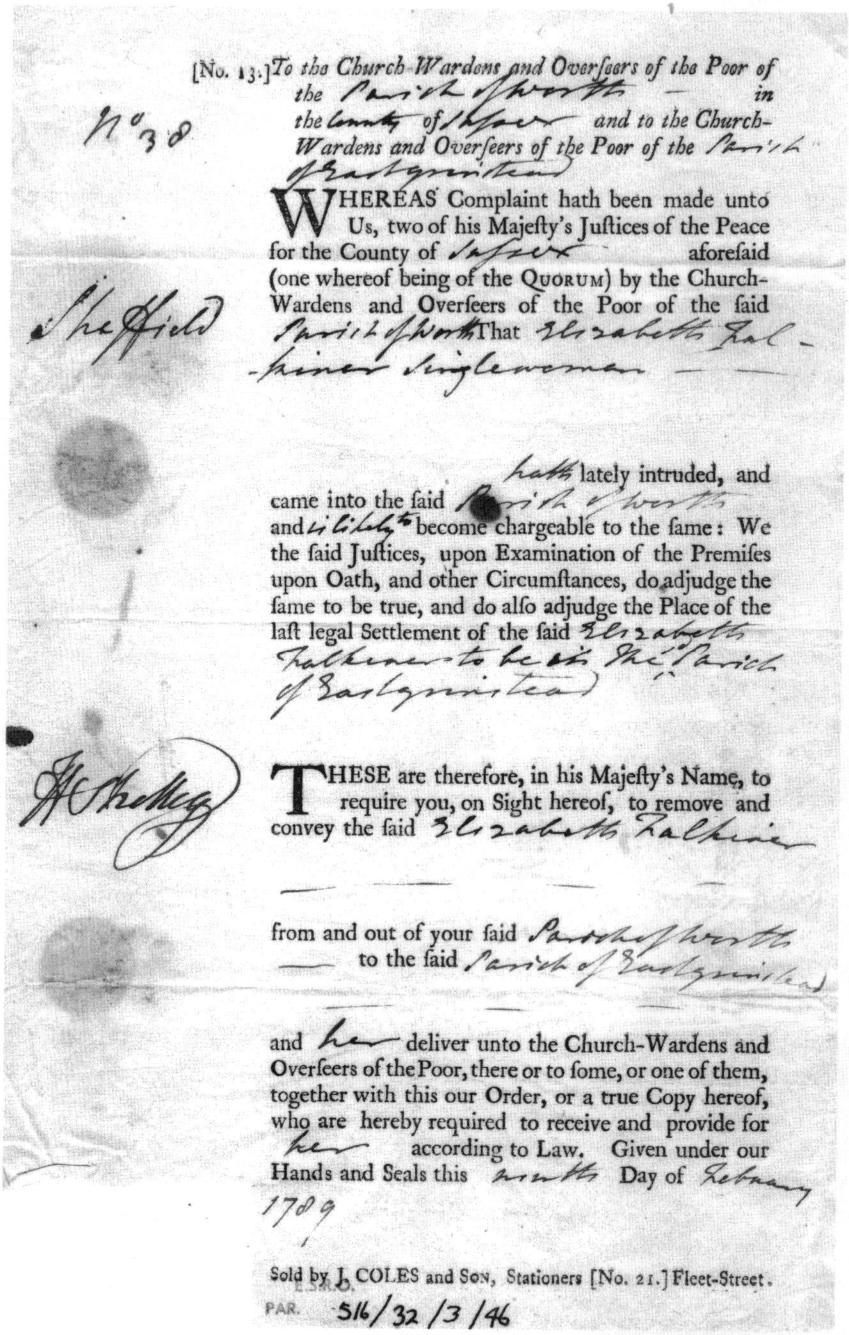

[No. 13.] *To the Church-Wardens and Overſeers of the Poor of the* Parish of Worth *in the* County *of* Sussex *and to the Church-Wardens and Overſeers of the Poor of the* Parish of East grinstead

No 38

WHEREAS Complaint hath been made unto Us, two of his Majeſty's Juſtices of the Peace for the County of Sussex aforeſaid (one whereof being of the QUORUM) by the Church-Wardens and Overſeers of the Poor of the ſaid Parish of Worth That Elizabeth Fal-kiner Singlewoman

hath lately intruded, and came into the ſaid Parish of Worth and is likely to become chargeable to the ſame: We the ſaid Juſtices, upon Examination of the Premiſes upon Oath, and other Circumſtances, do adjudge the ſame to be true, and do alſo adjudge the Place of the laſt legal Settlement of the ſaid Elizabeth Falkiner to be in the Parish of East grinstead

THESE are therefore, in his Majeſty's Name, to require you, on Sight hereof, to remove and convey the ſaid Elizabeth Falkiner

from and out of your ſaid Parish of Worth to the ſaid Parish of East grinstead

and her deliver unto the Church-Wardens and Overſeers of the Poor, there or to ſome, or one of them, together with this our Order, or a true Copy hereof, who are hereby required to receive and provide for her according to Law. Given under our Hands and Seals this ninth Day of February 1789

Sheffield

Sold by J. COLES and SON, Stationers [No. 21.] Fleet-Street.

E.S.R.O. PAR. 516/32/3/46

Fig. 5. Removal order of Elizabeth Falkiner from Worth to East Grinstead, 1789. (WSRO Par 516/32/3/46)

One might expect the 'strenuous efforts' of the parish officers to be shown by items in the overseers' accounts recording the actual costs of removal. Again the picture is patchy. For example, Cowfold has a considerable number of settlement certificates and removal orders. The available overseers' accounts show entries relating to removal on only four occasions, and only one precisely corresponding to an order.[26] Conversely, Ifield has no removal orders, but 27 entries in the overseers' accounts for 1784-1800 which clearly indicate much activity in this aspect of pauper control.[27] A check of the account books and papers of the overseers of the poor for the parishes covered by this publication has revealed that Ardingly, Cowfold, East Grinstead, Hurstpierpoint, Lindfield and Worth have a considerable number of accounts documents; Balcombe, Bolney, Henfield, Horsted Keynes, Ifield, Twineham and West Hoathly have fewer; Albourne, Clayton, Crawley, Keymer, Shermanbury, Slaugham and Woodmancote none.

Other parishes have recorded details of investigations carried out on their behalf by solicitors. In 1822 Bolney received an account from Kell & Son 'regarding notice of appeal served by Brighton against order of removal of Holloway and his family'. From 10 April several journeys were made to Brighton in order to examine the said family and to view the house in Circus Court, where they had been living. Two builders were asked to value the house, a Mr Willee valued it at a rent of £7 per annum, but a local builder, Mr Slater, said it was not worth £7 a year. A further journey was made to Brighton, to try and prove the pauper's settlement in Brighton by evidence of the landlords of houses in John Street & Cumberland Street. One of these landlords, Mr Pratt, considered the house in Circus Court worth £10 a year and it was also found that Mr Akehurst, the other landlord, was one of the overseers of Brighton parish. The Court ruled in favour of Bolney by confirming the removal order to Brighton. Total cost £30.18s 0d.[28]

Vagrancy:

Before 1531 placement in the stocks was a common summary punishment; after that date until 1572 whipping was used more frequently. Neither of these deterrents necessarily occasioned the production of documentary evidence. This means that we have no way of knowing accurately how the numbers then compared with later periods. From 1572 until 1593 committal to gaol, together with Quarter Sessions or Assize hearings, provided some papers, while the most prolific records relate to the first part of the seventeenth century. During this latter period the Sussex Bench appointed provost marshals to combat vagrancy over a wider area than that of the hundred constables. They were deemed to have been successful in Bramber rape, in that they had 'rid the country of such wanderers'.[29]

The Act of 1744 (17 Geo II c.5), which covered vagrancy and bastardy, classified vagrants into three groups: 'idle and disorderly persons', those who abandoned their dependants, ignored a removal order, or begged in their own parishes; 'rogues and vagabonds', those who were perpetually itinerant, including those claiming to be entertainers of many kinds, pedlars without licences, and beggars; 'incorrigible rogues', those who had escaped from custody and those refusing examination.

The documents include orders to convey vagabonds from one overseer to the next (through a series of parishes, as with removal orders, until the place of settlement was reached), warrants for apprehension and orders for committal to a house of correction.

Examination of many of the available documents does not support the contemporary official view that vagrancy equated with crime, particularly with the perceived existence of organised bands. While some of these may have been operating in other parts of the country, the evidence in Mid Sussex is mainly of individuals or families seeking means of survival after personal disasters in a period of population increase and reduced opportunities for work. Begging, stealing and working were equally useful to this end.[30] As in other areas of parish control, the local officers were concerned with one thing, to reduce the burden on the rate payers to its absolute minimum.

Bastardy:

Illegitimacy increased in the seventeenth and eighteenth centuries as enclosure reduced the labourer's chances to set up on his own, and also limited the accommodation available. The resultant overcrowding either encouraged or combined with a freer moral attitude among the working class. Furthermore, pregnancy brought the possibility of increased relief.

Legally an illegitimate child was settled in the parish of its birth, not in that of either its father or its mother, which would have been the case if legitimate. The inevitable reaction of the parish officers was to try to reduce the burden on the poor rate, either by moving the mother on to another settlement before giving birth or by using every endeavour to make the father or his family pay.

As with strict settlement matters, the legal process often started with an examination of the circumstances. The pregnant woman was required on oath to identify the father. He, often together with his father, would be asked to enter into a bond of indemnification by which either a lump sum or a weekly maintenance would be paid to the overseers; or alternatively an affiliation order would be issued against him (Fig. 6).

ORDER OF FILIATION.

SUSSEX } THE ORDER of Thomas Partington &
TO WIT. } Henry Campion Esquires, two of his Majesty's Justices of the Peace, in and for the said County of Sussex, one whereof is of the Quorum, and both residing next unto the Limits of the Parish Church, within the Parish of Lindfield in the said County, made the twenty eighth day of February in the Year of our Lord one thousand eight hundred and Twenty concerning a female Bastard Child, lately born in the Parish of Lindfield aforesaid, of the Body of Mary Staines single Woman.

WHEREAS it hath appeared unto us the said Justices, as well upon the Complaint of the Churchwardens and Overseers of the Poor of the said Parish of Lindfield as upon the Oath of the said Mary Staines that she the said Mary Staines on the twenty second Day of February now last past, was delivered of a female Bastard Child in the Parish of Lindfield aforesaid, and that the said Bastard Child is become chargeable to the said Parish of Lindfield and further that John King of the Parish of Uckfield in the said County, Labourer did beget the said Bastard Child, on the Body of her the said Mary Staines And Whereas it duly appeareth to us that the said John King hath been duly summoned to appear before us, to the end that we might examine into the Cause and Circumstances of the premises. And whereas the said John King hath not appeared before us according to such summons, and hath not shewn to us any sufficient cause why he should not be adjudged the reputed Father of the said Bastard Child.
We therefore, upon Examination of the Cause and Circumstance of the Premises, as well upon the Oath of the said Mary Staines as otherwise, do hereby adjudge him the said John King to be the reputed Father of the said Bastard Child.

And thereupon we do ORDER, as well for the better Relief of the said Parish of Lindfield as for the Sustentation and Relief of the said Bastard Child, that the said John King shall and do forthwith, upon Notice of this our Order, pay or cause to be paid to the said Churchwardens and Overseers of the Poor of the said Parish of Lindfield or to some or one of them, the Sum of three pounds fourteen shillings & sixpence which hath been duly assertained by us, and which we do adjudge to be the reasonable Charges and Expences attending the Birth of such Bastard Child; that is to say, part thereof, to wit, the Sum of Three pounds two shillings & sixpence are the Charges and Expences of the Lying-in of the said Mary Staines of the said Bastard Child, and the Maintenance of the said Bastard Child, to the time of making this our Order, and other part thereof, to wit, the Sum of Twelve Shillings are the Costs of this our Order of Filiation.

And we do also hereby further Order, that the said John King shall likewise pay, or cause to be paid to the Churchwardens and Overseers of the Poor of the said Parish of Lindfield for the time being, or to some or one of them, the Sum of two shillings & sixpence Weekly and every Week from the present time, for and towards the Keeping, Sustentation, and Maintenance of the said Bastard Child for and during so long time as the said Bastard Child shall be chargeable to the said Parish of Lindfield

And we do further Order, that the said Mary Staines shall also pay, or cause to be paid to the said Churchwardens and Overseers of the Poor of the said Parish of Lindfield for the time being, or to some or one of them, the Sum of Six pence Weekly and every Week, from the present time so long as the said Bastard Child shall be chargeable to the said Parish of Lindfield in case she shall not nurse and take care of the said Child herself.

Given under our Hands and Seals the Day and Year first above written.

T Partington

H Campion

Fig. 6. Affiliation order of John King of Uckfield, father of the bastard daughter of Mary Staines of Lindfield, 1820. (WSRO Par 416/34/3/22)

A seventeenth century volume dealing with the work of the Justices of the Peace invoked 'the Law of God' as written in Exodus Ch.22,v.16 and Deuteronomy Ch.22, vv.28,29, to the effect that 'the reputed Father.... was to give unto the Maids Father fifty shekels of silver, and he also was to take her to his wife'.[31] If this approach failed, an order from the magistrates could be obtained to enforce the appearance of the father. In some cases, the father absconded, and a warrant for his apprehension would be issued.

Sometimes the legal processes were anticipated, and gangs of local men, without the warrant of a removal order, even during labour itself, would ensure that birth took place in another parish.[32] If this failed, the justices often ruled that bastard children should be sent to the place of their birth, even if this meant separation from their parents. In 1657 a family of father, mother and three children were split between three of the Mid Sussex parishes.[33]

Apprenticeship:

The medieval system of apprenticeship was municipal, not national, although centres such as London and Norwich set standards which were followed generally. In the sixteenth century this system broke down and was reorganised on national lines by the Statute of Artificers 1563 (5 Eliz I c 4). The earlier seven year terms continued, and for some specialist trades apprentices travelled considerable distances to join a suitable master, often someone known to the father. In the Mid-Sussex parishes in the years 1710-1752 several hundred young people were apprenticed in this way.[34]

For the parish officers this was a convenient way of disposing of a pauper child, generally in another parish because, whether voluntarily or through the intervention of the parish officers, apprenticeship gave legal settlement. The legality of the arrangement was established in one of three ways: before 1758 (31 Geo III c.11) an indentured deed was required (Fig. 7); after that date a stamped deed was deemed sufficient; both before and after 1758 lists of pauper children 'placed out' were entered in other parish records such as the vestry minutes.

By the 1536 Act (27 Hen VIII c.25) referred to earlier, vagrant children between the ages of 5 and 14 could be arrested and apprenticed, not to learn a trade but to receive board and training similar to the boarding-out system operated within parishes. In Worth indentured apprenticeships start in 1614, with a printed form being used 11 years later, but numbers increased, and became general throughout the area in the 1630s. Because not every master was willing to take a pauper child, in 1697 compulsion was introduced with a fine of £10 for refusal (8 & 9 W III c.30). Masters who failed to instruct their charges in their craft or trade, or who

This Indenture Witnesseth, That William Devall of East Grinstead in ye County of Sussex by ye Consent of his Aunt Mary Burgis of Cowden in ye County of Kent puts him-self Apprentice to Henry Bewman of Aylesford in the said County of Kent Miller and with him - after the manner of an Apprentice to serve from the Twentieth Ninth day of September now last past - unto the full end and term of Five Years from thence next ensuing, to be fully compleat and ended: During which Term, the said Apprentice his - said Master - faithfully shall and will serve, his - Secrets keep, his Lawful Commands every where gladly do he - shall do no Damage to his said Master - nor see it to be done of others, but to his Power shall let or forthwith give Notice to his said Master - of the same, the Goods of his said Master shall not waste, nor the same without License of his said Master to any give or lend: Hurt to his said Master - shall not do, cause or procure to be done, he shall neither Buy nor Sell, without his Masters License; Taverns, Inns, or Ale-Houses, he - shall not haunt at Cards, Dice, Tables, or any other unlawful Game, he - shall not play he shall not Commit fornication nor Contract marraig within ye sd term - nor from the Service of his - said Master - Day nor Night absent himself, but in all things as an honest and faithful Apprentice shall and will demean and behave himself towards his - said Master - and all his - during the said term. And the said Master - his said Apprentice in the Art, Mystery, or Occupation of a miller - which he now useth, shall Teach, and Instruct, or cause to be Taught and Instructed, the best way and manner that he - can; finding and allowing unto his said Apprentice, sufficient wholesome Meat, Drink, Apparel, Washing, Lodging, and all other Necessaries during the said term and at ye said term shall & will give & allow unto his said Apprentice two good Suits of apparell whereof one to be good and new for hollodays and ye other for working days fitt for such a Servant to wheare - And for the true performance of all and every the said Covenants and Agreements, either of the said Parties abovesaid, bindeth him-self unto the other firmly by these Presents. *In Witness* whereof, the said Parties to these Indentures interchangeably have set their Hands and Seals, the Twentieth Ninth Day of January - in the Tenth - Year of the Reign of our Sovereign Lady Anne by ye grace of god of Great Britain, &c. Anno Dom. 1711/12

Sealled and delivered in ye presents of

Edward Rumons

Thos: Bonniwell

his - marke

Henry O Bewman

E.S.R.O.

PAR. 348/33/1/49.

Fig. 7 Apprenticeship indenture of William Devall of East Grinstead, to Henry Bewman of Aylesford, Kent, miller, 1712. (WSRO Par 348/33/1/49) ventured beyond the strict terms of the agreement into such matters as religious observance, were dealt with by the bench. If the constable or headborough failed to implement any warrant issued by the Justices without good cause, he was himself liable to punishment.

To quote again the 1677 treatise on the activities of the JPs:

> 'Poor, are here to be understood (not Vagabond Beggers and Rogues but) those that labor to live, and such as are old and decrepit, unable to work, Poor Widows, and Fatherless Children, and Tenants driven to Poverty; not by Riot, expence or carelessness, but by mischance.'[35]

THE PAROCHIAL SYSTEM IN CRISIS 1795-1834

Notwithstanding the strenuous efforts of the parish officers to minimise the cost to the payers of the Poor Rate, by restricting relief of indigence to those who could not be denied it, those whose claim to lawful settlement was irrefutable, the cost of such relief increased exponentially during the last quarter of the eighteenth and the first quarter of the nineteenth centuries. The causes of this disastrous drain on the resources of a relatively small number of occupiers have been long debated, although some are fairly clear.

In the second half of the eighteenth century both prices and population were rising, the latter producing an increase in the so-called dependency ratio, that is the number of people, mainly children, who had to be supported by the 'breadwinners'. This necessitated supplementary payments, mainly to labourers, at a time when quality of life expectations were themselves advancing.

As has been said, the 1662 Act of Settlement had given power to remove potentially indigent newcomers. Later amendments, in particular the 1795 Act (35 Geo III c.101), allowed a migrant continued residence until he or she became chargeable, if the 'home' parish had issued a certificate, or if bound as an apprentice. This whole system, with all its bureaucratic ramifications, increased the work load for JPs and parish overseers, and limited the movement of labour to areas where it might be needed. The result was that often it was the women and men with families who were removed, while young single male labourers were dealt with in a more flexible manner. For example, it was common practice for agricultural workers to be hired for less than a year, thus making use of their labour without giving them settlement status.

The poor themselves had two options. They could deny themselves the chance of relief for fear of removal, or they could seek out an acknowledged settlement in order to be sure of support by one parish if not another. Sometimes, for example, the settlement parish would pay relief to their poor in other parishes.

While the settlement laws enabled parishes to control mobility in a flexible manner, a more rigid approach was adopted if vagrancy could be established. The whippings of the sixteenth century gave way to the issue of passes, or hard labour in houses of correction, while the cost of removal was borne by a county rate rather than the parish. As the seventeenth century passed, those subject to control by this means were not only the 'idle and disorderly', but increasingly the women and the elderly. In other words, laws which had been enacted to deal with an earlier perceived security threat were now being used to reduce relief costs.

The final stages of enclosure (although Mid Sussex was not greatly affected by this, most enclosure having occurred long before), the development of agricultural mechanisation, the institution of Speenhamland and 'roundsman' practices, the deterrent effects of the 1723 Workhouse Test Act (9 Geo I c.7) in denying relief to those who refused indoor support, and of course the rapidly rising costs, all exercised their cumulative influence on the situation. It meant that most parishes were increasingly active on the settlement issue in desperate efforts as well as dealing with that part of the problem that they could not shift on to someone else. For example, from the Mid-Sussex parishes involved in these records, no less than 83 individuals in 26 families were the subjects of Removal Orders on one day, 18th April 1817. The result was mounting agitation for reform, reinforced by the extra problems caused by soldiers returning from the Napoleonic Wars in a period of shortage, and moves towards the 1834 Poor Law Amendment Act (4 & 5 W IV c.76). However, it must be remembered that the 1834 legislation did not affect settlement as such. There are occasional examples of attempts at settlement enforcement after this date, and the law itself was not substantially altered until 1876 (39 & 40 Vic c.61).

Quite apart from the increasingly uncontrollable costs, which were the concern of both central and local government, there was mounting adverse comment in the last quarter of the eighteenth century against the principle behind settlement. For example, Adam Smith wrote: 'To remove a man who has committed no misdemeanour, from a parish where he chuses to reside, is an evident violation of natural liberty and justice'.[36] An opinion from the early years of the twentieth century is that Settlement did not stop the flow of labour, but regulated it in the interest of the employing class.[37]

Perhaps the official documents, explicit as they are, may fail to evoke the full extent of the problems lived through by officials and victims alike. For the most part, no attempt has been made to include private letters in the parish entries; they are too few and too far between. But mention has been made earlier to the Appendix containing some samples. This is a small group which comprises all the letters retained in the settlement archives of one parish, Worth. Apart from eliminating the conventional opening and closing formulae, they are quoted in their entirety. They speak for themselves of the desperate straits of the paupers and their families, of the efforts of the parish officers to minimise hardship while maintaining some attempts at cost control, of the almost inevitable activities of informers and complainants. Also included is one year's account (Easter 1821 - Easter 1822) from a firm of solicitors acting on behalf of this same parish. It shows very clearly the range of legal procedures needed to implement the provisions of the poor law.[38]

Echoes of the settlement problems and attitudes can be heard even today at the end of the twentieth century, in Mid Sussex as well as in inner cities. Great concern is being expressed about the possibility of large scale housing development in the area. The perceived parish problem is no longer merely one of rate costs, but of environmental upheaval, of 'changing the character of the countryside', and of 'incomers'. The particular subject may be different, but the very understandable wish to maintain a vestige of local control still exists. And at national level the debate continues about economic migrants versus asylum seekers.

CONCLUSIONS

In summary, this volume records all relevant official documents known to be extant which relate to parish management of the problem of pauperism in Mid Sussex. These documents provide the family historian with specific data regarding individuals, with record office reference numbers for those wanting further details. They indicate the special problems of the area and the scope of the efforts at control, thus offering information for studies at both parish and county level. The range of types of document involved demonstrates the important part played by pauper settlement issues in a changing rural economy, and should prove useful as evidence in more general research in this field.

However, there are several significant reservations to be noted. The documents deposited in record offices are clearly only a fraction of those originally raised. To take the varying numbers of documents at face value would risk assuming that some parishes had problems on a larger scale than others, or were more active in their management methods. The fragmented extent of the archives means that this is not a conclusion which should be drawn. Even where we can trace a reasonably coherent story on paper, we cannot always be sure how efficiently the provisions were implemented. Records relating to more than one parish have often been discovered in the deposited archive of only one, leading to the possibility that parts of the evidence may be lodged in other parts of the country. One of the parishes deposited material with the record office long after the research for this book had started; further discoveries may be made in the future, with the potential for distorting the whole picture.

The fraction we have available only emphasises that survival of documents does not necessarily relate to the extent of the problem. The sources themselves are scattered, both among the parishes and between the parishes and the courts. We are always left with only a fragment of the story. Even within the documents listed it is important not to rely on only one set.

Table 1 AVAILABLE MID SUSSEX POOR LAW RECORDS

	1	2	3	4	5	6	7	8	9	10	11	12	13
	Pop.	Settlement		Removal		App.	Bastardy			Warr.	Misc.	Total	Tot. less QS
		Exam.	*Cert.*	*Par.*	*QS*		*Exam.*	*Bond*	*Ord.*				
Albourne	253	-	-	-	27	4	-	-	1	-	-	31	4
Ardingly	506	3	1	34	43	-	1	1	3	4	-	90	47
Balcombe	451	-	-	1	35	-	-	-	-	-	-	36	1
Bolney	497	26	59	40	86	6	-	8	6	5	1	237	151
Clayton	337	-	-	-	40	-	-	-	-	-	-	40	-
Cowfold	601	51	45	112	58	1	9	3	29	39	-	347	289
Crawley	210	-	-	-	28	-	-	-	-	-	-	28	-
Cuckfield	1693	14	133	92	190	131	8	24	1	5	5	603	413
Ditchling	706	-	-	-	89	-	-	-	-	-	1	90	1
East Grinstead	2659	84	240	370	270	74	26	66	21	72	-	1223	953
Henfield	1037	19	17	62	105	63	2	9	10	20	-	307	202
Horsted Keynes	627	-	-	-	52	-	-	-	-	-	-	52	-
Hurstpierpoint	101	5	57	59	119	10	2	19	6	19	-	296	177
Ifield	637	-	-	-	46	1	-	-	-	-	-	47	1
Keymer	465	-	-	-	57	-	-	-	1	-	-	58	1
Lindfield	1077	21	80	143	120	11	2	9	23	13	-	422	302
Shermanbury	274	-	-	-	40	-	-	-	-	-	-	40	-
Slaugham	560	-	-	-	96	-	-	-	-	-	-	96	-
Twineham	238	-	-	2	45	1	-	-	-	1	-	49	4
West Hoathly	794	10	43	62	104	12	4	7	6	7	-	255	151
Wivelsfield	442	-	1	-	89	-	-	-	-	-	-	90	1
Woodmancote	231	-	1	-	26	-	-	-	-	-	-	27	1
Worth	1501	24	140	174	147	76	7	10	27	11	1	617	470
TOTAL	16857	257	817	1151	1912	390	61	156	133	196	8	5081	3169

For explanation of the column numbers see below.

Columns in the table opposite:

1 1801 population
2 Settlement examinations
3 Settlement certificates
4 Parish removal papers
5 Quarter Sessions entries
6 Apprenticeships
7 Bastardy examinations
8 Bastardy bonds
9 Bastardy orders
10. Warrants
11. Miscellaneous
12. Total records
13. Total without QS entries (i.e.in parish papers)

Having entered all these caveats, it is still the case that we have sufficient evidence to show how the lives of the poor were rigidly controlled by the 'middling sort' in their roles as parish officers and magistrates. While posing further interesting questions, the book, with its variety of interrelated records, does show the operation of all aspects of poor law and poor relief in a small area.

Table 2 MID SUSSEX LANDOWNERSHIP 1785

Parish	Total Rental £	Total no of Taxpayers	Larger Landowners	% of Taxpayers	% of Rental
Albourne	710.05	13	5	38.5	61.7
Ardingly	1080.50	46	5	10.7	61.3
Balcombe	965.50	33	6	18.2	70.0
Bolney	1079.00	44	5	11.4	41.9
Clayton	838.50	41	6	14.6	54.8
Cowfold	1370.53	42	7	16.7	51.4
Crawley	259.00	27	0	-	-
Cuckfield	3808.50	153	15	9.8	57.8
Ditchling	1542.25	62	8	12.9	57.5
E Grinstead	1684.11	181	6	3.3	54.8
Henfield	2242.00	80	7	8.8	51.2
Horsted Keynes	859.25	58	3	5.2	38.3
Hurstpierpoint	2616.00	82	11	13.4	88.8
Ifield	1583.00	52	6	11.5	58.9
Keymer	1111.50	54	7	13.0	59.9
Lindfield	2031.88	96	11	11.5	64.2
Shermanbury	748.76	23	6	26.1	77.7
Slaugham	859.00	69	0	-	-
Twineham	870.00	15	5	33.3	87.9
W Hoathly	1434.25	76	6	7.9	44.3
Wivelsfield	1051.25	50	6	12.0	48.4
Woodmancote	634.50	21	5	23.8	64.1
Worth	2305.00	134	10	7.5	62.4
Falmer	797.58	13	3	23.1	84.2

(Larger landowners: those with annual rents of £50+)

Sources: Sussex Record Society Vols 77 & 82

EDITORIAL PRACTICE

Conventions of Extraction and Calendaring

Almost all the different types of documents which make up this volume follow strict legal forms prescribed by the legislation which created them. This means that they can be calendared rather than transcribed; and the calendaring will present the data in a consistent and simple style, without losing significant information. For all the individuals involved, all personal details have been extracted (names, occupations, relationships, ages) together with all places mentioned. Names of officials, such as parish officers and justices, however, have normally been omitted.

Conventions of spelling and abbreviation

Readers should be aware of the somewhat erratic spelling in documents such as these, particularly with regard to surnames. Surnames and christian names have been transcribed *litteratim.* Place names are given in their modern form - although in the examinations both original and conventional versions have been included. Surname variants may be found in the index; but in the listings the first spelling encountered has been recorded, with any significant variations shown in brackets.

Ages of children are shown thus: "6y" and "6m" for years and months respectively. Weeks and days are given in full.

Settlement and Bastardy Examinations:

In the case of examinations, a fuller style of precis has been adopted, to reflect their more discursive and narrative style Evidence was taken on oath and the documents of course use the present tense, the witness signing or making a mark immediately on completion. In recording these much repetition has been omitted, and reported speech used to make them more relevant to later readers.

Officials

Documents refer variously to Churchwardens, Churchwardens and Overseers, Overseers, or Parish Officers. For the sake of uniformity, the latter term has been used throughout.

Damaged documents:

Many papers have been damaged to a greater or lesser extent. Where there is no doubt about a word, square brackets have been used to complete it, e.g. Kn[ight - torn]; in other instances, square brackets indicate either total loss [missing] or inability to transcribe [indecipherable].

Pre 1752 Dates:

With the change from the Julian to the Gregorian Calendar, New Year's Day was moved from 25 March to 1 January. In this volume all pre 1752 entries between those dates have been standardised to agree with the modern system. For example, 12 February 1646 Old Style has been entered as 12 February 1647.

County Identification:

Where no county name is given Sussex is to be understood.

Counties other than Sussex are given in full in the text of documents; in lists they are identified by three letters (the Chapman Code):

Bdf	Bedfordshire	Lin	Lincolnshire
Bkm	Buckinghamshire	Lnd	London
Brk	Berkshire	Mdx	Middlesex
Cam	Cambridgeshire	Mon	Monmouthshire
Chs	Cheshire	Nfk	Norfolk
Con	Cornwall	Nth	Northamptonshire
Dby	Derbyshire	Oxf	Oxfordshire
Dev	Devon	Sal	Shropshire (Salop)
Dor	Dorset	Sct	Scotland
Ess	Essex	Som	Somerset
Gls	Gloucestershire	Sry	Surrey
Ham	Hampshire	War	Warwickshire
Hrt	Hertfordshire	Wil	Wiltshire
Iow	Isle of Wight	Wor	Worcestershire
Ken	Kent	Yks	Yks
Lei	Leicestershire		

Record Office Cataloguing:

The parishes involved in this compilation are numbered in the Record Offices as follows:

Albourne	226	Hurstpierpoint	400
Ardingly	231	Ifield	109
Balcombe	234	Keymer	407
Bolney	252	Lindfield	416
Clayton	294	Shermanbury	167
Cowfold	59	Slaugham	483
Crawley	60	Twineham	495
Cuckfield	301	West Hoathly	379
Ditchling	308	Wivelsfield	514
East Grinstead	348	Woodmancote	214
Henfield	100	Worth	516
Horsted Keynes	384		

The classification used in the Record Offices for the documents listed is shown at the head of each list as follows.

29	Constables - miscellaneous
32	Settlement
32/1	Indemnity Bonds and Certificates
32/2,3	Removal Orders
32/4	Examinations
33	Apprenticeship
34	Bastardy
34/1	Bonds
34/2	Orders
34/3	Examinations
35	Settlement - miscellaneous
37	Poor Law Miscellaneous - pre 1834

The catalogue mark is made up of the prefix "Par" followed by the parish number, the class number(s), and the piece number (e.g. Par 400/29/1) - often followed by a further number when each individual document has been given a separate reference. Unless there is a particular problem of identification, this last number has been omitted.

Wherever possible, documents catalogued as "miscellaneous", i.e. under (35) or (37), have been listed with similar items and a specific note added.

Parish descriptions and Population figures:

Very brief descriptions are given at the head of each parish entry. These consist of the topography, superficial geology, type of agriculture and other occupations, and population. They are derived mainly from the relevant information in the Victoria County History and the Census Returns.

The population totals have been calculated on the following principles:

1. 1676 Compton Census returns of communicants were made on a national basis by parish priests. The wording of the relevant question required clarification. The intention was to record numbers of communicants (in practical terms those over 16), but not all dioceses or individual parishes interpreted the requirement in a consistent manner. There are some suspiciously round figures; some instances where those under 16 were incorrectly included; others where only males were counted. It has been calculated that two thirds of the population were over 16, but in view of the inconsistencies the multiplier used in the following entries (1.5) must be treated with considerable reserve. (see Whiteman A: 'Compton Census', in Schurer K and Arkell T (1992): *Surveying the People*).

2. 1724 population figures represent the Bowers Survey totals multiplied by 4.73, the so-called English standard mean household size (Laslett P & Wall R (1972): *Household and Family in Past Time*, p.133)]

Quarter Sessions Records:

As has been indicated in the Introduction, many documents held in the parishes have been lost or damaged, and Court records have been used to supplement information. The Quarter Sessions Order Books are held at East Sussex Record Office, the relevant catalogue entries being the following:

QO/EW 19-54 and QM/EW 10 (to cover a gap in the QO volumes).
Microfilm copies of the Order Books are available at the West Sussex Record (MF 1526-1546).

Many of the Quarter Sessions orders are respites, referring a case to a later sitting of the court. In cases where a final decision is recorded, these respites have normally been omitted.

In many cases a document among the parish collections is a copy of a Quarter Sessions order, and for simplicity and completeness we decided to include both records. We had originally planned to provide cross references between the two copies, but eventually abandoned a scheme which would have added substantially to the labour of editing. The Personal Names Index, however, will enable the reader to identify references in the two series with relative ease.

The following abbreviations have been used in the abstracts for the venues for the Quarter Sessions:

A - Arundel	L - Lewes
B - Battle	M - Midhurst
C - Chichester	P - Petworth
H - Horsham	S - Steyning

NOTES AND REFERENCES

1. Hale M (1683): *A Discourse Touching Provision for the Poor*, pp 2-3
2. Wilkins D (1737): *Concilia III*, p 790, cited in Slack P (1990): *The English Poor Law 1531-1782*, p 12
3. Slack P (1988): *Poverty and Policy in Tudor and Stuart England*, p.39
4. Brigden S (1984): 'Religion and Social Obligation in Early Sixteenth-Century London', in *Past and Present* 103, p.106
5. Slack P (1988): *op. cit..*, p.24
6. Sampson G (ed)(1910): *Utopia*, p.53
7. Thirsk J & Cooper JP (1972): *Seventeenth -Century Economic Documents*, p.103
8. Sharpe JA (1984): *Crime in Early Modern England* 1550-1750, p 118
9. Tate W E (1983): *The Parish Chest*, pp 323-327
10. ESRO, Sessions Rolls 33/2
11. Slack P (1988): *op. cit.*, p.195
12. Slack P (1988): *Ibid.*, p.63
13. Sharpe JA (1984): *op. cit.*, pp 68-9
14. Snell KDM (1985): *Annals of the Labouring Poor*, p.107, n9
15. Brandon P (1974): *The Sussex Landscape*, pp 30-31
16. Brandon P & Short B (1990): *The South East from AD 1000*, p 6
17. Mills DR (1980): *Lord and Peasant in 19th Century Britain*, ch.6
18. Wrightson K: 'Aspects of social differentiation in rural England c. 1580-1660', *Journal of Peasant Studies*, **5**, pp 33-47
19. Schurer K & Arkell T (eds)(1992): *Surveying the People*, p.40
20. PRO/MH12/12829
21. Smith A (1776): *The Wealth of Nations*, vol i, p.18,
22. Thomas E G (1979): Pauper Migration to Worth, in *West Sussex Archives Society Newsletter* No.13, pp 3-4
23. Hobsbawm EJ (1964): *Labouring Men*, p 38
24. Fletcher A (1975): *A County Community in Peace and War: Sussex 1600-1660*, pp 168-9
25. ESRO QO/EW
26. WSRO Par 59/31/2,6
27. WSRO Par 109/31/1
28. WSRO Par 252/35/1
29. PRO, SP 16/426/19, cited in Fletcher A: *op cit.*, p 167
30. Sharpe JA (1984): *op. cit.*, pp 99-103
31. Dalton M (1677): *The County Justice: containing the Practice of the Justices of the Peace out of their Sessions*, p. 40
32. Snell KDM (1985): *op. cit.*, p 107
33. ESRO, QSOB 1655-60, f.35v
34. SRS Volume 28: *Sussex Apprentices and Masters* 1710-1752
35. Dalton M: *op. cit.*, p.146
36. Smith A (1776): *The Wealth of Nations*, vol. i, p.194
37. Hammond JL & B (1911): *The Village Labourer 1760-1832*, p.115
38. WSRO Par 516/31/22/6

BIBLIOGRAPHY:

Beckett J V (1990): *The Agricultural Revolution.*
Arguing that the process was more gradual and more complex than traditionally assumed.

Beier A L (1985): *Masterless Men.*
The vagrancy in England 1560-1640. Full reliable treatment of the perceived problem.

Blaug M (1963): 'The myth of the old poor law and the making of the new', *Journal of Economic History*, 23.
A defence of the system.

Boyer G R (1986): 'The old poor law and the agricultural labour market in southern England: an empirical analysis', *Journal of Economic History,* 46.

Brandon P & Short B (1990): *The South East from AD 1000*, ch 5.
One chapter in a wide ranging general history devoted to the stresses in developing communities.

Brent C E (1976): 'Rural employment and population in Sussex 1550-1640', *Sussex Archaeological Collections*, vol 114, pp27-48.

Burchall M J (1977, 1978, 1982): *Catalogue of Sussex Quarter Sessions Settlement Orders and Cases,1661-1700, 1701-1729, 1730-1749.* (Three volumes)

Burchall M J (1979): *Eastern Sussex Settlement Certificates 1670-1832.*

Burnett J (1994): *Idle Hands, The Experience of Unemployment 1790-1990*, ch 1: 'Unemployment in the countryside 1790-1834'.
Focus on the problems of working people, with personal biographies.

Clark P & Souden D (eds) (1987): *Migration and Society in early modern England.*
Essays covering seventeenth and eighteenth centuries.

Clay C (ed) (1990): *Rural Society: Landowners, Peasants and Labourers 1500-1750*, ch 3 (Everitt A): 'Farm labourers 1500-1640'.
Deals with the condition of the farm labourer within the context of the agrarian history of England and Wales.

Coats A W (1960): 'Economic thought and poor law policy in the eighteenth century', *Economic History Review*, 2nd series, 13.
Discussion of public concerns.

Coward B (1988): *Social Change and Continuity in early modern England 1550-1750.*
Covers the main themes of social history.

Emsley C (1987): *Crime and Society in England 1750-1900.*
Looks at changes in perception and management of crime.

Fletcher A (1975): *A County Community in Peace and War: Sussex 1600-1660*, pp 165-170.
A small section on the local enforcement of order.

Fletcher A & Stevenson J (eds) (1985): *Order and Disorder in early modern England.*
Several contributions to the debate on social control.

Hobsbawm E.J (1964): *Labouring Men.*

Hammond J L & B (1911): *The Village Labourer 1760-1832. A study of the government of England before the Reform Bill.*
Impassioned approach to the plight of the rural poor.

Horn P (1987): *Life and Labour in rural England 1760-1850.*
The influence of industrialisation on rural trades and crafts.

Marshall J D (1985): *The old Poor Law 1795-1834.*
Good short guide.

Oxley G W (1974): *Poor Relief in England and Wales 1601-1834.*
Guide concentrating on eighteenth century.

Sharpe J A (1984): *Crime in early modern England 1550-1750.*
Looks at different ways of studying crime; deals with 'social' crime and elite attitudes.

Short B (ed) (1992): *The English Rural Community; Image and analysis.*
Examines the variety of contrasting and developing communities.

Slack P (1990): *The English Poor Law 1531-1782.*
Excellent introduction to the subject.

Slack P (1988): *Poverty and Policy in Tudor and Stuart England.*
A synthesis of recent scholarship on definitions, social attitudes, economic realities and the legal framework.

Snell K D M (1985): *Annals of the Labouring Poor. Social change in agrarian England 1660-1900.*
Settlement records used to discuss the labouring poor.

Taylor J S (1976): 'The impact of pauper settlement 1691-1834', *Past and Present*, 73.
The effects of legal control.

Webb S & B (1927): *English Poor Law History; Part 1. The Old Poor Law.*
The standard work before the recent increased interest.

ACKNOWLEDGEMENTS

The long gestation of this volume has left us with many debts of thanks. The first must be to Mick Reed, who initially joined Norma Pilbeam in the task of arranging and editing the vast collection of material she had transcribed.. It was his enthusiasm that made it clear that the volume was viable and valuable. His decision to move to Australia meant that he was forced to withdraw from the editorial team; but he had provided the initial impetus which has enabled Ian Nelson, as his successor, to carry the project through its long journey to fruition.

We must also acknowledge the pioneering work of Michael Burchall who had published some of the material in his genealogical articles. It has been most useful to be able to compare his transcriptions where they cover the same ground; but the editors must emphasise that they are responsible for all the transcription work in this volume - and of course for any errors.

Many individuals have made valuable contributions to the complex task of putting the material into published (and we hope simple and user-friendly) form. We are particularly grateful to Chris Leighton's meticulous skill in taking on the massive task of the Personal Names index, and to Rosie Ritchie for tackling, with speed and patience, the Places index. Additionally we must thank Sarah Farrell who undertook part of the typesetting. Mr Bill Parrott deserves special thanks for producing the delightful illustration on the dustjacket - his must be the first artistic commission to be acknowledged in one of the Society's volumes. Andrew Foster has provided valuable advice in the preparation of the Introduction. The staff at both the West and East Sussex Record Offices have been unfailingly helpful. Throughout the project Peter Pilbeam has provided unceasing encouragement and support, in addition to a vast amount of practical help with the research and checking. Above all, we wish to record our thanks to Peter Wilkinson, who has shown dedicated nursing of this volume through the lengthy gestation, and for his expert guidance with the text, the lists themselves, and the type-setting.

The majority of the original documents are held in the West Sussex Record Office, and we are grateful to the County Archivist, Richard Childs, for his positive support for the project. The remaining material is at the East Sussex Record Office, and we are glad to make similar acknowledgement to Roger Davey. To both we are further indebted for permission to publish the documents in their custody - as we are of course to the incumbents of the 23 parishes. For permission to reproduce items as illustrations we should mention more specifically the incumbents of East Grinstead, Hurstpierpoint, Lindfield and Worth.

The cost of publishing a volume of this size and scope could not have been met by the normal subscription income of the Society. The Council of the Sussex Record Society is pleased to have this opportunity to express its thanks to the Marc Fitch Foundation for a substantial grant, and to the West Sussex Archives Society and the West Sussex County Council for generous financial assistance.

MID SUSSEX POOR LAW RECORDS

1601-1835

The records are calendared separately for each parish.

The types of record have been included in the following order:-

Settlement examinations;
Settlement certificates;
Removal orders from the parish (Parish Records);
Removal orders from the parish (Quarter Sessions records);
Removal orders to the parish (Parish Records);
Removal orders to the parish (Quarter Sessions records);
Bastardy examinations;
Bastardy bonds and orders;
Warrants;
Apprenticeship indentures and bonds.

ALBOURNE

Albourne: 1763 acres, 2 miles north of South Downs. S boundary 150 ft; S half on Gault & Lower Greensand, which forms 2 ridges, one carrying Albourne Place & Bishops Place, the other Albourne Street. N half Weald clay, mostly below 100ft. Drains N & W to river Adur. Soil better than most in Weald, for pasture & arable. Church 1 mile SW of main settlement at Albourne Street; no evidence of medieval settlement, but later remains nearby. Albourne Place emparked from 16th to 20th century. The Street and Albourne Green have several 17th century buildings; scattered farm settlements, some recorded in 13th century. Roman Greensand Way crossed S end of parish.

Population: 1676 147; 1724 118; 1801 253; 1811 293; 1821 360; 1831 362.

QUARTER SESSIONS REMOVAL ORDERS FROM ALBOURNE

		To
C 1670 Jan.10	William ADAMS; order defective, new one to be obtained.	Steyning
C 1675 Apr.12	John SMYTH; on appeal order respited.	Henfield
L 1675 Jul.15	John SMYTH; confirmed.	Henfield
L 1676 Jul.13	John STURT; on appeal he is to be returned to Albourne.	Hurstpierpoint
L 1688 Oct. 4	Edward MOORE and wife; respited.	Ditchling
L 1693 Jul.13	John BUTCHER; Chailey appealed for him to be sent to Albourne; order respited and meanwhile J.B. to be sent to Albourne.	Chailey
L 1693 Oct. 5	John BUTCHER; ordered that, as it did plainly appear that he is not an inhabitant of Albourne, he is to be settled at Chailey until they can find another place of habitation.	Chailey
P 1716 Jan. 9	Mary READ; confirmed.	Westmeston
L 1730 Jan.15	William CHAPMAN; discharged.	Wivelsfield
P 1744 Oct. 1	Frances PELHAM, singlewoman; confirmed.	Slaugham
C 1756 Apr.26	Thomas PUTTOCK, and wife Ann; confirmed.	Lancing
H 1762 Jul.12	John MILES and wife Mary; confirmed.	Woodmancote
M 1772 Jan.13	Ann OTTIVE; quashed.	Withyham
C 1772 Apr.27	Ann COMBER and child Sarah 5m; confirmed.	East Grinstead
P 1810 May 1	Elizabeth MITCHELL, singlewoman; confirmed.	Hurstpierpoint
H 1810 Jul.10	Elizabeth BURT, singlewoman; confirmed.	Henfield
P 1811 Apr.23	Susannah BLAKER; confirmed.	Beeding
P 1811 Oct. 8	Henry MARTIN and wife Ann; confirmed.	Woodmancote
C 1813 Jan.12	James BATCHELOR, wife Elizabeth and children James 2y and Mary 10m; confirmed.	Twineham
C 1814 Jan.11	John GATLAND and wife Phoebe; confirmed.	Sompting
P 1816 Jan. 9	William HYDER, wife Mary and son Henry 6m; confirmed.	Hurstpierpoint
P 1816 Jan. 9	Philip GROVES and wife Martha; confirmed.	Woodmancote

P 1819 Jan.11	James ROBINSON, wife Lydia and children Elizabeth 5y, Mary 2y and James 9m; confirmed.	Rudgwick

QUARTER SESSIONS REMOVAL ORDERS TO ALBOURNE

		From
L 1764 Jan.12	John BLABER and wife Ann; confirmed.	Westmeston
C 1812 Jan.14	Thomas BURRELL, wife Harriet and children William 6y, John 4y and Harriet 4m. Confirmed.	Steyning
L 1821 Jan.12	William MASCALL, wife Sarah and children William 5y, George 3y, Charles 2y and Louisa 8m; respited.	Patcham
H 1828 Jul.15	Mary Ann SHARP 7y; confirmed.	Steyning

ALBOURNE APPRENTICESHIP AGREEMENTS Par 226/1/1/1

1701 Jun. 16 HUBBER'S girl to Peter HILL for 3 years last Easter. Consideration £5: £3 for 1st year and 20s for next 2 years.
Par 226/1/1/1 f32v

1701 Jun. 16 HAIR'S boy to John BOX for 3 years last Easter. Consideration £4 and 2 pairs of new shoes: £2 for 1st year and 20s for next 2 years.
Par 226/1/1/1 f32v

1713 May 3 Thomas HUBBART to be taken care of and maintained for 7 years from 3 May for sum of £5. Consideration £5 to be paid at 40s per year for first 2 years and 20s for third year.
Par 226/1/1/1 f43v

1713 May 3 Edward HUBBART to be taken care of and maintained by John BOX and William BALCOMBE for 7 years. Consideration £5 to be paid at 40s per year for first 2 years and 20s for third year.
Par 226/1/1/1 f43v

ARDINGLY

Ardingly: 3,841 acres. Church at 398ft in centre, sloping down S to Ouse valley at 125ft and up to 500ft in N. Streams on E & W boundaries. Roman road ran N-S through centre of parish. Ironworks with hammer pond. Hamlet of Hapstead on E side now main settlement. Wakehurst Place (1590) now part of Kew Gardens. 1 inn and 14 shops.

Population: 1724 189; 1801 506; 1811 553; 1821 579; 1831 587.

ARDINGLY SETTLEMENT EXAMINATIONS Par 231/32/4

1796 Apr. 1 John JENNER, now residing in Ardingly, said that, fifteen years ago Ladyday last, he hired himself to John SNASHALL of Balcombe, yeoman, for a year at wages of £5.10s 0d, which term he served and received his wages, and that he continued in the same service for another two and a half years under separate hirings, since which he has done no act to gain a settlement. [Mark of J.J.]

1803 Sep.13 John EDEE, now residing in Ardingly, said that, about ten years ago Ladyday last, he hired himself to William JENNINGS of Cuckfield, yeoman, for a year at wages of four guineas, which term he served and continued with the same master for five years more under separate and distinct hirings of one year each, and has not gained a settlement in any other parish. [Mark of J.E.]

1821 Oct.20 John MITCHELL, now residing in Reigate, Surrey, said that he was born in Reigate and that he lived as a groom with the Revd. Mr. RAMSDON at Ardingly for sixteen months at the wages of 25 guineas per annum, and received his full wages. That he quitted this service six years ago and has not done anything to gain a settlement since.

ARDINGLY SETTLEMENT CERTIFICATE Par 231/32/1

		From
1742 Jan.24	John WOODMAN, wife Mary and daughters, Elizabeth and Sarah	East Grinstead

REMOVAL ORDERS FROM ARDINGLY Par 231/32/2/1

		To
1812 Jan.17	John DOWNER and wife Mary. Confirmation.	Goudhurst, Ken
1812 Apr.10	John TULLEY, wife Hannah and children Benjamin 2y and an infant, unbaptised. Confirmation.	Worth
1815 Mar.31	Mary TESTER, singlewoman, being with child.	West Hoathly
1815 Mar.31	John COOK, wife Sarah and children Richard 3y and Harriot 1y 6m. [Endorsed: Delivered 1 April].	West Hoathly

1815 Dec.15	George ELLSEY and wife Elizabeth.	West Hoathly
1817 Apr.18	John HOBDEN and wife Mary. Confirmation.	Hamsey
1817 Aug.22	Lydia BASHFORD. [Endorsed: Delivered 22 Aug]	Cuckfield
1818 Oct.30	Thomas HENLEY, wife Phoebe and children Caroline 5y , Mary 3y and Harriot 2y. [Endorsed: Delivered the family 30 Oct.]	Balcombe
1821 Dec.14	William TINGLEY and wife Elizabeth. [Endorsed: Delivered 14 Dec.]	Horsted Keynes
1822 Nov. 8	William BOX, wife Charity and son Richard 1m. [Endorsed: This order executed on 11 Nov.]	East Grinstead
1823 Dec. 5	Edward BROWNE, wife Catherine and son William, 13y. [Endorsed: Delivered 10 Dec.]	Charlwood, Sry

QUARTER SESSIONS REMOVAL ORDERS FROM ARDINGLY

		To
L 1705 Jan.11	Henry ROBOROW; confirmed.	Cuckfield
L 1711 Jul.12	Anne BAKER, widow; discharged.	West Hoathly
L 1714 Jul.15	Mary GRATWICKE; discharged.	Eastbourne
L 1723 Oct.10	Thomas DAWSON and wife Sarah; confirmed.	Warborough, Oxf
L 1747 Apr.30	John SYMMONS and son Thomas 10y; confirmed.	Worth
L 1750 Jul.12	John MARCHANT and wife Elizabeth; respited.	Cuckfield
L 1750 Oct. 4	John MARCHANT and wife Elizabeth; discharged.	Cuckfield
L 1752 Oct. 5	Ann AWCOCK, singlewoman; discharged.	West Hoathly
L 1755 Apr.10	John TOOTH; respited.	Cuckfield
L 1755 Jul.17	John TOOTH; confirmed.	Cuckfield
L 1757 Apr.21	William TOOTH, wife Mary and children William and Sarah, both under 7y; discharged.	Shermanbury
L 1760 Apr.17	Thomas AWCOCK, wife Sarah and daughter Ann aged 14 weeks; confirmed.	Lingfield, Sry
L 1760 Apr.17	Nathanial COPPARD, wife Sarah and infant son; confirmed.	Cuckfield
L 1760 Jul.17	Samuel AMON; confirmed.	Holybourne, Ham
L 1761 Apr. 2	John BOWELL and wife Mary; confirmed.	Storrington
L 1764 May 3	George WILLIAMS, wife Mary and children George 7y, John 6y, Mary 3y, and William 11m; discharged.	Worth
L 1765 Oct.10	John ROSAR and wife Elizabeth; confirmed.	Horsted Keynes
L 1768 Jan.14	Elizabeth JACKSON, singlewoman; confirmed.	Cuckfield
L 1810 May 4	William KNIGHT, wife Sarah and children Mary, Sarah, Ann and William; confirmed.	Hackney, Mdx
L 1812 Jan.17	John DOWNER, wife Mary; confirmed.	Goudhurst, Ken
L 1812 Apr.10	John TULLEY, wife Hannah and children Benjamin 2y and an infant not yet baptised;	Worth

	confirmed.	
L 1817 Apr.18	John HOBDEN and wife Mary; confirmed.	Hamsey
L 1817 Apr.18	John STEDMAN; respited.	Marylebone, Mdx
L 1818 Oct.23	Abraham CHERRIMAN and wife Elizabeth; respited.	Lindfield
L 1819 Jan.15	Abraham CHERRIMAN and wife Elizabeth; quashed.	Lindfield
L 1819 Apr.23	Abraham CHERRIMAN, wife Elizabeth, and child Mildred 3m; confirmed.	Henfield
L 1824 Jan.16	Jane PHILCOX; confirmed.	Maresfield
L 1827 Jan.11	William HOLLOWAY and wife Celia; confirmed.	Brighton
L 1827 Apr.26	George TESTER, the younger, wife Elizabeth and daughter Maria Louisa 1y; confirmed.	Balcombe
L 1827 Apr.26	Sarah EVANS; confirmed.	Godstone, Sry
L 1827 Oct.18	John LEDWARD, wife Hope and son John 6m; confirmed.	Uckfield
L 1828 Jan.17	John MARCHANT and wife Sarah; confirmed.	Lindfield
L 1828 Jan.17	Richard TAYLOR; confirmed.	Worth
L 1828 Jul.17	Robert RUDDOCK, wife Hannah and children Maria 13y, William 10y, Robert 6y and Charles 2y; confirmed.	Bramfield, Hrt
L 1834 Jul. 3	Henry TESTER, wife Sarah and son George 8m; confirmed.	Fletching
L 1834 Jul. 3	Susannah BACKSHELL; respited.	West Hoathly

REMOVAL ORDERS TO ARDINGLY Par 231/32/3

		From
1791 Aug.10	William CARR, wife Hannah and son William aged 6 weeks.	East Grinstead
1792 Mar.21	John CHILD and wife Mary.	Penshurst, Ken
1793 Dec. 7	Sarah WALES.	Brighton
1794 Jan. 6	Thomas BUDGEN, wife Elizabeth and children Ann 2y and Thomas 6m.	Fletching
1801 May 26	Mary FAULKNER, singlewoman.	Horsted Keynes
1812 Nov.19	Keziah FURNER, was apprehended in Brighton as a rogue and vagabond, duly convicted and sent to the House of Correction for seven days as she did, on 1 October last, commit acts of vagrancy by wandering abroad without visible means of gaining a livelihood, lodging in alehouses and not giving a good account of herself. On examination she said she was born in Ardingly where her father was legally settled and she has never gained a settlement elsewhere. [Mark of K.F.]	House of Correction, Lewes.

1813 Jan.14	Richard HOLMAN, wife Phobe and sons John 3y, Richard 11m. R.H. unable to travel due to sickness and infirmity; order suspended until it may be safely executed without danger.	Warnham
1813 Mar. 6	Mary MEW, singlewoman.	Horsted Keynes
1816 Jan. 1	Ann CORK, singlewoman, who is with child.	Fletching
1816 Apr.30	Jane HENDLEY was at Quarter Sessions, Lewes, on 26 April last, adjudged a rogue and vagabond and ordered to be recommitted to the House of Correction, Lewes. Her sentence being discharged, she is to be passed home to Ardingly, the place of her last legal settlement. On examination she said she was born in Chislehurst, Kent, where her father was legally settled. That 45 years ago she was legally married at Salisbury, Wiltshire, to her late husband, Thomas HENDLEY, then a Private in the Surrey militia who, she believes, was legally settled in Ardingly and that she has been kept in the workhouse of Ardingly and, very lately, received relief therefrom. [Mark of J.H.]	House of Correction, Lewes.
1816 Jul.18	William CARR, wife Mary and sons James 3y and. Thomas 5m.	Brighton
1817 Mar.21	James MILES, wife Mildred and children Mary 4y and John 2y.	Lindfield
1817 May 9	Elizabeth BATCHELOR, the wife of Henry BATCHELOR the younger, and her daughter Elizabeth 8y 6m.	Lindfield
1817 Jun. 7	James DAWES, wife Ann and daughter Ann 4m. [Endorsed: Received 25 June]	Croydon, Sry
1817 Nov.15	Elizabeth NICHOLAS, singlewoman.	Keymer
1817 Dec.22	Henry WILLIAMS and wife Jane.	East Grinstead
1819 Mar. 5	Luke BUDGEN, wife Charlotte and son Edward 10m.	Wivelsfield
1820 May 8	William LEPPARD.	Lower Beeding
1822 Mar. 7	Harriet HARMAN, singlewoman.	Goudhurst, Ken
1823 Aug.11	Sarah MAY otherwise Sarah HESKETH. [Endorsed: Received 12 Aug.]	Sevenoaks, Ken
1823 Dec.15	Jane HILLS, singlewoman.	Brighton
1826 Oct. 2	Celia BASHFORD, who is with child.	Brighton
1827 Mar.23	Martha MARCHANT, an unmarried woman who is with child.	Balcombe

QUARTER SESSIONS REMOVAL ORDERS TO ARDINGLY

		From
C 1733 Apr. 2	John JUPP, wife Mary and son John; confirmed.	Itchingfield
L 1785 Apr. 7	James BALCOMBE, wife Esther and daughter Margaret; respited.	Fletching
L 1785 Jul.14	James BALCOMBE, wife Esther and daughter Margaret; quashed.	Fletching
L 1789 Jul.16	Brie SCRASE; confirmed.	Hailsham
L 1804 Apr.13	Richard BOTTING, wife Jane and children Elizabeth 3y and Friend 1y; respited.	Chailey
L 1804 Jul.13	Richard BOTTING, wife Jane and children Elizabeth 3y and Friend 1y; quashed.	Chailey
L 1832 Oct.18	Thomas RADFORD and wife Ann; respited.	Chiddingly

ARDINGLY BASTARDY EXAMINATION Par 231/34/3

1818 Jun. 4 Mary CHILDS of Ardingly, singlewoman, said that she is now with child and that Richard LEPPARD of West Hoathly, labourer, is the father. [Mark of M.C.]

ARDINGLY BASTARDY BOND Par 231/34/1

1790 Jul.11 Richard SIMMONDS of Ardingly, labourer, bound to the parish officers of Ardingly in £50, in respect of Sarah WARINER of Ardingly, singlewoman, who has lately been delivered of a male bastard child in Ardingly, R.S. being the putative father. [Mark of R.S.]

ARDINGLY BASTARDY ORDERS Par 231/34/2

1815 May 31 Mary WEBBER, singlewoman, was delivered of a male bastard child at the house of her father in Ardingly, on 21 March last, and John TULLEY of Ardingly, servant, is the father. J.T. to pay £1.10s 0d towards costs and £2.10s 0d for charges and expenses incident to the birth, and 3s 0d a week; the mother to pay 1s 0d a week. [Endorsed: 21 [?March] 1815 to 21 Feb.1817 - 100 weeks at 1s 0d a week = £5.]

1816 Mar. 8 Charlotte PATTENDEN, singlewoman, was delivered of a female child at the house of her father, William PATTENDEN, in Ardingly, on 1 January last, and Benjamin BEAL of Ardingly, carpenter, is the father. B.B. to pay 12s 6d towards costs and £2.10s 0d expenses incident to the birth and 2s 6d a week; the mother to pay 6d a week.

1821 Oct.30 Sophia PILBEAM, singlewoman, was delivered of a male bastard child at the Workhouse in Ardingly on 3 October last and John JENNER of Ardingly, labourer, is the father. J.J. to pay 8s 0d costs and 40s 0d expenses incident to the birth and 2s 0d a week; the mother to pay 6d a week.

ARDINGLY WARRANTS Par 231/29/1

1815 Apr.29 Mary WEBBER, late of Ardingly, singlewoman, has been delivered of two bastard children in Ardingly, which are likely to become chargeable to that parish. M.W. to be apprehended and brought before a Justice to answer the charge and to be further dealt with.

1816 Feb.16 Charlotte PATTENDEN of Ardingly, singlewoman, was delivered of a female bastard child at her father's house in Ardingly, on 1 January last, and Benjamin BEAL of Ardingly, carpenter is the father. C.P. to appear before the Justices at The Talbot Inn, Cuckfield on Friday 8 March next; notice to be given to B.B. so that he may also be present.

1823 Jan. 7 Mildred DAWES of Ardingly, singlewoman, has declared that she is with child and that William AGATE of Cuckfield, servant, is the father. W.A. to be apprehended.

1826 Feb. 3 Harriett PATTENDEN of Ardingly, singlewoman, was delivered of a female bastard child at the house of John TULLEY on 21 December last, and John Tulley of Ardingly, labourer, is the father. H.P. to appear before the justices at the house of Faulkner BEST in Cuckfield on 17 February next and notice to be given to J.T. so that he may also be present.

BALCOMBE

Balcombe: 4,795 acres from river Ouse in S to forest ridge, 460ft in N. Chalybeate springs, stone quarries. 1 inn and 11 shopkeepers.

Population: 1724 237; 1801 451; 1811 559; 1821 606; 1831 641.

QUARTER SESSIONS REMOVAL ORDERS FROM BALCOMBE

		To
L 1674 Jan.15	Edward HYDE, under 7y.	Worth
L 1683 Apr.19	Mary GARDINER, a poor child; respited.	Horsham
L 1694 Apr.19	William SAYERS; discharged.	Ardingly
L 1705 Jan.11	Richard VENNALL [VERRALL]; on his appeal order discharged.	Ardingly
B 1711 Apr.12	John FAULKONER; discharged.	Slaugham
L 1718 Jan.16	Edward STEPHENS, wife Elizabeth and son Stephen; confirmed as to Edward Stephens and wife and discharged as to son Stephen.	Carshalton, Sry
L 1721 Jul.13	Thomas GIBSON, wife Sarah and son Abraham; confirmed.	Portslade
L 1726 Jul.14	Richard JENNER, wife Elizabeth and children William, Mary, Elizabeth and Richard; confirmed.	Burwash
L 1732 Jan.13	John GILLIAM; discharged as he was a certificate man and not actually chargeable.	Maresfield
L 1764 May 3	John PATERSON; confirmed.	Lewisham, Ken
L 1771 Apr.11	Edward TATE, wife Mary and child aged 5 weeks; confirmed.	Cuckfield
L 1773 Apr.22	George WATSON and wife Elizabeth; respited.	Horsted Keynes
L 1774 Jan.13	George WATSON, and wife Elizabeth; confirmed	Horsted Keynes
L 1778 Jul.16	Ruth WHARTON, wife of John WHARTON, late Ruth WHEELER, singlewoman, together with Samuel 3y, a bastard child born to her at Alfold, Surrey, on 22 March 1775; confirmed. [But see next entry]	Alfold, Sry
L 1778 Jul.16	Ruth WHARTON, wife of John WHARTON, late Ruth WHEELER, singlewoman, together with William 5y, a bastard child born to her at Horley, Surrey, on 3 December 1772; confirmed. [But see previous entry]	Horley, Sry
L 1783 Jul.17	George CHERRIMAN, wife Martha and children Martha 8y, John 6y, George 4y, and Rachel 1y; quashed.	Wiston
L 1801 Jan.15	Richard BOTTING and wife Jane; respited.	Ardingly
L 1801 Apr.16	Richard BOTTING and wife Jane; quashed.	Ardingly

L 1808 Jul.15	James MARCHANT, wife Sarah and children Mary 9y, James 7y, Henry 5y and Martha 1y; confirmed.	Ardingly
L 1811 Oct.11	Hannah STAMMER; respited.	Cuckfield
L 1812 Jan.17	Hannah STAMMER, singlewoman; confirmed.	Cuckfield
L 1812 Jan.17	Mary BOURNE, singlewoman; confirmed.	Horne, Sry
L 1816 Apr.26	Ambrose HARBOUR, wife Jane and children Esther 5y and William 2y; confirmed.	Withyham
L 1816 Jul.19	Joseph HOLMAN and wife Elizabeth; respited.	Brighton
L 1827 Jan.11	James WELLS and wife Sophia; confirmed.	Washington
L 1827 Apr.26	William TESTER and wife Elizabeth; quashed.	Nuthurst
L 1829 Oct.22	James BOURNE, wife Elizabeth and children Mary 8y and James 2y; confirmed.	Worth
L 1830 Apr.22	Thomas GARDNER, wife Jane and children William 13y, Henry 10y, Elizabeth 6y, Johanna 5y and Mary 3y; quashed.	East Grinstead
L 1830 Jul.15	Thomas GARDNER, wife Jane and children William 13y, Henry 10y, Elizabeth 6y, Johanna 5y and Mary 3y; confirmed.	Worth
L 1831 Apr. 7	Henry BOTTING, wife Mary and children Sarah Susannah 3y and Harry 1y; confirmed.	Chiddingstone, Ken

REMOVAL ORDER TO BALCOMBE — Par 234/32/3/1

		From
1834 Dec. 9	John LASFORD, wife Mary and children William 5y and Frederick 2y. On examination J.L. said that, when a singleman, he lived as a yearly hired servant for about three years on twenty guineas per annum, with Rev. Henry SEARLE in Balcombe, and left there about twelve years [ago] and has done no act to gain a legal settlement since.	Lambeth, Sry

QUARTER SESSIONS REMOVAL ORDERS TO BALCOMBE

		From
M 1741 Jan.12	Thomas TESTER, wife Mary and children Thomas 4y, Mary 3y and Jenny 1m; respited.	Ferring
C 1741 Apr. 6	Thomas TESTER, wife Mary and children Thomas 4y, Mary 3y and Jenny 1m; confirmed as to Thomas senior, as he has a former wife, and discharged as to Mary and children Thomas, Mary and Jenny.	Ferring
C 1776 Apr.15	John WARTON and wife Ruth; confirmed.	Easebourne

M 1800 Apr.22	Barbara SANDERS, (wife of John SANDERS, a private in West Essex Regiment of Militia), and son Thomas aged 6 weeks; respited.	Horsham
H 1800 Jul.15	Barbara SANDERS, (wife of John SANDERS, a private in West Essex Regiment of Militia) and son Thomas aged 6 weeks; quashed.	Horsham

BOLNEY

Bolney: 3,557 acres from 50ft in Adur valley to 392 on N boundary. Clay and gravel on clay and sandstone. Common enclosed 1841.

Population: 1676 318; 1724 416; 1801 497; 1811 510; 1821 560; 1831 635.

BOLNEY SETTLEMENT EXAMINATIONS Par 252/32/4/1

1729 May 5 Benjamin STRINGER, husbandman, said that, in 1722, he was hired by James MORETON esq., deceased of Slaugham, to live with him as a yearly servant at thirty shillings, which term he served and received his year's wages and that he has not lived with any other person as a yearly servant nor has he acquired a legal settlement elsewhere. [Signature of B.S.]

1770 Jul.20 James PAINE, now residing in Bolney, cordwainer, late a mariner belonging to HMS Southampton, said that he believes he was born in Amberley and that, when he was 14 years of age, his parents bound him an apprentice to John SCRAGG of Ridgewick [Rudgwick], cordwainer, by indentures for the term of seven years, which term he served, and he has done no act whereby to gain a settlement in any other parish. [Mark of J.P.]

1778 Nov.26 James OCKENDEAN, now residing in Bolney, said that he was born in Hurstpierpoint where, he believes, his father, John OCKENDEAN, was legally settled. That, ten or twelve years agone, his father came and resided in Bolney under a certificate from Hurstpierpoint to Bolney for himself and this examinant and other part of his family and that he, this examinant, has done no act since his birth to gain a settlement. [Mark of J.O.]

1779 May 3 James PHILLARY, now residing in Bolney, labourer, said that he was born in Hurstpierpoint and that, in 1765, he removed with his father as part of his family to Bolney and there resided since, under a certificate granted by Hurstpierpoint to Bolney, and that last Lady Day, twelve months agone, he hired himself to Richard KNIGHT of Bolney, farmer, for one whole year and performed the entire year's service, and has done no act since to gain a settlement. [Mark of J.P.]

1787 Jan. 9 Henry HEASMAN, now residing in Bolney, labourer, said that he was born in Horsham but that his father, Barnard HEASMAN, was a settled inhabitant of Bolney. That, twelve years since, he hired himself to Thomas AGATE of Cowfold, farmer, for a year and, without quitting, hired and performed one or two more years service with him, and has done no act to gain a settlement in any other parish. [Signature of H.H.]

1790 Feb.15 John GIBBS, now residing in Bolney, said that he was born in Edburton where his father was legally settled and that, in 1743, he removed with his father and family to Keymer, when he was a year and a half old, into a tenement above ten pounds a year, where he resided with the rest of the family for about one year. That, 22 years agone, he went to reside in Ditchling, being then married, in a house rented by the Countess of Huntingdon, in which he lived for 3 years but paid no rent although he paid the poor rate, and has done no act to gain a settlement in any other parish. [Signature of J.G.]

1790 Feb.15 John OCKENDEN, now residing in Bolney, said that he was born in Bolney where he believes his father was legally settled. That, in March 1776, he hired himself to Thomas STEELE of Nuthurst, farmer, as a carter for one year, which year he served and received his full wages, and that he has done no act to gain a settlement in any other parish. [Signature of J.O.]

1790 Feb.15 Henry EDWARDS said that he was born in Cranley [Cranleigh], Surrey, where his father was legally settled. That, in November 1787, he paid the King's tax for his dwelling house in which he is now resident in Bolney and has continued to pay tax ever since, conceiving himself to be rated and obliged to pay the tax although it was outset by his landlord as part of his rent. [Signature of H.E.]

1790 Feb 15 Jasper STILL, now residing in Bolney, said that he was born in Bolney where his father was legally settled but that, when he was a child, he removed with his father to Slaugham and gained a settlement there. That, in 1783, he hired himself to William LAMB of Slaugham, farmer, as a carter for one year, which he served and received his full wages, and has done no act to gain a settlement in any other parish since. [Mark of J.S.]

1790 Feb.15 John WHITEING, now residing in Bolney, said that he was born in Bolney where, he believes, his father was legally settled and that, in March 1773, he hired himself to John KELSEY of Cuckfield, farmer, as an oxman for one year and received his full wages and has done no act to gain a settlement since. [Mark of J.W.]

1790 Feb.15 Abraham SANDERS, now residing in Bolney, said that he was born in Bolney where, he believes, his father was legally settled and that, in April 1771, he hired himself to William TURNER of Twineham, farmer, as servant in husbandry for one year, which he served and received full wages, and has done no act to gain a settlement in any other parish. [Mark of A.S.]

1790 Feb.15 John BATCHELOR said that he was born in Cowfold, where his father was legally settled, and that, in April 1769, he hired himself to Edward DOWLEN the elder of Cowfold, farmer, as a servant in husbandry for one year, which term he served and received full wages, and he has done no act to gain a settlement in any other parish. [Mark of J.B.]

1790 Feb.15 James FAIRALL, now residing in Bolney, said that he was born in Chailey but, he believes, his father was legally settled in Ditchling. That, in October 1768, he hired himself to Thomas DODD of Newtimber, bailiff to John

BULL, an infant, to serve him as his oxman for one year, which he served and received full wages, and has done no act to gain a settlement in any other parish. [Signature of J.F.]

1792 May 15 Mary ROADS, now residing in Bolney, said that she was born in Shipley where, she believes, her father, William ROADS, was legally settled and that, four years agone last May day, she hired herself to Stephen STOFFELD of Bolney, farmer, at wages of one shilling a week and served until the following Lady Day, when she hired herself again to Stephen Stofell (sic) by the week at £3 for a year's wages, then served a further year at three guineas and, in like manner, a further year expiring last Lady Day, and she has done no act to gain a settlement in any other parish. [Mark of M.R.]

1793 Jan. 3 Harry GLAZEBROOK, now residing in Shermanbury, said that he was born in Shermanbury, where his father was legally settled, and that he, this deponent, has not, since his birth, done any act to gain a settlement in any other parish. [Mark of H.G.]

1793 Aug.23 John PIERCE, a private in Sussex Militia now on actual service and serving as a substitute for Thomas ATTREE of Bolney, blacksmith, said that he was born in Bolney where his father, John PIERCE, was residing under a certificate from Slaugham. That, five years agone Michaelmas last, he hired himself to John WELCH of Slaugham, farmer, for a year at £3 and served the entire year and has done no act to gain a settlement in any other parish. That his late wife Elizabeth is dead and he has one child by her living named Mary, aged two months. [Mark of J.P.]

1794 May 20 Edward HARWOOD the younger, now residing in Bolney, said that he was born in Ashington where his father, Edward HARWOOD the elder, was and now is legally settled. That, in August 1781, he was put out to service with Richard DREWETT of Ashington, farmer, as parish boy and served him for 3 years and had no wages, the parish finding him in clothes. [Mark of E.H.]

1795 Oct.16 John GILLHAM, now residing in Bolney, said that he was born in Bolney, where his father was an inhabitant legally settled.. That, twelve years ago Ladyday last, he hired himself to Thomas AGATE of Cowfold, yeoman, for a year at wages of £3 and continued there for 2 years and received full wages, and has done no act since to gain a settlement. [Mark of J.G.]

1796 Feb. 3 Memorandum of John TAYLOR overseer of Bolney concerning Richard KING, labourer of Bolney, and Thomas DIVALL, labourer of Cuckfield, who were living together with Mr. WARREN, farmer of Cheem [Cheam] Surrey, 30 years ago. Richard King said that he lived with Mr. Warren as a servant for a year, excepting one week, and that Thomas Divall lived there before him and was still there when he came away and he always thought that Thomas Divall was a servant the same as he, as they both worked together in all sorts of husbandry work and he never heard him say he worked by the Great or by the day, neither did Thomas Divall find himself in any working tools except a flail, which was usual for servants to find themselves. That once, when they were to thresh out a wheat rick, their master did expect them to work long hours in the barn a threshing, and it was agreed that all they earned above 8s 0d a week each they should have to themselves, 2s 6d per quarter of wheat and 1s 0d per load for binding the straw, which amounted, for him, to about 2s 6d for every week. That Richard King did not see his master make any settlement with Thomas Divall or any money pass to him whilst they lived together with Mr Warren.

1796 Feb. 6 Michael GODSMARK, now residing in Bolney, said that he was born in Cuckfield where his father was legally settled and has done no act to gain a settlement elsewhere. [Mark of M.G.]

1796 Mar.16 Thomas GRAVELEY of Bolney, said that he was born in Slaugham where his father was legally settled and has done no act to gain a settlement elsewhere, and that he has a wife named Ann and two children namely John aged 2 years and Thomas 6 months. [Signature of T.G.]

1796 Apr. 1 Thomas ATTREE, now residing in Bolney, said that he believes he was born in Newick, where his father was residing under a certificate from Wivelsfield and that, since his birth, he has not done any act to gain a settlement in any parish or place. [Mark of T.A.]

1796 Oct.14 Daniel WELLS, now residing in Bolney, said that he believes he was born in Slaugham, where his father was legally settled and that, since his birth, he has done no act to gain a settlement in any parish or place. [Signature of D.W.]

1796 Oct.14 John SIMMONDS of Bolney said that he was born in Twineham where his father was legally settled, and that he has not gained a settlement in any parish whatever out of the parish of Twineham. [Signature of John Simons (sic)]

1800 Apr.18 Richard LONGLEY, now residing in Bolney, said that he was born in Cuckfield, where his parents were legally settled. That, at Lady Day four years ago, he hired himself to Mary STONE of Worth for a year at £8, which year he served and received his wages. That, afterwards, he hired himself to James BUNN, gentleman, of Cuckfield for a year at £8.8s 0d but agreed to go felling timber during the season and to return when it was over, which he did and served the remainder of the year, and received his wages. That, since that time, he has done no act to gain a settlement in any other parish. [Mark of R.L.]

1809 Nov.28 Henry STARLEY, now residing in Cuckfield, said that he was born in Cowfold but that his father, Thomas STARLEY, was legally settled in Bolney, and that he has not done any act to gain a settlement out of Bolney by hiring and services or otherwise. [Mark of H.S.]

BOLNEY SETTLEMENT CERTIFICATES. Par 252/32/1/1

		From
1717 Jul. 8	William BENNET and family.	Ifield
1717 Jul.16	William MOSE and wife.	Twineham
1718 Feb. 9	Thomas WALLER, wheelwright, wife and children.	Portslade
1719 Mar.30	Thomas BUCKMAN, wife and family.	Warnham
1728 Mar.17	Anthony WOOD and wife Elizabeth.	Wivelsfield
1731 Jan. 7	Richard RUSSELL, tailor, wife and family	Slaugham
1736 Apr.26	John SCUTT, husbandman, wife Elizabeth and family.	Cowfold
1736 Apr.26	Richard SCUTT, wife and family.	Henfield
1736 Jul. 8	John GOLDSMITH, wheelwright, wife Mary and sons John and William.	Henfield
1737 Oct. 2	Catharine COATES.	Cowfold
1738 Jan. 8	Thomas WEST and wife Dorcas.	Shipley
1738 Nov. 6	Thomas JARRETT, wife Jane and daughter Jane aged 6 weeks.	Maresfield
1739 Apr.28	Elizabeth MARTEN, widow.	Twineham
1739 Oct. 1	Henry GEAREN wife Sarah, children Henry, Tomas and Sarah, and William King his apprentice.	Clayton
1743 Feb.16	Giles WEEDING and wife Mary.	Ifield
1743 Mar. 5	William TIDY, wife Elizabeth and family.	Cowfold
1743 May 30	Thomas LUTMAN and wife Mary.	Shermanbury
1743 Dec.11	Philip MICHELL, shoemaker, and wife Hannah.	Uckfield
1747 Jan. 9	Richard NYE, wife Hannah and children James 14y, Jane 13y, Mary 7y, Sarah 3y and John 1y 6m	Cuckfield
1749 Mar.31	Richard GEARING, wife Ann and daughter Susannah.	Twineham
1750 Feb.19	Richard KNIGHT and wife Mary.	Twineham
1753 Jul. 2	Henry PIERCE and wife Sarah.	Slaugham
1755 Oct.25	John KING and wife Elizabeth.	Streat
1756 Jan.25	Charles SMITH and wife Mary.	Cuckfield
1756 Oct. 3	James THORP and wife Katherine.	West Grinstead
1760 Oct. 6	William BURCHELE, wife Ann and children William 4y, and Mary 2y.	Sullington
1761 Jan. 1	Thomas COOK, wife Ann and children Ann 4y, Elizabeth 2y and Thomas 3m.	Shermanbury
1761 Oct.20	William GIBSON, wife Elizabeth, and children William 12y and John 6y.	Slaugham
1762 Apr.16	William WICKHAM otherwise BLANK, wife Mary and daughter Elizabeth, infant.	Slaugham
1762 Nov. 6	John CHATFIELD, wife Mary and children Mary 9y, John 7y and Henry 4y.	Cuckfield
1762 Dec. 5	Thomas MILES and wife.	Cowfold
1762 Dec. 5	William CHATFIELD, wife Elizabeth and	Cowfold

	daughters.	
1763 Jan.28	John LEWRY and wife Jane.	Cuckfield
1763 Mar. 7	James VALLANCE and wife Sarah.	Hurstpierpoint
1763 Apr. 3	John NYE and wife Mary.	Cuckfield
1763 Apr.10	Thomas MORRIS, wife Ann and children John, Ann, Susannah and Sarah.	Cowfold
1763 Jul.23	William TURRLE, wife Elizabeth and daughter Mary.	Cowfold
1763 Jul.23	Edward PETERS, wife Mary and children Sarah, Henry, James, Samuel and Charles.	Cowfold
1764 Apr.10	Hannah MARTIN, wife of John MARTIN, clerk, and children John 4y, Mary 2y and Elizabeth 1y.	Reigate, Sry
1766 Mar.31	John PHILLARY, wife Mary and children James and Lydia 7y.	Hurstpierpoint
1766 May 17	William BURLEY, wife Susanna and children Mary, Susanna, William and Thomas	Cuckfield
1766 May 23	Richard COOK, wife Sarah and children Richard 1y 9m and William 2m.	Cuckfield
1766 May 23	James SMITH, wife Lucy and daughter Catherine 15y.	Cuckfield
1768 Oct.17	George STILL, wife Sarah and children Mary 10y and William 8y.	Slaugham
1768 Oct.17	William JUPP, wife Mary and daughter Mary 15m.	Slaugham
1768 Nov.23	Thomas UWINS, wife Mary and children Sarah 14y, Ann 11y and Thomas 4y.	Shermanbury
1769 Jan.14	Philip STONYER and wife Ann.	West Grinstead
1769 Feb. 5	Thomas RENFIELD and wife Piercy.	Pyecombe
1769 Feb.18	John HENLEY and wife Sarah.	Nuthurst
1770 May 19	Joseph JUPP, wife Mary and children Jenny 10y, and John 7y.	Cowfold
1770 Jul.18	Thomas GODMAN, wife Hannah and son Thomas 3y.	Brighton
1770 Nov.23	Sarah DEDMAN, singlewoman, and son John 1y.	Crawley
1771 Apr. 6	John FAULCONER, wife Mary and children Mary 3y, John 2y and Ann 1y.	Cuckfield
1771 Oct.19	James BIRCHFELL, wife Philadelphia and son James 10y.	Cuckfield
1774 Aug.20	Jenny RICHARDSON, singlewoman.	Cowfold
1774 Nov. 3	Edward PURSER, wife Dianah and children Ann 3y and Thomas 1y.	Cuckfield
1778 Apr. 6	John GREEN and wife Catherine	Cuckfield
1778 Aug.26	Joseph PAGE and wife Lydia.	Leigh, Sry
1782 Aug.31	Francis RICHARDSON, wife Susan and children John, Henry, Francis and William. Ack.	Cuckfield

LIST OF BOLNEY INHABITANTS POSSESSING CERTIFICATES OF SETTLEMENT 1763 Par 252/32/1/2
WITH ADDITIONS TO 1774.

[Covering dates 1717-1774 - Note numbers 3, 12, 15, 26, 28, 29, 34, 41, 48 and 56 do not appear under Bolney settlement certificates Par 252/32/1/1]

"A List of People who have certificates in Bolney, which was taken April 1763, and the List has been continued till May 1766, and is intended to be so as Certificates become necessary."

1.	Richard NYE, wife and children. "N.B. He has since gained a setlement in Bolney by virtue of having rented above £10 a year."	Cuckfield
2.	Philip MICHELL and wife. "N.B. They have left the Parish many years."	Uckfield
3.	Samuel REEVE and wife.	Beeding
4.	Anthony WOOD and wife." N.B. Dead or gone several years."	Wivelsfield
5.	James THORP and wife.	West Grinstead
6.	John KING and wife.	Streat
7.	Charles SMITH and wife.	Cuckfield
8.	Thomas WALLER and wife." N.B. They have left the Parish many years."	Portslade
9.	Giles WEEDING and wife." N.B. They have left the Parish many years."	Ifield
10.	Catherine COATES. "N.B. She has been dead many years."	Cowfold
11.	Thomas LUTMAN and wife.	Shermanbury
12.	William BERNARD and wife." N.B. He has since gained a legal settlement in Bolney by virtue of having rented above £10 a year."	Cowfold
13.	Richard KNIGHT and wife." N.B. They have left the Parish many years."	Twineham
14.	Henry GEAREN and wife." N.B. They have left the Parish many years"	Clayton
15.	Joseph TERRELL and wife." N.B. They have been gone or dead many years."	Cowfold
16.	John SCUTT and wife. "Settlement."	Cowfold
17.	Richard RUSSEL, wife and family. "N.B. They have left the Parish many years."	Slaugham
18.	William TIDY and wife.	Cowfold
19.	William MOSE and wife." N.B. Dead or gone many years."	Twineham
20.	Richard GEARING and wife." N.B. Gone some years."	Twineham
21.	Henry PIERCE and wife.	Slaugham
22.	Richard SCUTT and wife.	Henfield
23.	Elizabeth MARTIN, widow." N.B. Dead."	Twineham
24.	Thomas WEST and wife Dorcas. "N.B. Gone from the Parish"	Shipley

25.	John GOLDSMITH and wife." He has been dead some years and his widow gone."	Henfield
26.	William AKEHURST and wife "N.B. Gone many years."	Cowfold
27.	William BENNET and family.	Ifield
28.	John COALY and wife.	Wivelsfield
29.	William KING and wife.	Hurstpierpoint
30.	Thomas BUCKMAN and wife." N.B. Dead."	Warnham
31.	Thomas COOK and family.	Shermanbury
32.	William BURCHELL and family.	Sullington
33.	William WICKHAM otherwise BLANK, wife and family.	Slaugham
34.	Richard HAYLER and wife.	Beeding
35.	William GIBSON, wife and family.	Slaugham
36.	Thomas MILES and wife.	Cowfold
37.	John LEWRY and wife.	Cuckfield
38.	John CHATFIELD, wife and family.	Cuckfield
39.	William CHATFIELD wife and family.	Cowfold
40.	[? John NYE and wife - document torn]	Cuckfield
41.	Peter EMERY and family.	Twineham
42.	James VALLANCE and wife Sarah.	Hurstpierpoint
43.	Thomas MORRIS, wife and family.	Cowfold
44.	Hannah MARTIN wife of John Martin, clerk, with several children. "N.B. She is now the wife of Thomas GODMAN, see below."	Reigate, Sry
45.	Edward PETERS, wife and family.	Cowfold
46.	William TURRLE, wife and family.	Cowfold
47.	John PHILLARY, wife and family.	Hurstpierpoint
48.	John OCKENDEN, wife and family.	Hurstpierpoint
49.	James SMITH, wife and family.	Cuckfield
50.	William BURLEY, wife and family.	Cuckfield
51.	Richard COOK, wife and family.	Cuckfield
52.	William JUPP, wife and family.	Slaugham
53.	George STILL, wife and family.	Slaugham
54.	Thomas RENFIELD and wife Piercy.	Pyecombe
55.	Thomas and Hannah GODMAN and Thomas his son.	Brighton
56.	Elizabeth DEDMAN.	Crawley
57.	Thomas UWINS and wife Mary with several children.	Shermanbury
58.	Philip and Ann STONYER.	West Grinstead
59.	Joseph JUPP and wife Mary with their children.	Cowfold
60.	Sarah DEDMAN and son John.	Crawley
61.	James BIRCHFELL and wife Philadelphia and child.	Cuckfield
62.	Jenny RICHARDSON, singlewoman.	Cowfold
63.	Edward PURSER, wife and family.	Cuckfield
64.	John FAULCONER, wife and family.	Cuckfield
65.	John HENLEY and wife Sarah.	Nuthurst

REMOVAL ORDERS FROM BOLNEY Par 252/32/2/1

		To
1727 Jul.19	Thomas GODMAN and wife Mary.	Plumpton
1737 Nov. 3	Thomas JENNER, wife Elizabeth and daughter Elizabeth 15y.	Beeding
1739 Jan.11	James CHASEMERE, wife Sarah and daughter Sarah. Confirmation.	Twineham
1747 Jan.15	William SHIRLEY and wife Hannah. Confirmation.	Peper Harow, Sry
1756 Jan.15	Charles SMITH and wife Mary. Confirmation.	Cuckfield
1758 Mar.28	Penelope WILLETT.	Cowfold
1759 Mar.12	Richard HAYLOR and wife Ann.	Beeding
1760 Mar.22	Jane PARSONS, singlewoman.	Horsted Keynes
1761 Mar. 7	John BRIGGS, husbandman, and wife Hannah. [Delivered 7 March]	Dorking, Sry
1768 Mar.12	Elizabeth DEDMAN, widow and children Sarah, Elizabeth, Mary and Thomas. [Delivered 14 March]	Crawley
1794 Mar. 7	Cassandra BOORN, singlewoman.	Cuckfield
1795 Oct.16	Sarah TULLEY, singlewoman. [Delivered 20 Oct]	Mortlake, Sry
1798 Jan. 6	Watt HEASMAN and wife Mary. [Delivered 2 Feb]	Speldhurst, Ken
1802 Sep.25	Elizabeth HEASMAN, singlewoman.	Cuckfield
1811 Sep.19	Jane EDE, singlewoman, now with child.	Warnham
1812 Jan.17	Barbara COMBER, singlewoman. Confirmation.	Cuckfield
1812 Jan.17	Elizabeth SAYER, singlewoman. Confirmation.	Ditchling
1812 Apr.10	Edward VINE. Confirmation.	Lindfield
1812 Aug. 7	James KEMPE, wife Lydia and children Lucy 3y 6m, William 2y and Elizabeth 6m.	South Malling
1813 Feb.26	Frances WHITE, wife of John WHITE a private soldier in H.M. 35th Reg. of Foot, and children John 9y and Mary 6y.	Godstone, Sry
1813 Apr.30	Charlotte HEASMAN, singlewoman. Confirmation.	Worth
1813 Apr.30	John BENNETT [BURNETT]. Confirmation.	Steyning
1815 Jan.13	Henry STARLEY. Confirmation	Cowfold.
1815 Jul.14	John WHITEING the younger, wife Mary and children Mary 3y, John 2y and Sarah 4m. Confirmation.	Cuckfield
1816 Jan.12	Richard BOURNE, wife Martha and son John. Confirmation.	Balcombe
1816 Jan.12	Richard CHERRYMAN and wife Sarah. Confirmation.	Henfield
1816 Jan.12	John WEEKES and wife Elizabeth.	Rolvenden, Ken
1822 Apr.19	Nicholas PARSONS, wife Caroline and son Edward 3m. Confirmation.	Twineham

1822 Apr.19	John HOLLOWAY, wife Rachel and children Moses 19y, William 18y and Jane 16y. Confirmation.	Brighton

QUARTER SESSIONS REMOVAL ORDERS FROM BOLNEY

		To
L 1688 Jan.12	Robert LAGG; case between Bolney and Nuthurst referred to next sessions.	Nuthurst
L 1688 Apr.26	Robert LAGG; confirmed.	Nuthurst.
L 1689 Jul.18	Edward BARTLEE, wife and children; respited.	Preston
L 1689 Jul.18	John BENNETT, wife and family; respited.	Cowfold
L 1689 Jul.18	Jerrard POULTER; respited.	Worth
L 1689 Oct.10	John BENNETT; discharged.	Cowfold
C 1694 Apr.16	John DENMAN, son of Isaac DENMAN deceased and Anne his wife; discharged.	Shermanbury
L 1694 Oct. 4	[?] HOLFORD and family; confirmed.	Keymer
L 1706 Apr. 4	Robert STURT; discharged.	Cuckfield
L 1707 Apr.24	Anne WOOD; discharged.	Ardingly
L 1709 Jul.14	Thomas ROWLAND, wife and children Thomas, James, Nathaniel and two daughters; discharged as to Thomas Rowland the son and confirmed for Thomas Rowland the father, his wife and rest of children.	Cowfold
B 1711 Apr.12	John BATCHELLER, wife Sarah and children William and Sarah; confirmed.	Newick
L 1717 Jul.18	Benjamin NYE; discharged.	Horsted Keynes
L 1721 Jul.13	Sarah MITCHELL, widow; discharged.	Shermanbury
L 1739 Jan.11	Richard STEDMAN, wife Anne and children Anne, Richard and Thomas; confirmed.	Slaugham
L 1739 Jan.11	John CHASEMORE, wife Sarah and daughter Sarah; confirmed.	Twineham
L 1743 Apr.14	Philip MITCHELL and wife Anne; confirmed.	Uckfield
L 1746 Oct. 9	William SHIRLEY and wife Hannah; discharged.	Compton, Sry
L 1747 Jan.15	William SHIRLEY and wife Hannah; confirmed.	Peper Harow, Sry
L 1750 Apr.26	Ann MOORE, singlewoman; confirmed.	Lindfield
L 1754 Jan.17	Henry SANDERS and wife Sarah; discharged.	Slaugham
L 1755 Oct. 9	Charles SMITH and wife Mary; respited.	Cuckfield
L 1756 Jan.15	Charles SMITH and wife Mary; confirmed.	Cuckfield
L 1763 Apr.14	Elizabeth CHASMORE, widow; confirmed.	Horley, Sry
L 1766 Oct. 9	Philip KNOWLES, wife Ann and children Fanny 2y 6m and William 1y; confirmed.	Balcombe
L 1770 Jul.12	William STENING, wife Jane and child Elizabeth 5m; respited.	Cowfold
L 1770 Oct. 4	William STENNING, wife Jane and child Elizabeth 5m; respited.	Cowfold

L 1774 Jan.13	Sarah FRENCH, singlewoman; respited.	Cuckfield
L 1777 Jul.17	James PAYNE, wife Ann and children Susanna 6y and Walter 1y; quashed.	Rudgwick
L 1777 Oct. 9	James PAIN, wife Ann and children Susanna 7y and Walter 18m; confirmed.	Tillington
L 1785 Jan.13	John HEASMAN; respited.	Twineham
L 1787 Apr.19	Frances SMITH, wife of John Peter SMITH, and children Elizabeth 3y, Mary 18m and an infant 2m not yet baptised; quashed.	West Grinstead
L 1787 Apr.19	Richard MITCHELL, wife Catherine and children Catherine 6y, Stephen 5y, Sarah 3y and Elizabeth 6m; quashed.	Balcombe
L 1790 Jan.14	Henry OCKENDEN, wife Mary and his three children (by his former wife also Mary) Samuel 6y, Edward 4y and Henry 18m; confirmed.	Sevenoaks, Ken
L 1796 Apr. 8	Elizabeth SMITH 12y, Mary SMITH 11y and Henry SMITH 9y, the 3 children of Frances SMITH and husband Johannes Petrus SMITH, a foreigner (that is to say) a native of Switzerland; confirmed.	West Grinstead
L 1801 Jan.15	Mary WICKHAM, singlewoman; respited.	Twineham
L 1801 Apr.16	Mary WICKHAM, singlewoman; confirmed.	Twineham
L 1802 Oct. 8	Elizabeth HEASMAN, singlewoman; respited.	Cuckfield
L 1805 Jan.18	William MARCHANT, wife Mary and children John and Mary; confirmed.	Shermanbury
L 1805 Oct.11	Frances SMITH, wife of Johannes Petrus SMITH and children Thomas 10y and Stephen 7y; quashed as to Frances and confirmed as to Thomas and Stephen her children.	West Grinstead
L 1805 Oct.11	Elizabeth KING, singlewoman; confirmed.	Brighton
L 1805 Oct.11	Benjamin BOURNE and wife Lydia; confirmed.	Cuckfield
L 1806 Oct.10	William COMBER and wife Sarah; confirmed.	Nuthurst
L 1810 Jan.12	Bett HEASMAN, singlewoman; respited.	Cowfold
L 1810 May 4	Bett HEASMAN, singlewoman; quashed.	Cowfold
L 1811 Jan.18	James ETHERTON, wife Sarah and child John 2y; confirmed.	Rudgwick
L 1811 Jan.18	James ROWLAND, wife Sarah and child Henry 9m; confirmed.	Cuckfield
L 1811 Jan.18	Edward RIDLEY and wife Ann; confirmed.	Worth
L 1812 Jan.17	Elizabeth SAYER, singlewoman; confirmed.	Ditchling
L 1812 Jan.17	Barbara COMBER, singlewoman; confirmed.	Cuckfield
L 1812 Apr.10	William MITCHELL, wife Jane and child Sarah aged 13 weeks; confirmed.	Woodmancote
L 1812 Apr.10	Edward VINE; confirmed.	Lindfield
L 1813 Apr.30	Charlotte HEASMAN, singlewoman; confirmed.	Worth
L 1813 Apr.30	John BURNETT; confirmed.	Steyning

L 1815 Jan.13	Henry STARLEY; confirmed.	Cowfold
L 1815 Jul.14	John WHITEING, the younger, wife Mary and children Mary 3y, John 2y and Sarah 4m; confirmed.	Cuckfield
L 1816 Jan.12	Richard CHERRYMAN and wife Sarah; confirmed.	Henfield
L 1816 Jan.12	John WEEKES and wife Elizabeth; confirmed.	Rolvenden, Ken
L 1816 Jan.12	Richard BOURNE, wife Martha and son John; confirmed.	Balcombe
L 1818 Jan.16	John STONER and wife Jane; confirmed.	Clayton
L 1818 Jan.16	James LINDFIELD and wife Mary; confirmed.	Isfield
L 1818 Jul.17	John UWINS and children Elizabeth 14y and George 11y; confirmed.	Woodmancote
L 1819 Apr.23	James KNIGHT, wife Catherine and children Eliza 5y, Thomas 3y and Barbara 1y; confirmed.	Twineham
L 1820 Jan.14	Joseph SIMMONDS and wife Kitty; quashed.	Albourne
L 1820 Apr.14	Joseph SIMMONDS and wife Kitty; confirmed.	Woodmancote
L 1820 Apr.14	Mary ANSCOMB, singlewoman; respited.	Cowfold
L 1820 Jul.14	Mary ANSCOMB, singlewoman; confirmed.	Cowfold
L 1822 Apr.19	John HOLLOWAY and wife Rachel; children Moses 19y, William 18y and Jane 16y; confirmed.	Brighton
L 1822 Apr.19	Nicholas PARSONS, wife Caroline and son Edward 3m; confirmed.	Twineham
L 1824 Jan.16	Daniel PAINE and wife Ann; confirmed.	Twineham
L 1825 Jul.14	Ann PETERS otherwise HEASMAN, singlewoman; confirmed.	Brighton
L 1827 Apr.26	Rebecca MITCHELL, singlewoman, who is with child; confirmed.	Charlwood, Sry
L 1828 Jan.17	William MANSBRIDGE, wife Sarah and children James 9y, Thomas 7y, Henry 3y and William 5m; confirmed.	Cowfold
L 1831 Apr. 7	George EVANS; confirmed.	Woodmancote
L 1831 Apr. 7	Sarah FAIRHALL; confirmed.	Woodmancote
L 1832 Oct.18	Henry ORAM, wife Susannah and son John aged 6 weeks; confirmed.	Keymer
L 1833 Apr.11	John DENNETT, wife Mary and children Charles 10y, Emma 9y, Henry 5y, Charlotte 3y 6m, Arthur 2y and Alfred George aged 11 weeks; confirmed.	Hurstpierpoint
L 1834 Apr.11	William GATFORD, wife Rebecca and children John 5y, Sarah 2y and Lucy aged 13 weeks; quashed.	Twineham

REMOVAL ORDERS TO BOLNEY

Par 252/32/3/1

		From
1721 Jan.24	John PERCE and his wife Elizabeth. On examination J.P. said that he was last a yearly servant to John STONE, who lived then at Bolney.	Slaugham
1751 Dec. 7	William SCRACE, wife Mary and child aged 2 weeks.	Brighton
1793 Jan. 4	Mary GODMAN, singlewoman, was apprehended in Ringmer as a rogue and vagabond, wandering abroad and begging there. As she has said that her place of birth is Bolney she is to be conveyed to that parish. On 26 December 1792 she was examined and said that she was born in Bolney and had once lived as a servant with a tanner in the City of Chichester for a year but cannot now recollect his name or where he lived. That she has never gained a settlement but, for many years past, has travelled about the country and lived by making matches and begging. *Catalogued under Par 252/32/4/2*	House of Correction, Lewes.
1793 Aug. 5	Thomas EAGER, wife Ann and daughter Ann 14y.	Newdigate, Sry
1793 Aug.19	William SHIRLEY and wife Ann.	Cuckfield
1794 Jul.12	Elizabeth DAWES, widow of Edward DAWES.	Brighton
1822 Oct. 1	John STEERLY, wife Sarah and children James 5y, John 2y and Stephen 10m.	Chiltington
1831 Apr.21	Sarah PICKNELL, widow of Thomas PICKNELL.	Brighton
1831 Nov.11	William COOKE, wife Elizabeth and children Henry 2y 6m and Elizabeth 5m.	Rotherfield
1831 Dec. 6	Elizabeth KING, otherwise TIDY, singlewoman.	Hurstpierpoint
1832 Mar. 1	Elizabeth WILMORE. Unable to travel due to sickness, fit to do so by 22 March. Bolney to pay £2.1s 0d for her keep.	Brighton

QUARTER SESSIONS REMOVAL ORDERS TO BOLNEY

		From
S 1705 Oct. 1	Robert STURT; confirmed.	Horsham
A 1710 Jan. 9	Sarah SAVADGE, wife of John SAVADGE; discharged.	Horsham
L 1812 Jan.17	Mary PETERS, singlewoman; confirmed.	All Saints, Lewes
L 1813 Oct. 8	James BROWN, wife Martha and children Catherine 13y, Martha 11y, John 9y, Elizabeth 7y, James 5y and Thomas 2y; quashed.	Brighton
L 1826 Jul.13	Mary POTTER, singlewoman, confirmed.	Brighton

L 1828 Jan.17	Elizabeth NAILARD, widow, and daughter Jane 13y; respited.	Patcham
L 1828 Apr.17	Elizabeth NAILARD, widow, and daughter Jane 13y; confirmed.	Patcham
L 1833 Apr.11	Joseph FIEST; respited.	Brighton

BOLNEY BASTARDY BONDS Par 252/34/1/1

1744 Jul.12 John LOCK, of Worth, labourer, Thomas LOCK, of Ifield, husbandman, and John LOCK, of Crowhurst, Surrey, labourer, bound to the parish officers of Bolney in £100 in respect of Sarah PARSONS, singlewoman, who is now big with child, the father being John Lock of Worth. [Marks of J.L., T.L. and J.L.]

1752 Feb.21 John MURRELL, the younger, of Bolney, yeoman, and John MURRELL, the elder, of Bolney, yeoman, bound to the parish officers of Bolney in £100 in respect of Ann STONER of Bolney, singlewoman, who is big with child. [Signatures of J.M. the younger and J.M. the elder.]

1755 Oct. 7 Richard STAPLEY of Hickstead, Twineham, gent., bound to the parish officers of Bolney in £100 in respect of Mary BROWN, singlewoman, who has declared that she was delivered of a male bastard child on 9 August last and that James WOOD, son of John WOOD of Twineham, gent., is the father. John Wood junior to pay 2s 0d a week maintenance. [Signature of R.S.]

1761 Jul.23 Thomas CREASEY, the younger of East Grinstead, husbandman, and John COMBRIDGE of Hartfield, yeoman, are bound to the parish officers of Bolney in £100 in respect of Sarah BROWNE, widow, who was lately delivered of a female bastard child in Bolney, baptised Susannah Creasey, to which child Thomas Creasey the younger stands charged to be the reputed father. [Signatures of T.C. and J.C.]

1762 Mar.19 Richard VINCENT of Bolney, yeoman, bound to the parish officers of Bolney in £100 in respect of Mary BARDEN, singlewoman, who was lately delivered of a female bastard child, baptised Mary BARDEN, of which child Richard Vincent is the reputed father. [Signature of R.V.]

1783 May 17 The parish officers of West Grinstead are bound to the parish officers of Bolney in £30. As Mary WOOLLVEN of West Grinstead, now enscient [enceinte] with child has charged James PETERS late of Bolney, husbandman, with having gotten her with child, the parish officers of West Grinstead have agreed that, in consideration of £15 paid by the parish officers of Bolney, they will provide for and maintain the child and keep indemnified the said James Peters from all expenses for the birth and maintenance and that Mary Woolven (sic) shall, after she shall have been brought to bed of the child, be examined as to the father of the child.

1798 Oct.27 Agreement between William DUDENEY, timber hewer of Twineham the one part and the parish officers of Bolney on the other part. W.D. paid John TAYLOR, overseer of the said parish, £10 in consequence of getting Catherine MITCHELL with child in Bolney, which child was likely to be born a bastard; the said £10 to remain in the parish officers hands, paying W.D. interest of five per cent until the child be brought up, so that it is not chargeable to the parish.
Catalogued under Par 252/12/1 f42v

1802 Aug. 7 John ANSCOMB of Bolney, yeoman, bound to the parish officers of Bolney in £100 in respect of Mary POTTER of Bolney, singlewoman, who was lately delivered of a female bastard child and has declared that John Anscomb is the father, which he acknowledges and agrees to indemnify Bolney parish for 20 years from the birth of the child. [Mark of J.A.]

BOLNEY BASTARDY ORDERS Par 252/34/2/1

1747 Jan.16 Katherine MILLS, singlewoman, has declared that Henry GEARING of Bolney, tailor, is the father of a female bastard child lately born to her in Bolney. H.G. to pay £2.15s 0d for expenses at the birth and 1s 0d a week maintenance; the mother to pay 6d a week.

1793 Aug.19 Jane HEASMAN, singlewoman, has declared that Joseph JOHNSON of Crawley, chaise driver, is the father of a female bastard child born to her on 9 September last, at the house of Thomas NYE of Bolney. J.J. to pay £6.10s 0d towards the cost of lying-in and 2s 0d a week maintenance; the mother to pay 1s 0d a week.

1799 Jun. 1 Catherine MITCHELL, singlewoman, has declared that William DEWDNEY late of Twineham, timber hewer, is the father of a female bastard child born to her on 29 March last at the house of Michael GODSMARK in Bolney. W.D. to pay £2.10s 0d costs of lying-in and 2s 0d a week; the mother to pay 6d a week.

1823 Apr.11 Martha SHIRLEY of Bolney, singlewoman, has declared that Daniel OREHAM of Slaugham, labourer, is the father of a female bastard child born to her on 7 March last in Bolney. D.O. to pay £3 (£2.8s 0d expenses of lying in and 12s 0d cost of filiation order), and 2s 0d a week; the mother to pay 1s 0d a week.

1826 Jan.20 Mary GODSMARK of Bolney, singlewoman, has declared that John PARSONS of Bolney, wheelwright, is the father of a female bastard child born to her on 5 December last, at the house of William GODSMARK. J.P. to pay £2 expenses and 2s 6d a week; the mother to pay 6d a week.

1826 Apr.28 Ann KING, singlewoman, has declared that Thomas PENFOLD of Hurstpierpoint, labourer, is the father of a female bastard child born to her on 25 March, at her father's house in Bolney. T.P. to pay £2.7s 6d expenses at birth, £1.2s 0d cost of apprehending him and 2s 6d a week; the mother to pay 6d a week.

BOLNEY WARRANTS Par 252/29/1

1757 Oct.28 Bond for appearance of the reputed father of a bastard child. The parish officers of Hurstpierpoint are bound to the parish officers of Bolney in the sum of £40. As Jenny PARSONS of Bolney, spinster, has declared that she is with child and that Thomas HEASLEGROVE of Keymer, cordwainer, is the father, a warrant has been granted for apprehending T.H. The officers of Hurstpierpoint agree to deliver T.H. to Bolney when demanded, and to pay all costs.
Catalogued under Par 252/34/1/1

1821 Jun.11 Caroline INGS of Bolney, singlewoman, has declared that she is with child and that Nicholas PARSONS of Bolney, servant, is the father; and he is to be apprehended.

1821 Jun.29 Mary SCUTT of Bolney, singlewoman, has declared that she is with child and that Allen ANSCOMBE of Bolney, servant, is the father; and he is to be apprehended.

1826 Jun. 9 Louisa BURTENSHAW, singlewoman, has declared that she was, on 16 September last, delivered of a male bastard child, at the workhouse in Bolney, and that Edmund HARWOOD late of Pulborough, servant, is the father. L.B. to appear before the Justices at Cuckfield on 23 June, and notice is to be given to E.H. that he may also attend.
Catalogued under Par 252/34/3/1

1826 Jul.21 Mary POTTER of Bolney, singlewoman, has declared that she was delivered of a male bastard child on 22 May last at the house of John PARSONS and that Thomas POCOCK of Brighton, builder, is the father. M.P. to appear at the house of Faulkener BEST of Cuckfield, called the Talbot, on 4 August next, and notice is to be given to T.P. that he may also attend.
Catalogued under Par 252/34/3/1

BOLNEY APPRENTICESHIP AGREEMENTS Par 252/33/1/1

1676 Apr. 1 Mary NYE apprenticed to Humphrey KILLINGBANK of Bolney until the age of 21 years. [Signature of Humphrey Killingbeck (sic)]

1700 Jul. 2 Thomas PERRY apprenticed to William LINTOT junior of Bolney, until the age of 24 years; husbandry. [Signature of William Lintott (sic)].

1707 Apr.18 Susanna DAVEY apprenticed to John TILLEY until the age of 21 years; housewifery.

1728 Apr. 22 James TERRY apprenticed to Michael HARMES until the age of 21 years during which time M.H. shall not be obliged to take any other apprentice. Consideration 40s.
Catalogued under Par 252/12/1 f11v.

1737 Jul.13 William KING, aged 14 years, son of Thomas KING of Bolney, labourer, apprenticed to Henry GEARING of Clayton, tailor, for seven years from 13 April 1736; trade of tailor. Consideration; £6. [Endorsed: 6 Aug.1737 Duty paid = 3s 0d. Signature of Henry Gearen (sic)]

1800 Nov.14 Thomas MITCHELL, aged 15 years, apprenticed to Richard WOOD of Bolney, cordwainer, until the age of 21 years; trade of cordwainer. [Signature of R.W.]

CLAYTON

Clayton: 2459 acres, long, narrow parish from South Downs 700ft to N end of present day Burgess Hill. Loam and sand on clay and sand. Mainly arable. Buttinghill Hundred Courts held behind Ham Farm; Roman settlement near Stone Pound. Church contains 13/14th century wall paintings.

Population: 1676 162; 1724 (with Keymer) 237; 1801 337; 1811 425; 1821 453; 1831 489.

QUARTER SESSIONS REMOVAL ORDERS FROM CLAYTON

		To
L 1684 Apr.10	Abraham SAYERS, wife and children have lately come from Streat to Clayton, and got into a house there without the consent of the owner. They are to remain there until next sessions when an order is to be made returning them to Streat.	Streat
L 1718 Jan.16	Richard GREVATT, wife Hannah and daughter; confirmed.	Patcham
L 1737 Jul.14	Edward PARKER; confirmed.	Keymer
L 1741 Jan.15	George MORLEY and wife Elizabeth; confirmed.	Cuckfield
L 1741 Jan.15	Elizabeth SHEPPARD, singlewoman; respited.	Cowfold
L 1741 Apr. 9	Elizabeth SHEPPARD, singlewoman; confirmed.	Cowfold
L 1742 Jan.14	Edward HOLLINGDALE, wife Mary and children Mary and Edward; confirmed.	Ditchling
L 1747 Jul.16	Sampson BAGNALL and wife Susanna; confirmed.	St. Andrew, Holborn, Mdx
L 1750 Oct. 4	William IFOLD, wife Elizabeth and son William; confirmed.	Hurstpierpoint
L 1751 Apr.18	Thomas TOMSETT, wife Jane and daughter Sarah 2y; confirmed.	Cuckfield
L 1753 May 3	Sarah SMITH, singlewoman; confirmed.	Cuckfield
L 1762 Jul.15	Mary HASELGROVE, singlewoman; respited.	Ditchling
L 1762 Oct. 7	Mary HASELGROVE, singlewoman; quashed.	Ditchling
L 1763 Apr.14	Martha FURLONGER, singlewoman; confirmed.	Burpham
L 1770 Jan.11	Henry PETER, wife Elizabeth and children Mary 7y, Henry 5y, Thomas 4y, Elizabeth 3y, Ann 1y and William 3m; confirmed.	Hurstpierpoint
L 1773 Oct. 7	Mary REEVES, singlewoman; confirmed.	Preston
L 1801 Apr.16	Edmund PRONGER, wife Sarah and children Susannah 2y and Peter 3m; respited.	Twineham
L 1801 Jul.16	Edmund PRONGER, wife Sarah and children Susannah 2y and Peter 3m; quashed.	Twineham
L 1802 Jan.14	Robert BIGNALL and wife Ann; quashed.	Ovingdean
L 1805 Jul.19	Henry ORAM, wife Lydia and children Henry 2y 6m and Lucy 10m; confirmed.	Hurstpierpoint

L 1808 Apr.29	Elizabeth ACKNEY, (wife of William ACKNEY, a private in 38th Regiment of Foot); confirmed.	Hurstpierpoint
L 1809 Apr.14	Joseph ELLIS and wife Ann; quashed.	Rye
L 1809 Jul.14	Joseph ELLIS and wife Ann; confirmed.	Barking, Ess
L 1812 Jan.17	Stephen ORAM, wife Ann and children Sarah 3y and Henry 2y; quashed.	Hurstpierpoint
L 1812 Jan.17	Henry DURTNALL, wife Sarah and son Henry aged 5 weeks; respited.	Keymer
L 1812 Apr.10	Henry DURTNALL, wife Sarah and son Henry aged 5 weeks; confirmed.	Keymer

QUARTER SESSIONS REMOVAL ORDERS TO CLAYTON

		From
L 1676 Jan.13	Anne CHANDLER. On appeal by Clayton, concerning an order for settling A.C. in Clayton, that order to be vacated and made void; Clayton discharged from providing for her.	Not given
L 1697 Oct. 7	Ann LEGATE, widow, and child; discharged as, on appeal, they are to be returned to Streat.	Streat
P 1723 Oct. 8	William BERRY and wife Ann; discharged.	Steyning
L 1724 Jul.16	Elizabeth SCRIVENS; discharged.	Fletching
M 1754 Jan.14	Richard DIVALL, wife Mary and children John 13y, Thomas 7y, George 3y and an unbaptised infant 1m; discharged.	Steyning
L 1765 Jan.17	John REEVES; quashed.	Maresfield
L 1775 Jul.13	Rebecca ALLFREY, singlewoman; confirmed.	Pyecombe
L 1795 Apr.17	Elizabeth ARNALL, singlewoman; confirmed.	Brighton
L 1805 Jan.18	Charity FULLER, wife of John FULLER, and children Sarah 4y and John 2y; respited.	Brighton
L 1805 Jul.19	Charity FULLER, wife of John FULLER, and children Sarah 4y and John 2y; quashed.	Brighton
L 1808 Jul.15	Jane GEERING and children Mary 5y, Sarah 2y and Ann aged 5 weeks; respited.	Brighton
L 1808 Oct. 7	Jane GEERING and children Mary 5y, Sarah 2y, and Ann 5 weeks; confirmed.	Brighton
L 1818 Oct.23	William MILES, wife Barbara and children Barbara 18y, William 15y and Maria 13y; confirmed.	St. Michael, Lewes
P 1825 Apr.12	Mary WELLER, singlewoman; respited.	Broadwater

COWFOLD

Cowfold: 4,501 acres in Weald 8 1/2 miles SSE of Horsham. Gently undulating from 300ft in NE to 25ft in S; Weald clay overlies Upper Tunbridge Wells Sand, with 2 patches of gravel and 5 narrow E-W bands of Horsham Stone; quarried in the past; also brickfields and brickworks. Cowfold stream flows S to river Adur. Woodland pasture in scattered 13th and 14th settlements from manors to S; hunting; woodland in NE. Church separated from roads by houses built on roadside waste encroachments. St Hugh's monastery (1873) at Parkminster S of village. Cricket was being played in 1721 .

Population: 1676 450 (probably one of the parishes whose Compton returns were grossly inaccurate); 1724 284; 1801 601; 1811 614; 1821 822; 1831 809.

COWFOLD SETTLEMENT EXAMINATIONS Par 59/32/4

1723 May 31 William JESTED, carpenter, said that he was born in Alborn [Albourne], where he lived until the age of 13 years and then went to service with William BALCOMBE of Woodmancote, with whom he lived for ten years as a yearly servant viz: six and a half years in Woodmancote and three and a half years in Alborn, and received, for his last year's service, £6. That, afterwards, he lived with John NEWNHAM of Wiston, from 11 days after Michaelmas to the following Michaelmas, but, as he was not well in health, he was forced to quit his service for a fortnight and allowed his master 5s 0d for his loss of time. That he then lived in Alborn for 4 years but not as a yearly servant, then went to live in Cowfold, where he has lived till this time, and has married and has 3 children. That, since quitting the service of William Balcombe, he has not gained a settlement elsewhere. [Signature W.J.]

1764 Nov. 21. Thomas ANDREWS said that he was born in Cowfold, in a barn belonging to a farm called East Ridge, and that his father, Robert ANDREWS, and his mother, Frances ANDREWS, were, at that time, vagrants travelling about the country and had not any legal settlement in any place but, as his father died before this examinant was 5 years old, he can remember very little concerning him. That, 23 years ago, his mother received, from the overseers of Cowfold, 30s a year for his maintenance for two years, and that then they refused to pay her any more money, whereupon his mother took him to Cowfold and left him at the workhouse there for the space of half an hour but, he being dissatisfied, his mother came and took him away again. He further said that, in February 1758, he enlisted in the Chatham division of H.M. Marines and continued in that service till June 1763, when he was discharged, and he has not gained a legal settlement since his birth in Cowfold. [Mark of T.A.]

1767 Dec. 12 Mary LANGFORD, widow of John LANGFORD late of West Dean, said that she was legally married to John Langford, and that he died on or about 3 October 1764 at West Dean, and that she does not know in which parish he was legally settled but has heard him say that he was born in Cowfold.
[Mark of M.L.]

1774 Dec. 30 William WHITE, now residing in Cowfold, cooper, said that he was born in Bolney where, he believes, his father was a parishioner and that, in February 1763, he was put out apprentice by the parish officers of Bolney for seven years, by indenture, to Henry and Thomas DOWNER of Horsham, hoopmakers, which term he served but that, one and a quarter years of this time near the middle of the term, he served, by appointment of his master, with Thomas BENNETT of Chailey, cooper. That he believes Henry and Thomas Downer resided in Horsham with a certificate from Henley-upon-Thames [Oxfordshire] to Horsham and that his apprenticeship was never assented to or signed by any magistrate, and he has not done, since his birth, any act to gain a settlement in any place save as aforesaid. [Mark of W.W.]

1775 Apr. 28 James SHAW, now residing in Cowfold, labourer, said that he was born in Cowfold where, he believes, his father was a settled parishioner and that, last Michaelmas two years agone, he hired himself to Richard WARDS of West Grinstead, farmer, for one year, which term he served and he has not done any act to gain a settlement in any other parish. [Mark of J.S.]

1775 Apr. 28 Richard PENFOLD said that he was born in West Grinstead where, he believes, his father was a settled parishioner and that, last Lady Day six years agone, he hired himself to William GRATWICK of West Grinstead, farmer, for one year and performed the whole year's service, and has not since done any act to gain a settlement in any other parish. [Mark of R.P.]

1775 Oct. 18 James BRIGGS said that he was born in Slinfold, where he lived and in several other places till 1768, when he hired himself to Joseph STANDEN of Sullington, yeoman, for one year, from Michaelmas to Michaelmas, for £5 wages, which year he served, and that he has not done any act whereby to gain a settlement in any other parish. [Mark of J.B.]

1778 Feb. 21 Richard TERRELL said that he took a lease from his father of a house, mill pond and premises in Cowfold, from Ladyday last for 11 years, and that, soon afterwards, he entered on the said premises in which he now resides, and that he is to give more than £10 a year for the same. [Signature of R.T.]

1779 Oct. 18 William TULETT, now residing in Cowfold, labourer, said that he was born in Nuthurst where, he believes, his father, William TULETT, was a legally settled inhabitant and that, six years agone last Michaelmas, he hired himself to John LEE of Cowfold, farmer, for a year, which term he served, and that he has done no act to gain a settlement in any other parish. [Mark of W.T.]

1780 Feb. 10 James SMITH of Cowfold, labourer, said that, 13 years ago, he hired himself to John ELLIS of Washington, farmer, for one year from the Michaelmas day following, which term he served, since which he has done no act to gain a settlement in any other parish. [Signature of J.S.]

1780 Nov. 13 John CHATE, now residing in Cowfold, labourer, said that, seven years agone last Michaelmas, he hired himself to Richard PIERCE of Shermanbury, farmer, for one year, which term he served and has not done any act to gain a settlement in any other parish. [Signature of J.C.]

1783 Apr. 5 John VINALL, now residing in Cowfold, bricklayer, said that his parents are legally settled in Cowfold and that he has not gained a settlement in any other parish. [Signature of J.V.]

1783 May 10 John BATEUP, now residing in Cowfold, timber hewer, said that he was born in Cowfold where, he believes, his father, Thomas BATEUP, is a legally settled inhabitant and has been so for upwards of 20 years and before he, this examinant, left his father's family and went out to service. That, 16 or 17 years agone last Ladyday, he hired himself to Edmund COBBY of West Grinstead, farmer, for a year, which term he served and then, for two more successive years, made a like hiring to this master, and he has done no act to gain a settlement in any other parish. [Signature of John Baytup (sic)]

1783 May 29 Joseph HUMPHREY, now residing in West Grinstead, labourer, said that he was born in Slinfold, an illegitimate child of Elizabeth HUMPHREY, and that, on Lady Day 1776, he hired himself to John READS of Horsham, farmer, for one year, which term he served, since which time he has done no act to gain a settlement in any other parish. [Mark of J.H.]

1783 Oct. 31 William RICHARDSON, now residing in Cowfold, labourer, said that he was born in Shermanbury but that his father, Henry RICHARDSON, was then and now is a legally settled inhabitant of Cowfold. That, six years agone last Lady Day, he hired himself to John STANFORD of Ivorys, West Grinstead, farmer, for a year, which term he served, since which he has done no act to gain a settlement in any other parish. [Signature of W.R.]

1783 Oct. 31 Richard STANDING, now residing in Cowfold, labourer, said that he was born in Bolney but that his father, John STANDING, was then and now is a legally settled inhabitant of Slaugham. That, two years agone last Ladyday, he hired himself to Richard WARD of Westlands, West Grinstead, gentleman, for a year, which term he served, since which he has done no act to gain a settlement in any other parish. [Signature of Richard Standen (sic)]

1783 Nov. 4 John BANFIELD, now residing in Woodmancote, cordwainer, said that he was born in Albourne where, at the time of his birth, he believes his father, George BANFIELD, was a legally settled inhabitant. That, eight years agone last Ladyday, he hired himself to Thomas HUGHES of Cowfold, farmer, for a year, which term he served, since which he has done no act to gain a settlement in any other parish. [Signature of J.B.]

1785 Aug. 15 James HEDGCOCK, now residing in Cowfold, said that he was lately a mariner in H.M. service, on board the Dragon Guardship in Portsmouth harbour, from whence he was discharged about two years agone last spring, and is now a traveller about the country seeking for employment. That he was born in St. Mary's, Dover, Kent, where, he believes, his father, William HEDGCOCK, was a legally settled inhabitant, and that he has never done anything to gain a settlement in any other parish. That, on 4 July last, he was married at Haslemere, Surrey, to Mary FROGLEY, then of Haslemere, and that she is now resident with him in Cowfold with Elizabeth their daughter, an infant about a fortnight old last Friday. [Mark of J.H.]

1787 Oct. 3 Thomas FISHER, now residing in Cowfold, labourer, said that he was born in Dorking, Surrey, where, he believes, his father, Thomas FISHER, was a legally settled inhabitant. That, after living in various services and in different places, about three years agone last Michaelmas, he hired himself to John CHESMAN of Dorking, brandy merchant, for a year, which term he served, since which he has done no act to gain a settlement in any other parish. [Signature of T.F.]

1790 Jun. 5 Peter NEWNHAM, now residing in Cowfold, said that he was born in West Grinstead, where his parents were legally settled and that, when he was ten years of age, he was put out to George BURGESS of West Grinstead, farmer, by the parish officers of Cowfold but not by indentures, for two and a half years and then, Mr. Burgess removing to Nuthurst he, this examinant, went with him and remained one and a half years but, since then, has never done any act to gain a settlement in any other place. That he is married and his wife's name is Jane. [Mark of P.N.]

1790 Sep. 23 Thomas PIERCE, now residing in Cowfold, blacksmith, said that he was born in Lindfield where, he believes, his father was a legally settled inhabitant. That, in July 1779, he was bound an apprentice by legal indenture to Thomas LEOPARD of Cuckfield, blacksmith, then a legally settled inhabitant of Cuckfield, for the term of seven years, which he duly served. That he is married to Mary, late Mary EDE. [Signature of T.P.]

1791 Feb. 24 Benjamin TERRY, now residing in Cowfold, said that he was born in Woodmancote where, he believes, his parents were legally settled. That he has done no act to gain a settlement and that he is married and his wife's name is Elizabeth. [Mark of B.T.]

1792 Jan. 7 Thomas STAYLEY of Cowfold said that, just before Lady Day fifteen or sixteen years ago, he hired himself to Richard KNIGHT of Bolney, farmer, for a year at wages of £5.10s 0d, which term he served, since which he has done no act to gain a settlement elsewhere. That he is married and his wife's name is Martha and they have four children: John 7 years, Elizabeth 5 years, James 3 years and Eleanor 6 months. [Mark of T.S.]

1792 Feb. 14 John HOLLINGHAM, now residing in Cowfold, tailor, said that he was born in Lancing where, he believes, his father, John HOLLINGHAM, was a legally settled inhabitant and that, since his birth, he has done no act to gain a legal settlement in any other parish. [Signature of J.H.]

1793 Jan. 2 John STANFORD the younger, of Cowfold,labourer, said that he was born in Cowfold where his father, JOHN STANFORD the elder, resided under a certificate from Nuthurst. That, 17 years ago, he hired himself to Richard MILLS of Nuthurst, farmer, for a year, which term he served and then served another year with the same master. [Mark of J.S.the younger]

1793 Oct. 14 Elizabeth MATTHEW, singlewoman, now residing in Cowfold, said that she was born in Cowfold where her father, Thomas MATTHEW, was and is a settled inhabitant and that, since her birth, she has done no act to gain a settlement in any other parish. [Mark of E.M.]

1793 Nov. 25 Henry LINDFIELD, now residing in Cowfold, labourer, said that he was born in Slaugham where his father, Henry LINDFIELD, was and now is a legally settled inhabitant. That he has done no act to gain a settlement in any other parish, and is married to his present wife Ann and has no children. [Signature of H.L.]

1793 Nov. 25 William MITCHELL, now residing in Cowfold, labourer, said that he was born in West Grinstead where his father, John MITCHELL, was and now is legally settled. That he has done no act to gain a legal settlement in any other parish, and is married to his present wife Sarah and has 3 children born in wedlock. [Mark of W.M.]

1793 Nov. 25 William COMBER, now residing in Cowfold, labourer, said that he was born in Nuthurst where his father, Thomas COMBER, was and now is a legally settled inhabitant. That he has done no act to gain a settlement in any other parish, and is married to his present wife, Ann, and has no children. [Mark of W.C.]

1794 May 9 Thomas HANSHET now residing in Cowfold, said that he was born in Birmingham, Warwickshire, and that his father, George HANSHET, was legally settled in St. Martins in the Fields, Westminster, Middlesex. That, in 1787, he put himself apprentice to John TURLEY of St. Giles in the Fields, hairdresser, for the term of 5 years, which term he served, and that he is now a private in the East Middlesex Militia. [Mark of T.H.] [Endorsed: Married Sarah Mathews]

1794 Oct. 18 James WHITING, now residing in Cowfold, labourer, said that he was born in Henfield where, he believes, his parents were legally settled. That he has never done any act to gain a settlement in any other parish and that he is married and his wife's name is Charlotte. [Signature of J.W.]

1796 Feb. 6 Richard WALES, now residing in Cowfold, said that he was born in Ifield and that, 10 years agone, he hired himself to Thomas MITCHELL of Cowfold, farmer, for a year at nine guineas wages, which term he served, since which he has done no act to gain a settlement in any other parish. That he is married and his wife's name is Lydia by whom he has one child named William, aged 3 years. [Mark of R.W.]

1799 Dec. 4 William BOUND of Shermanbury, servant, said that he was born in Henfield where his parents were legally settled, and he has never done any act to gain a settlement in any other parish. [Mark of W.B.]

1799 Dec. 28 James ATTREE now living in Cobham, Surrey, labourer, said that, 21 years ago, he hired himself for a year to Thomas MARTIN of Cowfold, farmer, at wages of £3 or 3 guineas, which term he served and that he has done no act to gain a settlement since. That he has a wife named Elizabeth and four children namely:- Hannah 8 years, James 5 years, William 3 years and John 2 years. [Mark of J.A.]

1801 Mar. 7 John SAYERS, now residing in Slaugham, labourer, said that he was born in Cuckfield where his parents were legally settled. That, 20 or 21 years ago last Ladyday, he hired himself to Robert UWINS of Cowfold, farmer, for a year at wages of 9 guineas, which year he served. That, for 2 years, he lived in different places by half yearly hirings, and then hired himself to William HEAVER of Slaugham, miller, for half a year at wages of 5 guineas, which time he served, then hired again for half a year at £4, after which he lived with William Heaver for two and a half years more without making any fresh agreement. That he is married and his wife's name is Jane by whom he has one child born in wedlock namely Nanny, aged 13 years. [Signature of John Sayears (sic)]

1801 May 19 John ELSEY, now residing in Cowfold, labourer, said that he was born in Ardingly where his parents were legally settled, as he believes. That he has never done any act to gain a settlement elsewhere, and that he is married and his wife's name is Elizabeth. [Mark of J.E.]

1801 Jul. 4 William STRINGER, now residing in Cowfold, wheelwright, said that he was born in Ashington but that his parents then were and now are legally settled in Steyning. That, when he was fourteen or fifteen years of age, he went to live with his uncle, William STRINGER of Adversane, Billingshurst, to learn the business of a wheelwright, without any binding agreement. That he stayed with his uncle for two years, when they disagreed and parted, and his uncle charged this examinant's father £20 for the time he had been there, since which he has never done any act to gain a settlement in any other parish. That he is married and his wife's name is Sarah. [Signature of W.S.]

1801 Dec. 5 Francis MASON, now residing in Cowfold, labourer, said that, nine years ago last July, he was removed by an order from Wiston to Abinger, Surrey, since which he has done no act to gain a settlement in any other parish. That he is married and his wife's name is Sarah by whom he has two children born in wedlock, Ann 7 years and William 5 years. [Signature of F.M.]

1803 Nov. 5 Philip STONER, of Cowfold, labourer, said that he was born in Shermanbury but his parents were then and now are legally settled in Nuthurst, since which he has never done any act to gain a settlement in any other parish. That he is married and his wife's name is Elizabeth, by whom he has one child born in wedlock, namely: John aged 10 weeks. [Mark of P.S.]

1804 Dec. 26 Mary WOOLVEN, wife of James WOOLVEN of Cowfold, said that, 20 years ago, she was married to James Woolven, who belonged to West Grinstead and that, soon after their marriage, they removed to West Grinstead as the place of their settlement, and that her husband left her 18 years ago and, to the best of her knowledge, he has never done any act to gain a settlement since. That she has frequently been relieved by the parish officers of West Grinstead, as their parishioner, and has also been relieved by the officers of Cowfold. [Mark of M.W.]

1805 Jan. 11 John Richardson STANDING, now residing in Henfield, labourer, said that he was born in Henfield, where his parents were legally settled, as he believes. That he has not done any act to gain a settlement in any other parish, and that he is married and his wife's name is Mary Ann. [Mark of J.R.S.]

1805 Sep. 16 John JOHNSON, now residing in Cowfold, labourer, said that he was born in Wivelsfield where his parents were, and now are, legally settled. That he has never done any act to gain a settlement elsewhere and is married and his wife's name is Mary. [Signature of J.J.]

1807 Sep. 5 William LAUNDERS, now residing in Twineham, labourer, said that he was born in Albourne but that his parents then were and now are legally settled in Hurstpierpoint. That, 3 years ago last Michaelmas day, he was bound apprentice by indenture regularly executed, for 3 years, to Joseph BAKER of Albourne, wheelwright, but served him only one year when they agreed to part, the master not having sufficient employ for him; but that the indenture was not cancelled or delivered up to him, and he served the last 40 days of his apprenticeship in Twineham. That he has done no act to gain a settlement in any other parish, that he is married and his wife's name is Elizabeth, by whom he has one child born in wedlock named William. [Mark of W.L.]

1808 Jan. 9 The joint and several information of Jane SHOUBRIDGE wife of William SHOUBRIDGE of Horsham, cordwainer, and John KNOWLES, overseer of Cowfold. Ann (sic) Shoubridge said that the person now before her, whose name is Harriot ALDRIDGE, daughter of Ann ALDRIDGE, late wife of James ALDRIDGE of Horsham, labourer, was born at her house situate in Horsham. John Knowles said that Harriot Aldridge has been relieved by Cowfold parish for some years past but does not belong to them, as he has heard and believes. [Mark of Ann (sic) Shoubridge and signature of J.K.]

1810 May 12 Charles SAUNDERS, of Cowfold, labourer, said that he was born in Hurstpierpoint but that his parents then and now belong to Twineham

and that he has never done any act to gain a settlement in his own right. That he is married and his wife's name is Mary, by whom he has two children born in wedlock, namely: Mary 2 years 6 months and John seven months.
[Signature of C.S.]

1811 Feb. 2 Thomas MITCHELL, of Cowfold, carpenter, said that he has, for the past 5 years, rented of Mr. William PHILLIPS of the Borough of Southward [?Southwark, Surrey], grocer, a house, garden and orchard in Cowfold at the rent of £16 a year, which rent he has regularly paid. [Signature of T.M.]

1811 Oct. 5 Thomas HAYBITTLE, now residing in Cowfold, labourer, said that he was born in Washington but that his parents were legally settled in Ashurst, as they have been relieved by that parish. That he has never done any act to gain a settlement in his own right, and that he is married and his wife's name is Barbara, by whom he has 2 children, Barbara 3 years 6 months and Mary 6 months, and has received relief from Cowfold. [Mark of T.H.]

1813 Jan. 4 Henry WOOLVEN of Horsham, labourer, said that he was born in the hamlet of Lower Beeding, where his parents were legally settled. That, nineteen years ago, he hired himself to Mr. John HUES of Cowfold, farmer, to serve for a year at wages of 2 guineas, which time he served, and that he has never done any act to gain a settlement in any other parish. That he is married and his wife's name is Elizabeth but he has no child. [Signature of H.W.]

1815 Nov. 4 James NEWMAN of Cowfold, labourer, said that he was born in Cowfold but that his parents were settled in West Grinstead. That he has never done any act to gain a settlement in his own right and is married and his wife's name is Mary, by whom he has 3 children born in wedlock namely: Mary 5 years, James 3 years and William 6 months. [Mark of J.N.]

1817 Mar. 6 William FREEMAN, carpenter, said that his father was settled in Slinfold, and that he was bound apprentice to Allen HULL, carpenter of Slinfold, for 4 years but Allen Hull, failing in business, he served with him only 2 years and then went to live with SAVAGE, carpenter, at Horsham, to whom he hired himself at 15s 0d a week and remained in his service for 2 years but never engaged himself to Savage for a year, and considered himself at liberty to quit him at any time. That he never hired himself for a year to any other master nor ever took any lodging of higher value than one shilling per week nor ever did any act to gain a settlement in any other parish. [Signature of W.F.]

1823 Feb.12 Case for the opinion of Mr. NOLAN. Samuel SAYERS, a poor boy of Shermanbury, when about 10 years old was employed by Mr. WHITE of Cowfold as a knife boy. He boarded him in his house and gave him clothes but made no hiring till two years later when the pauper wanted wages and was hired for half a year, which continued for several years, making fresh bargains every half year. Mr. White said that he took the pauper when a little boy for board only and it was quite at his option to

give him clothes. The pauper's father said it was agreed Mr. White should give him clothes as well as board when he first took him, Shermanbury at first fitting him with two shirts. The pauper has been removed to Shermanbury from Cowfold but an appeal has been lodged, intending to set up the two year's service with Mr. White as a settlement. Opinion: If Mr. White made any agreement whereby he engaged this boy as his servant and did not mention that it should be only during his pleasure it was an indefinite agreement as to time; this the law considers as a hiring for a year sufficient to give a placement; and this result would follow whether White had agreed to find the pauper in clothes or board only. But, if Mr. White's account is credited that there was no agreement for this boy's service during the first two years, the pauper has not gained a settlement in Cowfold. It seems a question of fact for the sessions.
Catalogued under Par 59/35/1

COWFOLD SETTLEMENT CERTIFICATES Par 59/32/1

		From
1695 Nov.28	Richard PURVEY, blacksmith, wife and children.	Nuthurst
1699 Jul. 1	Thomas HOADLY, son of Thomas HOADLY of Shermanbury blacksmith, with wife and child.	Shermanbury
1700 Feb.12	Edmand GARDNER, husbandman, wife and family.	Shermanbury
1703 Apr.21	John JENCKS and Ann DAVEY, wife of John DAVY, "his harlett & her children and his family".	Beeding
1707 Sep.21	Widow West and "the child that is with the widow we do also freely own".	West Grinstead
1708 Sep.10	Joseph TERRY, wife and child.	Ifield
1711 Nov.10	Nicholas FEIST, husbandman, wife and family. *Catalogued under Par 59/32/3*	Billingshurst
1719 Mar.30	Mary GATFORD widow.	Beeding
1729 Jul.27	Thomas TURNER, wife Sarah and child.	Horsham
1731 Sep.18	John REEVE.	West Grinstead
1731 Sep.18	Ann NEWMAN widow and son William 2y.	Nuthurst
1735 Jan.25	Thomas WASHER, wife Mary and son John.	Horsham
1744 Jan.29	Stephen DAVEY and children.	Shermanbury
1749 Mar.27	William BATCHELOR, wife Mary and children William and Mary.	Capel, Sry
1749 May 31	John VINALL, wife Ann and son John.	Henfield
1749 Oct.15	Richard BROAD wife Elizabeth and children William, Richard, Elizabeth, Mary and Anne.	Shermanbury
1749 Oct.30	Thomas DENCH, wife Mary and children Thomas, Mary, John, Sarah, Elizabeth and Daniel.	Shermanbury
1750 Feb. 3	James KNOWLES and wife Elizabeth.	St. John sub Castro, Lewes
1750 Apr.15	John COMBER, wife Jane and children Richard, Ann, John and Elizabeth.	Nuthurst
1756 Oct.26	Thomas SNOW and wife Mary.	Poling

1760 Jan.26	Thomas KNOWLES, wife Jane and children James, Elizabeth and Thomas.	Steyning
1763 Jan.30	Thomas FEAST, wife Fanny and six children.	West Grinstead
1763 Apr. 2	Thomas POLLARD, wife Ann and children John 3y and Thomas 1y.	West Grinstead
1764 May 13	John STANFORD, wife Ann and children William 7y, Mary 4y, Sarah 3y and John 6m.	Nuthurst
1765 Mar.10	William SHEARLOCK and wife Mary.	Shipley
1769 Feb.25	William GATFORD, wife Susannah and children John 5y, Susan 3y and Mary an infant.	Bolney
1769 Sep.23	George SHERLOCK and wife Sarah.	Henfield
1771 Dec 28	John COOK, wife Mary and children William 6y, Charlotte 7m.	Bolney
1776 Feb.21	John FLINT, wife Ann and daughters Mary, Abbigial, Elizabeth and Francis.	Charlwood, Sry
1777 Jul. 7	Philip STONER, wife Ann and daughter Sarah.	West Grinstead
1777 Oct. 7	James SHAW the younger, wife Sarah and children Thomas and Charlotte.	West Grinstead
1780 Mar. 4	Richard WIGHTING and wife Sarah.	Ifield
1780 Sep.29	Isaac MICHELL, wife Ann and children Stephen 5y, Ann 4y, Allen 3y, Hannah 2y and Lucy 6m.	Cuckfield
1780 Nov. 3	James MILES, wife Sarah and son John under 1y.	West Grinstead
1782 Apr.28	David CHILD, wife Mary and children Ann, Hannah and Robert. Ack.	Henfield
1782 Dec.29	James COATES wife Ann and son Edward 10y.	West Grinstead
1783 May 4	Jobe BETS, labourer, wife Cattern and daughter Cattern. Ack.	Nuthurst
1784 Jun.20	Edward STRINGER, wife Amy and children Mary and Benjamin. Ack.	West Grinstead
1785 Apr.11	William WHITE wife and family. Ack.	Bolney
1786 Apr.17	John WOOLVEN, wife Mary and children Mary 20y and Mildred 17y.	West Grinstead
1786 Jun.24	James ELPHICK, wife and children Sarah 3y, and Hannah 9m.	Shipley
1786 Jul.23	John BAYTUP, wife Mary and children John 4y and Mary 1y 6m.	West Grinstead
1786 Oct.29	John POLLARD and wife Sarah.	Ashurst
1790 Mar.27	James BOTTING, wife Elizabeth and children James 3y, Elizabeth 2y, and Richard 6m.	West Grinstead
1790 May 4	William BATCHELOR, wife Mary and son William	Wisborough Green

REMOVAL ORDERS FROM COWFOLD Par 59/32/2/1.

		To
1701 Apr.28	Charity SEAGRAVE.	Amberley
1701 Oct.11	William WELLER.	Beeding
1722 Jul.30	Jonathan HODGKINS and wife Mary.	Eckington, Dby.
1723 Jun. 1	William JESTED, wife and 3 children.	Albourne
1728 May.13	Rebaccah MUZZALE, female bastard child of Susannah LILLIOT.	Albourne
1728 Oct. 7	John WILLETT and wife Ann. On appeal, order discharged.	Bolney
1741 Feb.16	Thomas FOX, wife Elizabeth and Margarett her daughter, an infant under 7 years.	Moreton, Sry [Morden]
1741 Sep.26	John COMBER, wife Jane and children Richard, Ann and John.	Nuthurst
1756 Dec.16	Charles HARDING, labourer, wife Ann and daughter Sarah 2y.	Speldhurst, Ken
1765 Mar. 2	William SHEARLOCK and wife Mary.	Shipley
1769 Sep. 9	Elizabeth FOREMAN, singlewoman. *Catalogued under Par 59/32/3/1*	Nuthurst
1769 Sep.16	Jane FIST [FEIST], singlewoman.	Shipley
1775 Oct.18	James BRIGGS and wife Thezia.	Sullington
1783 May 14	Sarah WIGHTING, wife of Richard WIGHTING who has gone away and left her, and children Elizabeth 9y, James 3y 6m and Thomas 9 weeks. [Delivered 14 May]	Ifield
1783 Nov. 1	Mary MOSE [MOSSE], wife of James MOSE	Horsham
1785 Apr. 2	John UPTON and wife Jane.	Horsted Keynes
1785 Jul.12	Ann TERRELL, singlewoman. *Catalogued under Par 59/32/4*	Epsom, Sry
1786 Mar. 4	David KING and wife Jenny. [Delivered 3 April]	Hurstpierpoint
1786 Mar. 4	William BURRELE and wife Ann. [Delivered Sat. 4 March at 5 o'clock in the afternoon]	Steyning
1786 Jun. 5	James ELPHICK, wife Sarah and children Sarah 2y 6m and Hannah 6m.	Shipley
1786 Jul. 1	Edward TURNER, wife Mary Elizabeth and son Henry 8y. [Delivered 1 July]	Horsham
1786 Oct.14	Martha WHITE, singlewoman, apprehended in Cowfold as a rogue and vagabond found wandering and begging. On examination M.W., said that she was born in Henfield, where her parents were legally settled. [Mark of M.W.] [Delivered 16 Oct]	Henfield
1786 Nov. 4	John BENNETT, wife Martha and son John 1y 9m. [Delivered 20 Nov]	Hurstpierpoint
1786 Nov. 4	Henry STONER, wife Elizabeth and children Thomas 10y, William 9y, Ann 8y, Hannah 4y and Philip 1y. [Delivered 12 Dec]	Nuthurst

1787 Oct.24	Thomas WOOLVEN, wife Mary and children Edward 14y and Richard 10y. [Delivered 9 Nov]	West Grinstead
1791 Aug. 4	John PURVEY and wife Sarah.	Cuckfield
1791 Aug. 6	Sarah and Elizabeth GREENFIELD, children of John GREENFIELD by Elizabeth his late wife deceased.	Epsom, Sry
1793 Dec. 7	Nanny MATTHEWS, singlewoman. [Delivered 9 Dec.]	Woodmancote
1795 Dec. 5	Mary MICHELL. [Delivered 7 Dec.]	Beeding
1800 Feb. 1	Elizabeth WADY, singlewoman, being with child.	Newtimber
1800 Jul. 5	Ann MESSER, wife of Peter MESSER who has deserted and run away from her	Nuthurst
1801 Feb. 7	John NYE, the younger, wife Ann and children John 2y 9m and Ann 19 weeks	Shermanbury
1801 May 2	John NYE, wife Ann and children John 3y and Ann 7m [Delivered 25 May]	Woodmancote
1802 Sep. 4	Lydia WALLER, singlewoman, being with child. [Delivered 4 Sep.]	West Grinstead
1802 Oct.28	Jemima TULLETT, singlewoman, being with child. [Delivered 3 Nov.]	Westmeston
1802 Dec. 4	Jane BUCKWELL, singlewoman. [Delivered 31 Jan. 1803]	St. George, Bloomsbury, Mdx
1803 Oct.15	Lydia MATTHEWS, singlewoman.	Cuckfield
1805 Oct.19	Mary JOHNSON, wife of John JOHNSON, who has absconded and left her.	Wivelsfield
1810 Oct.13	Sarah WILLETT, singlewoman, being with child. [Delivered 27 Oct]	Brighton
1812 Sep. 5	Ann BROWNE, singlewoman. [Delivered 7 Sep]	West Grinstead
1815 Nov. 4	James NEWMAN [NEWNHAM], wife Mary and children Mary 5y, James 3y and William 6m.	West Grinstead
1815 Nov.18	Charles TIDY and wife Sarah. [Delivered 21 Nov.]	Ewhurst, Sry.
1815 Nov.28	William MORLEY and his 8 children, Catherine 17y, James 15y, William 14y, Henry 12y, Richard 10y, Sarah 9y, Jane 8y and Elizabeth 5y. Suspended till 2 Dec. as Catherine and Jane ill. Southwick to pay £1 costs. [Delivered whole family 4 Dec.]	Southwick
1816 Jun.15	Richard WHITE, wife Rebecca and children David 5y, John 2y and an unbaptised infant. [Delivered 17 June]	Hurstpierpoint
1816 Jul.20	Sarah POLLARD, wife of James POLLARD, who has deserted her, and children Frances 9y and Mary 7y. [Delivered 22 July]	Shermanbury
1816 Oct. 2	John WILLETT and wife Rebecca. [Delivered 2 Oct.]	Cuckfield
1817 Apr. 5	George LANDER and wife Elizabeth.	Hurstpierpoint

1817 Apr.12	Thomas FIEAST, wife Ann and children John 7y, Mary 5y, Ann 3y, Elizabeth 2y and an unbaptised infant. [Delivered 22 April]	Ashurst
1817 May 3	Thomas LANGFORD and wife Sarah. Order suspended until 21 June due to Sarah's sickness. [Delivered 25 June]	West Wittering
1817 May 24	Lydia MOORE, singlewoman. [Delivered 28 May]	Seaford
1817 Oct. 4	Francis SHORTER and wife Mary. [Delivered 9 Oct]	Stokenchurch, Bkm
1819 Nov. 6	James HUGHES, wife Elizabeth and unbaptised infant.	Kirdford
1822 Dec. 7	Samuel SAYERS, wife Jane and son John 6m. [Delivered 9 Dec.]	Shermanbury
1823 Jan.13	James CAFFYN, wife Sarah and children Eliza 7y, Richard 4y, Ann 3y and William 2y. Confirmation.	Withyham
1823 Jan.13	Aaron SAYERS, wife Mary and unbaptised infant. Confirmation.	Twineham
1825 Jan.11	Edward PANNELL [POWELL in QS], wife Mary and children Mary 9y, Rebecca 7y and William 4y. Confirmation.	Buckland, Sry
1826 Apr.15	Thomas STONER, wife Sophia and children Martha 14y and Thomas 10y.	Beeding
1830 Sep.18	Ann HILLS, singlewoman. Sick, unable to travel until 16 Oct. [Endorsed: Child by William SHAW belonging to Cowfold. Shaw must be made to keep child or Cowfold parish must]	Brighton
1830 Dec.18	William FOWLER and wife Sarah. [Delivered William Fowler 21 Dec., his wife ill and unable to move]	Henfield

QUARTER SESSIONS REMOVAL ORDERS FROM COWFOLD

		To
L 1678 Apr. -	Ann GREAVELY, singlewoman, and child; respited.	Twineham
P 1701 Apr.28	Charity SEAGRAVE; confirmed.	Amberley
H 1713 Jul.13	John EASTON; confirmed.	Beeding
S 1715 Oct. 3	William STONER and wife Ann; discharged.	Woodmancote
M 1727 Jan. 9	Richard PRONGER, wife and three children; discharged.	West Grinstead
P 1728 Oct. 7	John WILLETT and wife Anne; discharged.	Bolney
M 1744 Jan. 9	Hugh BARRETT and wife Jane; discharged.	Folkington
H 1755 Jul.14	John KING and wife Elizabeth; confirmed.	Streat
C 1769 Apr. 3	William MARTIN, wife Mary and children William 4y and an infant newly born; respited.	Cuckfield

H 1769 Jul.10	William MARTIN, wife Mary and children William 4y and an infant; discharged.	Cuckfield
H 1771 Jul.15	Richard MORE, wife Christian and children John 10y, Elizabeth 8y, Stephen 6y, Richard 3y and an infant not yet baptised; confirmed.	Penshurst, Ken
H 1777 Jul.14	Edward BOTTING, the younger, and wife Elizabeth; confirmed.	Sullington
H 1777 Jul.14	Sarah WHITING, wife of Richard WHITING, and child 1y; respited.	Ifield
P 1777 Oct. 6	Sarah WHITING, wife of Richard WHITING, and child 1y; quashed.	Ifield
M 1778 Jan.12	Sarah WHITING, wife of Richard WHITING, and child 1y; confirmed.	Ifield
H 1778 Jul.13	William FRANCIS and wife Ann; confirmed.	Frinsted, Ken
C 1800 Jan.14	Stephen SAYERS, wife Ann and children Richard 3y, Jane 2y and an infant son; confirmed.	Beeding
M 1801 Apr.14	John NYE, the younger, wife Ann and children John 2y and Ann aged 19 weeks; quashed.	Shermanbury
P 1810 May 1	James BROWNE, wife Sarah and children James 9y, Thomas 7y, Keziah 3y, and John 5m; respited.	Sts.Peter & Mary, Lewes
H 1810 Jul.10	James BROWNE, wife Sarah and children James 9y, Thomas 7y, Keziah 3y, and John 5m; confirmed.	Sts.Peter & Mary, Lewes
P 1812 Oct. 6	Mary COMBER, singlewoman; quashed.	Bolney
P 1812 Oct. 6	Ann BROWNE, singlewoman; respited.	West Grinstead
P 1812 Oct. 6	George GIBBS, wife Sarah and children Jane 3y 11m, John and William 1y 5m; respited.	East Grinstead
P 1813 Apr.27	George GIBBS, wife Sarah and children Jane 3y 11m, John and William 1y 5m; confirmed.	East Grinstead
P 1813 Apr.27	Ann BROWNE, singlewoman; quashed.	West Grinstead
H 1817 Jul.14	Thomas FIEST, wife Ann and children John 7y, Mary 5y, Ann 3y, Elizabeth 2y and an infant not yet baptised; quashed.	Ashurst
H 1817 Jul.14	Thomas LANGFORD and wife Sarah; quashed.	West Wittering
H 1817 Jul.14	Lydia MOORE, singlewoman; respited.	Seaford
C 1817 Oct.13	Lydia MOORE, singlewoman; quashed.	Seaford
P 1819 Jan.11	Thomas STURT and wife Hannah; confirmed.	West Grinstead
H 1822 Jul.15	Mary WOOD, wife of William WOOD (who has deserted her); quashed.	Twineham
P 1823 Jan.13	Samuel SAYERS, wife Jane and son John 6m; respited.	Shermanbury
P 1823 Jan.13	James CAFFYN, wife Sarah and children Eliza 7y, Richard 4y, Ann 3y and William 2y; confirmed.	Withyham

P 1823 Jan.13	Aaron SAYERS, wife Mary and a child not yet baptised; confirmed.	Twineham
P 1823 Apr. 7	Samuel SAYERS, wife Jane and son John 6m; quashed.	Shermanbury
P 1825 Jan.11	Edward POWELL [PANNELL in parish records], wife Mary and children Mary 9y, Rebecca 7y and William 4y; confirmed.	Buckland, Sry
P 1827 Jan. 9	James TULLETT and wife Susannah; confirmed.	Hurstpierpoint
P 1830 Apr.20	John SAYERS, wife Sarah and children Thomas 3y and Frances 1y; confirmed.	Shermanbury
P 1830 Apr.20	Elizabeth LANGFORD, an unmarried woman who is with child; confirmed.	Shipley

REMOVAL ORDERS TO COWFOLD Par 59/32/3/1.

		From
1709 Jul.14	Thomas ROWLAND, wife and sons Thomas, James and Nathaniel and 2 small daughters. On appeal, order discharged as to Thomas Rowland the son and confirmed as to Thomas Rowland the father, his wife and the rest of the children.	Bolney
1717 May 1	Thomas WHITE, settled in Cowfold by serving apprenticeship of 7 years to Richard STOFFALL.	Twineham
1727 Oct. 6	Susannah LILLIOT, wife of William LILLIOT of Cowfold, husbandman, who has run away from his family, has lately intruded herself into Albourne. S.L., and her bastard child, Rebecca aged 1m, who is at nurse with her mother till age of 7y, to be removed to Cowfold. [Endorsed: Infant chargeable to Albourne where born and must be maintained by them]	Albourne
1728 Jul.18	Edward SAYERS, wheelwright, and wife Mary.	Beeding
1729 Jan. 2	John COLES and wife Mary.	Rudgwick
1739 Dec.10	Catherine PLUMMER, singlewoman.	Beeding
1743 Apr.23	Thomas WITTEN aged 4y and James WITTEN 3y, sons of Thomas WITTEN late of Cowfold, husbandman, deceased, by Elizabeth his late wife. Upon oath of Elizabeth TOMPSETT, now the wife of Joseph TOMPSETT of Shermanbury, husbandman, and mother of said children, the legal place of settlement of Thomas and James Witten is Cowfold.	Shermanbury

1764 Nov.27	Joseph FIGLESS aged 11y. Upon oath of Margaret, now the wife of Richard CROCKER, late Margaret FIGLESS, singlewoman, and mother of Joseph Figless, it is adjudged that he was born a bastard in Cowfold.	Easebourne
1776 Feb. 3	Richard TEIDEY and wife Amy.	Rye
1783 Apr.14	Susannah TUGWELL, singlewoman.	Horsham
1783 Dec.20	James PAGE, aged 8y.	Withyham
1786 Feb. 4	Edward STRINGER, wife Amy and children Benjamin 3y, Stephen 15m and Edward 8 weeks.	West Grinstead
1786 Dec. 6	James FIEST, wife Elizabeth and children John 2y and Francis 6m.	Old Shoreham
1792 Sep.17	Mary ATTREE, wife of Richard ATTREE.	West Hoathly
1794 Feb. 3	Mary Ann PILBEAM 11y and Sarah PILBEAM 8y. Their mother, Ann MARTIN on remarriage, said on oath that their place of settlement is Cowfold. [Endorsed:William PILBEAM'S two children from Epsom].	Epsom, Sry
1795 Jan. 3	Mildred WOOLVEN.	West Grinstead
1795 Jan. 7	Thomas PIERCE and wife Mary.	Ashurst
1798 Mar.21	William CHAMPION, wife Jenny and children William 3y and Harriet 5m.	Beddingham
1798 Oct.13	Sarah TIDY, wife of Stephen TIDY, and child Lucy 14m.	Slaugham
1799 Feb. 2	William BOTTING, and wife Hannah.	West Grinstead
1799 Nov.23	William PESKITT, wife Ann and children Rebecca 2y and James 1y.	Pulborough
1799 Dec. -	James ATTREE, wife Elizabeth and children Hannah 8, James 5y, William 3y and John 2y.	Cobham, Sry
1801 Jan.10	John BONNIFACE, wife Elizabeth and son Henry aged 16 weeks.	Nuthurst
1804 Jan.12	Ann AGATE, singlewoman.	Bolney
1805 Nov. 9	Bet HESMAN, singlewoman, being with child.	Bolney
1806 Nov.12	William DEWDNEY, wife Mary and children Samuel 3y, Ann 2y and Sarah 6m.	Shermanbury
1808 Oct.29	Mary TERELL, singlewoman, being with child.	Brighton
1809 Jul. 7	Sarah TIDEY, wife of Stephen TIDEY.	Bolney
1809 Jul.11	William BURTON, wife Elizabeth and child Amy 2y. Upon appeal, order quashed. Bobbing to pay £6.10s 0d maintenance.	Bobbing, Ken
1810 May 4	Bett HEASMAN, singlewoman. Upon appeal, order quashed and Bolney to pay £7.17s 0d towards relief of the pauper (and the two bastard children of which she has been delivered in Cowfold pending appeal).	Bolney
1812 Aug.24	William AYNSCOMB and wife Martha.	East Grinstead

1813 Jan. 4	Thomas Blake MANSBRIDGE, wife Elizabeth and children James 4y, and William 1y.	Barming, Ken
1813 Oct. 7	Sarah PILLVEN, singlewoman.	Brighton
1814 Dec. 6	Henry STARLEY.	Bolney
1815 Jun.10	Henry BONIFACE.	Nuthurst
1816 Aug.24	James LANGFORD, wife Sarah and children Stephen 5y, James 3y and Maria Ann 1y.	Chidham
1816 Dec.13	John TIDEY, wife Jane and children James, Mary and Charlotte.	Isfield
1817 Jan. 1	Henry STIRLEY and wife Sarah.	Speldhurst, Ken
1818 Sep.16	Thomas MITCHELL, wife Elizabeth and daughter Eliza 4y.	Berwick
1819 Apr.19	Stephen TIDEY, wife Mary and daughter Lucy 1y. Upon appeal, order quashed and Nuthurst to pay £2.9s 6d maintenance.	Nuthurst
1820 Jan.15	Richard FREEMAN.	Horsham
1820 Apr. 3	Sarah STONER wife of John STONER who has deserted her.	Nuthurst
1821 Jan.21	Thomas JENDEN and wife Lucy.	Nuthurst
1821 May 26	Charlotte PALMER aged 14y. On examination of Mary DAVIS otherwise ARNOLD, late Mary PALMER, singlewoman, the mother of Charlotte.	Edenbridge, Ken
1825 Mar. 5	Elizabeth WOOLLVIN, an unmarried woman who is with child.	Horsham
1825 Nov.25	Elizabeth HEASMAN als BATCHELOR, singlewoman, who is with child.	Cuckfield
1828 May 5	Abigail ANSCOMBE, singlewoman.	Brighton
1828 May 31	Ann TESTER, widow of Matthew TESTER, and children Ann 6y, Matthew 4y 6m and Lucy 2y 6m.	St. Leonard, Shoreditch, Mdx
1830 Dec.27	John KNIGHT, wife Avis and daughter Mary 6y.	Henfield
1831 Jan.28	Sarah FAIRHALL. [Endorsed: Order withdrawn 25 Feb]	Bolney
1831 Nov.14	John MATTHEWS and wife Sarah.	Steyning
1834 Aug.16	Elizabeth TERRELL.	Horsham
1835 May 12	Edward BOTTEN and wife Hannah. On examination Edward Botten said that he was born in Cowfold where his father was legally settled and that his first place of service, out of Cowfold, was with his Uncle, John BOTTEN of West Grinstead, under half yearly agreements. That, when he married, he returned to Cowfold and has done no other act to gain a settlement. [Mark of E.B.]	Mountfield

QUARTER SESSIONS REMOVAL ORDERS TO COWFOLD

		From
C 1698 May 2	Edward LONGHURST; confirmed.	Beeding
S 1699 Jul.11	Edward LONGHURST; respited on appeal.	Beeding
M 1699 Oct. 2	Edward LONGHURST; confirmed.	Beeding
A 1701 Jan.13	Charity SEAGRAVE; confirmed.	West Grinstead
S 1719 Jul.13	John HARDING; confirmed.	Beeding
M 1729 Jan.13	John COLES and wife Mary; confirmed.	Rudgwick
H 1735 Jul.14	Susan LYLLIOTT; confirmed.	West Grinstead
H 1738 Jul.10	Susan LILLIOTT and children Susan, Abraham and James; confirmed.	Nuthurst
C 1776 Apr.15	Thomas BAYTUP, wife Martha and children Thomas, Henry, Martha, William, Edward and James; respited.	West Grinstead
H 1776 Jul.15	Thomas BAYTUP, wife Martha and children Thomas, Henry, Martha, William, Edward and James; confirmed.	West Grinstead
P 1819 Jan.11	Stephen TIDEY, wife Mary and daughter Lucy 1y; respited.	Nuthurst
P 1819 Apr.19	Stephen TIDEY, wife Mary and daughter Lucy 1y; quashed.	Nuthurst
H 1825 Jul.12	John TERELL, wife Sarah and daughter Elizabeth 14y; respited.	Horsham
L 1825 Jul.14	Ann Bradford PAGE, widow, and son John 1y 8m; confirmed.	Frant
C 1825 Oct.18	John TERRELL, wife Sarah and daughter Elizabeth 14y; confirmed.	Horsham
H 1827 Jul.10	Lucy JENDEN, (wife of Steele JENDEN, transported beyond the seas for felony), and children John 6y and Richard 4y; respited.	Horsham
P 1828 Jan.15	Lucy JENDEN, (wife of Steele JENDEN, transported beyond the seas for felony) and children John 6y and Richard 4y; quashed as respects the mother removed by the name of Lucy, the wife of Steele Jenden, it having been proved that she was married, in February 1827, to William MITCHELL, and confirmed as to children John and Richard.	Horsham
L 1831 Apr. 7	James MARTIN, wife Ann and son William 4y; respited.	Brighton
L 1831 Jun.30	James MARTIN, wife Ann and son William 4y; quashed.	Brighton

COWFOLD BASTARDY EXAMINATIONS Par 59/34/3/1.

1755 Feb. 17 Hannah STRINGER, singlewoman, said that on Ladyday 1751 she came to live with John PILBEAM of Cowfold as a yearly servant, with whom she hired herself for one whole year for the wages of forty shillings, which term she served and received her wages and that since then she has not done any act to gain a settlement in any other parish. That she is now resident in Cowfold and with child, and that the said J.P.is the putative father. [Mark of H.S.]
Catalogued under Par 59/32/4

1771 Mar. 23 Elizabeth WILLETT of Cowfold, singlewoman, has declared that she is with child and that John FORD of Lancing, farmer, is the father. [Mark of E.W.]

1800 Jun. 28 Ann MITCHELL of Cowfold, singlewoman, has declared that she is with child and that the father is Peter MESSER, servantman of Cowfold. [Mark of A.M.]

1800 Nov. 13 Sarah STONER of Cowfold, singlewoman, has declared that she is with child and that John FAIRES late of Twineham, servant, is the father. [Mark of S.S.]

1803 Jun. 18 Sarah TULLETT of Cowfold, singlewoman, has declared that she is with child and that Henry MOBSBY of Cowfold, servant, is the father. [Mark of S.T.]

1808 May 11 Sarah KING of Cowfold, singlewoman, has declared that she is with child and that George GIBB of Twineham, servant, is the father. [Mark of S.K.]

1809 Feb. 3 Mary BANFIELD of Cowfold, singlewoman, has declared that she is with child and that Richard Weeks VINCENT of Cowfold, is the father. [Signature of M.B.]

1821 Mar. 3 Susannah ANSCOMB, of Cowfold, singlewoman, has declared that she is with child and that James JENNER otherwise MARTIN, labourer, is the father. [Mark of S.A.]

1822 Jan. 19 Ann MOORE of Cowfold, singlewoman, said that she was born in Cowfold, where her father is legally settled. That nearly three years ago she hired herself to Mrs. NAILARD of Westlands, West Grinstead, for 6s 0d a month, month's wages, month's warning. That she served one and three quarter years and made no other hiring with her. That she received her wages by 2 or 3 shillings at a time, as she wanted it, until she came away and then her wages were fully settled. That she has done no other act to gain a settlement and that she is with child. [Mark of A.M.]
Catalogued under Par 59/32/4

COWFOLD BASTARDY BONDS Par 59/34/1/1

1771 Apr. 12. John FORD of Lancing, yeoman, bound to the parish officers of Cowfold in £100 in respect of Elizabeth WILLETT of Cowfold, singlewoman, who has declared that she is with child and that J.F. is the father. [Signature of J.F.]

1771 May. 25. Thomas AGATE of Cowfold, farmer, bound to the parish officers of Cowfold in £100 in respect of Elizabeth WALDER of Cowfold, singlewoman, who has declared that she was lately delivered of a male bastard child in Cowfold and that T.A. is the father. [Mark of T.A.]

1809 Mar. 11. Richard VINCENT of Cowfold, yeoman, bound to the parish officers of Cowfold in £200 in respect of Mary BAMFIELD of Cowfold, singlewoman, who has declared that she is with child and that the father is R.V. [Signature of R.V.]

COWFOLD BASTARDY ORDERS Par 59/34/2

1741 Jan. 19 Elizabeth SHERLOCK, singlewoman, has declared that Thomas FOX of Moreton [Morden], Surrey, husbandman, is the father of the female bastard child born to her in Cowfold. T.F. to pay 1s 6d a week and the mother shall, from 20 December last, the day of the birth, pay 6d a week.

1782 Mar. 2 Mary MANSBRIDGE, singlewoman, has declared that Thomas BLAKE, late of Cowfold, servant, is the father of a male bastard child born to her on 25 December last at the house of Arthur FOREMAN in Cowfold. T.B. to pay £2.7s 6d towards the lying-in and 1s 6d a week; the mother to pay 1s a week.

1786 Jul. 10 Hannah PETERS was delivered of a male bastard child named James Stevens on 11 February 1784 at the dwelling house of John NIXON in Croydon, Surrey, and, six months after, went and resided in Cowfold, which is the place of her last legal settlement, with the child as a nurse child. H.P. has been relieved by Cowfold parish officers and as she is very poor and unable to support the child, the parish officers of Croydon are ordered to pay 2s 0d a week to Cowfold as long as she shall reside in that parish.
Catalogued under Par 59/35/1/1

1786 Sep. 2 Susanna TUGWELL, singlewoman, has declared that Edward TURNER, late of Horsham, labourer, is the father of a female bastard child born to her on 11 July 1783 at the Poor House in Cowfold. E.T. to pay £17.18s 0d towards the lying-in and 2s 0d a week; the mother to pay 6d a week.

1791 Aug. 6 Sarah ANSCOMB has declared that Joseph HOLMAN, of Cowfold, labourer, is the father of a female bastard child born to her on 14 June last at the house of Thomas KNOWLES of Cowfold. J.H. to pay £2.6s 0d towards the lying-in and 2s 0d a week; the mother to pay 6d a week.

1800 Aug. 2 Elizabeth MATTHEWS, singlewoman, has declared that James POPEY late of Horsham and now of Stony Stratford, Buckinghamshire, is the father of a female bastard child born to her on 17 November 1794 at her father's house in Cowfold. J.P. to pay costs of £42.5s 0d and 3s 0d a week; the mother to pay 6d a week.

1801 Apr. 4 Sarah STONER has declared that John FAIRES of Twineham, is the father of a female bastard child born to her on 3 February last at the poorhouse in Cowfold. J.F. to pay £2.9s 0d towards the lying-in and 2s 0d a week; the mother to pay 6d a week.

1801 Aug. 1 Sarah STRINGER, wife of William STRINGER of Cowfold, wheelwright, heretofore Sarah MITCHELL, singlewoman, has declared that James MORGAN, late of Handcross, wheelwright, is the father of a male bastard child born to her on 17 November 1799 at her mother's house in Cowfold. J.M. to pay £10.13s 0d towards the lying-in and 2s 0d a week; the mother to pay 6d a week.

1802 Aug. 7 Rosamond GOWER, widow, has declared that John LEOPARD of Nuthurst, blacksmith, is the father of a male bastard child born to her on 12 May last at the poorhouse in Cowfold. J.L. to pay £3 towards the lying-in and 2s 6d a week; the mother to pay 6d a week.

1802 Sep. 4 Elizabeth KNIGHT, singlewoman, has declared that John SAWYER late of Cowfold, journeyman shopkeeper, is the father of a male bastard child born to her on 19 June last at the poorhouse, Cowfold. J.S. to pay £3 towards the lying-in and 3s 0d a week; the mother to pay 6d a week. [Endorsed: List of payments made by John Sawyer from 4 September 1802 to 10 January 1810]

1803 Jul. 12 Mary PETERS, singlewoman, has declared that James STONER, late of Cowfold, servantman, is the father of a male bastard child, born to her on 5 April last at the workhouse in Cowfold. J.S. to pay £3 towards the lying-in and 2s 0d a week; the mother to pay 6d a week.

1804 Jun. 2 Ann AGATE, singlewoman, has declared that William ANSCOMB late of Cowfold, labourer, is the father of a male bastard child born to her on 14 January last. W.A. to pay £3.12s 0d towards the lying-in and 2s 0d a week, the mother to pay 6d a week.

1805 Jan. 5 Mary Ann PILBEAM, singlewoman, has declared that John STANDEN late of Henfield, labourer, is the father of a male bastard child born to her on 11 October last at the poorhouse in Cowfold. J.S. to pay £3.16s 0d towards the lying-in and 3s 0d a week; the mother to pay 6d a week.

1805 Mar. 2 Elizabeth BAYTOP, singlewoman, has declared that John TUCKER of Handcross, bailiff, is the father of a female bastard child, born to her on 16 July at house of Thomas WOOD in Cowfold. J.T. to pay £1.11s 6d towards the lying-in and 3s 0d a week; the mother to pay 6d a week.

1806 Apr. 12 Ann BATES of Cowfold, singlewoman, has declared that Isaac MICHELL late of West Grinstead, labourer, is the father of a male bastard child born to her on 27 November last at the poorhouse in Cowfold. I.M. to pay £5.8s 0d towards the lying-in and 3s 0d a week; the mother to pay 6d a week. [Endorsed: Received 13 April 1807 £13.4s 0d, 5 August 1808 £10.4s.0d, Oct. 1809 £9.6s 0d for 62 weeks pay.]

1806 Apr. 12 Bet HEASMAN has declared that Thomas BATCHELOR of Bolney, servantman, is the father of a female bastard child born to her on 1 January last in the poorhouse, Cowfold. T.B. to pay £4.13s 0d towards the lying-in and 3s 0d a week; mother to pay 6d a week. [Endorsed: Received £15 on 6 August, 1807, £4.13s 0d on 11 March, 1808, £5.4s 0d on 7 Jan. 1810. Due on this order up to 16 June 1821 £98.5s 0d.]

1807 Feb. 7 Mary WOOLVEN, singlewoman, has declared that Philip ANSCOMBE of Cowfold is the father of a female bastard child born to her on 1 October last in the poorhouse in Cowfold. P.A. to pay £4.6s 0d towards the lying-in and 3s 0d a week; the mother to pay 6d a week.

1816 Mar. 2 Ann MOORE, singlewoman, has declared that Philip HEDGCOCK of Henfield, butcher, is the father of a male bastard child born to her on 30 Nov. last, at her father's dwelling house in Cowfold. P.H. to pay costs of 12s 0d for maintenance, £2.10s 0d for charges incident to the birth, 14s 0d for cost of filiation order, and then 4s 0d a week; the mother to pay 6d a week. [Endorsed: List of payments made to 17 March 1823]

1816 Jul. 6 Catherine TULLETT, singlewoman, has declared that James FRANCIS of Cowfold, labourer, is the father of a female bastard child born to her on 21 April last at the poorhouse in Cowfold. J.F. to pay 15s 0d for maintenance, £2 for birth expenses, 9s 0d for cost of filiation order and 2s 6d a week; the mother to pay 6d a week. [Endorsed: 1816 Paid till 30 June £3.4s 0d, Oct. 13 paid 15 weeks £1.17s 6d, 8 Dec. 8 weeks due £1.0s 0d. Child dead]

1818 Oct. 3 Elizabeth MOORE, singlewoman, has declared that Thomas STEELE of Cowfold, labourer, is the father of a female bastard child, born to her on 24 July last at the poorhouse in Cowfold. T.S. to pay costs of £1 for maintenance, 13s 0d cost of obtaining this order and 2s 6d a week; the mother to pay 6d a week.

1819 Mar. 27 Ann MOORE, singlewoman, has declared that James FILLERY of Henfield, labourer, is the father of a male bastard child born to her on 14 February last at the poorhouse in Cowfold. J.F. to pay 14s 0d for maintenance, £2 for expenses incident to the birth, 13s 0d cost of this order and 3s 6d a week; the mother to pay 6d a week. [Endorsed: David Moore buried 23 March 1824]

1821 Jun. 2 Ann TIDY, singlewoman, has declared that James JENDEN, labourer, is the father of a female bastard child born to her on 7 August last at the poorhouse in Cowfold. J.J. to pay £5.8s 0d expenses, £2 for charges incident to the birth, £2 for cost of his apprehension, 9s 0d for cost of order and 3s 0d a week; the mother to pay 6d a week.

1821 Oct. 6 Susan ANSCOMB, singlewoman, has declared that James MARTIN JENNER of Bolney, labourer, is the father of a female bastard child born to her on 6 July last at the poorhouse in Cowfold. J.M.J. to pay £1 costs, £2 expenses incident to the birth, 13s 0d cost of this order and 2s 6d a week; the mother to pay 6d a week. [Endorsed: £3 received 21 Oct. 1821, £1 on Jan. 1 1822, and £2 up to Michaelmas 1824]

1824 Sep. 4 Ann POOLEY of Cowfold, singlewoman, has declared that Richard WHITEMAN late of Leeds, Kent, carpenter, is the father of a male bastard child born to her on 8 April last at the house of Mrs. PARKER in Cowfold. R.W. to pay £2.13s 6d for costs, £2 expenses incident to the birth, £7.10s 0d costs of summoning him, 13s 0d cost of order and 2s 6d a week; the mother to pay 6d a week.

1825 Nov. 19 Sarah LANGFORD, wife of Thomas LANGFORD who was transported beyond the seas two years ago, has declared that James PARSONS of Bolney, labourer, is the father of a male bastard child, born to her on the 18 September last at the workhouse in Cowfold. J.P. to pay to pay 2s 0d a week and 13s 0d for the cost of order; the mother to pay 6d a week.

1826 May 6 Elizabeth HEASMAN of Cowfold, singlewoman, has declared that John VINALL of Henfield, bricklayer, is the father of a male bastard child born to her on 19 March last at the poorhouse in Cowfold. J.V. to pay 15s 0d charges, £2 expenses incident to the birth, £2.12s 0d and 13s 0d for cost of order and 2s 6d a week; the mother to pay 6d a week.

1829 Jul. 4 Mary MATTHEWS of Cowfold, singlewoman, has declared that Charles PARSONS, labourer of Cowfold, is the father of a male bastard child born to her on 25 February last at her father's house. C.P. to pay 2s 6d a week and 12s 0d for cost of order; the mother to pay 6d a week.

1830 Sep. 4 Lucy MOBSLY of Cowfold, singlewoman, has declared that Richard HALL of Worth, labourer, is the father of a female bastard child born to her on 20 January last. R.H. to pay 3s 0d a week and shall also pay 6d a week in case the mother shall not nurse the child, also £3 cost of order.

1830 Oct. 16 Ann HILLS of Cowfold, singlewoman, has declared that William SHAW, labourer, is the father of a male bastard child born to her on 14

September last at the house of William GRATWICKE. W.S. to pay £2 expenses incident to the birth, 15s 0d costs of apprehending him, 12s 0d cost of obtaining the order and 2s 6d a week; the mother to pay 6d a week.

COWFOLD WARRANTS Par 59/34/2

1774 Feb. 7 Thezia STONER of Cowfold, singlewoman, has declared that she is with child and that James BRIGS, now or late of West Chiltington, labourer, is the father; and he is to be apprehended.

1783 Mar.20 Sarah WHITEING and three children was said by her father, William BATCHELOR, to be very poor and he applied to the overseers of Cowfold for relief for her but was refused. As one of the overseers for that parish is unable to show cause why relief was refused it is ordered that Cowfold pay to Sarah Whiteing 5s 0d a week. Note signed by J. CHALLEN, J.P.
Catalogued under Par 59/37/1.

1783 May 13 Sarah WHITEING, the wife of [Richard] WHITEING, and their three children are now chargeable to Cowfold, is to be brought before a Justice to be examined concerning their last legal settlement.
Catalogued under Par 59/32/2.

1786 Feb.18 Hannah PETERS of Cowfold, widow, has declared that she is with child and that Henry YOUNG late of Cowfold, carpenter, is the father; and he is to be apprehended.

1786 Sep. 2 Edward TURNER late of Horsham, labourer, the reputed father of a female bastard child born to Susanna TUGWELL on 11 July 1783, at the poorhouse, Cowfold, was ordered to pay £17.18s 0d towards the lying-in and 2s 0d a week. As he has refused to pay he is to be apprehended and delivered to the keeper of H.M. Prison, Horsham, until he obeys the order or appears at the next Quarter Sessions.

1799 Dec. 3 Ann WILLETT, singlewoman, has declared that she is with child and that William BOUNDY otherwise BOUND of Shermanbury, servantman, is the father; and he is to be apprehended.

1800 Jan. 4 Sarah MITCHELL of Cowfold, singlewoman, has declared that she was delivered of a male bastard child on 17 November last, at the house of her mother in Cowfold, and that James MORGAN late of Handcross in the parish of Slaugham, blacksmith, is the father; and he is to be apprehended.

1800 Jun. 28 Ann MITCHELL of Cowfold, singlewoman, has declared that she is with child and that Peter MESSER of Cowfold, servantman, is the father; and he is to be apprehended.

1802 Mar. 6 Elizabeth KNIGHT of Cowfold, singlewoman, has declared that she is with child likely to be born a bastard and that John SAWYER of Cowfold, shopkeeper, is the father; and he is to be apprehended.

1802 Mar. 6 Rosamond GOWER of Cowfold, has declared that she is with child and that John LEOPARD late of Cowfold, blacksmith, is the father; and he is to be apprehended.

1802 Jul. 3 Rosemond GOWER of Cowfold, widow, has declared that she was delivered of a male bastard child on 12 May last, at the workhouse in Cowfold, and that John LEPPARD late of Cowfold, blacksmith, is the father. R.G., to be apprehended and brought before a Justice at the house of Susannah LEE bearing the sign of the Kings Head, Horsham, on 3 August, and notice is to be given to J.L., that he may also be present.

1802 Aug. 7 Elizabeth KNIGHT, singlewoman, has declared that she was delivered of a male bastard child on 17 August last at the poorhouse, Cowfold, and that John SAWYER late of Cowfold, journeyman shopkeeper, is the father. E.K. to be apprehended and brought before a Justice at the house of Susannah LEE at the sign of the Kings Head, Horsham, on 4 September, and notice is to be given to J.S. so that he may also attend.

1805 Nov.11 Bet HEASMAN of Cowfold, singlewoman, has declared that she is with child and that Thomas BATCHELOR of Bolney, servantman, is the father; and he is to be apprehended.

1807 May 2 Barbara POOLEY, singlewoman, has declared that she is with child and that Henry STOPFORD of Cowfold, servantman, is the father; and he is to be apprehended. [Endorsed: To pay £20 immediately, £10 more when the child is 12 months old but not otherwise]

1808 Mar. 9 Bet HEASMAN, singlewoman, has declared that she has been delivered of a female bastard child on 1 January 1806, at the poorhouse in Cowfold, and that Thomas BATCHELOR late of Bolney, servantman, is the father; and he is to be apprehended.

1808 May 11 Sarah KING of Cowfold, singlewoman, has declared that she is with child and that George GIBB of Twineham, servant, is the father; and he is to be apprehended.

1808 Jul. 2 George GIBBS, late of Twineham, labourer, has run away and left Sarah GIBBS, his wife, chargeable to Cowfold; and he is to be apprehended.
Catalogued under Par 59/35/1.

1808 Aug. 6 John TUCKER, adjudged to be the father of a female bastard child delivered to Elizabeth BAYTOP, singlewoman, at the house of Thomas WOOD in Cowfold, was, on 2 March 1805, ordered to pay £1.11s 6d for the lying-in and 3s 0d a week maintenance. As he has not performed this order he is to be apprehended and conveyed to the Common Gaol at Horsham.

1808 Dec. 6 Anne BATES, singlewoman, has declared that she is with child and that Richard DUFFLE or DUFFIELD of West Grinstead, labourer, is the father; and he is to be apprehended.

1808 Dec. 6 Sarah TULLETT of Cowfold, singlewoman, has declared that she is with child and that Richard BATCHELOR late of West Grinstead, servant, is the father; and he is to be apprehended.

1810 Jan. 6 James BROWN, late of Cowfold, has run away and left his wife and three children chargeable to the parish; and he is to be apprehended.
Catalogued under Par 59/35/1.

1816 Feb.17 Catherine TULLETT of Cowfold, singlewoman, has declared that she is with child and that James FRANCIS of Cowfold, labourer, is the father; and he is to be apprehended. [Endorsed: Child since dead]

1817 Aug. 4 Harriet VINALL of Cowfold, singlewoman, has declared that she is with child and that William FREEMAN, carpenter, of Horsham is the father; and he is to be apprehended.

1817 Nov. 1 Lydia MOORE of Cowfold, singlewoman, has declared that she was delivered of a male bastard child on 31 July last, at Seaford, where she had been removed from Cowfold by an order since quashed, and that James PELHAM of Seaford, labourer, is the father. L.M. is to be apprehended to appear before a Justice at the Kings Head Inn, Horsham on Saturday 15 November and notice to be given to J.P., that he may also attend.

1818 May 21 Joseph RAILTON late of Cowfold, carpenter, has run away and left his wife and child whereby they are become chargeable to Cowfold; and he is to be apprehended.
Catalogued under Par 59/35/1.

1818 Dec.19 Thomas STEELE of Cowfold, labourer, was adjudged to be the father of a female bastard child lately born to Elizabeth MOORE, in Cowfold, and ordered to pay £1 maintenance to time of order, 13s 0d for cost of obtaining the order and 2s 6d a week. As he has not paid the £2.13s 0d now due, he is to be apprehended. [Endorsed: Received on 19 Dec.1818 sum of £2.13s 0d being the amount due from Thomas Steele up to this day, Sept. 23 1820: Thomas Steele committed to Petworth House of Correction for three months. 1820: Paid up to 23 December by 3 months imprisonment in Petworth]

1819 May 24 Ann MOORE late of Cowfold, singlewoman, above the space of one month last was delivered of a bastard child, at the poorhouse in Cowfold, which child is now living and chargeable to the parish; and she is to be apprehended.

1820 Apr.22 Ann TYDAY of Cowfold, singlewoman, has declared that she is with child and that James JENDEN of Shermanbury, farmer, is the father; and he is to be apprehended.

1820 May 6 John STONER, late of Cowfold, labourer, has run away and left his wife who is pregnant and very near being delivered, whereby she has become chargeable to Cowfold; and he is to be apprehended.
Catalogued under Par 59/35/1.

1821 Mar. 3 Susannah ANSCOMBE of Cowfold, singlewoman, has declared that she is with child and that James JENNER otherwise MARTIN of Bolney, labourer, is the father; and he is to be apprehended.

1821 May 5 Ann TIDY of Cowfold, singlewoman, has declared that she was delivered of a female bastard child on 7 August last, at the poorhouse, and that James JENDEN of Shermanbury, labourer, is the father; and he is to be apprehended.

1821 Sep.15 Susan ANSCOMB of Cowfold, singlewoman, has declared that she was delivered of a female bastard child on 6 July last, at the poorhouse, Cowfold, and that James MARTIN JENNER late of Bolney is the father. S.A. to appear at the Kings Head Inn, Horsham, on Saturday 6 October and notice is to be given to J.M.J. that he may also attend.

1822 Jan.19 Ann MOORE of Cowfold, singlewoman, has declared that she is with child and that James WOOD of Twineham, labourer, is the father; and he is to be apprehended.

1825 Feb.19 Richard WHITEMAN of Leeds, Kent, carpenter, was adjudged to be the father of a male bastard child delivered to Ann POOLEY, singlewoman, in Cowfold and ordered to pay £12.6s 6d for the expenses incident to the birth and of obtaining order of filiation and for the maintenance of the child. As he has absconded, he is to be apprehended.

1825 Mar. 5 Elizabeth WOOLLVIN of Cowfold, widow, has declared that she is with child and that John TAYLOR of Worthing, currier, is the father; and he is to be apprehended.

1825 Mar. 5 James FILLERY of Henfield, labourer, adjudged to be the father of a bastard child born to Ann MOORE of Cowfold, singlewoman, was ordered to pay 3s 6d a week maintenance. As 258 weeks of the sum of 3s 6d, amounting to £48.10s 0d, is due and J.F. has left his usual place of abode and failed to appear after being summoned, he is to be apprehended.

1826 Oct. 7 James PARSONS of Bolney, labourer, the reputed father of a male bastard child by Sarah LANGFORD, singlewoman, was ordered to pay 2s 0d weekly and 13s 0d for cost of order; and 50 weeks at 2s 0d, amounting to £5.13s 0d, is due. As he has not appeared to answer a summons he is to be apprehended.

1826 Dec. 2 The parish officers of Hurstpierpoint are summoned to appear at the Kings Head Inn in Horsham on Saturday 16 December to show cause why James TULLETT should not be removed from Cowfold to Hurstpierpoint.
Catalogued under Par 59/32/2.

1827 May 19 Harriet PEARCE of Cowfold, singlewoman, has declared that she is with child and that Peter TOURLE of West Grinstead, labourer, is the father; and he is to be apprehended.

COWFOLD APPRENTICESHIP AGREEMENT Par 59/33/1

1631 Jul. 5 Thomas GEERES of Hurstpierpoint, farmer, bound to the parish officers of Cowfold in the sum of 20 marks agrees to take Margaret TURNER, the daughter of Thomasin TURNER of Cowfold, widow, to dwell and serve as an apprentice for the term of nine years and has received from the parish officers of Cowfold the sum of £7 in consideration of the keeping and teaching of M.T., during her term of apprenticeship. [Elizabeth GEERES also mentioned as the wife of Thomas Geeres] [Mark of T.G.]

CRAWLEY

Crawley: 780 acres from 200ft on Surrey border through Tilgate and Pease Pottage Forests to 468ft in S. Clay and marl on clay. Arable. Small market town mainly in Ifield parish (see below) on main road between London and Brighton, with three inns (one a posting house) and some 30 shopkeepers and traders. Coaches and carriers to London and Brighton.

Population: 1724 95; 1801 210; 1811 234; 1821 334; 1831 394.

QUARTER SESSIONS REMOVAL ORDERS FROM CRAWLEY

		To
L 1670 Jul.14	Thomas MICHELL and wife. Recites order 7 April, removing them from Crawley to Horsham; on appeal they are to be settled at Crawley.	Horsham
L 1684 Jan.17	Samuel STONE.	Worth.
L 1688 Jan.12	Robert BATTELL alias BINION; discharged.	Ifield
L 1718 Oct. 9	Richard BANKS; discharged.	Brighton
L 1756 Apr.29	James CHAPMAN, husbandman; respited.	Worth
L 1758 Oct. 5	William ATTREE, wife Mary and daughter Elizabeth 10y; quashed.	Ditchling
L 1811 Jan.18	Philadelphia MITCHELL, wife of Edmund MITCHELL, and daughter Mary 1y; quashed.	Ditchling
L 1811 Jul.19	Martha WATSON, widow of Thomas WATSON, and children Thomas 4y and James 2y; confirmed.	Leadenham, Lin
L 1818 Jan.16	Wheeler WELLING, wife Susannah and children Henry 7y, Susannah 4y and Benjamin 8m; confirmed.	Beeding
L 1818 Jan.16	William STEDMAN, wife Lucy and children William 6y, Lucy 4y, Mary 2y and Sarah 7m; confirmed.	Ewhurst
L 1819 Apr.23	Richard BERRYMAN 9y; respited.	Brighton
L 1819 Jul.16	Richard BERRYMAN 9y; quashed.	Brighton
L 1826 Apr. 6	Amy DENMAN; respited.	Charlwood, Sry
L 1826 Jul.13	Amy DENMAN; quashed.	Charlwood, Sry
L 1827 Jul.12	John GOLDSMITH, the younger, and wife Frances; confirmed.	Hurstpierpoint
L 1830 Jan.14	Philip KENT, wife Mary and children Mary 3y and Elizabeth 5 weeks; confirmed.	Charlwood, Sry
L 1831 Apr. 7	Martha HUMPHREY; confirmed.	Charlwood, Sry
L 1831 Oct.20	William GORING and wife Ann; confirmed.	Banstead, Sry

QUARTER SESSIONS REMOVALS ORDERS TO CRAWLEY

		From
L 1666 Apr.26	Ann DANIELL, a poor child now at Crawley; case between this parish and Nuthurst respited.	Nuthurst
L 1666 Jul.12	Elizabeth DANIELL; respited.	Nuthurst
L 1667 Jan.17	Elizabeth DANIELL, a poor child; confirmed.	Nuthurst
H 1742 Jul.12	William BOXSHELL, wife Deborah, and daughter Mary 1y; discharged.	Horsham
L 1805 Apr.26	James SAYERS, wife Sarah and children Sarah 4y, Mary 3y, Joseph 1y and Elizabeth aged 6 weeks; quashed.	Brighton
L 1816 Jul.19	Richard BARNHAM and children Richard 6y, Mary Ann 4y and Amelia 2y; adjourned.	Salehurst
L 1817 Jan.17	Richard BARNHAM and children Richard 6y, Mary Ann 4y and Amelia 2y; quashed, but without prejudice as to the respondents insisting on the same settlement in case, upon further enquiry, it should turn out that the Land Tax was deducted from the pauper's salary as an officer of excise, in which case the respondents are to be at liberty to remove to Crawley, subject to appeal.	Salehurst
L 1820 Jan.14	Ann FRAMPTON, wife of George FRAMPTON, and an unbaptised child 2m; confirmed.	Brighton
L 1828 Jul.17	Richard PHILP, wife Esther and children John 13y, William 11y, Emily 7y, Joseph 5y 6m and Henry 2y; respited.	Brighton
L 1828 Oct.16	Richard PHILP, wife Esther and children John 13y, William 11y, Emily 7y, Joseph 5y 6m and Henry 2y; quashed.	Brighton

CUCKFIELD

Cuckfield: 11,275 acres, rises from Ouse valley in N to 400ft in centre and falls to 100ft in S. Loam on clay. Arable and pasture. Ironworks with hammer ponds. Includes villages of Staplefield 3 miles NW of church, and Ansty to S. Small market town (weekly market from 1255); free grammar school; over 70 shopkeepers and traders. Coaches to London and Brighton, carrier to London.

Population: 1676 1200; 1724 1277; 1801 1693; 1811 2088; 1821 2385; 1831 2586.

CUCKFIELD VAGRANTS. 1618-1638, 1693-1698 Par 301/7/2 f8

1618 Memorandum that William ROBERTS, being taken as a vagrant person was whipt heere, according to the law in that behalfe, the xvith day of August 1618, and had a passe made thence to travayle to Llangefnye, [Llangefni] Anglesey, Wales, and thirtye dayes allowed him to travayle thither.

1627 Memorandum that Mary DIXON, being taken as a vagrant person was whipt heere, according to the law in that behalfe, the xxiiii day of March 1627, and had a passe made thence to travayle to Hardingstone, Northamptonshire, and twenty and twoo dayes allowed her to travayle thither.

1627 Memorandum that Edward PRICE vagrant, aged about 11 yeares, was whipped the 7 July 1627, and had a passe to travaile to Shorum [Shoreham], Kent, and had 4 dayes allowed him to travaile thither.

1630 Alexander SYLLIBAN and wife Jane, taken as vagrant persons and whipped 26 August 1630, and had a pass to travell to Pensance [Penzance], Cornwall where (they said) they were born.

1630 Jo.[?JONES], whipped the same day and year and passed to Plymouth, Devonshire.

1630 Godfrey PIERCE, whipped the same year and day, and passed to Asburnham [Ashburnham]

1630 Jeremie, a woman whipt and sent to Street [Streat].

1630 Walter PAINE, 12 years old, passed to Romsey, Hampshire.

1630 John BOATS, 20 yeares, whipped 25 October 1630 and passed to Wenlock [Much Wenlock], Shropshire.

1630 Marie ANTHONY, an Irish woman, whipped 28 November 1630 and passed to Shoram [Shoreham], for Ireland.

1632	John SMITH, a counterfeit, whipped 22 July 1632, and passed to Highgate, Middlesex.
1632	Richard PIERCIEFIELD, whipped 3 December 1632, and passed to Frindsbury, Rochester, Kent.
1632	Elizabeth BURLEIGH, whipped the same day, and passed to Angmering in this County.
1632	Marie [?MANSON], whipped the same day, and passed to Angmering in this County.
1632	Marie FRANNCIS, whipped the same day, and passed to Angmering.
1632	Richard LEIGH, whipped 4 December 1632, and passed to St. Lawrence, Reading, Berkshire.
1632	Adam FARMER, whipped the same day, and passed to Minster, Isle of Shepey [Sheppey], Kent.
1632	Marie COO, whipped the same day, and passed to Rochford, Essex.
1632	Elizabeth SPRAG, with a child Gaman Sprag, passed to Stening [Steyning], in this county, where she was born.
1632	Agnes DIER, whipped 7 December 1632, and passed to Havant, Hantshire [Hampshire].
1632	Anne MERIFIELDS, whipped the same day, and passed to the same place.
1634	Walter PERIMAN, whipped 30 June 1634, and passed to Milton, Kent.
1634	Robert KENTFICK, whipped the same day, and passed to Sittingburne, [Sittingbourne], Kent.
1635	Margaret CLARK, whipped 23 March 1635, and passed to Haslemore, [Haslemere], Surrey.
1635	Anne CLARK, her daughter, whipped the same day, and passed to the same place.
1635	Elisabeth PHILPOTT, whipped 15 April 1635 and passed to Chichester.
1635	Will CLARK and Phil CLARK, brothers, whipped 19 April and passed to Pool [Poole], Dorsetshire.

1635 Elizabeth DAVYS, Joan DAVYS, and Thom DAVYS, whipped 20 May, 1635 and passed to Charleton, [Charlton], Kent.

1636 Thomas CARGILL, a Scot, whipped 23 January 1636, and passed to Stramiglo [?Strathmiglo], Fife, Scotland.

1636 James FINE, Irish, whipped 29 January 1636, and passed to Waterford, Ireland.

1636 Joan, wife of David BREAD, whipped the same day and passed thither too, with three children.

1636 Tobias ROBINS whipped 9 June 1636 and passed [place not given].

1637 Joan GUESS and Thomas PHILIPS whipped 20 May 1637 and passed to South Hampton [Southampton].

1638 Joh. WILLIAMS and wife Elisabeth, wife whipped 12 July 1638 and passed to Little Dean, Gloucestershire.

1638 Roger O'REYLY, an Irish boy, whipped 23 July 1638 and passed to Cornwall, for Ireland.

1693 Margaret LONGHURST, widow and vagrant, was sent from Cuckfield, by the Minister and officers and other inhabitants, to Brighthelmston, the place where she says she last lived [but saved from whipping as being mad], and sent thither by a pass from tithing to tithing the next way thither 29 July 1693, and allowed two or three days for to travail thither.

1693 Barbara WINCHESTER, singlewoman, a vagrant aged about one and twenty years, was passed from hence to Chimer [?Keymer] in the County of Sussex 6 December 1693 and allowed a day or two for the said passage.

1698 Feb.19 Elizabeth GRIMES, wife of Francis GRIMES, with two children William and Elizabeth, was passt from Cockfield [Cuckfield], from tything to tything to the said Francis, a souldyer in Capt. Dennis, his Company of Col. Seymour's Reg. at Steyning, or to the next officer.

CUCKFIELD SETTLEMENT EXAMINATIONS Par 301/32/4/1

1713 Jun. 15 Leonard HASELGROVE said that he hired himself for a year, about seven years since, to Thomas MERCHANT in Hurstpierpoint, which term he served. That he was bound as apprentice by Hurstpierpoint to one NEWLAND in Chealy [Chailey] with whom he continued near a twelve month and then came away without the consent of Newland, which time of binding was about 4 years before he hired himself to aforesaid Marchant (sic). That he believes he is now about the age of 26 years and has not, since this time, hired himself for the space of a year. [Mark of L.H.]

1714 Mar. 27 John OVELL said that he was last settled in Horsted Keynes as a yearly servant to Joseph HAMLYN of Horsted Keynes. [Letter from L. GALE states that John Ovell served a full year with Joseph HAMBLEDON (sic) of Horsted Keynes about six years ago and had his full wages at the rate of £4.15.0, and he has never served a full year or gained any legal settlement since.]

1714 Sep. 6 Lodwicke GARDNER said that he was born at Lynn [Kings Lynn] in Norfolk and has not gained a legal settlement in any place since his birth and that he has, for some years, used the sea and now belongs to the ship called the "Lyon", Captain WALLPOLE Commander. That Katherine is his wife and they married in St. Mary Sumersetts [Somerset] als Broken Wall, [London] and, on examination, Katherine said that the last place of her settlement (before her marriage) was with Mr. HOWELL, victualler, in St. Katherines, London, with whom she lived as a servant for one whole year, and received her full year's wages.

1714 Dec. 5 Gibbon MATHER said that he was born in Canterbury [Kent] and that he served an apprenticeship to one Phillip REASON of St. Georges, Canterbury and has never had any legal settlement since. [Signature of G.M.]

1728 Mar. 10 John PICKNALL said that he was legally hired by John ROBERTS of Cowfold, yeoman, as a husbandman, from Lady Day 1723 to Lady Day 1724 for £5, which time he served and received his wages, and then served the following year for £6, and further saith not. [Signature of J.P.]

1728 Dec. 10 William FILLARE, labourer, said that under a certificate from parish of Sundrich [Sundridge] in Kent, dated 4 March last, "he came with Mary his wife and Jesse his son, now about the age of 3 years, into Cuckfield where he had born of the body of Mary his wife, William his son now about 8 months old," and further said that he has not, since the date of the certificate, gained any legal settlement in Cuckfield or elsewhere. [Mark of W.F.]

1730 Jan. 14 John HATTEN, weaver, said that he was born in Ewhurst, Surrey, of parents who were likely to be there chargeable, to prevent which this examinant was bound apprentice, by the officers of Ewhurst, to Henry BENNETT, late of Horsham, weaver, till J.H. should attain the age of 24 years. J.H. lived with H.B. for 7 years when his master, for want of work, gave this examinant the remaining part of his time, with liberty to dwell wheresoever he pleased. That he has never lived with his master out of Horsham or gained any legal settlement elsewhere. [Signature of J.H.] [Endorsed: Wife's name Jane, child's name Mary]

1730 Feb. 11 Robert FIELD said that, some years ago, he was bound apprentice to John THARP of East Grinstead, glazier and plumber, for 5 years and he served his master for one year in part of his time in East Grinstead and that his apprenticeship is now expired.

1730 Apr. 3 John SMITH said that, 18 years ago, he lived in Steyning and rented a house in that parish and was taxed and did pay to the poor and church rates for the said lease, and has not paid any taxes or rates in any other parish since or done any act to gain a settlement elsewhere. [Signature of J.S.]

1744 Jul. 9 Joseph GALYON of the 2nd Regiment of Foot, commanded by the Hon. Lord John SACKVILLE, said that, about 12 years ago, he hired himself as a yearly servant to John BOWYER of Lingfield, Surrey, miller and millwright, at wages of £7.10s 0d for the space of a year, which term he served and received his wages, since which time he has not gained a settlement in any other parish. [Signature of J.G.]

1756 Oct. 29 Ann WEBB, apprehended in Camberwell, Surrey, as a rogue and vagabond, said that she is a singlewoman and never gained a settlement by any act of her own and that she was born in Cuckfield, where her father was an inhabitant legally settled. [Mark of A.W.]

1766 Jul. 25 Francis JENNER said that, between thirty and forty years ago, he hired himself as a servant to Stephen BYNE of Hurstpierpoint, farmer, for a year at £8.5s 0d wages, which time he served and since then he has done no act to gain a settlement in any other parish. [Mark of F.J.] [Endorsed: Mary his wife]

1766 Nov. 20 John COX, labourer, now residing in Cuckfield, said that about 1752 he went to Mr. Thomas TUARTS, a tanner at Tunbridge Town, Kent, with whom his uncle, John BOTTING, then lived as a foreman in the yard, and his uncle bargained with Tuart for this examinant to serve him from then (about Whitsuntide) to the Michaelmas day old style following upon liking, and Mr. Tuart was to give him what money he pleased for such service, which term he served and then served a further year at wages of 2 guineas. That he continued to live with his master at Tunbridge till 1756 when Mr. Tuart hired a tanyard at Westerham in Kent, and went to live there in midsummer 1756, and this examinant went to live with his master at Westerham for the remainder of that year's hiring. That then he made a new agreement for a year at Westerham at wages of four and half guineas, which term he served but since has done no act whereby to gain a settlement in any other parish. [Signature of J.C.] [Endorsed: Mary his wife, John Cox an infant, about one and a quarter years.]

1771 Apr. 24 William JUPP, now residing in Cuckfield, husbandman said that, six years ago last Lady Day old style, he hired himself to Thomas YOUNG of Slaugham, farmer, to serve him for a year at wages of £6, and lived and served his master in Slaugham one whole year, since which he has done no act whereby to gain a settlement in any other parish. [Mark of W.J.] [Endorsed: Wm. Jupp, Mary his wife, Mary their daughter aged about 3 years and 9 months and John son aged about 9 weeks]

CUCKFIELD SETTLEMENT CERTIFICATES Par 301/32/1/4

N.B. A few certificates issued by Cuckfield to other parishes are listed separately immediately following the main series.

* Indicates items catalogued under Par 301/32/1/1

\+ Indicates items catalogued under Par 301/32/1/2

		From
1665 May 18	Thomas NORRIS and family who lately came to dwell in Cuckfield, have been ordered to be removed to Horsted Keynes, where he formerly dwelt, but the officers there now declare that, as T.N. has taken a chamber in the house of John LANGRIDGE at Horsted Green and has goods and household stuff there, he is accepted as an inhabitant of Horsted Keynes.	Horsted Keynes
1666 Apr. -	Widow ARCHPOOLE.	Slaugham
1673 Oct.13*	BOND. Richard DRINKWATER of Trinity Minor, Middlesex, bound to William BOARD of Cuckfield in £40 in respect of John MARSHALL, wife and family, late of Alton, turner, now of Cuckfield and employed by R.D. as his workman. [Signature of R.D.]	Alton, Ham
1686 Apr.24*	BOND. The parish officers of Bolney bound to Cuckfield parish in £100 in respect of Joan DUNTON, widow, who is now resident in Cuckfield.	Bolney
1686 Nov.30+	BOND. The parish officers of Slaugham bound to Cuckfield parish in £20 in respect of Elizabeth NAYLOR, spinster, late of Slaugham, who has lately come to settle with one Henry WATERMAN, a poor man of Cuckfield, as his apprentice.	Slaugham
1688 Mar.20*	BOND. The parish officers of Worth bound to Cuckfield parish in £100 in respect of John WOOD, tailor, wife Elizabeth and children John and Stephen who are now residing in Cuckfield.	Worth
1692 Jan.10*	Thomas WEST, wife and family. Ack.	Hurstpierpoint
1697 Sep.11*	Robert HOLMES and wife Ann. Ack.	Reigate, Sry
1698 Apr.16*	Thomas BARDEN. Ack.	Itchingfield
1700 Jan.10	William PHILLERY, wife and children.	Twineham
1703 Mar.29	Joan WIN, widow.	Balcombe
1707 Jul. 4	James TASTER, wife and family.	Balcombe
1707 Nov. 1	Henry WATERMAN, wife Jone and family.	Iford
1710 May 5	Thomas UPTON, wife and family.	Balcombe
1712 Dec. 5	John STENING, wife and children.	Capel, Sry
1713 Jan.15	John MARTIN, wife Elizabeth and child.	Twineham
1713 Jan.15	John DUNTON, husbandman, wife and children.	Twineham

1713 Feb.27	William SHERLOCK, wife and daughter.	Balcombe
1713 May 30	John BURTENSHAW, husbandman, wife and family.	West Hoathly
1713 Dec.30	John KING, son of Edward KING of Plumpton, and wife and children.	Plumpton
1714 Jan. 28	Henry HEASMAN, wheeler, and family.	Chailey
1714 Mar. 3	Thomas JENNER, blacksmith, wife and child.	Slaugham
1714 Nov 15	William BURNELL and wife.	Itchingfield
1715 Apr.26	Mary, Catherine and George PILBEAM, the three youngest children of Mary, wife of John TITKELL. Slaugham parish having already removed John Titkell, wife Mary and her four children, Anne, Mary, Catherine and George Pilbeam to Cuckfield, are now bound to the parish officers of Cuckfield in £200. In order to avoid a charge, which might arise upon an appeal by Cuckfield, Slaugham parish agree to provide for Mary, Catherine and George Pilbeam the three youngest children of Mary Titkell.	Slaugham
1717 Jan.12	John PHILLIPPS, cooper.	Haslemere, Sry
1717 Oct.22	William GREEN and wife.	Godstone, Sry
1718 Mar. 3*	Samuel CURTIS, wife and family.	Bolney
1720 Mar.19	John ANSCOMBE, wife Anne and family.	Wivelsfield
1720 Dec.30	Thomas CHALLENOR, cordwainer, and wife Elizabeth.	Hurstpierpoint
1721 Jan.22	Thomas GLASBROCK of Westmeston, wife Ann and children acknowledged as inhabitants of hamlet of Chiltington.	Chiltington
1721 Jun. 4	John TURNER, wife Joanna and children.	Betchworth, Sry
1723 Jan. 9	John CASLEDEN, wife Judith and family.	Ditchling
1723 Jan.10	James DAVY, wife Joan and children Mary, James, John, George, Ann and Thomas.	Clayton
1723 Apr.26	Richard JENNER and wife Mary.	Beddingham
1724 Sep.19	John CONSTABLE, bricklayer, wife and children to have indemnity for two years.	Newick
1725 Aug.18	Isaac HARMAN, butcher, and wife Elizabeth.	St. Michaels, Lewes
1728 Mar. 4	John GATLAND, wife and family.	Cowfold
1728 Mar. 4	William FILLARE, wife and children.	Sundridge, Ken
1728 Sep.16	John PAGE, wife and children.	Ockley, Sry
1729 Apr. 2	John BEARD, wife Mary and daughter Ruth.	Twineham
1729 Apr.26	Daniel HOBORN, wife Ann and children Ann and Walter.	West Hoathly
1729 Jul. 8	Thomas PURSER and wife.	Steyning
1730 Mar. 8	Thomas COLCHIN and wife Alice.	Withyham
1730 Mar.30	Robert FEILD, wife and family.	East Grinstead

1731 Apr.19	Richard CURTES, cripple, and wife.	Slaugham
1731 Oct.16	John FRENCH and wife Mary.	Croydon, Sry
1733 Feb. 1	Thomas GREEN and children Sarah and Edward.	Brighton
1733 Dec. 6	Robert NAPPER, butcher, having lately married, in Cuckfield, to Sarah PARROTT.	Horsham
1735 Apr.24	John HUMPHRYS, wife and family. [N.B. The certificate is addressed to "Henfield or any other parish".]	Hambledon, Ham
1735 Oct.25	Joseph SIMMINS and wife Sarah.	Worth
1736 Sep.13	William SHIRLEY and wife Susan.	Bolney
1737 Dec. 4	James EDWARDS, wife Sarah and children Thomas, James and Sarah.	Wivelsfield
1739 Jun.24	William TERRY, wife Mary and children Mary and Elizabeth.	Slaugham
1739 Jun.24	Richard HORDLEE, wife Sarah and children Richard, Sarah and Thomas.	Slaugham
1739 Jul. 1	James BROOKER, wife Frances and children George, James, John and Jane.	West Hoathly
1740 Mar. 1	Stephen SCRASE, wife Dorcas and son John 1y.	Telscombe
1741 Mar.21	Thomas RENFIELD and wife Piercy.	Pycombe
1741 Mar.30	John HALL, labourer, wife Anne and infant daughter Mary.	Slaugham
1744 Jan. 3	Moses ENGLISH and wife Mary.	Horsham
1744 May 6	John OWEN and wife Susan.	Warnham
1746 Mar. 9	Stephen PETERS, cordwainer.	Horsham
1746 Mar.15	Edward TIPPING.	Glynde
1747 Mar. 8	Henry HAMPER, wife Jane and children John, Henry, Sarah and Jane.	Lindfield
1748 Mar 19+	William SHIRLEY and wife Hannah.	Peper Harow, Sry
1750 Jan.17	William PARSON, wife Mary and children Sarah, Mary and John.	Steyning
1750 May 15	John CURTIS and wife Ann.	Billingshurst
1750 Nov.11	William CHATFIELD, wife Elizabeth and son Benjamin.	Cowfold
1752 Feb. 4	William TAYLOR and wife Mary.	Shipley
1752 Mar.11	William CHAMPION, wife Mary and children Thomas, William and Betty.	Horsham
1753 May 28	Charles BROWN, blacksmith.	Hamsey
1754 Aug. 6	Mary BENTLY and the child which she may have.	Lingfield, Sry
1754 Oct.26	John BATCHELOR, wife Elizabeth and son John.	Rusper
1755 Aug.31	John PENTICOURST, wife Ruth and children Elizabeth and Thomas.	Ringmer
1755 Nov.22	John JUPP, blacksmith, and wife Barbara.	Horsham
1756 Feb. 3	Richard OLDER, bricklayer, and wife Sarah.	Lindfield
1757 Nov.14	Thomas BLAND, wife Judeth and children Judeth 6y and John 4y.	Lindfield

1757 Nov.14	George EADE, wife Elizabeth and children Elizabeth and Sarah each aged 1y 9m.	Lindfield
1758 Jan. 3	Thomas SIMMONDS, flaxman, and wife Susanna.	Hurstpierpoint
1760 Feb. 3	John BISHOP, wife Elizabeth and son James 1y.	Reigate, Sry
1760 Apr.17	William HILLS and wife Elizabeth.	Poling
1760 Apr.21	Robert RISBRIDGER and wife Sarah.	Horsham
1761 Apr. 7*	Henry FAIRHALL, labourer, and wife Jane.	Lindfield
1761 Aug.31	Matthew GREEN, cordwainer, wife Mary and children Mary 3y, Sarah 2y and John 1y.	Brighton
1761 Dec.26	John DEAN, wife Sarah and children Sarah 14y, John 12y, Thomas 9y and Isaac 6y.	Horsted Keynes
1762 Sep.18	William DEADMAN, husbandman, wife Elizabeth and children Sarah, Elizabeth, Mary and Thomas.	Crawley
1763 Jan.15	William MASON and wife Ann.	Hurstpierpoint
1763 Mar.10	Michael WALLER, wife Ann and daughter Ann 11y.	Bolney
1764 Jan. 4	John SHOULDER and wife Ann.	Woodmancote
1766 Jan.13	Henry BROOKFIELD and wife Sussannah.	Midhurst
1766 Jan. 29	John COOK, wife Sarah and daughter Mary 8y.	Bolney
1766 Mar.31	Thomas CARTER, wife and children; John RIST, wife and children; and John WARRENER, wife and children. Ack. [all on the one document]	Balcombe
1766 Jul. 5	Thomas STONER, wife Phebe and daughter Phebe 14m.	Cowfold
1766 Oct.15	Guy RIVERS, wife Elizabeth and daughter Elizabeth 9m.	Godstone, Sry
1766 Dec. 2	James RAPLEY, labourer, and wife Ann.	Lindfield
1767 Apr. 7	Nicholas VINALL, labourer, wife Elizabeth and children Richard 4y, Elizabeth 3y and Nicholas 7m.	Lindfield
1767 May 3	Francis JENNER and wife Mary.	Hurstpierpoint
1768 Nov.13	Richard MIHILL, labourer, wife Judeth and children Sarah 14y and Susannah 11y.	Horsted Keynes
1769 Feb. 6	George PARSON and wife Elizabeth.	Wivelsfield
1769 Feb.12	John HART fellmonger, wife Mary and children John 5y and Mary 5m.	Lindfield
1769 Apr.23	Thomas THOMSETT, labourer, and wife Elizabeth.	Lindfield
1770 Apr.18+	James HOLDEN, blacksmith.	Woodmancote
1770 Jun.10	William POBGEE and wife Hannah.	Horsham
1771 Mar.13	William BOOKER and wife Ann.	Lingfield, Sry
1771 Oct.21	Hanah NYE, widow, and children Jane and John.	Bolney
1771 Nov.26	John TRIGGS, wife Mary and daughter Ann 1y.	Rogate
1772 Feb. 3	Thomas PECKHAM and wife Mary. Ack.	Wivelsfield
1773 Jul.19	John HOWELL and wife Sarah.	St. Michael, Lewes

1774 Apr. 4	Francis HARDING, wife Sarah and child Susanna 7y.	Cowfold
1774 Dec.27	John NEWICK and wife Hannah.	Steyning
1775 Mar.13	William SUMNER, wife Sarah and children James 3y and Mary 1y.	Slaugham
1776 Feb.18	Thomas LEPPARD and wife Sarah.	Nuthurst
1776 Apr. 2	John GREENFIELD, wife Ann and children Thomas 3y and Ann 6 weeks.	Lindfield
1777 Dec.31	Thomas HEASMAN, wife Frances and children Frances 7y, Thomas 6y, Ann 4y and John 1y. Ack.	Balcombe
1779 Mar.31	Henry MERCHANT, wife Susannah and children Ann, Elizabeth, James and John. Ack.	Balcombe
1779 Mar.31	John RICE, wife Sarah and children Susannah, John and Elizabeth. Ack.	Balcombe
1779 Apr.14	George WELLS and wife Elizabeth.	Ashington
1779 Oct.24	Edward TYLER, wife Mary and children John 5y, Sarah 3y and Edward 1y.	Warnham
1779 Nov. 6	John PENNIFOLD.	Slaugham
1781 Apr.19	Richard LASHFORD.	Gatton, Sry
1787 Jan.27	John TOLLHURST, wife Mary and daughter Elizabeth 8m.	Newick
1787 Jan.31	John HOLLINGHAM and wife Sarah.	Lancing
1787 Mar.20	Richard STEDMAN and wife Sarah.	Slaugham
1787 Oct. 9	John LEOPARD, wife Elizabeth and children Mary 17y, Thomas 11y, James 8y, Ann 6y, and Jenny 3y.	Beeding
1788 Feb.28	Edmund DAVEY and wife Lucy.	Brighton
[-] May 4	John RANDAL, wife and family.	East Grinstead

Catalogued under Par 301/32/1/3

CERTIFICATES OF SETTLEMENT IN CUCKFIELD — Par 301/32/1/4

		To
1694 Jan.15*	Ann HALL, widow, and children John and Mary. Ack.	Slaugham
1694 Mar.15*	Thomas TITLE, wife Mary and children Elizabeth and Mary. Ack.	Slaugham
1694 Jul.30*	Robert HALL, wife Jane and three children. Ack.	Slaugham
1695 Jul.29	Leonard POTTER, labourer and wife.	Clayton
1704 May 20*	Edward HILLMAN and family.	Tonbridge, Ken
1732 Apr.20	Thomas HOLLYBONE, wife Mary and children Mary and Elizabeth. [Document not signed]	Hurstpierpoint

1744 Jan. 6	BOND. John EDWARDS and William EDWARDS both of Cuckfield, cordwainers, bound to Henry GATLAND of Cuckfield, gent., in £50 in respect of above named William Edwards and wife Katherine, who have obtained a settlement certificate from Cuckfield, W.E. agreeing not to take any apprentice whilst settled in Westmeston. [Mark of W.E.]	Westmeston
1776 Jan. 5	William VARNES otherwise VAUGHANS.	Not given
1781 May 29	James BUCKMAN, wife Mary and children Mary 12y, James 9y, Edward 7y, Elizabeth 4y and Sarah 1y.	Slaugham

REMOVAL ORDERS FROM CUCKFIELD — Par 301/32/2/3

		To
1696 Apr.14	Henry NYE. *Catalogued under Par 301/32/2/1*	Hurstpierpoint
1696 Oct. 9	Edward DOBLE, a bastard child, was born in Newick, son of Jane DOBLE who was afterwards, by an order, settled in Cuckfield, and E.D., as a nurse child, went with his mother to Cuckfield. As Edward Doble is now beyond the capacity of a nurse child and ought to be settled in Newick where he was born, he is to be removed to that parish.	Newick
1697 Jan.14	Edward DOBLE. On appeal, order confirmed.	Newick
1710 May 9	[Henry LONGE], wife Mary LONGE and son Henry.	Beeding
1711 Apr.12	Robert NIGHTINGALE. On appeal, order confirmed.	Slaugham
1712 Apr.24	John STENING, wife and family. Last legal place was Capel, where he was a yearly servant.	Capel, Sry
1712 Dec.29	John DUNTON, husbandman, and wife.	Twineham
1712 Dec.29	Elizabeth MARTIN.	Twineham
1713 Apr.16	Thomas WELFARE and wife. On appeal, order confirmed.	Lindfield
1713 Jul. 1	Leonard HASLEGROVE and wife.	Chailey
1713 Jul.16	Mary BLABER, singlewoman, and son George. Confirmation.	St. Michaels, Lewes
1713 Nov.26	Fredricke FRENCH.	Brighton

1714 Jun. 3	William BERRY was, by indenture, bound apprentice by Cuckfield to Henry GEERING of Keymer, tailor, till age of 24. As W.B. has since returned to Cuckfield and likely to become chargeable, he is to be removed to Keymer, the place of his lawful settlement and, if he returns again to Cuckfield after his removal, he is to be conveyed to the House of Correction to be punished as a vagrant.	Keymer
1714 Jul.12	William BURNELL.	Itchingfield
1714 Oct. 7	Thomas STANNING. On appeal, order discharged.	Bolney
1714 Dec.	Gibbon MATHER and wife and children.	St. George, Canterbury, Ken
1717 Oct.10	John JENNER and wife Frances. On appeal, order confirmed.	Twineham
1719 Apr.22	James PICKE and wife Elizabeth. On examination, J.P. said that he was last legally settled in St. Margarets, Rochester, being bound apprentice to John LADBURY of that parish.	Rochester, Ken
1719 Sep.21	William FRENCH and wife Elizabeth.	Hurstpierpoint
1719 Dec.26	Mary PRING, wife of Isaac PRING of Lindfield, husbandman, and Isaac her child 9m.	Lindfield
1720 Nov.23	Thomas CHALLONER and wife Elizabeth.	Hurstpierpoint
1724 Apr.10	Thomas SAVAGE. On examination, it appears that he was born in St. Martins, Leicester, where his father was legally settled at the time of his birth, and T.S. has not gained a settlement elsewhere.	Leicester, Lei
1724 May 30	Male bastard child, aged seven weeks, born to Elizabeth HILLS, singlewoman.	Wivelsfield
1728 Dec.10	William FILLARE, and infants Jesse and William, under age of 7 years, born to his wife Mary. W.F. and wife came into Cuckfield with a certificate dated 4 March 1728 from Sundrich [Sundridge], Kent, which has been produced but, as W.F. and children have become chargeable, they are to be removed to Sundrich.	Sundridge, Ken
1729 Oct. 9	Elizabeth TYDEY, widow, and daughters Mary 10y and Elizabeth 8y. On appeal, order discharged.	Slaugham
1730 Feb.23	Robert FIELD and wife Mary.	East Grinstead
1730 Jul.16	John SMITH the younger. Confirmation.	Steyning
1731 Jan.14	Richard CURTIS and wife Jane. Confirmation.	Slaugham
1731 May 25	Isaac HARMAN, butcher, wife Elizabeth and son Josiah 5y have dwelt in Cuckfield for some time by a certificate dated 18 Aug. 1725 from St. Michaels, Lewes but, having become chargeable, they are to be returned to that parish.	St. Michaels, Lewes

1735 Oct. 9	Thomas LUTMAN and wife Mary. Confirmation.	Shermanbury
1736 Jan.15	William PETERS, wife Mary and son William. Confirmation.	Slaugham
1736 Oct. 7	Richard HOADLEY, wife Sarah and children Richard and Sarah. On appeal, order confirmed.	Slaugham
1736 Oct 7	Humphrey MORRIS and wife Mary. Confirmation.	Ditchling
1737 Jul.14	Mary DUMBRELL. On appeal, order confirmed and Hurstpierpoint to pay Cuckfield 20s 0d costs.	Hurstpierpoint
1737 Sep. 2	James EDWARDS, wife Sarah and children Thomas 5y, Sarah 4y and James 2y.	Wivelsfield
1737 Oct. 6	Joseph HOLDEN and wife Ann. Confirmation.	Kirdford
1738 Jan.12	Thomas EDWARDS and wife Elizabeth. Confirmation.	Horley, Sry
1739 May 3	Charles SHIRLEY, wife Mary and daughter Anne. Confirmation.	Reigate, Sry
1739 Oct. 4	Thomas LASHMORE. Confirmation.	West Hoathly
1740 Jul.17	George NYE. Confirmation.	Shipley
1741 Jan.15	William STANDEN and wife Mary. Confirmation.	St. Sepulchre, Mdx.
1741 Oct. 8	Sarah LONGLEY. Confirmation.	Slaugham
1741 Oct. 8	Richard LASHMER and wife Mary. Confirmation. *Catalogued under Par 301/32/2/1*	Ditchling
1745 Jul.18	Robert NAPPER, wife Sarah and children Elizabeth, Henry and Phillis. Confirmation.	Horsham
1746 Jan. 9	Sarah DAVY, singlewoman.	East Grinstead
1746 Apr. 4	Thomas LUTEMAN and wife Mary.	Shermanbury
1756 Sep.10	William LONGHURST, labourer.	Pulborough
1756 Nov. 1	William SHIRLEY, wife Hannah and children Richard, John and Thomas. The family have dwelt for some time in Cuckfield by reason of a certificate, dated 19 March 1747, from Peperharow.	Peper Harow, Sry
1757 Jan.13	Ann WEST, singlewoman. Confirmation.	Albourne
1757 Jan.13	William LONGHURST and wife Ann. Confirmation.	Pulborough
1757 Oct.14	John BISHOP and wife Elizabeth.	Reigate, Sry
1759 Feb.20	Mary SHEPHERD, singlewoman.	Cowfold
1759 Apr.20	George MOCKFORD.	Hawkhurst, Ken
1763 Nov.21	John SHOULDER and wife Ann.	Woodmancote
1764 Jul.12	Mary SMITH. Confirmation.	Goudhurst, Ken
1765 Apr.12	Elizabeth PETTIT, singlewoman.	Slaugham
1766 Apr. 4	Henry WEST and wife Sarah.	Worth
1766 Jul.25	Francis JENNER and wife Mary.	Hurstpierpoint
1766 Oct. 6	James RAPLEY and wife Ann. On appeal, order confirmed.	Lindfield
1766 Nov.20	John COX, wife Mary and son John 1y 3m.	Westerham, Ken
1768 Jan.26	John BOXELL.	Lurgashall

1770 Jan.11	Thomas MATTHEW and wife Elizabeth. Confirmation.	Cowfold
1771 Apr.24	William JUPP, wife Mary and children Mary 3y 9m and John 9 weeks.	Slaugham
1771 Nov.20	John TRIGGS, wife Mary and daughter Ann about 11m.	Rogate
	Catalogued under Par 301/32/2/2	

QUARTER SESSIONS REMOVAL ORDERS FROM CUCKFIELD

		To
L 1659 Jul.14	Richard COLMAN removed to Hartfield, this being the place of his last habitation.	Hartfield
L 1666 Oct. 4	Edward OSBORNE.	Lindfield
L 1671 May 4	- RANDALL, wife and family.	East Grinstead
L 1671 Oct. 5	Thomas GREENE was, on 2 October, brought from Cuckfield to Horsham, without an order; he is to be returned to Cuckfield until an order showing cause for removal is given to Horsham.	Horsham
L 1677 Jan.11	Richard COX; on his appeal order respited.	Lindfield
L 1681 Apr.14	Elizabeth GARDYNER 5y, whose parents are vagrant persons; respited.	Balcombe
L 1690 May 1	Thomas BUTTON and wife; on appeal they are to be settled at Cuckfield.	Slaugham
L 1690 May 1	John PASSELL, wife and family; confirmed.	Balcombe
L 1697 Jan.14	Edward DOBLE; confirmed.	Newick
L 1699 Jan.12	- TITLE. Male bastard child of Ann TITLE; discharged as he is to be settled at Cuckfield, where he was born.	Lindfield
L 1703 Jul.15	Elizabeth NAYLOR; discharged.	Ditchling
B 1711 Apr.12	Robert NIGHTINGALE; confirmed.	Slaugham
L 1713 Apr.16	Thomas WELFARE and wife; confirmed.	Lindfield
L 1713 Jul.16	Mary BLABER, singlewoman; and son George; confirmed.	St. Michaels, Lewes
L 1714 Oct. 7	Thomas STANNING; discharged.	Bolney
L 1714 Oct. 7	Thomas MITCHELL; discharged.	Hurstpierpoint
L 1714 Oct. 7	Edward JENNER; discharged.	Cowfold
L 1717 Oct.10	John JENNER and wife Frances; confirmed.	Twineham
L 1722 Jan.11	Thomas CARE and wife Frances; discharged.	Ardingly
L 1724 Oct. 8	Timothy HUMPHRES, singlewoman; confirmed.	Slaugham
L 1729 Jan.16	John UPTON and wife Susannah; discharged.	Ardingly
L 1729 Oct. 9	Elizabeth TYDEY, widow, and children Mary 10y and Elizabeth 8y; discharged.	Slaugham
L 1730 Jul.16	John SMITH, the younger; confirmed.	Steyning
L 1730 Oct. 8	Allen PARSONS and wife; confirmed.	St. James, Clerkenwell,Mdx

L 1731 Jan.14	Richard CURTIS and wife Jane; confirmed.	Slaugham
L 1731 Oct. 7	Allen PARSONS, wife Mary and children Philip and James, both under 7y; discharged. A.P. served apprenticeship to James WRIGHT in Mead's Court, Old Bond Street for 3 years, which place was then in St. George, Hanover Square, Middlesex.	St. Martin in the Fields, Mdx
L 1732 Jan.13	Allen PARSONS, wife Mary and children Philip and Allen; confirmed.	St. George, Hanover Square, Mdx.
L 1735 Oct. 9	Thomas LUTMAN and wife Mary; confirmed.	Shermanbury
L 1736 Jan.15	William PETERS, wife Mary and son William; confirmed.	Slaugham
L 1736 Jan.15	Richard HOADLY, wife Sarah and children Richard and Sarah; respited.	Slaugham
L 1736 Oct. 7	Humphrey MORRIS and wife Mary; confirmed.	Ditchling
L 1736 Oct. 7	Richard HOADLEY, wife Sarah and children Richard and Sarah; confirmed.	Slaugham
L 1737 Jan.13	Mary DUMBRELL; respited.	Hurstpierpoint
L 1737 Apr.21	James BROOKER, wife Frances and three children under 7y; confirmed.	West Hoathly
L 1737 Jul.14	Mary DUMBRELL; confirmed.	Hurstpierpoint
L 1737 Oct. 6	Joseph HOLDEN and wife Anne; confirmed.	Kirdford
L 1738 Jan.12	Thomas EDWARDS and wife Elizabeth; confirmed.	Horley, Sry
L 1739 May 3	Charles SHERLEY, wife Mary and daughter Ann 6m; confirmed.	Reigate, Sry
L 1739 Oct. 4	Thomas LASHMORE; confirmed.	West Hoathly
L 1740 Jan.17	William WHITEING and wife Sarah; confirmed.	Henfield
L 1740 Jul.17	George NYE; confirmed.	Shipley
L 1741 Jan.15	William STANDEN and wife Mary; confirmed.	St. Sepulchre, Mdx
L 1741 Oct. 8	Sarah LONGLEY; confirmed.	Slaugham
L 1741 Oct. 8	Richard LASHMER and wife Mary; confirmed.	Ditchling
L 1743 Jan.13	Richard WICKES and wife Hanah; confirmed.	Portslade
L 1745 Jul.18	Robert NAPPER, wife Sarah and children Elizabeth, Henry and Phillis; confirmed.	Horsham
L 1745 Oct.10	Joseph INGRAM and wife Elizabeth; confirmed.	St. James Westminster,Mdx
L 1749 Jan.12	Turner BRISTOW, wife Elizabeth and children Scipio 9y and Anne 1y; confirmed as to Turner and discharged as to Elizabeth the wife and children Scipio and Anne.	Edenbridge, Ken
L 1750 Jan.11	John WOOD and wife Joanah; discharged.	Falmer
L 1750 Apr.26	Elizabeth COOK; confirmed.	Henfield
L 1750 Apr.26	John WOOD and wife Joanah; confirmed.	Brighton

L 1750 Jul.12	John CURTIS and wife Ann; confirmed.	Billingshurst
L 1750 Oct. 4	John TOMSON and wife Mary;confirmed.	Wiston
L 1753 Oct. 4	Mary FARMER, singlewoman; confirmed.	Horsham
L 1757 Jan.13	Ann WEST, singlewoman; confirmed.	Albourne
L 1757 Jan.13	William LONGHURST and wife Ann; confirmed.	Pulborough
L 1757 Apr.21	John SHIRLEY and wife Sarah; confirmed.	Bolney
L 1758 Jul.13	Elizabeth DENMAN, singlewoman; respited.	Shermanbury
L 1758 Oct. 5	Elizabeth DENMAN, singlewoman; confirmed.	Shermanbury
L 1759 Apr.26	James PRIOR and wife Elizabeth; confirmed.	Willingdon
L 1762 Apr.22	Thomas GILLHAM and wife Katherine; confirmed.	Newick
L 1764 Jul.12	Mary SMITH; confirmed.	Goudhurst, Ken
L 1766 Oct. 9	James RAPLEY and wife Ann; confirmed.	Lindfield
L 1770 Jan.11	Thomas MATTHEW and wife Elizabeth; confirmed.	Cowfold
L 1771 Jul.18	William SUMNER and wife Sarah; confirmed.	Slaugham
L 1773 Apr.22	Henry SMITH and wife Sarah; confirmed.	Wadhurst
L 1775 Oct. 5	William PERRY; confirmed.	Croydon, Sry
L 1785 Jan.13	George ROWLAND the younger, and wife Charity; confirmed.	Hurstpierpoint
L 1787 Jan.11	John ROGERS and wife Sarah; confirmed.	Lingfield, Sry
L 1787 Jan.11	John TOLLHURST, wife Mary and daughter Elizabeth 3m; confirmed.	Newick
L 1788 Jan.17	John SIDFORD and wife Ann; confirmed.	Romsey, Ham
L 1788 Jan.17	George HEASMAN, wife Mary and children Elizabeth 9y, Henry 5y and James 2y; respited.	West Grinstead
L 1788 Apr. 3	George HEASMAN, wife Mary and children Elizabeth 9y, Henry 5y and James 2y; confirmed.	West Grinstead
L 1789 Jan.15	Jane MORTON, singlewoman; confirmed.	Battersea, Sry
L 1791 Oct. 6	Moses RAPLEY; confirmed.	Chailey
L 1792 Apr.19	James LONGLEY, wife Ann and son 5m; confirmed.	Stratford, Ess
L 1794 Jul.17	John PENFOLD, wife Sarah and son Frank 1y; confirmed.	Dorking, Sry
L 1794 Oct. 9	James LENEY, wife Maria Grace and son James 1y; confirmed.	Newick
L 1795 Apr.17	William SAYER, wife Mary and an infant not yet baptised; respited.	Slaugham
L 1795 Apr.17	Edmund STANDEN, wife Ann and children Joseph 6y, Philidelphia 5y, Henry 4y and Edmund 6m; confirmed.	Clapham
L 1795 Jul.17	William SAYER, wife Mary and an infant child; confirmed.	Slaugham
L 1795 Oct. 9	Christopher DENMAN and wife Ann; confirmed.	Worth

L 1799 Oct.10	Mary DALE, (wife of John DALE, a private in the 11th Regiment of Light Dragoons now abroad), and son John 12y; confirmed.	Clayton
L 1801 Jan.15	James HEMSLEY, wife Sarah and children Philadelphia 5y and Mary 3y; confirmed.	Brighton
L 1801 Apr.16	Michael WALDER, wife Martha and son Michael 3m; confirmed.	Brighton
L 1801 Apr.16	Michael FIELD, wife Sarah and children Michael 3y and an infant not yet baptised; confirmed.	Chiddingstone, Ken
L 1801 Jul.16	Susanna GREEN 6y and William GREEN 3y; confirmed.	Warminghurst
L 1801 Oct. 8	Stephen Browne CHATFIELD 7y; confirmed.	Lindfield
L 1801 Oct. 8	Ann WELLER, singlewoman; confirmed.	Lindfield
L 1801 Oct. 8	John LINDFIELD, wife Elizabeth and children Samuel 4y, Elizabeth 2y and Sarah 3m; confirmed.	Slaugham
L 1803 Apr.22	William HARDS and wife Mary; confirmed.	Slaugham
L 1803 Apr.22	Fanny MITCHELL, singlewoman; confirmed.	Hurstpierpoint
L 1804 Jan.13	Mary MITCHELL, singlewoman; confirmed.	Croydon, Sry
L 1804 Apr.13	James HOLDEN, the younger, wife Elizabeth and children Elizabeth 7y, Mary 6y, Jane 4y and James 1y; confirmed.	Woodmancote
L 1804 Apr.13	Fanny PACKHAM, singlewoman; confirmed.	Chatham, Ken
L 1805 Jan.18	John BURGESS, wife Mary and children Thomas 5y, Mary 3y, and John 1y; confirmed.	Ditchling
L 1805 Apr.26	Richard SIMMONS, wife Mary and children Caroline 5y, Mary 3y and Richard 9m; respited.	Ardingly
L 1805 Jul.19	Richard SIMMONS, wife Mary and children Caroline 5y, Mary 3y and Richard 9m; confirmed.	Ardingly
L 1805 Jul.19	John AGATE and wife Sarah; confirmed.	Brighton
L 1805 Oct.11	Charles BURSTOW; confirmed.	Itchingfield
L 1806 Apr.18	Sarah HAZELGROVE, singlewoman; confirmed.	Friern[Barnet] Mdx
L 1807 Oct. 9	Emina HARDING, singlewoman; confirmed.	Brighton
L 1808 Jan.15	Mary PACKHAM, wife of Peter PACKHAM the younger, and son Thomas 9m; confirmed.	Gillingham, Ken
L 1808 Jan.15	Kaziah SNATT, (wife of James SNATT, now confined in Horsham gaol for debt), and children Mary 8y, Ann 6y, Susannah 4y, Sarah 12m; confirmed.	Chailey
L 1808 Apr.29	Elizabeth PARKER, (wife of William PARKER, a private in the Sussex Regiment of Militia), and children Elizabeth 10y, Ann 8y, William 5y, Amos 4y and Mary 2y; confirmed.	Shipley

L 1808 Oct. 7	Philadelphia PENTECOST; respited	St. Michaels, Lewes
L 1809 Jan.13	Philadelphia PENTECOST; confirmed.	St. Michaels, Lewes
L 1809 Jul.14	John MIALL and wife Amy; respited.	Lindfield
L 1809 Oct. 6	John MIALL and wife Amy; confirmed.	Lindfield
L 1810 Jan.12	Ann MARCHANT, singlewoman; confirmed.	Wivelsfield
L 1810 Jul.13	John SHARP and wife Elizabeth, children Harriet 6y, Sophia 3y 6m and Fanny 2y; confirmed.	Stansted, Ess
L 1811 Apr.26	Charles TULLEY; confirmed.	Hurstpierpoint
L 1811 Oct.11	Ruth POLLARD, (wife of Joseph POLLARD, a private in the 39th Regiment of Foot), and son William 4y; respited.	Horsham
L 1812 Jan.17	Ruth POLLARD, (wife of Joseph POLLARD, a private in the 39th Regiment of Foot), and son William 4y; confirmed.	Horsham
L 1812 Apr.10	Thomas SANDFORD, wife Sarah and daughter Mary 6y; confirmed.	Wisborough Green
L 1812 Apr.10	William PAYNE, wife Bet and children Robert 14y, Mary Ann 12y, Cornelious 10y, Rhoda 9y, Matilda 6y, Harriet 4y and Samuel 8m; confirmed.	Hambledon, Ham
L 1812 Oct. 9	John COATES 11y; confirmed.	St. Michaels, Lewes
L 1813 Oct. 8	Susan MASON, singlewoman; confirmed.	Paddington, Mdx
L 1814 Oct.21	William SAYER, wife Mary and children John 11y, Mary 8y, Ann 5y and Harriet 3y; confirmed.	Slaugham
L 1815 Apr. 7	Isaac SAYER and wife Ann; confirmed.	Brighton
L 1815 Apr. 7	George NYE, wife Susannah and children Martha 2y and Benjamin 7 weeks; confirmed.	Henfield
L 1815 Apr. 7	Ann AYRES, wife of Henry AYRES and children Charles 3y and John 8m; confirmed.	West Hoathly
L 1815 Apr. 7	Richard TOURLE, wife Hannah and son Edward 6m; confirmed.	Eastbourne
L 1815 Apr. 7	Thomas SAYER and wife Mary; confirmed.	Hurstpierpoint
L 1816 Jan.12	William HUGHES and wife Lucy; confirmed.	Wisborough Green
L 1816 Oct.18	William WALLS and wife Elizabeth; confirmed.	Ifield
L 1817 Apr.18	John WHITE, wife Elizabeth and daughter Mary 1m; respited.	Westmeston
L 1817 Jul.18	John WHITE, wife Elizabeth and daughter Mary 1m; quashed.	Westmeston
L 1817 Jul.18	Thomas WRIGHT; confirmed.	Dorking, Sry
L 1817 Oct.18	William ARNOLD; confirmed.	Horley, Sry
L 1818 Jan.16	William WILDS and wife Susan; confirmed.	Hadlow, Ken
L 1818 Jan.16	Sarah MITCHELL, singlewoman; confirmed.	Hurstpierpoint

L 1818 Jan.16	Charlotte GOWER, wife of John GOWER and children Charlotte 11y, Ann 6y, Elizabeth 3y and Harriet 4m; quashed.	Keymer
L 1818 Jul.17	Phillis LEE, singlewoman; confirmed.	Hurstpierpoint
L 1818 Oct.23	George GORRINGE and daughter Sarah 9m; confirmed.	Hurstpierpoint
L 1821 May 4	James ELLIS, wife Mary and children George 7y, Mary Ann 5y, Catherine 3y and Elizabeth 11m; confirmed.	Maresfield
L 1822 Jul.19	William KNIGHT, wife Mary and children James 5y, Sarah 3y and George 1y; confirmed.	Lindfield
L 1822 Jul.19	Ann STEDMAN, widow; confirmed.	Charlwood, Sry
L 1822 Jul.19	William ARNOLD otherwise Stedman, the illegitimate son of Ann STEDMAN, widow, formerly Ann ARNOLD, widow; confirmed.	Worth
L 1824 Jul.15	William KING, wife Mary and children Henry 5y and Sarah 2y; confirmed.	Hurstpierpoint
L 1824 Oct.21	Henry FOWLER, wife Mary and children Mary 12y, Henry 11y, Charlotte 9y, Louisa 7y, Elizabeth 3y and George 10m; confirmed.	Henfield
L 1825 Apr.14	John FIELDERS, wife Mary and children Sophia 3y, Eliza 2y and James 6m; respited.	Chailey
L 1825 Apr.14	William FIELDERS, wife Mary and children Martha 7y, Ann 6y, John 4y and William 1y 6m; respited.	Chailey
L 1825 Jul.14	William FIELDERS, wife Mary and children Martha 7y, Ann 6y, John 4y and William 1y 6m; confirmed.	Chailey
L 1825 Jul.14	John FIELDERS, wife Mary and children Sophia 3y, Eliza 2y and James 6m; confirmed.	Chailey
L 1825 Oct.20	Hannah PATTENDEN; confirmed.	Heathfield
L 1826 Jan.12	Elizabeth HEASMAN otherwise BATCHELOR; confirmed.	Cowfold
L 1826 Apr. 6	Sarah CARTER otherwise HARLAND; confirmed.	Clayton
L 1826 Jul.13	Mary Ann HARDS; confirmed.	Slaugham
L 1826 Oct.19	Thomas HOWE and wife Sarah; confirmed.	Ifield
L 1827 Apr.26	Mary KNIGHT, wife of John KNIGHT; respited	Ifield
L 1827 Apr.26	Mary Ann STEVENS, singlewoman, who is with child; confirmed.	Tring, Hrt
L 1827 Jul.12	Mary KNIGHT, wife of John KNIGHT; quashed.	Ifield
L 1830 Apr.22	Samuel PICKNELL; quashed.	Lindfield
L 1831 Jun.30	Elizabeth PUTTOCK and daughters Elizabeth 6y and Mary Ann 3y; confirmed.	Brighton

L 1835 Oct.19	William NOBLE, wife Charlotte and children Julia 13y, Horace 11y, Sarah 9y, Walter 7y, Susan 5y, Ambrose 3y and Charles 12m; confirmed.	Brighton

REMOVAL ORDERS TO CUCKFIELD — Par 301/32/3/3

* Indicates item catalogued under Par 301/32/3/2

		From
1694 Apr.19	The wife of John BUTTON, sawyer, and child are now resident in Horsham and refuse to inhabit in Cuckfield parish, being the place of residence and legal settlement of John Button. Horsham to remove the wife of J.B. and her child to Cuckfield and deliver them to J.B. or, in his absence, to the parish officers there.	Horsham
1696 Apr. 6	Richard VENALL [VERRALL], labourer, wife and child. R.V. having been servant to William BEDLE *Catalogued under Par 301/32/1/1*	Ifield
1696 Apr.23	Richard VERRALL and wife. On appeal it appears that the inhabitants of Ifield did, fraudently and by misinformation, get an order for removing R.V. and wife from Ifield to Cuckfield, and the court does think fit that this order be discharged.	Ifield
1708 Nov. 8	Ann SCRIVEN, singlewoman, now great with child. *Catalogued under Par 301/32/3/1*	Balcombe
1712 Dec. 1*	Henry Finch TYNE, aged 14y, the bastard son of Ann TYNE, singlewoman, was born in Cuckfield but has lived, since his birth, in Horsham.	Horsham
1723 Jul.18*	Jane PEIRCE. On appeal, order discharged.	Fletching
1733 Nov.16*	Ann STAPLEY, singlewoman.	Balcombe
1737 Jun.16*	Elizabeth FILLERY.	Ditchling
1738 Apr. 6	William STEPNEY, wife Rachele and son William *Document displayed in Cuckfield church*	Ratcliff in St. Dunstans, Stepney, Mdx
1738 Jun. 2	William STEPNEY, wife Rachell and son William. Cuckfield give notice that they intend to appeal, at next Quarter Sessions for Middlesex, against removal of W.S. and family.	Ratcliff, St. Dunstan, Stepney, Mdx
1739 Aug. 3	Sarah and Mary FRENCH, spinsters, and Charles FRENCH aged 9y, the illegitimate children, born in Cuckfield, to Mary FRENCH, singlewoman, who is now the wife of Thomas LUTMAN, of Shermanbury. Notice of appeal.	Shermanbury

1740 Mar.28	Richard KNIGHT.	Clayton
1741 Jul.13	Joane STEVENS. On appeal, order discharged.	Steyning
1741 Dec.23	Edward HILLMAN and family, came to Tonbridge by virtue of a certificate dated 18 [or 20] May, 1704. As E.W. and family have now become chargeable they are to be returned to Cuckfield.	Tonbridge, Ken
1742 Jan. 7	Robert OWDEN, wife Hannah and children John 4y and Susan under 1y. *Catalogued under Par 301/32/3/1*	Keymer
1745 Aug. 7	Joan LINDFIELD.	Balcombe
1749 Sep. 2	Sarah BUTTENSHAW, singlewoman.	Sundridge, Ken
1751 Feb. 2	Benjamin MASCALL, husbandman, and wife Sarah.	Penshurst, Ken
1751 Nov. 4	Francis JUNIPER.	Maresfield
1756 Oct.29	Ann WEBB, singlewoman, was apprehended in Camberwell as a rogue and vagabond. A.W. who, on examination, said that her last legal settlement was at Cuckfield, is to be conveyed to Crawley, that being the first parish in the next precinct through which she ought to pass in the direct way to Cuckfield. *Catalogued under Par 301/29/3*	Camberwell, Sry
1763 Mar. 9	John WALTER.	Wrotham, Ken
1763 Dec.24	Edward CHATFIELD, wife Ann and children Mary 11y, Anna-Maria 6y, Martha 5y and Ann 9 weeks.	Framfield
1767 Sep.21	Elizabeth JACKSON, singlewoman.	Ardingly
1768 Jan.16	Susanah GALLARD 13y, Elizabeth GALLARD 10y, and Sarah GALLARD 3y, the children of Edward GALLARD, lately deceased.	Fulham, Mdx
1768 Mar.10	Elizabeth FINCH, aged 19y, daughter of Thomas FINCH deceased.	St. Luke, Mdx
1769 Jun.23	William MARTIN, wife Mary and son William 4y and an infant, newly born. An order for their removal from Cowfold to Cuckfield cannot be proceeded with as, despite a diligent search, William Martin cannot be found.	Cowfold
1769 Nov. 29	Henry GALLARD and wife Ann.	Barcombe
1771 Nov. 1	Elizabeth PARSONS, daughter of John PARSONS. John Parsons with wife Dorothy and daughters Ann 12y and Elizabeth 10y were allowed, for some time past, to live in Steyning by a certificate, dated 7 August 1763 from Cuckfield. Now E.P., having become chargeable to Steyning, is to be removed to Cuckfield, the place of her last legal settlement.	Steyning
1783 Oct.18	George ELLIS and wife Elizabeth.	Clayton

QUARTER SESSIONS REMOVAL ORDERS TO CUCKFIELD

		From
L 1665 Jul.13	Edward BRAY; on appeal ordered that he is to be settled at Maresfield; Cuckfield parish discharged from providing for him.	Maresfield
L 1666 Jan.11	Edward BRAY, wife and family.	Maresfield
L 1666 Apr.26	Edward BRAY, wife and family; recites previous order, which is now confirmed.	Maresfield
L 1676 Jul.13	George BALCOMBE; discharged.	New Shoreham
L 1689 Oct.10	Jane DOBELL, a bastard child.	Newick
L 1705 Apr.19	Allen DAW and family; confirmed.	Heathfield
A 1707 Apr.21	Sarah MABSBY; confirmed.	Horsham
L 1723 Jul.18	Jane PEIRCE; discharged.	Fletching
L 1740 Jan.14	Mary WEBB, Ann WEBB and Thomas WEBB; respited.	Horsham
C 1740 Apr.14	Mary WEBB, Ann WEBB and Thomas WEBB; On examination, Jane WEBB states that she married Thomas WEBB over six years ago and that the Thomas named in the order is not her son; respited.	Horsham
L 1740 Apr.17	Mary WEBB, Ann WEBB and Thomas WEBB; confirmed as to Mary Webb and Ann Webb, quashed as to Thomas Webb.	Horsham
H 1741 Jul.13	Joane STEVENS; discharged.	Steyning
H 1748 Jul.11	Thomas BUTTON, wife Sarah and son Thomas over 2y; discharged.	St. Peter the Great, Chichester
L 1754 Jul.18	Martha PARKER, widow; confirmed.	Fletching
L 1770 Jan.11	Henry GALLARD and wife Ann; confirmed.	Barcombe
L 1771 Apr.11	Edward APPS; quashed.	Rotherfield
C 1789 Apr.20	William SMITH, wife Sarah and son William; quashed.	Angmering
L 1793 Jul.26	George BUCKWELL and wife Pricilla; respited.	Chailey
L 1793 Oct.10	George BUCKWELL and wife Pricilla; respited.	Chailey
L 1794 May 1	Mary QUAIFE, widow, and daughter Henrietta; respited.	Catsfield
P 1797 Oct. 3	Jenny SAUNDERS, wife of James SAUNDERS, and children Margaret 11y, James 9y, William 7y, Sarah 5y, Elizabeth 4y and Charlotte 3y; respited.	Beeding
L 1798 Apr.20	Rebecca WILLIS, widow; respited.	Brighton
L 1798 Oct. 5	Rebecca WILLIS, widow; confirmed.	Brighton
L 1804 Jul.13	John MILLER, wife Ann and children Mary 12y, Thomas 10y and Ann 5y; respited.	Brighton
L 1804 Oct. 5	John MILLER, wife Ann and children Mary 12y, Thomas 10y and Ann 5y; confirmed.	Brighton
L 1810 Jan.12	Mary EVENDEN, singlewoman; respited.	Westmeston

L 1810 May 4	Mary EVENDEN, singlewoman; confirmed.	Westmeston
L 1811 Jan.18	Mary RICHARDSON, widow, and children William 5y, Richard 3y and Henry aged 10 weeks; confirmed.	All Saints, Lewes
L 1816 Jul.19	William FALKNER, wife Lydia and children William 20y, Charles 19y, John 17y, Martha 12y, George 10y, Henry 8y, Thomas 6y and Lydia 3y; quashed as to children William, Charles and John and confirmed as to William Falkner senior, wife Lydia and children Martha, George, Henry, Thomas and Lydia.	Brighton
L 1817 Apr.18	Henry HAYLER and wife Ann; confirmed.	Hailsham
L 1817 Apr.18	James TURNER; confirmed.	Barcombe
L 1817 Apr.18	John MITCHELL, wife Jane and children Thomas 14y, Sarah 12y, Elizabeth 10y, Jane 8y and Mary 5y; respited.	Brighton
L 1817 Jul.18	John MITCHELL, wife Jane and children Thomas 14y, Sarah 12y, Elizabeth 10y, Jane 8y and Mary 5y 6m; confirmed.	Brighton
L 1822 Jan.18	Richard PECKHAM and wife Jane; confirmed.	Westmeston

CUCKFIELD BASTARDY EXAMINATIONS Par 301/34/3/1

1717 May 3 Goody DAY said that she has not lived with her husband for the space of a year or longer. That she has lived and served with Mary FRYER of Hellsome [?Hailsham] and the said Widow Fryer's son, John FRYER, is the father of her child. [Mark of Jane Day (sic)]

1719 Jan.13 Mary MILES has declared that she is quick with child and that Isaac PRING of Lindfield is the father of her child. [Mark of M.M.]

1720 Nov.19 Susan HOLMES of Cuckfield, widow, has declared that Henry MICHELL of Cuckfield, husbandman, did, about June 1709, beget her with child and that, on the 30 April following, she was delivered of a male bastard child, H.M. being the father. [Mark of S.H.]

1730 Feb.11 Mary FRENCH, junior, of Cuckfield, singlewoman, has declared that Thomas TIDY of Keymer, labourer, is the father of a male bastard child born to her on Sunday 11 January last, in Cuckfield.
[Signature of M.F. junior]

1732 Apr. 19 Mary GILLAM, singlewoman, was delivered of a male bastard child in Cuckfield the last Thursday of January, being 29 [or 7] January and she says that John PROCTOR, servant to Charles SERGISON, is the father of the said child. [Mark of M.G.] *Document displayed in Cuckfield church.*

1733 Nov.16 Ann STAPLEY, singlewoman, now residing in Balcombe, has declared herself to be with child. On examination, she said that she lived as a servant with Michael FULLER of Southease, from near Ladyday last till the latter end of last harvest and, during this time, she became familiarly acquainted with Thomas WHITE, her fellow servant, and that she is now with child, the said T.W. being the father of the child. [Mark of A.S.]

1759 Feb.20 Mary SHEPHARD of Cuckfield, singlewoman, said that, last Maytide, 12 months ago, she hired herself as servant to Robert UNWINS of Cowfold, yeoman, to serve him from that time to new Ladyday following at wages of 55s, which term she served. That, before her time was out, she made a fresh bargain with her mistress, the wife of R.U. for a further year at the same wages and she served until 19th instant when, she being with child, her mistress turned her away. [Mark of M.S.]
Catalogued under Par 301/32/4/1.

1768 Jan. 6 Susannah GEERING of Cuckfield, singlewoman, has declared that she is with child and charges Thomas HARLAND of Cuckfield, labourer, with being the father. [Mark of S.G]

1772 Apr.25 Sarah BARTHOLOMEW of Cuckfield, has declared that she is with child and charges Richard MIGHELL, otherwise MIALL, with being the father. [Mark of S.B.]

CUCKFIELD BASTARDY BONDS Par 301/34/1/3.

1607 Dec.17 Henry DAVYE of Cowfold, yeoman, bound to the parish officers of Cuckfield in £30 in respect of Dorothy SAVADGE, who was lately delivered of a bastard child in Cuckfield, the father being John DAVY (sic), son of the above Henry Davye. [Mark of H.D.]
Catalogued under Par 301/34/1/2

1680 Oct.20 Edward BURT of West Grinstead, yeoman, Nicholas BURT of Cuckfield yeoman, and Henry BURT of Cuckfield, husbandman, bound to the parish officers of Cuckfield in £100 in respect of Thomasine DAWSE, singlewoman, daughter of Richard DAWSE of Cuckfield, labourer, who is with child and has named E.B. as the father. [Signatures of E.B.,N.B.and H.B.]
Catalogued under Par 301/34/1/1

1704 Apr. 1 Richard LUCKIN of Horsham, gent., bound to the parish officers of Cuckfield in £20 in respect of Henry FINCH of Ifield, husbandman, who, as the father of a bastard child born to Ann TITLE, singlewoman, was ordered, on 18 July 1701, to pay 1s 6d a week maintenance, which sum R.L. has undertaken to pay. [Signature of R.L.]

1721 Mar. 7 Henry MICHELL of Hoo, Kent, bound to the parish officers of Cuckfield in £200 in respect of Susanna HOLMES of Cuckfield, widow, who, several years ago, was delivered of a male bastard child in Cuckfield, called Jeptha HOLMES, and has declared that H.M. is the father. [Mark of H.M.]

1723 Sep. 4 John MILLS of Slaugham, husbandman, bound to William HEASMAN of Cowfold in £100, agrees that he will appear at the next Quarter Sessions regarding Sarah BANNISTER, singlewoman, who is with child and has named him as the father. [Signature of J.M.]

1723 Oct. 7 John MILLS of Slaugham, husbandman, bound to the parish officers of Cuckfield in £100 in respect of Sarah BANNISTER, singlewoman, who has lately been delivered of a male bastard child in Cuckfield, and has declared that J.M. is the father. [Signature of J.M.]

1727 Apr.13 Peter HILL junior, and Thomas FOWLE both of Albourne, yeomen, bound to the parish officers of Cuckfield in £200 in respect of Mary FRENCH, singlewoman, who was delivered of a female bastard child on 16 March last, in Cuckfield, P.H. junior being the father. [Signatures of P.H. and T.F.]

1728 Jun.15 Richard WHITE of Cuckfield, yeoman, bound to the parish officers of Cuckfield in £100 in respect of Sarah KNIGHT, singlewoman, who is with child and names R.W. as the father. [Mark of R.W.]

1731 Jan.11 John PILBEAM junior of Cuckfield, yeoman, and John PILBEAM senior bound to the parish officers of Cuckfield in £100 in respect of Mary MORRIS, singlewoman and late servant to John Pilbeam the elder, who is with child and names J.P. the younger as the father. [Mark of J.P. the elder and signature of J.P. the younger]

1734 Feb.20 Ann STEAPLEY of Ardingly, widow, bound to the parish officers of Cuckfield in £10, agrees to pay 9d a week towards the keeping of a child lately born to her daughter, Ann STEAPLY (sic), who is now in the workhouse at Cuckfield. [Mark of A.S.]
Catalogued under Par 301/34/1/1

1740 Jan.18 Turner BRISTOW of Ardingly, practitioner in physick, and Edward MILES of Balcombe, higler, bound to the parish officers of Cuckfield in £100 in respect of Elizabeth DUMBRELL, singlewoman, who was delivered of a male bastard child on 1 July last, in Cuckfield and T.B. acknowledges that he is the father. [Signatures of T.B. and Edward Mills (sic)]

1741 Mar. 7 James WEEKS, labourer, Michael HARMES the elder, yeoman, Michael HARMES the younger, yeoman, and Thomas JEFFERY, yeoman, all of Bolney, bound to the parish officers of Cuckfield in £100 in respect of Hannah STRINGER, singlewoman, who was delivered of a female bastard child on 6

November last, in Cuckfield, and has declared J.W. to be the father. [Mark of J.W. and signatures of M.H. senior, M.H. junior, and T.J.]
Catalogued under Par 301/34/1/1

1744 Jan.14 William STEDMAN, the elder, and William STEDMAN, the younger, both of Balcombe, yeomen, bound to the parish officers of Cuckfield in £100 in respect of Sarah BEACHLY of Balcombe, singlewoman, who is now big with child, and W.S. the younger acknowledges himself to be the father. [Mark of W.S. and signature of W.S.]

1749 Sep. 2 Turner BRISTOW of Edenbridge, Kent, practitioner in physick, bound to the parish officers of Cuckfield in £100 in respect of Elizabeth DUMBRELL, singlewoman, who has been delivered of a female bastard child in Cuckfield and has declared that T.B. is the father. [Signature of T.B.]

1759 Mar.23 Elizabeth FELDWICK of Balcombe, widow, bound to parish officers of Cuckfield in £100 in respect of Ann SNELL, singlewoman, who is with child and has charged William FELDWICK of Balcombe, yeoman, with being the father. [Signatures of E.F. and James (sic) Feldwick]

1761 May 4 John MARCHANT of Streat, gent., bound to the parish officers of Cuckfield in £100 in respect of Sarah VAUGHAN, singlewoman, now of Cuckfield, who is with child. [Signature of J.M.]

1763 Mar.28 Michael FIELD of Cuckfield, yeoman, bound to the parish officers of Cuckfield in £100 in respect of Mary HARDHAM, singlewoman of Cuckfield, who has lately been delivered of a female bastard child in Cuckfield and has declared that M.F. is the father. [Signature of M.F.]

1764 May 18 John MARCHANT of Streat, gent., bound to the parish officers of Cuckfield in £100 in respect of Sarah VAUGHAN, singlewoman, who was, sometime in or about November last, delivered of a male bastard child in Cuckfield, baptised John, and J.M. is the father. [Signature of J.M.]

1765 Jun.13 William HARDS of Beeding, yeoman, bound to the parish officers of Cuckfield in £100 in respect of Ann HEASMAN, singlewoman, who is with child. [Signature of W.H.]

1765 Oct.25 Peter GENDRE of Charlwood, Surrey, weaver, and George MICHELL of Cuckfield, weaver, bound to the parish officers of Cuckfield in £100 in respect of Jane COSTER, otherwise Jane GENDRE, daughter of the above P.G., who has lately intruded herself into Cuckfield parish, not being an inhabitant, and is now with child and not capable of being removed to her place of settlement. [Signature of P.G. and mark of G.M.]

1766 Jan.18 George THOMAS, the elder, and George THOMAS, the younger, both of Cuckfield, husbandmen, bound to the parish officers of Cuckfield in £100 in respect of Sarah OCKENDEN, singlewoman, who is with child and has declared that G.T. the younger is the father. [Signature of G.T. senior and mark of G.T. the younger]

1767 Jul.10 Thomas MARTEN of Cuckfield, yeoman, bound to the parish officers of Cuckfield in £80 in respect of Mary HERIOTT of Cuckfield, singlewoman, who is with child and names T.M. as the father. [Signature of T.M.]

1769 Sep.16 Charles CROUCHER and John CROUCHER both of Cuckfield, yeomen, bound to the parish officers of Cuckfield in £100 in respect of Jane HAMPER of Cuckfield, singlewoman, who was delivered of a female bastard child on or about 9 March last, in Cuckfield, baptised Phebe. C.C. acknowledges that he is the father. [Signatures of C.C. and J.C.]

1786 Apr.14 William BURTENSHAW of Cuckfield, yeoman, bound to the parish officers of Cuckfield in £100 in respect of Mary BURTENSHAW, singlewoman and daughter of above W.B., who has declared that she was delivered of a female bastard child on 27 May 1784 at her father's house, in Cuckfield, and that William COPPARD of Cuckfield, servant, is the father. W.C. has paid to W.B. £21 for maintenance of the child. [Signature of W.B.]

CUCKFIELD BASTARDY ORDER Par 301/34/2/1

1730 Feb.14 Mary FRENCH junior, singlewoman, has lately given birth to a male bastard child in Cuckfield, and Thomas TIDY of Keymer, labourer, is adjudged to be the father of the child. T.D. to pay 2s 6d a week maintenance; the mother to pay 6d a week.

CUCKFIELD WARRANTS Par 301/29/1

1610 Feb.21 Richard AYLMOR at Offord [?Alfold], Surrey, be taken at Cuckfield as a vagrant and punished according to the law.
Catalogued under Par 301/7/2 f99v

1610 Feb.21 John STEVENS of Eltam, Kent, being used accordingly as aforesaid.
Catalogued under Par 301/7/2 f99v

30 Chas.II [1678-1679] Margaret BRYANT aged 13 years or thereabouts, a poor child of Cuckfield, placed by the churchwardens and overseers of Cuckfield to John BARTLETT until she is aged 21 years.
Document displayed in Cuckfield church

1719 Jan.13 Mary MILES of Cuckfield, singlewoman, has declared that she is now with child and that Isaac PRING of Lindfield is the father; and he is to be apprehended.

1768 Jan. 6 Susannah GEERING of Cuckfield, singlewoman, has declared that she is with child and that Thomas HARLAND of Cuckfield, labourer, is the father; and he is to be apprehended.

1772 Apr.25 Sarah BARTHOLOMEW of Cuckfield, singlewoman, has declared that she is with child and that Richard MIGHELL otherwise MIALL, late of Cuckfield, huntsman, is the father; and he is to be apprehended.

CUCKFIELD APPRENTICESHIP INDENTURES Par 301/33/3

A Catalogue of the names of the Apprentices put out in parish of Cuckfield with their master's names. 21 January 1634.

MASTERS	APPRENTICES
1. John ASHFOLD	1. Mary WARD
2. Walter BURRELL, esq.	2. Thomas HERYET
3. Walter BURT, senior.	3. Francis BURT
4. John BEACHELY	4. Joan RANDOLL
5. Walter BURT, junior.	5. William RUSSELL
6. William DUMBRELL	6. Richard VILDERS
7. Richard FILLERY	7. Agnes VILDERS
8. John GARSTON	8. Richard FRENCH
9. Nicholas GENNER	9. Richard HOLCOMBE
10. Thomas HURST	10. John TESTER
11. Walter HOLCOMB	11. Thomas GEERE
12. Edward HARFIE	12. Nicholas SALTER
13. Edward JENNER	13. Thomas LEWES
14. Thomas JENNER	14. Edward BURRELL
15. George JENKINS	15. Richard HERYET
16. William JUPP	16. Henry NUTLEY
17. William KEMPSHALL	17. Richard MILES
18. John LASHMER	18. Thomas BURRELL
19. Richard MILES, car[rier?]	19. Richard ILMAN
20. Mrs. Anne MOORE	20. Anne HOWARD
21. Richard MILES, bricklayer	21. George HOLCOMBE
22. Henry MITCHEL	22. Thomas WELLER
23. Thomas PAGE	23. Edmund RENDALL
24. Edward STEELE	24. Robert CHELSAM
25. John SHOULDER	25. Judith GUNTER
26. Robert STANDBRIDGE	26. Thomas PELLING
27. Mr.John SKEFFINGTON	27. Thomas MILES
28. Francis SCRACE	28. Richard VERALL

29. Alan SAVAGE	29. Mary MILES
30. Edward SHERMAN	30. George BALCOMB
31. Thomas TOMPSON	31. Susan TERRY
32. Henry VENNE	32. Walter HOCKHAM
33. Thomas VINCENT	33. Agnes GYNNER
34. Thomas WOOLDRED	34. William FRANCIS
35. John WARDEN	35. John COLLINGS
36. John WELLER	36. Richard PELLING
37. James WORNUT	37. Margery LANE
38. Thomas WEST	38. Susan HOLCOMB
39. Edward WICKHAM	39. Agnes PELLING
40. Stephen WICKHAM	40. Thomas STEPHENS

CUCKFIELD APPRENTICESHIP AGREEMENTS Par 301/33/4

* Indicates item catalogued under Par 301/33/1
+ Indicates item catalogued under Par 301/33/2

1599 Oct. 7 Mary SMITH, daughter of Robert SMYTH (sic), apprenticed to John SKINNER of Slaugham for five years. Consideration £5.
Catalogued under Par 301/7/2 f128v

1599 Oct. 7 Jo[?hn] MORLEY son of Jo[?hn] MORLEY apprenticed to William WELLER, weaver, to be taught his trade of weaver and kept with 40s 0d. *Catalogued under Par 301/7/2 f128v*

1607 Jul. 4* John COWLSTOCK and John BURTENSHAWE both of Cuckfield, husbandmen, bound to the parish officers of Cuckfield in £40. Condition: John Cowlstock agrees to take as apprentice Johne MORLEY, daughter of John MORLEY late of Cuckfield, deceased, until age of 21 years. Consideration 20s 0d. [Signatures of John Coulestock (sic) and J.B.]

1609 May 1 Frances KEARRIE, bastard daughter of Joan KEARRIE, apprenticed to John UMPHRIE of Cuckfield, sadler, for her to dwell with him from 17 July 1608 until she is aged 21 years; housewifery. Consideration £6.13s 4d. [Mark of J.U.] [Endorsed: Frances Kearrie was baptised the 2nd February 1607]

1611 Feb.10 Thomas MILLS, son of William MILLS of Cuckfield, collier, deceased, apprenticed to Thomas PAGE of Cuckfield, yeoman, until age of 24 years; husbandry. [Mark of T.P.]

1613 Jun.13* Jerrard WINTON, of Bolney, weaver, and John DUNSTELL of Covehould [?Cowfold], yeoman, bound to the parish officers of Cuckfield in £5. Condition: Jerrard Winton agrees to take as an apprentice Mercy FORWOODE, daughter of Thomas FORWOOD (sic), late of Cuckfield, deceased, until age of 21 years. Consideration 53s 4d. [Marks of J.W. and J.D.]

1614 Mar.20* William MEWE, bastard son of Margerie MEWE of Cuckfield, widow, apprenticed to Richard BLAKER of Cuckfield, yeoman, until age of 24 years. Consideration £3.6s 8d. [Signature of R.B.] [Endorsed: 10 April 1603 was baptised William Mewe, bastard son of Margerie Mewe, widow]

1614 Sep.30 Elizabeth NORMAN, daughter of Richard NORMAN of Cuckfield, forgeman, apprenticed to Roger BUTLER, gent., and Elizabeth his wife, of Cuckfield, until age of 21 years; housewifery. [Endorsed: Elizabeth, daughter of Richard and Joahn Norman, was baptised 27 April 1606]

1617 Jun.22 John GEALLE, son of John GEALE (sic) of Cuckfield, labourer, deceased, apprenticed to Anthony MORTTEN, husbandman, until age of 24 years; husbandry. [Endorsed: Baptised 24 January 1602]

1617 Jun.22 William GATTEN, son of John GATTEN of Cuckfield, labourer, apprenticed to John WARDEN of Cuckfield, yeoman, until age of 24 years; husbandry. [Signature of J.W.] [Endorsed: Baptised 3 April 1603]

1617 -- John PEPPER, son of Richard PEPPER of Cuckfield, deceased, apprenticed to Thomas PEPPER of Southover, Lewes, husbandman, until age of 24 years; husbandry. [Endorsed: John Pepper, son of Richard Pepper, was baptised 29 January 1608, being born 8 days before Candlemas, 1608]

1620 Jun.11 Joane FRENCHE, daughter of Joane FRENCHE of Cuckfield, widow, apprenticed to Richard PARKES of Cuckfield, yeoman, until age of 21 years. [Signature of Richard Parke (sic)]

1620 Jun.15 Henry MITTEN apprenticed to Richard PARKES of Cuckfield, yeoman, until age of 24 years; husbandry. [Signature of Richard Parke (sic)]

1621 Mar.16 Henry HOVER, a bastard child (the supposed son of Henry BAILY, tanner) apprenticed to John JENNER of Cuckfield, yeoman, until age of 24 years; trade of husbandman. Bond of same date: John Jenner with Richard BLAKER junior of Cuckfield, yeoman, bound to the parish officers of Cuckfield in £6. [Mark of J.J. and signature of R.B.]

1622 May 23 Joane WOODS, daughter of Richard WOODS, late of Cuckfield, shoemaker, deceased, apprenticed to William BARBER of Fletching, husbandman, until age of 21 years. [Mark of W.B.]

1624 Jan.15 Ann AVERYE [AVERY], daughter of Bridget AVERIE (sic) late of Cuckfield, apprenticed to Thomas GURR of Balcombe, husbandman, until the age of 21 years or till she shall be married. Consideration £4.10s 0d. Bond of same date: Thomas Gurr bound to the parish officers of Cuckfield in £9. [Mark of T.G.]

1625 Feb.27 Thomas WEST of Cuckfield, blacksmith, bound to Nathaniel HUSSEE of Cuckfield, gent., in £10, agrees to take as an apprentice Edward LASHMER. [Term not given] [Mark of T.W.]

1625 Dec.18 William NUTLEY, aged 9 years, apprenticed to Thomas GINNER of Cuckfield, yeoman, until age of 24 years. [Signature of Thomas Jenner (sic)]

1625 Dec.18 Thomas STEVENS, aged 10 years, apprenticed to Abraham PELHAM of Cuckfield, yeoman, until age of 24 years. [Signature of A.P.]

1626 Aug.20 Francis FRENCH, apprenticed to Richard HAMMOND of Cuckfield, thatcher, until age of 24 years; trade of thatcher. [Mark of R.H.]

1627 Jun. 1 Francis BRYAN, son of Francis BRYAN of Cuckfield, apprenticed to John STEELE of Slaugham, yeoman, and wife Joan, until age of 24 years; husbandry. [Signature of John Steell (sic)]

1627 Oct.23 Jane HART, daughter of Richard HART, late of Cuckfield deceased, apprenticed to Richard MYLES and wife Elizabeth, of Cuckfield, bricklayer, until age of 21 years; "huswiferie and spinstring" [spinning]. Consideration 50s 0d. Bond of same date: Richard Myles bound to the parish officers of Cuckfield in £5. [Signature of R.Miles (sic)]

1628 Mar. 9 Katherine ANSTY als HOLCOMBE, daughter of Phillipe ANSTYE (sic) als HOLCOMBE, late of Cuckfield, husbandman, deceased, apprenticed to Stephen ANSTY als HOLCOMBE of Cuckfield, husbandman, with wife Dorothy, until age of 21 years; housewifery. Consideration 50s 0d. [Marks of S.A. and D.A.]

1628 Oct. 4 Richard COLLINS, son of Richard COLLINS, late of Cuckfield, deceased, apprenticed to Walter ANSTY als HOLCOMBE of Cuckfield, yeoman, until age of 24 years; husbandry. Consideration £4.10s 0d. [Signature of Walter Holcom (sic)]

1630 Jun.14* William STONE of Cuckfield, husbandman, bound to the parish officers of Cuckfield in £70, agrees to take as apprentice Jane HEATH until age of 21 years. Consideration 30s 0d. [Mark of W.S.]

1634 Jan.21 Mary WARD, aged 12 years, apprenticed to John ASHFOLD of Cuckfield, yeoman, until age of 21 years. [Mark of J.A.]

1634 Jan.21 Joane RENDALL, aged 13 years, apprenticed to John BETCHLEY of Cuckfield, yeoman, until age of 21 years.
[Signature of John Beachely (sic)]

1634 Jan.21 Francis BURT, aged 12 years, apprenticed to Walter BURT of Cuckfield, until age of 24 years. [Signature of W.B.]

1634 Jan.21 Thomas HERYET, aged 13 years, apprenticed to Walter BURRELL esq., until age of 24 years. [Signature of W.B.]

1634 Jan.21 Susan TERRY, aged 9 years, apprenticed to Thomas TOMPSETT of Cuckfield, yeoman, until age of 21 years.
[Signature Thomas Tomson (sic)]

1634 Jan.21 Richard VILDERS, apprenticed to William DUMBRELL of Cuckfield, yeoman, until age of 24 years. [Signature of W.B.]

1634 Jan.21 Richard FRENCH, aged 13 years, apprenticed to John GARTON of Cuckfield, yeoman, until age of 24 years.

1634 Jan.21 Thomas WELLER, aged 8 years, apprenticed to Henry MICHELL of Cuckfield, yeoman, until age of 24 years. [Signature of H.M.]

1634 Jan.21 Richard ILMAN, aged 12 years, apprenticed to Richard MYLES, of Cuckfield, carrier, until age of 24 years. [Mark of R.M.]

1634 Jan.21 Henry NUTLEY, aged 11 years, apprenticed to William JUPP of Cuckfield, yeoman, until age of 24 years. [Signature of W.J.]

1634 Jan.21 Nicholas SALTER, aged 16 years, apprenticed to Edward HARFIE of Cuckfield, yeoman, until age of 24 years. [Document not signed]

1634 Jan.21 William FRANCIS [age not given] apprenticed to Thomas WOLDRIDGE, until age of 24 years. [Signature of Thomas Wolldrd (sic)]

1634 Jan.21 George BAWLCOME [BALCOMBE] aged 15 years, apprenticed to Edward SHERMAN of Cuckfield, innholder, until age of 24 years.

1634 Jan.21 Judith GUNTER, aged 14 years, apprenticed to John SHOULDER of Cuckfield, yeoman, until age of 21 years. [Mark of J.S.]

1634 Jan.21 Mary MYLES, aged 12 years, apprenticed to Allen SAVADGE of Cuckfield, yeoman, until age of 24 years. [Mark of A.S.]

1634 Jan.21 Susan HOLCOMB, aged 14 years, apprenticed to Thomas WEST of Cuckfield, yeoman, until age of 21 years. [Signature of T.W.]

1634 Jan.21 Richard PELING, aged 9 years, apprenticed to John WELLER of Cuckfield, yeoman, until age of 24 years. [Mark of J.W.]

1634 Jan.21 John COLLINS, aged 12 years, apprenticed to John WARDEN of Cuckfield, gent., until age of 24 years. [Signature of J.W.]

1634 Jan.21 Agnes GYINNER, aged 9 years, apprenticed to Thomas VINCENT of Cuckfield, yeoman, until age of 21 years. [Signature of T.V.]

1634 Jan.21 Thomas PELLING, aged 12 years, apprenticed to Robert STANDBRIDGE of Cuckfield, yeoman, until age of 24 years. [Signature of R.S.]

1634 Jan.21 Walter HOCKHAM [HALCOMB] aged 10 years, apprenticed to Henry VENNE of Cuckfield, schoolmaster, until age of 24 years. [Signature of H.V.]

1637 Feb.27 Edward BRISTOWE, son of Edward BRISTOWE, late of Cuckfield, tailor, deceased, apprenticed to Drewe BURSTOWE of Porchmouth [Portsmouth], Hampshire, tailor, until age of 24 years; trade of tailor. Consideration 30s 0d now and 30s 0d more to be paid on 27 February 1637 (being the £3 which was given by Mr. Allen, late of Cuckfield, towards the putting out of an apprentice). Bond of same date: Drewe Burstowe bound to the parish officers of Cuckfield in £6. [Signature of D.B.]
[*See under Par 301/33/1 for the bond*]

1637 Jul.4+ Henry MOORE, son of Henry MOORE late of Cuckfield, husbandman, deceased, apprenticed to Edward BYSHE esq., of Burstow, Surrey, until age of 24 years. [Signature of E.B.]

1642 May 6 James BLUET, son of John BLUET, forgeman, deceased, with the consent of his mother and the overseers of Cuckfield, has put himself apprentice with John BARTLEMEW of Nuthurst, forgeman, until age of 24 years; trade of forgeman. Bond of same date, John Bartlemew and Henry BOTTING of Beeding, husbandman, bound in £6. [Signatures of John Bartholme (sic) and H.B.]

1643 Mar.27 Elizabeth HARLAND, daughter of Thomas HARLAND of Cuckfield, tailor, deceased, apprenticed to William LASHMER of Cuckfield, yeoman, for seven years. [Mark of W.L.]

1643 Mar.27 Stephen JENNER, son of Francis JENNER of Cuckfield, husbandman, deceased, apprenticed to William STEEDMAN of Cuckfield, wheelmaker, until age of 24 years; trade of wheelmaker. [Mark of W.S.]

1643 Dec. - Robert YOUNG, son of Robert YOUNG of Cuckfield, husbandman, deceased, apprenticed to Richard BURT of Cuckfield, tanner, until age of 24 years; trade of tanning. [Endorsed: Young indenture never executed]

1644 Dec. 1 Grace JENNER of Cuckfield, a poor child, being born in the said parish and destitute of maintenance, aged 15 years, apprenticed to Henry GATLAND of Cuckfield and wife Ann, until age of 21 years.

1648 Mar.10 Edward TILTMAN, son of Thomas TILTMAN late of Cuckfield, deceased, apprenticed to Edward STEELL, until age of 24 years; husbandry. [Signature of Edward Steele (sic)]

1652 Dec.27 Thomas BLAKER, son of Richard BLAKER late of Cuckfield, tailor, with the consent of his mother, Elizabeth BLAKER and the parish officers of Cuckfield, apprenticed to Allen SAVAGE, until age of 24 years; husbandry. [Signature of Allen Savidg (sic)]

1652 Dec.27 Mary GEERE, daughter of Eve GEERE of Cuckfield, deceased, apprenticed to William SMYTH of Cuckfield and wife Elizabeth SMYTH, until age of 21 years; housewifery. [Marks of M.G.,W.S., and E.S.]

1653 Apr.12 Thymothy BURCH, daughter of - BURCH of Cuckfield, tailor, late deceased, apprenticed to Edward STEELE of Cuckfield, yeoman, and wife Joan STEELE, until age of 24 years. [Signature of E.S.]

1654 Feb.17 Mary MICHELL, daughter of Richard MICHELL late of Cuckfield, yeoman, apprenticed to William BURSTOW of Horley, Surrey, yeoman, for 13 years; housewifery. [Signature of W.B.]

1655 Sep. 4 James TESTER, apprenticed to Edward WICKHAM until age of 24 years; husbandry. [Mark of E.W.]

1655 Sep. 8 John TESTER, apprenticed to Thomas WEST of Cuckfield yeoman, until age of 24 years; husbandry. [Signature of T.W.]

1656 Mar.26 Edward PEPPER, apprenticed to Richard BARTLEE of Cuckfield, yeoman, until age of 24 years; husbandry. [Signature of R.B.]

1656 Mar.26 Elizabeth PECKHAM, apprenticed to George WARD of Cuckfield, until age of 21 years. [Signature of G.W.]

1656 Apr. 8 Anne BRIANT, apprenticed to Allen SAVAGE of Cuckfield, yeoman, until age of 21 years or day of marriage. [Signature of Allen Savadg (sic)]

1661 Mar.25 Frances OUSLEY, one of the daughters of Edward OUSLEY of Cuckfield, labourer, apprenticed to Jane BURRELL of Cuckfield, spinster, until age of 21 years. [Signature of J.B.]

1661 Apr. 9 Mary HARDING, apprenticed to Edward STEELE of Cuckfield, yeoman, until age of 21 years. [Signature of E.S.]

1662 Sep.27 Alice BRYANT, apprenticed to Richard PARSONS of Cuckfield, until age of 21 years. [Signature of R.P.]

1662 Sep.27 James RAPLEY, apprenticed to William BOARD esq., of Cuckfield, until age of 24 years. [Signature of W.B.]

1662 Sep.27 Mary STANDLEY, apprenticed to Mychaell MARTIN of Cuckfield, until age of 21 years. [Signature of Michaell Marten (sic)]

1662 Sep.27 Mary KING, apprenticed to Richard BURT of Cuckfield, until age of 21 years.

1670 Jan.24 Edward BERRICK, apprenticed to John JENNER of Horsgate, until age of 24 years. [Signature of J.J.]

1680 Jul. 9 George MICHELL, apprenticed to Jonathan BETCHLEY until age of 24 years; husbandry. [Signature of Jonathan Bechely (sic)]

1680 Jul. 9 Francis JENNER, apprenticed to John DUMBERELL of Cuckfield until age of 21 years; housewifery. [Signature of John Dumbrell (sic)]

1680 Jul. 9 Edward JUPPE apprenticed to John GASSON of Cuckfield, until age of 24 years; husbandry. [Mark of J.G.]

1680 Jul. 9 Martin PASSELL, apprenticed to George JENNINGS of Cuckfield, husbandman, until age of 24 years; husbandry. [Signature of Georg Jenings (sic)]

1680 Jul. 9 John ASHFEILD, apprenticed to Walter BURTT of Cuckfield, until age of 24 years; husbandry. [Signature of Walter Burt (sic)]

1680 Jul. 9 Joane STAMMER, apprenticed to Thomas GASSON of Cuckfield, until age of 21 years; housewifery. [Mark of T.G.]

1690 Jun.24 John PARSON, apprenticed to Henry SHARPE for seven years; trade of cordwainer. [Signature of Henry Sharp (sic)]

1696 Jun.24 Henry HEATH, apprenticed to Richard HAMMONDS of Cuckfield, thatcher, for seven years; trade of thatcher. Consideration 15s 0d yearly for first 4 years of term. [Signature of Richard Hamond (sic)]

1697 Mar.19+ Edward GATLAND, apprenticed to James COX of Lindfield, weaver, until age of 24 years; trade of weaving. [Signature of J.C.]

1699 Mar. 6 William WOOD, apprenticed to William BOARD of Cuckfield, gent., until age of 24 years; husbandry. [Signature of W.B.]

1699 Mar. 6 James TILT, apprenticed to Walter BURT of Cuckfield, tanner, until age of 24 years; trade of tanner. [Signature of W.B.]

1699 Mar. 6 William JENNER, apprenticed to Walter BURT of Cuckfield, gent., until age of 24 years; husbandry. [Signature of W.B.]

1699 Mar. 6 Henry MARCHANT, apprenticed to Richard BURT of Cuckfield, tanner, until age of 24 years; trade of tanner. [Signature of R.B.]

1699 Mar. 6 Thomas GATES, apprenticed to Thomas GATES of Cuckfield, yeoman, until age of 24 years; husbandry. [Signature of T.G.]

1699 Mar. 6 Richard HUMPHRY, apprenticed to Marrian JARRETT of Cuckfield, yeoman, until age of 24 years; husbandry. [Mark of M.J.]

1699 Mar. 6 Frances HAMBLIN, apprenticed to Joseph WEBB of Cuckfield, yeoman, until age of 21 years or day of marriage; housekeeping and housewifery. [Signature of J.W.]

1699 Mar. 6 Mary WINTER, apprenticed to Stephen COMBER of Cuckfield, yeoman, until age of 21 years or day of marriage; housekeeping and housewifery. [Signature of S.C.]

1699 Mar. 6 Ann BURTENSHAWE, apprenticed to Thomas NYE of Cuckfield, yeoman, until age of 21 years or day of marriage; housekeeping and housewifery. [Signature of T.N.]

1699 Mar. 6 Thomas STALEY, apprenticed to Richard WICKHAM of Cuckfield, yeoman, until age of 24 years; husbandry. [Signature of R.W.]

1699 Mar. 6 Elizabeth FRENCH, apprenticed to Richard COOPER of Cuckfield, yeoman, until age 21 years or day of marriage; housekeeping and housewifery. [Mark of R.C.]

1699 Mar. 6 Thomas SHURLEY, apprenticed to William JUPPE, of Cuckfield, yeoman, until age of 24 years; husbandry. [Signature of W.J.]

1699 Mar. 6 John HUMPHEREY, apprenticed to Charles SAVAGE, of Cuckfield, yeoman, until age of 24 years; husbandry. [Signature of C.S.]

1699 Mar. 6 Richard MARTEN, apprenticed to Robert CHATFEILD of Cuckfield, yeoman, until age of 24 years; husbandry. [Signature of R.C.]

1699 Mar. 6 Mary WARNETT, apprenticed to Thomas UWINS, yeoman, until age 21 years or day of marriage; housekeeping and housewifery. [Signature of T.U.]

1699 Mar. 6 Elizabeth WALES, apprenticed to Thomas HOLCOMBE of Cuckfield, yeoman, until age of 21 years or day of marriage; housekeeping and housewifery. [Signature of Thomas Holcomb (sic)]

1699 Mar. 6 Thomas PEETERS, apprenticed to Richard HARLAND of Cuckfield, yeoman, until age of 24 years; husbandry. [Signature of R.H.]

1699 Mar. 6 Henry WATERMAN, apprenticed to Anthony HUGGETT of Cuckfield, yeoman, until age of 24 years; husbandry. [Signature of A.H.]

1699 Mar. 6 Richard VILDERS, apprenticed to Samuel SAVAGE, of Cuckfield, yeoman, until age of 24 years; husbandry. [Signature of S.S.]

1699 Mar. 6 Christopher HILTON, apprenticed to John ATTREE of Cuckfield, yeoman, until age of 24 years; husbandry. [Signature of J.A.]

1699 Mar. 6 Elizabeth KEALE, apprenticed to Jonathan BETCHLEY of Cuckfield, yeoman, until age of 21 years or day of marriage; housekeeping and housewifery. [Signature of Jonathan Bethely (sic)]

1699 Mar. 6 Katharine PEPPER, apprenticed to Stephen WEST of Cuckfield, yeoman, until age of 21 years or day of marriage; housekeeping and housewifery.

1699 Mar. 6 Thomas HOLIBONE, apprenticed to Henry BURTENSHAWE of Cuckfield, yeoman, until age of 24 years; husbandry. [Signature of H.B.]

1699 Mar. 6 Edmund KING, apprenticed to Edward JENNER of Cuckfield, yeoman, until age of 24 years; husbandry. [Signature of E.J.]

1699 Mar. 6 Thomasine JENNER, apprenticed to Ellis GEERE of Cuckfield, yeoman, until age of 21 years or day of marriage; housekeeping and housewifery. [Signature of E.G.]

1699 Mar. 6 Thomas HAMBLINE, apprenticed to Thomas BURTENSHAWE of Cuckfield, yeoman, until age of 24 years; husbandry. [Signature of Thomas Burtenshaw (sic)]

1699 Mar.10 John BUTTEN, apprenticed to George AGATES of Cuckfield, yeoman, until age of 24 years; husbandry. [Signature of G.A.]

1699 Mar.10 Thomas RICHARDSON, apprenticed to Thomas CHALKER of Cuckfield, husbandman, until age of 24 years; husbandry. [Mark of T.C.]

1699 Apr.19 John MICHELL, apprenticed to Henry GATES of Cuckfield, yeoman, until age of 24 years; husbandry. [Signature of H.G.]

1699 Apr.19 Katharine PEPPER, apprenticed to John HERRING of Cuckfield, yeoman, until age of 21 years or day of marriage; housekeeping and housewifery. [Mark of J.H.]

1699 Apr.19 Anne BROWNING, apprenticed to William BANISTER the elder of Cuckfield, yeoman, until age of 21 years or day of marriage; housewifery. [Mark of W.B.]

1699 Apr.19 James HEATH, apprenticed to Samuel HIDER of Cuckfield, yeoman, until age of 24 years; husbandry. [Signature of S.H.]

1699 Apr.19 Ann WEST, apprenticed to Timothy BURRELL of Cuckfield, gent., until age of 21 years or day of marriage; housewifery. [Signature of T.B.]

1700 Mar.10 Richard SAUNDERS, apprenticed to William SAUNDERS of Cuckfield, bucket maker, until age of 24 years; trade of bucket maker. [Mark of W.S.]

1700 Mar.14 Richard MICHELL als TAILOR, apprenticed to Stephen WATTS, of Cuckfield, weaver, until age of 24 years; trade of weaver. [Mark of S.W.]

1700 Oct.25+ Edward WARNETT, apprenticed to John JENNER of Thorndeane, Cuckfield, yeoman, until age of 24 years; husbandry. [Signature of J.J.]

1707 Jan. 3 Thomas BUTTEN, aged 10 years, apprenticed to Richard SLEECH of Brighthelmston, mariner, and at present master of the "Reformation Pink" of Brighthelmston, about 150 tons burthen, until age of 21 years; occupation of mariner. [Signature of R.S.]

1707 Jan.20+ Frederick FRENCH, aged 14 years, apprenticed to John PEIRCEY of Brighthelmston, mariner and at present the master of the good pinck or vessel called the "Elizabeth and Mary" of Brighthelmston, burthen about 130 tunns, until age of 21 years; occupation of mariner. [Signature of John Peircy (sic)]

1708 Jan.15 Thomas COSENS, apprentice to James SMITH, is discharged of his apprenticeship, the master having no employment for him.

1708 Sep.17* John KEALE, apprenticed to James STORRER of Hurstpierpoint, baker, until age of 24 years; trade of baker. [Signature of James Storer (sic)]

1709 Jan. 7* Edward BERRY, apprenticed to Henry BERRY and William BERRY son of above Henry Berry, both of Cuckfield, cleavers, until age of 24 years; trade of cleaver. [Signatures of H.B. and W.B.]

1709 Jan.20* Thomas GLASS, aged twelve years, apprenticed to Dighton ELLGATE of Brighthelmstone, mariner, until age of 21 years; occupation of mariner. [Signature of D.E.]

1709 Nov. 4 John MITCHELL, apprenticed to Stephen WATES, weaver, until age of 24 years; trade of weaver. [Mark of S.W.]

1709 Jul. 1 William BERRY, apprenticed to Henry GEERING of Keymer, tailor, until age of 24 years; trade of tailor. [Signature of Henry Gearen (sic)]

1709 Nov.11 Henry PILBEAM, apprenticed to John CHATFIELD of Cuckfield, carpenter, until age of 24 years; trade of carpenter. Consideration £7 (20s on 11 May 1710, 20s on 11 November 1710 and to pay 20s in like manner until the £7 be paid.)

1714 Jun.25* Jeremyah PAIN, son of Jeremyah PAIN of Cuckfield, husbandman, apprenticed to John PAINE of Rygate [Reigate], Surrey, husbandman, for ten years; trade of husbandman. Consideration £4. [Signature of John Pain (sic)]

1724 Mar.26 John SCRACE, son of Thomas SCRASE (sic) deceased, apprenticed to John LUXFORD of Whittersham, [Wittersham], Island of Oxney, Kent, carpenter, until age of 24 years; trade of carpenter. [Signature of J.L.]

1731 May 29 Sarah CARE, aged 12 years, apprenticed to Thomas PARSONS of Thornden, Cuckfield, farmer, until age of 21 years or day of marriage. [Signature of Thomas Parson (sic)]

1737 Sep. 2+ Ruth OLIVER, aged about nine years, apprenticed to Henry ELLIS of Lingfield, Surrey, husbandman, until age of 21 years or day of marriage. Consideration £3.10s 0d. [Signature of H.E.]

1739 Apr.13 John TOOTH, eldest son of John TOOTH of Ardingly, yeoman, with the consent of John Tooth the father, apprenticed to Michael GODSMARKE of Cuckfield, millwright, for seven years; trade of millwright. Consideration £7, paid by John Tooth the elder. [Signatures of M.G., J.T. and J.T.] [Endorsed: 3 July 1739, 3s 6d paid of H.M. Duty at 6d in the £]

1739 Dec.14 Richard KNIGHT, aged 11 years, apprenticed to John SISLY of Clayton, fellmonger, until age of 21 years; trade of fellmonger. Consideration: £8, i.e. £4 now and £4 at the end of five years. [Signature of J.S.]

1747 Dec.28 Joseph WALTER, aged 15 years, apprenticed to Thomas GEERING of Keymer, flaxdresser and farmer, until age of 24 years; trade of flaxdresser and farmer. [Signature of Thomas Gearin (sic)]

DITCHLING

Ditchling: 4,265 acres, long, narrow strip little more than 1 mile wide, 6 miles long from Ditchling Beacon, 813ft in the South Downs to 124ft on the extensive common at the N boundary, with a ridge, Lodge Hill 275ft immediately NW of the village. Southern third is downland, whole parish agricultural; earlier market discontinued by 19th century. Manor belonged to Alfred the Great and later to Edward the Confessor. Well established Baptist and Independent places of worship as well as parish church. 27 shopkeepers and tradesmen. Coaches to London and Brighton, carriers to London.

Population: 1676 207; 1724 378; 1801 706; 1811 740; 1821 844; 1831 917.

REMOVAL ORDER FROM DITCHLING
This Removal Order, framed under glass, is on display in Ditchling Museum.

		To
c1790	James FELDWICK, wife Jane and their children Jane 5y, Elizabeth 4y, Ann 3y and James 8m.	Lindfield

QUARTER SESSIONS REMOVALS ORDERS FROM DITCHLING

		To
L 1663 Jan.15	Dorothy TIPPING, spinster.	Southover
L 1667 Jan.17	Thomas ROBINS.	Maresfield
L 1673 Apr.10	John NUTTLEY, wife and family.	Lindfield
L 1677 Apr.26	-- KAYNE; respited.	Westmeston
L 1680 Apr.22	John NUTLEY, wife and family. Sessions order 10 April 1673. Since making this order John Nutley has died and his widow and three children have returned to Ditchling, and are now to be removed to Lindfield.	Lindfield
L 1687 Oct. 6	Elizabeth DYER.	Clayton
L 1688 Jul.12	Henry CHAMBERS and wife came from Ditchling to Clayton; they are to remain at Clayton, without prejudice.	Clayton
L 1691 Apr.23	Mary COMBER; complaint of Ditchling for her removal to Clayton continued, as an order has not been obtained.	Clayton
L 1700 Apr.11	Sarah DWITE; confirmed.	Steyning
L 1703 Jan.14	Thomas CLARK, wife and three children; discharged.	Wivelsfield
L 1704 Jul.13	William BURSTY; discharged.	Plumpton
L 1704 Jul.13	Thomas OLLY; discharged.	Seddlescombe
L 1708 Jan.15	Anne BROOKER; confirmed.	Westmeston
L 1736 Oct. 7	Lucy HALLETT; confirmed.	Hurstpierpoint
L 1737 Jul.14	Elizabeth FILLERY; confirmed.	Cuckfield
L 1742 Apr.29	Mary HEMSLEY, singlewoman; confirmed.	Keymer

L 1748 Jul.14	James PARSON and son James under 3y, now residing in Ditchling, by virtue of a certificate from Horsham, with Isaac PARSON, father of the first named James Parson; confirmed.	Horsham
L 1750 Apr.26	William WARD and wife Anne; confirmed.	Henfield
L 1757 Apr.21	Edward GEERE and wife Sarah; confirmed.	East Grinstead
L 1761 Jul.16	John MILLS, wife Mary and children Henry, Mary, Christian, Piercy and Elizabeth; confirmed.	Broadwater
L 1785 Oct. 6	John WELFARE; confirmed.	Halden, Ken
L 1788 Jan.17	William BAKER and wife Elizabeth; confirmed.	Keymer
L 1789 Jul.16	William HOW, wife Barbara and son William aged 22 weeks; confirmed.	St. Cuthberts, [Wells], Som
L 1796 Jan.15	Ambrose GLAZEBROOK, wife Charity, and children Ann 13y, Thomas 11y, John 8y, Sarah 6y, Ambrose 4y, Elizabeth 3y, Esther 20m and a son 1m not yet baptised; quashed.	Wivelsfield
L 1796 Apr. 8	Ambrose GLAZEBROOK, wife Charity and children Ann 13y, Thomas 11y, John 8y, Sarah 6y, Ambrose 4y, Elizabeth 3y, Esther 20m and Benjamin 5m; confirmed.	Plumpton
L 1797 Jul.14	Thomas EAGER, wife Elizabeth and children Elizabeth 5y, Thomas 3y 6m and William 1y; quashed.	Keymer
L 1800 Apr.24	Richard MITCHELL, wife Elizabeth and children Frances 17y, Ann 10y, Mary 8y, Sarah 6y and Richard 9m; respited.	Lindfield
L 1800 Jul.17	Richard MITCHELL, wife Elizabeth and children Frances 17y, Ann 10y, Mary 8y, Sarah 6y and Richard 9m; quashed.	Lindfield
L 1804 Apr.13	George STEPNEY and wife Ann; confirmed.	St. Michaels, Lewes
L 1806 Oct.10	Harding PANFOLD 7y, a male bastard child born to Lucy PANFOLD at Rodmell; confirmed.	Rodmell
L 1808 Apr.29	Richard MASKALL, wife Sarah and children William 6y, Thomas 4y, Sarah 2y and John 2m; confirmed.	Brighton
L 1809 Apr.14	Edmund MITCHELL and wife Philadelphia; quashed.	Ifield
L 1810 Jan.12	John BUCKWELL, wife Sarah and children Harriet 2y and Sarah 5m; respited.	Plumpton
L 1811 Apr.26	Edmund MITCHELL, wife Philadelphia and daughter Mary 2y; respited.	Reigate, Sry
L 1811 Jul.19	Edmund MITCHELL, wife Philadelphia and daughter Mary 2y; confirmed.	Reigate, Sry

L 1812 Jan.17	William BROAD, wife Jane and children Mary 7y, William 6y, John 4y, James 3y, and Elizabeth 1y; confirmed.	Wivelsfield
L 1812 Oct. 9	Elizabeth PRITCHARD, wife of Edward PRITCHARD, and son Edward 8m; confirmed.	Brighton
L 1813 Apr.30	George THOMAS, wife Elizabeth and daughter Elizabeth 2y and a female child 2m, not yet baptised; respited.	Wivelsfield
L 1813 Apr.30	James HOLLINGDALE, wife Charlotte and son James 4m; confirmed.	Keymer
L 1813 Jul.16	George THOMAS, wife Elizabeth and daughter Elizabeth 2y and a female child 2m, not yet baptised; confirmed.	Wivelsfield
L 1814 Jan.14	Martha THORPE, wife of James THORPE; confirmed.	Rottingdean
L 1814 Jul.15	Ann HALLETT, singlewoman; confirmed.	Keymer
L 1815 Jan.13	Ann PECKHAM, singlewoman; confirmed.	Cuckfield
L 1815 Jul.14	Samuel DENMAN, wife Elizabeth and children Eleanor 4y, Joseph 2y and an infant son not yet baptised; confirmed.	Hurstpierpoint
L 1815 Jul.14	William EAGER; confirmed.	Hurstpierpoint
L 1816 Jan.12	Mary HAMPER, singlewoman; confirmed.	Streat
L 1816 Jan.12	Edward ILLMAN; confirmed.	Lingfield, Sry
L 1816 Jul.19	Thomas LINDFIELD, wife Sophia and children Frances 2y and John 1y; confirmed.	Keymer
L 1816 Jul.19	Esther MILLER and son William 4y; confirmed.	Chailey
L 1817 Jan.17	Richard UWINS, wife Elizabeth and children John 11y, Lucy 9y, James 7y, Harriet 5y, Ruth 3y and Reuben 9m; confirmed.	Chailey
L 1817 Apr.18	John PORT and wife Elizabeth; confirmed.	All Saints, Lewes
L 1817 Apr.18	William CHATFIELD; confirmed.	Hurstpierpoint
L 1818 Apr. 3	Thomas UWINS, wife Mary and son James 1y; confirmed.	Chailey
L 1820 Jan.14	William SADLER; quashed.	Ifield
L 1820 Apr.14	Sarah MEW, wife of William MEW, and daughter Mary Ann 7m; confirmed.	Whippingham, Iow
L 1824 Jul.15	Frances PACKET aged 7y; confirmed.	Chailey
L 1825 Jan.13	Edward GODDARD, wife Lydia and son John 4m; confirmed.	Brighton
L 1825 Jul.14	Ann SLATER, wife of Henry SLATER, the younger, and son Henry 4m; confirmed.	Steyning
L 1825 Oct.20	James BROOKER; confirmed.	Brighton
L 1825 Oct.20	Henry MORLEY, wife Sarah and children Henry 10y, Sarah Ann 7y, Edwin 4y, Louisa 3y and Elizabeth 9m; confirmed.	New Shoreham
L 1826 Jan.12	Naomi TATE, singlewoman; respited.	Brighton

L 1826 Apr. 6	Naomi TATE, singlewoman; quashed.	Brighton
L 1829 Jan.15	Jesse LIKEMAN, wife Susan and daughter Harriet 3m; confirmed.	Westmeston
L 1830 Jul.15	Sarah EAGER, wife of James EAGER, and daughter Lucy 8m; quashed.	Keymer

QUARTER SESSIONS REMOVAL ORDERS TO DITCHLING

		From
L 1650 Jul.18	Henry WEBB and wife.	Poynings
A 1667 Jan.14	CHAMBERS. So many of the children of William CHAMBERS as are above the age of 7y to be removed to Ditchling.	Horsham
L 1734 Jan.17	William DUDDEN; confirmed.	Brighton
L 1748 Jan.14	Thomas MEERES and wife Elizabeth; discharged	Barcombe
L 1762 Jan.14	Joseph SMITH, the younger, and wife Mary; confirmed.	Piddinghoe
L 1764 May 3	William MABB; confirmed.	Lewes
L 1769 Jan.12	James SANDERS, wife Elizabeth and son James 6m; confirmed.	Hellingly
L 1771 Jul.18	Edward COLLINS and wife Ann; confirmed.	Brighton
L 1786 Apr.27	Edward DUDLEY, wife Jane and sons Samuel 2y and Edward 5m; respited.	St. John sub Castro, Lewes
L 1786 Jul.13	Edward DUDLEY, wife Jane and sons Samuel 2y and Edward 5m; confirmed.	St. John sub Castro, Lewes
L 1789 Apr.23	Benjamin LULHAM and wife Lucy; confirmed	Berwick
L 1791 May 5	James FENNER and wife Elizabeth; confirmed.	Ringmer
L 1794 Oct. 9	Ann SIMMONS, singlewoman; respited.	Pyecombe
L 1799 Jul.18	John HEMSLEY and wife Sarah; quashed.	Streat
L 1813 Jan.15	Robert ALDRIDGE and children Mary 11y, Ann 9y, Susannah 6y and Robert 4y; quashed.	Bexhill
L 1815 Jan.13	Samuel TOWNSHEND, batchelor; confirmed.	Framfield
L 1815 Jan.13	William FORSTER and wife Mary; confirmed.	All Saints, Lewes
L 1816 Apr.26	William DAY, wife Sarah and daughter Charlotte; quashed.	Hooe
L 1816 Apr.26	George BOOKER, wife Sarah and daughters Mary 7y, Ann 5y, Sarah 4y, Jane 2y and Maria 6 weeks; respited.	Eastbourne
L 1817 Apr.18	John HAYLEY, commonly called HAYLER, and wife Jane; respited.	Burwash
L 1817 Jul.18	John HAYLEY, commonly called HAYLER, and wife Jane; quashed.	Burwash
L 1818 Jul.17	John ASHDOWN, wife Mary and son Benjamin 2y; confirmed.	Patcham
L 1823 Jan.17	Thomas PAINE and wife Hannah; confirmed.	Streat
L 1826 Jan.12	James SOUTER and wife Sarah; confirmed.	Plumpton

L 1827 Oct.18	Thomas CHAMBERS, wife Phoebe and son Richard aged 6 weeks; respited.	Ovingdean

EAST GRINSTEAD

East Grinstead: 15,128 acres on Surrey border, in Weald just N of Forest Ridge. Borough 1235, by 16th century 300 in town of 48 burgages; Assizes in 17th and 18th centuries; market town with 12 inns in 18th century (7 in 19th), wide range of over 100 tradesmen and shopkeepers. Coaches to London, Eastbourne and Lewes, carriers to London and Lewes. Surrounded by arable, pasture and woodland. Roman roads ENE and W.

Population: 1724 1466; 1801 2659; 1811 2804; 1821 3153; 1831 3364.

EAST GRINSTEAD SETTLEMENT EXAMINATIONS Par 348/32/4/1
* Indicates catalogued under Par 348/32/4/54

1686? Settlement Statement. George SWAN, father of Jane SWAN, came from Eatonbridge [Edenbridge], Kent, to live in East Grinstead before Lady Day 1686 and lived in a house which he rented off one Edward WOODGATE for rent of 40s 0d a year for three and a half years, and there died without having told the parish officers about his house and the number of his family, as required by law. He buried his wife in his lifetime and married again and lived with her till he died, about a fortnight [ago], and never served any office or paid poor tax. Jane Swan, his daughter, was put to nurse in Eatonbridge but was sent back to East Grinstead for default of payment, Jane being under the age of seven years. [Signature of Thomas BODLE, churchwarden of East Grinstead and William ALLEN, churchwarden of Edenbridge]
Catalogued under Par 348/37/5/1

1714 Mar.27 John OVELL, said that he hired himself as a yearly servant to Joseph HAMLYN of Horsted Keynes. [Endorsed: A separate letter dated 17 March, 1714 from L. GALE states that John Ovell served a full year with Joseph HAMBLEDEN (sic) of Horsted Keynes about six years ago and had his full wages at the rate of £4.15s 0d but he never served a full year or gained any legal settlement since in any other parish]

1715 Jan.27 Ruth FINCH alias FIN said that she was last a servant to Mr. Francis ALLIN, mariner, in Meacham [Mitcham], Surrey, for one whole year or more and received a full year's wages, and has not gained a settlement elsewhere. [Mark of R.F. alias F.]

1715 Mar.15 William PRINCE said that he was born in Clift [?Cliffe], Kent, and from thence was bound out an apprentice to Henry MILLAMS of Chatham, Kent, victualler. [Mark of W.P.]

1715 Mar.29 Edward HARPER, turner, said that he is the son of Edward HARPER who lived at Wells, Somerset, by trade a turner, and that his father lived there many years in a house of his own. That he was never apprenticed to anyone or a yearly servant and never rented for £10 a year or paid to church or poor in any parish. [Signature of E.H.]

1715 Jul.22 Edward PRICE said that he was born in Llanunogg [Llanwnog], Mongumrishire [Montgomeryshire], and has a freehold estate there, and has not acquired a settlement elsewhere. [Signature of E.P.]

1715 Nov.25 Ann FALKNER, widow, said that she is an inhabitant of Worth and that her husband rented a farm there and paid to the church and poor, and that her husband had not, before his death nor she since, acquired a settlement elsewhere. That the parish of Worth buried her husband and have since relieved her as occasion required. [Mark of A.F.]

1717 Nov.25 Alice LEE said that her son Thomas LEE was born at Tatnam [Tottenham] High Cross, Middlesex, at one FANGES house, a blacksmith, and was baptised there about 27 years ago. [Mark of A.L.]

1717 Dec. 6 Thomas LEE said that he was born at Totnam [Tottenham] High Cross, Middlesex and has not had any legal settlement since. That he was married last Easter Sunday, seven years ago, to Mary HAINES, servant to Mr. FISH, in St. George's, Southwark, [Surrey] and has three children now living viz: Frances born at Hellingly 6 years ago last Michaelmas, Mary born at Warbleton three years ago the 30 May last, and Thomas born at Alciston on 13 March last. [Mark of T.L.]

1718 Sep. 5 William BARHAM, husbandman, said that he was last a yearly servant to John BEST, yeoman in Lingfield, Surrey, and received a full year's wages, and has not acquired a legal settlement elsewhere. [Mark of W.B.]

1719 Feb.17 William COLLENS, late soldier in the Company of Col. John COAPE in the 2nd Regiment of Foot Guards, said that he was last a yearly servant for five whole years to Mr. Charles BLAKE, in Halts [Halse], near Tanton [Taunton], Somerset, and received full wages and has done no act to gain a settlement elsewhere. That he was married to Jane his wife at Bridgwater, Somerset, having the banns made public. [Mark of W.C.]

1719 Feb.18 George SPARKES said that he lived as a yearly servant for 3 full years with Mr. John MAY in Shervill [?Sherfield], Hampshire, and received a full year's wages for his last year's service and has not gained a legal settlement elsewhere. [Mark of G.S.]

1719 Feb.18 Elizabeth SPARKES said that she was married to George SPARKES (her fellow servant at Mr. HEWITS), by the minster of the parish of Streat, by licence. [Mark of E.S.]

1722 Jan. 2 William HULAT, hatmaker, said that he served an apprenticeship of seven years to William FRAMPTON, hatmaker, in Fordingbridge, Hampshire, and has never gained any other settlement. [Signature of W.H.] [Endorsed: Eliz. his wife, Eliz. and Mary their children]

1722 Jan. 3 Elizabeth HULAT alias GALE said that she was last a yearly servant to Mr. Henry TAPSELL at Cliffe, Lewes, and received full wages for such service. That, at the beginning of June 1717, she was married to William HULAT of Fordingbridge, Hampshire, hatmaker, by licence at Stammer [?Stanmer] Church upon the Hill, and her eldest daughter, Elizabeth, was born at Midhurst, on 9 March 1719 and the youngest daughter was born at East Grinstead on 6 April 1721, christened Mary. [Signature of E.H. alias Gale]

1722 Jan.20* William WOODMAN said that he has lived in Godstone, Surrey for two years and not gained a legal settlement since. [Mark of W.W.]

1722 Jan.20* William BASSETT said that he has lived about 5 years in Godstone, Surrey, and not gained a legal settlement since. [Mark of W.B.]

1723 Jan.19 Settlement Statement. Temperance TOOTH, who was married to Isaac PRING, did not gain a settlement by this marriage as he already had a wife living at the time of marriage. If the first marriage cannot be proved then she (if her marriage is proved) will be settled in the parish of Isaac Pring. If he served out his whole year in Rash [?Ryarsh, Kent], he gained a settlement there, notwithstanding he married within the year, and such was determined in the Court of the Kings Bench between the parishes of Faringdon, Berkshire and Wilcot, Oxfordshire, that, if a person unmarried be hired for a year and marries within the year, that he gains a settlement if he serve out his year, notwithstanding such marriage, and if no other settlement can be found for Pring, then he must be settled at Lindfield.
Catalogued under Par 348/37/5/5

1725 Jan.12 Henry PRESTON said that he was born at Martin [Merton], Oxfordshire, and has not gained a legal settlement elsewhere. That he was married to Susanna MASON at St. Dunstans, Canterbury, Kent, on 2 February last, and his wife was delivered of a male child on 26 December last, in East Grinstead. [Mark of H.P.]

1725 Jan.22 John PUPLETT, regarding his marriage with Sara POCOCK and his last legal settlement said that he was lawfully married to his wife in St. George, Southwark, Surrey, and that, for several years, he served Thomas RELFE, the elder, and Thomas RELFE, the younger, of Buxted, as a yearly servant, hired by the year, and has not served elsewhere. [Mark of J.P.]

1727 Sep.11 Thomas LOVELIDGE said that, about 20 years ago, he hired a farm in Duxford, Cambridgeshire at the yearly rent of £30, where he lived 3 years, and paid rent to the church and the poor. That, about Bartholomewtide 1720, he was hired by John WEBSTER esq., of Bromley, Kent, as a bailiff at £25, with whom he lived at Bromley for near 9 months and, when a farm called Tablehurst came into Mr. Webster's hands he, this deponent, was sent to East Grinstead, where the farm lay, to look after it and there he served for over two years. [Endorsed: 16 Feb.1728. The examinant, being further examined, said that he was married, 11 years ago, at Southampton, Hampshire, to his present wife Elizabeth.] [Signature of T.L.]

1727 Sep.16 Joseph HOLMES, being a quaker, said upon his affirmation, that he was bound apprentice, by indenture dated 1 November 1708, to Gamaliel INGRAM of Croydon, Surrey, cordwainer, to be taught the trade of cordwainer, with him to serve and dwell for 7 years and he served the full term, and knows of no other settlement. [Signature of J.H.]

1729 Aug. 7 John WORNHAM said that he was born in All Saints, Lewes, and bound an apprentice, by indenture, to William RICHARDSON of Sevenoaks, Kent, saddle treemaker, for seven years, to be taught his master's trade but did not serve above 3 years. That, afterwards, he hired himself to George COURTHOPE of Ticehurst, at £5 a year, and lived there as a yearly servant for 4 years and received his wages, which time followed after the 7 years were expired. That he then hired himself to his father, John WORNHAM of All Saints, for one year at 40s 0d wages, which he received, and hired £10 a year of Mr. Charles PAIN of East Grinstead, and of Mary BUTCHING 35s 0d a year. [Signature of J.W.]

1729 Nov.13* John ROKES said that he was born in Withyham and his friends bound him apprentice to Alexander AULCORNE of East Grinstead for two years, which term he served, and further sayeth not. [Mark of J.R.]

1729 Dec.27 Thomas NEWNHAM said he was born in Lingfield, Surrey, and knows nothing further of his last legal settlement. [Signature of Thomas Newnam (sic)]

1729 Dec.29 John UNDAY said that he was born in St. [?Giles], Norwich, Norfolk, and was bound apprentice to John PEARSEN of St. Michaels, Cousney to whom he served half his time, afterwards being turned over to Micall GREENWOOD of St. Saviours and there served the remainder of his time. That, after he came from thence, he gained no legal settlement till he came to East Grinstead and bargained with Daved DUDLEY the 9 November 1728, for a year at £1.10s 0d and to have privileges of the shop and the stable, which time he served and received full wages. [Signature of J.U.]

1732 Mar.23* Elizabeth COSHAM said that she gained a settlement in Ringmer, being the daughter of Thomas COSHAM, and has not gained a legal settlement in any other parish. [Mark of E.C.]

1732 Oct.24* William SIBLEY said that he was bound apprentice to Robert HOLMAN of St. Catherine Colman, in Fan Church [Fenchurch] Street, London, cloth scourer, for 8 years beginning 4 October 1714 and served his master until 4 October 1722, and has not, since that apprenticeship, gained a legal settlement. [Signature of W.S.]

1732 Nov. 4* Robert HOOK said that he hired himself to Thomas PYEPER of Mayfield, yeoman, as a yearly servant for £3 per annum, where he served a full year and received his wages and he, now being very aged and infirm, cannot remember when that service expired but he has not gained a legal settlement since. [Mark of R.H.]

1732 Nov.13* Bartholomew CROSS said that, in 1711, he was bound apprentice to John WELTCH of Axminster, Devonshire, blacksmith, for 7 years and served his master for 5 years, then listed himself a soldier, and has not gained a legal settlement since that apprenticeship. [Mark of B.C.]

1735 Feb.14* Jowel BOWRA said that, about 18 years ago, he bargained with Edward BAKER of Betchworth, Surrey, to live with him as his servant for a year from the 3 May following, which year he served. That he has not lived as a yearly servant since but, two years after the expiration of the above service, he was married and, about 4 years ago, went to live in East Grinstead, during which time he was appointed and served the office of Headborough of the Borough of Wardleigh in East Grinstead (where he now dwells), for the space of a year.

1736 Jul. 3* Thomas EDWARDS said that, 14 or 15 years ago, he bargained with Gervase LONG of Chatham, Kent, farmer, to serve him for one year from Michaelmas to the Michaelmas following for £6 and upwards, he cannot exactly set forth the same, but served out his time and received his wages. [Mark of T.E.]

1737 Aug.23* Anne TAYLOR, spinster, said that she was hired as a yearly servant to the Rt. Hon. Marquis of CARNARVON in April, 1731, and served out that hiring upwards of a year and received her wages at £7 per annum, and she further said that the last 40 days of such service was in St. James, Westminster, Middlesex, and that she has not since gained a legal settlement in any other parish. [Signature of A.T.]

1738 Feb. 6* Joseph MEARS said that he was born in Byfleet, Surrey, and, at the age of about 11 or 12 years, went as a servant to Ensign FLOYD in Col. STRINGER'S Regiment of Foot, and served him for four years till his master was killed in Flanders. That he then listed himself in the said regiment as a soldier and served 5 years and was then drafted into Lord MONTJOY'S regiment, where he served 2 years. That he then was drafted into Col. MOLESWORTH'S regiment and served in that for seven years, at the end of which the regiment was disbanded and he settled in Byfleet and has been there near 14 years, and has not gained a settlement in any other parish. [Mark of J.M.]

1738 Sep.19* Elizabeth JARRATT, spinster, said that she hired herself as a yearly servant to John PIGOTT of Lingfield, Surrey, sometime before Michaelmas 1736, and served a whole year, receiving £3.5s 0d in wages and has not gained a legal settlement since. [Mark of E.J.]

1738 Nov.27* James GLOVER said that, in May 1731, he hired himself as a yearly servant to Rt. Hon. the Countess Dowager of Northampton in Great St.Georges, Bloomsbury, Middlesex, for £7 per year. That he served the said Lady 3 years and received his full wages, the last 40 days of the service being in Great St.

Georges, Bloomsbury, and he has not since gained a legal settlement in any other parish. [Mark of J.G.]

1739 Jan. 1* Mary BUTLER said that she hired herself as a yearly servant to Andrew FURMINGER of Hartfield, in April 1735 at 55s per year, where she served one whole year and received her wages, and then began another year with her master for the same wages, and served till six weeks of the expiration thereof and received 50s 0d, and has not gained a settlement in any other parish since this service. [Mark of M.B.]

1739 Jan. 1* Easter CUMBER, singlewoman, said that she was born in Horsted Cains [Keynes] and was never hired as a yearly servant or ever gained a legal settlement in any other parish. [Mark of E.C.]

1739 Jul.26* William BROOKER said that he served William HOSKINS esq., of Oxted, Surrey, as a yearly servant for 14 years, without any intermission, and received full wages, and has not gained a settlement in any other parish since the above service. [Signature of W.B.]

1739 Sep.26* Richard BROOKER said that he hired himself as a yearly servant to Robert SAXBYE of Prinkham, Lingfield, Surrey, from before Michaelmas 1736 at £8 per year, which he served and received his full wages, and has not gained a legal settlement in any other parish. [Mark of R.B.]

1740 Mar. 6* Mary BRIANT, singlewoman, said that, about 3 weeks before Christmas 1738, she contracted with Elizabeth, the wife of Samuel FLOYD of Addington in Surrey, to serve as a domestic servant from the Friday next after Christmas for one year, with condition that the contract be void if, at any time, either of the parties should give to the other one month's notice of his or her dislike of or to the other, or if Mr. Floyd should, before the expiration of the year, pay to her one month's wages more than she was due, but no such dislike, notice or payment having been taken, given or made, this examinant did serve one year and received £3, being her full wages. [Mark of M.B.]

1740 Mar. 26 Mary MARTEN, singlewoman, said that, 6 years ago, she hired herself as a servant to George HUGGETT of Wivelsfield, farmer, for a year from Lady Day next, lived there for a full year and received her full wages, and then served another full year with the same master. [Mark of M.M.]

1740 May 12 Examination of Katherine READY, wife of Lewes READY of East Grinstead, regarding the birth of Elizabeth and Thomas GANDY, children of Edward GANDY of East Grinstead, labourer, and his wife Jane. Katherine Ready said that she had, for about 16 years, followed and used the business of a midwife in East Grinstead and that she was sent for, about six and a half years ago, to be employed in that capacity of the bringing to bed of Jane, the wife of Edward Gandy, whom she delivered of a daughter who was, soon afterwards, baptised Elizabeth in East

Grinstead where she has, ever since, resided. She further said that she did also deliver a son which, about three and a half years ago, was born to Jane at East Grinstead, where he was soon baptised Thomas, and that he still resides in that parish. [Mark of K.R.]

1741 Jan.12 Thomas EDWARDS said that, nineteen years ago, he gained a legal settlement in Chatham, Kent, by having served Gervice LONG for one year, and receiving full wages. That later he went, with Mary his wife, to live in East Grinstead and obtained a settlement certificate from Chatham parish. [Mark of T.E.]

1741 Sep.22 Robert STREATFIELD said that he hired himself as a yearly servant to Edward EVERIST of Chittingstone, [Chiddingstone], Kent, from Michaelmas day 1736 to Michaelmas 1737, and received £4.4s 0d in wages. That he then hired himself, as a yearly servant, to Anne MEDHURST of Chittingstone, widow, from Michaelmas day 1737, served a full year and received his wages, and then served her a second year, and received £5.10s 0d wages for the last whole year ending Michaelmas 1739, and has not worked a full year since to gain a settlement anywhere else. [Signature of R.S.]

1742 Mar.24 Susannah HARDS, widow, said that 8 or 9 years ago she married Robert HARDS of Hartfield, cordwainer, who, she often heard declare, was last legally settled in Hartfield and that she lived with her husband at Hartfield for several years, until his death, since which time she has been a sojourner in East Grinstead and, since the death of her husband, she has not gained a legal settlement for herself. [Mark of S.H.]

1742 Mar.24 James MITCHELL said that, by an indenture dated 23 June 1736, he took an assignment of a farm in Godstone and Tandridge, Surrey, whereby an indenture, dated 12 June 1731, was demised by Edward EVELYN esq., to Adam RICHARDSON for 21 years at the yearly rent of £9 and 2 fat pulletts. That he purchased the assignment of Adam Richardson and paid to him, as an income for the same for the residue of the term, being 16 years, the sum of £23.10s 0d, and he lived at this farm for 5 years, then assigned the indenture for the residue of the term of about 11 years, to Robert TILT and received of the said Tilt an income of £21.3s 0d. That he hired, in the year 1737, of Edward EVELYN, other lands in Godstone at the yearly rent of £3, from 15 April 1737 for 1 year and paid £12 to Mr. Evelyn, being the year's rent due, and he has not gained a settlement elsewhere. [Signature of J.M.]

1742 Apr.26 Timothy PRUDDEN otherwise HARTOP said that, on 2 May 1732, she was married, at the Fleet in London, to Caleb HARTOP of Dorking, Surrey, turner, who, dying on 3 October 1739 and leaving her a widow and childless, she, about a month later, hired herself to John FOWLER of Lingfield, Surrey, victualler, to serve him a year for £4 wages, which term she served. That, soon after Easter 1741, she hired herself to MR ATTWOOD of Sanderstead, Surrey, for a year but served only until a few days before Christmas last and that, two months before she left Mr. Attwood's service, to wit at the beginning of October last, she was married at the Fleet in St.

Sepulchre, London, to John PRUDDEN of Wooton [Wootton] in Bedfordshire, blacksmith. [Mark of T.P.]

1742 Apr.27 John PRUDDEN, blacksmith, said that he was born at Elstow, Bedfordshire and, at about a year old, was removed by his father who went with a certificate to Wooton [Wootton], Bedfordshire, where, near 20 years ago, his father was made Constable and executed that office during a year at Wooton. That this examinant resided with his father, as part of his family, till he was 17 years of age, when he departed and went to London where, and at divers other places, he has continued to work as a journeyman blacksmith by weekly contracts from that time to this. That he married on 2 October 1741 in that part of the Fleet which lies in St. Sepulchre, London, by Robert CUTHBERT, Minister Keeper of the Register of the said marriage, as mentioned in a certificate of the celebration of the marriage, signed by Robert Cuthbert and now produced, and that he has not acquired a legal settlement since his departure from Wooton. [Signature of J.P.]

1742 Oct.11 John GORRINGE said that, 14 years ago, he hired a farm in Pembury, otherwise Pipinbury, Kent, at the yearly rent of £14 a year for 12 years, and paid taxes to the church and poor, and has not gained any legal settlement since renting the above farm. [Mark of J.G.]

1743 Feb. 1 Mary WILLSON, late of East Grinstead, widow, said that, in 1722 or 1723, being then a singlewoman, she hired herself to Daniel CLARE at his late coffee house in Great George Street in St. George, Middlesex, to serve a year at wages of £4 and that she served her master, in the coffee house, the said year, for which she was so retained for successive years at different wages. That, from thence, she hired herself to - HOWARD in Newport Street, near Long Acre, goldsmith, in Westminster, Middlesex, whom she served about 11 months, and from thence to Mr. POWEL in St. James Street, Westminster, for 9 months, and voluntarily departing from her service, was thereupon married to James WILLSON a Scotsman, then a soldier in Col. Bing's Coy. of Foot Guards until his death, which happened, she was informed and believes, in March 1741 at the siege of Carthergina, in the West Indies. That she believes her husband never acquired any legal settlement in England or Wales and that she has two children by her late husband, the youngest, (named William) born in Whitechapel without the gate of the City of London, called Aldgate, Middlesex, who is now near 5 years old and residing, she believes, in East Grinstead. [Signature of M.W.]

1743 Mar.24 John DUMSDAY said that he was born in Lingfield, Surrey, 27 or 28 years ago, his father, John DUMSDAY, dwelling there by virtue of a certificate from Shipley. That he lived, as part of his father's family, as a journeyman to him by the week in Lingfield, from the time of his birth until Christmas last four years ago, about which time he married and continued to dwell and to work as aforesaid, sometimes as a master for a year, and then came to live in East Grinstead, where he has ever since resided without acquiring any legal settlement for himself there. [Signature of J.D.]

1743 Mar.28 John YEOMANS, labourer, said that he believes he was born in Horley, Surrey, and that he has been married over 14 years and that, before his marriage, he never lived as a yearly servant or apprentice out of Horley and, since his marriage, has done no act to gain a settlement in any other parish.
[Mark of J.Y.]

1743 Aug.12 Lawrence SUTTON said that he was apprenticed by indenture, 9 years ago, to William MILES of East Grinstead, glazier, and that he has served 5 years with him and has not been hired to any person since. [Signature of L.S.]

1743 Oct.11 John HARR[IS?] of East Grinstead, labourer, said that, four years ago last Michaelmas, he hired a farm at Hartfield of Robert CHIPPING of Bletchingley, Surrey, for a year at the yearly rent of £24, and occupied the farm until about July next following when the landlord, distraining his goods for non-payment of the rent of the farm, he then quitted the possesson of the farm and has not acquired any legal settlement in any other parish. [Part of this document is missing]

1743 Oct.11 John OVELL, labourer of East Grinstead, said that, six years ago, he hired himself to JOHN COWDREY of Crowhurst, Surrey, farmer, to live and serve him as a menial servant for a year, and that he lived with and served his master the whole year in Crowhurst and received his wages, since which he has not acquired a legal settlement elsewhere. [Signature of J.O.]

1744 Feb.20 John CUFFTREE, shovelmaker, said that he believes he was born at Chesham, Buckinghamshire, and has never acquired a legal settlement elsewhere. [Mark of J.C.]

1744 Feb.20 Francis BENNETT, weaver of East Grinstead, said that he was born at Horsham where, he believes, his father, Thomas BENNETT, was last legally settled and so continued till his death, and he further said that he has not, since he left Horsham, gained any settlement elsewhere. [Signature of F.B.]

1746 Jun.20 Anne WRIGHT said that she is 21 years of age, that she is the wife of William WRIGHT, a soldier in General Skelton's Regiment of Foot, and that the place of her husband's legal settlement, as he informed her, is East Grinstead, and that she was apprehended in Boroughbridge, Yorkshire, wandering and begging, and further sayeth not.

1752 Oct.21* George MEDHURST, now residing in East Grinstead, husbandman, said that the place of his last legal settlement is in Limpsfield, Surrey, by hiring himself to the service of Abraham BROWNE of Limpsfield, farmer, for one year at four guineas wages, from 3 days after Michaelmas 1739 to the next Michaelmas, as far as he can remember, but he received full wages and agreed to serve another year at £4.15s 0d, which he served out and received his wages. [Mark of G.M.]

1753 Mar. 8* Winifred SMITH late OVELL, said that, about 12 years ago, she was married to Samuel SMITH, late of Crowhurst, Surrey, in the parish church of East Grinstead, with whom she lived about 3 years after the marriage, when he left her and was gone for about [torn] or 5 years, during which time she [torn] served with Thomas MARTEN of East Grinstead, husbandman. That, about a year after which last marriage, Samuel Smith came to East Grinstead about the receipt of money which Winifred's father had left to her by his will, nearly £15, that S.S. did then receive £5 of this money, and she had the remaining £10, and, after this transaction, S.S. left her again and she has not seen anything of him since. W.S. said that she had one son by S.S., who has been sent, sometime since, to Crowhurst, it being the last legal settlement of her husband, and the parish officers there have provided for her son ever since. [Mark of W.S. late Ovell]

1754 Dec. 9* William STILLWELL, said that his last legal settlement was in Dunsfold, Surrey, by serving Thomas MELLEISH of that place, farmer, for one year, as he best remembers, from Michaelmas 1747 to the following Michaelmas for wages of £6, which he duly served and received full wages, and has not gained a legal settlement since. [Mark of W.S.]

1755 Feb. 8* Richard AWCOCK, now living in West Hoathly, said that his father was settled in Ardingly and that, 20 years ago, he had obtained a certificate from Ardingly to remove and dwell in West Hoathly, where he followed the trade of a butcher till he died about 3 years ago, without having gained a settlement there. This examinant said that he was born in West Hoathly and lived with his father chiefly but never had a settlement there or anywhere, and knows of no settlement but that of Ardingly. [Signature of Richard Alcock (sic)]

1759 Feb. 2* George STILLER said that he bargained with Richard MARTIN of East Grinstead to serve him from Michaelmas 1757 to Michaelmas 1758 for wages of £4.10s 0d, which term he served and received his full wages, and has not gained a settlement in any other parish. [Signature of George Stiler (sic)]

1761 Dec.12 Thomas EDWARDS said that he was born in East Grinstead about 29 years ago, and that his father dwelt there until his death. That soon after this his mother, self and two sisters were removed, by an order, to Chatham, Kent, as it was the last legal settlement of his deceased father, Thomas EDWARDS. That he remained at Chatham for one and a half years when his grandfather, Richard EDWARDS of East Grinstead, took him from Chatham workhouse and hired him to serve for a year at wages of 30s 0d, which time he served and then served his grandfather for four years, and knows nothing further as to a settlement elsewhere. [Mark of T.E.]

1763 Jan.18 Thomas MERRITT said that he was born in Dorking, Surrey, about 23 years ago, and believes his last place of settlement is in Walkhamstead otherwise Godstone, Surrey. That, a month before Christmas 1761, he hired himself to John RUSSELL of Godstone, farmer, to serve him to the feast of St. Michael next, receiving wages of four guineas, which time he served and then was hired to serve John

Russell for another year at wages of five guineas but served only 3 months and some days of this last hiring, being prevented by the parish officers apprehending him to answer concerning his getting one Mary LAMBERT with child, which Mary he has now married. [Signature of T.M.]

1775 Oct.17 Elizabeth KING, singlewoman, said that, five and a half years ago, she was hired by Dame PUTHAM of the Green Dragon at East Grinstead, for a year and served there two whole years and received 2 year's wages. That, afterwards, she was hired by WILLIAM MOON, shoemaker, of the same parish for a year and received her wages and she has not been hired or served a whole year in any place since that time. [Mark of E.K.]

1778 Mar. 2* Winny OVELL, singlewoman, said that she was born in East Grinstead where her father, John OVELL, did and now does reside by virtue of a certificate granted by Crowhurst, Surrey, to East Grinstead and she has not gained a settlement elsewhere. [Mark of W.O.]

1778 Apr.13* James TOWES, husbandman, said that he is aged 24 years and was born in Horsted Keynes and that he hired himself to Mr. Richard WESTON of West Hoathly, farmer, from old Lady Day 1777 to Old Lady Day 1778 at £6.6s 0d wages, which time he served and received his wages. That he married Elizabeth, his now wife, at the parish church of East Grinstead. [Mark of J.T.]

1778 Jul.21* James GARRETT said that he was born in Orsett, Essex, the residence of Thomas GARRETT, his father, who is a legal inhabitant of the parish of Orsett, and he has done no act to gain settlement in any other parish. [Signature of J.G.]

1778 Jul.21* John REDDY, labourer, said that, 4 years ago last Michaelmas, he hired himself to Sarah KNIGHT of Lingfield, Surrey, widow, for one year in husbandry business, at wages of six and a half guineas, which term he served and received his full wages, since which he has done no act to gain a settlement in any other parish. [Mark of J.R.] [Endorsed: Jenny his wife, Bett an infant aged 9 weeks]

1779 Nov. 1 Thomas PELLATT of East Grinstead, mariner, said that he was born in Penhill in Bletchingley, Surrey, he believes, and has not gained a legal settlement in any other parish. [Signature of T.P.]
Catalogued under Par 348/34/1/11

1781 Jan. 7 James READY said that he was he was born in East Grinstead where his father was legally settled. That he was hired to [torn] BANKS of East Grinstead for a year at wages of three [torn] a week, which year he served and received [his wages] and has not done any other [torn] to gain a settlement. [Mark of J.R.]

1797 Feb. 4 Thomas PRYER, now residing in Carshalton, Surrey, said that, ten years ago, he was bound apprentice to William MARTIN of East Grinstead, cordwainer, for seven years in the trade of a cordwainer, and that he had served for about five years when he and his master agreed to discontinue the apprenticeship, and indentures were exchanged by them accordingly, and he has not gained a settlement in any other parish. That, a year ago, he married at Chipstead, Surrey, to Susannah, his now wife, by whom he has one child named Susannah, aged 8 months.

1798 Apr.11 John SIMMONS, now residing in Godstone, [Surrey], said that he was born in East Grinstead where his father's settlement is, and that he has done no act whereby a settlement might be gained in his own right, and that, about 9 months ago, he married Henrietta his present wife.

1801 Sep.12 James MILES, now residing in Westmeston, said that he was born in that parish but that his father was legally settled in East Grinstead. That he lived by half yearly hirings with Mr. HODSON of Westmeston and Mr. MOTT of the same parish, and also lived two separate half year's with Mr. HAMSHAR and Mr. Thomas HODSON of Streat. That he has not been hired separate from that he derived from his father in East Grinstead, and that this examinant was married at Westmeston to Amy PECKHAM on 13 October last, by whom he has one child, baptised Ann. [Mark of J.M.]

1802 Jul.10 William ISTED, now residing in Slaugham, said that he was born in East Grinstead where his parents were legally settled and that he has not gained a settlement since. [Mark of W.I.]

1803 Jun. 1* Elizabeth AGENT, now residing in East Grinstead, singlewoman, said that, at Ladytide 1800, she hired herself to William TURNER of Crowhurst, Surrey, farmer, for a year at wages of £3, from old Lady Day 1800 to the following Old Lady Day, when she received her wages and then hired herself to the same master for another year at £3.10s 0d, which year she served and then quitted his service, and has done no act to gain a settlement in any other parish. [Mark of E.A.]

1804 Apr. 5* Elijah WEST, now residing in Nuthurst, labourer, and lately discharged from Sussex Regiment of Militia, said that he was born in Horsham where his parents then resided, but that they belonged to Rudgwick, as he believes. That, 18 years ago, he hired himself to William ISTED of East Grinstead, farmer, for a year at wages of £3.3s 0d, which he completed and received full wages. That, after living at 2 other places in the parish for a year and receiving his wages, he worked at his own hand for 2 years in the parish, then hired himself to Robert HEATH of East Grinstead, farmer, for a year at wages of £9, which term he served, and has not gained a settlement in any other parish. That he is married and his wife's name is Zelpha, by whom he has two children born in wedlock: Elijah 9 years and Zelpha 6 years. [Mark of E.W.]

1805 Apr.6* Bannister TRUELOCK said that, at Lady Day, six years ago, he hired a house and garden in Nowels Row, Pentonville, Islington, Middlesex, of Mr. LEWIS of Grub Street, the landlord, at the yearly rent of £10, and he continued to occupy the house for 4 years (paying the rent quarterly). When his wife died he quitted the same, since which he has done no act to gain a settlement. [Signature of Bannister Trulock (sic)]

1806 May 28* Simon WHITE said that he was born in Slinfold, where his father and mother were legally settled and that, since his birth, he has done no act to gain a settlement. That he has this day married Jane, his present wife, late JANE TINGLEY, widow. [Mark of S.W.]

1812 Dec.26* William BRIDGER, now residing in Tunbridge, Kent, labourer, said that he believes he was born in wedlock in Rotherfield, where his father was legally settled. That, in 1800 about a month before old Michaelmas day, he hired himself to William BROWN of East Grinstead, farmer, for a year to old Michaelmas Day 1801, at wages of 10 guineas, which time he served and received his full wages. That, soon afterwards, he married and has one child born in wedlock, named William aged 10 years, and his wife's name is Mary, and that he has not gained legal settlement in any other parish. [Mark of W.B.]

1815 Sep. 2* James STONER said that he was born in Cowfold and that, at about 10 or 12 years of age, he hired himself to Mr. James HUGHES, farmer, by the year at wages of 2 guineas per annum, serving the time out and received his wages, and has not hired himself for a year at any other place. [Mark of J.S.]

1815 Sep. 30* Letter to Mr. HEAD of East Grinstead. Benjamin GROVES having lately resided in our parish wished to be examined as to his place of settlement which was done yesterday. It appears he is settled in your parish. I have therefore sent him with the order to save expense but if you have any doubt as to his settlement, we will deliver him in approved way. I am your obed. servant Philip TURNER, East Hoathly.

CERTIFICATES OF SETTLEMENT OUTSIDE EAST GRINSTEAD Par 348/32/1/1

N.B. A few certificates issued by East Grinstead to other parishes are listed separately immediately following the main series.

* Indicates items catalogued under Par 348/32/1/168

		From
1699 Jul.30*	William BURSTOWE, wife Rose and family.	Godstone, Sry
1699 Nov. 4*	William HEAD, wife and family.	Hartfield
1700 Aug. 5*	Henry WOOD and wife.	West Hoathly
1701 Sep.27*	John BRINKHURST and wife Jane.	Chailey
1701 Oct.25*	Andrew HIBBEN, wife Anne and children George, John, Elizabeth and Anne.	North Cray, Ken
1702 Jun. 3*	Thomas CAREW, wife and family.	Burstow, Sry
1702 Jul.24*	William HOYDEN, wife and male child.	Ewell, Sry
1703Aug 30*	Edward MIDHURST, trunkmaker, and wife Susan.	Guildford, Sry

1705 Jul.24*	Richard DAY, carpenter, wife Mary and children Elizabeth, David, John, James, Susanna. [Names deleted and "family" substituted].	West Hoathly
1706 Apr.17*	Henry BATEMAN, surgeon, wife and children.	Reigate, Sry
1707 Jun. 7*	Richard LEOFORD and wife.	Bletchingley, Sry
1710 Oct.28*	Richard NELSON, blacksmith, wife and family.	Godstone, Sry
1711 Sep. 6*	William DEANE and wife.	Horne, Sry
1712 Oct.14*	Elizabeth WILKINS.	St. Lawrence, Pountney, Lnd
1712 Dec. 8*	William LOCK, weaver, wife Anne and children.	Lingfield, Sry
1713 Feb.21*	Francis BISH and wife Elizabeth.	Lingfield, Sry
1714 Mar.26	William MUDDLE, cooper, wife and family.	Ardingly
1715 Jul.22*	Richard MARTEN, collarmaker, wife and family.	Horsham
1715 Sep. 3*	Robart CRIPPS, weaver.	Rotherfield
1715 Sep. 3*	John GILBART, husbandman, wife and child.	Rotherfield
1715 Sep. 9*	William ILMAN.	Horsham
1715 Sep.24*	John COOMBER and wife.	West Hoathly
1716 Mar.30*	Nynnion CREASIE, husbandman, wife and children.	Rotherfield
1717 Jan.26*	Robert PETTET, shoemaker.	Hartfield
1720 Apr.18	William BARRAM, wife Sarah and children.	Lingfield, Sry
1720 Apr.21	John BEARD, wife Mary and children Mary, Sarah and Ruth.	Twineham
1721 Mar.10	Joseph MERCHANT, wife and family.	Oxted, Sry
1722 Mar.26	Thomas CHAPMAN, tailor, wife Catharine.	Speldhurst, Ken
1722 Jun.19	William NASH and wife Anne.	West Hoathly
1722 Jul.19	Robert STREATFEILD, wife Mary and family.	Speldhurst, Ken
1722 Nov.27	James WILLARD and wife Elizabeth.	Kemsing, Ken
1723 Apr.13	John CAUGHT, wife and children.	Godstone, Sry
1724 Aug.18	Isaac PRING, wife Temperance and son John.	Ryarsh, Ken
1725 Jun.28	Robert PITMAN, currier, wife Katharine and son Robert also Elizabeth and Anne WIMARK daughters of Katharine by a former husband.	Brighton
1726 Feb.20	William VARGE, shoemaker.	Nutfield, Sry
1726 Jul. 2	Robert GOODWIN, wife and family.	Cowden, Ken
1726 Oct. 3	George KEMP and wife Elizabeth.	Findon
1726 Oct. 8	William BEST, wife Mary and family [Elizabeth and Mary their children - crossed through].	Snodland, Ken
1727 Feb.13	Philip MOATT, wife Mary.	Pulborough
1728 Feb.20	Joseph HOLMES and wife Ruth.	Croydon, Sry
1728 Mar.18	Timothy HOWARD and wife Mary.	Bicester, Oxf
1728 Apr.27	Richard PAINE, wife Jane and son John.	Lingfield, Sry
1728 Dec. 5	Thomas BAILEY and wife Elizabeth.	Mayfield
1729 Jan. 5	John BELCHAMBER.	Lindfield
1729 Feb.27	John VAUGHAN, brickmaker, and wife Jude.	New Fishbourne
1729 Apr.22	Richard BIRCH, hoopmaker, and family.	Penn, Bkm

1729 Jul.25	William NORMAN and his children.	Godstone, Sry
1729 Oct. 1	John WORNHAM.	All Saints, Lewes
1730 Feb.11	John ORGLES and wife Sarah.	West Hoathly
1730 Mar. 3	Thomas NEWNAM and wife Elizabeth.	Lingfield, Sry
1730 Mar.11	John FARMER, wife Mary and daughter Mary 1y.	Woodmancote
1731 May 24	Robert LEWICE, labourer, wife Jane and daughter Mary.	Dorney, Bkm
1731 Jul.29	Griffith CURTHOYS [CURTIS], labourer, wife Anne and son George 4y.	Thornbury, Gls
1731 Sep.24	John SMITH, wife and children.	Colchester, Ess
1732 Jan.23	Samuel RIVERS wife Jane, son Henry and daughter Elizabeth Tamar.	Worth
1732 Feb.28	John BROWN, wife and family.	Lingfield, Sry
1732 Apr. 1	Samuel SMITH, labourer and wife Elizabeth.	Crowhurst, Sry
1732 May 7*	John BROOKER and wife Elizabeth.	Sevenoaks, Ken
1732 Aug.14	Nicholas PALMER, blacksmith, wife Alice and son William 2y.	Brighton
1732 Oct. 9	Valentine TREE, labourer, and wife Anne.	Firle
1734 Sep.14	Thomas POCKNELL and wife Barbara.	Edenbridge, Ken
1735 Jan.24*	Robert TILT and wife Elizabeth.	Horsham
1735 Jul. 5	George DEW and wife Mary.	Lingfield, Sry
1735 Oct.26	Richard BAKER and wife Frances.	Hartfield
1735 Dec.26	Edward TAPSELL. Ack.	Worth
1736 Feb. 1	Robert DINNES [DENNESS], wife and children.	Lingfield, Sry
1736 Mar.26	Edward TAPSELL, wife Hannah and 3 children.	Worth
1736 Mar.30	William TAYLER and wife Hannah.	Horne, Sry
1736 Apr. 1	Ralf KILLICK and wife Mary.	Rotherfield
1736 Apr. 5	Jacob PRING, tailor, who served an apprenticeship in Lindfield, wife Jane and daughter Elizabeth.	Lindfield
1736 Jun. 6	Thomas EVEREST, blacksmith.	Hever, Ken
1736 Sep.19	Thomas KEMP.	Faversham, Ken
1736 Sep.25	Mathew REEVES and wife Susan.	Astley, Sal
1736 Oct.21	Thomas EDWARDS, wife and children.	Chatham, Ken
1737 Apr. 8	William PAINE and wife Elizabeth.	Lingfield, Sry
1737 Jul. 5	John HISTED, wife Ann and son John 6m.	Horsted Keynes
1737 Oct.27	Robert DINNIS, wife Amey and children.	Lingfield, Sry
1738 Apr.13	Edward HOLLANDS, wife Mary and children.	Edenbridge, Ken
1739 Apr. 2	Thomas BUTLER and wife Esther.	Withyham
1739 Apr. 5	George TAYLER and wife Grace.	Dorking, Sry
1739 Oct.12	Richard BROOKER, wife Praxed and son Richard.	Lingfield, Sry
1740 Jan.10	William BROOKER, wife Mary and children Sarah 8y and Elizabeth 6y.	Oxted, Sry
1740 Feb. 8*	Thomas BURLEY, husbandman, and Mercy BURLEY, his mother.	West Hoathly
1740 Feb.20	John HUMPHERY, wife and children Ann 3y and John 1y.	West Hoathly

1740 Apr. 7	Henry FARLEY, wife Elizabeth and children Elizabeth and Henry.	Barcombe
1740 Apr. 7	William FARRANT, wife Elizabeth and children Thomas, Sarah, Mary and Philadelphia.	Fletching
1740 Oct.19	William MUDDLE, wife and child.	Crowhurst, Sry
1740 Nov. 3	Edward GANDY, wife Jane and Elizabeth 7y and Thomas 4y.	Albourne
1741 Nov.29	Robert STREATFIELD, husbandman, and wife Susanah.	Chiddingstone, Ken
1742 Apr.16	Susanna HARDS, widow of Robert HARDS late of Hartfield, cordwainer.	Hartfield
1742 Apr.19	Francis HOBLEY, flaxdresser.	Alcester, War
1742 Nov. 3	James MITCHELL, wife Mary and children John 11y, Mary 10y, Elizabeth 4y and Sarah 2y.	Godstone, Sry
1742 Nov. 9	George CHILDREN, wife Arabella and children Sarah 13y, George 9y, Barbara 6y, Thomas 3y and Isabella 11m.	Hartfield
1743 Jul.10	Thomas BURT.	Cuckfield
1743 Aug. 1	James MILES, wife Sarah and children Thomas, Sarah, James, John, William, Richard and Elizabeth.	Shipley
1743 Aug.13	John DUMSDAY and wife Jane.	Shipley
1743 Oct. 6	William DALE, wife Elizabeth and children William and Sarah.	Dorking, Sry
1743 Oct.17	John EARLE, perukemaker.	Cranbrook, Ken
1744 Jan. 4	John MEPHAM and wife Susannah.	Salehurst
1744 Mar.23	John HARRIS, wife Ann and son Edward.	Hartfield
1744 Apr.21	Francis BENNETT and wife Mary.	Horsham
1744 May 29	John OVAL, wife Sarah and children John, Sarah and Elizabeth.	Crowhurst, Sry
1744 Aug. 7	John OSBORN, butcher, and wife Ann.	Lindfield
1744 Dec. 3	John HOATH and family. Ack.	Crowhurst, Sry
1744 Dec.20	Richard GIB and family. Ack.	Lingfield, Sry
1745 Oct. 6	Thomas HISTED, wife Sarah and children John, Elisabeth and Michael.	West Hoathly
1746 Jun. 4	John LOCK, wife Anne and daughter Anne.	Horne, Sry
1746 Jul. 8	John BENNETT, wife Ann and son Noah.	Horsham
1747 Jan.29	Henry BURNET, wife Margarett and child Elizabeth.	Limpsfield, Sry
1747 May 24	Acknowledgement. "This is to let you know to hom it dus consarn that Tho MARTAIN the sun of the wid MARTAIN was bornd in the parish of Hucking and we own him a prishar. Witness our hans. Daniel WISE Courchworden, William STAPLE, oversear, Robart ATTWOOD". Reply on	Hucking, Ken

	same document "Gentlemen, Notwithstanding the Widow Martain has brought us a note from the officers of Hucking signd by one Daniel Wise, churchwarden and Willm. Staple, overseer, upon the boy's returning again with the said Martain making us believe her to be an imposter, therefore we beg the favour of you to let us know what you allow her for keeping the said boy and likewise whether you ever signed any note which will be a satisfaction to the parish of East Grinstead."	
1747 Nov. 2	Richard KILLNER and wife Elisabeth.	West Hoathly
1748 Apr.13	Thomas VENTERMAN and wife Ann.	Speldhurst, Ken
1748 Apr.15	John CRIPPS and wife Mary.	Bolney
1748 May 16	Robert LOCK and wife Elizabeth.	Lingfield, Sry
1748 Jun.29	Richard BEST wife Ann and children Isaac 4y and Anne 1y.	West Hoathly
1749 Feb. 3	Richard SIPPETS, poulterer, and wife Elizabeth.	Westerham, Ken
1749 Mar. 6	John WEBB, wife Jane and Mary [?MARTIN] his daughter-in-law.	Lingfield, Sry
1749 Mar. 6	John COOCK and wife Susan.	Worth
1749 Mar.13	John STACY, wife Elizabeth and son-in-law William.	Lingfield, Sry
1749 Jun.10	Edward BROWNE and wife Mary.	Horne, Sry
1750 Dec. 9	Thomas CARPENTER, husbandman, wife and children	Lingfield, Sry
1751 Mar.16	Francis BURT.	Keymer
1751 Apr.13	Richard HEAD wife Jane and children Elisabeth 5y, Jane 2y and Mary 1y.	Horsted Keynes
1751 Apr.20	Richard DEVALL wife Sarah and children Mary and Sarah.	Coulsdon, Sry
1751 May 12	Thomas YOUNG, mason and stonecutter, wife Mary and son Thomas 15m.	Hartfield
1751 May 12	George GUNNER, wife Elizabeth and children Jane 6y, George 3y and William 10m.	Burstow, Sry
1751 May 26	Edward SIMMANS, son Thomas 18y and daughter Rose 16y.	Worth
1751 Sep.22	Edward MARTIN, wife Ann and daughter Elizabeth 10y.	Godstone, Sry
1752 Jan 25	George STONE and wife Rose.	Withyham
1752 Feb. 1	Edward MERCHANT and wife Elizabeth.	Hartfield
1752 May 1	Walter CARD and wife Catherine.	St. George the Martyr, Mdx
1752 Jul.20	William SERLES, wife Mary and daughter Mary 8m.	Horsted Keynes
1752 Oct. 9	James FREIND, wife Amy and children Elizabeth 9y, William 6y, James 4y and Amy 2y.	Oxted, Sry

1752 Nov.12	George MEDHURST, wife Abigail, and children Margaret, George and Sarah.	Limpsfield, Sry
1753 Mar.26	John EVARIST, wife Ann and son William.	Lingfield, Sry
1753 Apr. 1	John FAULKNER, wife Ann and son John, newly born.	Withyham
1754 Feb.18	Thomas WEARE, wheelwright.	Lingfield, Sry
1754 Apr. 6	Henry GANDER.	Lingfield, Sry
1754 May 14	John AUSTIN and wife Sarah.	Cowden, Ken
1755 Jan. 5	John BEARD and wife Philiadelphia.	Crowhurst, Sry
1755 Jan.13	William STILWELL and wife Sarah.	Dunsfold, Sry
1756 Mar. 7	John OTTAWAY, wheelwright, wife Hannah and daughter Mary aged 11 weeks.	Horsted Keynes
1756 Apr.16	Richard KNIGHT, wife Timothy, and children Robert and Richard.	Lingfield, Sry
1756 Jul.10	Thomas JESSUP and wife.	Sundridge, Ken
1756 Sep.23	Thomas EVARIST and daughter Elizabeth.	Lingfield, Sry
1756 Nov.25	Isaac SHEPPEARD, tailor and wife.	Penton Mewsey, Ham
1757 Apr.11	Michael BURGESS, wife Elizabeth and daughter Mary aged 6 weeks.	Godstone, Sry
1757 Jul.31	Richard ALCOCK, wife Elizabeth, and children John 2y and Mary 9m.	Ardingly
1757 Dec. 7	Thomas CHAPMAN and wife Mary.	Godstone, Sry
1758 Jan. 1	Richard WELLS, wife Elizabeth and son Thomas 2y.	Cowden, Ken
1758 Mar.27	Isaac DURRANT, wife Elizabeth and children Elizabeth 9y, Richard 7y, Mary 5y, James 3y 6m and Sarah 1y 6m.	Godstone, Sry
1758 Apr. 2	Thomas WALLS, wife Ann and son Martin.	Chiddingstone, Ken
1758 Jul.23	John SHOVE, wife Mary and children Jane and Elizabeth.	Horley, Sry
1758 Dec. 4	William CLARKE, wife Sarah and children Sarah, Ann, Mary and Thomas.	Horne, Sry
1759 Jan.13	James MARNER and wife Sarah.	Hartfield
1759 Mar.10	John STENT and wife Mary.	Hartfield
1759 Mar 24	George HUMPHERY, wife Elizabeth and daughter Susana.	Horne, Sry
1759 Apr. 2	Francis LANE and wife Hannah.	Horley, Sry
1759 Apr.20	William MILES and wife Jane.	Cuckfield
1759 Nov. 5	William ROBERTS, wife Elizabeth and son William.	Fletching
1760 Jun. 7	Richard BARRETT and wife Sarah.	Ashford, Ken
1760 Jun.15	William POBGEE.	Horsham
1760 Jul.10*	Richard GRAYLING, wife Charity and daughter Elizabeth.	Dallington

1760 Dec. 7	William KNIGHT and wife Elizabeth.	Cowden, Ken
1761 Mar.23	John MARDEN, husbandman, wife Mary and children John, James, William, Joseph, Henry and Elizabeth.	Penshurst, Ken
1761 Jul. 7	John WELLER, labourer, and wife Elizabeth.	Lindfield
1761 Dec. 6	Joseph DAVY and wife Elizabeth. Ack. [Endorsed: There shall be no charge while staying in East Grinstead for some considerable time until they can give a certificate or take him home to their parish.]	Hever, Ken
1762 Apr.12	Edward MARTIN, wife Susannah and children Sarah 5y and William 2y.	West Grinstead
1762 Jun.10	James NASH and wife Mary.	Ashburnham
1762 Aug.29	Richard KING and wife Rosanna.	Worth
1762 Dec.26	Thomas MARCHENT, wife Elizabeth and son Michael.	Burstow, Sry
1764 Jan. 1	Harber MAYNARD, wife Sarah and children James, John and Mary.	Horley, Sry
1764 Jan. 1	Isaac CHARLWOOD, wife Elizabeth and daughter Amy.	Horley, Sry
1764 Jan. 7	William HOLLANDS, wife Elizabeth and son William 11m.	Godstone, Sry
1764 Jan. 7	Edward KILNER, wife Mary and children Jenny 2y and William 10m.	Horsted Keynes
1764 Feb.12	Thomas BLACKSTONE, wife Hannah and children Thomas 13y, Elizabeth 11y, Mary 9y, Ann 7y, Hannah 5y, and Henry 2y.	Chailey
1764 May 7	John MILLER, wife Mary and son William.	Wilmington
1765 Sep. 2	John GOURD and children Thomas, Anne, and William.	Fletching
1767 Feb.14	Anthony HARDING, wife Jane and children Jenny, Sarah and Frank.	Cowfold
1767 Dec.13	John CARPENTER, husbandman, wife Ann and son John 9m.	Hartfield
1768 Mar.13	Thomas PRITCHETT, cordwainer.	Lindfield
1769 Jul. 9	Thomas FOWLE, clocksmith.	Uckfield
1770 Oct. 3*	Edward TURNER, wife and children. Ack.	Lingfield, Sry
1772 Oct.22*	James CHURCHER, wife Grace and infant child.	Arundel
1774 Jan. 7*	William ROACH, wife Rachel and children Mary, Jenny, Thomas, Sall and Philley.	Hurstpierpoint
1775 Apr.15*	Richard JENNER, wife Mary and daughter Mary 1y.	Godstone, Sry
1775 Dec.26*	Francis DAVIS, wife Ann and children Elizabeth 7y, Francis 3y and David 6 weeks.	Withyham
1776 May 3*	William GUNNER, wife Hannah and children Jane and Sarah.	Penshurst, Ken

1776 Jun.17*	James HOLMAN and wife Mary.	Worth
1776 Jul.14*	Joseph FAIRCLOTH, wife Sarah and children Joseph, Elizabeth and William.	Tonbridge, Ken
1778 Mar.11*	Daniel SANDERS and wife Sarah.	Coulsdon, Sry
1778 Apr.20*	Robert SKINNER, wife Elizabeth and son John 1y 6m.	West Hoathly
1778 Oct.24*	Thomas GIBB, wife Elizabeth and sons Thomas 3y and John 22 weeks.	Lingfield, Sry
1778 Oct.24	John READY, wife Jenny and daughter Elizabeth 6m.	Lingfield, Sry
1778 Oct.24*	William HOLDER, wife Mary and sons Henry 6y and John 1y.	Lingfield, Sry
1778 Nov. 2*	John JESAP, wife Ann and son John 2y.	Fletching
1778 Nov.18*	Nathaniel COOK, wife Ann and children Hannah, Nathaniel, John and Ann.	Godstone, Sry
1778 Nov.24*	John ROBERSON. Ack.	Crawley
1779 Mar.18*	Richard FLORANCE, wife Sarah and son James.	Rumboldswhyke
1779 May 2*	William WILLSON and wife Mary.	Rotherfield
1779 Jun.21*	Thomas SIMMONS, wife Elizabeth and child Sarah.	Tonbridge, Ken
1779 Sep 25*	William GARDNER and wife Joanna.	West Hoathly
1779 Oct. 1*	Richard JEWELE the younger.	Lingfield, Sry
1780 Jan.22*	Thomas WELLER and wife Elizabeth.	Lingfield, Sry
1780 Mar. 1*	James ISTED, wife Fanny and daughter Philadelphia 9m.	Horsted Keynes
1780 Mar. 6*	William MITCHEL, wife Sarah and daughters Ann and Lucy. Ack.	Hartfield
1780 Mar.27*	William BROOKER, wife Hannah and children John 14y, Ann 8y, Benjamin 3y, Elizabeth 2y and Hannah 3m.	Wadhurst
1780 Aug. 1*	James WALKER, wife Margaret and children Nancy 11y, Elizabeth 9y, Margaret, Susannah, Hannah and Martha, all under seven years.	Chingford, Ess
1780 Aug. 6*	Richard SAWYER, wife Elizabeth and daughter Ann Baker.	Rotherfield
1781 Feb.11*	William MICHELL, wife and family. Ack.	Hartfield
1781 Nov.19*	Edward COOPER and wife.	Lingfield, Sry
1782 Jul.28*	Richard BUDGEN, wife Mary and son John 6m. Ack.	Maresfield
1783 Apr.27*	Richard BUDGEN, wife Mary and son John 1y 3m. Ack.	Maresfield
1783 Jul. 7*	Thomas LANGDEN and wife Ann.	Hartfield
1784 Apr 13*	Joseph ENGLISH, wife Ann and children William 3y, Joseph 2y and Harriot 1y.	St. John sub Castro, Lewes
1784 Apr.25*	Richard BUDGEN wife Mary and son John. Ack.	Maresfield

1784 Jun.18*	William UNDERWOOD, wife Mary and sons William and James. Ack.	Cowden, Ken
1784 Sep.27*	Edward EVEREST, wife Sarah and son John. Ack.	Hartfield
1785 Mar. 9*	William READY and wife Elizabeth.	Penshurst, Ken
1786 Apr 3*	William TURNER, wife Sarah and daughter Ann. Ack.	Hartfield
1786 Apr.18*	John HEWETT and wife Margaret.	Horne, Sry
1786 Sep.27*	John AGATE, wife Mary and children Elizabeth 9y, Mary 7y, Philadelphia 4y, Ann 2y and John 2m. [For ages of children see also Removal Order dated 28 January 1786 under Par 348/32/2/1.]	Lingfield, Sry
1786 Dec.15*	John PAGE and wife Mary.	Uckfield
1787 Mar. 3*	John JOHNSON, wife Elizabeth and daughter Elizabeth 5m.	Cuckfield
1787 Jun.16*	Francis BELLCHAMBER, wife Anne and children James 12y, Mary 10y, Francis 7y, Jane 5y, Anne 2y and William 2m.	Horsted Keynes
1787 Jul. 31*	William UNDERWOOD, wife Mary and children William 6y, James 3y and Ann 6m.	Cowden, Ken
1787 Oct.20	Thomas ASHBY, wife Sarah and children Thomas, Sarah, William and James. Ack.	Lamberhurst, Ken
1787 Dec. 1*	Edward WELLFARE, wife Philadelphia and children Edward 5y and William 3y.	Horsted Keynes
1787 Dec.15	Thomas WEST, husbandman, and wife Elizabeth.	Rudgwick
1788 Feb.23*	Cooper COOPER, wife Hannah and children Edward 2y 9m and John 9m.	Wilmington
1788 Oct.16*	Richard EVERSHED, his wife and infant child.	Arundel
1789 Mar. 1*	Thomas PAYNE, wife Martha and children Mary 4y and Jane 2y.	Tandridge, Sry
1792 Mar. 4	Susanna LANGLEY, a poor child now staying in East Grinstead until they can take her home and provide for her. Ack.	Hever, Ken
1793 Apr.13	Joseph HORTEN and wife Elizabeth.	Sts. Peter and Mary, Lewes
1793 May 6	Francis BYSH, wife Ann and children Francis, Philip, Elizabeth, Mary and John.	Lindfield
No date	John HAYWARD, flaxdresser, wife Mary and daughter Anne.	Godstone, Sry

CERTICATES OF SETTLEMENT IN EAST GRINSTEAD — Par 348/32/1/1

		To
1703 Apr. 7	Thomas GARDENER, carpenter, and family.	Brasted, Ken
1718 Oct.11	Thomas BEVIS, wife and children.	Camberwell, Sry

1726 Oct. 1*	Richard MILLS, collarmaker, wife Mary and daughter Mary. [Endorsed: Letter of 9 Dec.1774 from Joseph SIDWELL, Clerk of the Vestry, Battle. "Gentlemen, In answer to yours of 28 Nov. I am desired to acquaint you that Richard Mills is 73 and his wife 74 years of age; they have very little to support them, he says if you will allow him something this winter he will try and support himself in the summer but if you require him to come home, if you let him know, he will come without giving any trouble or charge to you; he hath had about 4 shillings of this parish".]	Battle
1732 Oct.31	Thomas ENGERFIELD, wife Elizabeth and son Thomas 9m.	Cowden, Ken

REMOVALS ORDERS FROM EAST GRINSTEAD — Par 348/32/2/1

* Indicates catalogued under Par 348/32/2/169
\+ Indicates catalogued under Par 348/32/3/1

		To
1693 Jan.13	Henry CHEALL, wife and family.	West Hoathly
1693 Jan.13	George UNDERHILL, wife and family.	Lingfield, Sry
1694 Sep. 8	James WESTON and wife. On examination, J.W. said that he was last legally settled as an apprentice with one John CHERIHOLME.	Fellchurch, [?Felkirk], Yks.
1695 Jan.17	James WESTON, and wife. On appeal, order confirmed.	Fellchurch, [?Felkirk], Yks.
1695 Mar.12	Samuel WATTS, to be removed to Berkshire [place not given] where he was last legally settled with one Henry COB, as an apprentice.	Not given, Brk
1696 Jan.14	Mary ATTFIELD. Last legally settled in Withyham, in service.	Withyham
1698 Jul.14	Mary ALLEN. On appeal, ordered that she be settled as an inhabitant in Isfield parish as she was hired as a yearly servant there with one CHATFIELD.	Isfield
1699 Dec.22*	Mary WILSON, who came into West Hoathly being great with child and was there delivered of a male bastard child, has now departed from that parish. As the child has since, illegally, been brought into East Grinstead by the officers of West Hoathly, the child is to be conveyed back to that parish, his place of birth.	West Hoathly
1700 Jan.23*	John WORGER and family.	Tandridge, Sry
1701 Jul.10	William FASSELL.	Godstone, Sry

1701 Aug.25	Jane COOPER, spinster, having been a servant in Clayton.	Clayton
1701 Oct.11	John BRINKHURST and wife Jane.	Chailey
1703 Oct. 8	Edward MIDHURST, taken as a vagrant in East Grinstead and punished, ordered to be sent back to his parish of St. Mary's, Guildford, via Horne, Surrey.	Guildford, Sry
1709 Jan.14	Rebecca CHANTLER removed to St. Olaves.	Southwark, Sry
1710 May 5	Rebecca CHANTLER, who was removed on 14 January 1709 to St. Olave, Southwark, Surrey, has since returned to East Grinstead, big with child. She ought to be sent to the House of Correction and whipped as a vagabond but cannot be sent thither till the child is born. R.C. to be conveyed to Godstone, Surrey, through which she is to pass to the place of her lawful settlement. *Catalogued under Par 348/32/1/3*	Southwark, Sry
1710 Dec.18	Edger BOWYER.	Lingfield, Sry
1712 May 17	Anne BANISTER.	Lingfield, Sry
1712 Sep 15	Elizabeth WILKINS.	St. Lawrence, Pountney, Lnd
1712 Sep.16	Francis BISH, a yearly servant to Walter WOODGATE in Lingfield.	Lingfield, Sry
1713 Mar.24	Elizabeth CONNER.	All Saints, Lewes
1714 Mar.17	John OVELL, wife and two children.	Horsted Keynes
1714 Oct.30+	Thomas LEE, a vagrant aged 26y and daughter Mary. On examination T.L. said that he was born in Totnam [Tottenham] High Cross.	Tottenham, Mdx
1714 Nov. 6	Mary LEE and infant daughter Mary.	Tottenham, Mdx
1715 Mar.15	William PRINCE, apprenticeship to Henry MILLAMS, victualler of Chatham.	Chatham, Ken
1715 Apr.28+	John HUMPHREY, wife and family. On appeal, order discharged.	Chailey
1715 Jul.20	John COMBER and wife Sarah. J.C. having been a yearly servant to John BROWNING at Tickeredge.	West Hoathly
1715 Jul.20	Richard CHEALE, husbandman. R.C. having been a yearly servant to Benjamin CHEALE of Godstone.	Godstone, Sry
1718 Jan.16	Thomas LEE, wife Mary and children Frances, Mary and Thomas. Confirmation.	Tottenham, Mdx
1719 Feb.20	George SPARKES and wife Elizabeth. G.S. having been a yearly servant to John MAY, gent., of Shervill [?Sherfield] for 3 full years.	Shervill, Ham (sic)
1720 Apr.28+	John CHEAL. On appeal, order discharged.	Rotherfield
1722 Jan.26	Robert BRAN, wife Martha and child Susanna 6m.	Godstone, Sry

1722 Sep 3	Elizabeth GEALE and bastard child Elizabeth Hulett 3y.	Midhurst
1724 Jul.27	Thomas RICH, wife Mary and children Sarah 22y, Thomas 12y and William 6y.	Rotherfield
1725 Apr. 8+	William BROWNE and wife Mary. On appeal, order discharged.	Lingfield, Sry
1726 Feb.17	John PUPLETT, wife Sara and son Thomas under 3y.	Buxted
1727 Dec. 4	Richard URIDGE.	Tatsfield, Sry
1727 Dec. 5	Susanna HUMPHREY, living as a hired servant for a whole year with John JEALE.	Worth
1728 Feb.16	Thomas LOVELIDGE, and wife Elizabeth, by hiring and using a farm of £30 per annum in Duxford.	Duxford, Cam
1730 Feb.21*	Thomas NEWNAM and wife Elizabeth.	Lingfield, Sry
1730 Feb.21*	John CUMBER and wife Mary.	West Hoathly
1732 Jul.13	Nicholas BROXHAM als BROXCELE, wife Sara and children John, William, Anne, Mary and Hestor. On appeal, order confirmed. [Delivered 1 Aug.]	Godstone, Sry
1732 Nov. 4*	Robert HOOK. [Delivered 8 Nov.]	Mayfield
1733 Jan.11*	Edward GANDY and wife Jane.	Albourne
1733 Jan.11	Margarett ANDREWS. Confirmation.	St. Osyth, Ess
1735 Feb.15*	George DEWE and wife Mary.	Lingfield, Sry
1736 Jan. 6*	Robert DENNIS, wife Amy and children William 2y, Robert 1y 3m. [Delivered 20 April.]	Lingfield, Sry
1736 Jan. 6*	Mary BENNET, widow. [Delivered 5 July]	Lingfield, Sry
1736 Mar. 1*	Thomas EVEREST.	Hever, Ken
1736 Apr.11*	William STAPLEY, wife Elizabeth and son Joseph 1y. [Delivered 20 April.]	Rotherfield
1736 Nov. 1*	Mordecai DOUCH.	Corscombe, Dor
1737 Feb.22*	William BEST, with wife Mary and daughters, Elizabeth and Mary, came to this parish 10 years ago, by a certificate dated 8 October 1726, and has since had 4 more children born in East Grinstead, Susannah, Sarah, William and John. W.B., wife Mary, and five of their children: Elizabeth 14y. Mary 12y, William 7y, Sarah 4y and John 2m to be removed to Snodland.	Snodland, Ken
1737 Apr.14*	John HISTED, wife Ann and son John under 7y.	Horsted Keynes
1737 Aug.23*	Anne TAYLOR, spinster. On examination A.T. said that she served the Rt. Hon. Marquis of Caernarvon as a yearly servant for a year and received full wages. and that the last 40 days of such service was in the parish of St. James, Westminster.	Westminster, Mdx

1738 Feb. 6*	Joseph MEARS, wife Anne and children Joseph, Mary, Elizabeth and a female infant, unbaptised.	Byfleet, Sry
1738 Sep.19*	Elizabeth JARRATT, spinster, who served John PIGOTT of Lingfield one full year and received £3 5s 0d for such services.	Lingfield, Sry
1738 Nov.27*	James GLOVER and wife Betty.	Gt. St. George, Bloomsbury, Mdx
1739 Jan. 1*	Easter CUMBER.	Horsted Keynes
1739 Jan.16*	Mary BUTLER.	Hartfield
1740 Feb.12*	Thomas and Esther BUTLER came to East Grinstead with a certificate from Withyham but, as Thomas Butler has run away and left his wife Esther behind in a sick and weak condition of health, she has now become chargeable. E.B. to be returned to Withyham. [Delivered 16 February]	Withyham
1740 Feb.12*	Henry ILLMAN otherwise HILLMAN, wife Susannah and son John 10m.	Worth
1740 Feb.12*	George CREASY, wife Mary and son John 8m.	Worth
1740 Apr.17	John PARIS, wife Elizabeth and son John. On appeal, order confirmed.	Hartfield
1740 Jul.17	Mary MARTIN, singlewoman. Confirmation.	Wivelsfield
1740 Jul.17	Elizabeth GANDY and Thomas GANDY. On appeal order confirmed.	Albourne
1740 Jul.17	Mary BRIANT, singlewoman. Confirmation.	Addington, Sry
1740 Oct. 9	Richard BROOKER, wife Practice and son Richard. Confirmation.	Lingfield, Sry
1740 Oct. 9	Robert NORMAN. Confirmation.	Beeding
1741 Jan.15	William MUDDLE, wife Susannah and daughter Susannah. Confirmation.	Crowhurst
1741 Mar.19	Mary EDWARDS, widow, and children Thomas, Elizabeth and Mary, certificate persons from Chatham to East Grinstead and now chargeable.	Chatham, Ken
1742 Jan.14	Susanah PAINE. Confirmation.	Horley, Sry
1742 Mar.27	Susannah HARDS, widow. [Delivered 10 Apr.]	Hartfield
1742 Apr.26	James MITCHELL, wife Mary and children John 11y, Mary 10y, Elizabeth 4y and Sarah 1y. Confirmation.	Godstone, Sry
1742 Apr.27	John PRUDDEN and wife Timothy.	Wootton, Bdf
1743 Mar.24	John DUMSDAY and wife Jane. [Delivered 11 Jul.]	Shipley
1743 Mar.28	John YEOMANS, wife Frances and daughter Sarah 1y.	Horley, Sry
1743 Oct. 6	John DUMSDAY and wife Jane. On appeal, order confirmed.	Shipley

1744 Jan.12	John HARRIS, wife Anne and son Edward under 1y. Confirmation.	Hartfield
1744 Apr. 5	John LULHAM, an infant. Confirmation.	Chevening, Ken
1746 Jan.16	John POPE. Confirmation.	Godstone, Sry
1746 Feb 3	Richard FEILDER, shovelwood maker and turner, and wife Anne, are rogues and vagabonds to be conveyed to Speldhurst, Kent, there to be taken to Bidborough, for which the constable of East Grinstead to be allowed £1.4s 0d and no more.	Bidborough, Ken
1747 Jul.16	Simon COCKERELL and wife Mary. Confirmation.	Chiddingstone, Ken
1748 Apr. 7	Thomas VENTIMAN and wife Anne. [Delivered 9 Apr]	Speldhurst, Ken
1749 Apr.10	Edward BROWNE and wife Mary. [Delivered 12 May]	Horne, Sry
1749 Sep.18	John DENYER and wife Mary. [Delivered 19 Sept]	Wiggonholt
1751 Aug.10	Edward SMITH aged 7y, son of Samuel SMITH deceased (sic) [see Par 348/32/4/54 settlement examination of Winifred SMITH late OVELL, dated 8 March 1753] and wife Winifred. On examination W.S. said that the last legal settlement of E.S. was Crowhurst.	Crowhurst, Sry
1752 Feb.25	Charles POST.	Tandridge, Sry
1752 Oct. 4*	Anne COOKE.	Rotherfield
1753 Mar.19*	Samuel SMITH and wife Winifred. [Endorsed: Winifred Smith [only] delivered 30 [?March] 1754]	Crowhurst, Sry
1755 Jan.25*	Thomas BUTLER.	Withyham
1755 Apr.12*	William TURLE and wife Elizabeth.	Cowfold
1755 Apr.17*	Mary SCOTT, singlewoman, and sons Thomas 10y and James 4y.	Salisbury, Wil
1755 Jul.29*	John DIVALL, aged 8y, bastard son of Sara, now wife of John DIVALL, late Sara FARNS, who gives Hartfield as J.D.'s place of birth.	Hartfield
1756 Jan.15	William TOOTH and wife Mary. On appeal, order confirmed.	Telscombe
1757 Jan. 4*	Edward EDWARDS.	Cowden, Ken
1757 Dec. 1*	Edward TOOTH, aged 14y, son of William TOOTH.	Hartfield
1757 Dec. 1*	Sarah TOOTH, aged 15y, daughter of William TOOTH.	Hartfield
1757 Dec.29*	Mary CREASY, singlewoman.	Addington, Sry
1759 Jun.28*	Richard GIB, wife Mary and children Richard, Anne and Sarah.	Worth
1760 May 12	Richard BARRETT and wife Sara.	Ashford, Ken

1760 Jul. 8	Richard GRAYLING, wife Charity and daughter Elizabeth 1y.	Dallington
1760 Dec. 9	Winifred JARRETT, singlewoman.	Lingfield, Sry
1761 Jan.12+	Sarah BROWN, widow.	Bolney
1761 Mar.19	William JUP and wife Mary.	Edenbridge, Ken
1761 Oct.27	Rose SYMOND, singlewoman.	Worth
1762 May 18	James NASH and wife Mary. [Delivered 21 May]	Ashburnham
1763 Mar. 7	William BROOKER and children Ann 18y and Richard 11y.	Oxted, Sry
1766 Oct.11	John DALE, wife Elizabeth and children Michael 9y and Sarah 6y.	Lamberhurst
1770 Dec. 3	John WEBB, wife Martha and daughter Ann 6m.	Frampton, Gls
1770 Dec. 3*	Jane SMITH, widow, and daughter Elizabeth 5y.	Fletching
1771 Nov.12*	Edward SCRASE, blacksmith.	Newick
1772 Feb.21*	Mary HISTED. [Endorsed: with note concerning examination of reputed father of her child, Richard HARLING the younger, shoemaker.]	Newick
1773 May 14*	Elizabeth MIDHURST.	Limpsfield, Sry
1774 Mar.23*	Philadelphia FARNE alias STANDEN, daughter of Sarah STANDEN, late of Rotherfield, deceased.	Rotherfield
1774 Mar.23	William LUCAS, an infant, on examination of Elizabeth GREENWAY, grandmother of child.	Crowhurst, Sry
1774 Jun. 6*	John HOADLY, wife Elizabeth and son Thomas 2y.	Billingshurst
1777 Jan. 6*	Ann HARMAN, singlewoman.	Lingfield, Sry
1777 Sep. 1*	Robert SKINNER, wife Elizabeth and son John 1y 6m.	West Hoathly
1777 Sep. 1	Thomas BREDEN, wife Elizabeth and children Elizabeth 6y, Charles 5y and son Craven 1y 6m.	Balcombe
1778 Mar. 2*	Winny OVELL, singlewoman.	Crowhurst, Sry
1778 Apr.13*	James TOWES and wife Elizabeth.	West Hoathly
1778 Apr.27*	Charles POPE, wife Betty and children Thomas 2y and Betty 1y.	Ilchester, Som
1778 Jul.21*	Nathaniel COOK, wife Ann and children Hannah, Nathaniel, John and Ann all under 7y.	Godstone, Sry
1778 Jul.21*	John JESSUP, wife Ann and son John 1y 9m.	Fletching
1779 Mar.17*	William WILSON and wife Mary.	Rotherfield
1779 May 3*	Richard GREENFIELD, wife Rebecca and daughter Rebecca 9m.	Ashurst, Ken
1779 Jun. 7*	Henry HUMFRY, wife Elizabeth and son John 14m.	Hartfield
1779 Jun. 8*	John TAYLER and wife Mary.	Worth
1785 Jan.24	Mary GIBB, singlewoman.	Lingfield, Sry
1785 Apr. 2	Henry HUMPHERY and son John 6y.	Hartfield

1786 Jan.28	John AGATE, wife Mary and children Elizabeth 13y, Mary 4y, Philadelphia 2y 6m and Ann 1y 6m. [For ages of children see Settlement Certificate dated 27 Sep.1786 under Par 348/32/1/168] [Delivered 1 April.]	Lingfield, Sry
1786 Jan.28	John PAGE and wife Mary.	Uckfield
1786 Jan.28	Susannah STILLER.	Cowden, Ken
1786 Jul. 3	John LAKER and wife Ann.	Tonbridge, Ken
1787 Nov. 5	Thomas WEST and wife Elizabeth. [Delivered 30 Nov.]	Rudgwick
1787 Nov. 5	Edward WELFARE, wife Philadelphia and children Edward 4y and William 2y.	Horsted Keynes
1787 Nov.19	Cooper COOPER, wife Hannah and children Edward 2y and John 6m.	Wilmington
1788 May 5	Thomas ASHBY, wife Sarah and children Thomas 8y, Sarah 6y, William 3y and James 1y. [Delivered 21 May]	Lamberhurst
1788 Jun. 2	Francis POTTER and wife Catherine. [Delivered 4 June.]	Slinfold
1788 Jul. 7	Richard EVERSHED, wife Philadelphia and Richard 2y and Elizabeth 7m.	Wisborough Green
1788 Jul. 7	Sarah ROFEY. [Delivered 7 July.]	Horne, Sry
1788 Jul. 7	Edward BALCOMB and wife Mary.	Isfield
1788 Jul.22	Elizabeth KILNER, singlewoman. [Delivered 22 July]	Hartfield
1788 Jul.22	Mary MARTIN, singlewoman.	Croydon, Sry
1788 Aug. 4	John EDWARDS and wife Sarah.	Speldhurst, Ken
1788 Dec. 1	Ann BURTON, singlewoman. [Delivered 1 Dec.]	Rottingdean
1789 Oct.19	Charles RUSSELL and wife Mary. [Delivered 20 Oct]	Withyham
1792 Oct. 4+	George ELLIS, wife Sarah and children George 8y, Anthony 6y, Thomas 4y and Martin 2y. On appeal, order quashed.	St. George, Southwark, Sry
1802 Jan.14	Edward GILES and wife Sarah. Confirmation.	Mayfield
1803 May 16*	Cravey BREDEN and wife Sarah. [Delivered 17 May]	Lingfield, Sry
1804 Dec. 8*	Mathew BOURNE and wife Lydia. [Delivered 10 Dec.]	Charlwood, Sry
1804 Dec.24	Thomas GATLAND, wife Sarah and children Mary 2y 6m and Fanny 4m. [Delivered 26 Dec.]	Godstone, Sry
1805 Feb.11*	James BUTLER and wife Ann. [Delivered 11 Feb.]	Hartfield
1805 Apr. 8*	Bannister TRUELOCK. [Delivered 30 April]	Islington, Mdx

1805 May 24*	Receipt. Received of Mr. George SAWYER churchwarden of East Grinstead, an order for the removal of Catherine MASCOE, wife of John MASCOE, from East Grinstead to Lewisham, Kent, dated 29 Dec. 1800, which order Edward LATTER, attorney of Bromley, Kent, promises to return.	Lewisham, Ken
1808 Jan.15	Simon WHITE, the younger, and wife Jane. Confirmation.	Slinfold
1808 Jan.15	Thomas BROOKSBANK and wife Mildred. Confirmation.	St. Margaret, Westminster, Mdx
1808 Apr.29	William GORRINGE, wife Elizabeth and children William 3y and James 14m. Confirmation.	Worth
1809 Jan.13	Thomas HOLMAN and wife Mary. Confirmation	Worth
1809 Jan.13	Reuben SNASHALL, wife Sarah and children John 4y and James 2y. Confirmation.	Rotherfield
1810 Jan.12	James CAMPBELL and wife Susannah. Confirmation	Leigh, Ken
1810 Jan.12	Richard TAYLOR, wife Elizabeth and children James 3y 6m and Mary Ann 2y 3m. Confirmation.	Addington, Sry
1810 Oct.15*	John TAYLOR, wife Nahomi and children Mary 11y, John 8y and William 5y.	Battersea, Sry
1811 Jan.18	Lucy MONTAGUE, widow. Confirmation.	Hammersmith, Mdx
1811 Jan.18	John TAYLOR, wife Naomi and children Mary 11y, John 8y and William 5y. Confirmation.	Battersea, Sry
1811 Jan.18	Thomas RICE wife Mary and children Elizabeth 6y, Mary 4y and Thomas 3m. Confirmation.	Worth
1811 Jan.18	Ann CREW, wife of Nathaniel CREW. Confirmation.	Lingfield, Sry
1811 Oct.11	Mary MEAD, singlewoman. Confirmation.	West Hoathly
1811 Oct.11	William SHERLOCK wife Elizabeth and children Elizabeth 6y, Mary 4y, Martha 3y and Sarah 1y 4m. Confirmation.	Rusper
1812 Jan.17	Henry ROFFEY wife Sarah and children Maria 9y, William 7y and John 5y. Confirmation.	Merstham, Sry
1812 Apr.10	Thomas CHAPMAN and wife Lucy. Confirmation.	Horsted Keynes
1812 Jul.17	Thomas DAWSON wife Sarah and children Mary 6y and James and Jane aged 2y. Confirmation.	Woking, Sry
1812 Oct. 9	William AYNSCOMB and wife Martha. Confirmation.	Cowfold
1814 Apr.22	John SKINNER and wife Ann. Confirmation.	Warnham

1814 Apr.22	Edward BEARD wife Mary and children Edward 3y and John 3m. Confirmation.	Fletching
1814 Nov.28*	John LEOPARD and wife Hester.	West Hoathly
1814 Dec.26	Louisa SPENCER, singlewoman. Unable to travel due to sickness, until 13 March 1815. Hartfield to pay expenses of £2.12s 6d.	Hartfield
1815 Feb.27	Sarah PAINTER, wife of John PAINTER, and children John 7y, Sarah 4y and Mary 16m.	Hambledon, Ham
1815 Aug.14	Elizabeth MARCHANT, singlewoman.	West Hoathly
1815 Dec.18	Mary BUTCHER, singlewoman.	West Hoathly
1816 Jan. 8*	James ARNOLD and wife Mary.	Worth
1816 May 27	Lewis READY and wife Elizabeth.	Crowhurst, Sry
1816 May 27	Mary HOOKER, singlewoman.	Lingfield, Sry
1817 Jan.17	Elizabeth CAMFIELD, widow. Confirmation.	Fletching
1817 Jan.17	Sarah VINES, singlewoman. Confirmation.	Balcombe
1817 Jan 27	Joseph DANCY and wife Ann.	Cuckfield
1817 Jan.27	Thomas GASSON and wife Sarah.	Chevening, Ken
1817 Apr. 7	John GARDNER, wife Jane and children Ann 6y, John 3y and William 1y.	West Hoathly
1817 Apr.18	Thomas GASSON and wife Sarah. Confirmation.	Chevening, Ken
1817 Apr.18	John PAYNE, wife Rebecca and children William 9y and Mary Ann 5y. Confirmation.	Warnham
1817 Apr.28	James SNOW and wife Susannah.	Preston
1817 Apr.28	James SETFORD and wife Ann.	Lindfield
1817 May 28	James LINCOLN and wife Ann.	Ditchingham, Nfk
1817 Jul.18	James SETFORD and wife Ann. Confirmation.	Lindfield
1817 Jul.18	Joseph DANCY and wife Ann. Confirmation.	Cuckfield
1817 Jul.18	John GARDNER, wife Jane and children Ann 6y, John 3y and William 1y. Confirmation.	West Hoathly
1818 Jan.16	James KILLICK, wife Ann and children Sarah 2y and a female infant not yet baptised. Confirmation.	Godstone, Sry
1818 Jan.16	Thomas NORMAN. Confirmation.	Worth
1818 Apr. 3	John EDWARDS, wife Harriet and children Jane 6y, Joseph 4y, Mary 2y and Hester 3m. Confirmation.	Hartfield
1818 Apr. 3	John BISH and wife Lydia. Confirmation.	Lindfield
1818 Apr. 3	Henry WILLIAMS and wife Jane. Confirmation.	Ardingly

QUARTER SESSIONS REMOVAL ORDERS FROM EAST GRINSTEAD

		To
L 1667 Jan.17	Bastard child of Anne COOPER. Recites order 26 July 1666; child to be sent to Poynings.	Poynings

L 1668 Jul.16	Thomas BROMLEY and wife; on appeal against an order to remove them from East Grinstead, they are to be settled in that parish.	Not given
L 1671 Jan.12	Mary WHITTINGTON and child, left in East Grinstead by her husband, Thomas WHITTINGTON, are to be sent to him at Maidstone.	Maidstone, Ken
L 1671 May 4	Mary WHITTINGTON, wife of Thomas WHITTINGTON, and child are to be sent to T.W. at Maidstone.	Maidstone, Ken
L 1677 Oct. 4	William GOWER, formerly of East Grinstead, and wife Mary, in whose right he is seized of an estate in Horne, has now acquired a legal settlement there.	Horne, Sry
L 1680 Oct. 7	Widow WHITE.	Horne, Sry
L 1680 Oct. 7	Nicholas MORGAN.	Worth
L 1682 Oct. 5	Samuel COMBER, wife and children.	Chailey
L 1683 Apr.19	Nicholas WHITE; respited.	Beeding
L 1684 Jan.17	Jane MATHEWS, (wife of Richard MATHEWS of Lingfield, Surrey, who has now run away), is to be sent to Lingfield, the place of her legal settlement.	Lingfield, Sry
L 1684 Oct. 4	John STEPHENS.	Westerham, Ken
L 1685 Oct.19	Thomas OSBOURNE and wife.	Alfriston
L 1694 Jul.12	Mary COMFORT; to be returned to East Grinstead as she was last in that parish.	West Hoathly
L 1695 Jan.17	James WESTON and wife; confirmed.	Felchurch, [?Felkirk],Yks.
L 1698 May 5	William FASSELL; confirmed.	Godstone, Sry
L 1698 Jul. 14	Mary ALLEN; confirmed as she was a yearly servant to CHATFIELD of Isfield.	Isfield
L 1698 Oct. 6	Edward SHARPE and family; order quashed as it is defective in form.	Godstone, Sry
L 1709 Oct. 6	Richard YOUNG and children Mary and Sarah; discharged.	Pevensey
L 1713 Jan.15	Robert FARMER; confirmed.	Waldron
L 1715 Apr.28	John HOVENDEN, wife Mary and two children; discharged.	Cranbrook, Ken
L 1715 Apr.28	John HUMPHREY, wife and family; discharged.	Chailey
L 1715 Apr.28	John GILBERT, wife and family; respited as J.G. bargained for a year at Wadhurst, served half his time and then his master moved to Rotherfield, where he served the other half year.	Rotherfield
L 1715 Oct. 6	John GILBERT, wife and family; confirmed.	Rotherfield,
L 1718 Jan.16	Thomas LEE, wife Mary and children Frances, Mary and Thomas; confirmed.	Tottenham High Cross, Mdx

L 1718 Apr.24	Arthur GILBERT; discharged.	Newington Butts, Sry
L 1720 Apr.28	John CHEAL; discharged.	Rotherfield
L 1722 Jan.11	Robert BRANE, wife Martha and daughter Susanna; discharged.	Horsted Keynes
L 1725 Apr. 8	William BROWNE and wife Maria; confirmed.	Lingfield, Sry
L 1729 Jul.17	John BURSTOW; discharged.	Lye [Leigh], Ken
L 1731 Jul.15	John KILNER and wife Elizabeth; discharged.	Lindfield
L 1732 Jan.13	Nicholas BROXHAM, wife Sarah and children John 8y, William 6y, Ann 4y, Mary 3y and Hester 1y; discharged.	St. Thomas, Cliffe, Lewes
L 1732 Apr.20	Nicholas BROXHAM otherwise BROXCELL, wife Sarah and children John, William, Ann, Mary and Hester; respited.	Godstone, Sry
L 1732 Jul.13	Nicholas BROXHAM otherwise BROXCELL, wife Sarah and children John, William, Ann, Mary and Hester; confirmed.	Godstone, Sry
L 1733 Jan.11	Margaret ANDREWS; confirmed.	St. Osyth, Ess
L 1733 Jan.11	Edward GANDY and wife Jane; confirmed.	Albourne
L 1740 Apr.17	John PARIS, wife Elizabeth and son John; confirmed.	Hartfield
L 1740 Jul.17	Elizabeth GANDY and Thomas GANDY; confirmed.	Albourne
L 1740 Jul.17	Mary MARTIN, singlewoman; confirmed.	Wivelsfield
L 1740 Jul.17	Mary BRIANT, singlewoman; confirmed.	Addington, Sry
L 1740 Oct. 9	Robert NORMAN, labourer; confirmed.	Beeding
L 1740 Oct. 9	Richard BROOKER, wife Practice and son Richard; confirmed.	Lingfield, Sry
L 1741 Jan.15	William MUDDLE, the younger, wife Susannah and daughter Susannah; confirmed.	Crowhurst
L 1742 Jan.14	Susannah PAINE; confirmed.	Horley, Sry
L 1742 Apr.29	James MITCHELL, wife Mary and children John 11y, Mary 10y, Elizabeth 4y and Sarah 1y; confirmed.	Godstone, Sry
L 1743 Apr.14	James BUTLER and wife Sarah; discharged.	Hartfield
L 1743 Jul.14	William WILSON; confirmed.	St. George, Mdx
L 1743 Oct. 6	John DUMSDAY and wife Jane; confirmed.	Shipley
L 1744 Jan.12	John HARRIS, wife Anne and son Edward under 1y; confirmed.	Hartfield
L 1744 Apr. 5	John LULHAM, infant; confirmed.	Chevening, Ken
L 1746 Jan.16	John POPE; confirmed.	Godstone, Sry
L 1747 Jul.16	Simon COCKERELL and wife Mary; confirmed.	Chiddingstone, Ken
L 1751 Apr.18	Mary TOOTH, singlewoman; discharged.	Hartfield
L 1755 Jan.16	Amy daughter of Elizabeth PARRIS; confirmed.	Nutfield, Sry
L 1755 Jul.17	Mary STANFORD, singlewoman; respited.	Hartfield

L 1755 Oct. 9	Mary STANFORD, singlewoman; discharged.	Hartfield
L 1756 Jan.15	William TOOTH and wife Mary; confirmed.	Telscombe
L 1761 Apr. 2	Sarah BROWNE, widow; confirmed.	Bolney
L 1767 Jan.15	John DALE, wife Elizabeth and children Michael 9y and Sarah 6y; respited.	Lamberhurst
L 1767 Apr.30	John DALE, wife Elizabeth and children Michael 9y and Sarah 6y; discharged.	Lamberhurst
L 1772 Jul.16	Joseph TERRY and wife Catherine; quashed.	Worth
L 1772 Jul.16	George BURR, wife Ann and children Ann 2y and Elizabeth aged 9 weeks; respited.	Rotherfield
L 1773 Jan.14	George BURR, wife Ann and children Ann 2y and Elizabeth aged 9 weeks; quashed.	Rotherfield
L 1775 Apr.27	Thomas WOOD, wife Mary and son Thomas 12m; quashed.	Worth
L 1776 Jan.11	James MARTIN and wife Ann; confirmed.	Chart Sutton, Ken
L 1778 Apr.30	William HOLDER, wife Mary and sons Henry 5y and John 2y; respited.	Lingfield, Sry
L 1778 Jul.16	William HOLDER, wife Mary and sons Henry 5y and John 2y; confirmed.	Lingfield, Sry
L 1782 Apr.11	Thomas TERRY, wife Hannah and children Sarah 1y and Mary aged 7 days; respited.	Worth
L 1782 Jul.18	Thomas TERRY, wife Hannah and children Sarah 1y and Mary aged 7 days; quashed.	Worth
L 1784 Oct. 7	John JENNER and wife Ann; confirmed.	Sevenoaks, Ken
L 1787 Apr.19	John LAKER and wife Ann; confirmed.	Tonbridge, Ken
L 1787 Jul.12	Susanna MILL, singlewoman; confirmed.	Edenbridge, Ken
L 1787 Jul.12	William UNDERWOOD, wife Mary and children William 6y, James 3y and Ann 6m; confirmed.	Cowden, Ken
L 1787 Jul.12	William WELLER, wife Elizabeth and children Sarah 3y and an infant son, not yet baptised; confirmed.	Godstone, Sry
L 1787 Oct. 4	Robert PAYNE and wife Lucy; confirmed.	Hartfield
L 1788 Jan.17	Ann GIBB, singlewoman; confirmed.	Lingfield, Sry
L 1788 Jan.17	John RUSSELL and wife Ann; respited.	Ardingly
L 1788 Apr. 3	John RUSSELL and wife Ann; confirmed.	Ardingly
L 1788 Oct. 9	Joseph HOLMES and wife Elizabeth; quashed.	Newbury, Brk
L 1791 Jul.14	Philadelphia GOLDSMITH, singlewoman; quashed.	St. Thomas, Cliffe, Lewes
L 1792 Apr.19	Henry EDWARDS and wife Hannah; respited.	Compton
L 1792 Oct. 4	George ELLIS, wife Sarah and children George 8y, Anthony 6y, Thomas 4y and Martin 2y; quashed.	St. George, Southwark, Sry
L 1792 Oct. 4	John CHAPMAN, wife Catherine and children Hannah 13y, Lucy 11y, Thomas 8y, James 8y and William 6y; respited.	Horsted Keynes

L 1793 Jan.17	John CHAPMAN, wife Catherine and children Hannah 13y, Lucy 11y, Thomas 8y, James 8y and William 6y; confirmed.	Horsted Keynes
L 1801 Jul.16	John NOYS, wife Elizabeth and children Mary Ann and John; confirmed.	Horsmonden, Ken
L 1801 Jul.16	William MARTIN, wife Mary and son John 18m; confirmed.	Chiddingstone, Ken
L 1801 Jul.16	Robert WHITE, wife Ann and son John 18m; confirmed.	Lingfield, Sry
L 1801 Jul.16	Thomas SHAW and children Mary 19y, Ann 18y, Susannah 16y, Elizabeth 13y and Sarah 11y; confirmed.	St. George, Hanover Square, Mdx
L 1801 Oct. 8	Sarah JENNER; singlewoman; confirmed.	Battle
L 1801 Oct. 8	Humphrey HEAD, wife Jane and children Susannah 8y, Jane 8y, John 4y, Mary 2y and an infant 1m; confirmed.	Reigate, Sry
L 1802 Jan.14	Edward GILES and wife Sarah; confirmed.	Mayfield
L 1803 Jan.14	John DUNN, wife Mary and children Mary 11y, Philadelphia 8y, William 6y and John 4y; confirmed.	Altrincham, Chs
L 1804 Jan.13	Ann STANFORD, wife of John STANFORD; quashed.	Edenbridge, Ken
L 1804 Jan.13	Sarah SPENCER, singlewoman; confirmed.	Hartfield
L 1804 Jan.13	John WOOD, wife Mary and children Lucy 6y, Ann 5y and Elias 3y; confirmed.	Godalming, Sry
L 1808 Jan.15	Simon WHITE, the younger, and wife Jane; confirmed.	Slinfold
L 1808 Jan.15	Thomas BROOKSBANK and wife Mildred; confirmed.	St. Margaret, Westminster, Mdx
L 1808 Apr.29	William GORRINGE, wife Elizabeth and children William 3y and James 14m; confirmed.	Worth
L 1809 Jan.13	Thomas HOLMAN and wife Mary; confirmed.	Worth
L 1809 Jan.13	Reuben SNASHALL, wife Sarah and children John 4y and James 2y; confirmed.	Rotherfield
L 1810 Jan.12	Richard TAYLOR, wife Elizabeth and children James 3y 6m and Mary Ann 2y 3m; confirmed.	Addington, Sry
L 1810 Jan.12	James CAMPBELL and wife Susannah; confirmed.	Leigh, Ken
L 1811 Jan.18	Ann CREW, wife of Nathaniel CREW; confirmed.	Lingfield, Sry
L 1811 Jan.18	Thomas RICE, wife Mary and children Elizabeth 6y, Mary 4y and Thomas 3y (sic) confirmed.	Worth
L 1811 Jan.18	Lucy MONTAGUE, widow; confirmed.	Hammersmith, Mdx

L 1811 Jan.18	John TAYLOR, wife Naomi and children Mary 11y, John 8y and William 5y; confirmed.	Hamlet of Penge, Battersea, Sry
L 1811 Oct.11	William SHERLOCK, wife Elizabeth and children Elizabeth 6y, Mary 4y, Martha 3y and Sarah 1y; confirmed.	Rusper
L 1811 Oct.11	Mary MEAD, singlewoman; confirmed.	West Hoathly
L 1812 Jan.17	Henry ROFFEY, wife Sarah and children Maria 9y, William 7y and John 5y; confirmed.	Merstham, Sry
L 1812 Apr.10	Thomas CHAPMAN and wife Lucy; confirmed.	Horsted Keynes
L 1812 Jul.17	Thomas DAWSON, wife Sarah and children Mary 6y, James 2y and Jane 2y; confirmed.	Woking, Sry
L 1812 Oct. 9	William AYNSCOMB and wife Martha; confirmed.	Cowfold
L 1814 Jan.14	John SKINNER and wife Ann; respited.	Warnham
L 1814 Apr.22	John SKINNER and wife Ann; confirmed.	Warnham
L 1814 Apr.22	Mary SKINNER, singlewoman; quashed.	Bidborough, Ken
L 1814 Apr.22	Edward BEARD, wife Mary and sons Edward 3y and John 3m; confirmed.	Fletching
L 1814 Jul.15	Ann BORRER, singlewoman; quashed.	Coulsdon, Sry
L 1814 Jul.15	Thomas CAREY, wife Catherine and children Ann 8y, Elizabeth 6y and Mary 2y; respited.	Horley, Sry
L 1815 Jan.13	Thomas CAREY, wife Catherine and children Ann 8y, Elizabeth 6y and Mary 2y; confirmed.	Horley, Sry
L 1815 Apr. 7	Louisa SPENCER, singlewoman; confirmed.	Hartfield
L 1815 Apr. 7	Elizabeth RICHARDSON, (wife of James RICHARDSON, who has lately been transported to places beyond the seas), and children Mary Ann 5y and Hannah 2y; confirmed.	Maresfield
L 1815 Apr. 7	Sarah PAINTER, wife of John PAINTER, and children John 7y, Sarah 4y and Mary 16m; confirmed.	Hambledon, Ham
L 1815 Jul.14	Martha LUCAS, (wife of Edward LUCAS, a private in the Royal Artillery now serving abroad) and children Elizabeth 2y and Edward 4m; respited.	Fletching
L 1816 Jan.12	Mary BUTCHER, singlewoman; confirmed.	West Hoathly
L 1816 Jan.12	John SMITH and wife Sarah; confirmed.	Lingfield, Sry
L 1816 Jan.12	Thomas HOLMAN; confirmed.	Worth
L 1816 Apr.26	Martha LUCAS, (wife of Edward LUCAS, a private in the Royal Artillery now serving abroad) and children Elizabeth 2y and Edward 4m; quashed.	Fletching
L 1816 Jul.19	Mary HOOKER, singlewoman; confirmed.	Lingfield, Sry
L 1816 Jul.19	Lewis READY and wife Elizabeth; confirmed.	Crowhurst, Sry
L 1817 Jan.17	Sarah VINES, singlewoman; confirmed.	Balcombe
L 1817 Jan.17	Elizabeth CAMFIELD, widow; confirmed.	Fletching

L 1817 Apr.18	John PAYNE, wife Rebecca and children William 9y and Mary Ann 5y; confirmed.	Warnham
L 1817 Apr.18	Stephen MUDDLE, wife Elizabeth and children Edmund 5y, Phoebe 3y, Mary 2y and an infant not yet baptised; quashed.	Lindfield
L 1817 Apr.18	John GARDNER, wife Jane and children Ann 6y, John 3y and William 1y; respited.	West Hoathly
L 1817 Apr.18	Thomas GASSON and wife Sarah; confirmed.	Chevening, Ken
L 1817 Jul.18	James SNOW and wife Susannah; respited.	Preston
L 1817 Jul.18	James LINCOLN and wife Ann; confirmed.	Ditchingham,Nfk
L 1817 Jul.18	Storer GIBB and wife Susannah; confirmed.	Lingfield, Sry
L 1817 Jul.18	John GARDNER, wife Jane and children Ann 6y, John 3y and William 1y; confirmed.	West Hoathly
L 1817 Jul.18	Joseph DAVEY (?DANCY) and wife Ann; confirmed.	Cuckfield
L 1817 Jul.18	James SETFORD and wife Ann; confirmed.	Lindfield
L 1817 Oct.18	Charles GATTON, wife Elizabeth and children John 5y and Elizabeth 18m; quashed.	Beddingham
L 1817 Oct.18	James SNOW and wife Susannah; confirmed.	Preston
L 1818 Jan.16	Thomas NORMAN; confirmed.	Worth
L 1818 Jan.16	James KILLICK, wife Ann and daughter Sarah 2y and an infant daughter not yet baptised; confirmed.	Godstone, Sry
L 1818 Jan.16	George ELLIS, wife Elizabeth and children George 12y, Mary 8y, Charlotte 7y, Martin 5y and Henry 3y; confirmed.	St. Mary Magdalene, Bermondsey, Sry
L 1818 Apr. 3	John BISH and wife Lydia; confirmed.	Lindfield
L 1818 Apr. 3	Henry WILLIAMS and wife Jane; confirmed.	Ardingly
L 1818 Apr. 3	John EDWARDS, wife Harriet and children Jane 6y, Joseph 4y, Mary 2y and Hester 3m; confirmed.	Hartfield
L 1818 Oct.23	Susan BRISTER, singlewoman; confirmed.	Crowhurst
L 1819 Apr.23	William STANFORD; confirmed.	Beeding
L 1819 Jul.16	Sarah BRIGGS, wife of William BRIGGS and children Elizabeth 4y and Henry 11m; respited.	Horsham
L 1820 Jan.14	Sarah BRIGGS, [wife of William BRIGGS], and children Elizabeth 4y and Henry 11m; confirmed.	Horsham
L 1821 May 4	Robert AVES and wife Frances; confirmed.	Hartfield
L 1821 May 4	William CANDLE, wife Mary and children William 16y, John 14y, Beatrice 12y, Frederick 10y, Adolphus 8y, Edward 6y, Robert 3y, Samuel 3y and Priscilla 2y; respited.	St. Thomas, Cliffe, Lewes

L 1821 Jul.13	William CANDLE, wife Mary and children William 16y, John 14y, Beatrice 12y, Frederick 10y, Adolphus 8y, Edward 6y, Robert 3y, Samuel 3y and Priscilla 2y; quashed as W.C. is in possession of a house in East Grinstead at rental of over £10 a year.	St. Thomas, Cliffe, Lewes
L 1821 Oct.19	William ANSTON; confirmed.	St. John sub Castro, Lewes
L 1821 Oct.19	Mary BROOKER, singlewoman; confirmed.	Tandridge, Sry
L 1822 Apr.19	Thomas HOATH, wife Elizabeth and daughter Mary Ann 14m; confirmed.	Edenbridge, Ken
L 1822 Oct.18	George PERRIER; confirmed.	Rudgwick
L 1822 Oct.18	James LINCOLN and wife Ann; confirmed.	Ditchingham,Nfk
L 1822 Oct.18	Mary HARTFIELD, singlewoman, and son not yet baptised; confirmed.	Buxted
L 1823 Jan.17	William CHART; confirmed.	Godstone, Sry
L 1823 Jan.17	William LEWRY; confirmed.	Lingfield, Sry
L 1823 Apr.11	Thomas HOLMAN, wife Amelia and children John 9y, Thomas 7y, Sarah 4y and James 2y; confirmed.	Tandridge, Sry
L 1823 Jul.18	Sarah HEASMAN; confirmed.	Chailey
L 1824 Jan.16	Edward ROFFE and wife Sarah; confirmed.	Leigh, Ken
L 1824 Jan.16	John HAYWARD, wife Sarah and children John 15y, William 12y, Robert 10y, Mary 7y, Elizabeth 5y, Sarah 3y and Edward 7m; respited.	Lingfield, Sry
L 1824 Jan.16	Edward TAYLOR, wife Jemima and children Harriet 3y and Mary Ann 1y; confirmed.	Horsted Keynes
L 1824 Jan.16	William BARTON, wife Mary and children Susannah 7y, Ann 5y, Mary 3y and William 1y; confirmed.	Withyham
L 1824 Jan.16	Peter TURNER, wife Sarah and children Charles 10y, William 8y, Ann 5y, Mary 3y and Eliza 4m; confirmed.	St. Margaret, Westminster, Mdx
L 1824 Jan.16	Edward DADSWELL, wife Martha and children Edward 5y, James 3y and John 6m; confirmed.	Rotherfield
L 1824 Apr.30	John HAYWARD, wife Sarah and children John 15y, William 12y, Robert 10y, Mary 7y, Elizabeth 5y, Sarah 3y and Edward 7m; confirmed.	Lingfield, Sry
L 1825 Jan.13	Sarah HUNTLEY, singlewoman; confirmed.	St. Marylebone, Mdx
L 1825 Apr.14	John JACKSON, wife Kitty and children Thomas 6y, Ann 4y, Eliza 2y and Mary 4m; respited.	West Hoathly
L 1825 Jul.14	John JACKSON, wife Kitty and children Thomas 6y, Ann 4y, Eliza 2y and Mary 4m; confirmed.	West Hoathly

L 1825 Oct.20	Sarah DOWNING, widow, and daughter Mary Ann 3m; confirmed.	Werrington, Dev
L 1826 Jan.12	Nathaniel JOHNSON otherwise called Charles JOHNSON; confirmed.	Basingstoke, Ham
L 1826 Jan.12	Susannah JOHNSON, singlewoman; confirmed.	Faversham, Ken
L 1826 Jan.12	John Boghurst JOHNSON 7y; confirmed.	Catsfield
L 1826 Jan.12	Ann JOHNSON 5y; confirmed.	Hawkhurst, Ken
L 1826 Jan.12	William PAINE, wife Hannah and son Charles Newnham PAINE 8m; confirmed.	Chiddingstone, Ken
L 1826 Jan.12	Sophia JOHNSON, singlewoman; confirmed.	Betchworth, Sry
L 1826 Jan.12	Henry JOHNSON; confirmed.	Salehurst
L 1827 Jan.11	Mary BUTCHER, singlewoman; confirmed.	Camberwell, Sry
L 1827 Jul.12	James LINKEN and wife Sarah; confirmed.	Ditchingham, Nfk
L 1827 Jul.12	Robert WATERS; confirmed.	St. Andrew, Holborn, Mdx
L 1827 Jul.12	George BALDWIN; confirmed.	Godstone, Sry
L 1831 Oct.20	William SHERLOCK, the younger; confirmed.	West Hoathly
L 1832 Apr. 5	Joseph COOMBER alias POWELL; confirmed.	Warlingham, Sry
L 1832 Apr. 5	Creasy UNICUM; confirmed.	Battle
L 1832 Apr. 5	Henry HEMSLEY, wife Tirzah and children Tirzah Fanny 4y and Agnes 2y 9m; confirmed.	Horsted Keynes
L 1833 Jan. 3	William AVIS; confirmed.	Lingfield, Sry
L 1833 Jan. 3	Mary DEARLING; confirmed.	Godstone, Sry
L 1833 Jan. 3	William YATEMAN and wife Sarah; confirmed.	Cowden, Ken
L 1833 Jan. 3	Frederick PICKETT, wife Sarah and children Eliza 10y, Ellen 8y, Benjamin 5y, Thomas 3y, Esther 2y and Martha 3m;quashed.	Streatham, Sry
L 1833 Jan. 3	Mary MILES; respited.	Hartfield
L 1833 Jan. 3	William AVERY, wife Ann and children Louisa 5y, Ann 3y and George 2y; confirmed.	Wandsworth, Sry
L 1833 Apr.11	Mary MILES; quashed.	Hartfield
L 1833 Apr.11	William HEMSLEY, the younger, wife Eliza and children Fanny 4y, Eliza 2y and Charles William 4m; confirmed.	Ringmer
L 1833 Apr.11	Ambrose DRAPER; confirmed.	St. George the Martyr, Southwark, Sry
L 1833 Oct.17	William SUTFORD; confirmed.	Lindfield
L 1833 Oct.17	Henry DANN; confirmed.	Heathfield
L 1834 Apr.11	Hannah SIMMONS, wife of Thomas SIMMONS, and children Ann 9y, George 7y, Hannah 5y, John 3y and Mary 1y; confirmed.	Speldhurst, Ken
L 1834 Apr.11	Adam GRINHAM, wife Charlotte and children Ann 4y and William 2y; confirmed.	Frant
L 1834 Jul. 3	Mary GIBB; confirmed.	Lingfield, Sry

L 1834 Jul. 3	Thomas DEARLING, wife Catherine and children Amelia 8y, Catherine 5y, Eliza 4y and William 2y; confirmed.	Worth
L 1834 Oct.16	Richard GIBB, wife Rachel and children James 14y, William 12y, John 7y, George 5y, Mary Ann 3y, Thomas 2y and Jane 8m; respited.	Lingfield, Sry
L 1835 Jan. 5	Richard GIBB, wife Rachel and children James 14y, William 12y, John 7y, George 5y, Mary Ann 3y, Thomas 2y and Jane 8m; confirmed.	Lingfield, Sry
L 1835 Jun.29	Philadelphia GATES; confirmed.	Wandsworth, Sry
L 1835 Jun.29	Edward LAMBTON otherwise DODSWELL; confirmed.	Rotherfield
L 1835 Jun.29	Ann PAYNE; confirmed.	West Hoathly

REMOVALS ORDERS TO EAST GRINSTEAD Par 348/32/3/1

* Indicates catalogued under Par 348/32/3/77
+ Indicates catalogued under Par 348/32/2/1
# Indicates catalogued under Par 348/32/4/54

		From
1690 Jul.15+	John BORER. On appeal, it is agreed that J.B. is an inhabitant of Hartfield as he rents a tenement in that parish at yearly rent of £10. East Grinstead discharged from providing for him.	Hartfield
1693 May 8	Edward SHARPE and wife.	Maresfield
1698 Jan.15	Edward SHARPE, wife and family were removed, by an order dated 8 May 1693, to East Grinstead, the place of the last legal settlement of E.S. As East Grinstead refuse to provide for them, and the order has not been discharged, Maresfield are again to convey the family to East Grinstead, who are to provide for them.	Maresfield
1698 Aug.22*	Robert BUTCHER. [Endorsed: Seven years A.COOPER, not likely to be chargeable.]	West Hoathly
1698 Oct. 6+	John WATERS. On appeal, order discharged, as J.W. has an estate in lands of his own and not likely to become chargeable to Hartfield.	Hartfield
1699May 30+	William FASSELL. On appeal, order confirmed and East Grinstead to pay 24s 0d maintenance.	Godstone, Sry
1700 May 18	Edward FULLER.	Cowden, Ken
1700 May 18	Edward FULLER. The parish officers of East Grinstead give notice of appeal against the removal of E.F. as he was in service with William STEER in East Grinstead for one year from 14 October 1696 but served only one quarter and 2 weeks and then ran away. E.F. has since been unsettled but	Cowden, Ken

	had been in service in Cowden two full years before he came to East Grinstead. *Catalogued under Par 348/37/5/1*	
1702 Oct. 6+	Richard TAYL0R and wife. On appeal, order quashed. *See Appendix*	Cowden, Ken
1702 Nov.24	Elizabeth STONESTREET, a bastard child born in East Grinstead was allowed by agreement with Withyham overseers, to remain in Withyham with her mother in consideration of 30s 0d a year for the term of 7 years from 7 August 1695. As that term has now expired the child to be conveyed to East Grinstead. *Catalogued under Par 348/34/3/1*	Withyham
1702 Dec.19	Edward RUSSELL, wife Elizabeth and infant child, have a settlement dated 24 September 1702 from East Grinstead but, as E.R. has now gone away leaving his wife and child, he (when found) and his family are to be removed to East Grinstead	Appledore, Ken
1706 Jan.17+	John PAGE, an infant. On appeal, order discharged.	Keymer
1710 Apr.18+	William GROVE and wife Rachel. On appeal, order quashed.	Crayford, Ken
1711 Jan.23	Thomas SHERMAN and wife Anne.	Worth
1711 Mar. 20	William BUDGING, wife Elizabeth and children Anne and Elizabeth.	West Hoathly
1712 Sep. 1	Jane CHAPMAN.	Hartfield
1712 Oct. 9+	Jane CHAPMAN. On appeal, order discharged.	Hartfield
1712 Dec. 17	Thomas HARWOOD, wife Susanna and children.	Maresfield
1713 Jan.15+	Thomas HARWOOD. On appeal, order quashed.	Maresfield
1714 Nov. 4	Mary LEE, an infant aged 20 weeks, was brought to the Constables of Lingfield, Surrey, from East Grinstead with a pass for her to be conveyed on as a vagrant to Tottenham High Cross, Middlesex. Upon examination it appears that the child cannot, by law, be any further conveyed as a vagrant and Lingfield are to reconvey M.L. to East Grinstead, and from there she is to be conveyed to the place of her last legal settlement.	Lingfield, Sry
1715 Jul.14+	Mary WELLS, widow, and children Nicholas and Simeon. On appeal, order discharged.	Hartfield
1716 Feb. 4	Joseph DANIEL, now apprentice to John ELVEY of East Grinstead, weaver.	Edenbridge, Ken
1716 May 26	James JARRETT, wife Mary and child.	Hever, Ken
1717 Jan.17+	John PUTLAND, wife Ann and children Lydia, Thomas and William. On appeal, order discharged.	Uckfield

1717 May 3	Henry WILLINGTON, wife Ann and child Sarah 6m.	Horley, Sry
1717 Jul 18	Richard ROSE, wife Sarah and children. On appeal, warrant quashed for want of form.	Maresfield
1717 Oct.10+	Richard ROSE, wife Sarah and children Richard and Elizabeth. On appeal, order discharged.	Maresfield
1717 Dec.31	John MARTIN, wife and family. J.M. has been settled in East Grinstead as a yearly servant to Anthony BURNETT of that parish for 2 years.	West Hoathly
1721 Sep. 4	Henry COCKRELL and wife Clements. [Received 20 Oct]	Hartfield
1722 Jan.15*	William DUGLAS.	Lingfield, Sry
1723 Feb.12	William DUGLAS was removed from Lingfield by an order dated 15 January last. As his wife, Elizabeth DUGLAS, has lately come into Lingfield to settle and is likely to become chargeable, she is to be conveyed to East Grinstead.	Lingfield, Sry
1723 Nov.29	Thomas FRENCH and wife Margarett.	Burwash
1724 Mar.28	William HOLMES, wife Elizabeth and child.	Edenbridge, Ken
1724 Apr.14	William HOLMES, wife Elizabeth and child. On appeal, Maidstone Court ordered that so much of the order, as relates to the settlement of the child, shall be quashed and the residue of the order, relating to the settlement of William Holmes and wife Elizabeth, shall be confirmed.	Edenbridge, Ken
1724 Oct. 7	Robert COMBRIDGE and wife Mary.	West Hoathly
1725 Apr. 5	George SKINNER and wife Jane.	Cuckfield
1725 Apr.26	Ann MUNKTON, wife of John MUNKTON whose last legal settlement was in East Grinstead by living as a hired servant for 3 years successively with Edward CHAPMAN at the Bull in East Grinstead. *See Appendix*	Brentwood, Ess
1725 Aug.27	Mary and Ann BEAVER [?BEVIS].	St. Saviour, Southwark, Sry
1726 Jan.13+	Ann LASHMER, spinster. On appeal, order discharged.	West Hoathly
1728 Apr.11	Edward LINN, whose last legal settlement was in East Grinstead by living there as a hired servant for one whole year.	Fletching
1736 Feb.27*	Fortune JENNER, singlewoman.	Lingfield, Sry
1736 Sep. 6*	John FARNES, wife Mary and son James 2y.	Hartfield
1737 Nov.26*	Rebecca ROODE. Elizabeth ROODE als SIBLEY, being, as she informs, about the age of 50y, was apprehended in Ticehurst, with children Richard 10y, Rebecca 5y, Ann 2y and Susanna 6m, there wandering and begging. On examination, Elizabeth	Ticehurst

	said that daughter Rebecca is a bastard child born in East Grinstead. As R.R. has not gained a legal settlement since her birth, she is to be conveyed to East Grinstead and delivered to the parish officers there "who are not to suffer her to wander about again".	
1738 Jul.20*	William SMALL and wife Mary.	Hartfield
1738 Nov. 2*	Winifred OVEL, singlewoman.	Horsted Keynes
1738 Dec.30*	William HARRIS, wife Ann and son William 2y.	Cowden, Ken
1739 May 1+	Elizabeth WILLIX, wife of James WILLIX, drummer, and her child Mary 1m were removed from Lingfield by order dated 3 April last. On appeal order is hereby vacated, discharged and set aside.	Lingfield, Sry
1739 Sep.25*	Hester POTTER, wife of Joshua POTTER late of East Grinstead and daughter Hallamsby 6 or 7y, on oath of Joshua POTTER, the father of the above mentioned Joshua Potter.	West Hoathly
1739 Nov. 5*	Sarah RUSSELL.	Maresfield
1740 Apr. 2*	Mary FARNES, singlewoman.	Hartfield
1740 Nov. 3*	Mary FEAST, wife of William FEAST, was apprehended in West Hoathly as a rogue and vagabond who was last found begging in East Grinstead, and passed through the same unapprehended. As the place of her legal settlement, birth or parents abode cannot be discovered, she is to be returned to East Grinstead.	West Hoathly
1741 Jan.29+	Elizabeth CHART, singlewoman,	Lingfield, Sry
1741 Feb. 5	William BUTCHER, husbandman and wife Elizabeth.	Edenbridge, Ken
1741 Feb.20	Rebecca THEOBALD, wife of William THEOBALD who has lately gone into His Majesty's Service, and son William 2y 9m. James THEOBALD (father of the above said William) and wife and family were owned inhabitants legally settled in East Grinstead by a certificate dated 29 June 1711. On examination and the certificate being produced and no subsequent settlement appearing, it is ordered that East Grinstead is the place of legal settlement for Rebecca Theobald and child.	Croydon, Sry
1742 Nov. 1	George BASSET, son of William BASSET, baker, late of East Grinstead. A certificate dated 20 Jan.1722 acknowledged William Basset and children to be settled in East Grinstead.	Godstone, Sry
1743 Oct. 8	Thomas WEAKLING.	Seal, Ken

1744 Mar.12	James MARNER and wife Sarah.	Horne, Sry
1745 Jan.17+	Thomas HUTCHINSON and wife Jane. On appeal, order discharged.	Hartfield
1746 Jun.20	Anne WRIGHT, aged 21 years, was apprehended in Boroughbridge as a rogue and vagabond wandering and begging there. A.W. to be conveyed to Nottingham, the first town in the next precinct. [Endorsed: June 26 Rutland - allowed to pass this county. L. DAWES. June 26 Stamford Borough, Lincoln. Allowed to pass this borough. Chas. SHIPLEY, mayor. June 26, Liberty of Peterborough, County of Northampton, allowed to pass this liberty, John TILLEY, constable. 27 June Huntingdonshire, allowed to pass this County. R. EDWARDS. 27 June To Constable of Papworth, County of Cambridge. Convey this vagrant to Royston in County of Hertford in order to be further conveyed. Will. LUNN. 29 June Hertfordshire. Allowed to pass this County by me Fran. [?GULSTON] 30 June Middlesex. Allowed to pass this county. Will UNDERWOOD.	Boroughbridge, Yks
1748 Jan. 8	Hannah ILLMAN, singlewoman,	Worth
1748 Apr.12	John MASCALL, son of William MASCALL and Mary WOODGATE. Upon oath of Ann WALLS, wife of John WALLS, J.M. is chargeable to East Grinstead.	Hartfield
1751 Mar. 2*	Robert PAYNE, cordwainer.	Sevenoaks, Ken
1751 Mar 2*	Robert MALYAN, cordwainer and wife Mary.	Sevenoaks, Ken
1751 Jun.29*	Daniel COOPER, wife Ann and son Joseph. [Received 30 July]	Dorking, Sry
1753 Feb.23*	John DIVEALL, wife Sarah and children John and Elizabeth.	Hartfield
1754 Jul. 9*	Ann EDWARDS, singlewoman.	Etchingham
1755 Jun. -*	John GEER and wife Mary.	Arlington
1758 Nov.15	Thomas WELLER, husbandman, and wife Judith.	Worth
1760 Jun.16	Nicholas PAIN and wife Frances.	Horsted Keynes
1760 Aug.20	Jane ATTWOOLL, wife of George ATTWOOLL, a soldier in the 23rd Regiment of Foot Guards, with her son John 4y, to be removed to East Grinstead, it being the place of her husband's settlement.	Fletching
1760 Sep.17	Edward COOPER and wife Mary.	Horley, Sry
1760 Nov.25	Jane SHOEBRIDGE, singlewoman.	Hartfield
1761 May 30	Edward POST and wife Sarah.	West Hoathly
1761 May 30	Nicholas PAYNE and wife Frances.	West Hoathly
1761 Aug. 3	John VINE and wife Susannah.	Waldron
1762 Apr.12	Mary STEVENS, singlewoman.	Maidstone, Ken

1764 May 3	William BROWN, labourer, and wife Sarah.	Edenbridge, Ken
1765 Dec.12	Richard EDWARDS, wife Mary and son Richard 3y.	Dorking, Sry
1766 Jan. 6	Betty otherwise Elizabeth ARIDGE, singlewoman.	Fletching
1766 Nov.11	Edmund Eabs HOLMES and wife Philadelphia.	Fletching
1770 Dec. 5	Richard SANDERS and wife Sarah.	Horne, Sry
1770 Dec. 8+	Elizabeth MAY, singlewoman.	Sevenoaks, Ken
1775 Oct.17*	Elizabeth KING.	Worth
1776 Feb. 3*	Ann ARCHER, singlewoman.	West Ham, Ess
1777 May 17	Henry JOHNSON, was apprehended in Borzeat, Northampton, as a rogue and vagabond wandering and begging. H.J. who, on examination, said that he was born in East Grinstead, [mark of H.J.] is to be returned there, via Olney, Buckinghamshire.	Bozeat, Nth
1777 Aug.11#	Elizabeth JENNER was apprehended in St. James, Westminster, as a rogue and vagabond, wandering abroad and lodging in the open air. E.J. to be conveyed to St. Mary, Lambeth, Surrey, being the first parish through which she ought to pass to East Grinstead. On examination E.J. said that she was 52 years old, wife of James JENNER (gone from her) to whom she was married at the parish church of Stoke, Gosport, Hampshire, about 17 years ago. That her husband was bound apprentice to John PRING, a linen weaver in East Grinstead, where he served for 3 years, and never gained another settlement. [Signature of E.J.]	Westminster, Mdx
1778 Mar. 5*	Mary PAGE.	Withyham
1778 Aug. 5	William LASHMORE and wife Ann.	Horsted Keynes
1779 Mar.13*	Henry WALLER and wife Sarah.	Hamsey
1779 Mar.23*	James BACKSHALL and wife Mary.	Ringmer
1779 Apr.27*	James MILLS, wife Ann and daughter Mary 6m.	Seddlescombe
1779 Jul.17*	John MAYNARD, husbandman.	Horne, Sry
1779 Oct.25*	Thomas BALCOMB, wife Sarah and son William 9m.	West Hoathly
1783 Jan.10	Daniel FINCH, bricklayer, wife Mary and son Robert 4m.	Dover, Ken
1786 Nov.23	Hetty BLEACH was apprehended as a rogue and vagabond in St. Martin in the Fields, Westminster, wandering abroad and lodging in the open air. H.B. to be conveyed to East Grinstead, via St. Dunstan, London, together with this pass and duplicate of her examination, in which she said that she is aged 25 years, the wife of John BLEACH (gone from	Westminster, Mdx

	her) to whom she was married at East Grinstead parish church, five and a half years ago, and that her husband was bound apprentice for seven years to Edward JORDAN, carpenter of East Grinstead, which term he served. [Mark of H.B.] *Catalogued under Par 348/32/4/1*	
1787 Jan. 1	Charles GIBB, wife Lydia and son Joseph.	Penshurst, Ken
1788 Jan.14	Thomas PARKER, wife Sarah and children Henry and Sarah.	Worth
1788 Feb.11	Thomas BROOKER, husbandman, and wife Mary.	Worth
1788 Feb. 18	Jane SHOOSMITH, singlewoman.	Hartfield
1788 May 5	Benjamin HARRIS and wife Elizabeth.	Tonbridge, Ken
1788 Aug.14	Mary JENNER, wife of James JENNER, hatter, who on Tuesday the 5 August deserted and left her, and children William 7y, Ann 6y and Sarah 2y.	Southover
1789 Feb. 9	Elizabeth FALKENER, singlewoman.	Worth
1789 Feb.10	John FOSTER, wife Elizabeth and child 1m.	Warbleton
1789 Mar.31	John MITCHELL and wife Mary.	Leigh, Ken
1789 Apr.20	Mary EVERIST.	Withyham
1789 Jun. 8	Ann BROOKER, singlewoman.	Hartfield
1789 Jul.18	Eleanor BASHFORD, singlewoman.	Burstow, Sry
1801 May 9*	Thomas PRYER, wife Susanna and children Susanna 4y and Sampson 2y.	Carshalton, Sry
1801 Nov.30	William FRANKS was, on 24 November 1801, apprehended in the parish of St. Mary Woolchurch, London, wandering abroad and begging. W.F. was convicted as a rogue and vagabond and confined in the Hospital of Bridewell, being the House of Correction in London, for seven days and is now to be conveyed to St. Olave, Southwark, Surrey, that being the first parish in the next precinct through which he ought to pass in the direct road to East Grinstead. On examination, W.F. said that he served seven years as apprentice to William Moon, shoemaker, in East Grinstead. [Mark of W.F.]	Bridewell, Ldn
1802 Oct.13*	Alexander HOLMS and wife Sarah.	Hamsey
1803 Sep. 1#	Sarah TURNER was, on 25 Aug. last, apprehended in Alverstoke, Hampshire, as a rogue and a vagabond wandering abroad in the open air and not giving a good account of herself, for which offence she has been convicted and imprisoned in the Bridewell of Gosport for 7 days and is to be conveyed to Portsea, being the next parish to pass on her way to East Grinstead. On examination S.T.	Alverstoke, Ham

	said that she was born in East Grinstead and was 19 years of age and that, two and a half years ago, she hired herself as a yearly servant to Mr. BETSLEY of East Grinstead at 30s 0d a year, which wages she received and she has not gained a settlement in any other parish. [Mark of S.T.]	
1803 Oct.31*	Robert HUGHES, wife Catherine and son George 2y.	Stone, Ken
1803 Nov. 7*	William HARRIS, wife Mary and children Sarah 12y, Ann 10y, William 8y, Mary 6y, Elizabeth 4y and Thomas 1y.	Otham, Ken
1804 Mar. 3*	Martha COMBER, spinster.	Balcombe
1804 Jul.21*	Richard WINCHESTER.	Eastchurch, Ken
1804 Nov.17*	Lydia LONGHURST, singlewoman, being with child.	Rusper
1804 Dec.14*	Hannah PAGE, wife of John PAGE, who has deserted and left her, and daughter Eliza aged 7 weeks.	Lindfield
1805 Feb. 6*	James JENNER and wife Sarah.	Sts.Peter & Mary, Westout, Lewes
1805 Apr.18*	Joseph MIALL, wife Mary and son Richard 2y.	West Hoathly
1805 Apr.30#	Sarah KILDARE was apprehended in Brighthelmstone as a rogue and vagabond, wandering about, committing acts of vagrancy, and has been confined in the House of Correction for seven days. On examination S.K. said that she was born in East Grinstead, where her father was legally settled and she has not gained a settlement in any other parish. [Mark of S.K.]	House of Correction, Lewes
1806 Mar.18*	Ernest GROVES, wife Philadelphia and children Lucy 4y 10m, Caroline, 3y, George 13m, and Henny 3 weeks. Philadelphia unfit to travel due to sickness until 17 June; East Grinstead to pay £2.17s 6d maintenance.	Ticehurst
1806 Jul.23*	Emilia HODGES, singlewoman.	Lingfield, Sry
1806 Oct.25#	Mary EVERSHED was apprehended in Ore as a rogue and vagabond lodging in outhouses etc., and has been confined in the House of Correction for 7 days. On examination M.E. said that she was born in East Grinstead, where her father was legally settled, and that she has not done any act to gain a settlement elsewhere. [Signature of M.E.]	House of Correction, Lewes
1807 Jan.13*	Elizabeth RIDLEY, singlewoman.	Reigate, Sry
1807 Mar.13*	James WICKENS.	Lambeth, Sry
1807 Mar.14*	James MILES, wife Emy and children Ann 6y, Harriet 4y, William 3y and Henry 1y.	Westmeston

1808 Apr.22*	Jane PAYNE, wife of Thomas PAYNE a private in the 95th Regiment of Foot. [Endorsed: Lives with Mr. Turner.]	West Hoathly
1808 Apr.29*	William WOOLGAR, wife Ann and children James 6y and William 3y.	Tonbridge, Ken
1808 Dec. 5*	William BROOKER.	Wrotham, Ken
1809 Aug.12#	Amy RODDELL, apprehended in Alverstoke, Hampshire, as a rogue and vagabond wandering abroad and begging, has been imprisoned in the House of Correction at Winchester, Hampshire, for seven days and is now to be removed to East Grinstead via Farnham, Surrey. On examination A.R. said that she is the wife of John RODDELL, an Irishman now in one of H.M.'s Regiment of Foot, at this time abroad and not having any legal place of settlement in England. That her place of settlement, before her marriage, was East Grinstead, which she gained by birth. [Mark of A.R.]	House of Correction, Winchester, Ham
1810 Jan.16*	Elizabeth DUNGATE, singlewoman.	Burwash
1810 Mar.16*	James MEADS, the infant son of William MEADS, on examination of Sarah DAY and others.	West Hoathly
1810 May 8*	William LUCAS. Unable to travel due to sickness, fit to do so 8 Aug.1811. East Grinstead to pay £36.4s 0d maintenance.	St. Mary, Newington, Sry
1810 Jun.19*	Samuel LUSTED, wife Susannah and children Rebecca 14y, Mary 11y 6m, Lucy 9y 6m, Hannah 8y, Jane 6y and Ann 2y 9m.	Heathfield
1810 Jun.25*	Elizabeth CHAPMAN, singlewoman. Unable to travel, due to sickness, until 23 July 1810; East Grinstead to pay £3.15s 6d maintenance.	Ewell, Sry
1810 Oct. 2*	John MORRIS, widower and children Jane 5y and John 4y.	East Peckham, Ken
1811 Jun.24*	William MORLEY and wife Anne. W.M. unable to travel due to sickness. [Endorsed: William has since died from the sickness and infirmity under which he lately laboured. Anne Morley now to be conveyed to East Grinstead, who are to pay £3.5s 0d.]	Dartford, Ken
1811 Jul. 1*	James PATCHING. Unfit to travel due to sickness. [Endorsed: Warrant dated 6 Jan.1812 orders East Grinstead to pay £2.12s 6d, as James Patching "was to be removed but is since dead".]	Epsom, Sry
1811 Jul.19+	Mary GATTON, wife of Charles GATTON the younger. On appeal, order confirmed.	Ringmer
1811 Oct.25*	Mary MARTIN, singlewoman and insane.	St. Pancras, Mdx

1812 Apr. 3*	Jonathan COOKE and wife Rebecca.	West Hoathly
1812 Apr.25*	Elizabeth BURGESS, singlewoman.	Cowden, Ken
1812 Jun.10*	Caroline TURNER, singlewoman.	Withyham
1812 Sep.16*	Stephen SERJEANT and child Susannah 14y.	Nutfield, Sry
1812 Nov.14*	Robert HUNT wife Jemima and children Henry 10y and Mary 7y.	Shoreham, Ken
1812 Nov.17*	John Watson NEWNHAM. Unable to travel due to sickness, fit to do so by 7 December; East Grinstead to pay £9.11s 6d.	Ewell, Sry
1813 Jan. 2*	Samuel JENNER, wife Elizabeth and son William 18m.	Capel, Ken
1814 Feb.14#	Charles JOHNSON was apprehended in the parish of St. Michael, Lewes and charged that, on 24 October, he did commit acts of vagancy by wandering abroad and begging and was confined in the House of Correction for seven days and is now to be removed to East Grinstead. On examination C.J. said that he was born in East Grinstead, where his father was legally settled, and that he has never done any act to gain a settlement elsewhere. [Mark of C.J.]	House of Correction, Lewes
1814 Apr. 2*	Benjamin DAY and wife Elizabeth.	Horsted Keynes
1815 Jan. 9*	Sarah CRITTENDEN, singlewoman.	Withyham
1815 Aug. 9	Mary WOOD singlewoman.	Eastbourne
1815 Sep.29	Benjamin GROVE, wife Francis and children Robert, George, William and Obediah.	East Hoathly
1815 Oct. 6	Ann HEAD, wife of William HEAD.	Slaugham
1815 Dec.19*	Martha EDWARDS, widow of Thomas EDWARDS, late a Sergeant in the Waggon Train, deceased. On examination of Thomas Edwards in his life time, the lawful settlement for his wife is given as East Grinstead.	Wootton Bassett, Wil.
1816 Jan.12*	Richard TOWSE, wife Jane and daughter Harriet aged 9 weeks.	West Hoathly
1816 Nov.25*	Edward RYE. Unable to travel by reason of his leg having been broken; fit to do so by 10 January 1817; East Grinstead to pay £12.7s 0d	Maresfield
1817 Feb. 3*	James YOUNG, wife Amey and children Lucy 6y, Mary 3y and an infant girl aged 3 weeks.	Godstone, Sry
1817 Mar. 8*	John OLLIVE, wife Elizabeth and children Ann, Eliza, William, Mary, Caley and Elizabeth.	Mayfield
1817 Mar.13	Jane BAILY, singlewoman.	Camberwell, Sry
1817 Mar 18*	Richard JENNER, wife Jane and child Maria 13m.	Burwash
1817 May31*	Ann MORLEY, widow.	Portsea, Ham

1817 Jun.28*	Edward BUTCHER, wife Susan and children Francis 6y, Sophia 3y 6m and Frederick 14m. Edward Butcher sick and unable to attend Petty Sessions. [Endorsed: 6 Sep. 1817 Edward Butcher has, since the above date, departed this life and it appears that Susan Butcher, his widow, and children may now be conveyed to East Grinstead, who are to pay £9.12s 0d.]	Croydon, Sry
1817 Jul.18+	John PRICE and wife Maria. Confirmation. [Order made out to Rotherfield or any other parish]	Withyham
1817 Jul.18+	John STEVENS and wife Ann. Confirmation. [Order made out to Rotherfield or any other parish].	Withyham
1817 Dec.18*	John NEALE, wife Elizabeth and children James 2y 6m and Mary 3m.	Crowhurst, Sry
1818 Jan. 2*	Daniel FINCH, wife Elizabeth and child Elizabeth Rachel 18m.	Charlton, Ken
1820 Oct.14	Sarah WICKS, singlewoman, now pregnant with an illegitimate child.	Croydon, Sry
1820 Oct.17	Sarah WICKS, singlewoman, being with child, ordered to be removed from Croydon to East Grinstead. On appeal at Kingston Quarter Sessions, order respited.	Croydon, Sry

QUARTER SESSIONS REMOVALS TO EAST GRINSTEAD

		From
L 1644 May 3	Ann PAYNE under 7y, daughter of William PAYNE deceased was, in October last, removed by the wife of one CLARKSON to Chiddingly and left at Thomas GILBERT'S for two days, and then returned to Chalvington who are to give notice to East Grinstead, Chiddingly, Ringmer and Arlington, to attend a hearing.	-
L 1644 Jul.11	Ann PAYNE, daughter of William PAYNE, deceased.	Chalvington
L 1644 Oct. 3	Ann PAYNE, daughter of William PAYNE, deceased. Appeal by East Grinstead that they were not given timely notice of hearing and that Anne was only put out as a nurse child to them; respited.	Chalvington
L 1645 Jul.15	Ann PAYNE, daughter of William PAYNE, deceased; respited.	Chalvington
L 1666 Apr.26	Ann COOPER and child. To be sent by Poynings from House of Correction.	Poynings

L 1666 Jul.12	Ann COOPER, about last Christmas, had a bastard child born to her at Poynings, which child is to stay with its mother at East Grinstead until 7y, and then to be sent back to the place of its birth.	Poynings
L 1698 May 5	Edward SHARPE; confirmed.	Maresfield
L 1698 Oct. 6	John WATERS. As he has an estate in lands of his own and is not likely to become chargeable to Hartfield, he is to be allowed to settle there.	Hartfield
C 1701 Jul.14	William WOOLGAR, wife Elizabeth; discharged.	Rusper
B 1712 Oct.9	Jane CHAPMAN; discharged.	Hartfield
L 1713 Jan.15	Thomas HARWOOD; quashed.	Maresfield
L 1715 Jul.14	Mary WELLS, widow, and children Nicholas and Simeon; discharged	Hartfield
L 1717 Jan.17	John PUTLAND, wife Ann and children Lydia, Thomas and William; discharged.	Uckfield
L 1717 Jul.18	Richard ROSE, wife Sarah and children; quashed for want of form.	Maresfield
L 1717 Oct.10	Richard ROSE, wife Sarah and children Richard and Elizabeth; discharged.	Maresfield
S 1719 Jul.13	Ruben BORER; discharged.	Rusper
L 1726 Jan.13	Ann LASMER, spinster; discharged.	West Hoathly
L 1740 Jan.17	Sarah RUSSELL; confirmed.	Maresfield
L 1745 Jan.17	Thomas HUTCHINSON and wife Jane; discharged.	Hartfield
L 1755 Jul.17	John GEER and wife Mary; confirmed.	Arlington
L 1756 Jan.15	Jeremiah PATTENDEN and wife Hannah; confirmed.	Hailsham
L 1759 Apr.26	Anthony RUSSELL and wife Elizabeth; confirmed.	Hartfield
L 1763 Apr.14	Elizabeth CHAPMAN, widow, and son James 5y; confirmed.	Fletching
L 1766 Jan.16	Elizabeth ARIDGE; confirmed.	Fletching
L 1769 Jul.13	Thomas CLARK, wife Elizabeth and children Edward 7y, Mary 3y, Sarah 2y and an infant aged 1 week; confirmed.	Withyham
L 1774 Jan.13	Edward DICKER and wife Ann; respited.	Fletching
L 1774 Jul.14	Edward DICKER and wife Ann; confirmed.	Fletching
L 1779 Apr.15	Henry WALLER and wife Sarah; confirmed.	Hamsey
L 1781 Apr.26	James JENNER; confirmed.	Ringmer
L 1785 Apr. 7	John TOMSET, wife Jane and son John; confirmed.	Fletching
L 1785 Oct. 6	Charles GATTON and wife Elizabeth; respited.	Ringmer
L 1799 Jan.17	Samuel LUSTED, wife Susannah and children John 8y 6m, William 6y 6m, Rebecca 4y 6m and Mary 2y; confirmed.	Heathfield
L 1807 Apr.10	James MILES, wife Emy and children Ann 6y, Harriet 4y, William 3y and Henry 1y; confirmed.	Westmeston
P 1810 May 1	Mary BAKER, wife of Stephen BAKER, and children Caroline 7y and William 18m; respited.	Arundel

L 1810 May 4	Mary GATTON, wife of Charles GATTON, the younger; respited.	Ringmer
L 1810 May 4	Edward BATCHELOR, wife Mary and children Ann and Susannah; respited.	Withyham
H 1810 Jul.10	Mary BAKER, wife of Stephen BAKER and children Caroline 7y and William 18m; confirmed.	Arundel
L 1811 Apr.26	William STEPNEY, wife Catherine and daughter Catherine 1y; respited.	Laughton
L 1811 Jul.19	Mary GATTON, wife of Charles GATTON, the younger; recites appeal of 4 May 1810, which order is now confirmed.	Ringmer
L 1811 Jul.19	William STEPNEY, wife Catherine and daughter Catherine 1y; confirmed.	Laughton
L 1814 Oct.21	Penelope CAREY, singlewoman; respited.	Jevington
L 1815 Jan.13	Penelope CAREY, singlewoman; quashed.	Jevington
L 1815 Oct.20	Mary WOOD, singlewoman, respited;	Eastbourne
L 1815 Oct.20	Benjamin GROVE, wife Frances and children Robert, George, William and Obediah; respited.	East Hoathly
H 1816 Jul.16	Edward PENTECOST, wife Sarah and children William 14y, Edward 12y, Thomas 10y, Isaac 8y, Henry 6y and Martha 4y; confirmed.	Beeding
L 1817 Jan.17	Henry THORPE, wife Lucy and children Mary and Jane; confirmed.	Maresfield
L 1817 Apr.18	John OLLIVE, wife Elizabeth and children Ann, Eliza, William, Mary, Caley and Elizabeth; confirmed.	Mayfield
L 1818 Jul.17	William BROWN, wife Ansley and children Mary Annis 17y, Nancy Caroline 14y, Leah Ascuith 12y, Eliza Agnes 3y and Emma Harriet 1y; respited.	Bishopstone
L 1818 Oct.23	William BROWN, wife Ansley and children Mary Annis 17y, Nancy Caroline 14y, Leah Ascuith 12y, Eliza Agnes 3y and Emma Harriet 1y; confirmed.	Bishopstone
L 1819 Apr.23	George COATES, wife Mary and son George 11m; confirmed.	Alfriston
L 1822 Jan.18	William DAW and wife Mary; respited.	Buxted
L 1822 Apr.19	Mary HARTFIELD, singlewoman; respited.	Buxted
L 1822 Jul.19	Mary HARTFIELD, singlewoman; quashed.	Buxted
L 1823 Jan.17	Sophia SCOTT, singlewoman; confirmed.	Fletching
L 1823 Jul.18	James AVIS and wife Susan; quashed.	Hartfield
L 1824 Jul.15	Henry PARKER and children Harriet 11y, Sarah 8y, Caroline 6y, Susannah 4y, and Eliza Ann 1y 6m; respited.	Stanmer
L 1824 Oct.21	Henry PARKER and children Harriet 11y; Sarah 8y, Caroline 6y, Susannah 4y, and Eliza Ann 1y 6m; confirmed as to Henry and quashed as to the five children.	Stanmer

L 1828 Oct.16	Harriet FORD; respited.	Withyham
L 1832 Jan. 5	Luke TURNER, wife Martha and children George 8y and Martha 4m; respited.	Fletching

EAST GRINSTEAD BASTARDY EXAMINATIONS Par 348/34/1/1
* Indicates catalogued under Par 348/34/1/11.

1700 Jan. 1 Jane BURLEY said that she is with child and that Henry CHEESMAN of Horsham, blacksmith, is the father of the child.
Catalogued under Par 348/34/3/18

1701 Aug. 25 Anne RUSSELL said that, about Christmas two years ago, she was delivered of a male bastard child in East Grinstead and that John ERIDGE of Worth, husbandman, is the father of the child, and that he promised her marriage.

1719 Mar. 23 Mary WIMSETT, spinster of East Grinstead, said that she was delivered of a male bastard child on 28 February last, and that William PUTLAND of East Grinstead, cutler, is the father of the child. [Mark of M.W.]
Catalogued under Par 348/32/4/1.

1721 Sep. 21 Ann SAVAGE of East Grinstead, spinster, said that she is with child and that William HOLMES of East Grinstead, mason, is the father of her child. [Mark of A.S.]
Catalogued under Par 348/32/4/1

1723 Dec. 23 Anne MONKTON, the wife of John MONKTON, was examined touching marriage with the said John Monkton and the place of birth of a male infant born to Anne before her marriage. A.M. said that she was married to John Monkton at South Weald, Essex, on 15 October last, and that the male infant was born to her at the White Hart Inn in South Weald, out of wedlock, on 6 October last and before her marriage with John Monkton. [Signature of A.M.]
See Appendix 2

1725 Sep. 16 Ann SHARP, spinster, said that she is now with child and that Oliver GROVE, her fellow servant at her master Abraham HUGGET'S house, is the father of her child. [Mark of A.S.]

1732 Sep .12* Honor STYLEING said that, about February 1730, she was delivered of a female bastard child in Fittleworth, which child was baptised Diana in Fittleworth parish church and is now called Diana QUINELL, and that one Richard QUINEL, who is since dead, was the father of the child and that she, this examinant, has no place of legal settlement. [Mark of H.S.] [Endorsed: 14 September: Delivered Diana to Fittleworth.]

1732 Sep 12* Honor STYLEING said that, about 12 or 13 years ago, she was delivered of a male bastard child in Rogate, baptised Richard in Rogate parish church and now going by the name of Richard QUINEL. That the child has not gained a settlement since his birth, and Richard QUINEL, who is since dead, was the father of the child. [Mark of H.S.] [Endorsed: 15 September. Richard Quinel delivered to Rogate.]

1738 Nov 3* Winifred OVEL, spinster, said that she is quick with child and that John MARTIN, a servant to John COWDERY of Crowhurst, Surrey, is the father of her child. [Mark of W.O.]

1739 Jan. 1* Mary BUTLER said that, on 7 December last, she was delivered of a female bastard child and that Thomas GROVES, late of East Grinstead, is the father. [Mark of M.B.]

1741 May 12 Elizabeth CHART said that, on 21 April last, she was delivered of a male bastard child in East Grinstead, and that John FLETCHER of East Grinstead, yeoman, is the father of her child. [Mark of E.C.]

1754 Jun 24* Mary EDWARDS, singlewoman, said that she is now quick with child, and that Robert KNIGHT of East Grinstead, miller, is the father of her child. [Mark of M.E.]

1760 Oct 8 Hannah CHANTLER of East Grinstead, singlewoman, said that she is with child and that Lazarus ROFFEE of Worth, husbandman, is the father of her child. [Signature of H.C.]

1762 Oct 14 Sara EDWARDS, singlewoman, said that on, 15th September last, she was delivered of a male bastard child in the house of William WICKING, called the Blue Anchor, in Godstone, Surrey, which child is not yet baptised. S.E. further said that one BROOKS (an out-rider to a linen draper in the Strand, as she is informed), who came to the house of her master, William BROOKS at Forest Row, a little before Christmas last, is the father of her child. [Mark of S.E.]

1763 Mar 11 Elizabeth CHAPMAN was examined touching the place of the last legal settlement of the reputed father of a male bastard child born to her and of another with which she is now pregnant. E.C. said that she was lawfully married, in the parish church at Lindfield, to John CHAPMAN, who was legally settled in East Grinstead, by whom she has one child named James aged about five years, and that she has not seen her husband for these four years past, and has lately heard his mother say that he was dead. That, about two years ago, she was delivered of a male bastard child in Fletching, since baptised there by the name of George, who is now with her, and that William WESTON, now or late of Rotherfield, is the father of the said child. She further said that she is now quick with child and that Thomas TAYLOR of Fletching, husbandman, is the father of the child. [Mark of E.C.]

1767 Oct 20 Ann OSBORNE of Wilmington, singlewoman, said that, on 15 September last in Wilmington, she was delivered of a female bastard child and that Charles COLEMAN of Wilmington, shoemaker, is the father of the child. [Signature of Ann Osborn (sic)]

1806 Apr 22* Jane TINGLEY, widow, said that she is with child and that Simon WHITE, late of East Grinstead, hoop shaver, is the father of her child. [Mark of J.T.]

1807 Jan 16* Elizabeth RIDLEY of East Grinstead, singlewoman, said that she is with child and that Alexander PETERS of Horley, Surrey, blacksmith, is the father of her child. [Mark of E.R.]

1809 Dec 11* Ann PAYNE, singlewoman, now living in East Grinstead, being at this time pregnant of a child likely to be born a bastard, said that she is the daughter of John PAYNE now of High Easter, Essex, and that she has never, by servitude or otherwise, acquired a settlement in her own right separate from that of her father. [Mark of A.P.]

[1809 Dec 11*] John PAYNE of High Easter, Essex, regarding the settlement of his daughter, said that he is the father of the above Ann Payne and that he is residing in the parish of High Easter under the certificate of his father, William PAYNE from East Grinstead, and that he has never acquired a settlement in his own right, independant of the settlement of his father. [Mark of J.P.]
[*The examinations of Ann Payne and John Payne are written on one document.*]

1809 Dec 29* Susannah TERRY of East Grinstead, said that she is with child and that James CAMMEL of Leigh, Kent, farmer's servant, is the father of her child. [Mark of S.T.]

1811 Sep 28* Elizabeth MORLEY, singlewoman, said that she is with child and that John DIPLOCK, now of Hastings but lately living as an apprentice to Mr. HEAD, shopkeeper of East Grinstead, is the father of her child. [Signature of E.M.]

1814 Dec 7* Anne GORINGE of East Grinstead, singlewoman, said that she is with child and Thomas WEAIRE of East Grinstead, labourer, is the father of her child. [Mark of A.G.]

1815 Aug 23* Susannah JENNER of East Grinstead, singlewoman, said that she is now with child and that James STONEHAM, by trade an underdrainer and labourer, is the father of her child.

1815 Oct 19* Sarah EDWARDS of East Grinstead, singlewoman, said that she is with child and that Richard PAYNE, Corporal in the Sussex Regiment of Militia, is the father of her child. [Mark of S.E.]

1816 Feb 1* Elizabeth GATES of East Grinstead, singlewoman, said that she is with child and that Abraham AWCOCK of Edenbridge, Kent, is the father of her child. [Mark of E.G.]

1816 Feb. 2* Mary HEAVER of East Grinstead, singlewoman, said that she is with child and that William LYEWOOD of Worth is the father of her child.

EAST GRINSTEAD BASTARDY BONDS Par 348/34/4/1
* Indicates catalogued under Par 348/34/4/43

1690 Jul.17 William PARKER of East Grinstead, innholder, bound to the parish officers of East Grinstead in £50 in respect of Sarah MONCKE, singlewoman, who has of late been delivered of a male bastard child in that parish, and W.P. acknowledges himself to be the father. [Mark of W.P.]

1691 Jun. 1 Edmund HEATHFIELD of Reigate, Surrey, tanner, and John MORGEN of Worth, farmer, bound to the parish officers of East Grinstead in £40. E.H. has, for a consideration of £7.12s.6d, undertaken to educate and bring up one Richard RAMTON, a child of five years. [Signature of E.Hethfield (sic) and mark of J.M.]

1695 Sep.10* The parish officers of East Grinstead are bound to Withyham parish in respect of Anne STONSTREETE, a parishioner of Withyham, who was lately delivered of a bastard child in East Grinstead. The officers of East Grinstead shall pay to Withyham, from 7 August last for seven years, 30s 0d a year for the upbringing of the child, so allowing the child to stay with its mother in Withyham until the age of seven years.

1701 Jul.24 Henry CHEESMAN of Horsham, blacksmith, and John CHEESMAN of Worth, carpenter, bound to the parish officers of East Grinstead in £100 in respect of Jane BURLEY, singlewoman, who was delivered of a female bastard child and H.C. is adjudged to be the father. [Signatures of H.C. and J.C.]

1702 Dec.24 Edward CRUNDWELL, George WEEKS, yeoman, and Robert BENNETT, husbandman, of Withyham bound to the parish officers of East Grinstead in £100 in respect of Anne STONESTREET of Withyham, spinster, who has been delivered of a female bastard child in East Grinstead, R.B. acknowledging himself to be the father. [Signatures of E.C., George Wikes (sic), and the mark of R.B.]

1703 Apr. 6 Edward GIBSON of East Grinstead, farmer, William BORER of Fletching, farmer and Nicholas TOOTH of East Grinstead, farmer, bound to the parish officers of East Grinstead in £50 as E.G. is charged to be the reputed father of a bastard child born to one Jane BURLEY. [Marks of E.G., W.B. and N.T.]

1710 Aug.14 William BRASTED, merchant, James WESTON, tailor, both of East Grinstead, bound to the parish officers of that parish in £100 in respect of Frances BRASTED, singlewoman, who has lately been delivered of a female bastard child, baptised Elizabeth, and W.B. (father of the said Frances), and J.W. will indemnify East Grinstead parish. [Signatures of W.B. and J.W.]

1712 Feb. 5 Richard DAY of West Hoathly, carpenter, bound to the parish officers of East Grinstead in £100, in respect of Mary WILLINGTON, singlewoman, who has lately been delivered of a female bastard child, R.D. being the father of the child, and he agrees to pay 2s 0d a week maintenance. [Signature of R.D.]

1713 Jan.28 Edward PRICE of Hartfield, gent., and Sara LINDFEILD of East Grinstead, spinster, bound to the parish officers of that parish in £100, as E.P. is the reputed father of a bastard child, called Betty, lately born to Mary LINDFEILD, now the wife of the said E.P. [Signature of Edward Pryce (sic) and mark of S.L.]

1713 Sep. 5 Thomas TURNER of Petworth, blacksmith, and Robert SEERES of East Grinstead, innholder, bound to the parish officers of East Grinstead in £200, as a certain person is lately come into the parish who goes by the name of Katherine BICKLEY of Petworth, singlewoman, and is now at the house of the said R.S. in East Grinstead and was, very lately, delivered of a female bastard child called or known as Katt. [Signatures of T.T. and Robert Seare (sic)]

1715 Dec.12 William WINTON, senior, of Southover, Lewes, yeoman, bound to the parish officers of East Grinstead in £100 in respect of Mary BURGISS who has lately been delivered of a female bastard child in East Grinstead, and W.W. stands charged to be the reputed father. [Signature of W.W.]

1718 Aug.21 Anthony RUSSELL, farmer, and John RUSSELL senior, yeoman, both of East Grinstead, bound to the parish officers of that parish in £200 in respect of Elizabeth STEVENS, singlewoman, who has lately been delivered of a male bastard child, and A.R. is esteemed and looked upon to be the reputed father. [Signature of A.R. and Mark of J.R.]

1720 Mar.30 Thomas PAINE of Burwash, yeoman, bound to the parish officers of East Grinstead in £100 in respect of Thomas PAYNE, son of Henry PAYNE, late of East Grinstead, cooper, deceased, who is now an inhabitant of that parish. Thomas Paine, in consideration of £6.10s 0d, has agreed to indemnify the parish of East Grinstead until the said Thomas Payne shall attain the age of thirty years. [Signature of Thomas Payne (sic)]

1721[torn]29 Thomas WISEMAN of East Grinstead, bart., bound to the parish officers of that parish in £40 as there is a male bastard child born of the body of Ann HASLEDEN, of East Grinstead, widow, which may happen to be chargeable to the parish and the above bounden Sir Thomas Wiseman has agreed to give security. [Signature of T.W.]

1722 Mar. 6 William LAWRENCE, weaver, John TURNER, sawyer, Robert BURGESS junior, butcher, and Edward LATTER, weaver, all of Hartfield, bound to the parish officers of East Grinstead in £100 in respect of Margarett BUTCHER of East Grinstead, spinster, who is with child, to which child the above bounden Edward Latter stands charged to be the reputed father. [Mark of W.L. and signatures of J.T., R.B., and E.L.]

1724 Apr.22 William CAPELL, periwig maker and Andrew CAPELL, cheesemonger, both of Croydon, Surrey, bound to the parish officers of East Grinstead in £100 in respect of Mary PARSONS, singlewoman, who has lately been delivered of a male bastard child in East Grinstead, baptised Capell, and M.P. has declared that W.C. is the father of the child. [Signatures of W. Capel and A. Capel (sic)]

1724 Jun.17 Thomas DENTON and William DENTON both of East Grinstead, farmers, bound to the officers of that parish in £50 in respect of Elizabeth SMITH, singlewoman, who is with child by the said W.D., as appears by her examination and upon the open confession of W.D., who has agreed to marry Elizabeth Smith as soon as maybe after the banns of matrimony can be published in the parish church. [Signature of T.D. and Mark of W.D]

1724 Dec.18 Charles LUXFORD of East Grinstead, gent., bound to the parish officers of East Grinstead in £100 in respect of Anne HASLEDEN, widow, who is with child and C.L., for divers good causes and considerations, has agreed to indemnify East Grinstead parish. [Signature of C.L]

1725 Jul.10 James BAKER, innholder, and Samuel BOKKOM, farmer, both of Godstone, Surrey, bound to the parish officers of East Grinstead in £100 in respect of Margaret BUTCHER, singlewoman, who has been lately delivered of a male bastard child, called John, in East Grinstead and has declared that J.B. is the father of the child. [Signature of J.B. and Mark of S.B.]

1727 Apr. 1 Anthony ELLIS of East Grinstead, farmer, bound to the parish officers of East Grinstead in £100 in respect of Anne WICKERSHAM of Lingfield, Surrey, (daughter of Anne, now wife of above A.E.), who is with child, to which child James LINDFEILD of Lingfield stands charged to be the reputed father. Whereas A.W. is lately come from Lingfield, where she was last legally settled and, in case she shall be delivered of the child in East Grinstead, Anthony Ellis agrees to indemnify East Grinstead parish. [Signature of Anthony Elliass (sic)]

1728 Jan.29 Thomas QUENNELL of Crowhurst, Surrey, farmer, Edward WHITE of Godstone, Surrey, farmer, and Jane QUENNELL of Lingfield, Surrey, spinster, bound to the parish officers of East Grinstead in £100 in respect of Anne

PECKHAM, spinster, who is with child, of which child T.Q. stands charged to be the reputed father. [Marks of T.Q., E.W. and J.Q.]

1728 Jul.11 James LINDFEILD junior of Lingfield, Surrey, gent., and Henry ISTED of Horne, Surrey, yeoman, bound to the parish officers of East Grinstead in £100, agree to pay 2s 0d a week towards the maintenance of Elizabeth, a female bastard child lately born to Anne, now the wife of Thomas WEST of Tenterden, Kent, husbandman, (late Anne WICKERSHAM), in persuance of an order made 3 June last. [Signatures of J.F. junior and H.I.]

1729 Nov.14 John BAYLEY, yeoman, Thomas BAYLEY, yeoman, and Thomas Wood junior, blacksmith, all of East Grinstead, bound to the parish officers of East Grinstead in £30 in respect of Edee CARD, singlewoman, who was lately delivered of a male bastard child and who has declared that J.B. is the father of the child. J.B. summoned to appear at the next monthly meeting of the parish officers to enter into further security for the maintenance of the child. [Signatures of John Bally (sic) and T.W. and Mark of T.B.]

1730 Feb.21* John PAYNE of East Grinstead, carpenter, bound to the parish officers of East Grinstead in £60 in respect of Mary SMITH, singlewoman, who is now big with child. [Signature of J.P.]

1733 Mar.15* Thomas WICKERSHAM, yeoman, and Robert GOODWIN, tailor, both of East Grinstead, bound to the parish officers of East Grinstead in £50 in respect of Ann WISDOM, singlewoman, who is with child. [Marks of T.W. and R.G.]

1735 Dec.23* John SAWYER, mercer, and Charles LUXFORD, gent., both of East Grinstead, bound to the parish officers of East Grinstead in £100 in respect of Elizabeth WHEELER, who has lately been delivered of a female bastard child in East Grinstead. [Signatures of J.S. & C.L.]

1740 Mar.10* Daniell PIPER the younger of Addington, Surrey, husbandman, Daniell PIPER the elder of Croydon, Surrey, blacksmith, and Samuel FLOYD of Addington, yeoman, bound to the parish officers of East Grinstead in £60 in respect of Mary BRYANT of Addington, singlewoman, who has lately been delivered of a male bastard child in East Grinstead, baptised Daniell, D.P., the younger, being the father. [Mark of D.P. the younger and signatures of D.P. and S.F.]

1744 Apr. 4 John PIPER of Withyham, labourer, and John RASTRIGG of Cuckfield, husbandman, bound to the parish officers of East Grinstead in £100 in respect of Mary TULLEY, spinster, who has lately been delivered of a male child, J.P. acknowledging himself to be the father. [Marks of J.P. and J.R.]

1746 Nov. 4 John WHEATLEY, warrener, and Edward WHEATLEY, weaver, both of Maresfield, bound to the parish officers of East Grinstead in £100 in respect of Ann BURTENSHAW, singlewoman, who has declared herself to be with child and that J.W. is the father, which he acknowledges himself so to be. [Signatures of John and Edward Wheatly (sic)]

1749 Jul. 6 George KNIGHT, warrener, Thomas MILLS, gent., and Abraham OSBORNE, miller, all of Withyham bound to the parish officers of East Grinstead in £40 in respect of Ruth WESTON, singlewoman, who has been lately delivered of a male bastard child in East Grinstead. G.K. stands charged to be the reputed father, and is to pay 18d a week maintenance. [Mark of G.K. and signatures of T.M. and A.O.].

1751 Sep. 5* Edward JEFFERY, husbandman, and John BALLARD, husbandman, both of East Grinstead, bound to the parish officers of that parish in £50 in respect of Mary DEVALL, daughter of Richard DEVALL of East Grinstead, collier, who has lately been delivered of a female bastard child, of which child E.J. acknowledges himself to be the father. [Signature of Edward Jeffrey (sic) and mark of J.B.]

1752 Jan.21* Jeremiah PATTENDEN of East Grinstead, husbandman, and Thomas PATTENDEN of West Hoathly, yeoman, bound to the parish officers of East Grinstead in £50 in respect of a male bastard child born in East Grinstead on 2 September last to Sara BATCHELOR, singlewoman. J.P. to indemnify the parish in accordance with order dated 10 January 1752. [Signatures of J.P. and T.P.]

1752 Oct.16* William CHATFIELD of Rotherfield, tanner, and John CHATFIELD of Mayfield, butcher, bound to the parish officers of East Grinstead in £40 in respect of Anne COOKE, singlewoman, who has been lately delivered of a male bastard child in East Grinstead, baptised William, of which child W.C. stands charged to be the reputed father. [Signatures of W.C. and J.C.]

1753 Mar. 9* Edward HENTY of East Grinstead, husbandman, bound to the parish officers of that parish in £50 in respect of Mary EDWARDS who has been lately delivered of a male bastard child in East Grinstead, baptised Richard, and M.E has declared that E.H. is the father of the child. [Mark of E.H.]

1756 Dec.23* William BLEACH of Maresfield, pedlar, and William BLEACH, son of the aforesaid William Bleach are bound to the parish officers of East Grinstead in £100 in respect of Mary EDWARDS, singlewoman, who has lately been delivered of a male bastard child in East Grinstead, baptised John Bleach, of which child, William Bleach the son, stands charged to be the reputed father. [Mark of W.B. and signature of W.B.]

1757 Jan.25* John PAYNE, yeoman, and William BOOKER, wheelwright, both of East Grinstead, bound to the parish officers of that parish in £100 in respect of Elizabeth WHEATLEY, singlewoman, who has declared that she is now with child and that J.P. is the father of her child. [Signatures of J.P. and W.B.]

1757 Nov.14* Thomas MILLS and Thomas MILLS the younger, both of Limpsfield, Surrey, yeomen, bound to the parish officers of East Grinstead in £100 in respect of Anne CHANDLER, singlewoman, who has declared that she is now with child and that T.M., the younger, is the father of her child. [Signature of T.M. and mark of T.M.]

1758 Nov.28* William SOANE, miller, and John SIMMONS, bricklayer, both of East Grinstead bound to the parish officers of that parish in £100 in respect of Elizabeth MICHELL, singlewoman, who has declared that she is with child, and that W.S. is the father of her child. [Signatures of W.S. and J.S.]

1758 Dec.19* Nicholas FRANCES the younger of East Grinstead, collier, and John FRANCES of Godstone, Surrey, husbandman, bound to the parish officers of East Grinstead in £20 in respect of Elizabeth CARPENTER'S male bastard child, born in East Grinstead on or about 4 October last, she being a singlewoman. [Signature of N.F. and mark of J.F.]

1759 May 30* John LULHAM, maltster, William FARMER, fellmonger, and Thomas WOOD, fellmonger, all of East Grinstead, bound to the parish officers of that parish in £50 in respect of Elizabeth BATCHELOR, singlewoman, who has been lately delivered of a male bastard child in East Grinstead, baptised John, of which child J.L. stands charged to be the reputed father. [Signatures of J.L., W.F. and T.W.]

1759 Aug. 3* William BISH the younger of Worth, coachman, and William BISH the elder of Burstow, Surrey, blacksmith, bound to the parish officers of East Grinstead in £50 in respect of Elizabeth SANDERS, singlewoman, now big with child, who has declared that W.B., the younger, is the father of her child. [Signature of William Bysh (sic) and mark of W.B.]

1760 Jan. 9 Isaac JENNER and Edward JENNER both of Withyham, husbandmen, bound to the parish officers of East Grinstead in £50 in respect of Mary BAKER, singlewoman, who has declared that she is now with child and that I.J. is the father. [Marks of I.J. and E.J.]

1760 Jul. 8 Robert DANE of East Grinstead, servant, bound to parish officers of that parish in £50 in respect of Sara JARRETT, singlewoman, who was delivered of a male bastard child in East Grinstead on or about 21 May last, and R.D. agrees to abide by an order concerning maintenance of the child. [Signature of R.D.]

1760 Jul.31 William WATERS of East Grinstead, husbandman, bound to the parish officers of that parish in £50 in respect of Hannah BROWNE, singlewoman, who was delivered of a male bastard child in East Grinstead on or about 4 August last and W.W. agrees to abide by an order concerning the maintenance of the child. [Signature of William Wattlers (sic)]

1760 Sep.27 John JESSOP and Robert JESSOP both of East Grinstead, husbandmen, bound to the parish officers of East Grinstead in £50 in respect of Elizabeth TOURL, singlewoman, who has declared that she is now with child, and that J.J. is the father of her child. [Mark of J.J. and signature of R.J.]

1761 Jan. 1 William BEECH of Hartfield, husbandman, son of William BEECH of Isfield, yeoman, and the said William BEECH the father, bound to the parish officers of East Grinstead in £100 in respect of Jane SHOOEBRIDGE, singlewoman, who has declared that she is now with child, and that W.B. the son, is the father of her child. [Marks of W.B. junior and W.B.]

1761 Jan. 3 James HALLAWAY of Catsfield, yeoman, bound to the parish officers of East Grinstead in £50 in respect of Mary PECKHAM, singlewoman, who was, in December last, delivered of a male bastard child in East Grinstead, baptised James. [Signature of J.H.]

1761 Nov.20 Christopher Arthur MIDDLETON and John MIDDLETON both of East Grinstead, peruke makers, bound to the parish officers of that parish in £50 in respect of Mary MARTIN, singlewoman, who has lately been delivered of a male bastard child in East Grinstead, baptised Christopher Middleton, of which child J.M. stands charged to be the reputed father. [Signatures of C.A.M. and J.M.]

1762 Jul. 6 John WEST of [?Ayriff], near Woolwich, Kent, husbandman, Thomas WEST of East Grinstead, husbandman, and John DISMORE of Plumstreet, [?Plumstead] near Woolwich, ship carpenter, bound to the parish officers of East Grinstead in £50 in respect of Elizabeth HUGGETT who was delivered of a male bastard child on 10 May last, in East Grinstead, and J.W. agrees to abide by an order, dated 9 June last, concerning the maintenance of the child. [Signatures of J.W. and T.W.]

1762 Aug.27. James GORRENGE of East Grinstead, husbandman, bound to the parish officers of East Grinstead in £50 in respect of Hannah MITCHELL, singlewoman, who has declared that she is now with child and that J.G.is the father. [Mark of J.G.]

1763 Apr.21 Joseph CHEESMAN of East Grinstead, husbandman, bound to the parish officers of East Grinstead in £50 in respect of Sarah PEACY, widow, who has declared that she is now with child and that J.C. is the reputed father. [Mark of J.C.]

1765 May 25 Stephen SAWYER of East Grinstead, mercer, bound to the parish officers of East Grinstead in £50 in respect of Susannah UNDERHILL, singlewoman, who has been lately delivered of a male bastard child in East Grinstead, baptised Abraham, of which child S.S. is charged to be the reputed father. [Signature of S.S.]

1765 Oct. 7 John FINCH of East Grinstead, blacksmith, bound to the parish officers of East Grinstead in £100 in respect of Sarah LOCKYER, singlewoman, who has been lately delivered of a female bastard child in East Grinstead, baptised Jane, of which child J.F. stands charged to be the reputed father. [Signature of J.F.]

1766 Feb. 8 John EDWARDS, butcher, and William MASON, salesman, both of East Grinstead, bound to the parish officers of East Grinstead in £50 in respect of Hannah EDWARDS, singlewoman, who has been lately delivered of a female bastard child, baptised Mary, and has charged Daniel DOUBELL of East Grinstead, a minor, to be the father, which he acknowledges. [Mark of J.E. and signature of W.M.]

1771 Aug.21* John BAKER of Sevenoaks, Kent, watchmaker, bound to the parish officers of East Grinstead in £100 in respect of Rebecca FRY, singlewoman, who is with child, J.B. acknowledging that he is the father. [Signature of J.B.]

1772 Oct. 3* Richard DODD of Tandridge, Surrey, yeoman, and John DODD of Croydon Surrey, yeoman, bound to the parish officers of East Grinstead in £100 in respect of Elizabeth LULHAM, widow, who has declared that she was lately delivered of a male bastard child, and that John Dodd is the father. J.D. ordered to pay 1s 6d a week from 29 May last and 40s 0d for lying-in costs. [Mark of R.D. and signature of J.D.]

1774 Jan. 1* John MARDEN junior of East Grinstead, husbandman, John MARDEN senior of Penshurst, Kent, husbandman, and William KEMBER of East Grinstead, farmer, bound to the parish officers of East Grinstead in £100 in respect of Mary WICKING, singlewoman, who has been lately delivered of a male bastard child in East Grinstead, of which child J.M. is the reputed father. [Marks of J.M. junior, J.M. senior and W.K.] [Endorsed: Agreed by parish that John Marden is to pay 1s 3d a week only.]

1774 Mar.11* Thomas HAYWARD of Etchingham, gent., bound to the parish officers of East Grinstead in £100 in respect of Sarah STEPHENS, who is with child, and T.H. acknowledges that he is the father of her child. [Signature of T.H.]

1775 Feb. 7* Thomas FARMER of East Grinstead, yeoman, bound to the parish officers of that parish in £100 in respect of Sarah WALLS, who was lately delivered of a female bastard child named Sarah, T.F. acknowledging himself to be the father. [Signature of T.F.]

1778 Jun.27* Robert JESSOP, the younger, of East Grinstead, husbandman, bound to the parish officers of that parish in £100 in respect of Mary FINCH who was lately delivered of a male bastard child named William, and R.J. acknowledges himself to be the father. [Signature of R.J.]

1778 Sep.30* George EEDE of Leigh, Surrey and John CAPLIN of Worth, bound to the parish officers of East Grinstead in £100 in respect of Ann HARRIS of East Grinstead who is with child, and G.E. acknowledges that he is the father of her child. [Mark of G.E. and signature of J.C.]

1806 Nov.24 William FAULKNER and William FAULKNER, the younger, both of Lingfield, Surrey, yeomen, bound to the parish officers of East Grinstead in £50 in respect of Mary BRIDGLAND, singlewoman, who has declared that, on 6 October last, she was delivered of a female bastard child in East Grinstead and that W.F., the younger, is the father. [Marks of W.F. senior and junior.]

1806 Nov.26* William JUPP of Lingfield, Surrey, blacksmith, and William WREN of the same place, blacksmith, bound to the parish officers of East Grinstead in £50 in respect of Emila HODGES, singlewoman, who has declared that, on 5 October last, she was delivered of a male bastard child in East Grinstead and that W.J. is the father. [Signatures of W.J. and W.W.]

1812 Sep.28 Henry HISTED the younger of Forest Row, butcher, bound to the parish officers of East Grinstead in £50 in respect of Jane WELLER of Forest Row, singlewoman, who was, on 21 February last, delivered of a male bastard child at East Grinstead, baptised Henry, of which child H.H. acknowledges himself to be the father and agrees to pay 3s 0d a week towards maintenance of the child. [Signature of H.H.]

1816 Mar.12* Abraham AWCOCK promises to pay to the parish officers of East Grinstead £15 for a male bastard child sworn to him by Elis[abeth] GATES, the first payment of £5 on Michaelmas day 1816, the second payment of £5 on Ladyday 1817, and the third payment of £5 at Michaelmas 1817. [Mark of A.A.] [Endorsed: Abraham Awcock shall have all the money that has not been expended in the maintenance of the said child if he marries the girl before he gains a settlement in the said parish of East Grinstead.]

1824 Jan.21 Thomas PALEY of Reigate, Surrey, maltster bound, to the parish officers of East Grinstead in £100 in respect of Mary BAKER, singlewoman, who was, on 31 July last, at the house of Hugh SIMMONS in East Grinstead, delivered of a female bastard child and who has declared that T.P. is the father of her child. [Signature of T.P.]

EAST GRINSTEAD BASTARDY ORDERS Par 348/34/3/1
* Indicates catalogued under Par 348/34/3/18
+ Indicates catalogued under Par 348/32/3/1

1701 Jun. 13* Jane BURLEY of East Grinstead, singlewoman, has declared that Henry CHEESMAN of Horsham, blacksmith, is the father of a female bastard child lately born to her in East Grinstead. H.C. to pay, within six days next after notice of this order, 40s 0d maintenance and 18d a week; the mother to pay 6d a week.

1701 Jul. 17 Jane BURLEY, singlewoman. On appeal of Henry CHEESMAN from an order adjudging him to be the father of a female bastard child born to above Jane Burly, order confirmed.

1703 Oct. 7+ Ann RUSSELL was delivered of a male bastard child in East Grinstead and, by an order dated 8 September 1703, John ERRIDGE of Worth is adjudged to be the father. Confirmation.

1711 Jul. 26 Mary WILLINGTON of East Grinstead, singlewoman, has declared that Richard DAY is the father of a female bastard child lately born to her in East Grinstead. R.D. to pay 2s 0d a week; the mother to pay 6d a week.

1741 Jul. 6 Elizabeth CHART, singlewoman, has declared that John FLETCHER of East Grinstead, yeoman, is the father of a male bastard child born to her on 21 April last, in East Grinstead, baptised John on the 26th of the same month. J.F. to pay 1s 6d a week and £2.5s 0d, being money expended, horse hire, journeys and other charges in relation to the child; the mother to pay 6d a week.

1745 Oct. 11 Ruth WESTON, singlewoman, has declared that William BARDEN of East Grinstead, blacksmith, is the father of a male bastard child born to her on or about 11 August last, in East Grinstead. W.B. to pay £4.5s 7d charges and 1s 6d a week; the mother to pay 6d a week.

1752 Jan. 10* Sara BATCHELOR has declared that Jeremiah PATTENDEN of East Grinstead, servant, is the father of a male bastard child born to her on 2 September last in East Grinstead. J.P. to pay 40s 0d charges and 18d a week; the mother to pay 6d a week.

1752 Jul. 6* Elizabeth BUTCHER, singlewoman, has declared that Richard GILES, of East Grinstead, husbandman, is the father of a female bastard child born to her on 17 May last in East Grinstead. R.G. to pay 18d [a week]; the mother to pay 6d [a week.] [Document torn]

1752 Oct. 4* Anne COOKE has declared that William CHATFIELD of Rotherfield, tanner, is the father of a male bastard child born to her on 29 August last in East Grinstead. W.C. to pay 29s 0d costs and 18d a week; the mother to pay 6d a week.

1758 Dec. 19* Elizabeth CARPENTER, singlewoman, has declared that Nicholas FRANCES, the younger, collier, is the father of a male bastard child born to her on 4 October last in East Grinstead. N.F. to pay 18d a week; the mother to pay 6d a week.

1769 Jun. 10 Ann MITCHELL, singlewoman, has declared that Richard HOUNSOME of East Grinstead, is the father of a female bastard child born to her on 26 February last, at the house of James LYNN in East Grinstead. R.H. to pay £2.16s 6d towards the cost of lying-in and 18d a week; the mother to pay 6d a week.

1788 Feb. 18 Deborah EASTWOOD, singlewoman, has declared that Thomas BROMLEY of East Grinstead, labourer, is the father of a female bastard child born to her on 24 October last, at the house of Michael BROMLEY in East Grinstead. T.B. to pay 40s 0d towards the cost of lying-in and 2s 0d a week; the mother to pay 6d a week.

1788 Apr. 4 Maria LINDLEY, singlewoman, has declared that Thomas ALCOCK of East Grinstead, butcher, is the father of a male bastard child born to her on 1 January last, in East Grinstead. T.A. to pay £4.8s 0d towards the cost of lying-in and 2s 0d a week; the mother to pay 6d a week.

1788 Jun. 2 Jane SHOOSMITH, singlewoman, has declared that Thomas ATHERFOLD, late of Clayton, miller, is the father of a male bastard child born to her on 2 November 1779 in East Grinstead. T.A. to pay £2.16s 0d towards the cost of lying-in and 1s 6d a week; the mother to pay 6d a week.

1788 Aug. - Sarah GIBB, singlewoman, has declared that George WOOD, late of East Grinstead, labourer, is the father of a male bastard child born to her on 16 April last, in East Grinstead. G.W. to pay £3.12s.0d towards the cost of lying-in and 2s 0d a week; the mother to pay 6d a week.

1803 May 16* Sarah HOLMES was, on Saturday 5 December 1801, at the poorhouse, Hamsey, delivered of a female bastard child and, about one year afterwards, she went into and has ever since resided in East Grinstead (which is the place of her last legal settlement) with the child as a nurse child, and been relieved by that parish. The parish officers of Hamsey have been ordered to pay 2s 0d a week maintenance for the child.

1806 Sep. 22* Hannah PAYNE, singlewoman, has declared that Joseph TRAINFIELD, late of East Grinstead, labourer, is the father of a male bastard child born to her on 29 March 1805, in East Grinstead. J.T. to pay £8.18s 0d towards the cost of lying-in and 2s 0d a week; the mother to pay 6d a week.

1811 Dec. 23* Harriet PARKER, singlewoman, has declared that William HEATH of Withyham, yeoman, is the father of a male bastard child born to her on 8

November last in East Grinstead. W.H. to pay £5.7s 0d towards the cost of lying-in and 3s 0d weekly; the mother to pay 6d a week.

1812 Sep. 14 Elizabeth TESTER, singlewoman, has declared that Stephen ROBERTS of Hailsham, labourer, is the father of a female bastard child born to her on 15 June last in East Grinstead. S.R. to pay £3.19s 0d towards the cost of lying-in and 3s 0d a week; the mother to pay 6d a week.

1812 Sep. 14 Elizabeth ASHDOWN, singlewoman, has declared that Mathias ANDERSON of Hartfield, labourer, is the father of a female bastard child born to her on 18 May last in East Grinstead. M.A. to pay £4.11s 0d towards the cost of lying-in and 3s 0d a week; the mother to pay 6d a week.

1814 Nov. 28 Mary HISTED, singlewoman, has declared that William PAYNE of East Grinstead, labourer, is the father of a male bastard child born to her on 8 October last in East Grinstead. W.P. to pay £3.16s 6d towards the cost of lying-in and 2s 6d a week; the mother to pay 6d a week.

EAST GRINSTEAD WARRANTS Par 348/29/1

+ Indicates catalogued under Par 348/29/2
# Indicates catalogued under Par 348/34/1/1
* Indicates catalogued under Par 348/34/2/1

1692 Mar. 5 William PEINE, George UNDERHILL, John CHANNELL, George STACEY and Henry CHEALE, who are lately come into the parish to get their living and are likely to become chargeable, are to be apprehended and taken before a Justice to be examined as to their settlements.
Catalogued under Par 348/32/4/55

1696 Mar. 5 William WALLICE of East Grinstead, turner, is lately run away, leaving his family upon the parish; and he is to be apprehended.
Catalogued under Par 348/32/5/1

1697 Mar. 5 John TURNER of East Grinstead, who has run away out of the parish leaving his family, is to be apprehended.
Catalogued under Par 348/32/2/1

1701 Sep. 9 John BRINCKHURST to be apprehended in order to be examined regarding his settlement.
Catalogued under Par 348/32/4/1

1710 Jun.12 Rebecca CHANTLER, being in February last legally settled in St. Olave, Southwark, Surrey, did, afterwards, come into East Grinstead and was removed back to St. Olave. As she has now returned to East Grinstead, in contempt of the law, she is to be apprehended and conveyed to the House of Correction at Lewes

and delivered to the keeper thereof, who is to receive her but not to correct or punish her until further ordered.
Catalogued under Par 348/34/3/1

1713 Aug.10* Elizabeth MIRGEN of East Grinstead, singlewoman, has declared that Henry PARKER of East Grinstead, husbandman, is the father of the child she now goes with; and he is to be apprehended.

1719 Feb. 2 Mary WIMSET of East Grinstead to appear before the Court to answer to what shall be laid to her charge by the overseers.
Catalogued under Par 348/32/4/1

1729 Dec. 1 John FARMER, John ORGLES, - JACKSON, John COMBER, John UNDAY, William NICHOLAS and Thomas NUNHAM to be apprehended and brought before the Justices to answer regarding their settlements.
Catalogued under Par 348/32/4/1

1736 May 4 Fortune JENNER of East Grinstead, singlewoman, has declared that she was, on 28 March last, delivered of a male bastard child in East Grinstead and that John COMBER, late of Lingfield, Surrey, is the father of her child; and he is to be apprehended.

1738 Nov. 23+ Catherine GROVE to be apprehended to answer things as she shall be objected against by the parish officers.

1738 Dec. 1+ Mary BUTLER to be apprehended to answer things as shall be objected against her by the parish officers.

1739 Jan. 16 Mary BUTLER of Hartfield has declared that she was delivered, on 7 December last, of a female bastard child in East Grinstead and that Thomas GROVES, late of East Grinstead, is the father of her child; and he is to be apprehended.

1741 May 12# Elizabeth CHART of East Grinstead, singlewoman, has declared that, on 21 April last, she was delivered of a male bastard child in East Grinstead, the father being John FLETCHER of East Grinstead, yeoman; and he is to be apprehended.

1752 Oct. 4 Ann COOKE of East Grinstead, singlewoman, has declared that, on 29 August last, she was delivered of a male bastard child, named William, in East Grinstead, and that William CHATFEILD of Rotherfield, tanner, is the father of her child; and he is to be apprehended.

1753 Feb. 24 Elizabeth BROWN of East Grinstead, singlewoman, has declared that she was, on 8 January last, delivered of a bastard child in East Grinstead, named Orson, and that John KEMP of Bletchingley, Surrey, is the father; and he is to be apprehended.

1753 Feb. 28 Mary EDWARDS of East Grinstead, singlewoman, has declared that on 12 January last she was delivered of a bastard child named Richard and that Edward HENTY of East Grinstead is the father; and he is to be apprehended.

1761 May 27# Anne POST, singlewoman, has declared that she was delivered of a male bastard child, named Edward, on 19 February last, in East Grinstead, and that William VIRGOE late of East Grinstead, husbandman is the father of her child; and he is to be apprehended.

1774 Mar. 23 Mary MARTIN of East Grinstead, singlewoman, has declared herself to be with child and that Thomas SIMMONS, son of William SIMMONS, of East Grinstead, gardener, is the father of her child; and he is to be apprehended.

1774 Apr. 11 Ann SIMMONS of East Grinstead, singlewoman, has declared that, sometime in the month of May last, at Forest Row, she was delivered of a male bastard child and that David CONNER of Midhurst, clockmaker, is the father of her child; and he is to be apprehended.

1774 Jun. 6+ John CARMAN of East Grinstead, husbandman, to be apprehended for running away and leaving his wife and family chargeable to the parish.

1775 Mar. 13* Lydia BURR of East Grinstead, singlewoman, has declared that she is with child and that Henry TODMAN of East Grinstead, husbandman, is the father; and he is to be apprehended.

1786 Aug. 14* Sarah GIBB of East Grinstead, singlewoman, has declared that she was delivered of a female bastard child on 21 July last at Dean Farm House, East Grinstead, and that George WOOD, late servant to David JENNER of East Grinstead, miller, is the father; and G.W.is to be apprehended.

1787 Aug. 20* Sarah BOTTING of East Grinstead, singlewoman, has declared that she is with child and that Joseph SEALY, now or late of Old Bond Street, London, servant, is the father; and he is to be apprehended.

1787 Sep. 17 Robert PAYNE and wife Lucy PAYNE have come to inhabit the parish of East Grinstead and are likely to become chargeable, and James PAYNE, the father of the said R.P. is to be brought before a Justice to be examined concerning the place of the last legal settlement of Robert Payne and wife Lucy.
Catalogued under Par 348/32/4/1

1788 Feb. 8* Hanah TOOTH of East Grinstead, singlewoman, has declared that she is with child and that Richard TURL is the father; and he is to be apprehended.

1788 Feb. 8* Mary CARPENTER of East Grinstead, who was, some time past, delivered of a bastard child likely to become chargeable to East Grinstead is to be apprehended.

1788 Jul. 3* Mary TODMAN and Lucy WOOD, late of East Grinstead, who were lately delivered of bastard children likely to become chargeable, are to be apprehended.

1788 Oct.28* Ann JORDAN of East Grinstead, singlewoman, has declared that she is with child and that Robert WAKEFORD, now living with William POBGEE of East Grinstead, currier, is the father; and R.W. is to be apprehended.

1788 Dec. 1* George WOOD of East Grinstead, labourer, stands charged with the payment of a certain weekly sum for the female bastard child born to Sarah GIBB, singlewoman, he being the father of the child. As G.W. has not paid anything and £5.6s 0d is now due, he is to be apprehended.

1789 Jan.12* Sarah ALLCOCK of East Grinstead, singlewoman, has declared that she was delivered of a male bastard child on Sunday 14 December last in East Grinstead and that John POTTER of East Grinstead is the father; and he is to be apprehended.

1789 Jan.12 William KING of East Grinstead, labourer, has lately run away from the parish and left his family chargeable thereto, he being of sufficient ability to maintain them therein; and he is to be apprehended.
Catalogued under Par 348/32/5/1

1789 Feb. 3* Sarah WALLES of East Grinstead, singlewoman, has declared that, six weeks ago, she was delivered of a female bastard child at East Grinstead and that Benjamin HUGGETT is the father. S.W.is to be brought before the Justices at the house of Jethrow TURNER at the Sheffield Arms, Fletching, on 2 March, and notice is to be given to B.H. so that he may also attend.

1789 Mar. 2* Mary CARPENTER of East Grinstead, singlewoman, has declared that on 18 June 1782 she was delivered of a female bastard child in East Grinstead and she has also declared that, on 27 June 1787, she was delivered of a male bastard child in East Grinstead, and that William CURTIS is the father of these children. M.C. to appear before the Justices at Jethro TURNER'S house, bearing the sign of Sheffield Arms, Fletching, on 20 April, and notice is to be given to W.C. so that he may also attend. [Two documents of same date, one for each child]

1789 Jun. 8 William MOON of East Grinstead, cordwainer, has neglected and refused to maintain his family, he being of sufficient ability so to do, and he is to be apprehended.
Catalogued under Par 348/32/5/1

1789 Aug.25* Ann HEASMAN of East Grinstead, singlewoman, who was delivered of a female bastard child on 15 July last at the workhouse, East Grinstead, has declared that William PARSONS, late servant to Mr. MOOR of the Washways, Lambeth, Surrey, nurseryman, is the father; and W.P. is to be apprehended.

1789 Oct.16* Ann BROOKER of East Grinstead, singlewoman, has declared that she was delivered of a female bastard child on 25 August last, at the workhouse, East Grinstead, and that James DOWNWARD of Rotherfield, glazier, is the father. A.B. to be brought before the Justices at Jethro TURNER'S house at the Sheffield Arms, Fletching on 28 December, and notice is to be given to James Downard that he may also attend.

1803 Feb. 21 Sarah HOLMES, wife of Alexander HOLMES of East Grinstead, yeoman, was, on Saturday 5 December 1801, delivered of a bastard child at Hamsey and, about Thursday last, she came to East Grinstead (the place of her last legal settlement) with the child as a nurse child, and received relief. The parish offiers of Hamsey to appear before the Justices on Monday 4 April at the Swan, Forest Row, to say why they should not support the child.
Catalogued under Par 348/34/3/1

1803 Nov. 28 Jane BUCKLAND, singlewoman, has declared that on, 20 October last, she was delivered of a female bastard child at the poorhouse in East Grinstead and that William SKINNER, late of East Grinstead, blacksmith, is the father, and he is to appear before the Justices at the Swan, Forest Row, on Monday 26 December.

1804 Jun. 6 Ann SETFORD of East Grinstead, singlewoman, has declared that she is with child and that George GATES of East Grinstead, labourer, is the father of the child. [Endorsed: Separate document dated 7 June 1804. As George Gates has refused to give security to indemnify the parish and refused to enter into a recognizance with sufficient surety upon condition he appears at the next general quarter sessions for this county, he is to be conveyed to the House of Correction at Lewes]

1805 Jan.16 Elizabeth SETFORD of East Grinstead, singlewoman, has declared herself to be with child and that George WATSON of West Hoathly, farmer's servant, is the father; and he is to be apprehended.

1805 Apr. 8 Alice WILDISH of East Grinstead, singlewoman, has declared that, on 24 February last, she was delivered of a female bastard child and that John MITCHELLBORNE is the father; and he is to be apprehended. [Endorsed: John Mitchellborne senior and John Mitchellborne junior to pay £25 to the parish by three instalments - £8.10s 0d at Michaelmas 1805, £8.5s 0d at Midsummer 1806 and £8. 5s 0d at Ladyday 1807.]

1807 Jan.16 Elizabeth RIDLEY of East Grinstead, singlewoman, has declared that she is with child and that Alexander PETERS of Horley, Surrey, blacksmith, is the father; and he is to be apprehended.

1808 Jan. 4 Ann STANFORD of East Grinstead [singlewoman crossed through] has declared that, on 5 October 1806, she was delivered of a male bastard child and that William HUGGETT, late of East Grinstead, baker, is the father; and he is to be apprehended.

1808 Jan.11 Mary MITCHELL of East Grinstead, singlewoman, has declared that she is with child and that Edward PAYNE of East Grinstead, cordwainer, is the father; and he is to be apprehended.

1808 Apr.25 Mary LUCAS, singlewoman, was on a Saturday in November last, delivered of a bastard child in Steyning and, about a month afterwards, came to East Grinstead (which is the place of her last legal settlement) with the child as a nurse child and has been relieved by East Grinstead. The parish officers of Steyning are to appear at the Swan, Forest Row, on Monday 13 June to show cause why an order should not be made on them for a weekly sum to support the child. [Endorsed 29 May 1808, copy delivered to Steyning workhouse]
Catalogued under Par 348/34/3/1

1808 Jul.11 Elizabeth ALLCOCK of East Grinstead, singlewoman, has declared that, on 21 November last, she was delivered of a male bastard child and that William WALLER, late of East Grinstead, farmer's servant, is the father; and he is to be apprehended.

1808 Oct.24 Emila HODGES of East Grinstead has declared that she is with child and that James KING of Bexhill, labourer, is the father; and he is to be apprehended.

1808 Dec.14 Ann AKEHURST of East Grinstead, singlewoman, has declared that she is with child and that James FRENCH, late of Godstone, Surrey, collar maker, is the father of her child; and he is to be apprehended.

1809 May 22 Mary PACKHAM of East Grinstead, spinster, has declared that, on 13 May last, at her mother's parish of East Grinstead, she was delivered of a female bastard child and that Mr. Thomas WELLS, late of Newhaven, is the father; and he is to be apprehended.

1809 Dec.27 Sarah JORDAN of East Grinstead, singlewoman, has declared that, on 4 November last, she was delivered of a male bastard child at the house of Henry JORDAN in East Grinstead, and that Richard LEVENS of Croydon, Surrey, calico printer, is the father; and he is to be apprehended.

1809 Dec.29 Susannah TERRY has declared that she is with child and that James CAMMEL otherwise SMITH of Leigh, Kent, labourer, is the father, and he is to be brought before a Justice, at the Swan at Forest Row, on Monday 8 January next.

1810 Jan.29 Sarah GODLEY of East Grinstead, singlewoman, has declared that she is with child and that Henry CHAPMAN of East Grinstead is the father; and he is to be apprehended.

1810 Jun.18 Emily HODGE of East Grinstead, singlewoman, has declared that she is with child and that Thomas WHITEBREAD of Hever, Kent, yeoman, is the father; and he is to be apprehended.

1810 Sep. 5 Mary BEST of East Grinstead, singlewoman, has declared that she is with child and that James BUDGEN, late of West Hoathly, stonemason, is the father; and he is to be apprehended.

1810 Sep.14 Mary HOOKER of East Grinstead, singlewoman, has declared that she is with child and that William BRIGDEN, miller, late of East Grinstead, miller is the father; and he is to be apprehended.

1811 Jan.14 Thomas DAWSON, late of East Grinstead, tailor, to appear before the Justices at the Swan, East Grinstead, on Monday 28 January, to answer charges of refusing and neglecting to maintain his wife and family and running away, leaving them chargeable to the parish.

1811 Apr. 1 John WORSLEY, late of East Grinstead, to appear before the Justices at the Swan at Forest Row on Monday 15 April to answer charges of running away and leaving his wife and family chargeable to the parish.

1811 Jul.29 Amy JENNER of East Grinstead, singlewoman, has declared that she is with child and that Richard ALFREY of Norwood, Surrey, farmer's servant, is the father; and he is to be apprehended.

1811 Dec.23 Jane PAYNE the wife of Thomas PAYNE of East Grinstead, has declared that, on 11 November last, at the house of William BUDGEN of East Grinstead, she was delivered of a male bastard child and that Thomas HAYLER of Cuckfield, labourer, is the father; and he is to be apprehended.

1812 Jan. 9 Jane BORER of East Grinstead, singlewoman, has declared that she is with child and that Thomas CHAPMAN of Lingfield, Surrey, servant, is the father; and he is to be apprehended.

1812 Sep.14 Susannah CREASEY of East Grinstead, singlewoman, has declared that she is with child and that John VINCENT, now or late of Worth, labourer, is the father; and he is to be apprehended.

1814 Sep. 22 William FALCONER of Lingfield, Surrey, labourer, is to appear before the Justices at the Crown in East Grinstead on Monday 26 September to answer complaint for neglecting and refusing to maintain Mary BRIDGLAND, the bastard daughter of Mary, formerly Mary BRIDGLAND, of which he, the said W.F. is the reputed father.

1814 Dec. 3 Sarah CRITTENDEN of East Grinstead, singlewoman, has declared herself to be with child and that George TERRY of Withyham, is the father. G.T. has been apprehended by a warrant dated 28 November last but, as he has refused to give security to indemnify the parish and also refused to enter into a recognizance with sufficient security that he will appear at the next general quarter sessions, he is to be conveyed to the House of Correction at Lewes.

1814 Sep.26 Ann BORER of East Grinstead, singlewoman, has declared that, on 17 August last, she was delivered of a male bastard child at the poorhouse in East Grinstead and that Charles MILLER otherwise SERGEANT, late of East Grinstead, is the father; and he is to be apprehended.

1815 Apr.24 Lydia GATTON of East Grinstead, singlewoman, has declared that she is with child and that Thomas CHAPMAN the younger of East Grinstead, yeoman, is the father; and he is to be apprehended.

1815 Jun.26 Sarah CRITTENDEN of East Grinstead, singlewoman, has declared that, on 16 May last, at the house of Elizabeth ELLIS, she was delivered of a male bastard child and that George TERRY of Withyham, servant, is the father; and he is to be apprehended.

1815 Aug.14 Mary WHEELER of East Grinstead, singlewoman, has declared that she is with child and that James ARNOLD of Worth, is the father; and he is to be apprehended.

1815 Aug.23 Susannah JENNER, singlewoman, has declared that she is with child and that James STONEHAM, late of East Grinstead, labourer, is the father; and he is to be apprehended.

1815 Sep. 2 Mary MARTIN of East Grinstead, singlewoman, has declared that she is with child and that John TAYLOR, footman in service of Lord Hervey, of No.9 Portland Place, Middlesex, is the father; and he is to be apprehended.

1815 Oct.19 Sarah EDWARDS, singlewoman, has declared that she is with child and that Richard PAYNE, Corporal in the Sussex Militia, is the father; and he is to be apprehended.

1816 Feb. 1 Elizabeth GATES of East Grinstead, singlewoman, has declared that she is with child and that Abraham AWCOCK of Edenbridge, Kent, is the father; and he is to be apprehended. [Endorsed: Separate document dated 11 March 1816. Elizabeth Gates was delivered of a male bastard child on 3rd February last.]

1816 Feb. 2 Mary HEAVER of East Grinstead, singlewoman, has declared that she is with child and that William LYEWOOD of Worth, is the father; and he is to be apprehended.

EAST GRINSTEAD APPRENTICESHIP AGREEMENTS Par. 348/33/1

+ Indicates catalogued under Par 348/33/2/1
* Indicates catalogued under Par 348/33/3
# Indicates catalogued under Par 348/33/1/72

1678 Apr. 1 Thomas WALTER, apprenticed to Richard PAGE of East Grinstead, innholder, until age of 24 years.

1679 Jun.18 William TINKER, apprenticed to William BROWNE of East Grinstead, yeoman, until age of 24 years; husbandry. [Signature of W.B.]

1682 Sep.29 Thomas LEVITT, apprenticed to Robert STILL of Cowden, Kent, tailor, until age of 24 years; trade of tailor. [Mark of R.S.]

1682 Nov. 9 George RENOLDS als FOX, apprenticed to John STENNING of East Grinstead, yeoman, until age of 24 years; husbandry. [Mark of J.S.]

1683 Apr.30 Frances GOORD, a poor bastard child, apprenticed to John DIVOLE of East Grinstead, collier, until she is aged 21 years or day of marriage. Bond: John Divole bound to the parish officers of East Grinstead in £20. [Mark of J.D.]

1683 Oct. 4+ William THOMAS was apprenticed to John BARTHOLOMEW the younger, of East Grinstead, shoemaker, but as his master has run away and left him in East Grinstead, solely without employment, W.T. is discharged of his apprenticeship.

1683 Oct.15 Phillip STONESTREETE, apprenticed to John STONESTREET of Betchworth, Surrey, until age of 24 years. [Mark of J.S.]

1683 Nov.12 John BARTHOLOMEW, apprenticed to John BARTHOLOMEW of East Grinstead, until age of 24 years. [Signature of J.B.]

1683 Nov.12 Abraham BARTHOLOMEW, apprenticed to George TYNETT of East Grinstead, until age of 24 years. [Signature of Gorrg Tinet (sic)]

1683 Nov.15 Mary BEST, apprenticed to Thomas POCKNELL of East Grinstead, until age of 21 years or day of marriage; housewifery. [Mark of T.P.]

1684 Feb.19 John LEVET, apprenticed to John POLLARD of East Grinstead, until age of 24 years; husbandry. [Mark of J.P.]

1684 Mar.11 Edward PAYNE, apprenticed to Edward NICHOLL, senior, and Edward NICHOLL junior, both of East Grinstead, until age of 24 years; trade of wheelwright. [Signatures of Edw. Nycoll (sic) senior and Edw.Nycoll (sic) junior]

1684 Apr. 2 Mary BEST, apprenticed to Thomas POCKNELL of Lingfield, Surrey, husbandman, until age of 21 years or day of marriage. Bond: Thomas Pocknell and Francis POCKNELL of East Grinstead, husbandman, bound to the parish officers of East Grinstead in £40. [Marks of T.P. and F.P.]

1684 Apr.21 William THOMAS has put himself apprentice to Thomas WENBORNE of Woodhurst [?Wadhurst], Sussex, cordwainer, until age of 24 years.

1684 Jun. 2 John RENNOLDS, apprenticed to Thomas JENNER of East Grinstead, tailor, until age of 24 years. [Signature of T.J.]

1684 Nov. 6 Ann LEVETT, the daughter of Thomas LEVETT, a poor man of East Grinstead, apprenticed to John ELLIS and Richard DENTON, both of East Grinstead, coopers, until age of 21 years or day of marriage. [Marks of J.E. and R.D.]

1684 Nov.12 John BROOKER, son of John BROOKER of East Grinstead, labourer, of his own free will and with the consent of his father, has put himself apprentice to Robert CORNISH of East Grinstead, blacksmith, until age of 22 years; trade of blacksmith. [Mark of R.C.]

1685 Dec.30 Elizabeth BATCHELER alias BOWRA, apprenticed to John BAZELY of East Grinstead, husbandman, and wife Elizabeth, until age of 21 years; housewifery.

1685 Dec.31 Ann STONSTREAT, apprenticed to William FREEMAN of Horne, Surrey, mason, until age of 21 years; housewifery. [Mark of W.F.]

1689 Oct. 1 William FOX alias REYNOLDS, apprenticed to Anthony BURNUPP of East Grinstead, until age of 24 years; husbandry. [Signature of A.B.]

1690 Feb.20 John COSTER, apprenticed to John BURTON of Edenbridge, Kent, until age of 24 years. [Signature of J.B.]

1691 Apr.30 Richard LEVETT, apprenticed to Thomas DIVALL of East Grinstead, collier, until age of 24 years; husbandry. [Mark of T.D.]

1692 Feb. 2 Thomas GOURE, apprenticed to Francis COOK of Hever, Kent, until age of 24 years; trade of tailor. [Signature of F.C.]

1694 Oct.11 Edward PAYNE, apprenticed to William AUSTEN of East Grinstead, blacksmith, until age of 24 years; trade of blacksmith. [Signature of W.A.]

1695 Feb.11 Mary BROOKER, apprenticed to Henry COOPER of East Grinstead, husbandman, until age of 21 years or day of marriage; housewifery. [Mark of H.C.]

1695 Oct.17* John CHANTLER, apprenticed to Josuah HOWARD of Horne, Surrey, weaver, until age of 24 years; trade of weaver. [Signature of Joshua (sic) Howard]

1696 Jan. 6 William WALLIS, apprenticed to George HOLMES of East Grinstead, mason, until age of 24 years; trade of mason. [Signature of G.H.]

1696 Jan.10 Edward RIDGWAY, apprenticed to John BODLE of East Grinstead, yeoman, until age of 24 years; husbandry. [Signature of J.B.]

1696 Apr.10 Richard BATTES, apprenticed to Andrew LEDGER of Withyham, warrener, until age of 24 years; husbandry. [Signature of A.L.]

1697 Jun.29# Susana MORGAN, apprenticed to Anne GANDER of East Grinstead, spinster, until age of 21 years; housewifery.

1698 Jun. -* Elizabeth BATTES, apprenticed to John DANE of East Grinstead, gardener, until age of 21 years or day of marriage; housewifery. [Signature of J.D.]

1698 Jun.24 Elizabeth MORGAN, apprenticed to John KNIGHT, butcher, until age of 21 years; housewifery. [Signature of J.K.]

1698 Jun.24* Mary BROWNE, apprenticed to William BARTHOLOMEW of East Grinstead, cordwainer, until age of 21 years or day of marriage; housewifery.

1698 Sep.28 Mary RAMTON, apprenticed to Richard GROVE of East Grinstead, husbandman, until age of 21 years or day of marriage; housewifery. [Mark of R.G.]

1698 Oct.14 Katherin COCKETT, apprenticed to Richard BROUGHTON of East Grinstead, husbandman, until age of 21 years or day of marriage; housewifery.

1699 Dec.15 John PAICE, apprenticed to Henry PICKE of East Grinstead, farmer, until age of 24 years; husbandry. Bond: Henry Picke bound to the parish officers of East Grinstead in £20. [Mark of H.P.]

1699 Dec.15 Mary RIDGWAY, apprenticed to James LEVETT until the age of 21 years or day of marriage; houswifery. [Signature of J.L.]

1700 Jul.20 Robert LUSHER, apprenticed to John MONKE of East Grinstead, carpenter, until age of 24 years; trade of carpenter. [Signature of J.Monk (sic)]

1700 Jul.20 Richard KNIGHT, apprenticed to John UNDERHILL of Frith in Lingfield, Surrey, yeoman, until age of 24 years; husbandry. [Signature of J.U.]

1710 Aug. 3 John TURNER, apprenticed to Phillip ESEGATE of Godstone, Surrey, blacksmith, until age of 24 years; trade of blacksmith. [Signature of Phillip Esgate (sic)]

1711 May 3 Elizabeth BROWNE of East Grinstead, spinster, daughter of Sara now wife of William BARHAM of Lingfield, Surrey, husbandman, and late wife of William BROWNE of East Grinstead, butcher, deceased, apprenticed to William Barham, until age of 21 years or day of marriage. Consideration: 47s 0d and a shift cloth, to him in hand paid and delivered by the parish officers before the ensealing. [Mark of W.B.]

1711 May 31 William GROVE, apprenticed to William TESTER of Worth, husbandman, until age of 24 years; husbandry. [Mark of W.T.]

1711 May 31 Cornelius ERRIDG, apprenticed to Thomas MARTEN of Worth, carpenter, until age of 24 years; trade of carpenter. [Mark of T.M.]

1711 Jun.28 Richard ROSE, apprenticed to Grace WAKELIN, widow, and Thomas WAKELIN, both of West Hoathly, until age of 24 years; husbandry. [Signatures of G.W. and T.W.]

1712 Jan.29 William DEVALL, of East Grinstead, by the consent of his Aunt Mar[?y] BURGIS of Cowden, Kent, has put himself apprentice to Henry BEWMAN of Aylesford, Kent, miller, for 5 years; trade of miller. [Mark of H.B.]

1714 Jun. 7 Richard BENNETT, apprenticed to John HOMEWOOD of St. Saviours, Southwark, Surrey, glassgrinder, until age of 24 years; trade of glassgrinder. Consideration £5.10s 0d. [Signature of J.H.]

1714 Nov.30 Richard MILLS, apprenticed to John MILLS of St. Thomas in the Cliff, Lewes, collarmaker, until age of 24 years; trade of collarmaker. [Signature of J.M.]

1717 Jun.24 Richard BOOKER, apprenticed to Jeremiah SEVENOAK of Rotherfield, until age of 24 years; husbandry. [Signature of Jeremy Sevenok (sic)]

1717 Sep.29 Ninion CREASY, apprenticed to George STEVENSON of East Grinstead, currier, until age of 24 years; trade of currier. [Signature of G.S.]

1718 Mar. 6 Harrington PAYNE, apprenticed to John KIDMAN of Horsham, bodiesmaker [bodicemaker] until age of 24 years; in said trade. [Signature of J.K.]

1722 Oct. 30 Mary PATTENDEN, daughter of Jeremiah PATTENDEN, brickmaker, apprenticed to Elizabeth STORER of Westminster, mantua maker, to serve from 1st September last for one year; trade of making and cutting mantuas and petticoats. Consideration £5. [Signature of M.P.]

1722 Dec.20 John WORGER, son of William WORGER of East Grinstead, husbandman, with the consent of his father, apprenticed to Edward HASELDEN of East Grinstead, glover, to serve from 19 July last until the end of the term of two years; trade of glover. [Endorsed: The parish officers of East Grinstead to give and allow unto the said William Worger twelve pence per week, during the two years of his apprenticeship, towards his board. The two years, within mentioned, is valued by the Commissioners at £5 per annum] [Signature of E.H.]

1725 Nov. 1 Anne HASLEDEN, apprenticed to Sara CREASY of East Grinstead, widow, until age of 21 years; trade of mantua maker. S.C. and the parish officers of East Grinstead have agreed to discharge A.H. from her service at the end of five years, and S.C. promises to deliver up unto her the parish officer's part of the indentures to be cancelled. [Signature of S.C.]

1726 Jun.24 Edward SMITH, apprenticed to William SMITH of St. Thomas in the Cliff, Lewes, saddler and collarmaker, until age of 24 years, in said trade. [Signature of W.S.]

1732 Mar.31* John PERRY, with the consent of Henry PERRY, his grandfather, apprenticed to Francis HAMLIN of East Grinstead, fellmonger, for seven years. Consideration £4.4s 0d. Bond: Francis Hamlin bound to the parish officers of East Grinstead in £10. [Signature of F.H.]

1744 Jul. 14 Thomas HEASMAN, son of William Heasman of East Grinstead, husbandman, with the consent of his father, has put himself apprentice to Christopher Arthur MIDDLETON of East Grinstead, barber and perukemaker, for seven years from 24 June last, in said trade. Consideration £5.5s 0d. [Signature of C.A.M.]

1747 Sep.29 Nathanial BUTCHING, son of John BUTCHING of East Grinstead, butcher, and the said John Butching of the one part and Francis HAMBLIN of East Grinstead, fellmonger and glover, of the other part, witnesseth that N.B. of his free and voluntary will and with the consent of J.B. his father, has put himself apprentice to Francis Hamblin in trade of fellmonger and glover, for seven years. Consideration 52s 6d. [Signature of F.H.]

1747 Nov.28 Felix ROAKS, apprenticed to John SMITH esq., of East Grinstead, until age of 24 years; husbandry. [Signature of J.S.]

1750 [torn]* Mary SMALL, aged [?12] years, apprenticed to Joseph SYMMONDS of Maresfield, until age of 21 years or day of marriage; "housewifery, spinning, knitting and sewing, and a maid servant's business". [Signature J.S.]

1750 ?Apr.25* James SOANE, son of [torn] apprenticed to William MORPHEW, of East Grinstead, weaver, until age of 24 years; trade of weaver. [Signature of W.M.]

1750 May 3* John COX, aged 11 years, son of Arthur COX deceased, apprenticed to Walter COX of Horsted Keynes, thatcher, until age of 24 years; trade of thatcher. [Mark of W.C.]

1754 Dec.31* Thomas TOOTH, son of William TOOTH of East Grinstead has, of his own free will, put himself apprentice to Thomas HASLEGROVE of Cuckfield, cordwainer for seven years; trade of cordwainer. Consideration £5 paid by Thomas Tooth. [Signature of Thomas Haselgrove (sic)] [Endorsed: 13 February, 1755, 6d duty, paid 2s 6d.]

1757 Apr.28* Edward TOOTH, aged 14 years, son of William TOOTH, apprenticed to William LONGLY of Hartfield, brickmaker, until age of 24 years; "art, trade or mystery of making bricks and tiles". [Signature of W.L.]

1783 Jul. 1 Bannester TRULOCK, son of Bannester TRULOCK of [torn], husbandman, apprenticed to John PAYNE, cordwainer, for seven years; trade of cordwainer. [Signature of J.P.]

1786 Sep.30 James BOTTEN, aged 14 years, apprenticed to William TOOTH of East Grinstead, hatter, until age of 21 years; trade of hatter. [Signature of W.T.]

1786 Nov.25 Charles BEARD, aged about 14 years, apprenticed to John ELVEY of East Grinstead weaver, until age of 21 years; trade of weaver. [Signature of J.E.]

1802 Sep.27 Joseph MARTIN, aged 16 years, apprenticed to William ISARD, tanner, of East Grinstead, until age of 21 years; trade of tanner. [Signature of W.I.]

1802 Nov. 3 John GIBB, aged 16 years, apprenticed to William SIMMANS, of East Grinstead, wheelwright, until age of 21 years; trade of wheelwright. [Signature of William Simmond (sic)]

1803 Jan.14* Richard PAYNE, aged 14 years, apprenticed to James MORRIS, currier, of East Grinstead, until age of 21 years; trade of currier. [Signature of J.M.]

1804 Jul.14* Richard EDWARDS, aged 12 years, apprenticed to Thomas Wood EDWARDS, cordwainer, of East Grinstead, until age of 21 years; trade of cordwainer. [Mark of T.W.E.]

1806 May 12* John JORDAN, aged 15 years, apprenticed to Thomas ELLIS of East Grinstead, collar and harnessmaker, until age of 21 years; in said trade. [Signature of T.E.]

1824 Jun.23 George WILKINS, with consent of his father, George WILKINS of East Grinstead, apprenticed to William WOOD of East Grinstead, blacksmith, for five and a half years; trade of blacksmith. Consideration £20 paid by George Wilkins the elder, ten pounds now and the rest at the expiration of half the period of apprenticeship. [Signatures of G.W. the elder and younger]

1824 Nov. 1 Thomas WEAIRE, with the consent of his father, William WEAIRE, of East Grinstead, wheelwright, apprenticed to Mary PAYNE of East Grinstead, cordwainer, for five and a half years; trade of cordwainer. M.P. to pay to T.W. in his first year the sum of 3s 0d a week, and in second year, 3s 6d a week and, at the end of the first two years, she agrees to find him sufficient meat and lodging, and to pay him £2 per annum towards finding him in cloth till the expiration of the term. [Signatures of T.W., William Wiear (sic) and M.P.]

1825 Mar.14 [torn] ?son of Edward EVERIST, apprenticed to Luke SNOW, bricklayer and mason of ?Brighthelmstone. Consideration £8 paid by E.E. [Marks of E.E. and L.S.]

HENFIELD

Henfield: 4,518 acres chiefly on east bank of River Adur 7 miles upstream from Shoreham. Weald clay with a central tongue of Lower Greensand with some steep slopes quarried for both sand and stone, just over 100ft in south and south-east. Market gardening on south-facing slopes, woodland and open common; two emparked areas, one until 17th century, the other since 19th. Roman Greensand Way passed throught Oreham Common in S. 5 inns and 42 shopkeepers and traders; hamlet of Nep Town S of church and village. Coaches to London, Brighton, Oxford and Windsor, carriers to London, Brighton and Lewes.

Population: 1724 473; 1801 1037; 1811 976; 1821 1404; 1831 1516

HENFIELD SETTLEMENT EXAMINATIONS Par 100/32/4.

1746 Oct.15 Susan BROWNING of Henfield said that, last summer, she was placed out, by Henfield parish, as apprentice to Thomas BENLETT, yeoman of Fletching, by indenture; that she stayed with her master one month and then he sent her to her father who, at that time, lived at St. John's Common, for a pair of shoes and that she stayed there two days and returned to her Master Benlett. That she stayed with her master one month more and then, her master beating her, she went away again for a quarter of a year but returned to T.B. before Christmas Day, on which day she remembers they had, for dinner, a shoulder of mutton, a plum pudding and some white cabbage and turnips. S.B. also said that she remained with her master from that time till within a fortnight of the fair at Henfield, which was on the 20th July last, without ever absenting herself, and then her master beat her again, very much, which made her run away from him and she has, ever since, worked about in several places. Since she went away from her master, he has gone away from Fletching, she knows not whither nor what is become of him, and further she saith not. [Mark of S.B.]
Catalogued under Par 100/33/1

1774 Feb. 9 John HOLT, sawyer, now residing in Henfield, said that he was born in Staplehurst, Kent, where he lived with his father until he was 17 years old, then he went to Goudhurst, Kent, for some time and then to Cranbrook, Kent, where he married. That, 14 years ago, he went to New Shoreham, where he worked under Mr. FOSTER for 5 years at 12s 0d a week, and then lived in Henfield, in a house belonging to Mr. BRIGGS but never hired £10 a year or lived as a yearly servant nor did any act to gain a settlement elsewhere since his birth. [Signature of J.H.]

1774 Feb.21 Joseph SELSBY, labourer, now residing in Henfield, said that he was born in Henfield and, about twelve years since last Lady Day, he was hired by Thomas BURTENSHAW of Shermanbury, farmer, to serve him from the then Lady Day for one whole year, which he performed and for which he received his full year's wages, and has not gained a settlement elsewhere. [Mark of J.S.]

1775 Jul.28 William COBBY, labourer, now residing in Henfield said that, on Michaelmas day 12 or 13 years ago, he hired himself to Thomas

COOPER of Kirdford, farmer, to serve one whole year for £7 wages, which he served and received his full year's wages, and then served him for one other year for £7.10s 0d or 7 guineas wages. About a week after Michaelmas Day, he hired himself to George KEENE of North Chapple [Northchapel], farmer, to serve till the following Michaelmas day but cannot recollect for what wages, which term he served, and he has not gained a settlement elsewhere. [Mark of W.C.]

1777 Feb. 3 Daniel COX said that he was was born in Wisborough Green, Sussex, where, he believes, his father, Jeremiah COX, resided under a certificate from the parish of Awfold [Alfold], Surrey. About Michaelmas old style 1769, he hired himself to John HARWOOD of Poolborough [Pulborough], farmer, for one year, which full year's service he performed and has not gained a settlement elsewhere. [Signature of D.C.]

1777 Dec.11 James FOICE, carpenter, now residing in Henfield, said that he was born in Billingshurst where, he believes, his father, John FOICE, was legally settled, and that he has not gained a settlement out of Billingshurst. [Mark of J.F.]

1781 Sep.12 James FOYCE, carpenter, now residing in Henfield, said that he was born in Billingshurst and that, about 14 or 15 years ago, he came to live in Woodmancote, Sussex, under a certificate from Billingshurst and has not gained a settlement elsewhere. [Mark of J.F.]

1781 Sep.12 Richard LIDBETTER, carpenter, now residing in Henfield, said that he was born in Ifield, Sussex, and, 14 or 15 years ago, went to live with his Uncle Richard LIDBETTER of Nuthurst, who told him he might live with him as long as he pleased, that he might go away when he pleased and that he should give him no money. This deponent then said that he stayed with his uncle about a year and a half but never received anything for his work at sawing and hewing timber, notwithstanding, he did whatever work his uncle ordered him to do, and has not gained a settlement, save as above, since his birth. [Signature of R.L.]

1782 Mar.13 William SHEPPARD, now residing in Henfield, said that he was hired to Thomas ELLIS of Henfield, farmer, three years ago, from 24 days before old Michaelmas to the next Lady Day, then again for half a year, then again for a year and served him until the New Year day following. That he has not gained a settlement elsewhere. [Mark W.S.]

1782 May 8 Joseph TOWSE, carpenter, said that he was born in Billingshurst, as he has often heard his father say, and to which parish his father belonged. That, eight or nine years ago last Michaelmas, he hired himself to Richard ELMS of Wisborough Green to serve him for a year, which he served and then hired himself, three days after Michaelmas Day, to Edward REDMAN of Pulborough, farmer, and served a year, except for the three days as aforesaid, and when he left Redman's service he put himself apprentice to William PESKETT of Henfield, carpenter, to serve for three years who, this deponent believes, then resided in Henfield under a certificate. That he served his master in Henfield for 13 months and then worked for Charles WARD in Henfield, by the consent of his master, with whom he worked until new Lady Day, according to Pesket and Ward's agreement for that purpose. That, while he lived with Charles Ward, his Master Peskett purchased a copyhold estate and came to this deponent and told him he must discharge him from his apprenticeship as, otherwise, he would belong to Henfield but this deponent told his Master Peskett that he must return half the money which was given upon his being bound apprentice and find him in a winter's work, which the said Peskett did. That he then lived with James TRIBE of Findon by the week, for about nine months, and then went to live in Ockley, [Surrey], where he has lived for five years but has never done any act to gain a settlement elsewhere.

1782 May 8 William PESKETT of Henfield, carpenter, said that, some years ago, he resided in Henfield under a certificate from the parish of Washington and, whilst he resided in Henfield under the certificate, Joseph TOWSE from Billingshurst, put himself apprentice to this deponent for three years by indenture dated 30 November 1774. That, after J.T. had been with him for eight months he, this deponent, purchased a copyhold estate in Henfield to the value of £30, which was surrendered to him on 12 November following and that, before admittance to the estate, he had consented that his apprentice might work with Charles WARD of Henfield, carpenter, from Michaelmas to Lady Day. That, 32 days after he was admitted to his estate, he told his apprentice he must be discharged for he did not like the parish should say that he had settled an apprentice in Henfield and, on the 16th December 1775, he went before John Challen esq., one of His Majesty's Justices, with his apprentice and they then exchanged their indentures by consent, and he returned to his apprentice half the money he had received, it being his agreement so to do in case he did not keep on the business at the time the indentures were executed.

1783 May 30 Peter PATCHING, now residing in Woodmancote, husbandman, said that, six years ago the 10 October last, he hired himself to William MARTIN of Telscombe, near Lewes, for one year, with whom he lived a full year and received his wages. That he then hired himself to W.M. for another year and, before his last year expired, he married and went from his service about a fortnight after he was married, and has not gained a settlement elsewhere. [Mark of P.P.]

1790 Jul. 2 John KING, now residing in Woodmancote, labourer, said that he was born in Woodmancote, an illigitimate child as he has been told and believes, and that he has not gained a settlement out of the parish of Woodmancote. [Mark of J.K.]

1795 Jun.11 Zachariah GREENFIELD, late of Hangleton, said that he was born in Sullington, Sussex, where his father was and is legally settled, and he has done nothing to gain a settlement elsewhere. [Mark of Z.G.]

1795 Nov.26 Henry PARKER, late of Clapham, Sussex, labourer, said that he was born at Washington and that he hired himself to Mr. HOLMES of North Farm and served him for a year in Washington. That, afterwards, he hired himself for a year to Mr. WYAT of Mitchelgrove in the parish of Clapham, and served a year in Clapham and has not gained a settlement elsewhere, and has a wife named Ann. [Mark of H.P.]

1796 Jan.23 William CHURCHER of Henfield, labourer, said that, at Michaelmas 1794, he hired himself to Mr. Richard PENFOLD of Steyning, to serve him for a year at wages of nine guineas, and served him in Steyning and Wiston the whole of the year and that, the last night of his service, he slept in Steyning and, in the morning, returned with his master's cattle to Buddington in the parish of Wiston and then returned to his master at Steyning, who paid him his wages. That Mr. Penfold was rated and occupied a house in Steyning and paid the poor rates for the same. That he has done no act whereby to gain a settlement since, and has a wife named Mary. [Mark of W.C.]
Catalogued under Par 100/34/1

1812 Nov.12 Henry COOK, residing in Mickleham, Surrey, said that he is 33 years of age, born in Mickleham, as he was informed by his parents, William and Hannah COOK, and where they then resided on a legal certificate granted to them by Effingham, Surrey. That he continued to live there until the death of W.C. eleven years ago last February, and under this certificate his mother Hannah continues to reside at Mickleham and, to his knowledge, William COOMBS [sic] and wife Hannah have not gained a legal settlement out of the parish of Effingham and he, this examinant, has not done any act to gain himself a settlement. [Signature of H.C.]

1833 Apr.29 Joseph SHOLDERS said that, 16 years ago, he hired himself with the Rev. W. RIDEOUT of Woodmancote, Sussex, for a year at wages of £30, with board and lodging. J.S. served the year and received his wages quarterly and lived with W.R. for several years under the same agreement, and has done no act to gain a settlement elsewhere.

1835 Jan.29 James FOSTER late of Brighton, labourer, said that he was born in Henfield, in lawful wedlock, where his father was legally settled by yearly renting a brickyard and occupying a dwelling house in Henfield and paying taxes, and that his father was removed from Brighthelmston to Henfield in 1827 by a removal order. That he has not gained a settlement in his own right and was married to Ann, his present wife, in the parish church of Brighthelmston in 1833, and now he and his wife are chargeable to that parish. [Signature of J.F.]

HENFIELD SETTLEMENT CERTIFICATES Par 100/32/1

A settlement certificate from Henfield to another parish is listed separately immediately following the main series.

		From
1698 Jul.13	Thomas WASE with his wife and four children.	Ashurst
1703 Feb.27	Richard YOCKHORST	St. Thomas, Cliffe, Lewes

1706 Mar.22	John PETER, a poor man of Steyning, husbandman, wife and family	Steyning
1709 Sep.24	James HOLDEN (or HOLDING), husbandman, his wife and one child	Beeding
1711 Apr.14	Bond. Parish officers of Ashington bound to parish officers of Henfield in £50 in respect of John EEDE, labourer, wife and family.	Ashington
1716 Mar.29	Benjamin HARMAN, wife Anne and children.	Brighton
1717 Jan.10	Richard SHERLOCK, husbandman, wife Elizabeth and children.	Preston
1734 Jul.10	John WOOLLGER (or WOOLGAR) and wife Jane	Hurstpierpoint
1738 Aug. 6	Thomas SERGEANT and wife Mary.	Hurstpierpoint
1747 Oct.12	John BATTMAN.	North Stoke
1756 Mar.13	Allen DAVY.	Twineham
1761 Aug. 2	William MITCHELL and wife Sarah.	Hartfield
1769 Dec.21	John STILL, wife Mary and daughter Mary..	Ifield
1775 Jul.17	Joseph BATMAN, wife Sarah and infant child.	North Stoke
1782 Nov.24	Edward TURNIS and wife Mary.	Maresfield
1788 Mar.25	Bond. John LEFFAN of Hove, husbandman, bound to the parish officers of Henfield in £100 in respect of Elizabeth LEFFAN, wife of John Leffan, and her three children now residing in Henfield, one of which children has, for some time, been chargeable to the parish. [Signature of J.L.]	Hove

HENFIELD SETTLEMENT CERTIFICATES — Par 100/32/1

		To
1717 Feb. 6	Bond. William GREVATE, late of Henfield but now of Slinfold, bound to parish officers of Henfield in £100, W.G. agreeing not to take an apprentice or hire servants whereby they gain a legal settlement in Henfield. [Mark of W.G.]	Slinfold

REMOVAL ORDERS FROM HENFIELD — Par 100/32/2

		To
1763 Jul.11	Susan KNIGHT, singlewoman. Confirmation	Steyning
1764 Oct.18	Thomas PATCHING and wife Susan. [Delivered 19 October]	Woodmancote
1772 Jan. 8	John PAIN, his wife and child.	Beeding
1772 Jan. 8	William GREEN and wife Ann.	West Grinstead
1776 Feb. 5	Joseph DICKER and wife Mary. [Delivered 7 Feb]	[Froyle], Ham
1776 Nov.13	Lydia BOUND and child. [Delivered Friday 15 Nov.]	Walton on the Hill, Sry

1777 Feb. 3	Daniel COX and wife Ann.	Pulborough
1778 Sep.23	Thomas CAIN, wife Hannah and daughter Hannah 2y. [Delivered 6 Oct.]	Sompting
1780 Oct.16	Henry BILINGHURST and wife Frances. [Delivered 16 October]	Ashurst
1780 Nov.22	Christian PATCHING, singlewoman. [Delivered 22 Nov.]	Steyning
1782 Jul.10	John MANSBY, wife Elizabeth and their children Elizabeth 9y, Sarah 8y, Ann 6y, John 5y, Jane 4y and Thomas 2y.	Shermanbury
1783 Sep.17	Thomas KNIGHT and wife Sarah [Delivered 23 Sep.]	Woodmancote
1785 Aug.26	Richard WHEATLAND, wife Mary and children Thomas 2y and Mary 6m.	Shipley
1786 May 24	Ann GOLDSMITH. [Delivered 25 May]	Hurstpierpoint
1814 Mar. 9	William STILLAWAY, otherwise COBBY.	Northchapel
1815 Dec. 6	James COMPER, wife Ann and children Edward 2y and Charles 7m.	Thakeham
1816 Jan.24	James STEER and his two children, Frances 6y and Sarah 4y.	Beeding
1816 Feb. 7	Philip GODDARD and wife Kitty.	Brighton
1819 Dec. 6	John KNIGHT, wife Elizabeth and children Edward 11y, Timothy 9y, Thomas 6y and Elizabeth 4y. [Sent home 10 Dec]	Brighton
1830 Jan.11	George VIRGOE.	Broadwater
1830 Jul.26	Caroline HOLDER, singlewoman. [Delivered 27 July]	Broadwater
1830 Nov.15	William PARRY, wife Mary and children Jane 11y, John 10y, Mary 8y, Elizabeth 6y, William 5y and Edward 4m. [Delivered 17 Nov]	Beeding
1830 Dec.13	Jeremiah JACKSON als COOK and wife Hannah. [Delivered 14 December]	Houghton
1830 Dec.13	Henry JENDEN and wife Frances. [Delivered 16 Dec]	Horsham
1831 Apr. 4	James STENNING, wife Rebecca and children Rebecca 9y, James 7y, Eliza 5y and Mary 2m. [Delivered 12 April]	Limpsfield, Sry
1831 Nov.28	Harriott LANGFORD, singlewoman. [Delivered 28 Nov]	Cowfold
1833 Feb. 4	Thomas NEWNHAM, wife Mary and children Mary Ann 2y and Thomas 3m.	West Grinstead
1833 Apr. 1	William VIRGO, wife Martha and child Fanny Elizabeth [age not given]	Broadwater
1833 Jun.10	Mary SHOULDERS and children David 6y, Thomas 4y.	Woodmancote
1833 Oct.28	Richard LAKER and wife Louisa.	Shipley

1834 Nov.24	Caroline HOLDER, singlewoman. [Delivered 20 Dec.]	Broadwater
1835 Mar.30	William PARSONS, wife Mary and children William 2y and Sarah 1y. [Delivered 28 April]	Edburton

QUARTER SESSIONS REMOVAL ORDERS FROM HENFIELD

		To
C 1666 Apr.23	John WHITE; to be settled in Beeding, unless that parish give security.	Beeding,
P 1667 Oct. 7	John WHITE, now at Henfield, refuses to move to Beeding and is to be taken into custody and conveyed to the House of Correction at Arundel, and his wife and children are to be sent to Beeding.	Beeding
A 1676 Jan.10	William HAMON[D]. Order removing him from Henfield; respited.	Not given
S 1676 Apr. 3	William HAMOND is to be settled at Henfield as he rents a house at £10 per annum.	Not given
C 1677 Apr.23	John WREN; discharged.	Ashurst
A 1679 Jan.13	John BROOKFIELD, son of Richard BROOKFIELD, late of Storrington, has come to Henfield; if he becomes chargeable he is to be sent back to Storrington to continue as an inhabitant there, nothwithstanding his now residency at Henfield.	Storrington
A 1687 Jan.10	Thomas SMITH, wife and family; on appeal they are to be returned to Henfield.	Shermanbury
C 1687 Apr. 4	Ralph MOORE and wife. Recites order 2 February 1686 but, as Henfield has not had the opportunity to remove R.M. and wife to Shermanbury, the order to be continued without prejudice to Henfield.	Shermanbury
P 1687 Jul.11	Ralph MOORE; discharged.	Shermanbury
M 1687 Oct. 3	Joseph CHEESMAN, in pursuance of the order to return to Henfield, has endeavoured to hire a house there but is obstructed and hindered by the overseers of Henfield, so that J.C. is now destitute of a house for himself and family; ordered that the parish officers of Henfield do, forthwith, provide a convenient house, for which J.C. is to pay the rent and all other charges.	None given
C 1709 May 2	James HOLDEN and family; confirmed.	Beeding
M 1712 Jul.14	Sarah TANNER; confirmed.	Lancing
A 1717 Jan.14	Elizabeth ILMAN; quashed for want of form.	Cowfold
M 1718 Jan.13	John JARVIS; confirmed.	Brighton

C 1718 Apr.21	Edward JERVICE; discharged.	Hurstpierpoint
H 1723 Jul.15	Ann LONG and children Edward and David; confirmed.	Trotton
C 1730 Apr. 6	Sarah alias Joane BOWELL; confirmed.	Shipley
L 1731 Oct. 7	Sarah BOWELL; confirmed.	Shipley
M 1746 Jan.13	John HAND, wife Anne and children William and John; discharged.	Sidlesham
H 1750 Jul. 9	John WARD 15m; respited.	Cuckfield
P 1750 Oct. 1	John WARD aged about 14m; discharged because he is under age of 7y and ought to be with his mother in Henfield for nurture.	Cuckfield
H 1757 Jul.11	Thomas GRANT, carpenter, wife Elizabeth and son Richard 27y, "an infirm person and one who hath not been able to get his living ever since his birth"; respited.	Slindon
H 1757 Oct. 3	Thomas GRANT, carpenter, wife Elizabeth and son Richard 27y, an infirm person; discharged.	Slindon
H 1761 Jul.13	Richard DIVALL and wife Ann; respited.	Clayton
M 1762 Jan.11	Richard DIVALL and wife Ann; confirmed.	Clayton
M 1762 Jan.11	William BANFIELD and wife; confirmed.	Merriworth [?Mereworth], Ken
H 1763 Jul.11	Susan KNIGHT, singlewoman; confirmed.	Steyning
M 1770 Jan. 8	John FLOAT, wife Elizabeth and children Henry 3y and Lidia 1y; quashed.	Bramber
H 1773 Jul.12	Andrew TYLER; confirmed.	Storrington
C 1775 Apr.24	William WOOLGAR and wife Jane; respited.	West Grinstead
H 1775 Jul.10	William WOOLGAR and wife Jane; confirmed.	West Grinstead
H 1782 Jul.15	John MANSBEY, wife Elizabeth and children Elizabeth 9y, Sarah 8y, Ann 6y, John 5y, Jane 4y and Thomas 2y; confirmed.	Shermanbury
H 1784 Jul.12	John SANDERS and wife Elizabeth; respited	East Tarring
P 1784 Oct. 7	John SANDERS and wife Elizabeth; discharged.	East Tarring
M 1785 Jan.10	John SANDERS and wife Elizabeth; discharged.	Woodmancote
C 1787 Apr.16	Ann NORMAN, singlewoman; respited.	Wisborough Green
H 1787 Jul. 9	Ann NORMAN, singlewoman; quashed.	Wisborough Green
P 1790 Apr.12	Ann APTED; singlewoman; respited.	West Grinstead
H 1790 Jul.12	Ann APTED, singlewoman; quashed.	West Grinstead
P 1790 Oct. 4	Ann APTED, singlewoman; confirmed.	Shermanbury
C 1791 Jan.10	Mary PAIN, singlewoman; respited.	Shermanbury
M 1791 May 2	Ann LISH, singlewoman; confirmed.	Woodmancote
M 1791 May 2	Mary PAIN; respited.	Shermanbury
H 1805 Jul.16	William BOWDIDGE, wife Patty and son John 1y; quashed.	Southover

P 1805 Oct. 8	William BOWDIDGE, wife Patty and sons John 1y 6m and Henry 6 weeks; confirmed.	Charmouth, Dor
C 1807 Jan.13	Thomas TAYLOR, wife Sarah and son William 1y; respited.	Cuckfield
P 1810 May 1	Frances NYE; confirmed.	Poynings
P 1810 Oct. 2	John HOLDEN, wife Elizabeth and son Thomas 3y; confirmed.	Steyning
P 1810 Oct. 2	James JUNIPER and wife Frances; confirmed.	Keymer
C 1811 Jan.15	Ann LANGLEY; confirmed.	Ashurst
C 1811 Jan.15	Ann EVANS, singlewoman; confirmed.	Brighton
H 1811 Jul.16	James HOADLEY, wife Sarah and children Mary Ann 8y, Henry 5y, Louisa 2y and James 3m; confirmed.	Shermanbury
P 1811 Oct. 8	John DAVEY, wife Sarah and child aged 6 weeks; confirmed.	Shermanbury
H 1812 Jul.14	William WEAVER, wife Sarah and children William 5y, Charlotte 3y and John 1y; confirmed.	Iford
H 1813 Jul.13	Isaac LULHAM, wife Charlotte and children Eliza 2y 6m and Isaac 11m; confirmed.	Lancing
H 1815 Jul.11	Thomas LANAWAY and daughter Mary Ann 12y; confirmed.	St. Olave, Chichester
H 1815 Jul.11	Thomas NYE, wife Sarah and children Sarah 7y, George 4y, Benjamin 2y and an infant aged 3 days, not yet baptised; confirmed.	Hadlow, Ken
H 1815 Jul.11	Jane COOKSEY, (wife of Daniel COOKSEY, a corporal in the 2nd Regiment of Foot Guards), and children Elizabeth 4y, and Penelope 1y; respited.	Brighton
P 1816 Apr.22	Ann MANVELL, singlewoman; confirmed.	Leatherhead, Sry
H 1816 Jul.16	Jane COOKSEY, (wife of Daniel COOKSEY, a corporal in the 2nd Regiment of Foot Guards), and children Elizabeth 4y and Penelope 1y; quashed.	Brighton
H 1816 Jul.16	Charles HOLDEN, wife Jane and son William 2m; confirmed.	Steyning
P 1831 Jan. 3	William PARRY, wife Mary and children Jane 11y, John 10y, Mary 8y, Elizabeth 6y, William 5y and Edward 4m; respited.	Beeding

REMOVAL ORDERS TO HENFIELD Par 100/32/3

		From
1694 Jan. 8	John BUTCHER. On appeal, order set aside as J.B. is settled in Chailey.	Chailey
1710 Apr.17	Thomas WHITEING, wife and family.	Woodmancote
1753 May 16	Christopher PARKS.	Lindfield
1765 Jun.25	Mary HOLLINGDALE, singlewoman.	Plumpton
1767 Jun.27	Ann WATSFORD and John her son 2y.	Beeding

1769 Nov. 3	Stephen FARLEY and wife Elizabeth.	Steyning
1775 Jan.11	Edward WARD, Mary his wife and their son James 2m.	Steyning
1781 Jun. 2	Richard MORGAN, an illegitimate child aged about eleven years, upon examination of John MORGAN, the father of the said child.	Send, Sry
1782 Apr.25	Joseph TOWES, wife Mary and children Mary 3y and Joseph 1y.	Ockley, Sry
1795 May 27	Francis FAIRS.	West Grinstead
1796 Feb.16	Ann SHERLOCK. Unable to travel due to sickness and other infirmity, fit to do so by 2 April. Charges of £5.19s 9d farthing to be paid by Henfield.	St. Thomas, Cliffe, Lewes
1796 Oct.15	Richard SAYERS and wife Elizabeth.	South Malling
1803 Dec.31	Benjamin HOGSFLESH and wife Jane.	Pulborough
1809 Oct.21	Martha WARD, singlewoman, being with child.	Brighton
1811 Feb.27	Hannah HARDS, singlewoman.	Edburton
1815 Jun.17	Isabel GODMAN, wife of William GODMAN, a private or gunner in the 1st Battalion of the Royal Artillery, now stationed at Woolwich under orders for embarkation for foreign service, and children Thomas 3y and Margaret 13m.	Hurstpierpoint
1816 May 11	William KINSETT, wife Elizabeth and child Mary Ann 1y.	Chailey
1831 Jan.31	John MUZZALL and wife Elizabeth.	Brighton
1831 Aug.22	Jane HOLDEN, singlewoman.	New Shoreham
1831 Nov.14	John THOMPSETT and wife Elizabeth.	Woodmancote
1832 Jan. 2	Edward TROWER, wife Eliza and child born in lawful wedlock, 9 weeks old, and not yet named.	Brighton
1832 Oct.29	Henry EDE, Martha his wife and Henry their son 2y.	Beeding
1833 Jan. 7	Edward HOLDER.	Dorking, Sry
1833 Apr.15	Edward SHOULDERS.	Brighton
1833 Oct.10	Philadelphia HILLYAR, wife of James HILLYAR.	Brighton
1834 Mar.15	Louisa HOLDEN, singlewoman.	Shermanbury
1834 Mar.17	Jane HOLDEN, pregnant of a child likely to be born a bastard. [Received 19 March]	Brighton
1834 Aug. 6	Frances NYE, singlewoman, being pregnant of a child likely to be born a bastard.	Hurstpierpoint
1835 Jan.29	James FOSTER and wife Ann.	Brighton
1835 Feb.26	Elizabeth PATCHING, singlewoman.	Brighton

QUARTER SESSIONS REMOVAL ORDERS TO HENFIELD

		From
A 1675 Jan.20	Edward WHISKEY; respited.	West Grinstead
C 1675 Apr.12	John SMYTH; respited.	Albourne
C 1675 Apr.12	Edward WHISKEY; confirmed.	West Grinstead
L 1675 Jul.15	John WHITTEN and family; discharged.	Old Shoreham
A 1676 Jan.10	Henry BROMFIELD; discharged.	Steyning
C 1678 Apr. 8	Richard LONGLEY. Case between Henfield and Ashurst; he is to be settled at Henfield.	Ashurst
A 1687 Jan.10	Joseph CHEESMAN, wife and family.	West Grinstead
A 1694 Jan. 8	John BUTCHER; discharged.	Chailey
M 1695 Oct. 7	Mary SHELLEY; discharged.	Shipley
A 1699 Jan. 9	Thomas GREENFIELD; confirmed.	Billingshurst
P 1706 Jan.14	John ASCALL; discharged.	Steyning
A 1708 Jan.12	John PELL; confirmed.	Washington
A 1717 Jan.14	William GREVATT; confirmed.	Slinfold
C 1719 Apr. 6	Richard SHERLOCKE, wife and child; confirmed.	Horsham
M 1723 Jan.14	Thomas RENFEILD; confirmed.	Lancing
H 1725 Jul.12	Thomas DURHAM, wife Mary and son John 1y; confirmed.	Storrington
P 1727 Oct. 2	Sarah HAYLER; discharged.	Bramber
M 1740 Jan.14	Elizabeth BURCHETT, bastard child of Jane BURCHETT, singlewoman; confirmed.	Kirdford
C 1749 Apr. 3	John JUDGEN, wife Mary and son Stephen; confirmed.	West Grinstead
L 1756 Jan.15	Hannah PATTENDEN, singlewoman; confirmed.	Hailsham
M 1764 Jan. 9	William BROWNING, labourer, and wife Ann; confirmed.	Horsham
M 1767 Jan.12	Thomas MUZZELL and wife Hannah; confirmed.	Ashurst
L 1767 Jul.13	Ann WATSFORD, singlewoman and son John 2y; confirmed.	Beeding
L 1775 Jul.13	Zillah ALLFREY, singlewoman; confirmed.	Pyecombe
C 1784 Apr.19	Robert PAGE, wife Ruth and daughter Mary 1m; respited.	Horsham
H 1784 Jul.12	Robert PAGE, wife Ruth and daughter Mary 1m; confirmed.	Horsham
M 1793 Apr. 8	John WEEKS and wife Mary; confirmed.	Angmering
P 1793 Oct. 7	Elizabeth BENNETT (wife of Thomas BENNETT, who has abandoned and left her), and son Thomas 2y; quashed.	Horsham
L 1800 Oct. 9	Harry WOOD, wife Sarah and children George 12y, Frederick 10y, Sarah 8y, Peter 7y, Eliza 5y and Sophia 4y; quashed.	Brighton

L 1805 Jan.18	Richard PAYNE; confirmed.	St. John Castro, Lewes
L 1806 Jan.17	Elizabeth WEST and daughter Mary Ann 18m; confirmed.	St. John Castro, Lewes
L 1808 Apr.29	Richard COMBER, wife Mary and children Sarah 22m and a male child 1m, not yet baptised; quashed.	Stanmer
P 1811 Oct.11	Charlotte COPPARD, singlewoman; confirmed.	Poynings
L 1812 Jan.17	John ALFREY, wife Susan and children Thomas 9y, Sarah 7y, John 4y and Edward 2y; confirmed.	Patcham
L 1814 Jan.14	Frances HEMSLEY (wife of William HEMSLEY, a private in the Guards) and children Susannah 6y and Emma 4y; quashed.	Brighton
L 1815 Jul.14	Maria HODGES, singlewoman; confirmed.	St. Michael, Lewes
P 1816 Apr.22	Henry WEST, wife Sarah and children Mary 15y, Barnard 11y, Henry 9y, William 7y, Ann 3y and John 3m; quashed.	Rackham
P 1817 Jan.14	William LISH, wife Elizabeth and children Mary 12y, Fanny 8y and Eliza 5y; quashed as to wife Elizabeth and three children, and confirmed as to William Lish.	Edburton
H 1817 Jul.14	Mary BENNETT alias LISH 12y, Frances BENNETT alias LISH 10y and Eliza BENNETT alias LISH 6y; confirmed.	Edburton
L 1829 Jan.15	John HELMSLEY, wife Mary and daughter Louisa 11m; confirmed.	Streat
P 1829 Apr.28	William CLARKE, wife Elizabeth and children William 9y, George 6y and Henry 3y; quashed.	Beeding
C 1831 Oct.17	Jane HOLDEN, singlewoman; confirmed.	New Shoreham
L 1832 Apr. 5	Jonathan FRANKS, wife Matilda and children Hannah 7y and Jonathan 5y; quashed.	Brighton

HENFIELD BASTARDY EXAMINATIONS Par 100/34/3

1736 Jun. 9 Sarah ABOTT of Henfield, singlewoman, said that in July last, she lived as a servant at the house of John HILL of Nutknowle, Woodmancote, and that Robert ADDS, then of Woodmancote, husbandman, is the father of the female bastard child born to her on 23 April last, in Henfield, which child is still living and has been, ever since its birth, chargeable to Henfield. [Mark of S.A.]

1796 Jan.[21] Mary TOWES of Henfield, singlewoman, said that she is with child and that William CHURCHER, now or late servant to Mr. Francis GELL of Coombes, is the father. [Signature of Mary Teewes (sic)]

HENFIELD BASTARDY BONDS Par 100/34/1.

1634 Jan. 3 George MOORE of Henfield, musician, bound to the parish officers of Henfield, in 80s 0d. G.M. agrees to pay 40s 0d as follows: 10s 0d on the feast of St. John the Baptist in the year 1637, 10s 0d on Feast of St. Michael the Archangel, 10s 0d more on feast of the birth of Jesus Christ next following, and 10s 0d more on feast of the annunciation of the Virgin Mary in year 1638. [Signature of G.M.] [*No indication given as to the reason for the loan. Also note that three copies of this document are catalogued under Henfield Apprenticeship Agreements, Par 100/33/1*]

1750 Jul. 7 James PARKER and his son Isaac PARKER, both of Keymer, brickmakers, bound to Richard WOOLVEN and John DURRANT, both of Henfield, yeomen, in £80 as [no name given] has lately been delivered of a bastard child in Henfield, and has charged I.P. with being the father.

1753 Feb. 8 Willard FRIEND, parish officer of Pycombe, bound to the parish officers of Henfield in £100, in respect of Elizabeth ALLFREY of Pycombe, singlewoman, now living in Henfield who was, about two and a half years ago, delivered of a female bastard child in Henfield and, as E.A. is now with child again, likely to be chargeable to Henfield, W.F., or his successor, agrees to indemnify Henfield parish. [Signature of Willard Freind (sic)]

1769 Jul. 1 Thomas PICKNOLD, the younger of Bolney, Sussex, husbandman, and Thomas PICKNOLD, the elder of Hurstpierpoint, husbandman, bound to the parish officers of Henfield in £50, in respect of Mary BANFIELD of Henfield, singlewoman, who has declared that she is with child and that T.P. the younger, is the father. [Signatures of both Thomas Picknall (sic)]

1774 Aug.27 Philip WARD and William WARD both of Henfield, carpenters, bound to the parish officers of South Malling in £100, in respect of Elizabeth HAILOR, late of South Malling, deceased, who was delivered of a male bastard child, in South Malling, and did charge P.W. with being the father. [Signatures of P.W. and W.W.]

1777 May 16 James BANFIELD of Woodmancote, husbandman, Thomas COPPARD, Edward BENNETT, Nicholas BURTENSHAW and John LEGG of Woodmancote, farmers, are bound to the parish officers of Henfield in £50, in respect of Hannah RENFIELD of Henfield, spinster, who states that she is great with child and that J.B. is the father.
Catalogued under Par 100/34/2.

1789 Jan. 6 Thomas ELLES of West Grinstead, farmer, bound to the parish officers of Henfield in £100, in respect of Elizabeth PENFOLD, singlewoman, who has declared that, on 27 September 1787 at Henfield, she was delivered of a female bastard child and that T.E. is the father. [Signature of Thomas Ellis (sic)]

1789 Apr.16 Edward STENNING and Edward STENNING, the younger, both of Henfield labourers, bound to the parish officers of Henfield in £100, in respect of Elizabeth WALLER of Henfield, singlewoman, who has declared herself to be with child. E.S. the younger, father of the child, to pay 40s 0d within one month next after her lying-in and 1s 6d a week. [Signatures of E.S. jun. and E.S.]

1790 Apr. 20 William VINALL and George VINALL, both of Henfield, wheelwrights, bound to the parish officers of Henfield in £200, in respect of Sarah BOTTING of Henfield, singlewoman, who was lately delivered of a bastard child, and has declared that W.V. is the father. [Signatures of W.V. and G.V.]

HENFIELD BASTARDY ORDERS Par 100/34/2

1763 Jul.11 Susan KNIGHT, singlewoman, has declared that Frank WINTON, the younger, of Sompting, farmer, is the father of a male bastard child born to her in Henfield. F.W. to pay 40s 0d for the expenses of lying-in and 2s 0d a week. [No sum given for the mother to pay]

1774 Sep.14 Mary LEFFEN of Henfield, singlewoman, has declared that William VINALL of Henfield, bricklayer, is the father of a male bastard child born to her on 7th August last, at Henfield. W.V. has now paid, into the hands of the overseer of Henfield, 40s 0d for the cost of lying-in and is to pay 2s 0d a week; the mother to pay 6d a week.

1775 Apr.26 Sarah WOODIN, singlewoman, has declared that Richard MITCHELL of Hurstpierpoint, labourer, is the father of a female bastard child born to her on 1 March last, at the poorhouse, Henfield. R.M. to pay 13s 0d costs and 2s 0d a week; the mother to pay 6d a week.

1775 Nov. 8 Elizabeth PARSONS, singlewoman, has declared that Richard TIDEY late of Henfield, labourer, is the father of a male bastard child born to her on 23 June last, at Henfield. R.T. who could not be found to be summoned to Court, is ordered to pay £3 towards cost of lying-in and 18d a week; the mother to pay 6d a week.

1777 Nov.26 Hannah RENFIELD, singlewoman, has declared that James BANFIELD of Woodmancote, is the father of a female bastard child born to her on 28 August last in Henfield. J.B. ordered to pay 52s 0d towards the cost of lying-in and 18d a week; the mother to pay 6d a week.

1778 Dec. 9 Annzilla BOUND, singlewoman, has declared that William COLLINS, late of Bansted, Surrey, is the father of a female bastard child born to her on 30 August last, at Henfield. W.C., who cannot be found, is ordered to pay £3.5s 0d towards cost of lying-in and 18d a week; the mother to pay 6d a week.

1781 Nov.28 Catherine LUXFORD has declared that William CARE, late of Woodmancote, is the father of a male bastard child born to her on 24 September last, at Henfield. W.C. to pay £2.7s 6d towards the cost of lying-in and 18d a week; the mother to pay 6d a week.

1781 Dec.12 Mary WHITE, singlewoman, has declared that James PRONGER, late servant to Henry WOOD of Henfield, gent., is the father of a male bastard child born to her on 24 November last, at her father's house. J.P. to pay £2.7s 0d towards cost of lying-in and 18d a week; the mother to pay 6d a week.

1795 Aug. 5 Sarah PAINE, singlewoman, has declared that Thomas HOAD, late of Henfield, labourer, is the father of a female bastard child born to her on 12 June last. T.H. to pay £2.8s 0d towards the cost of lying-in and 2s 0d a week; the mother to pay 6d a week.

1796 Dec.21 Elizabeth WOODLEY has declared that Daniel GOACHER, late of Hurstpierpoint, labourer, is the father of a female bastard child born to her on 15 November last, in the poorhouse, Henfield. D.G. to pay 42s towards the cost of lying-in and 2s 0d a week; the mother to pay 6d a week. [Endorsed: Received from D.G. £2.2s 0d and on 26 Dec. 2s 0d for week due 28 Dec. Also received 2s 0d from him on Jan.4, 8 and 17 and 8s 0d on Feb.12.]

HENFIELD WARRANTS Par 100/34/2

1726 Apr.15 Peter LILLIOTT, Hugh WHITE, Walter BUCKWELL, Thomas THORP, James HOLDEN, Thomas WEEDEN and William LANGLEY came lately to Henfield without bringing any legal certificates and are now to be brought before a Justice to be examined. [Endorsed: All of them warned by me - John BECKETT.]
Catalogued under Par 100/34/4

1767 May 30 Mary HODGES of Henfield, singlewoman, has declared that George HILLS, late of Henfield, labourer, is the father of a female bastard child born to her on 12 April last. at the house of Thomas HODGES in Henfield; and G.H. is to be apprehended.

1777 Feb. 1 Daniel COX, now living in Henfield without a certificate, to be examined regarding his place of settlement.
Catalogued under Par 100/34/4

1777 Apr.18 Sarah STENNING of Henfield, singlewoman, has declared herself to be with child and that Richard PRICE, late of Merstham, Surrey, labourer, is the father; and he is to be apprehended.

1778 Dec. 9 Anzilla BOUND, singlewoman, has declared that William COLLINS, late of Bansted, Surrey, is the father of a female bastard child born to her on 30 August last; and he is to be apprehended.

1781 Sep.20 In a letter addressed to Mr. Michael WARD, carpenter, Henfield, William ELLIS, Clerk of the Peace for Sussex, advises M.W. that unless he appears at the next quarter sessions at Lewes on Friday, 5th October next, on his recognizance for begetting a child born to Elizabeth CARTER, that the same will be presented, the consequence of which will be that the sureties must pay the penalties contained therein.

1795 Nov.25 Ann RINGFIELD of Henfield, singlewoman, has declared herself to be with child and that Henry PARKER, late of Washington, labourer, is the father; and he is to be apprehended.

1796 Jan.21 Mary TOWES of Henfield, singlewoman, has declared herself to be with child and that William CHURCHER, now or late servant to Francis GELL of Coombes, is the father; and he is to be apprehended.

1809 Oct.30 Sarah SLAUGHTER of Henfield, singlewoman, has declared that she is with child and that William TRIBE of Worthing, bricklayer, is the father; and he is to be apprehended.

1809 Oct.30 Martha WARD of Henfield, singlewoman, has declared that she is with child and that John PORTER, a Private in the South Gloucester Militia now at Brighton, is the father; and he is to be apprehended.

1809 Nov.10 Martha WARD of Henfield, singlewoman, is with child and has charged John PORTER, a Private in the South Gloucester Militia with being the father. As he has refused to give security to indemnify Henfield parish and refused to enter into a recognizance with sufficient suriety to appear at the next general Quarter Sessions, he is to be conveyed to the House of Correction at Petworth.

1811 Feb.27 Hannah HARDS of Henfield, singlewoman, has declared that she is with child and that Francis DEVAYNE, a Lieutenant in the Fifty First Regiment of Foot, is the father; and he is to be apprehended.

1815 Sep.20 Elizabeth FULLER of Henfield, singlewoman, has declared that she is with child and that Thomas BAKER, late of West Grinstead, labourer, is the father; and he is to be apprehended.

1830 May 3 William KNAPP of Twineham, shoemaker, is the reputed father of a female bastard child lately born to Ann MANSELL of Henfield and has been ordered to pay, among other things, the sum of 3s 0d a week but has refused to do so. As £5.17s 0d is now owing W.K. is to be apprehended and brought before a Justice at Steyning on 17 May.

1830 May 17 John BUTLAND of St. John's, Lewes, is reputed to be the father of a female bastard child born to Sarah DORRINGTON, singlewoman, and is ordered to pay 3s 0d a week. As £4. 2s 0d, up to 23 March last, is now due and J.B. has refused to pay, he is to appear before Justices at the White Horse Inn, Steyning, on 31 May.

1830 Jul.12 Thomas LELLIOTT of Henfield, bargeman, adjudged to be the father of a male bastard child born to Matilda HARDS, singlewoman, in Henfield, was ordered to pay 3s 0d a week. As 15 weeks are now due, amounting to £2.5s 0d, and T.L. has refused to pay, he is to be apprehended and brought to the White Horse Inn, Steyning on 26 July.

1832 Mar. 5 James LONGLEY of Broadwater, Sussex, labourer, adjudged to be the father of a male bastard child born to Caroline STILLAWAY, singlewoman, in Henfield, was ordered to pay 3s 0d a week. As 24 weeks pay is now due, amounting to £4.2s 0d, and J.L. has refused to pay, he is to appear at the White Horse Inn, Steyning on 19 March.

1832 Mar.19 Benjamin BIGNALL, adjudged to be the father of a male bastard child born to Jane HOLDEN of Henfield, was ordered to pay 3s 0d a week. As B.B. now owes £2.12s 0d for 18 weeks and refuses to pay, he is to be apprehended.

1834 Aug.12 Ann COFFIN, now residing in Henfield and believed to be with child, refuses to be examined as to her place of settlement and is to be apprehended in order to attend the White Horse Inn, Steyning on 1st September.
Catalogued under Par 100/29/1

1834 Aug.18 Jane HOLDEN of Henfield, singlewoman, has declared that Henry MORGAN of Brighthelmston is the father of a female bastard child born to her on 19 July last, at the poorhouse, and J.H. is to be brought before Justices at the house of James BROMHEAD, Steyning on 1 September next.

HENFIELD APPRENTICESHIP INDENTURES Par 100/33/1

1600 Oct. 3 William COOKE, aged 8 years, son of Will COOKE, apprenticed to Edward SEWER of Henfield, miller, until age of 24 years; husbandry. Consideration of £5 paid by parish officers, 50s 0d at [torn] and 50s 0d at Easter following, paying nothing to the poor in six years following, unless he come in greater occupying. [Mark of E.S.]

1600 May 1 John SEWBRIDGE, son of John SEWBRIDGE, late of Henfield, husbandman, deceased, with the consent of his mother, has put himself apprentice to William BAWCOM of Beeding, husbandman, for seven years; husbandry.

1612 Mar. 8 John BURNET, aged 12 years, son of Thomas BURNET late of Henfield, husbandman, deceased, apprenticed to Henry EASTON of Henfield, tailor, for 12 years; trade of tailor. [Mark of H.E.]

1612 Apr.14 John HARTE, aged 14 years, son of John HARTE, late of Henfield, deceased, apprenticed to Henry WILSON of [torn], shearman, for ten years.

1618 Apr.24 William BONNYFACE, apprenticed to Francis BRADFORD of Henfield, sawr [sawyer], until age of 24 years; trade of sawyer. [Mark of F.B.]

1620 Oct.15 Elizabeth BREAD, apprenticed to Edward PARSON of Henfield, tailor, for seven years. Consideration £8 (40s 0d now, 40s 0d at the Feast of St. Michael the Archangel 1621, 40s 0d in year 1622 and 40s 0d in year 1623). [Mark of E.P.]

1629 May 2 Antony BONNYFACE of Henfield, apprenticed to Thomas GOWARE of Henfield, thatcher, until age of 21 years. [Mark of T.G.]

1627 Jun.28 Thomas RIDLEY, son of Richard RIDLEY, late of Henfield, apprenticed to James ARNOLDE of Henfield, husbandman, until age of 21 years; husbandry. Consideration £3.15s 0d from parish officers.

1631 Sep.29 Edward COOPER, son of Edward COOPER, late of Henfield, deceased, has put himself as apprentice to Thomas COOPER, carpenter of Henfield, until age of 24 years; trade of carpenter. [Mark of T.C.]

1633 Mar.17 Elizabeth BRETHEN, daughter of Bridget BRETHEN of Henfield, spinster, apprenticed to Owen GRATWICKE, until age of 21 years; housewifery. [Mark of O.G.]

1634 Mar.17 Jone WHITE, daughter of William WHITE of Henfield, deceased, apprenticed to John TRENNELL of Henfield, yeoman, until age of 21 years; housewifery. [Mark of J.T.]

1635 Jan. 3 George MOORE of Horsham, musician, bound in 80s 0d, in respect of a loan of 40s 0d. [see Par 100/34/1 Bastardy Bonds for full details]

1635 Nov.22 William ALCOKE, apprenticed to John BARROW, yeoman, until age of 24 years; husbandry.

1637 Jul. 1 Geyles BAULDYN of Barkham [?Barcombe or Balcombe], Sussex, husbandman, bound to Jane DUKE, in £4 agrees to pay Jane Duke, his now apprentice, 40s 0d in the church porch of Henfield, if she shall live to age of 21 years. [Mark G.B.]

1643 Jul.25 Bond. John EARELAND of Stopham, farmer, and Richard CAPP of Shipley, farmer, bound to John LANKASTER, Edward GOFFE and Jacob GOLD, in £20, in respect of Elizabeth STOKES, put as apprentice to John Eareland dwelling now in Stopham. Consideration £10, paid to him by parish officers, to keep her until she is aged 21 years. [Mark of J.E.]

1643 Jul.25 Elizabeth STOKES, daughter of William STOKES of Henfield, lately deceased, apprenticed to John EARELAND of Stopham, husbandman, until age of 21 years. [Mark of J.E.]

1647 Oct.29 Allis HASLEGROVE, daughter of Richard HASLEGROVE of Henfield, deceased, apprenticed to Thomas ALLEN and wife Elizabeth ALLEN, until age of 21 years, in housewifery which Elizabeth Allen may or can teach and inform during that term. Consideration of 20s 0d to be paid at the ensealing, 20s 0d to be paid on the Annuniciation of the Blessed Virgin Mary next ensuing [1648], 20s 0d on Feast of St. Michael the Archangel 1648 and 20s 0d on Annunciation of the Blessed Virgin Mary in the year 1649. [Mark of T.A.]

1649 Oct.22 John ROKER, aged 12 years, apprenticed to John GRATWICKE until age of 24 years. [Signature of J.G.]

1649 Oct.22 Richard SCUTT, aged 8 years, apprenticed to John DUKE of Henfield, until age of 24 years. [Mark of J.D.]

1649 Oct.23 John MORLEY, aged 12 years, apprenticed to John MERCER of Henfield, until age of 24 years.

1649 Oct.23 Jane KILLICKE, aged 14 years, apprenticed to Stephen WOOLGER of Henfield, until age of 21 years.

1650 Jan. 7 Elizabeth GEERING, aged 12 years, apprenticed to Thomas BONIFACE until age of 21 years. [Mark of T.B.]

1650 Jan. 7 Henry STEMP, aged 9 years, apprenticed to Richard HAYNES of Henfield until age of 24 years. [Signature of Richard Heaine (sic)]

1651 Aug.13 John PARSON, aged 10 years, apprenticed to John GRATWICK of Eatons in Henfield, gent., until age of 24 years.

1652 Apr.10 Elizabeth KILLICK, aged nine years, apprenticed to John MIDHURST of Henfield, ploughmaker, until age of 21 years.

1654 Oct.20 Thomas LUCAS, aged nine years, apprenticed to Thomas HOLDEN of Henfield, until age of 24 years. [Signature of T.H.]

1655 Jul.13 James DAVIE, aged nine years, apprenticed to William WIATT of Henfield, gent., until age of 24 years. [Mark of W.W.]

1656 Jul.28 Elizabeth RAWLIE, aged nine years, apprenticed to Richard PELLETT of Henfield, until age of 21 years. [Mark of R.P.]

1658 Jun.21 Ann COALE, aged 11 years, apprenticed to Thomas WILLETT of Ashurst, gent., until age of 21 years. [Signature of T.W.]

1658 Oct.22 Richard ROFFE, aged eight years, apprenticed to John GARDNER of Henfield, miller, until age of 24 years. [Mark of J.G.]

1675 Sep.12 Edward BURRELL, apprenticed to John HAYNE of Henfield, until age of 24 years. [Signature of J.H.]

1675 Sep.12 John SMITH, apprenticed to Mr. Thomas PILFOLD of Henfield, until age of 24 years; husbandry. [Signature of T.P.]

1676 Jan.14 Thomas BLANIT, apprenticed to Nicholas BACKSHELL of Henfield, until age of 24 years; husbandry. [Signature of N.B.]

167[6]Apr.25 Richard FENALL, apprenticed to Thomas BONIFACE of Henfield, yeoman, until age of 24 years; husbandry.

1680 Sep. 20 Elizabeth DAVY, aged eleven years, apprenticed to Robert HOLDEN of Henfield, until age of 21 years. [Signature of R.H.]

1682 Jan.10 William SMYTH, apprenticed to William HONOUR, until age of 24 years; husbandry. [Signature of William Honor (sic)]

1686 Aug.14 William DEWNEY, apprenticed to William DEWNEY of Henfield, husbandman, until age of 24 years; husbandry. [Mark of W.D.]

1686 Aug.14 Richard PHILLIPS, apprenticed to John GOFFE of Henfield, yeoman, until age of 24 years; husbandry work. [Signature of J.G.]

1692 Dec.24 Jeremiah BONNER, apprenticed to John NORTON of Henfield, yeoman, until age of 24 years; in husbandry.

1693 Aug. 8 Dennis STONHAM, apprenticed to Thomas MIDHURST, of New Shoreham, until she is aged 21 years; "art and mystery of hussery" [housewifery].

1699 Oct.2[?] Thomas OLDER, apprenticed to John ELLIS of Henfield, gent., until age of 24 years; husbandry. [Signature of J.E.]

1704 Sep.29 Richard BRIDGER, apprenticed to John DALTON of Bolney, until age of 24 years; trade of cordwainer. [Signature of J.D.]

1707 Sep.10 Henry DOD, son of Henry DOD of Henfield, schoolmaster, has put himself apprentice to Thomas SNOOKE of New Shoreham, shipwright, to learn his art and to dwell and serve from 29 September ensuing for seven years, and to pay to Henry Dod a salary of £5, to be paid in seven equal yearly payments (that is to say) 14s 4d each year and, at the end, provide and deliver unto his apprentice a set of Shipwright's tools fit to do a day's work in a merchant yard. The said H.D. senior, his executors and assigns, shall find and provide for his son all sorts of clothes needful and convenient for him during the term above named. [Signature of Thomas Snook (sic)]

1709 Mar. 1 George SHERLOCK, apprenticed to Henry ATHER of Brighthelmston, mariner, until age of 21 years; consideration £6 from parish officers. [Signature of H.A.]

1715 Jan. 3 William BROWNINGS, son of Elizabeth BROWNINGS, now of Henfield, has, voluntarily and of his own free will, put himself apprentice to John SHOULDERS of Billingshurst but legally of Henfield, glazier or plumber, to learn that trade for seven years. [Signature of John Shoulder (sic)]

1717 Nov.12 James ROGERS, apprenticed to George PAGE of Burton, papermaker, until age of 24 years; trade of papermaker. [Mark of G.P.]

1718 Apr.25 William GRINAWAY, apprenticed to Thomas SNAT, tailor, until age of 24 years; trade of tailor. [Signature of Thomas Snatt (sic)]

1718 Sep.17 Mary BAKER of Henfield, widow, and William BAKER, her son, of the one part and Capt. William TUPPEN of New Shoreham, mariner, of the other part, witnesseth that W.B., by and with the consent of his mother, has put himself apprentice to W.T. to serve seven years; trade of mariner. [Signature W.T.]

1721 Jun.24 Agreed between the parishioners of Henfield and Edward WEST that he is to have ten pounds for the keeping of Thomas SHEPPARD and to teach him the trade of weaving and to receive the money yearly. [Mark of E.W.] [These details are written on a scrap of paper containing other items, and would appear to have been part of a Vestry book.]

1736 Oct.18 John BARBER, son of William BARBER late of Enfield [?Henfield] in Sussex, sawyer, deceased, put himself apprentice unto James LATHAM of St. John, Wapping, Middlesex., sawyer, until the end of seven years; trade of sawyer. [Signature of J.L.]

1742 Jun.14 Richard JERVIS, son of Edward JERVIS of Henfield, shoemaker, with the consent of his father has put himself apprentice to John SHEPPARD of New Shoreham, mariner, to serve from 1st June 1742 for nine years; occupation of sailor. Consideration: £7.7s 0d paid by E.J. [Endorsed: Duty paid 5 July, 1742 of 3s 0d.] [Signature of John Shepherd (sic)]

1745 Aug. 4 Thomas BROWNING, apprenticed to Robert BENLETT of Fletching, yeoman, with him to dwell and serve until age of 24 years; husbandry. [Mark of R.B.]

1745 Aug. 4 Susan BROWNING, apprenticed to Thomas BENLETT of Fletching, yeoman, until age of 21 years; housewifery. [Endorsed: May 18 1746. Received of John NORTON three pounds three shillings, by the order and for the use of the parish of Henfield for Susan Browning. [Signature of T.B.]

1746 Jul. 3 Edward JARVIS, son of Edward JARVIS of Henfield, cordwainer, voluntarily and of his own accord, by and with the consent of his father, apprenticed himself to William VINOR, the younger, of Brighthelmston, mariner and master, for seven years; occupation of mariner or sailor. Consideration: £2.10s 0d, paid by E.J. father of apprentice. [Endorsed: Duty paid 28 July 1746 of 1s 3d..] [Signature of W.V. Jnr.]

1746 - William BROWNING, apprenticed to Thomas BENLETT of Fletching, until age of 24 years. [Form not completed or signed]

1749 Nov.30 William BROWNING, apprenticed to John BULL of St. George, Middlesex, master and mariner, until age of 21 years; occupation of mariner. [Signature of J.B.]

1750 Jan. 1 Edward BRANSDEN, apprenticed to Richard STENT of Henfield, cordwainer, until age of 24 years; trade of cordwainer. [Signature of R.S.]

1752 Mar.30 John PHILLERY, apprenticed to James PHILLERY of Keymer, husbandman, until age of 24 years; trade of husbandman. [Mark of J.P.]

1756 Jul.18 Elizabeth TANNER, apprenticed to Thomas HAYNE of Henfield, tanner, until age of 21 years; housewifery.

1758 Sep.15 John DUNSTALL, apprenticed to Thomas GOBLE of Henfield, farmer, until age of 24 years; husbandry. [Signature of T.G.]

1758 Sep.15 John BARNETT, apprenticed to William BOUND of Henfield, farmer, until age of 24 years; husbandry. [Signature of W.B.]

1773 May 25 Benjamin HOGSFLESH, apprenticed to James WALLER of Henfield, farmer, until age of 24 years; husbandry.

1778 Apr.13 William STANDING, son of Thomas STANDING of Henfield, husbandman, put himself apprentice to George VINALL of Henfield, bricklayer and flaxdresser, from 9th June last, for 12 years; trade of bricklayer and flaxdresser. Consideration: £2. [Marks of W.S., T.S. and signature of G.V.]

HENFIELD MISCELLANEOUS. Par 100/35/1

1703 Nov.29 "I John ELLIS of Tharpe, in the Countye of Surrey heave Taken to keeper of the Church Wardens and Overseers or Majore part of them, and of sume more Inhabitants of the parish of Hendfeild in the Countye of Sussex one Jerimy PELLEN a Poore man of the said parish of Hendfeild from the Daye of the date heereof, from and dureing the Terme as long as the said Jerimy Pellen shall Live, both In Sickness and In health, If I the said John Ellis shall soe Long Live and Noe other wise, Att three shilling per week, to be pd me halfe yearlye by the overseers of the said parish, In Every halfe yeare for their time being, and I the said John Ellis am to find the said Jerimye Pelling for the Rate Above In All sorts of Cloths fitt and Deasent for his weare, Dureing the Time Mentioned Above from the Time Above. Wittness my hand John Ellis."

HORSTED KEYNES

Horsted Keynes: 4,232 acres at 328ft on Forest ridge; soil clay on Hastings sand. Earlier centre of Sussex iron workings.

Population: 1801 591; 1811 627; 1821 713; 1831 782

QUARTER SESSIONS REMOVAL ORDERS FROM HORSTED KEYNES

		To
L 1664 Jul.14	John HARDING, wife and child.	East Dean
L 1675 Jul.15	John SMYTH; confirmed.	Maresfield
L 1679 Jan.16	Sarah COLDEN, wife of Thomas COLDEN and John BURLEY, son of Sarah.	Isfield
L 1693 Jul.13	Thomas LEVIS. As he now rents and uses lands and tenements of over £10 per annum in Horsted Keynes, he is to be settled there.	Cuckfield
L 1700 Apr.11	Samuel COMBER; confirmed.	Lindfield
L 1706 Jul.18	William TEAGE; discharged.	Oxted, Sry
L 1710 Apr.20	Sarah REEDING; confirmed.	Charlwood, Sry
L 1713 Apr.16	John OVELL; discharged for want of form.	Hartfield
L 1718 Oct. 9	Walter DAVY and wife Mary; discharged.	Lindfield
L 1729 Jan.16	John CRIPPS and wife Mary; discharged.	West Hoathly
L 1746 Oct. 9	Mary STREET, widow; confirmed.	Burstow, Sry
L 1754 Apr.25	Jasper WHEELER, wife Elizabeth and son Jasper 10y; confirmed.	Croydon, Sry
L 1759 Jul.12	Thomas STANDEN, wife Mary and daughter Hannah 1y; confirmed.	Albourne
L 1763 Oct. 6	Sarah WELLER, singlewoman; discharged.	Lindfield
L 1774 Jan.13	William RIDLEY and wife Ann; quashed.	Wateringbury, Ken
L 1774 Apr.14	William RIDLEY, shoemaker, and wife Ann; confirmed.	Shipbourne, Ken
L 1775 Jan.12	Edward TULOTT and wife Hanah; confirmed.	Merstham, Sry
L 1800 Jan.16	Edward PATTENDEN, wife Frances and children John 2y and Thomas 10m; respited.	West Hoathly
L 1803 Apr.22	James FITNESS and wife Elizabeth; quashed.	Maresfield
L 1804 Jul.13	Michael WELLER, wife Sarah and infant daughter; confirmed.	Barcombe
L 1815 Jul.14	Mary FAULKNER, singlewoman; confirmed.	Ardingly
L 1822 Jul.19	John HILLS and wife Sarah Ann; quashed.	Burstow, Sry
L 1825 Apr.14	Henry SIMMONS; confirmed.	Tudely, Ken
L 1826 Oct.19	John KILNER, wife Lydia and children Caroline 6y, Anson 5y, Fanny 3y, Frederick 1y 8m and John 8m; respited.	Chailey
L 1827 Jan.11	John KILNER, wife Lydia and children Caroline 6y, Anson 5y, Fanny 3y, Frederick 1y 8m and	

	John 8m; quashed	
L 1827 Apr.26	John UPTON, wife Ann and daughter Susannah 11m; quashed.	Speldhurst, Ken
L 1829 Jan.15	Mary LUXFORD, singlewoman; quashed.	Lindfield
L 1832 Jan. 5	Henry RICHARDSON, wife Mary and children Fanny 15y, John 10y, Francis 8y, Matilda 6y and William 3y; respited.	Chailey

QUARTER SESSIONS REMOVAL ORDERS TO HORSTED KEYNES

		From
L 1685 Jan.15	Widow COOPER; respited.	Fletching
L 1685 Apr.30	Widow COOPER; respited.	Fletching
L 1688 Apr.26	William PILBEAME, wife and child; he is a certificate man from Horsted Keynes, and is to be allowed to remain at Fletching without prejudice.	Fletching
L 1690 May 1	Mathew CRAYFORD; on appeal he is to be returned to Fletching.	Fletching
H 1712 Oct. 6	Mary ENGLISH; confirmed.	Horsham
L 1728 Jul.18	Edward LONGLEY, wife Mary and daughters Mary, Elizabeth, Sarah and Frances, sons William and Robert; quashed for want of form.	Southover
L 1730 Oct. 8	Peter AUSTEN, wife Elizabeth and children Sarah, Martha, Catherine, Elizabeth, and Anne; confirmed.	Maresfield
L 1736 Jul.15	Elizabeth HOWELL; respited.	Friston
L 1736 Oct. 7	Elizabeth HOWELL; confirmed.	Friston
L 1741 Jan.15	Joseph WOOD, wife Anne and daughter Katherine 6y; confirmed.	Barcombe
L 1757 Jan.13	Thomas BEST, husbandman, wife and 5 children; confirmed.	Fletching
L 1757 Jul.14	Robert FURNER and wife Mary; discharged.	Mayfield
L 1758 Oct. 5	Robert FURNER and wife Mary; respited.	Mayfield
L 1759 Apr.26	Robert FURNER and wife Mary; confirmed.	Mayfield
H 1760 Jul.14	John DEANE, wife Sarah and children Sarah, John, Thomas and Isaac; confirmed.	Horsham
L 1783 Oct. 9	Charlotte MAY; confirmed.	Fletching
L 1801 Apr.16	John SANDELLS, wife Elizabeth and children Mary, Hester and Bett; quashed.	Fletching
L 1814 Apr.22	William MARTEN, wife Mary and children John, William and Thomas; respited.	Framfield
L 1814 Oct.21	William MARTEN, wife Mary and children John, William and Thomas; confirmed.	Framfield
L 1817 Apr.18	John BAKER, wife Lucy and children John 5y and Louisa 2y; quashed.	Brighton

H 1817 Jul.14	William TERRY, wife Hannah and son William aged 9 weeks; quashed.	Warnham
L 1826 Jul.13	Elizabeth NORMAN, (wife of John NORMAN, now a prisoner), and children Barbara 12y, Susannah 9y, John 6y, Sophia 4y, Sarah 3y and Elizabeth 9m; respited.	Brighton
L 1826 Oct.19	Elizabeth NORMAN, (wife of John NORMAN, now a prisoner) and children Barbara 12y, Susannah 9y, John 6y, Sophia 4y, Sarah 3y and Elizabeth 9m; quashed.	Brighton
H 1831 Jun.27	Henry LANHAM wife Amy and children Frances Ann 20y, Susan Sarah 18y, Catherine Amy 14y, Eliza Clara 7y, and Sophia an infant; confirmed.	Horsham

HURSTPIERPOINT

Hurstpierpoint: 5,088 acres from 225ft on lower slopes of Wolstonbury Hill (Saxon fort) through Danny Park to N portion below 100ft, with village on 145ft E-W ridge. Soil loam, varying to clay with subsoil of chalk and loam on understrata of sandstone in parts. Arable, including market gardening, and pasture; corn market. 3 inns and 76 shopkeepers and tradesmen. Carriers to Brighton and Lewes. Roman road NE-SW in S part.

Population: 1676 326; 1724 473; 1801 1101; 1811 1184; 1821 1321; 1831 1484.

HURSTPIERPOINT SETTLEMENT EXAMINATIONS Par 400/32/4/1

1728 Sep.18 John LONG, said that his late father, John LONG, served an apprenticeship in Trotton and never gained any other settlement before his death but died a certificate man of the said parish. This examinant has never gained a settlement by any act of his own since his birth but has been acknowledged by Trotton and relieved by that parish. [Signature of J.L.]

1781 Jul. 9 Mary DEAN said that she was born in Hurstpierpoint where, she believes, her father, Thomas DEAN, was legally settled. That, four years agone last Lady Day, she hired herself to John PECKHAM of Bolney, farmer, for one year, entering into his service a few days after old Lady Day and served until nine days before the following old Lady Day when, being desirous to quit, she applied for leave to do so, her master consenting providing she abated 1s 6d for the nine days short out of her wages, which was £2.5s 0d, to which she agreed. That she has done no act to gain a settlement elsewhere. [Mark of M.D.]

1781 Nov.28 Hannah JAY of Hurstpierpoint, singlewoman, said that she was born in Angmering where, she believes, her grandfather and grandmother resided under a certificate from the parish of Pulborough, and that she has done no act to gain a settlement since her birth. [Signature of H.J.]

1800 Nov.22 Edmund BUCKWELL said that he believes he was born in Hurstpierpoint where his father was legally settled, and that, forty years ago, John SMITH of Fletching died having, by his will, devised unto Sarah, the wife of this examinant, a house and three acres of land in Fletching forever, and this examinant and his wife resided thereon for some years, having built up another end in which he lived, and let the old end, paying regular taxes to the parish of Fletching. That, seventeen years ago, he removed with his wife and three children from Fletching to Hurstpierpoint, and hired himself to William LINDFIELD of Hurstpierpoint, miller, at wages of half a guinea a week, and slept in the Mill House, and lived there for ten years, settling with his master for wages once or twice a year, receiving money on account, in the mean time, when he wanted. That he then quitted the Mill House and was put into another house of William Lindfield in the same parish and, in other respects, lived on the same terms for another year. That he then quitted the service of William Lindfield as a miller and rented a tenement of William Lindfield in Hurstpierpoint at £3 a year and worked as a labourer in the same parish for some years, but did not pay any taxes or rates until after the year 1795, and has lived in the same parish to the present time. This examinant further said that, at the time of his quitting Fletching, he let the house in Fletching to one William HART by the year, at the rent of £6, keeping the old end on his own hands empty and, when Hart quitted it, he let it to William GROVER by the year at £6.10s 0d, reserving the old end of the house to himself. Grover continued tenant thereof for 2 years then this examinant let it to William HOBBS for a year at £6 10s 0d, reserving the old end of the house to himself as before. That, six or seven years ago, he took the premises in Fletching into his own hands (except the old end of the house which he let for two years to one Harry WESTON for 52s 0d per year) until the spring of 1800, when he sold the whole of the premises. [Signature of E.B.]

1823 Nov.25 John GEERE, labourer, said that he was born in Hurstpierpoint, where his father was legally settled, and when he was fourteen years of age, he was put out as a parish boy to Mr. WICKHAM of the same parish and served three years, and then lived in South Malling for half a year, from Lady Day to Michaelmas Day. That, a week afterwards, he hired himself to Mr. STANFORD of Preston until the following Christmas, for two pounds wages, which term he served and then bargained to the next Michaelmas, which he also served. That, after working on his own hands for a year or two, he lived with Mr. Stanford again for half a year, then worked on his own hands again for a year or more, and then lived with Mr. Stanford's bailiff, Richard KEY, at Preston for less than a year, when he received eleven pounds wages. That, since this time, he has not done any act to gain a settlement elsewhere; and he has a wife and two children. [Mark of J.G.]

HURSTPIERPOINT SETTLEMENT CERTIFICATES Par 400/32/1/1

Two settlement certificates from Hurstpierpont to other parishes is listed separately immediately following the main series.

		From
1704 Sep. 1	William REVET, cordwainer.	Brighton
1705 Apr. 9	Thomas COATES, hempdresser.	West Grinstead
1705 Sep.17	William ROACH	Alfriston
1709 Apr. 5	Richard CHRISTOPHER, wife Ruth and daughters Susan, Anne and Elizabeth, also Richard Christopher and John HOWARD.	Clayton
1729 Jul. 9	William SMITH, wife Mary and children Mary, Anne, Sarah and Elizabeth	Angmering
1731 Oct.17	Richard HUDSON, wife Sarah and son Richard.	Newtimber
1732 Apr.10	Thomas EDWARDS and wife Ann	Keymer
1733 Dec.15	Thomas HOLLIBONE, wife Mary and children Mary 8y and Elizabeth 4y.	Cuckfield
1737 Dec. 9	John PARSONS, wife [not named] and children Anne, John, Catherine, Edmund and Thomas	Steyning
1738 Feb. 7	Stephen ROBERTS, wife Anne and daughter Anne aged 8 weeks.	Chiddingfold, Sry

1738 Feb.19	William GANDER and wife Sarah.	Henfield
1740 Jan.26	William NASH and wife.	West Tarring
1740 Dec.29	Thomas SIMONS, wife Susanna and children Thomas, John, Mary and Ann.	Clayton
1741 May 19	George MORLEY, wife Elizabeth and family.	Cuckfield
1746 May 27	Silvester FRENCH, singlewoman.	Hailsham
1748 Apr.30	Abraham MUZZALL, wife Mary and children William, Henry, Abell and Elizabeth.	Newtimber
1749 May 2	Anne DUNTON.	Albourne
1751 Dec.20	John LINDFIELD, wife Sarah and son John 9m.	Plumpton
1752 Jan. 2	Mary HOLDEN, widow and son William 5y.	Clayton
1752 Mar.30	Thomas JERVIS and wife Sarah	Twineham
1752 Mar.30	Peter EMRAY, wife Mary and daughter Sarah 3y.	Twineham
1752 Jun.15	Edward DOWNARD	Uckfield
1753 Jan.20	John MICHELL and wife Mary.	Albourne
1753 Oct. 9	Thomas BROAD, labourer, and wife Mary.	Edburton
1756 Mar. 8	George WELLING, wife Abigail and daughter Ann.	Bramber
1756 Oct.24	John HAYLER, wife Ann and children Elizabeth and John.	Shermanbury
1759 Apr.16	Isaac BLINCK and wife Ann. Ditchling acknowledge them, as Hurstpierpoint has Thomas WHITE and family in Ditchling and they will take the same acknowledgment from Hurstpierpoint for them.	Ditchling
1760 Jul. 7	John HARRIS and wife Jane.	St. Pancras, Chichester
1761 Mar.23	Stephen REEVE, labourer, wife Sarah and children Thomas, James and Sarah	Twineham
1761 Mar.26	Jasper STILL and wife Elizabeth	Slaugham
1761 Apr. 6	James NYE, wife Mary and children Richard and Jane.	Newtimber
1762 Jan. 3	Isaac WOOLGER, wife Margaret and family.	Albourne
1762 Jan. 3	Thomas JUDIN, wife Mary and family.	Albourne
1764 Jan.16	William VENNALL, wife Elizabeth and children Mary and William.	Clayton
1764 Sep.19	Henry DALE, wife Sarah and children Henry 2y and Thomas 9 m.	Cuckfield
1765 Nov.19	William GANDER the younger and wife Mary.	Henfield
1767 May 12	Peter BIRD, wife Ann and daughter Mary 2 m.	Cuckfield
1767 Sep.13	Bernard BURTENSHAW, wife Elizabeth and daughter Ann.	Albourne
1774 Sep.26	William WHITE, wife Elizabeth and children William 2y 6m and Mary 6m.	Clayton
1775 Apr.17	Richard BURCHET, wife Ann and sons Richard 1y 6m and John 6m.	Shermanbury
1775 Apr.17	John LELLIOT and wife Ann.	Clayton

1780 Jun.11	James WOOD, wife Elizabeth and son James.	Woodmancote
1782 Mar. 6	Anthony HOLE, wife and child. Ack.	Uckfield
1783 Mar. 3	John RICHARDSON, blacksmith, wife Mary and children William, Ann and Mary. Ack.	Newtimber
1783 Apr.21	John SAUNDERS, wife Elizabeth and children John, Thomas and Elizabeth. Ack.	Twineham
1783 Dec.27	George GILES and wife Phoebe. Ack.	Ticehurst
1785 Jan. 3	Thomas PARSONS, wife Sarah and daughter Sarah. Ack.	Steyning
1785 Jan.12	Thomas PARSONS, wife Sarah and daughter Sarah.	Steyning
1785 Jan.15	George GILES and wife Pheby. Ack.	Ticehurst
1786 Nov.17	James WICKS and wife Elizabeth.	Cuckfield
1790 Nov.24	Letter to Mr. Crosskey, Hurstpierpoint. "Sir, The parish officers of Cranley are agreeable to give Thos. MERCER a certificate and send it to the Swan at Horsham as soon as confirmed. Your very obedient servant W. Martin, Cranley."	Cranleigh, Sry
1790 Dec. 5	Thomas MERCER, wife Sarah and daughter Sarah 17 m.	Cranleigh, Sry
1791 Mar.18	James PENFOLD, wife Susannah and children William and James. Ack.	Cuckfield
1792 Apr.11	William WHITE, wife Elizabeth and children Mary 17y, Henry 15y, John 14y, Ann 11y, James 9y, Kate 5y, Elizabeth 3y and Thomas 2y.	Clayton
1793 Mar.14	Luke HUMPHREY, wife Margaret and son William.	Arundel

HURSTPIERPOINT SETTLEMENT CERTIFICATES — Par 400/32/1/1

		To
1734 Jul.10	John WOOLGER and wife Jane.	Henfield
1751 May 5	William KING and wife Sarah.	Bolney

REMOVAL ORDERS FROM HURSTPIERPOINT — Par 400/32/2/1

		To
1728 Oct.10	John LONG and wife Mary. Confirmation.	Trotton
1758 Oct.30	George MOORE and wife Hanah.	Clapham
1775 Oct.30	James COOPER, wife Ann. [Delivered 4 Nov.]	Hadlow, Ken
1781 Oct. 4	Thomas VINCENT, wife Mary and son James 9m. On appeal, order quashed.	Keymer
1783 Mar. 1	John SAUNDERS, wife Elizabeth and children John 5y, Thomas 4y and Elizabeth 2y.	Twineham
1786 Oct.11	Isaac BLINK and wife Ann.	Ditchling
1790 Jun.28	John STREDWICK, wife Mary and son John. Kirdford to appeal against removal at next Q.S.	Kirdford
1790 Nov. 6	Thomas MERCER, wife Sarah and daughter Sarah	Cranleigh, Sry

	16m. [Sent home to Cranley on 23 Nov.]	
1790 Dec.29	Thomas ROWLAND and wife Sarah. [Sent home to Horsham 29 December]	Horsham
1791 Jul.15	William BURTENSHAW and wife Elizabeth. [Delivered 18 July]	Steyning
1792 Mar.13	William WHITE, wife Elizabeth and children Mary 17y, Henry 15y, John 14y, Ann 11y, James 9y, Kate 5y, Elizabeth 3y and Thomas 2y. [Delivered 17 March.	Clayton
1795 Apr. 4	Richard PETERS and wife Jane.	Twineham
1800 Jan.11	Richard TULLEY, wife Sarah and children Sarah 2y and Henry 4m. [Delivered 28 January].	Clayton
1801 Apr.11	John PANNETT and wife Sarah.	Hamsey
1801 Dec.19	Robert PRONGER and wife Sarah. Order suspended as Sarah is sick. [Endorsed: 6 Feb.1802: Sarah Pronger has died since date of the within order, which can now be executed.]	Dartford, Ken
1802 Apr.10	George WORSELL and wife Elizabeth. [Delivered 13 April]	Charlwood, Sry
1802 Jun. 5	Jane NYE, singlewoman. [Delivered 5 June]	Hailsham
1820 Jan.14	Sarah BANFIELD, wife of Thomas BANFIELD. Confirmation.	Edburton
1820 Apr.14	Ann CARD, singlewoman. Confirmation.	Clayton
1820 Jun.20	Charles WALLER. [Delivered 20 June]	Brighton
1820 Dec.26	Mary TIDY otherwise KING, and Elizabeth TIDY, otherwise KING. [Delivered 10 January 1821]	Bolney
1820 Dec.26	Sarah TIDY, wife of Stephen TIDY. [Delivered 9 January 1821]	Cowfold
1821 May 4	Mary TIDY, otherwise KING and Elizabeth TIDY, otherwise KING. On appeal, order confirmed.	Bolney
1821 May 4	Sarah TIDY, wife of Stephen TIDY. On appeal, order confirmed.	Cowfold
1822 Jul.19	Richard TIDY otherwise FLINT, Ann TIDY otherwise FLINT and James TIDY otherwise FLINT. Confirmation.	Newtimber
1824 Mar.30	Thomas HOLLINGDALE, wife Philadelphia and children Mary Ann 3y and William 7m. [Delivered 31 March]	Poynings

QUARTER SESSIONS REMOVAL ORDERS FROM HURSTPIERPOINT

		To
L 1646 Apr. 9	Edward MOORE of Pyecombe and impress as a soldier, having received hurt and become impotent, is to be sent from Hurstpierpoint, where he is at present, to Pyecombe.	Pyecombe

C 1651 Oct. 6	John BEARD.	Woodmancote
L 1663 Oct. 8	Ann CARTER, spinster. Hurstpierpoint to show cause, within one month, why A.C. should not be returned there.	Pyecombe
L 1664 Jul.14	Richard MACKARRALL.	Albourne
L 1664 Jul.14	Henry SYMONDS. To give security or be removed to Cowfold.	Cowfold
L 1674 Jan.15	Ann MARTIN, singlewoman.	Keymer
L 1678 Jan.17	George READE. On his appeal, order respited.	Steyning
L 1679 May 2	William MUTTON; confirmed.	Bolney
L 1680 Jan.15	WEBB. Case between Hurstpierpoint and Newtimber concerning the two children [names not given] of William WEBB is respited; meanwhile children to remain at Newtimber.	Newtimber
L 1682 Jan.12	Ann CARD, wife of James CARD; recites previous order which is respited.	East Grinstead
L 1700 Jul.18	- JENNER; discharged.	Cuckfield
L 1713 Jul.16	Mary MANFEILD, singlewoman; confirmed.	Albourne
L 1726 Apr.21	Joseph PARSONS, wife Susannah and children Sarah, Thomas and Joseph, all under 4y; confirmed.	Cuckfield
L 1727 Jan.12	Stephen REEVE, wife Ann and children Ann, Stephen, Samuel, Mary, Simon and Zephanah; confirmed.	Newtimber
L 1728 Oct.10	John LONG and wife Mary; confirmed.	Trotton
L 1732 Oct. 5	Thomas HOLIBONE, wife Mary and daughters Mary and Elizabeth; confirmed.	Cuckfield
L 1737 Apr.21	Anne DUNTON, widow of Thomas DUNTON, and children Thomas 9y, John 6y 9m, Henry 2y and Richard 4m; confirmed.	Albourne
L 1738 Jan.12	John CHASEMORE and wife Anne; respited.	Plumpton
L 1738 Jan.12	William BONIFACE, wife Elizabeth and daughter Anne; confirmed.	Woodmancote
L 1738 Apr.13	John CHASEMORE and wife Anne; confirmed.	Plumpton
L 1740 Oct. 9	Mary NICHOLAS, singlewoman, confirmed.	Albourne
L 1741 Apr. 9	Thomas VALLANCE, wife Elizabeth and children Ann 15y, Thomas 14y, David 12y, Margaret 10y, Elizabeth 8y, William 6y, James 4y and Mary 1y; discharged.	Preston
L 1753 Jul.12	John FOSTER; confirmed.	Keymer
L 1765 Jan.17	Thomas MARCHANT and wife Betty; confirmed.	Poynings
L 1770 Jul.12	John ROOK, wife Sarah and sons Thomas 8y and John lately born; confirmed.	Old Shoreham
L 1774 Jan.13	Charity BARNETT and daughter Martha; respited.	Cuckfield

L 1774 Jul.14	Charity BARNETT and daughter Martha; quashed.	Cuckfield
L 1776 Jan.11	Phoebe LENEY [?LEURY], singlewoman; respited.	Denton
L 1777 Jan.16	Phoebe LENEY [?LEURY] singlewoman; quashed.	Denton
L 1781 Jul.12	Thomas VINCENT, wife Mary and son James 9m; respited.	Keymer
L 1781 Oct. 4	Thomas VINCENT, wife Mary and son James 9m; quashed.	Keymer
L 1784 Apr.23	George HUGGETT, wife Hannah and daughter Mary 2m; quashed.	Ditchling
L 1790 Jul.15	John STREDWICK, wife Mary and son John 1m; quashed.	Kirdford
L 1791 Jul.14	William BURTENSHAW and wife Elizabeth; quashed.	Arundel
L 1791 Oct. 6	William BURTENSHAW; respited.	Steyning
L 1796 Jul.15	Mary GOODWIN, singlewoman; respited.	Henfield
L 1796 Oct. 7	Mary GOODWIN, singlewoman; quashed.	Henfield
L 1800 Apr.24	Thomas VIRGOE; quashed.	Old Shoreham
L 1802 Jul.16	William MILES, wife Barbarah and children John 7y, James 5y, Barbarah 2y and Esau 4m; confirmed.	Clayton
L 1805 Apr.26	George HARDS, wife Elizabeth and children George and Patience; confirmed.	Washington
L 1805 Oct.11	Barbara ELDRIDGE, wife of John Lloyd ELDRIDGE, and children Elizabeth Lloyd 6y, Mary 5y, Ann 3y, and Harriet 4m; confirmed.	Washington
L 1809 Apr.14	Anthony HOLE, wife Elizabeth and daughters Mary 2y and Elizabeth 1y; confirmed.	Bolney
L 1810 May 4	Mary GROVES, singlewoman; confirmed.	Poynings
L 1811 Jan.18	James GILES, wife Ann and son Thomas 1y; confirmed.	Ovingdean
L 1811 Apr.26	John BARBER, illegitimate child of Frances BARBER, singlewoman, deceased; confirmed.	Hamlet of Fulking, Edburton
L 1811 Apr.26	James HILLMAN, wife Sarah and daughter Susan 2y; confirmed.	West Grinstead
L 1811 Apr.26	Thomas SHAW, wife Elizabeth and sons William 5y and Thomas 2y; confirmed.	West Hoathly
L 1811 Oct.11	Ann EDWARDS, singlewoman; confirmed. confirmed.	Albourne,
L 1811 Oct.11	Jane GODLEY, singlewoman; confirmed.	Brighton
L 1812 Jan.17	Nathaniel PICKETT, wife Jane and children Sarah 15y, John 12y, William, [age not given] Ann 7y, Nathaniel 4y, and Henry 2y; confirmed.	Newick

L 1813 Oct. 8	James GODSMARK, wife Sarah and son Henry 2y; confirmed.	Balcombe
L 1814 Jan.14	Hannah BLABER, singlewoman; confirmed.	Albourne
L 1815 Apr. 7	John BURCHETT, wife Sarah and children John 9y, Sarah 6y, Mary 4y and Elizabeth 2y; respited.	Brighton
L 1815 Apr. 7	Charles HARDING, wife Mary and children Charles 11y, Mary 8y and Ann 3y; respited	Lambeth, Sry
L 1815 Apr. 7	Henry STREETON, wife Gany and daughter Barbara; confirmed.	Willingdon
L 1815 Jul.14	John BURCHETT, wife Sarah and children John 9y, Sarah 6y, Mary 4y and Elizabeth 2y; quashed.	Brighton
L 1815 Jul.14	Charles HARDING, wife Mary and children Charles 3y (sic), Mary 8y and Ann 3y; quashed.	Lambeth, Sry
L 1815 Jul.14	Isabella GODMAN, (wife of William GODMAN, a private gunner in lst Battalion R.A. now stationed at Woolwich, under orders for embarkation for foreign service), and children Thomas 3y and Margaret 13m; confirmed.	Henfield
L 1816 Jan.12	James GEERING, wife Prisilla and daughter Eliza 9m; confirmed.	Newtimber
L 1816 Apr.26	James MARSHALL; confirmed.	Uckfield
L 1816 Apr.26	Susannah BROWN, wife of Stephen BROWN and son Thomas 5m; confirmed.	Lindfield
L 1817 Jan.17	Lydia GEERE, singlewoman; confirmed.	Albourne
L 1817 Apr.18	Elizabeth HAZLEGROVE, singlewoman; confirmed.	Newtimber
L 1818 Apr. 3	John PAYNE, wife Mary and son John 5y; confirmed.	Herstmonceaux
L 1818 Jul.17	Susan PROVET, wife of Samuel PROVET; respited.	Lewknor, Oxf
L 1818 Jul.17	William TURNER, wife Mary and daughter Mary 1y, and an infant daughter not yet baptised; confirmed.	West Grinstead
L 1818 Oct.23	Susan PROVET, wife of Samuel PROVET; quashed.	Lewknor, Oxf
L 1819 Jul.16	John HOWARD, wife Mary and children Joseph 14y and Mary 11y; respited.	Wivelsfield
L 1819 Oct.22	Ann CARD, singlewoman; respited.	Edenbridge, Ken
L 1820 Jan.14	Ann CARD, singlewoman; quashed.	Edenbridge, Ken
L 1820 Jan.14	Sarah BANFIELD, wife of Thomas BANFIELD; confirmed.	Edburton
L 1820 Apr.14	Ann CARD, singlewoman; confirmed.	Clayton
L 1821 Jan.12	Sarah TIDY, wife of Stephen TIDY; respited.	Cowfold
L 1821 Jan.12	Mary TIDY otherwise KING and Elizabeth TIDY otherwise KING; respited.	Bolney
L 1821 May 4	Sarah TIDY, wife of Stephen TIDY; confirmed.	Cowfold

L 1821 May 4	Mary TIDY otherwise KING [and Elizabeth TIDY otherwise KING]; confirmed.	Bolney
L 1822 Jul.19	Richard TIDY otherwise FLINT, Ann TIDY otherwise FLINT and James TIDY otherwise FLINT; confirmed.	Newtimber
L 1826 Jan.12	Frances JENNER, wife of Daniel JENNER and son James 2m; confirmed.	Cuckfield
L 1826 Jul.13	John SINDEN and wife Ann; confirmed.	Cuckfield
L 1828 Jul.17	Sarah FULLER, wife of William FULLER who has deserted her) and son John 4m; confirmed.	Nuthurst
L 1828 Oct.16	Elizabeth WALLER, widow; respited.	Twineham
L 1828 Oct.16	John CHATFIELD and wife Eliza; respited.	Ditchling
L 1829 Oct.22	William Solomon PAMPLIN; quashed.	Brighton
L 1830 Jan.14	William Solomon PAMPLIN; confirmed.	Henfield
L 1834 Oct.16	Frances NYE, singlewoman; confirmed.	Henfield
L 1835 Apr. 6	William BURTENSHAW, wife Sarah and son William 16y; quashed.	Brighton

REMOVAL ORDERS TO HURSTPIERPOINT Par 400/32/3/1

		From
1718 Apr. 1	Edward JERVICE	Henfield
1718 Apr.21	Edward JERVICE. On appeal, order discharged	Henfield
1725 Jan.19	William STONEHAM and wife Mary.	Falmer
1791 Oct.14	Sarah TULLEY, singlewoman.	Clayton
1796 Apr.27	James GLAZBROOK and wife Jane.	Woodmancote
1801 Dec.10	Jane BENNETT, singlewoman, who has declared herself to be pregnant, the child likely to be born a bastard.	Ditchling
1819 Oct.25	John PARSONS, wife Jane and children Jane 7y, Eliza 3y and George 9m. [Received 1 Nov.]	Southwick
1819 Nov.13	Thomas NORMAN. [Received 3rd December]	St. Michael, Lewes
1819 Nov.29	Frances GOLDES, wife of George GOLDES, a Private in the Corps of Sappers and Miners.	Brighton
1820 Apr.14	Henry MANNERS. On appeal, order respited.	All Saints, Lewes
1821 Jan.12	Jane KING, apprehended in East Grinstead as a rogue and vagabond, was convicted as she did, on 16 December last, commit acts of vagrancy by wandering abroad, lodging in the open air and lighting fires under hedges and was ordered to be conveyed to Hurstpierpoint. On examination, J.K. said that she believes she was born in Bolney but that her father was legally settled in Hurstpierpoint, and that the parish officers put her out to service to Mrs. ALFORD in Hurstpierpoint, where she served	East Grinstead

	for upwards of a year, and has not gained a settlement elsewhere. [Mark of J.K.]	
1821 Feb.20	James RICHARDSON, wife Lydia and infant female child, not yet baptised. J.R. unable to travel due to sickness; fit to do by 15 March. £1.15s 0d to be paid to Streat. *Catalogued under Par 400/32/3/34*	Streat
1821 Feb.28	William SILSBY. On examination of W.S. and Mary SILSBY, his mother, his last settlement adjudged to be in Hurstpierpoint. [Received W.S. 1 March and ordered in the House]	Twineham
1821 Mar.28	Sarah GLAZEBROOK, wife of James GLAZEBROOK. [Received S. G. 6 April]	Woodmancote
1821 Apr.18	James HAMLETT, the son of Mary Ann HAMLETT, who was born illegitimate in Hurstpierpoint. [Received 25 April]	Warblington, Ham.
1821 Dec.14	John STANDING and wife Ann. [Received 15 December]	Twineham
1822 Mar. 8	Ann MASON, widow. [Received 9 March].	Cuckfield
1823 Jan.24	William BENNETT otherwise MITCHELL. [Received 24 January]	Keymer
1823 Jan.28	John MILES and wife Mary. [Received 30 January]	Patcham
1823 Jun.19	Elizabeth Lloyd ELDRIDGE, singlewoman, pregnant with child. [Received 20 June]	St. Margarets, Westminster, Lon
1823 Jul.26	David WHITE, wife Mary and children Peter 4y and Martha 1y. [Received 29 July]	Horsham
1823 Sep.15	Jane KING. [Received 15 September]	Brighton
1823 Sep.22	George GILES, wife Ann and children George 5y, William 3y and Mary 18m. [Received 25 September]	Brighton
1823 Nov.24	Mary HARMES.	Brighton
1824 Jan.20	Amelia SIMMONDS, wife of James SIMMONDS, now absent from her and a prisoner confined in the House of Correction at Lewes, and children John 2y and Francis 8m. [Endorsed: This is to certify that John Simmons [sic] named in this order is entered in error and not delivered with the other two [sic] 23 January 1824. Robert ACKERSON, churchwarden Brighton.]	Brighton
1824 Apr.23	William KING, wife Mary and children Henry 5y and Sarah 2y. [Received 30 April]	Cuckfield
1824 Jun. 7	Elizabeth JUPP, wife of Henry JUPP, labourer. [Received 7 June and left in the House]	Thakeham

1824 Sep. 7	Henry GEERE, wife Mary and children Frances 4y and William aged 6 weeks. Unable to travel due to H.G.'s sickness; fit to do so by 1 March 1825. Hurstpierpoint to pay £4.1s 0d.	St. John sub Castro, Lewes.
1824 Nov. 8	Harriet BURTENSHAW, singlewoman. [Received 11 November]	Brighton
1825 Mar. 1	Daniel HARLAND and wife Mary. [Received 5 March]	Preston
1825 Jun. 6	Martha WADEY. [Received 7 June]	Brighton
1826 Apr. 8	Mary EARLE, wife of George EARLE.	Slindon
1826 Dec.16	James TULLET and wife Susannah. [Received 18 December]	Cowfold

QUARTER SESSIONS REMOVAL ORDERS TO HURSTPIERPOINT

		From
L 1649 Oct. 4	Edward HOLLINGDALE, being a vagrant, is to be whipped and sent to Hurstpierpoint [it] being, as he confessed, the place of his birth.	Not given
L 1694 Apr.19	Richard WHITE and wife; to be settled at Hurstpierpoint.	Keymer
L 1708 Jul.15	- WALKETT; discharged.	Pyecombe
L 1745 Jul.18	Richard SURGION, wife Mary and daughter Elizabeth; discharged.	Beckley
L 1761 Jan.15	Ann BURTON otherwise ETHERINGTON; and son Thomas 1y 7 weeks; respited.	Edburton
L 1761 Apr. 2	Ann BURTON otherwise ETHERINGTON; and son Thomas 1y 7 weeks; confirmed as to Ann and discharged as to Thomas her son.	Edburton
L 1764 Jan.12	Elizabeth HOGSFLESH; confirmed.	Portslade
P 1771 Oct. 7	Richard WOOD, wife Elizabeth and daughter Ann aged 12 weeks; confirmed.	Horsham
L 1773 Jan.14	Phoebe LENEY; singlewoman; confirmed.	Hamsey
L 1805 Jan.18	Hannah MITCHELL; singlewoman; respited.	Brighton
L 1805 Jan.18	Henry LEWRY, wife Elizabeth and daughters Elizabeth 2y and Mary 8m; respited.	Brighton
L 1805 Apr.26	Hannah MITCHELL; singlewoman; confirmed.	Brighton
L 1805 Apr.26	Henry LEWRY, wife Elizabeth; and daughters Elizabeth 2y and Mary 8m; confirmed.	Brighton
L 1805 Oct.11	John BURT and wife Jane; confirmed.	Newtimber
M 1807 Apr. 7	Ann HOOD; confirmed.	Linchmere
L 1808 Jan.15	Addah FLINT; singlewoman; confirmed.	All Saints, Lewes
L 1810 Jan.12	Stephen HENLEY, wife Sarah and children William 3y and Susanna 1m; confirmed.	Rottingdean
L 1811 Jan.18	Elizabeth DUNTON, wife of Thomas DUNTON; confirmed.	Rottingdean

L 1814 Apr.22	Henry LEWRY, wife Elizabeth and children Elizabeth 11y, Maria 7y, William 6y, George 4y and David 8m; confirmed.	Brighton
P 1818 Jan.12	Sarah EDWARDS; confirmed.	Midhurst
L 1820 Jan.14	Frances GOLDS, (wife of George GOLDS, a private in the Corps of Sappers and Miners); confirmed.	Brighton
P 1820 Apr.11	John PARSONS, wife Jane and children Jane 7y, Eliza 3y and George 9m; confirmed.	Southwick
L 1820 Apr.14	Henry MANNERS; respited.	All Saints, Lewes
L 1820 Jul.14	Henry MANNERS; confirmed.	All Saints, Lewes
L 1821 May 4	James RICHARDSON, wife Lydia and an infant daughter not yet baptised; confirmed.	Streat
L 1823 Apr.11	John MILES and wife Mary; confirmed.	Patcham
L 1825 Apr.14	Daniel HARLAND and wife Mary; confirmed.	Preston
L 1825 Apr.14	Henry GEERE, wife Mary and children Frances 4y and William aged 6 weeks; confirmed.	St. John sub Castro, Lewes
L 1828 Jul.17	Susannah HENLEY; quashed.	Brighton
L 1830 Apr.22	William BROOMFIELD, wife Ann and children Mary 19y, William 18y, Stephen 10y, John 9y, Charles 7y and Ann 6y; respited.	Chailey
L 1830 Jul.15	William BROOMFIELD, wife Ann and children Mary 19y, William 18y, Stephen 10y, John 9y, Charles 7y and Ann 6y; quashed.	Chailey
L 1830 Oct.21	Eleanor DENMAN, singlewoman, who is with child; confirmed.	Falmer
L 1831 Jun.30	Mary SELCOMB, wife of Samuel SELCOMB, and daughters Sarah 6y and Mary 5y; quashed.	Brighton

HURSTPIERPOINT BASTARDY EXAMINATIONS Par 400/34/1/1

1776 Jan. 1 Elizabeth MITCHELL, singlewoman of Hurstpierpoint, is with child and has declared that Francis HEASMAN of Twineham, carpenter, is the father. [Mark of E.M.]

1803 Sep.16 Fanny MITCHELL, singlewoman, was delivered of a male bastard child on Sunday 24 July last, in Hurstpierpoint, and has declared that William AUSTIN of Oxted, Surrey, is the father. [Mark of F.M.]

HURSTPIERPOINT BASTARDY BONDS Par 400/34/4/1

1714 Jan. 6 William SMITH and Ambrose SMITH, his son, both of Ditchling, husbandmen, bound to the parish officers of Hurstpierpoint in £60 in respect of Mary SURGEON, singlewoman, who was lately delivered of a female bastard child, M.S. having declared that A.S. is the father. [Signature of W.S. and mark of A.S.]

1717 Jul.10 Thomas MUTTON of Rusper, butcher, and James MUTTON of Rusper, gent., bound to the parish officers of Hurstpierpoint in £30 in respect of Mary KING, who has declared that she was delivered of a bastard child in Hurstpierpoint, named Hanna KING, and that T.M. is the father. [Signatures of T.M. and J.M.]

1737 Dec. 5 Lucy HALLETT of Hurstpierpoint was delivered of a female bastard child on 30 September 1736, in Hurstpierpoint, and has charged Francis HOLCOMB with being the father. F.H. and John HOLCOMB of Cuckfield, father of F.H., do jointly promise to pay the parish officers of Hurstpierpoint 1s 6d a week, so long as the child shall be chargeable. [Signatures of F.H. and J.H.]

1744 Jan.13 The parish officers of Little Horsted are bound to the parish officers of Hurstpierpoint in £50 in respect of Elizabeth FALKNER, (a female bastard child born to Mary KNIGHT, late Mary FALKNER), and James FALKNER, (son of Mary Knight by William FALKNER, her late husband deceased), who were brought by their mother into Hurstpierpoint upon her marriage with John KNIGHT, a legal inhabitant of that parish. Mary Knight was, on 13 November 1742, granted 2s 0d a week each for her children to be paid by Little Horsted parish but, since the confirmation of that order on 6 October 1743, she has absconded and gone away from Hurstpierpoint, leaving the said Elizabeth and James behind. Therefore, it is agreed between all the above parties that Little Horsted shall, forthwith, receive the children into their parish and indemnify Hurstpierpoint from any further obligation.

1756 Nov.27 Joseph COLSTOCK of Hurstpierpoint, yeoman, bound to the parish officers of Hurstpierpoint in £60 in respect of Elizabeth PARSONS of Hurstpierpoint, singlewoman who, when examined on 13 May last, said that she was delivered of a female bastard child (named Ann) on 10 April last, and that J.C. is the father. [Signature of Joseph Coulstock (sic)]

1758 Oct.23 Thomas NYE, the younger, and Thomas NYE, the elder, both of Hurstpierpoint, husbandmen, bound to the parish officers of Hurstpierpoint in £200 in respect of Mary HERRIOT of Hurstpierpoint, who has declared that she is with child and that T.N., the younger, is the father. [Signature of T.N. and mark of T.N.]

1761 May 9 Edmund SAYERS of Steyning, labourer, and William SAYERS of Hurstpierpoint, husbandman, bound to the parish officers of Hurstpierpoint in £100 in respect of Sarah RENVELL of Hurstpierpoint, singlewoman, who has declared that she was delivered of a male bastard child on 8 December last at Hurstpierpoint and that E.S. is the father. [Signature of E.S. and mark of W.S.]

1761 Jul.24 Daniel LEWRY of Hurstpierpoint, yeoman, bound to the parish officers of Hurstpierpoint in £100 in respect of Elizabeth BARNARD, singlewoman, who has declared that she was delivered of a male bastard child on 24 May last, in Hurstpierpoint, and that D.L. is the father. [Signature of D.L.]

1766 Feb.18 James KNOWLS, Richard KNOWLES (sic) and Philip KNOWLS, all of Balcombe, husbandmen, bound to the parish officers of Hurstpierpoint in £100 in respect of Susannah WISE of Hurstpierpoint, singlewoman, who has declared that she is with child, and that James Knowls is the father. [Marks of J.K; R.K; and P.K.]

1768 Aug. 9 John WIX of Hurstpierpoint, husbandman, bound to the parish officers of Hurstpierpoint in £50, J.W. having agreed to maintain and educate a bastard child known by the name of John Wix [mother's name not given], and to pay 18d a week maintenance. [Signature of John Wicks (sic)]

1768 Nov. 8 Richard HAYNES of Hurstpierpoint, maltster, bound to the parish officers of Hurstpierpoint in £100 in respect of Sarah OLDER of Hurstpierpoint, singlewoman, who has declared that she is with child, and that R.H. is the father. [Signature of R.H.]

1774 Oct. 4 John PILBEAM of Hurstpierpoint, schoolmaster, and William PILBEAM of Plumpton, husbandman, son of John Pilbeam, bound to the parish officers of Hurstpierpoint in £100 in respect of Mary MAY of Hurstpierpoint, singlewoman, who has declared that she is with child and that W.P. is the father. [Signatures of J.P. and W.P.]

1774 Aug.19 Henry BURRY and Edward BURRY, father of Henry Burry, both of Hurstpierpoint, yeomen, bound to the parish officers of Hurstpierpoint in £200 in respect of Elizabeth JUPP, singlewoman, who was delivered of a female bastard child on 1 July last, in Hurstpierpoint, and has declared that H.B. is the father. [Signatures of H.B. and E.B.]

1778 Nov.16 James BROWNE of Lingfield, Surrey, husbandman, and Daniel WEST of Bolney, husbandman, bound to the parish officers of Hurstpierpoint in £100 in respect of Sarah BOWELL, singlewoman, who has declared that she was lately delivered of a male bastard child in Hurstpierpoint, and that J.B. is the father. J.B. agrees to pay £5, and a further £15 (£3.15s 0d on 16 November of each of the following years: 1779, 1780, 1781 and 1782). [Marks of J.B. and D.W.] [Endorsed: 16 Nov.1779 received £5.]

1780 Dec.23 Thomas MARCHANT, the elder, of Hurstpierpoint, surgeon, bound to the parish officers of Hurstpierpoint in £300 in respect of Jane MORRIS of Hurstpierpoint, spinster, who has declared that she is great with child and that T.M. is the father. [Signature of T.M.]

1782 Jan.16 Thomas HOLMAN of Albourne, yeoman, and John PIPER of Woodmancote, yeoman, bound to the parish officers of Hurstpierpoint in £100 in respect of Ann WHITE, now or late the wife of William WHITE, late of

Hurstpierpoint, husbandman, and now or late a soldier serving in one of His Majesty's regiments in North America, who has, since her husband's absence, been delivered of a female child christened by the name of Sarah. [Signatures of T.H. and J.P.]

1792 Aug.30 Francis LENEY of Danny in Hurstpierpoint, coachman, bound to the parish officers of Hurstpierpoint in £50 in respect of Elizabeth LEOPARD of Hurstpierpoint, spinster, who was delivered of a female bastard child on 26 May last in Hurstpierpoint. [Signature of F.L.] [Endorsed: £20 deposited.]

1792 Sep. 4 Richard KING of Hurstpierpoint, husbandman, and Thomas BARTLEY of Hurstpierpoint, collar maker, bound to the parish officers of Hurstpierpoint in £50 in respect of Sarah NYE of Hurstpierpoint, spinster, who was delivered of a male bastard child, baptised Richard, in Hurstpierpoint and S.N. has declared that the father is R.K. who is to pay 2s 0d a week maintenance. [Endorsed: On 5 Feb.1796 received of Richard King £3.6s 0d for 33 weeks pay due on 29th of last month.] [Signatures of R.K. and T.B.]

1800 - James BARTLEY of Patcham, labourer, bound to the parish officers of of Hurstpierpoint, in £30 in respect of Sarah BETTIE of Hurstpierpoint, spinster, who has declared that she is with child, and that J.B., the younger, servant to William John CAMPION of Danny, is the father but, as J.B. the younger is under age and unable to give security to the parish, J.B., the elder, is bound until J.B., the younger, shall arrive at the age of 21 years, when he can then enter into a bond himself.
[Mark of J.B.]

HURSTPIERPOINT BASTARDY ORDERS Par 400/34/3/1

1743 Jan.13 Elizabeth FALKNER, a female bastard child aged 9 months born to Mary KNIGHT, late Mary FALKNER, and James FALKNER aged 3 years, son of Mary Knight, by her late husband. Little Horsted appealed against an order dated 13 November 1742, whereby they are ordered to pay 2s 0d a week maintenance for each child, and the order is respited.

1743 Oct. 6 Elizabeth FAULKNER, aged 9 months, female bastard child of Mary KNIGHT, formerly FAULKNER, and James FAULKNER, aged 3 years, born to her by her late husband. On appeal against order to pay 2s 0d a week for each child, order is now confirmed.

1755 Apr. 4 Ann SIMMONDS, has declared that John BODLE of Hurstpierpoint, butcher, is the father of a male bastard child born to her on 28 December last, in Hurstpierpoint. J.B. to pay 1s 6d a week maintenance and to find surieties for his personal appearance at the next Quarter Sessions; the mother to pay 6d a week. [Endorsed: As it does not appear that John Bodle was ever served with a copy of this order it will be necessary to have Ann SIMMONS (sic), the mother of the child, re-examined and to have a warrant thereon to apprehend the said Bodle.]

1798 Jun. 9 Sarah DENMAN, widow, has declared that John MARSHALL of Hurstpierpoint, butcher, is the father of a female bastard child born to her on 1 April last, in Hurstpierpoint. J.M. to pay £3. 5s 0d for cost of lying-in and 2s 6d a week; the mother to pay 6d a week.

1821 Feb.20 Barbara BARTLEY of Hurstpierpoint, has declared that William NICHOLLS of Brighthelmstone, servant, is the father of a female bastard child born to her on 20 November last in Hurstpierpoint. W.N. to pay £4.4s 6d costs (£3.12s 6d for lying-in and 12s 0d for filiation order) and 2s 6d a week; the mother to pay 6d a week. [Endorsed: On 25 March 1826 demand was made for £37.5s 0d.]

1827 Apr.24 Naomi STANDEN, singlewoman, has declared that Peter KING of Hurstpierpoint, labourer, is the father of a female bastard child born to her on 1 February last. P.K. to pay £1.14s 0d (£1.2s 0d for lying in and 12s 0d for filiation order) and 2s 0d a week; the mother to pay 1s 0d a week. [Endorsed: Received 20s. Child died April, 1828.]

HURSTPIERPOINT WARRANTS Par 400/34/2/1

1759 Jan. 5 Mary BONIFACE of Hurstpierpoint, singlewoman, has declared that Jeremiah BANISTER of Hurstpierpoint, cordwainer, is the father of a female bastard child, named Mary, born to her on Friday 24 November last at Hurstpierpoint; and he is to be apprehended.

1759 Jan. 5 Mary VERRALL of Hurstpierpoint, singlewoman, has declared that Richard KNIGHT, of Woodmancote, labourer, is the father of the male bastard child, named Richard Knight, born to her on Thursday 5 October last, at Hurstpierpoint; and R.K. is to be apprehended.

1763 May 6 Mary VALLANCE, singlewoman, has declared that James CHAPMAN, late of Bletchingley, Surrey, blacksmith, is the father of a female bastard child born to her on 16th February last, at Hurstpierpoint. M.V. to appear before a Justice at the house of Henry VERRALL, in Lewes on Saturday 21 May, and notice is to be given to J.C. that he may attend.

1781 Oct. 5 Mary DEAN of Hurstpierpoint, singlewoman, who was, seven weeks agone, delivered of a female bastard child at Hurstpierpoint, refuses to be examined touching her child and charging the reputed father thereof; and M.D. is to be apprehended.

1784 Mar. 3 Sarah GODLEY of Hurstpierpoint, singlewoman, to be apprehended and brought before a Justice to be examined relative to the reputed father of a female bastard child, lately delivered to her in Hurstpierpoint.

1784 Mar. 3 George HUGGET, lately removed with wife and family from Hurstpierpoint to Ditchling by an order, has returned to reside in Hurstpierpoint, without producing any certificate of settlement; and he to be apprehended.
Catalogued under Par 400/37/106.

1785 Apr.13 Elizabeth EDWARDS of Hurstpierpoint, singlewoman, is to be apprehended and brought before a Justice to be examined as to the reputed father of a female bastard child lately born to her in Hurstpierpoint. [Endorsed: This summons is returnable at the Tiger Inn in Lindfield on Wednesday the 27th April, 1785.]

1801 Jan. 3 John HIDER, a pauper belonging to Hurstpierpoint, is charged with having, for a considerable time, absented himself from the parish leaving his family chargeable thereto; and he is to be apprehended.
Catalogued under Par 400/37/109.

1802 Apr.22 Jane BENNETT of Hurstpierpoint, singlewoman, has declared that James MITCHELL, late of Ditchling, labourer, is the father of a male bastard child born to her on 22 March last; and he is to be apprehended.

1818 Nov. 7 Philadelphia LEE of Hurstpierpoint, singlewoman, has declared that George MATTHEW of Hurstpierpoint, labourer, is the father of a female bastard child born to her on 20 July last in the poorhouse of Hurstpierpoint. P.L. to be apprehended and brought before Justices at County Hall, Lewes on 14 November, and notice to be given to G.M. that he may also attend.

1820 Jun.13 Ann TALMY of Hurstpierpoint, singlewoman, who is with child, has declared that Henry COSSUM of Ringmer, labourer, is the father; and he is to be apprehended. [Endorsed: Bail proposed are: Thomas COSSUM of Laughton, labourer, works for Mr. Morris of Stonecross, a housekeeper - has got [?80s] on Mortgage of a house at Laughton and [?90s] in the bank. Thomas HILLMAN of Ringmer, labourer, brother in law, housekeeper, has goods worth [?40s] but he receives 2s 0d a week of the parish.] [*Catalogued under Par 400/32/3/1*].

1824 Feb. 3 Edward KING of Hurstpierpoint, labourer, was, on 16 December 1823, ordered to pay a certain sum weekly for maintenance of a male bastard child, lately born to Elizabeth MARTIN, singlewoman, in Hurstpierpoint. £3.14s 0d is now due up to 3 February 1824 and, as E.K. has refused to pay, he is to be apprehended.

1825 Jun.14 Mary PORT of Hurstpierpoint, widow, has declared that Philip SAYERS of Hurstpierpoint, labourer, is the father of a female bastard child born to her on 16 September 1822, at her own house in Hurstpierpoint. M.P. to be apprehended and brought before a Justice at County Hall, Lewes, on 21 June, and notice is to be given to P.S. that he may also attend.

1825 Jun.14 Mary PORT of Hurstpierpoint, singlewoman, [sic] has declared that she is now with child and that Philip SAYERS of Hurstpierpoint, labourer, is the father; and he is to be apprehended.

1825 Oct.11 Ann KING of Hurstpierpoint, has declared that she is with child and that James PENFOLD of Brighton, bricklayer, is the father; and he is to be apprehended.

1826 Aug. 8 William NICHOLLS of Brighthelmston, servant, by an order of bastardy dated 20 February 1821, stands charged with the payment of a certain weekly sum for the relief of a female bastard child born to Barbara BARTLEY, singlewoman, of Hurstpierpoint, he being the father. [Endorsed: There is now £37.5s 0d owing up to 25 March 1826 and, as he has refused to pay the same, he is to be apprehended.]

1826 Sep.29 Mary MORLEY of Hurstpierpoint, singlewoman, has declared that she is with child and that Richard EAGER of Ditchling, labourer, is the father; and he is to be apprehended.

1826 Nov.28 Naomi STANDEN of Hurstpierpoint, singlewoman, has declared that she is with child, and that Peter KING of Hurstpierpoint, labourer, is the father; and he is to be apprehended.

Undated Lindfield parish request that Timothy BRIGDEN of Lindfield, carpenter, being charged as the reputed father of a female bastard child born to Mary THOMPSET in the workhouse of Hurstpierpoint on 26 December last, be allowed to continue on his recognizance till M.T. may go before the Justices in order to filiate the child.

HURSTPIERPOINT APPRENTICESHIP AGREEMENTS Par 400/33/1

1700 Jun. 7 Leonard HASELGROVE apprenticed to John NEWLAND of Chailey, cordwainer, until age of 24 years; trade of shoemaker. [Mark of J.N.]

1718 Apr. 7 BOND. Thomas AFFIELD of Hurstpierpoint, yeoman, bound to the parish officers of Hurstpierpoint in £50, agrees to take as an apprentice Henry HEATH als BALL, until age of 24 years; husbandry. [Signature of Thomas Affielld (sic)]

1718 Apr. 7 BOND. Richard WHITPAINE of Hurstpierpoint, gent., bound to the parish officers of Hurstpierpoint in £50, agrees to take as apprentice John BIGNULL until age of 18 years; husbandry. [Signature of R.W.]

1718 Jun. 3 Sarah LINDFIELD apprenticed to John WIGGENS of Hurstpierpoint, yeoman, until age of 21 years; housewifery. [Signature of John Wickins (sic)]

1751 Dec.23 John BALL, aged 11 years the 10 February last, apprenticed to Edward PAIGE of St. Michael, Lewes, cordwainer, until age of 24 years; trade of cordwainer.

1783 Jan.21 William MAY, aged 16 years, with the consent of his mother, Margaret MAY of Hurstpierpoint, widow, has put himself apprentice to Edward MAY of Alfriston, bricklayer, to serve from 25 March 1778, for seven years; trade of bricklayer. Consideration: £2.2s 0d. [Signatures of W.M.and M.M.] [Endorsed: 7 Feb. 1783: Duty paid at 6d in the £ = 1s 0d.]

1801 Nov. 9 John DUNTON of Hurstpierpoint, aged 17 years, with the consent of the parish officers, has put himself apprentice to William SHAW of Bolney, shoemaker, to serve from 10 October last until the end of term of three years; trade of shoemaker. Consideration: £30 to be paid by the parish officers. [Mark of J.D. and signature of W.S.] [Endorsed: 19 Nov.1801 Duty paid of 6d in the £ = 15s 0d.]

1802 Jan. 9 The parish officers of Hurstpierpoint promise to pay to William SHAW of Bolney £20 as follows: £10 on 10 October 1802 and £10 on 10 October 1803, being part of the £30 to be paid to William Shaw with John DUNTON his apprentice.

1809 Nov.20 John PACKHAM STONER otherwise PACKHAM, aged 18 years, apprenticed to Thomas PENNIFOLD of Clayton, weaver, until age of 21 years; trade of weaver. Consideration: £30 to be paid by the parish officers, £15 forthwith and £15 on 20th May 1811. [Signatures of J.P.S. otherwise P. and T.P.]

1829 May 19 Thomas PORT, aged 15 years, son of Mary PORT, widow, apprenticed by parish officers of Hurstpierpoint to George GREEN of Brighthelmstone, pipemaker, until age of 21 years; trade of pipemaker. Consideration: £7 at the time and a further £5 on 20 May 1830.

IFIELD

Ifield: 4,134 acres on northern border of Sussex, now within Crawley new town, 6 miles north-east of Horsham. Weald clay, overlaid in parts by river gravels or alluvium; some outcrops of sandstone, ironstone and limestone; between 200 and 300ft. Drains SW to NE by Ifield brook and others into river Mole; valleys marshy, fish bred in Ifield pond 1701. Much woodland and common, free warren. Crawley village within parish may have been medieval 'new town', accounted for most of population increase in 19th century.

Population: 1724 331; 1801 637.

QUARTER SESSIONS REMOVAL ORDERS FROM IFIELD

		To
P 1661 Jan. 9	COX. Two children [names not given] of Henry COX, late of Ifield, deceased; Steyning may appeal.	Steyning
L 1668 Jul. 9	William GREVATT; on appeal he is to be sent back of Ifield.	Bury
L 1691 Apr.23	William HOLLIS.	Worth
L 1696 Apr.23	Richard VERRALL and wife. Order was fraudently obtained by Ifield; discharged.	Cuckfield
L 1715 Oct. 6	Richard ESON and wife; quashed for want of form.	Bolney
L 1718 Oct. 9	William DORRIDGE; discharged.	Ditchling
H 1724 Jul.13	William ASHURST and wife Mary; quashed for want of form.	Cliffe, Lewes
L 1724 Jul.16	Richard ASHURST and wife Mary; quashed for want of form.	Cliffe, Lewes
P 1724 Oct. 5	Richard ASHURST and wife Mary; confirmed.	Wilmington
M 1725 Jan.11	John BROOKS and wife Elizabeth; confirmed.	Agmondesham, [Amersham, Bks]
M 1744 Jan. 9	Mary PARSONS; confirmed.	Horley, Sry
H 1744 Jul. 9	Sarah PARSONS, daughter of Samuel and Sarah PARSONS, certificate persons from Bolney to Ifield. Order removing her to Bolney, confirmed.	Bolney
P 1757 Oct. 3	William SIMMONS, wife Jane and a child under 7y; confirmed.	Worth
L 1766 Apr.10	Hannah TILLEY, singlewoman; confirmed.	Slaugham
C 1788 Mar.31	John TULLETT, wife Ann and sons William 4y and John 3y; respited.	Crawley
H 1788 Jul.14	John TULLETT, wife Ann and sons William 4y and John 3y; confirmed.	Crawley
C 1791 Jan.10	Ruth HOMWOOD, singlewoman; respited.	Crawley
M 1791 May 2	Ruth HOMWOOD, singlewoman; confirmed.	Crawley
M 1794 Apr.28	William EDE, wife Sarah and children Charlotte 6y, Edward 3y and Ann 6m; respited.	Bury

C 1797 Jan.10	Martha RAMSEY, singlewoman; confirmed.	Brighton
L 1806 Jul.18	William HEAVER respited.	Crawley
P 1811 Oct. 8	James CHANTLER, wife Sarah and children Mary 5y, William 3y and Thomas 1y; confirmed.	Worth
C 1815 Oct.17	Elizabeth HOMEWOOD, singlewoman; quashed.	Worth
P 1817 Jan.14	Mary CHARMAN, singlewoman; quashed.	Crawley
C 1818 Oct.13	John COMBER and wife Mary; respited.	West Hoathly
H 1825 Jul.12	Thomas PERRYER, wife Mary and child Mary 12y; confirmed.	Ockley, Sry
C 1827 Oct.16	John KNIGHT and wife Mary; confirmed.	Cuckfield
P 1830 Apr.20	Richard TAYLOR; quashed.	Bletchingley, Sry
H 1830 Jul.15	Robert COATES; quashed.	Withyham
P 1831 Jan. 3	Elizabeth TOBUTT, singlewoman, who is with child; respited.	Hurstpierpoint
P 1832 Dec.31	John GATTON; confirmed.	Thakeham

QUARTER SESSIONS REMOVAL ORDERS TO IFIELD

		From
C 1660 Oct. 1	COX. Two children [names not given] of Henry COX, late of Ifield, deceased.	Steyning
L 1696 Jul.16	John CHATFIELD; on appeal he is to be settled at Buxted.	Buxted
C 1707 Jul.14	Thomas FORMAN, wife and family; confirmed as to Thomas and his wife and discharged as to his family.	Horsham
M 1707 Oct. 6	Richard WRIGHT; discharged.	Warnham
L 1725 Jan.14	William CRIPPS, wife Elizabeth and children Edward and William; confirmed.	Ringmer
A 1728 Jan. 8	John MOUGRIDGE, wife and family; quashed for want of form.	Rusper
C 1728 Apr.29	John MOWGRIDGE, wife Mary and children Mary, Elizabeth, John, Thomas, James, Anne and Edward; confirmed.	Rusper
C 1732 Apr.17	Elizabeth MILLS and her bastard son; discharged.	Horsham
C 1733 Apr. 2	Joseph HOLLOWAY, children Richard and Mary; confirmed.	Billingshurst
M 1754 Jan.14	John GARTON and wife Sarah; confirmed.	Ashington
P 1781 Oct. 1	John GASTONE and wife Sarah; confirmed.	Burpham
L 1799 Jul.18	Ann MARTIN, singlewoman; quashed.	Brighton
L 1805 Jul.19	Lydia FORD wife of Robert FORD; confirmed.	Ringmer
L 1808 Jan.15	Henry SIMMONS and wife Mary; confirmed.	Ringmer
L 1825 Apr.14	William SMITH, wife Mary and children Richard 7y, Nathaniel 4y and Dedimier 2y; confirmed.	Pyecombe

IFIELD APPRENTICESHIP AGREEMENT Par 109/1/1/1

1620 Jul.6 Edward WILLSON, son of Edward WILLSON, late of Ifield, is apprenticed to William DODD of Crawley, gent. for the term of ten years. Consideration £7. [Mark of W.D.]

KEYMER

Keymer: 3,583 acres from 700ft on Downs to 100 ft further N; N portion now part of Burgess Hill. Downland chalk, loam and sand on sand and clay. Brick and tile works. Arable.

Population: 1676 216; 1724 (with Clayton) 237; 1801 465; 1811 536; 1821 679; 1831 681.

QUARTER SESSIONS REMOVAL ORDERS FROM KEYMER

		To
L 1663 Oct. 8	Thomas FRY and family.	Brighton
L 1694 Apr.19	Richard WHITE and wife.	Hurstpierpoint
L 1706 Jan.17	John PAGE, infant son of John PAGE; discharged.	East Grinstead
L 1706 Jul.18	John PAGE, infant son of John PAGE; discharged.	Hartfield
L 1706 Oct.10	John PAGE, infant son of John PAGE; discharged.	East Grinstead
L 1714 Oct. 7	Henry GEERING, wife and three children; confirmed.	Clayton
L 1715 Jan.13	John MILLS and wife; confirmed.	Wivelsfield
L 1734 Jan.17	Edward MURRALL and wife Eleanor; confirmed.	Hurstpierpoint
L 1735 Apr.17	Elizabeth GREEN and children Stephen 10y and Sarah 8y; confirmed.	Brighton
L 1741 Jan.15	Sarah DAWS; confirmed.	Cuckfield
L 1741 Jan.15	Sarah WOOLGAR, widow, and daughter Mary 5y; confirmed.	Woodmancote
L 1743 Jan.13	Anne GIBB, widow, and children Mary, Anne and John; discharged.	Edburton
L 1749 Jul.13	William CHATFIELD and wife Sarah; confirmed.	Cowfold
L 1749 Oct. 5	Thomas HASELGROVE and wife Mary; confirmed.	Cuckfield
L 1753 Jan.11	John MARTIN and wife Anne; confirmed.	Clayton
L 1767 Apr.30	John GEERING; respited.	Lindfield
L 1767 Jul.16	John GEERING; discharged.	Lindfield
L 1769 Apr. 6	Sampson BAGNALL, wife Susanna and sons Sampson 21y and James 20y; respited.	St. Andrew, Holborn, Ldn
H 1769 Jul.13	Sampson BAGNALL, wife Susanna and sons Sampson 21y and James 20; discharged.	St. Andrew, Holborn, Lnd
L 1775 Apr.27	Mary DAVEY, wife of Stephen DAVEY; respited.	Lindfield
L 1775 Oct.5	Mary DAVEY, wife of Stephen DAVEY; confirmed.	Lindfield

L 1786 Jan.12	Charles WATFORD, wife Ann and daughters Lucy 10y, Sealy 4y, and Teriah 2y, sons Charles 7y and James 5y; confirmed.	Ditchling
L 1798 Apr.20	William MITCHELL and wife Lucy; confirmed as to William Mitchell; quashed as to Lucy therein called his wife, it being proved that Lucy had a former husband now living.	Westmeston
L 1805 Jul.19	Jane GANDER; quashed.	Hurstpierpoint
L 1809 Jul.14	William PACKHAM, the younger, wife Elizabeth and children Henry 4y, Ann 2y and Mary 6m; quashed.	Wivelsfield
L 1812 Jan.17	Fanny LINDFIELD, singlewoman; confirmed.	Brighton
L 1812 Apr.10	Thomas BARNETT, wife Susannah and daughters Sarah 3y and Lucy 2y; confirmed.	Clayton
L 1819 Jan.15	Catherine GORRINGE, singlewoman; quashed.	Chiltington
L 1819 Apr.23	John POST and wife Lucy; confirmed.	Horsted Keynes
L 1819 Apr.23	John ILLMAN, wife Mary and children John 15y, Mary 12y, Alexander 10y, Rebecca 8y and William 2y 6m; confirmed.	Horsted Keynes
L 1821 Jan.12	Jane NORMAN, wife of James NORMAN; confirmed.	Brighton
L 1823 Oct.17	Milly CHAPMAN; confirmed.	Horsted Keynes
L 1825 Oct.2	Martha WICKENS; confirmed.	Wivelsfield

QUARTER SESSIONS REMOVAL ORDERS TO KEYMER

		From
L 1666 Jan.11	William STEVENS, son of Thomas STEVENS to be sent to his father at Keymer.	Arlington
L 1666 Apr.26	Thomas STEPHENS.	Arlington
L 1666 Jul.12	Thomas STEPHENS; respited.	Arlington
L 1689 Jul.18	Ann FARRELL; respited.	Stanmer
C 1698 May 2	Elizabeth DAVY; confirmed. Thomas ALCOCKE and Stephen POTTER, two of Beeding's parish officers, brought Elizabeth Davy on horseback to this sessions to be examined regarding her last settlement. On finding that E.D. should be settled at Keymer, they took away the horse and left her to beg her passage to Keymer, whereupon the court gave her money out of the charitable use money and ordered T.A. and S.P. to be apprehended.	Beeding
L 1702 Apr.16	John HEASMAN; confirmed.	Withyham
L 1736 May 6	John YOUNG, wife Elizabeth and children Sarah and John both under 7y; discharged.	Chiltington

L 1739 May 3	Elizabeth JUPP, widow, and son John under 3y; respited.	Alfriston
L 1739 May 3	Sarah POINTING; confirmed.	Maresfield
L 1739 Jul.12	Elizabeth JUPP and son John; discharged.	Alfriston
L 1775 Apr.27	Zillah ALLFREY, singlewoman; quashed.	Pyecombe
M 1777 Jan.13	John SERGENT; respited.	Broadwater
C 1777 Apr. 7	John SERGENT; respited.	Broadwater
L 1800 Apr.24	Philadelphia ORAM, singlewoman; respited.	Denton
L 1800 Jul.17	Philadelphia ORAM, singlewoman; quashed.	Denton
L 1802 Apr.29	James HARLAND, wife Martha and children Daniel 4y, Mary 2y and Sarah 1y; quashed.	Preston
L 1815 Jul.14	John SUMNER; quashed.	Southease
L 1818 Oct.23	Robert DENNETT and wife Sarah; confirmed.	Brighton
L 1819 Jul.16	David DENMAN; confirmed.	Brighton
L 1825 Jan.13	Henry MILLS, wife Frances and children Frederick 7y, William 3y and Charity 1y; confirmed.	Westmeston
L 1825 Oct.20	Ann TAYLOR, singlewoman; respited.	West Firle
L 1827 Jan.11	William GEERING, wife Sarah and children Caroline 7y, William 6y, Emily 2y and Sophia 10m; confirmed.	Newick
L 1827 Apr.26	Ann EDE, singlewoman; confirmed.	Westham
P 1830 Jan.12	William WIGGENS, wife Alice and children William 15m and Alice 4m; confirmed.	New Shoreham

KEYMER BASTARDY ORDER Par 400/34/3/1

1734 Jul.29 Ellenor MURRELL has requested, on behalf of James RIDDALLS, an infant under the age of one year, her male bastard child born in Keymer, for relief as she is unable to maintain and provide for him. As it does appear that J.R. ought to be relieved by Keymer, the parish officers of Keymer are ordered to pay to E.M. one shilling and three pence a week in Keymer, on demand from the date hereof, towards J.M.'s maintenance and relief, as long as the cause shall continue.

[*Note: The above document appears in the Hurstpierpoint Bastardy orders and the following entries appear in Keymer parish registers:*
1733 Aug. 19 James son of Eleanor Riddles.
1733 Sep. 13 Eleanor Riddles of this parish married to Edward MURRELL of Hurstpierpoint.]

LINDFIELD

Lindfield: 5,763 acres NE of present-day Haywards Heath, from 286ft in N to 91ft in Ouse valley, much common land liable to flood in winter; river navigable for barges during construction of Balcombe railway viaduct and even later as far as Sloop Inn. On route of one of main turnpikes from London to Brighton. 1344 sheep fair, largest in Sussex by 17th century. Following demise of iron smelting in 17th century, candles, paper, gloves and pianos were made. William Allen school of industry.

Population: 1717 (Archbishop Wake's Visitation) 776; 1801 1077; 1811 1237; 1821 1410; 1831 1485.

LINDFIELD SETTLEMENT EXAMINATIONS Par 416/32/4/1

1740 Oct.20 Thomas HOADER said that, 23 years ago, he hired himself as a menial servant to Charles GURR of Keymer and served him for one whole year and received his wages and that, the next year, he made the like bargain with Michael MARTIN of the same parish for a year, which year he served and received wages of £4 and has, ever since, worked as a flaxdresser. That he has not gained a legal settlement elsewhere. [Signature of T.H.]

1748 Feb.15 Ralph SAYERS, examined regarding the settlement of Mary SAYERS alias PARKER, said that she is a bastard child, born to Frances PARKER, in Clayton, and that she is the same person that he was, by order dated 13 January 1732, ordered to maintain and keep, he being adjudged the putative father thereof, and that she has not, to his knowledge, gained a settlement since her birth. [Signature of R.S.]

1748 Feb.19 Mary PARKER, singlewoman, now living in Lindfield, said that she believes she was born in Clayton and that it is the place of her last legal settlement, she not having gained a settlement elsewhere. [Mark of M.P.]

1758 Oct.19 Charles ROGERS said that he believes he was born in Beckenham, Kent, his parents then residing in that parish and that, soon after his birth, he and his parents were removed by an order to Item or Iteham [Ightham], Kent, as the place of their settlement. That he lived in that parish with his parents till he was 13 years of age and then hired himself, as a yearly servant, to William EDMUNDS of Item or Iteham, after which time he hired himself to Benjamin MORRICE of the same place, carrier, as a yearly servant and received his year's wages. That he has not gained a settlement elsewhere. [Mark of C.R.]

1774 Oct.18 John MEW, late of Buxted, husbandman, said that, on or before Lady Day old style 1773, he hired himself to Jeremiah GOWER of Horsted Keynes, yeoman, for a year at wages of £6 and that he lived with and served his master for one whole year and received his full wages, and has not gained a settlement elsewhere. [Signature of J.M.]

1775 Oct.11 John THARP, husbandman, said that, about 20 years ago last Lady Day, he hired himself to Thomas RENFIELD of Wivelsfield, yeoman, to serve him for a year at wages of six pounds, which he served and received his full wages, and that he has not gained a settlement elsewhere. [Mark of J.T.] [Endorsed: Wivelsfield acknowledge J.T. wife Lucy and their daughter, now unbaptised, to be legally settled in Wivelsfield and will provide for them if they become chargeable.]

1776 Apr. 4 Elizabeth CREASY, spinster, said that she is the daughter of Richard CREASY, late of Gravely in West Hoathly, farmer, and that, when she was about seven years old, she removed with her father to Ardingly, where he took a farm and paid taxes, and that she lived with him in Ardingly till she was 18 years of age, but since she left her father she has not gained a settlement elsewhere. [Mark of E.C.]

1778 Mar.10 Ann FALKINER, now residing in Lindfield, said that, to the best of her knowledge, she was born in Wivelsfield and that, about two years ago, she hired herself to Mrs. STANBRIDGE of Ardingly, from Lady Day 1776 for a year, which she served and received full wages, and has not since done any act whereby to gain a settlement. [Mark of A.F.]
Catalogued under Par 416/32/5/1

1785 Mar.30 Thomas BROAD, husbandman, said that, at Lady Day last two years ago, he hired two houses with about twelve acres of land of John PICKNELL, situate in Lindfield, at the yearly rent of twelve pounds. That he lets off one of the houses to Edward RIDLEY (and has done so ever since he took the same) at the yearly rent of two pounds, and one end of the house in which he resides, to Richard HALL at yearly rent of one pound six shillings, and that he has never paid any taxes for the premises, except the Land Tax. [Signature of T.B.]

1785 Sep. 6 Thomas HALL said that, in 1759, he was removed by an order from Lindfield to Fletching, to which order Fletching did not appeal. That, several years after he was removed, he went to hire himself to William BOARD esq., of Lindfield for a year but Mr. Board objected to hiring him for a year, as he did not choose to make him a parishioner. That he went into the service of Mr. Board and continued therein for three or four years, without anything further being said, and received money on account of wages as often as he had any occasion and that, at different times since, he has been in the service of Mr. Board, nine or ten years in the whole, under the same circumstances, and this examinant said that he has not done any other act to gain a settlement. [Signature of T.H.]

1786 Feb.20 William WATSON, residing in Lindfield, said that he believes he was born in St. Lukes, Chelsea, Middlesex, where his parents were legally settled. That, seven years ago, he purchased the lease of a house in St. Lukes, Chelsea, subject to the yearly rent of 14 guineas, in which house he resided for four years and paid all parochial taxes, since which time he has not gained a settlement elsewhere. [Endorsed: Jane als Jenny his wife and William his son.] [Signature of W.W.]

1788 Feb.29 Richard BROWN said that he was born in Kidderminster, Worcester, as he has been informed, and that, ten years ago, he rented a house, at six pounds a year for a year, in Lindfield and paid the Overseer's levies for the same and believes he was rated and assessed in his own name for the house, and that he has not gained a settlement elsewhere.

1794 Aug.18 James BUDGIN, now living in Lindfield, said that he believes he was born in Ardingly and that, four years ago, he hired himself to John SNASHELL of Newick, farmer, for a year, which term he served and received full wages. [Mark of J.B.]
Catalogued under Par 416/32/1

1794 Sep.22 Ann HOMEWOOD, now living in Chailey, said that she believes she was born in Rotherfield, where her father was legally settled, and remained with her father until she was aged about 11 years, when her father went to live at Chailey as under Bailiff to his brother, Francis HOMEWOOD, taking with him his wife, this examinant and the rest of his children. That she lived with her father at Chailey for 5 years, from whence her father took his family to Plumpton, where she resided with him for 12 months, at which time she went to service, according to her father's hiring, with William BULL of Barcombe for nine months and received her wages. That, from that time, she hired herself to John KENT of Lindfield, farmer, for a year at wages of 40s 0d and, by the desire of John Kent's wife (Martha KENT), she stopped with them five weeks after the expiry of her year, and received wages for same. That, afterwards, she was hired by Mr. WARRENER of Chailey, yeoman, for half a year, which time has not yet elapsed, and that she has done no act to gain a settlement elsewhere.

1803 Sep.28 William ANSCOMBE said that he believes he was born in Wivelsfield where his father was legally settled, and that he has not gained a settlement in his own right. [Mark of W.A.]

1807 Sep.16 John WOOD, now living in Lindfield, said that, nine years ago Lady Day last, he hired himself to John PARIS of Barcombe, yeoman, for a year at the wages of £10, which year he served and received his wages. That he has not gained a settlement elsewhere and that he, with wife Susanna, are now actually chargeable to Lindfield. [Mark of J.W.]

1807 Dec.15 Richard WELLFARE, late of Woolwich, Kent, now of Lindfield, labourer, said that he believes he was born in Lindfield, where his father was legally settled, and that, since his birth, he has not gained a settlement elsewhere. R.W. further said that he is married and has two children and that, during his residence in Woolwich, he was balloted to serve in the Kent Regiment of Militia. [Mark of R.W.]

1808 Dec.16 Edmund MARCHANT the younger, now living in Lindfield, said that he believes he was born in Lindfield, where his father was and still is legally settled. That, 19 or 20 years ago Lady Day last, he hired himself to Ambrose BRAY of Lindfield, yeoman, for a year, which year he served and received his wages of six pounds, and quitted his service at the end of the year. E.M. was absent for a month, then returned to A.B. until Lady Day following, and received his wages. E.M. then worked at his own hand for 18 months, then worked half a year with Mr. John BROAD of Hurst House, Wivelsfield, at wages of 3 guineas, and bargained another half year for the same man and worked for two years altogether, on separate six monthly hirings. That he has not, since his service in Wivelsfield, gained a settlement elsewhere; he has a wife and six children and is unable to support his family without parochial relief. [Signature of E.M.]

1810 Mar. 5 James BOTTEN, now living in Lindfield, said that he was born in Shipley, the place of the last legal settlment of his father, William BOTTEN, and that he has not gained a settlement elsewhere. [Mark of J.B.]

1810 Mar. 5 William CHERRIMAN, living in Lindfield, said that he believes he was born in Ringmer and that, about eight years ago, he hired himself to John FRANKS of Lindfield, farmer, for a year at nine guineas, which term he served and received full wages. That he has not gained a settlement elsewhere. [Mark of W.C.]

1814 Aug. 5 George ELLIOTT, a private soldier in the Royal Staff Corps (lately lying at Ham Street in Romney Marsh), who was examined by officials at Hythe, Kent, concerning his settlement, said that he was born in Worth, his father being a certificate man from Linworth [?Lindfield] to Worth and that, nine years ago, he hired himself to W. JOHNSON of Worth, farmer, for a year at six guineas, and lived in such service the whole year and received his full wages. That he has not gained a settlement elsewhere and is married to his present wife, Sarah, and has two children born in wedlock viz. Mary 4 years and George 12 months. [Mark of G.E.]

SETTLEMENT CERTIFICATES OUTSIDE LINDFIELD Par 416/32/1

A few settlement certificates from Lindfield to other parishes are listed separately immediately following the main series.

		From
1651 Jun. 3	William CHANTLER has one infant child living, kept at nurse with one George WICKENS of Lindfield, and Chailey shall be responsible for the child. *Catalogued under Par 416/32/2/1*	Chailey
1687 Oct.18	BOND. The parish officers of Slaugham bound to the parish officers of Lindfield in £50. At the special request of Slaugham, Lindfield have given their assent that Thomas WOODNUTT, an inhabitant of Slaugham, may come to Lindfield, there to sojourn so long as the inhabitants shall think fit and no longer, Slaugham acknowledging him to be an inhabitant of their parish. *Catalogued under Par 416/32/3/1*	Slaugham

1698 Dec. --	Richard PAGE, late of Brighton, wife and family	Brighton
1699 Mar. 8	John Glasington VINALL als TAPSELL, labourer, and wife.	Horsted Keynes
1700 Aug.30	Thomas TURNER, wife and family.	Hurstpierpoint
1700 Dec.22	Charles OSBORNE, husbandman.	East Peckham, Ken
1701 Sep.26	Anne BURY, widow of John BURY of Reigate, husbandman	Reigate, Sry
1706 May 20	Daniel BUTCHER, husbandman, of Chailey, wife and children Susanna and Thomas.	Chailey
1706 Nov. 1	William VYNALL, wife Elizabeth and child Richard. [Also John and Nicholas VYNALL but names struck out by agreement].	Ardingly
1712 Sep. 2	John PIPER, wife and children.	New Shoreham
1719 Mar.10	John VYNALL, cordwainer, and wife Sarah	Ditchling
1719 Apr.10	Stephen PARSONS.	Findon
1720 Apr.18	Thomas DAVEY, wife and children.	Cuckfield
1721 Mar. 26	Thomas DAVEY, husbandman, wife and children.	Cuckfield
1721 Aug.13	William COLEY and wife Mary.	Plumpton
1722 Apr.13	Thomas WATFORD, wife Sarah and child Richard.	Albury, Sry
1723 Sep.16	John WOOLL and wife Mary.	All Saints, Lewes
1724 Mar.14	Thomas BISHOP, wife Elizabeth and children.	Shipley
1725 Dec. 5	Joseph PEARSE and wife Frances.	Maresfield
1728 Jan.29	Joseph FUSON, wife Mary and children.	Bearsted, Ken
1729 Sep. 9	John YOUNG.	Ashford, Ken
1731 Sep.15	John MURRELL, wife and child under 1y.	Balcombe
1732 May 16	Edward COLLINS, wife Mary and children Edward 13y, Mary 11y, Jane 9y and Richard 6y.	Chailey
1732 Jun.24	George STANFORD and wife Mary.	Balcombe
1733 Mar.20	William HOLDEN and wife Susan.	Cuckfield
1734 Apr.13	John SMITH, wife Mary and children James and Mary.	Steyning
1735 Feb. 6	Benjamin FEWSON.	Bearsted, Ken
1736 Mar.21	Mary HILLS, (wife of John HILLS, now run away from his wife) and children John and Anne.	Ashurst, Ken
1739 Jul.23	Matthew LEWER, cleaver, and wife Susannah.	Billingshurst
1740 Sep.15	John VENNER and wife Sarah.	Lingfield, Sry
1741 Jul. 5	Edward WISKEY [WHISKEY], wife Frances and daughter Ann.	Cuckfield
1742 Jan. 9	William HESMAN [HEASMAN] and wife Mary.	Horne, Sry
1742 Nov.23	William HEAD	Lingfield, Sry
1746 Oct.16	Thomas COMBER, wife Mary and children Mary, Thomas and John.	Arlington
1749 May 15	James BUCKWELL, shoemaker, and wife Sarah.	Angmering
1749 Aug.26	George GEERE and wife Frances.	Cuckfield
1750 Mar.19	William COMBER, the elder.	Cuckfield

1750 Apr.20	William COMBER, the younger.	Cuckfield
1750 Apr.20	John MILES, wife Sarah and children Lydia and William.	Cuckfield
1750 Aug.13	John PAGE, hoopmaker, wife Elizabeth and family.	Leigh, Sry
1751 Dec.22	Richard POWELL, labourer, and wife Ann.	Ardingly
1752 May 19	John SEAGROVE, wife Elizabeth and children Mary 4y and Ann 1y.	Chailey
1752 Jun.28	Henry TYE, carpenter, and wife Elizabeth.	Penshurst, Ken
1752 Dec. 2	William GASSON, wife Mary and children Moses and Miriam.	Fletching
1753 Mar.17	Thomas FINCH. [Endorsed: The wife of Finch and their children's names with their respective ages must be inserted and added to his name in a fresh and new certificate.]	Pulborough
1753 Apr.20	Richard LEWERY and wife Sarah.	Rudgwick
1753 Aug.19	Benjamin BURT, wife Hannah and children Sarah 5y and Thomas 1y.	Keymer
1755 May 20	John VANDYKE and his children Henry about 8y, Thomas 7y and John 6y.	Battle
1756 Jun.12	Samuel BANISTER, wife Sarah and child Elizabeth 10m.	Hartfield
1756 Sep.13	Robert WOOD, tailor.	Horsted Keynes
1756 Sep.27	Thomas PERRIN, wife Ann and children Thomas, Mary, Richard and Susannah.	Slaugham
1757 Jan. 5	George VAN DYKE, wife Mary and child Elizabeth.	Steyning
1757 Jun. 6	Elizabeth SNELL, and daughter Susan 2y.	Chailey
1759 Aug.12	John SHIRLEY, labourer, wife Mary and children John 9y and Elizabeth 10y.	Ardingly
1760 Jan.28	Richard MUGRIDGE, labourer, and wife Sarah.	Uckfield
1760 Feb.10	James BLANCH [junior] wife Ann and James their infant son.	Chailey
1762 Dec.13	Thomas ELLES, labourer, wife Mary and son Thomas 2y 6m.	Chailey
1764 Oct.23	Richard MIHILL, labourer, wife Judeth and daughters Sarah 9y and Susannah 7y.	Horsted Keynes
1765 May 13	William RANDALS, labourer, wife Elizabeth and Jane 5m.	Horsted Keynes
1766 May 1	Edward ISTED, labourer, and wife Sarah.	East Grinstead
1768 Feb.14	William CARR, labourer, wife Susannah and son William 3m.	Horsted Keynes
1769 Feb. 9	William GANDER, tailor, and wife Mary.	Henfield
1769 May 21	Thomas THARPP, carpenter, and wife Sarah.	Ashurst
1769 Dec.17	Joseph DAVEY, labourer, wife Susanna and children Edmund, Allin, Abraham, Sarah, Martha and Jane. Ack.	Ardingly

1770 Feb. 2	John CHATE, wife Martha and sons Charles, John and Abraham.	Cuckfield
1772 Mar. 7	John BUCKMAN, wife Ann and sons William, Thomas and Edward. Ack.	Wivelsfield
1772 Dec.29	Thomas MASON, wife Sarah and children Henry and Thomas.	Chiddingstone, Ken
1773 Jun. 25	William WICKHAM and wife Ann.	Cowden, Ken
1774 May 11	Michael CURTIS, wife Barbara and children Sarah 13y and Elizabeth 4y.	Bolney
1774 Jun. 5	John RICHARDSON, wife Mary, daughter Riah and son Henry. Ack.	Cuckfield
1775 Jun.10	William GRIMES, wife Ann and children Prudence 4y, Mary 2y and Sarah 2m.	Findon
1778 Sep.27	William BIRCHFIELD, wife Jane and children William 6y 7m and Jane 4y 7m.	Worth
1779 Mar. 3	Isaac PARSONS, wife Susannah and son Isaac 1y.	Sompting
1789 May 4	Joseph DAVY, wife Susannah and children Susannah and Ann.	Ardingly
1790 Jan.13	William BUCKMAN, wife Ann and daughter Lidia.	St. Michael, Lewes
1790 Nov. 2	John HASLEGROVE, wife Elizabeth, now pregnant. Ack.	Ardingly
1793 Dec.14	John KNOLLS, wife Sarah and daughter Sarah 1y 6m.	Ardingly

SETTLEMENT CERTIFICATES IN LINDFIELD — Par 416/32/1

		To
1712 Feb.29	Mary BUCKWELL, singlewoman. Ack.	West Grinstead
1721 Apr.10	Memorandum. Simon WATSON of Etchingham agrees to bring his son-in-law George TAYLOR and wife Sarah to the parish of Lindfield if Salehurst require Lindfield to take and provide for them. *Catalogued under Par 416/37/3/5*	Salehurst
1723 Feb. 5	BOND. Stephen SCRACE of Lindfield, blacksmith, bound to the parish officers of Lindfield, in £50. As S.S. and wife Mary have been granted a certificate by Lindfield to satisfy Uckfield parish, S.S. agrees not to hire servants or apprentices such as to give them qualifications of settlement.	Uckfield

REMOVAL ORDERS FROM LINDFIELD Par 416/32/2/1

		To
1654 Mar. 2	Edward BELGRAVE, wife and children were, by an order, removed from Horton, Surrey, to Lindfield, who appealed saying that he is an inhabitant of the hamlet of Horton, where he has lands of his own and is able to live of himself.	Hamlet of Horton Epsom, Sry
1654 Mar.17	Edward BELGRAVE and family ordered, by Southwark assizes, to be returned to Horton.	Hamlet of Horton Epsom, Sry
1689 Oct.-	Edward MOORE and family. On appeal, order discharged.	Ditchling
1700 Nov.16	Margery ROSER of Ardingly, singlewoman, being great with child, was legally settled as a servant with John WHEELER of Ardingly.	Ardingly
1701 Mar. 7	George BURREDGE, [crocker*], and wife. [*OED potter]	Graffham
1707 Oct. 9	Richard SQUIRE. Confirmation. *Catalogued under Par 416/32/5/1*	Lingfield, Sry
1718 Oct. 9	William REYNOLDS and wife Sarah. Confirmation.	Ardingly
1718 Oct. 9	Thomas WALTER [junior], wife Elizabeth and son Thomas. Confirmation.	Cuckfield
1721 Jun. 8	William COLEY and wife Mary. W.C. was last a yearly servant to Thomas RICKWOOD of Plumpton and received full wages for such service.	Plumpton
1722 Sep.26	James ROFE.	Lingfield, Sry
1722 Oct. 4	Ann PARSONS. On appeal, order discharged. *Catalogued under Par 416/32/5/1*	Plumpton
1732 Sep. 2	Anne TABB, spinster.	Ardingly
1741 Jan.15	Thomas HODER and wife Sarah. On appeal, order confirmed. *Catalogued under Par 416/32/5/1*	Keymer
1752 Jan.30	John WARNETT, wife Elizabeth and son James aged 11 weeks. [Delivered 17 February]	West Hoathly
1753 May 16	Christopher PARKS. [Delivered 23 May]	Henfield
1754 Mar. 7	Jane COUMBER [COMBER], singlewoman. [Delivered 11 March]	Cuckfield
1758 Oct.19	Charles ROGERS and wife Mary.	Ightham, Ken
1758 Oct.31	John MORRIS and wife Mary.	Ditchling
1759 Oct.23	Thomas HALL. [Delivered 25 Oct.]	Fletching
1759 Oct.23	Sarah PLUMMER otherwise AYRES 8y. [Delivered 25 Oct]	Slaugham
1765 Sep.21	Mary STONSTREET [STONESTREET], singlewoman.	Horsted Keynes
1772 Oct. 6	Thomas MASON, wife Sarah and children Henry 1y 9m and Thomas 20 weeks.	Chiddingstone, Ken

1774 Apr.11	Sarah BUTCHER, singlewoman.	West Hoathly
1774 Oct.18	John MEW and wife Philadelphia. [Delivered 19 Oct]	Horsted Keynes
1776 Apr. 4	Elizabeth CREASEY, spinster.	Ardingly
1778 Jan.31	Robert LUCKEN and wife Hannah.	Fletching
1778 Mar.10	Ann FALKINER, singlewoman.	Ardingly
1778 May 12	James FULLER. [Delivered 9 July]	Streat
1778 May 12	Isaac PARSONS, wife Susannah and son Isaac aged 9 weeks. [Delivered 11 July.]	Sompting
1786 Feb.20	William WATSON, wife Jane alias Jenny and son William.	St. Luke, Chelsea, Mdx
1786 Sep. 4	Eden IRELAND, singlewoman.	Iford
1789 Mar. 2	William BUCKMAN and wife Anne.	St.Michael,Lewes
1789 Mar.23	Jacob DIX and wife Ann.	Pembury, Ken
1789 Aug. 3	John PIM and wife Ann.	Headley, Ham
1790 Nov. 1	John HASLEGROVE and wife Elizabeth.	Ardingly
1793 Oct.15	Elizabeth FUNNELL, widow, and children Thomas 6y, John 3y and William 9m.	Barcombe
1794 Aug.18	James BUDGEN and wife Sarah. [Delivered 18 Aug.]	Newick
1795 Feb. 7	Lydia LLOYD. [Delivered 9 Feb.]	Twineham
1796 Jun.16	Thomas PAINE and wife Mary. [Delivered 17 June]	Worth
1798 Dec.15	John KENNARD.	Plumpton
1803 Sep.28	William ANSCOMBE and wife Hannah. [Carried home to Wivelsfield 29 Sep.]	Wivelsfield
1805 Jul.19	Hannah PAGE, wife of John PAGE (who has deserted and left her), and daughter Eliza aged 7 weeks. Confirmation.	East Grinstead
1808 Jan.15	John WOOD and wife Susannah. Confirmation.	Barcombe
1808 Jan.15	Charles CARR, wife Jane and children Phebe 5y, Harriet 3y 6m and George 2y. Confirmation.	Horsted Keynes
1808 Apr.25	Jemima BUTCHER, the bastard child of Elizabeth, now the wife of Henry LANGRIDGE of Fletching, husbandman, (formerly Elizabeth BUTCHER, spinster).	Lamberhurst, Ken
1814 Apr.13	Fanny TYE, singlewoman. Sick and unable to travel. On 27 May 1814 she is stated to be dead; Preston to pay £3.14s 0d.	Preston
1815 Sep.12	Ann STANES.	Worth
1815 Oct.13	James BOTTING, wife Mary and children Jane and James. *Catalogued under Par 416/32/3/1*	Shipley
1815 Oct.13	Thomas BEAL and wife Rebecca.	Worth
1817 Jan.17	Charles BAKER and wife Barbara. Confirmation.	Rodmell
1817 Feb. 7	William PENFOLD and wife Ann.	Cuckfield

1817 Mar.21	James MILES, wife Mildred and children Mary 4y and John 2y.	Ardingly
1817 Apr. 1	James LAKER and wife Ann.	Hurstpierpoint
1817 Apr.18	John PARKER and wife Sarah. Confirmation.	Chailey
1819 Aug.23	Ann BLANCH, singlewoman. [Delivered 27 Aug.]	Cuckfield
1819 Nov.19	Temperance BARTLETT, wife of Richard BARTLETT, and children Charles 13y, John 11y and William 8y.	Budleigh, Dev
1823 Mar.10	Elizabeth GOWER, singlewoman. [Delivered to the poorhouse, Marylebone on 20 March.]	Marylebone, Mdx
1825 [--] 26	Fanny BARBER, singlewoman. [Delivered 4 Oct.]	Ticehurst
1827 Jan. 8	Thomas FULLER and wife Elizabeth. [Delivered 9 Jan.]	Westmeston
1827 Jun.11	Thomas GASSTON and children Thomas 8y, William 7y and Lucy Ann 3y.	Maresfield

QUARTER SESSIONS REMOVAL ORDERS FROM LINDFIELD

		To
L 1672 Apr.19	Moses LOVEWELL, wife Ann; on appeal they are to be settled at Lindfield.	Horsted Keynes
L 1674 Jan.15	Bennett BOWYER, wife of Mathew BOWYER who is now legally settled at West Dean.	West Dean
L 1674 Jan.15	Mary UNDERHILL. Recites order of 31 October 1672, removing her to Newick; respited.	Newick
L 1677 Jan.11	Robert JUPP; respited.	Shipley
L 1678 Apr. -	Anne JARRETT, over 7y, daughter of the now wife of Thomas OSBORNE of Lindfield.	Cuckfield
L 1685 Oct.19	Jane TOMPSETT, a poor person now residing at Lindfield, is likely to become chargeable there and - TOMPSETT, her father, an inhabitant of Wivelsfield, is to maintain and provide for her.	Wivelsfield
L 1689 Oct.1	Edward MOORE and family.	Ditchling
L 1698 Oct. 6	Ann TITLE, on appeal she is to be returned to Lindfield.	Cuckfield
L 1700 Apr.11	Abraham SAYERS; confirmed.	Clayton
L 1700 Apr.11	Gabriel WAKHAM; discharged.	Wivelsfield
L 1707 Oct. 9	Richard SQUIRE; confirmed.	Lingfield, Sry
L 1707 Oct. 9	John WHEELER, the younger; discharged.	Ditchling
L 1718 Oct. 9	William REYNOLDS and wife Sarah; confirmed.	Ardingly
L 1718 Oct. 9	Thomas WALTER, wife Elizabeth and son Thomas; confirmed.	Cuckfield
L 1722 Oct. 4	Ann PARSONS; discharged.	Plumpton
L 1727 Oct. 5	Daniel COLLEYER and wife Elizabeth; discharged as to Elizabeth Colleyer and confirmed as to Daniel Colleyer.	Billingshurst

L 1736 May 6	Thomas JARRETT and wife Mary; confirmed.	Buxted
L 1736 Jul.15	Mary PENTECOST, daughter of Priscilla PENTECOST; confirmed.	Nuthurst
L 1737 Jan.13	Thomas WALCH, wife Sarah and son Edmund 2m; confirmed.	Eastbourne
L 1741 Jan.15	Thomas HODER and wife Sarah; confirmed.	Keymer
L 1744 Jan.12	John PAGDEN under 12y and Anne PAGDEN under 7y; confirmed.	St. Clement, Hastings
L 1746 Oct. 9	Thomas COOMBER, wife Mary and children Mary 13y, John 10y and Thomas 7y; confirmed.	Arlington
L 1749 Jul.13	George GEERE and wife Frances; confirmed.	Cuckfield
L 1753 May 3	Richard LEWERY, wife Sarah and son Richard 6m; confirmed as to Richard Lewery and wife Sarah, discharged as to son Richard.	Rudgwick
L 1758 Oct. 5	John CHAPMAN and wife Elizabeth; confirmed.	East Grinstead
L 1760 Jan.17	Richard MUGGRIDGE and wife Sarah; confirmed.	Uckfield
L 1777 Jul.17	Thomas MARTIN and wife Jane; confirmed.	Beddingham
L 1794 Jul.17	John COOKE and wife Ann; confirmed.	Horsted Keynes
L 1798 Jan.12	Jane DUDLEY, wife of Thomas DUDLEY, and infant daughter Sarah; quashed.	Stalisfield, Ken
L 1798 Apr.20	Samuel POWELL; confirmed.	Clayton
L 1800 Jul.17	Elizabeth BROOKS, wife of John BROOKS, and children Elizabeth 9y, Thomas 7y, John 5y and William 2y; confirmed.	Petersfield, Ham
L 1801 Jul.16	Charity MITCHELL, singlewoman; confirmed.	Plumpton
L 1805 Apr.26	Philip SKINNER, wife Mary and children Mary 5y, Elizabeth 3y and Philip 1y; quashed.	Horsted Keynes
L 1805 Jul.19	Hannah PAGE, (wife of John PAGE, who has deserted and left her), and daughter Eliza aged seven weeks; confirmed.	East Grinstead
L 1808 Jan.15	John WOOD and wife Susannah; confirmed.	Barcombe
L 1808 Jan.15	Charles CARR, wife Jane and children Phebe 5y, Harriet 3y 6m and George 2y; confirmed.	Horsted Keynes
L 1809 Oct. 6	Thomas NORRIS, wife Sarah and children Elizabeth 8y, Faith 6y, Edward 4y, Thomas 3y and Sally aged 6 weeks; confirmed.	Reigate, Sry
L 1812 Apr.10	Edward PECKHAM, wife Elizabeth and children Martha 5y, James 3y and a son not yet baptised; confirmed.	Barcombe
L 1813 Jan.15	Edward GODLEE and wife Ann; quashed.	Clayton
L 1813 Jan.15	Jane WRIGHT, singlewoman; confirmed.	Dorking, Sry
L 1813 Jul.16	Elizabeth GOWER; confirmed.	Keymer
L 1814 Jan.14	Phildelphia DIX; confirmed.	Pembury, Ken
L 1814 Apr.22	Joseph STICKLAND, wife Emma and children John 2y and Ann 5m; respited.	Wadhurst

L 1814 Jul.15	Joseph STICKLAND, wife Emma and children John 2y and Ann 5m; quashed.	Wadhurst
L 1814 Oct.21	Joseph STICKLAND, wife Emma and children John 2y 6m and Ann 11m; confirmed.	Hawkhurst, Ken
L 1817 Jan.17	Charles BAKER and wife Barbara; confirmed.	Rodmell
L 1817 Apr.18	John PARKER and wife Sarah; confirmed.	Chailey
L 1817 Jul.18	John BAKEHURST and wife Mary; confirmed.	Fernhurst
L 1817 Jul.18	Elizabeth BATCHELOR, wife of Henry BATCHELOR, the younger, and daughter Elizabeth 8y 6m; confirmed.	Ardingly
L 1817 Oct.18	James SHELLEY, wife Mary and children Mary 10y, Frances 7y, Elizabeth 5y, James 3y, Ann 2y and a daughter born 18 April last, not yet baptised; quashed.	Brighton
L 1818 Apr. 3	Martha TEBBOTT, widow; confirmed.	St.Michael,Lewes
L 1819 Apr.23	Charles WHEELER and wife Sarah; respited.	Balcombe
L 1819 Jul.16	Charles WHEELER and wife Sarah; confirmed.	Balcombe
L 1819 Oct.22	Ann BLANCH, singlewoman; respited.	Cuckfield
L 1821 Oct.19	William WOOD, wife Sarah and son William 3y; confirmed.	Chailey
L 1830 Apr.22	Edward TESTER and wife Elizabeth; confirmed.	Horsted Keynes
L 1830 Apr.22	William ELLIOTT, wife Hannah and two children Louis 3y and the youngest not yet named; quashed.	Brighton
L 1831 Jun.30	William BOTTING; respited.	Worth
L 1831 Jun.30	Elizabeth DAVEY, singlewoman; confirmed.	Cuckfield
L 1831 Oct.20	William BOTTING; confirmed.	Worth
L 1832 Jan. 5	Eliza ELSEY 2y (the daughter of William ELSEY and Charity his late wife); confirmed.	Ardingly
L 1832 Oct.18	Harriet WOOD, singlewoman; confirmed.	Uckfield
L 1833 Jan. 3	Thomas ALDRIDGE, wife Elizabeth and children Ann 7y, Thomas 5y, Alfred 2y 6m and Allen 7m; confirmed.	Findon
L 1834 Apr.11	John COMBER; confirmed.	East Grinstead

REMOVAL ORDERS TO LINDFIELD — Par 416/32/3/1/1

		From
1639 May 4	William BACKSHELL and child removed to Lindfield by Ardingly. On appeal it is ordered that he and child be provided for in Ardingly, where he was born. *Catalogued under Par 416/35/1]*	Ardingly

1654 Jan.21	Edward BELGRAVE, wife and children. At Surrey Assizes, Croydon, on 10th instant, Edward Belgrave, who lately came to Horton and refused to give security for discharging the parish, was ordered to be sent back with his family to Lindfield, that being the place of their last abode.	Hamlet of Horton Epsom, Sry
1677 Jul. --	Robert JUPP. On appeal, order set aside and discharged. *Catalogued under Par 416/32/2/1*	Shipley
1695 Jan.17	Walter CHALLONER, wife and family. Appeal by W.C. who produced in court a bond entered into by him with three sureties to save the parish of Horsham from any charges. The security was declared to be good and sufficient and W.C. wife and family be settled inhabitants of Horsham. *Catalogued under Par 416/32/5/1*	Horsham
1696 May 6	Edward GILHAM.	Framfield
1699 May 10	William RIGLESFOORD.	Fletching
1699 Jul.13	William RIGGLESFOORD. Appeal by Lindfield. *Catalogued under Par 416/32/5/1*	Fletching
1701 Oct.27	Anthony LANE, wife and children were lately received into Dorking by a certificate from Lindfield. As he and his wife have since left Dorking, leaving behind them two of their children, daughters aged 7y and 4y, these children are to be conveyed to Lindfield.	Dorking, Sry
1713 Jan.12	James DUFFIELD. On appeal, order discharged. *Catalogued under Par 416/32/5/1*	Arundel
1716 Jul.14	Sarah BOYTON, singlewoman.	St. Katherine, Mdx
1718 Oct. 9	Walter DAVY and wife Mary. On appeal, order discharged.	Horsted Keynes
1723 Apr.27	William DAVY, wife Ann and child Mary.	Salehurst
1725 Jan.12	George TAYLER, wife Sarah and child Sarah.	Salehurst
1725 Apr. 6	Thomas RABSON. On appeal, order quashed.	Hawkhurst, Ken
1736 Jan. 5	John FOWLER and wife Mary.	Wadhurst
1747 Nov. 5	John HOADLEY and wife Elizabeth.	Withyham
1747 Dec.28	Elizabeth GEER, singlewoman.	Ditchling
1748 Mar.24	Thomas WALLER and wife Anne.	Ardingly
1748 Oct. 8	Francis TABB, bricklayer, wife Margaret and child Margaret 3y.	Tonbridge, Ken
1752 Oct.12	Mary HAMPTON and child Sarah 10y, were apprehended in St. James, Westminster, as rogues and vagabonds, there wandering in a loose, idle and	St.James, Westminster, Mdx

	disorderly manner. On examination, M.H. said that she is 33 years old, the widow of Robert HAMPTON, a linen draper, who served his apprenticeship with Timothy BROWN at Lindfield and never gained any other settlement. That she has one child now living by her husband, Sarah 10y. [Mark of M.H.] M.H. and Sarah to be removed to Lindfield via St. Mary, Lambeth. [Received into the Workhouse, Lindfield, 16 Oct.]	
1755 Jan. 6	Susanna SANDALLS, wife of Thomas SANDALLS, and son Thomas.	Hollington
1755 May 8	Henry ELLIKER, husbandman (since run away and cannot be found), wife Mary and children Robert, Mary, Prudence and Ann. All to be removed to Lindfield, (H.E. when found).	Farnham, Sry
1755 Jun.27	Sarah MICHELL, singlewoman.	Cuckfield
1774 Jun.13	Mary STONE, singlewoman.	Southover
1776 Sep.30	Richard BEARD and wife Elizabeth.	East Peckham, Ken
1777 Jul.22	Hester THOMPSETT, singlewoman.	Ditchling
1778 Jan. 5	John EVEREST, labourer, and wife Sarah.	Edenbridge, Ken
1778 Jan.12	John EVEREST. Lindfield having appealed against removal, are requested by Edenbridge to produce John Everest at the next General Quarter Sessions for Kent. *Catalogued under Par 416/32/5/1.*	Edenbridge, Ken
1778 Jan.15	John EVEREST. As Lindfield did not attend court to make their appeal, they are ordered to pay to Edenbridge £5 17s 6d costs. *Catalogued under Par 416/32/5/1*	Edenbridge, Ken
1778 Feb.25	Elizabeth VINSON.	Fletching
1778 Apr.27	Thomas HOADLEY and wife Mary.	Lamberhurst
1779 Feb. 4	Edward PAIN.	West Hoathly
1779 Feb.22	Richard BEST and wife Mary.	Horsted Keynes
1780 Aug.25	Richard BAKER, wife Jane and children Ann 8y and John 1y 6m.	West Firle
1784 May 26	Elizabeth BUCHER, singlewoman, who was apprehended in Bishops Tree, Leicestershire, as a rogue and vagabond wandering and begging there, is to be conveyed to Lindfield via Little Bowden, Northamptonshire, the first town in the next precinct. On examination, E.B. said that she was born at Lindfield where her father, Thomas Bucher, is now legally settled, and that she has not gained a settlement in her own right. [Mark of E.B.]	Bishops Tree (sic), Lei

1785 Mar. 5	William WILLE, wife Elizabeth and children Sarah 2y and Nathaniel 11m.	Chailey
1788 Feb.29	Richard BROWN, wife Frances and children Henry 11y, Sarah 10y, Richard 5y and Abraham 1y.	Lower Mitton, Wor
1788 Jun.14	William COOK wife Jane and daughter aged 8 weeks.	Keymer
1789 Mar. 2	Hannah PAGE, singlewoman.	Chailey
1789 Jun. 8	Richard LEE and wife Jane.	Buxted
1789 Oct.31	James COX, wife Elizabeth and children John 4y and James 2y.	Maresfield
1791 Sep. 3	Edward WOOD, wife Ann and children John 7y and Thomas 1y.	Horsted Keynes
	Catalogued under Par 416/32/2/1	
1804 Apr.23	Susannah SHAW, singlewoman. [Delivered 26 April]	Slaugham
1807 Jan.31	James SHORT and children Thomas 5y and John 6 weeks. [Wife not mentioned]	Hamsey
1807 Oct.31	Amelia BOTTING, wife of George BOTTING (he being in confinement in the House of Correction at Lewes), and son William about 7m.	Ardingly
1809 Jul.14	Lydia DURRANT, the wife of Benjamin DURRANT a Private in Corps of Royal Artillery Drivers, and daughter Sarah Ann born in lawful wedlock by her said husband. On appeal, order quashed.	Uckfield
	Catalogued under Par 416/32/5/1	
1810 Mar. 6	Charlotte ELLIS, who was apprehended in Brighton on 16 February last, as a rogue and vagabond and confined in the House of Correction, Lewes, for seven days, is now discharged and is to be conveyed to Lindfield. On examination, C.E. said that she believes she was born in Lindfield, where her father was legally settled, and she has never gained a settlement elsewhere. [Mark of C.E.]	House of Correction, Lewes
1810 May 18	Elizabeth ELLIS was convicted as a rogue and vagabond at the last General Quarter Sessions and recommitted to the House of Correction, Lewes, for 14 days and then to be passed home. On examination, E.E. said that she believes she was born in Lindfield, where her father was legally settled, and that she has never gained a settlement elsewhere. [Mark of E.E.]	House of Correction, Lewes
1810 Jun. 5	Ann MANNYWELL, singlewoman, now residing in Chailey, is with child which is likely to be born a bastard.	Chailey

1812 Feb. 3	Samuel SANDALLS, wife Elizabeth and children Stephen 5y and Samuel 4y.	Fletching
1812 May 22	George CHATFIELD. Unable to be removed owing to sickness but, by 27 June, was fit to travel. Lindfield to pay £8.1s 0d.	Chailey
1812 Aug.11	Thomas NICHOLLS, wife Lydia and children Thomas 4y, Walter 2y and Lydia 3m. [Endorsed: Agreed T.N. to have 3s 0d a week till otherwise ordered.]	Whatlington
1813 May 15	Thomas CHILDS, wife Elizabeth and daughter Sarah 1y 6m.	Horsted Keynes
1813 Nov.20	Anthony BLANCH and wife Sarah.	Ringmer
1814 Jul.12	Elizabeth BRIGDEN was removed from St. Giles, Camberwell to Lindfield, who appealed. Appeal allowed and order set aside. Further ordered that the respondents pay to the appellants the sum of 40s 0d costs together with the sum of £1.11s 6d for charges of maintenance of the said pauper. *Catalogued under Par 416/32/5/1*	St. Giles, Camberwell, Sry
1815 May 12	Susannah COLVEN.	Maresfield
1815 Sep. 6	Sarah MITCHELL (widow of Henry MITCHELL, deceased) and children Edward 14y, Ann 10y and John 4y.	All Saints, Hastings
1816 May 7	Henry WELLFARE. Unable to travel due to sickness, fit to do so by 13 June; Lindfield to pay £14.14s 2d.	Godstone, Sry
1816 Aug.24	Benjamin OLDER, wife Sarah and children Thomas 19y and John 13y. Thomas Older sick and unable to travel, fit to do so by 14 Sep. 1816. Lindfield to pay £3.16s 0d.	Sts. Peter and Mary, Westout Lewes
1817 Mar.10	James STEADMAN, wife Sarah and children Oby 2y 5m and Mary aged 5m.	Horsted Keynes
1817 Apr. 1	Robert BEARD, wife Sarah and children Elizabeth 7y, George 3y and William 1y.	Horsted Keynes
1818 Nov.20	Thomas Paine REED, wife Ann and son William 13m.	West Hoathly
1818 Dec. 4	William MARCHANT and wife Mary.	Maresfield
1818 Dec. 7	Mary VARNAM, singlewoman.	Fletching
1819 Apr.15	William SIMMONS, wife Naomi and children William 5y 6m, James 3y and Frederick 3m. Frederick unable to travel due to sickness, order suspended until he is fit. [Date of this not given]	Portslade
1819 Nov.20	Peter SANDAL. [Received 20 Nov.]	Speldhurst, Ken
1820 Mar.27	William VARNAM, wife Elizabeth and children Ann 3y, Elizabeth 2y and Sarah 6m.	Fletching

1820 Jun.13	Joseph MASTERS otherwise ROBERSON, aged 11y, upon examination of Ann LINNEY, mother of child.	Great Brickhill, Bkm
1821 May 9	Harriet HAYNES was, on 4 May, adjudged a rogue and vagabond and ordered to be recommitted to House of Correction at Lewes, till Wednesday then next, which time is now expired, and then to be passed home. On examination, H.H. said that she was born in Lindfield, where her father was legally settled, and that she has never gained a settlement in her own right. [Mark of H.H.]	House of Correction, Lewes
1821 Jun. 2	Catherine BOATES who was apprehended in Newport, Isle of Wight, convicted as a rogue and vagabond and confined in the House of Correction at Newport for seven days, is now to be conveyed to Lindfield via Portsmouth, Hampshire. On examination, C.B. said that she is the wife of John BOATES, a Private in the 35th Regiment now in Barbados, and she has often heard her husband say that he belonged to Lindfield, Essex (sic), that she came to the Isle of Wight to obtain a passage to her husband but, failing in that, she has been obliged to beg for relief. [Mark of C.B.]	Newport, Isle of Wight, Ham
1822 May 3	William KNIGHT, wife Mary and children James 5y, Sarah 3y and George 1y. [Removed 6 May.]	Cuckfield
1822 Oct.28	John TULLEY, wife Frances and children Frances 17y, Robert 15y, James 13y and Edwin 7y. Wife, daughter and 2 youngest children sick and unable to travel. On 6 January 1823, the removal to be put into execution accordingly. As the within named John Tulley has died since the making of the order, Lindfield is to pay £11.9s 6d costs incurred by the suspension of order and funeral of John Tulley.	Brighton
1822 Nov. 7	Edward CONSTABLE, wife Mary and son Mathias 2y 6m. Unable to travel as Mary sick. All able to do so by 21 November and Lindfield to pay £1.9s 6d. [Received the family 21 Nov.]	Brighton
1822 Dec. 9	James BUDGEN, wife Elizabeth and children John 16y, David 12y and James 10y.	East Grinstead
1823 Feb.21	James ELLIOTT and wife Harriett. [Received 21 Feb]	West Hoathly
1824 Jan.13	Henry RIDLEY, wife Sarah and daughter Mary 2y.	Hamlet of Chiltington, Westmeston
1825 Dec. 5	Ann MARCHANT, singlewoman.	Horsted Keynes

1827 Mar.31	Hannah NORRIS (widow of John NORRIS deceased) and her child John NORRIS 9y. [Received 13 Apr.]	Sevenoaks, Ken
1827 Jun.11	Mary PEARCE. [Received 13 June]	Horsted Keynes
1827 Dec.28	Charles MUDDLE, pauper. Unable to travel due to sickness; fit to do so by 16 April 1828. Lindfield to pay £21.4s 11d. [Endorsed: On 19 April sent to Waldron £10 Bank of England 7125, £10 Reigate 6120, £1 Lewes 15,239 and 2 half crowns.]	Waldron
1828 Apr.25	Ann MARCHANT, an unmarried woman with child likely to be born a bastard.	Worth
1828 Jul.28	William HOMEWOOD. [Received 1 Aug.]	Lewisham, Ken
1828 Aug. 9	Richard BROWN, wife Rhoda and female child aged 9 days, not yet baptised. Rhoda unable to travel because of sickness; fit to do so by 23 August. Lindfield to pay £2.17s 0d.	Deptford, Ken

QUARTER SESSIONS REMOVAL ORDERS TO LINDFIELD

		From
L 1649 Jan.11	John PORTER, falling sick in Lindfield and being destitute of habitation or relief, was unduly brought to Chailey and there left, where he was no inhabitant and likely to be a parish charge; to be returned to Lindfield.	Chailey
L 1662 Jan.16	William MORRELL and Mary MORRELL to be sent to Edward MASCALL of Lindfield, he having married their mother.	Fletching
L 1677 Jul.12	Robert JUPP. As it appears that he is not an inhabitant of Lindfield, order discharged.	Shipley
L 1688 Jan.12	Alice MASCALL and child; confirmed.	Edburton
L 1695 Jan.17	Walter CHALLENOR, wife and family. On appeal by W.C. he produced in court a bond entered into by himself, with three surieties, which was declared to be good, and he, wife and family are to be settled at Horsham.	Horsham
L 1697 Jan.14	John ATHERILL; order discharged; J.A. to be sent back to Horsham.	Horsham
L 1698 Oct. 6	Mary HYDER; confirmed as she was last settled as a hired servant for a year in Lindfield.	Fletching
L 1699 Jul.13	William RIGGLESFORD, on appeal, order discharged.	Fletching
L 1701 May 1	Mary LEOPARD; confirmed.	Framfield
L 1701 Jul.17	Joseph KING, wife Sarah and two children; discharged.	Battle
L 1704 Apr.27	Elizabeth MARCHANT; confirmed.	Brighton

S 1713 Jan.12	James DUFFIELD; discharged.	Arundel
L 1727 Jul.13	Samuel EDWARDS, wife Mary and children Mary and Samuel; confirmed.	Burwash
C 1734 Apr.22	Jethro WICKHAM, wife Sarah and son Isaac and an infant son not yet baptised; discharged.	Horsham
M 1736 Jan.12	Priscilla PENTECOST, singlewoman; respited.	Nuthurst
S 1736 May 3	Priscilla PENTECOST, singlewoman; discharged.	Nuthurst
P 1741 Oct. 5	Edward COULSTOCKE; respited.	Shipley
C 1742 Apr.26	Edward COULSTOCK; confirmed.	Shipley
L 1758 Jan.12	James DAVID and wife Elizabeth; confirmed	Fletching
L 1758 Jan.12	Anne MORETON, singlewoman; confirmed.	All Saints, Lewes
L 1762 Apr.22	Thomas AWCOCK, wife Mary and daughter Elizabeth 5m; confirmed.	Chalvington
L 1772 Jul.16	John STONE, Philadelphia STONE, Mary STONE and Maria STONE; confirmed.	Bishopstone
L 1793 Apr.11	Elizabeth TEELING and son Richard 1y; quashed.	Ringmer
L 1796 Jul.15	Thomas MITCHELL, wife Sarah and children Henry 5y and Mary an infant; quashed.	Fletching
L 1798 Apr.20	Sarah PARSONS, wife of William PARSONS, and sons William 3y 5m and George 1y 10m; respited.	Sts. Peter & Mary, Westout, Lewes
L 1798 Jul.13	Sarah PARSONS, wife of William PARSONS, and sons William 3y 5m and George 1y 10m; quashed.	Sts. Peter & Mary, Westout, Lewes
L 1801 Apr.16	Richard HALL, wife Sarah and daughters Sarah 11y and Elizabeth 7y; confirmed.	Plumpton
L 1803 Apr.22	George AWCOCK, wife Sarah and sons Thomas, Richard and George; quashed.	Fletching
L 1806 Jan.17	John HOLDER; confirmed.	Chailey
L 1809 Jul.14	Lydia DURRANT (wife of Benjamin DURRANT, a private in the Corps of Royal Artillery Drivers), and daughter Sarah Ann; quashed.	Uckfield
L 1812 Jan.17	John WOODGATE, wife Susannah and children Susannah 6y, Jane 4y and Charity 9m; confirmed.	Falmer
L 1812 Jan.17	Abraham KNIGHT, wife Lucy and children John 9y, James 6y, Elizabeth 3y and Caleb 14m; confirmed.	Ringmer
L 1812 Jan.17	Charlotte ELLIS, singlewoman; confirmed.	All Saints, Lewes
L 1812 Apr.10	Samuel SANDALLS, wife Elizabeth and sons Stephen 5y and Samuel 4y; confirmed.	Fletching
L 1812 Apr.10	John HOMEWOOD, wife Phoebe and children Henry 5y, Harriet 4y, Elizabeth 2y, and Richard aged 7 weeks; confirmed.	Chailey
L 1814 Jan.14	Anthony BLANCH and wife Sarah; confirmed	Ringmer

L 1815 Jan.13	Elizabeth WICKENS, widow; respited.	Brighton
L 1815 Jul.14	Susannah COLVEN; confirmed.	Maresfield
L 1816 Jul.19	Thomas TINGLEY 8y, illegitimate son born to Sarah RIDLEY deceased; confirmed.	Newick
L 1818 Apr. 3	Kitty CLUB, widow, and children Frances, Kitty and James; confirmed.	Chiddingly
L 1819 Apr.23	Mary VARNAM, singlewoman; confirmed.	Fletching
L 1820 Jul.14	William VARNAM, wife Elizabeth and daughters Ann 3y, Elizabeth 2y and Sarah 6m; confirmed.	Fletching
L 1824 Apr.30	Henry RIDLEY, wife Sarah and daughter Mary 2y; confirmed.	Hamlet of Chiltington, Westmeston
L 1825 Oct.20	Fanny BARBER, singlewoman; respited.	Ticehurst
L 1827 Apr.26	Joseph WOODGATE and children Edward 18y, John 16y, Jane 14y, George 12y, Joseph 10y, Mary 8y and Richard 5y; respited.	Brighton
L 1828 Jan.17	Philadelphia ELPHICK, singlewoman; respited.	Plumpton
L 1828 Jul.17	Philadelphia ELPHICK, singlewoman; confirmed.	Plumpton
L 1829 Apr.30	John Peckham HOLDER and wife Hannah; confirmed.	Chailey
L 1829 Oct.22	John Awcocke MICHELL, bastard child of Jane MICHELL, singlewoman; confirmed.	Fletching
L 1829 Oct.22	Jane MICHELL; confirmed.	Fletching
L 1831 Jun.30	Thomas FUNNELL, wife Ann and children Ann 6y and William 6m; confirmed.	Hove
L 1831 Oct.20	Mary SIMMONS, singlewoman, now pregnant; confirmed.	Barcombe
L 1831 Oct.20	Mary SALCOMBE wife of Samuel SALCOMBE and daughters Sarah 6y and Mary 5y; respited.	Brighton
L 1832 Apr. 5	James VARNHAM, wife Harriet and daughter Elizabeth 2y 6m; respited.	Maresfield
H 1834 Jun.30	Thomas EWINS, wife Charlotte and children John 8y, Jane 6y, Mary 3y and Thomas 8m; confirmed.	Southwick
L 1834 Jul. 3	Mary Ann JENNER wife of James JENNER and daughter Mary Ann 17y; quashed.	Brighton

LINDFIELD BASTARDY EXAMINATIONS Par 416/32/4/1

1807 May 4 Maria ROSER, widow of Lindfield, said that, on Monday 23 March last, she was delivered of a female bastard child at the poorhouse in Lindfield and that William RUSSELL of the said parish, blacksmith, is the father of the child. [Mark of M.R.]

1822 May 28 Mary BEARD of Lindfield, singlewoman, said that she is now with child likely to be born a bastard, and that William DAY, wheelwright, of West Hoathly is the father of her child. [Mark of M.B.]

LINDFIELD BASTARDY BONDS Par 416/34/1/1

1724 Oct. 9 Francis TRANSOME of Lindfield, husbandman, bound to the parish officers of Lindfield in £100 in respect of Mary CHRISTIAN, who was lately delivered of a female bastard child in Lindfield, and F.T. acknowledges himself to be the father. [Mark of F.T.]

1738 May 21 John PINION of Fletching, who married Mary VINALL, has at a vestry in our parish church of Lindfield, agreed with the parish officers and parishioners there present, to take home to his house, to keep and maintain (or to pay for the keeping and maintenance of) a male child born to his wife (begotten by John COMBER of Lindfield), at his own proper cost and charge and to free the parish of Lindfield from all charges thereof, except the 18d a week which he is to receive from the officers of Lindfield, as is paid by J.C. from 2nd May last, so long as the child is liable or may become chargeable.

1738 Oct.17 William KING of Albourne, yeoman, and Thomas MITCHELL of Albourne, wheelwright, bound to the parish officers in £100 in respect of Elizabeth IRELAND of Lindfield, spinster, who has declared that she is now with child and that W.K. is the father. [Signatures of W.K. and T.M.]

1750 Apr.21 John NYE of Pulborough, barber, Richard NYE of Henfield, weaver, and Caleb HACKMAN of Godalming, Surrey, gunsmith, bound to the parish officers of Lindfield in £100 in respect of Ann MOORE, singlewoman, who was delivered of a female bastard child in Lindfield, baptised Ann. [Signatures of J.N., R.N., and C.H.]

1755 Dec. 2 William WICKENS of Fletching, yeoman, bound to the parish officers of Lindfield in £100 in respect of Ann WICKENS of Lindfield, singlewoman, who was lately delivered of a female bastard child in Lindfield, and whereas she has not charged any person with being the reputed father, nevertheless, W.W. agrees to indemnify Lindfield parish. [Mark of W.W.] [Endorsed: Mr. William Wickens bond for a female bastard child born to Ann Wickens, his daughter.]

1771 Feb.13 Samuel CARTER of Lindfield, farmer, bound to the parish officers of Lindfield in £100 in respect of Ann HALL of Lindfield, singlewoman who was delivered of a female bastard child in Lindfield, baptised Ann Hall and now aged one year, S.C. being the father. [Mark of S.C.]

1775 Dec. 7 John CHILD of Lindfield, maltster, bound to the parish officers of Lindfield in £100 in respect of Alice HUBBARD, singlewoman, who was, in June last, delivered of a male bastard child in Lindfield, baptised John HUBBARD, J.C. being the reputed father. [Signature of J.C.]

1818 May 23 William POTTER of Lindfield, yeoman, bound to the parish officers of Lindfield in £200 in respect of Mary EDE of Lindfield, singlewoman, who was delivered of a male bastard child on 15 May last, at the house of William Potter, and M.E. has declared that W.P. is the father of the child. [Mark of W.P.]

1823 Jul. 2 John Burtenshaw COX and Richard Burtenshaw COX, both of Lindfield, yeomen, bound to the parish officers of Lindfield in £100 in respect of Sophia CONSTABLE of Lindfield, singlewoman, who is now with child, and has declared that J.B.C. is the father. [Signatures of J.B.C. and R.B.C.]
Catalogued under Par 416/34/3/1

LINDFIELD BASTARDY ORDERS Par 416/34/3/1

1672 Jul.10 Elizabeth MILLS of Lindfield, spinster, has been delivered of a bastard child and, on examination, she has declared that Abraham DUMBREL of Lindfield is the reputed father of the child, and he is to pay 2s 6d a week maintenance, so long as the child shall be chargeable to the parish.

1724 May 29 Mary CHRISTIAN, of Bittenden [Biddenden], Kent, singlewoman, was lately delivered of a female bastard child in Lindfield and, on examination of M.C. and Francis TRANSUM of Lindfield, labourer, it is adjudged that Francis Transum is the father of the child. F.T. shall, within 3 days notice of this order, pay to Lindfield the 6s 6d which the parish has already disbursed and 2s 0d a week maintenance and shall also pay £3, within three months after the child shall attain her age of 9 years, towards the putting forth of the child to be an apprentice, in case she shall then be chargeable to the parish. It is further ordered that M.C. shall, every week the child shall be chargeable and she shall not keep the same, pay 1s 0d towards the maintenance of the child and £3 towards putting forth the child to be an apprentice at the time and in manner as aforesaid. Lastly, it is ordered that F.T. and M.C. do, within six days notice of this order, give sufficient security to indemnify the parish against all charges.

1735 Mar.18 Mary VINALL, singlewoman, has declared that John COMBER of Lindfield, miller, is the father of a male bastard child born to her in Lindfield. J.C. to pay 1s 6d a week maintenance and £1.5s 0d already expended since the birth; the mother to pay 6d a week.

1786 Feb.20 Jenny BUDGEN, singlewoman, has declared that George STUCKEY is the father of the male bastard child born to her, on 8 December last in Lindfield, at the house of John WELLER. G.S. to pay 2s 0d a week maintenance; the mother to pay 6d a week.

1787 May 7 Mary OLDER, singlewoman, has declared that John PECKHAM of Chailey, tailor, is the father of the male bastard child born to her on 1 April last, at the house of her mother in Lindfield. J.P. to pay 2 guineas and 1s 0d costs for the lying-in and 3s 0d a week; the mother to pay 6d a week.

1788 Jan. 7 Mary TOURLE, of Lindfield, singlewoman, has declared that John WICKING of Lindfield is the father of the female bastard child born to her on 29 October last at Lindfield. J.W. to pay 40s 0d costs of the lying-in and 2s 0d a week; the mother to pay 6d a week.

1788 Oct.18 Elizabeth EYRE, singlewoman, has declared that Henry GEERING, now or late of Lindfield, labourer, is the father of a male bastard child born to her on 15 September last, in Lindfield. H.G. to pay £2.2s 0d towards the cost of lying-in and 2s 0d a week; the mother to pay 6d a week.

1788 Oct.18 Mary HARDS has declared that William HARDING, now or late of Lindfield, labourer, is the father of a male bastard child born to her on 7 August last, in Lindfield. W.H. to pay £2.13s 0d towards the cost of lying-in and 2s 0d a week; the mother to pay 6d a week.

1805 Jul. 1 Mercy POTTER, singlewoman, has declared that George BOTTING, servant, is the father of a female bastard child born to her on 10 April last, at the workhouse in Lindfield. G.B. to pay 12s 0d costs and 2s 0d a week; the mother to pay 6d a week. [Endorsed: 1 July 1805. Demanded of George Botting 12s 0d for the six weeks maintenance, which was duly paid.]

1807 May 4 Maria ROSER, singlewoman, has declared that William RUSSELL of Lindfield is the father of a female bastard child born to her at the workhouse in Lindfield. W.R. to pay 40s 0d towards the cost of lying-in and 3s 0d a week; the mother to pay 6d a week.

1808 Feb.18 George BOTTEN of Ardingly, labourer, agrees to pay 2s 0d a week towards the maintenance of a bastard child born to Mercy POTTER otherwise POTLETT and to pay the same weekly to the parish officers of Lindfield, from the date hereof. [Mark of G.B.]
Catalogued under Par 416/34/1/1

1811 Jan. 4 Margaret THOMPSETT, singlewoman, has declared that Richard ROSER late of Lindfield, labourer, is the father of a male bastard child born to her on 26 September last, at the house of Robert THOMPSETT. R.R. to pay £4.0s 0d towards the cost of lying-in and 3s 0d a week; the mother to pay 1s 0d a week. [Endorsed: Received of R.R. £3.12.0d up to 18 January 1811.]

1811 Jan. 4 Elizabeth RIDLEY has declared that John BEST of Chailey, thatcher, is the father of a female bastard child born to her on 1 December last, at the workhouse. J.B. to pay £2.13s 0d towards the cost of lying-in and 3s 0d a week; the mother to pay 1s 0d a week. [Endorsed: From 18 January 1811 to 12 April is 12 weeks at 3s 0d = £1.16.0d.]

1813 Oct.12 Sarah BATCHELOR, singlewoman, has declared that James BOYLAND of Worth, servant, is the father of a female bastard child born to her on 2 August last, at the workhouse. J.B. to pay 18s 0d costs, 50s 0d for expenses incident to the birth and 3s 0d a week; the mother to pay 1s 0d a week.

1813 Oct.12 Ann BLANCH, singlewoman, has declared that James WILLIAMS of Lindfield, servant, is the father of a male bastard child born to her on 22 March last, at the workhouse. J.W. to pay £3.15s 0d costs, 50s 0d for expenses incident to the birth and 3s 0d a week; the mother to pay 1s 0d a week.

1814 Mar.18 Ann HAYNES, singlewoman, has declared that William RUSSELL, late of Lindfield, blacksmith, is the father of a female bastard child born to her on 12 June last, at her mother's house in Lindfield. W.R. to pay £5.8s 0d costs, 50s 0d for expenses incident to the birth, and 3s 0d a week; the mother to pay 1s 0d a week.

1819 May 3 Mary VARNAM, singlewoman, has declared that Caleb FULLER of Fletching, glazier, is the father of a male bastard child born to her on 16 March last, at the house of Widow COX. C.F. to pay £5.11s 0d costs and 2s 6d a week; the mother to pay 6d a week. [Endorsed: Caleb Fuller's order, with warrant and bill of expenses, and his father's note of hand for £10, payable in 18 months from 31 Dec. 1822.]

1819 May 3 Sarah RIDLEY, singlewoman, was delivered of a male bastard child on 7 March 1808 at the poorhouse, Lindfield, and Thomas TINGLEY of Newick, labourer, adjudged to be the father. T.T. who did not appear at Court despite good warning, is ordered to pay 12s 0d costs and 2s 0d a week. [No order for payment by the mother.]

1819 Jun.21 Charity CHILD, singlewoman, has declared that George BUDGEN of Hamsey, labourer, is the father of a female bastard child born to her on 19 April last, at the poorhouse, Lindfield. G.B. to pay £3.14s 6d towards the cost of lying-in and 2s 0d a week; the mother to pay 6d a week. [Endorsed: 21 June 1819 Received of George Budgen by cash £3; 25 March 1820 cash £2; 30 September cash £2; by cash £1.]

1820 Feb.28 Mary STAINES, singlewoman, has declared that John KING of Uckfield, labourer, is the father of a female bastard child born to her on 22 February last, in Lindfield. J.K. to pay £3.14s 6d (£3.2s 6d for expenses of the lying-in and 12s 0d for costs of this order) and 2s 6d a week; the mother to pay 6d a week.

1820 Apr.14 Mary STANDING, singlewoman, has declared that William FARNCOMBE of Wivelsfield, labourer, is the father of a male bastard child born to her on 23 January last, in Lindfield, and that the child died on 25th of the same month. W.F. to pay £4 (£3.8s 0d towards the expenses of lying-in and his apprehension, and 12s 0d cost of filiation order).

1822 Sep. 9 Mary BEARD, singlewoman, has declared that William DAY of West Hoathly, wheelwright, is the father of a female bastard child born to her on 22 July last, at the house of Thomas BEARD of Lindfield. W.D. to pay 6s 0d expenses incident to the birth, 16s 6d apprehension costs, 10s 6d for costs of filiation order, and 2s 0d a week; the mother to pay 6d a week. [Endorsed: 9 Sept.1822 received £1.13s.0d]

1826 Apr. 3 Ann MARCHANT, singlewoman, has declared that Edward VIRGOE of Horsted Keynes, labourer, is the father of a female bastard child born to her on 9 March last, in Lindfield. E.V. to pay £2.18s 0d for expenses of lying-in and 2s 0d a week; the mother to pay 6d a week.

LINDFIELD WARRANTS Par 416/34/2/1

1701 Sep.23 Ann BURRY [BERRY], widow, to be apprehended and examined touching her last abode, in order for her removal from Lindfield.
Catalogued under Par 416/32/2/1

1732 Sep. 2 Ann TABB to be apprehended for intruding into Lindfield parish.
Catalogued under Par 416/29/1/1

1752 Dec. 1 Sarah REED of Lindfield, singlewoman, has declared that Richard LEWRY late of Lindfield, carpenter, is the father of her bastard child, William, born on 8 October last, in Lindfield; R.W. to be apprehended.

1753 Oct.27 Henry FAIRHALL of Lindfield, husbandman, to be apprehended for running away from his family, and leaving them to the charge of Lindfield parish.
Catalogued under Par 416/29/1/1

1778 Jan.29 Hannah KEMPTON of Lindfield, is with child and Robert LUCKINS als LUCKEN of Lindfield, the reputed father, is to be apprehended.
Catalogued under Par 416/34/1

1786 Sep.12 Ann WALES of Lindfield, singlewoman, has declared that she is with child, and that Charles BUTCHER of Lindfield, is the father; and he is to be apprehended.

1787 Dec.31 Edward WISE of Lindfield, to be apprehended as he has refused to perform an order for the maintenance of a female bastard child born to Mary CHILD. [Endorsed: Due on the order to 31 December 1787, £9.4s 0d.]
Catalogued under Par 416/29/1/1

1808 Sep.12 Sarah RIDLEY, singlewoman of Lindfield, has declared that Thomas TINGLEY of Newick, labourer, is the father of the male bastard child born to her on 7 March last, at the poorhouse, Lindfield; T.T.to be apprehended.

1813 Sep. 8 Ann BLANCH, of Lindfield, singlewoman, was delivered of a male child on 22nd March last, at the workhouse, Lindfield, the father said to be James WILLIAMS of Lindfield. A.B. to appear at the King's Head in Cuckfield on Tuesday 12 October to be examined and notice to be given to J.W. that he may also be present.

1813 Sep. 8 Philadelphia READ of Lindfield, singlewoman, was delivered of a male bastard child on 19 July last, at the workhouse, and William WILLIAMS, of West Hoathly, said to be the father. P.R. to appear at the King's Head, Cuckfield on Tuesday 12 October and notice given to W.W. that he may be present.

1818 Nov. 4 Philadelphia REED of Lindfield, singlewoman, has declared herself to be with child, and that Thomas HARRIOTT of Worth, husbandman, is the father; and he is to be apprehended.

1823 Jan.13 Ann LEPPARD of Lindfield, singlewoman, has named Philip SKINNER of Lindfield, labourer, as the father of a male bastard child born to her on Friday 28 November last, at the house of her father, Thomas LEPPARD, in Lindfield. P.S. to appear at Sheffield Arms Inn in Fletching on Monday 10 Feb.

1823 Jan.13 Mary VARNHAM, singlewoman, was lately delivered of a male bastard child at the house of Widow COX in Lindfield and Caleb FULLER, late of Fletching, glazier, is adjudged to be the father. C.F. was ordered to pay £5.11s 0d costs and 2s 6d a week but as he has not done so and £21.1s 0d is now owing, he is to be apprehended.

LINDFIELD APPRENTICESHIP AGREEMENTS Par 416/33/1/1

1589 May 20 BOND. John FROULD of Westmeston, husbandman, and John FROULD of Plumpton, husbandman, bound to the parish officers of Lindfield in £4. Condition: John Frould agrees to indemnify Lindfield for the bringing up and keeping of one boy born in the parish, named Francis BURTENSHAWE, until he shall accomplish the age of 18 years. Consideration 20s 0d, to be repaid to the parish officers if J.F. should die before F.B. reaches 18 years and also, if Francis should die before the age of 18 years, the 20s 0d to be given to the parish officers for the behoof of the brothers and sisters of Francis then living. [Mark of J.F.]
Catalogued under Par 416/3/1/1

1593 Nov.20 Edward JOHNSON son of - JOHNSON, late of Southease, has put himself apprentice to John TOWNESEND of Lewes, farrier, for nine years from 25 December next; trade of farrier. *Catalogued under Par 416/33/5*

1666 Dec.29 BOND. Samuel SAMMES of London bound to Thomas PURYOUR of St. George, Southwark, [Surrey], glazier, in £40. Condition: Whereas Henry PARSON, son of Francis PARSON of Lingwell [?Lindfield], Sussex, husbandman, by indentures of apprentice dated 3 December, has put himself out apprentice to Samuell Sammes for ten years, and whereas also Richard PARSON, son of Francis Parson, by indentures of apprentice dated the said 3 December, has put himself out apprentice to S.S. for nine years, T.P. (on behalf of the parish officers of Lingwell) has paid £3 to S.S. [Signature of Samuel Samms (sic)]

1692 Mar.15 Richard PAGE, apprenticed to John PAGE of Mayfield, until age of 24 years; husbandry. [Mark of J.P.]

1696 Jul. 3 Nathaniel GARDINER, apprenticed to Isaac AYRES of Brighthelmston, until age of 24 years. Bond. I.A. bound to parish officers of Lindfield in £100. [Signature of I.A.]
Catalogued under Par 416/37/3/1

1700 Feb. 1 Mary GODLY of Lindfield, apprenticed to George NEWTON of Lindfield, gent., until age of 21 years; housewifery. [Signature of G.N.]

1705 Sep.21 Thomas DAVIS apprenticed to George NEWTON of Mascalls, Lindfield, until age of 24 years; husbandry. [Signature of G.N.]

1705 Sep.21 William WALTER apprenticed to William ALLEN, one of the overseers of the parish of Lindfield, until age of 24 years; husbandry. [Signature of William Allin (sic)]

1711 Apr. 3 William BLAKER of Lindfield apprenticed to John BOARD of Lindfield, gent., until age of 24 years; husbandry. [Signature of J.B.]

1714 May 17 George BELCHAMBER apprenticed to Thomas HEATH of Godstone, Surrey, carpenter, until age of 24 years; "art, trade or manual occupation of a carpenter, millwright and pumpborer". [Signature of T.H.]

1714 May 17 George BELCHAMBER. Promissory note signed by Thomas YOUNG to pay Thomas HEATH of Godstone £4 immediately after Michaelmas next (which sum being the consideration money agreed upon to take George Belchamber as an apprentice).
Catalogued under Par 416/33/6

1739 Mar. 9 William MILES, apprenticed to Thomas MITCHELL of Cuckfield, linen weaver, until age of 24 years; trade of linen weaver. Consideration of 52s 0d paid by parish officers of Lindfield. [Signature of T.M.]

LINDFIELD MISCELLANEOUS Par 416/34/1/4

1740 Aug.30 RECEIPT. Received of the churchwardens and overseers of Lindfield the payment of Tho. BRIGDEN in the sum of £4 by virtue of an order made upon John RANDOLPH alias RANDALLS the father of a male bastard child born of the body of Elenor WOOD in Lindfield, for and towards putting out of the said bastard now living and of the age of 16 years, known by the name of Randolph WOOD and do promise to indemnify the officers on account of the payment thereof. [Signature of Thomas FENNER and mark of Joseph WOOD.]

SHERMANBURY

Shermanbury: 1915 acres on S side of Weald, between Cowfold and Henfield. Weald clay with alluvium along river Adur (tidal 600 yards above Mock bridge). Arable, warrens and chases; emparkment from 14th to 19th centuries; most older houses in eastern half of parish.

Population: 1724 137; 1801 274; 1811 270; 1821 320; 1831 345.

QUARTER SESSIONS REMOVAL ORDERS FROM SHERMANBURY

		To
C 1652 Apr.26	Richard BERRY, a lame, sick and impotent person who has lately come to Shermanbury, where he is a parish charge, is to be sent to Cliffe where he was last an inhabitant.	Cliffe, Lewes
L 1663 Jan.15	Edward WELLER, wife and children; respited to next sessions and family, meanwhile, to remain at Shermanbury.	West Firle
L 1663 Apr.30	Edward WELLER, wife and family; to remain at Shermanbury for one month.	West Firle
L 1679 Oct. 9	Eleanor JUPP, a poor child of Shermanbury sent to Beeding by pretending she was a nurse child under 7y, is to be sent back to Shermanbury as it appears she is 7y old.	Beeding
C 1687 Apr. 4	Joseph CHEESMAN, wife and children; confirmed.	Henfield
L 1693 Apr.27	Ann DENMAN, a poor widow of Shermanbury, has lately married William SMITH, a poor person of Bolney, and Shermanbury have since removed her children John, Ann and Isaac DENMAN, all under 7y, to Bolney, but when they reach 7y, or at their mother's death (whichever is the sooner), they are to be returned to Shermanbury.	Bolney
M 1701 Oct. 6	John LILLIOTT. On appeal, he is to be returned to Shermanbury.	Henfield
C 1706 Jul.15	Mark THOMAS; confirmed.	Albourne
P 1739 Oct. 1	Sarah FRENCH, Mary FRENCH, and Charles FRENCH aged 9y, children of Mary FRENCH, singlewoman, now the wife of Thomas LUTMAN of Shermanbury, tailor; confirmed.	Cuckfield
L 1739 Oct. 4	Sarah FRENCH, Mary FRENCH and Charles FRENCH; respited.	Cuckfield
S 1743 Jul.11	Thomas WITTEN 4y and James WITTEN 3y, the sons of Thomas WITTEN, (late of Cowfold, husbandman, deceased) by Elizabeth his late wife; confirmed.	Cowfold

S 1743 Jul.11	Anne DENMAN, singlewoman; confirmed.	Cowfold
C 1746 Apr. 7	Thomas GEERING, wife Rebeccah and children Richard, Sarah and Thomas, all under 7y; discharged.	Beeding
P 1750 Oct. 1	Sarah HAYLER, singlewoman; discharged.	Cowfold
C 1753 Apr.30	Mary HILLS, singlewoman; confirmed.	Amberley
P 1768 Jul.11	James GLAZBROOK, wife Mary and son James; respited.	East Chiltington
M 1769 Jan. 9	James GLAZBROOK, wife Mary and son James; discharged.	East Chiltington
C 1780 Apr. 3	Mary FINCH, widow; respited.	Balcombe
H 1780 Jul.10	Mary FINCH, widow; confirmed.	Balcombe
H 1781 Jul. 9	Elizabeth HENTY; respited.	Twineham
P 1781 Oct. 1	Elizabeth HENTY; quashed.	Twineham
M 1792 Apr.16	William DAVEY, wife Susannah and children John 7y, Henry and Elizabeth under 7y; respited.	West Grinstead
H 1792 Jul. 9	William DAVEY, wife Susannah and children John 7y, Henry and Elizabeth under 7y; quashed.	West Grinstead
M 1794 Apr.28	Benjamin CHATFIELD and wife Ann; quashed.	Horsham
P 1798 Oct. 2	Frances SAYERS, singlewoman; quashed.	Billingshurst
P 1810 May 1	John PEACOCK, wife Catherine and sons Peter 3y and William 1y; confirmed.	Albourne
P 1811 Oct. 8	Mary STURT; confirmed.	East Grinstead
P 1813 Apr.27	Ebenezer STREET 9y; quashed.	Twineham
H 1813 Jul.13	James MITCHELL, wife Mary and daughters Barbara 2y 6m and Harriet 6m; confirmed.	Slaugham
L 1814 Oct.21	Sarah HOLLOWAY, wife of John HOLLOWAY; respited.	Brighton
C 1815 Jan.10	Sarah HOLLOWAY, wife of John HOLLOWAY; quashed.	Brighton
P 1828 Jan.15	Richard SHARP and wife Ann; confirmed.	Woodmancote

QUARTER SESSIONS REMOVAL ORDERS TO SHERMANBURY

		From
P 1698 Jan.10	Elizabeth FOWLER, who was last settled at Burpham, being a yearly servant there, was removed to Shermanbury and whilst there she had a bastard child, which child is to remain at Shermanbury and E.F. is to be settled at Burpham.	Burpham
C 1746 Apr. 7	Mary PHILLPOTT, singlewoman; discharged.	West Grinstead
P 1756 Oct. 4	John MILES, wife Ann and daughters Ann 14y and Betty 5y; discharged.	Nuthurst
M 1796 Apr. 5	John HOLLOWAY, wife Rachael and children Ann 9y, James 7y, John 4y, Frances 2y, and Thomas 1y; respited.	West Grinstead

M 1796 Oct. 4	John HOLLOWAY, wife Rachael and children Ann 9y, James 7y, John 4y, Frances 2y and Thomas 1y; quashed.	West Grinstead
C 1812 Jan.14	Edward STENNING, wife Ann and son John 1y; respited.	West Grinstead
H 1819 Jul.12	Stephen TIDY, wife Mary and daughter Lucy 1y; confirmed.	Nuthurst
H 1830 Jul.13	William MITCHELL 13y, Mary Ann MITCHELL 8y and John MITCHELL 3y, the children of William and Charlotte MITCHELL deceased; confirmed.	New Shoreham

SLAUGHAM

Slaugham: 5,482 acres S of Crawley; 4 settlements from 200ft at Slaugham, 369ft at Warninglid to 504ft at Handcross and 270ft N of Pease Pottage. Sand and clay on clay, gravel and sand. Hammer ponds in SW woods. Arable.

Population: 1724 378; 1801 560; 1811 759; 1821 933; 1831 740.

QUARTER SESSIONS REMOVAL ORDERS FROM SLAUGHAM

		To
L 1646 Apr. 9	Richard DENCH of Worth, wife and child came to Slaugham intending to reside there; to be returned to Worth.	Worth
L 1650 Jan.16	John KNIGHT and wife, who lately came from Worth to Slaugham, to be settled in Worth, where his wife was a settled inhabitant at the time of their marriage.	Worth
L 1651 Jan.16	Henry KNIGHT, a covenant servant to Edward STENING of Horsham for the past 3 years, who was lately brought to Slaugham without an order, is to be returned to Horsham.	Horsham
L 1677 Jan.11	John MARLETT. Order removing him from Slaugham, discharged on his appeal, and he is to be settled at Slaugham where he rents lands of £10 per annum.	[Not given]
L 1681 Jun.13	Eleanor ELPHICKE.	Bolney
L 1708 Jul.15	Robert STANBRIDGE; confirmed.	Henfield
L 1709 Jan.13	William BOTTING; respited to next assizes.	West Hoathly
B 1711 Apr.12	Mary FEILD, wife of George FEILD, and child; confirmed.	[Wisborough] Green
B 1711 Apr.12	Nicholas FEIST, wife and children; confirmed.	Billingshurst
L 1721 Apr.20	John PERCE and wife Elizabeth; discharged.	Bolney
L 1723 Oct.10	Sarah BANISTER, spinster; discharged.	Cuckfield
L 1724 Jan.16	Sarah BANNISTER, spinster; discharged.	Cuckfield
L 1731 Jul.15	James BROOKER and wife Frances; discharged.	Burstow, Sry
C 1732 Apr.17	James BOTTING; confirmed.	Beeding
L 1745 Jul.18	John CRIPPS, wife Anne and children Anne 13y, Sarah 12y, Elizabeth 10y, Mary 8y and Susannah 5y; discharged.	Twineham
L 1749 Apr. 6	Frances ARES and wife Jane; discharged.	Horsted Keynes
L 1750 Apr.26	John WELCH, wife Elizabeth and children Amelia 6y and Charles 3y; respited.	Merstham, Sry
L 1750 Jul.12	John WELCH, wife Elizabeth and children Amelia 6y and Charles 3y; confirmed.	Merstham, Sry

L 1757 Apr.21	William CLARK, wife Sarah and children Thomas 7y, John 5y, Sarah 3y and Dinah 1y; discharged.	Tunbridge, Ken
L 1758 Jul.13	Thomas PERRIN and daughter Susan 7y; quashed.	Balcombe
L 1762 Jul.15	John DAY, wife Mary and children John and William under 1y; respited.	Beeding
L 1763 Jan.13	John DAY, wife Mary, children John and William under 1y; discharged.	Beeding
L 1764 May 3	Edward HILL, wife Elizabeth and children John 18y, William 10y, Elizabeth 7y and Jasper 5y; discharged.	Bolney
L 1774 Apr.14	Diana WHEELER, singlewoman; confirmed.	Horsham
L 1775 Apr.27	William CLARKE and wife Ann; quashed.	Waldron
L 1775 Jul.13	William CLARKE and wife Ann; confirmed.	Sullington
L 1776 Jul.18	Sarah WHEELER, bastard child born in Limpsfield to Sarah WHEELER, singlewoman, and now over 3y 6m old; confirmed.	Limpsfield, Sry
L 1777 Jul.17	William SNASHFOLD and wife Susanna; confirmed.	Cowfold
L 1781 Apr.26	James BUCKMAN, wife Mary and children Mary 12y, James 9y, Edward 7y, Elizabeth 4y and Sarah 1y; confirmed.	Cuckfield
L 1789 Jul.16	Thomas HOW and wife Sarah; respited.	Bolney
L 1789 Oct. 8	Thomas HOW and wife Sarah; quashed.	Bolney
L 1790 Jul.15	Mary STONER, singlewoman; quashed.	Cuckfield
L 1794 Jan.16	Ann IZZARD, singlewoman; respited.	Cuckfield
L 1794 May 1	Ann IZZARD, singlewoman; quashed.	Cuckfield
L 1807 Jan.16	James WELLER, wife Susannah and children James 4y, Joan 3y, Eliza 1y 5m and an infant, not yet baptised; confirmed.	Newdigate, Sry
L 1807 Apr.10	Caroline GATES, singlewoman; respited.	Lambeth, Sry
L 1807 Jul.17	Caroline GATES, singlewoman; on appeal the removal order to be amended by inserting, after the name "Caroline" and before the name of "Gates", the names "Catherine Bates"; order confirmed.	Lambeth, Sry
L 1810 Jul.13	Stephen BUCKWELL, wife Mary and children Jane 6y, Stephen 5y, George 3y and Mary 2y; confirmed.	Framfield
L 1811 Apr.26	Elizabeth TODMAN, widow of Richard TODMAN, and daughter Elizabeth 2y 9m; confirmed.	St.Peter the Great, Chichester
L 1813 Jul.16	William PIERCE and wife Sarah; respited.	Crawley
L 1814 Jan.14	William PIERCE and wife Sarah; quashed.	Crawley
L 1815 Oct.20	Ann HEAD, wife of William HEAD; respited.	East Grinstead

L 1815 Oct.20	Samuel MOTH, wife Phoebe and children Jemmima 14y, Harriet 13y, Hester 7y, Jane 5y, George 4y, William 3y and Eliza 14m; confirmed.	Frimley, Sry
L 1815 Oct.20	Ann KING, wife of David KING; respited.	Bolney
L 1816 Apr.26	Ann KING, wife of David KING; quashed.	Bolney
L 1816 Jul.19	David KING, wife Ann and son Robert 6m; confirmed.	Hurstpierpoint
L 1817 Jan.17	Sarah PESKETT, singlewoman; confirmed.	Hurstpierpoint
L 1817 Jan.17	Mary BALL otherwise JUPP; confirmed.	Nuthurst
L 1817 Jan.17	William JENNER and wife Ann; confirmed.	Dorking, Sry
L 1817 Jan.17	Louisa REEVES; confirmed.	Cuckfield
L 1817 Apr.18	Edward WENTUS; confirmed.	Botolphs
L 1817 Apr.18	Richard FARLEY, wife Ann and children Richard 5y, Mary 4y, Elizabeth 3y, Henry 1y and a son not yet baptised; confirmed.	Alfold, Sry
L 1817 Jul.18	William BURTENSHAW, wife Sarah and son Henry 1y; confirmed.	Hurstpierpoint
L 1818 Jan.16	William PUTTOCK and wife Phoebe; confirmed.	Easebourne
L 1818 Jul.17	Elizabeth BUCKMAN, singlewoman; confirmed.	All Saints, Lewes
L 1819 Apr.23	Obed OVERTON, wife Ann and children Ann 14y, James 12y, Mary 10y, Thomas 8y, William 6y, John 4y, Eliza 2y and Harriet 2m; respited.	Shere, Sry
L 1819 Oct.22	Obed OVERTON, wife Ann and children Ann 14y, James 12y, Mary 10y, Thomas 8y, William 6y, John 4y, Eliza 2y and Harriet 2m; quashed.	Shere, Sry
L 1820 Jan.14	John BOTTING; confirmed.	Godstone, Sry
L 1820 Apr.14	John CONSTABLE, wife Jane and son John 14m; confirmed.	Dorking, Sry
L 1820 Jul.14	James CHART, wife Charlotte; confirmed.	East Grinstead
L 1822 Jul.19	Richard ETHERTON, wife Ann and children Richard 9y, Jesse 7y, Hannah 3y and Parkhurst 7m; confirmed.	Rudgwick
L 1822 Oct.18	Thomas SMITHERS, wife Elizabeth and children Mary 21y, William 17y, Charles 15y and Seth 15y; confirmed.	Kirdford
L 1823 Jul.18	Ann JUPP, (wife of James JUPP, a prisoner in the House of Correction, Lewes), and children Mary Ann 11y, Frederick 9y, James 7y, William 5y and John 2y; quashed.	Beeding
L 1825 Apr.14	Elizabeth DRAPER; confirmed.	New Shoreham
L 1826 Apr. 6	Elizabeth BAKER otherwise COMBER; confirmed.	Bolney
L 1826 Jul.13	John COLEY and wife Ann; confirmed.	Brighton

L 1826 Jul.13	James WORNHAM, the younger, wife Mary and children Harriet 5y, Elizabeth 2y and a son 8 days old, not yet baptised; confirmed.	Cuckfield
L 1827 Apr.26	John JENNINGS, wife Sarah and son John 17m; confirmed.	Ightham, Ken
L 1827 Apr.26	Sarah ROVERY, wife of Thomas ROVERY, and son William 8m; confirmed.	Worth
L 1827 Apr.26	William WHITEING, wife Ann and children William 3y, Hannah 2y and James 11m; confirmed.	Reigate, Sry
L 1828 Oct.16	William LONGLEY and wife Elizabeth; confirmed.	Cuckfield
L 1829 Jan.15	William STOFFELL; confirmed.	Horsham
L 1829 Apr.30	James CONSTABLE and wife Harriet; confirmed.	Dorking, Sry
L 1829 Jul.16	Matilda IZARD, an unmarried woman, who is with child; confirmed.	Horsham
L 1830 Jul.15	Elizabeth JUPP, singlewoman; confirmed.	Cuckfield
L 1831 Jun.30	Job WELLS, wife Elizabeth and children Stephen 14y, Anne 11y, Thomas 7y, Benjamin 4y and Lydia 10m; confirmed.	Horsham
L 1833 Jan. 3	William SHEPHERD; respited.	Horsham
L 1833 Jan. 3	Keziah STONE; confirmed.	Newdigate, Sry
L 1833 Jul. 4	Edward PENFOLD, wife Elizabeth and children Jane 8y, Elizabeth 7y, Mary 5y, Ann 4y, Martha 2y and Phillis 3m; respited.	Ifield
L 1833 Jul. 4	Sarah WELCH; confirmed.	Horsham
L 1833 Oct.17	Edward PENFOLD, wife Elizabeth and children Jane 8y 6m, Elizabeth 7y, Mary 5y, Ann 4y, Martha 2y and Phillis 3m; confirmed.	Ifield
P 1834 Apr. 7	Henry SEARLE, wife Mary Ann and children Henry 14y, William 11y, James 9y, Charles 7y, Mary Ann 5y, George 3y and Eliza 7m; confirmed.	Broadwater
L 1834 Apr.11	Edward GATES, wife Eliza and sons William 8y and Richard 5y; confirmed.	Lower Beeding

QUARTER SESSIONS REMOVAL ORDERS TO SLAUGHAM

		From
H 1712 Oct. 6	Henry CHEESMAN and wife Anne; confirmed.	Nuthurst
H 1734 Jul.15	John MUNERY, wife Mary and children Anne 9y, Michael 5y and Edward 2y; discharged as J.M. has an equitable right in a house in Washington where he lives and so is not removable.	Washington

L 1750 Jan.11	Hannah PAGE, singlewoman; confirmed.	Chailey
L 1750 Oct. 4	John HARDING, wife Anne and daughter Sarah 8y; confirmed.	Withyham
L 1766 Apr.10	Joseph VERRALL, wife Mary and daughter Mary; confirmed.	Mayfield
L 1782 Jul.18	William STILL, wife Mary and son John 9y; quashed.	Pyecombe
L 1806 Jul.18	Abraham SHAW, wife Sarah and children Keziah, Isaac, Aesop, Jabez, Mary and Ebenezer; respited.	Isfield
L 1806 Oct.10	Abraham SHAW, wife Sarah and children Keziah, Isaac, Aesop, Jabez, Mary and Ebenezer; quashed.	Isfield
C 1812 Jan.14	Elizabeth CHARMAN, singlewoman; confirmed.	Beeding
P 1813 Apr.27	Mary SNASHALL; respited.	Lower Beeding
H 1813 Jul.13	Mary SNASHALL; confirmed.	Lower Beeding
L 1830 Jan.14	Susannah HARDING, singlewoman, who is with child; respited.	All Saints, Lewes
L 1830 Jul.15	Susannah HARDING, singlewoman, who is with child; confirmed.	All Saints, Lewes

TWINEHAM

Twineham: 1,937 acres, level below 100ft in Adur valley. Clay soil. Hickstead Place part of Saddlescombe manor of Order of St John of Jerusalem.

Population: 1676 107; 1724 123; 1801 238; 1811 234; 1821 275; 1831 337.

REMOVAL ORDER FROM TWINEHAM Par 495/32/5/1

		To
1801 Jul.16	John REEVES, wife Elizabeth and nine children:- Lucy, Richard, James, Stephen, Edward, Peter, William, Katherine and Harriott. On appeal, order quashed and Twineham to pay £15.0s 0d, being the money paid by Bolney for and towards the relief of the said paupers from time of removal to this present sessions. [Endorsed: Paid by cash £15. 0s 0d on Oct. 26, 1802.]	Bolney

QUARTER SESSIONS REMOVAL ORDERS FROM TWINEHAM

		To
L 1671 Jan.12	Richard WOOD, wife and child;	East Grinstead
L 1678 Jul.18	Bastard child of Anne GRAVELY to be removed to its birthplace at Cowfold.	Cowfold
L 1678 Oct.10	Bastard child of Ann GRAVELY; confirmed.	Cowfold
L 1688 Jan.12	Thomas PEACOCKE, infant son of Thomas PEACOCKE, to be sent to his father, who was last settled at Willingdon as a servant to John HOWELL.	Willingdon
L 1710 Apr.20	Joseph GRATWICKE, wife Elizabeth and children Mary and John; confirmed.	Ardingly
L 1737 Jan.13	John RICHARDSON, wife Ann and sons John 10y and Thomas 5y; confirmed.	Shermanbury
L 1751 Jan.17	John SYMONDS 8y, son of Henry SYMONDS deceased; discharged.	Bolney
L 1755 Jul.17	Mary BROWNE, singlewoman; confirmed.	Bolney
L 1757 Oct. 6	George VIRGOE, wife Mary and children David 7y, George 4y, Lydia 2y and an infant daughter, not yet baptised; discharged.	Ditchling
L 1762 Jan.14	Thomas HOADLY and wife Mary; confirmed.	Edburton
L 1764 Jul.12	Henry STREET and wife Elizabeth; confirmed.	Henfield
L 1765 Jul.18	Thomas SHIRLEY and wife Sarah; confirmed.	Bolney
L 1768 Jan.14	William HARLAND and wife Mary; quashed.	Clayton
L 1768 Apr.14	William HARLAND and wife Mary; confirmed.	Clayton
L 1771 Jul.18	Thomas BATCHELOR, labourer; quashed.	Ardingly
L 1790 Jan.14	Sarah TERRY, singlewoman; confirmed.	Hurstpierpoint

L 1792 Jan.12	Fanny WOOD, singlewoman; respited.	Henfield
L 1801 Apr.16	John REEVES, wife Elizabeth and children Lucy, Richard, James, Stephen, Edward, Peter, William, Katherine and Harriet; respited.	Bolney
L 1801 Jul.16	John REEVES, wife Elizabeth and children Lucy, Richard, James, Stephen, Edward, Peter, William, Katherine and Harriet; quashed.	Bolney
L 1806 Apr.18	Frances WHITE, (wife of John WHITE, a private in the Sussex Regiment of Militia), and son John 3y; quashed.	Hurstpierpoint
L 1806 Jul.18	Frances WHITE, (wife of John WHITE, a private in the Sussex Regiment of Militia), and son John 3y; quashed.	Tandridge, Sry
L 1807 Apr.10	Frances WHITE, (wife of John WHITE, a private in the Sussex Regiment of Militia), and children John 4y and Mary aged 14 weeks; confirmed.	Godstone, Sry
L 1815 Apr. 7	Charles MOORE and wife Mary; respited.	Cowfold
L 1821 May 4	William SILSBY; confirmed.	Hurstpierpoint
L 1822 Jul.19	Henry PACKHAM otherwise SIMMONDS 11y, the illegitimate son of Elizabeth the wife of John SIMMONDS of Twineham, labourer, formerly Elizabeth PACKHAM, spinster; confirmed.	Cuckfield
L 1825 Jul.14	Mary KING, wife of Thomas KING, and son William 10m; confirmed.	Bolney
L 1830 Jan.14	George Gerrard PICKARD 7y, illegitimate son of Mary STENNING formerly Mary PICKARD singlewoman; confirmed.	Cuckfield
L 1830 Jul.15	Ruth TIDY otherwise WOOD, the illegitimate daughter of Mary WOOD formerly Mary TIDY, singlewoman; confirmed.	Shermanbury

REMOVAL ORDER TO TWINEHAM. Par 495/32/3/1

		From
1818 Mar. 4	James PAINE, wife Catherine and two children, Catherine 2y and an infant female child aged about 3 weeks, not baptised.	Albourne

QUARTER SESSIONS REMOVAL ORDERS TO TWINEHAM

		From
A 1687 Jan.10	[Thomas] PEACOCKE, son of Thomas PEACOCKE who has gone to Twineham and there settled as a servant to James WOOD, is to be sent to his father at Twineham.	Sullington

C 1687 Apr. 4	Thomas PEACOCKE, infant son of Thomas PEACOCKE late of Twineham, is to be settled in Twineham unless they find out where his father was last settled, he being gone for several months to some parish unknown to Twineham.	Sullington
L 1707 Jan.16	John DUNTHON; confirmed.	Barcombe
H 1789 Jul.13	Sarah WOOSTER; respited.	Nuthurst
P 1789 Oct. 5	Sarah WOOSTER; quashed.	Nuthurst
L 1805 Apr.26	Thomas VIRGOE and wife Frances; respited.	Patcham
L 1805 Jul.19	Thomas VIRGOE and wife Frances; confirmed.	Patcham
L 1805 Jul.19	Edward HAMSHAR, wife Elizabeth and children Edward 4y and Mary 3m; quashed.	Plumpton
L 1811 Jan.18	Richard BRIGHT, wife Elizabeth and children Sarah 8y and John 6m; confirmed as to Richard, wife Elizabeth and son John and quashed as to daughter Sarah.	Brighton
L 1812 Jul.17	William ROWLAND, wife Rebecca and children James 8y, John 5y and Rebecca 4y; quashed.	Brighton
L 1817 Jan.17	James HIDER, wife Sarah and children Sarah 18m and Henry 2m; respited	Patcham
L 1817 Apr.18	James HIDER, wife Sarah and children Sarah 18m and Henry 2m; confirmed.	Patcham
H 1821 Jul.16	Jane GATES, singlewoman; quashed.	West Grinstead
L 1832 Jul. 5	John KNIGHT and wife Sarah; confirmed.	Brighton
L 1832 Oct.18	Elizabeth RICHARDSON; respited.	Brighton
L 1833 Jan. 3	Elizabeth RICHARDSON; confirmed.	Brighton
L 1833 Apr.11	William DENCH, wife Sarah and children William 8y, Harriet 6y and James 6m; respited.	Brighton

TWINEHAM WARRANT Par 495/34/1

1829 Dec.11 Susannah KNIGHT of Twineham, singlewoman, was delivered of a male bastard child on 2 November last, at the house of James KNIGHT, the father being John HOBDEN of West Hoathly, gamekeeper. S.K. to be brought to the King's Head, Cuckfield on 22nd January and John Hobden to be given notice to also attend.

TWINEHAM APPRENTICESHIP AGREEMENT Par 495/33/1

1827 Jun.25 Henry WOOD, aged 15 years, a poor child of Twineham, son of John WOOD, who is not able to maintain the child, apprenticed to William EKINS, tailor, of Brighthelmston until age of 21 years; consideration £30.

WEST HOATHLY

West Hoathly: 5,340 acres at between 400ft at Highbrook in S, 600ft on ridge of main settlement, and 602ft at Selsfield Common in NW. Clay on sand. Mainly pasture. 3 inns and 16 shopkeepers.

Population: 1724 473; 1801 794; 1811 840; 1821 943; 1831 980.

WEST HOATHLY SETTLEMENT EXAMINATIONS Par 379/32/4/1

1714 Dec. 9 Jane NELLSON, said that her daughter, Elizabeth, was born in May 1707 in Aylesford, Kent, and that her daughter, Jane HALL, was born at the parish of Pankridge [St. Pancras], Chichester, on 26 December 1709 [Mark of J.N.]

1720 May 30 John WOOD said that, in August 1719, he received relief from the parish officers of Ore, of 7s 6d and 5s 0d per week for 3 weeks together and, since last Easter, was again relieved by Ore, at 1s 6d a week for four weeks, one after the other. [Mark of J.W.]

1720 Oct.30 Johnathan BEACHLEY said that he served Richard WEEDING of Beeding, warrener, as a yearly servant for one whole year and received £5 wages, and since then he has not gained a settlement elsewhere. [Mark of J.B.]

1723 Oct.30 Thomas DANE of West Hoathly, labourer, said he lived with one Walter DANE, of Lindfield, for one whole year except for one week, but after that week he continued with Walter Dane for half a year, then went away and has not gained any other settlement. [Mark of T.D.]

1739 Nov.16 Thomas ISTED said that, ten years ago, he went with a certificate from Maresfield to Fletching, where he hired of Lady Abergavenny a tenement called Stephens, at the yearly rent of £6, which he occupied near two years. That he then hired another farm and lands called Brook House in Fletching, at the yearly rent of £8, and removed there from Stephens with his stock and goods. About the 24 June following, he [torn] Stephens to one BERRY who, on the payment of 2 guineas, was accepted by Lady Abergavenny as tenant of the same. That, five years ago last Lady Day, he hired and entered upon farm lands called Cranchesters land, lying in West Hoathly and Maresfield, at the rent of £8 per annum, all taxes to be paid by the tenant, and he resided on that part of the premises lying in [torn] where he has ever since [torn]. [Signature of Thomas Histed (sic)] [Endorsed: Jan.18 1740 Counsellor BURRELL has given his opinion that HYSTED (sic) has gained a legal settlement in West Hoathly. J. BOARD.]

1768 Feb. 8 James COBBY, said that, the day after Michaelmas day 1766, he hired himself to Benjamin BROADBRIDGE of Burton, farmer, for a year at £6. 15s 0d wages and continued there until the night before the next Michaelmas day, when his master gave him leave to go away and, since that time, he has not done any act to gain a legal settlement but had lived as a yearly servant with William BROADBRIDGE in Dunken [Duncton], for one year preceding the year with B.B. in Burton. [Mark of J.C.]

1769 Aug. 5 Joseph PARKER, now residing in West Hoathly, husbandman, said that four years ago last Michaelmas old style, he hired himself for a year to Francis WING of West Hoathly, yeoman, at the wages of £7, which he received after the end of a year's service. That, a fortnight after old Michaelmas 1755, he hired himself to John LUCAS of East Grinstead, yeoman, until the old Michaelmas day following, at the wage of 5 guineas, and served the full year, received his wages and came away, since which time he has done no act to gain a settlement. [Mark of J.P.]

1771 Mar.19 Ann HORSEY of West Hoathly, singlewoman, said that, a day or two before Lady Day old style 1768, her mother, Ann HORSEY, bargained with one OUTRIDGE of New Chappell, Godstone, Surrey, bailiff to Mr. RABY, for her to serve Outridge for a year at wages of £2.5s 0d, serving from Ladyday old style to next Lady Day new style, when her master told her she might go away if she liked and paid her full year's wages, and her mistress gave her, over and above her wages, a new checked apron and a pair of stockings for making of a bed for her. That since then she has done no act to gain a settlement. [Mark of A.H.]
Catalogued under Par 379/34/1/1

1793 Mar. 4 Thomas WELLER, said that about Lady Day (new style) 15 years ago, he hired himself to Edward ISTED of East Grinstead, farmer, at wages of £6 and worked from Lady Day to Lady Day and received his wages, and agreed to serve another year. That he continued to serve E.I. till Michaelmas following, when he removed with his master to a farm called Riceland in West Hoathly, where he served his master the rest of the year. That he then quitted, and ten days after old Lady Day 1780, hired himself to John ARNOLD of Horsted Keynes, farmer, for a year, served one more year and then quit. That, since then, he has done no act to gain a settlement, and has a wife Ann and children Elizabeth aged 10 years and Thomas 6 years. [Mark of T.W.]

1806 Apr. 9 John SAWYERS, now residing in Uckfield, said that he believes he was born in Little Horsted and that, 12 years ago, his father hired him to Mr. SEWELL of West Hoathly for a year at wages of £5, which service he completed and quitted his master, since which time he has done no act to gain a settlement. [Signature of J.S.]

WEST HOATHLY SETTLEMENT CERTIFICATES Par 379/32/1

N.B. A certificate issued by West Hoathly to another parish is listed separately immediately following the main series

		From
1693 Mar.29	Bond. Stephen Cox and wife Mary. The parish officers of Lindfield bound in £40 to indemnify West Hoathly parish. *Catalogued under Par 379/33/1*	Lindfield
1699 Jan.12	Robert BUTCHER, wife and family.	East Grinstead
1703 Jun. 1	William GIBB, husbandman, and wife Joane.	Worth
1704 May 10	Richard GARSTON.	Albourne
1707 Nov.24	John RICHBILL, wife Elizabeth and his daughter in law Mary ATTERSOLL *Document in pieces; catalogued under Par 379/32/3/1*	Horsted Keynes
1708 Apr. 3	William HUMPHRY. Ack.	Cowden, Ken
1709 Jul.30	Henry KING, wife and family.	East Grinstead
1716 Jun. 1	John BEST, wife and family.	East Grinstead
1718 Jan.29	John MARTIN, wife Mary and children.	East Grinstead
1720 Jun.13	John WOOD. Ack.	Ore
1721 Mar.27	William IFEILD, labourer, wife Mary and children Mary and Jane.	Horsted Keynes
1728 Nov. 9	Nicholas MEAD, wife Sarah and child Sarah.	Horsted Keynes
1728 Dec.22	Richard STREATER, wife Ann and children Ann, Mary, John, Sarah and Charity.	Ardingly
1732 Apr.19	Thomas BADCOCK, wife Elizabeth and child Thomas.	Wivelsfield
1732 Jun.24	Thomas BALCOMB, wife Elizabeth and John GODSMARK, her son.	Horsted Keynes
1734 Jan. 3	John ALCOCK, butcher, wife Mary and children Ann and John.	Ardingly
1734 Apr. 4	Bond. Daniel WARNETT, husbandman of West Hoathly, has, in order to secure the maintenance of wife, Anne Maria WARNETT, and five children John, Daniel, Hannah, Thomas and Edward, appointed the parish officers of West Hoathly to recover from William WARNETT of Horsted Keynes, yeoman, one annuity of £16 yearly, payable to D.W. out of certain lands in the occupation of W.W., called Buckhurst in Horsted Keynes. [Signature of D.W.]	
1742 Feb.27	James THORP, wife Mary and children Elizabeth 4 years and Frances 2 years.	Horsted Keynes
1746 Apr. 4	John HILL, wife Hannah and children John, Sarah, Richard, Hannah, William and James.	Worth

1747 --	John [ROSAR], wife [Barb]ara, and children Anne 14y, [John] 7y, Elizabeth 5y, Mary 2y and Susan 10 weeks. *Document in small pieces but parish registers show baptisms which correspond with the ages given.*	Horsted Keynes
1749 Nov. 3	Thomas LEOPARD, Mary [his wife?] and children. *Document damaged.*	Ardingly
1750 Jul.15	Bond. Daniel WARNETT of West Hoathly, husbandman, has, in order to secure the maintenance of wife Anne Maria WARNETT, and children John, Daniel and Hannah, appointed the parish officers of West Hoathly to recover from George WARNETT of Horsted Keynes, yeoman, his father, one annuity of £16 yearly payable to D.W., out of certain lands in the occupation of G.W., called Buckhurst in Horsted Keynes. [Signature of D.W.]	
1754 Jun. 6	Bond. Thomas PATTENDEN of West Hoathly, yeoman, bound to the parish officers of West Hoathly in £200. Condition: Whereas T.P. has, for sometime past, absented himself from the parish and left his wife, Sarah PATTENDEN, unprovided for so that the parish have advanced divers sums of money for her maintenance, T.P. on or before 1st July, is to pay these expenses and the cost of his apprehension and to indemnify the parish from all charges concerning the maintenance of his wife. [Signature of T.P.]	
1755 Nov. 3	John WELLS, wife Mary and children Mary, George and Henry.	Ashington
1757 Jan.29	Thomas HUMPHEREY, wife Elizabeth and son John.	Horne, Sry
1757 Jul. 3	Richard MATE, and wife Mathew.	Horsted Keynes
1757 Jul. 3	George GOUSE [GOOSE] and wife Mary.	Horsted Keynes
1758 [torn]	[torn] STREETER, wife Mary and daughter Ann 11y. *Document damaged.*	Worth
1758 May 21	John IZARD, wife Sarah and daughter Susan 6m.	Cuckfield
1759 Apr.16	William GROVES, wife Ann and son Jeremiah.	Speldhurst, Ken
1760 Apr. 7	Richard TESTER, wife Elizabeth.	Maresfield
1761 Mar.17	Jane BROWNE, daughter of William BROWNE (and Sarah his wife) late of Bolney, deceased.	Bolney
1761 Oct.11	Thomas COOPER, and wife Mary.	Worth
1765 Mar.14	Richard NUTLEY, and wife Esther.	Lindfield
1776 Jan.29	Thomas PACKHAM, and wife Judith.	Worth
1782 Jan.30	John BACKSHELL, wife Elizabeth and son William 7m.	Lindfield

1782 Nov.10	Richard AUSTIN, carpenter, wife Elizabeth and children Elizabeth and Mary.	Cowden, Ken
1782 Nov.19	Sarah WEAVER and daughter Fanny. Ack..	East Hoathly
1786 Feb.27	William TAYLOR, wife Mary and daughter Mary 1y.	Horsted Keynes
1792 Jun. 7	William PAYNE, wife Martha and children, Sarah, William and Sophia.	Ardingly
1793 Feb. 1	Benjamin BUDGEN, wife Mary and daughter Elizabeth 10m.	East Grinstead
[torn]	Ann DURRANT, widow, and three children. *Document damaged. Catalogued under Par 379/32/3/1*	Horsted Keynes

CERTIFICATE OF SETTLEMENT IN WEST HOATHLY — Par 379/32/1/1

		To
1715 Sep.24	John COMBER and wife. Acknowledged by West Hoathly.	[*Not given*]

REMOVAL ORDERS FROM WEST HOATHLY — Par 379/32/2/1

		To
1698 Oct. 6	Robert BUTCHER. Upon appeal order confirmed, R.B. having been an apprentice in East Grinstead..	East Grinstead
1711 Mar.20	William BUDGING, wife Eliza and daughters Anne and Elizabeth.	East Grinstead
1715 Jun. 1	Richard CHANTLER and wife Mary.	East Grinstead
1715 Sep.27	Sarah HAMMS, singlewoman.	Ardingly
1717 Mar.12	John BEST, wife and children. J.B. having been a yearly servant to William PAINE, of East Grinstead, for four years.	East Grinstead
[?1717] May 20	John BEST, wife and children, as above.	East Grinstead
1721 Apr. 5	Jonathan BEACHLEY and wife Elizabeth.	Beeding
1724 Jan. 16	Thomas DAVEY and wife Mary. Confirmation.	Lindfield
1724 Oct. 7	Robert COMBRIDGE, and wife Mary.	East Grinstead
1725 Apr. 8	Daniel WARNETT and wife Ann Maria. On appeal, order discharged. *Catalogued under Par 379/35/1/1*	Horsted Keynes
1725 Dec.20	Anne LASHMAR, singlewoman.	Cuckfield
1728 Feb. 5	Richard STREETER, weaver, wife Anne and children Anne 13y, Mary 10y, John 7y, Sarah 4y and Charity 2y.	Ardingly
1731 Jul.15	Phillip POLLARD, wife Mary and son Thomas. Confirmation.	Ardingly

1739 Jan.13	Anne LASHMER, spinster. On appeal, order discharged. *Catalogued under Par 379/35/1/1*	East Grinstead
1740 Jan.17	Hestor POTTER, wife of Joshua POTTER, and their daughter Hallamsby aged between 6 and 7y. Confirmation.	East Grinstead
1740 Jan.17	Richard SMITH and wife Sarah. Confirmation.	Uckfield
1744 Oct. 4	Francis ELLIS. Confirmation.	East Grinstead
1748 Mar.31	Margaret DEVALL, widow.	East Grinstead
1757 Jan.13	Walter WALLER, wife Mary and son William 1y. Confirmation.	Horsted Keynes
1757 Jan.13	Thomas H[UMPHRY], wife Elizabeth and son John 1y. Confirmation. [*Document damaged*]	Horne, Sry
1761 Jul.16	Nicholas PAYNE and wife Frances. Confirmation.	East Grinstead
1761 Jul.16	Edward POST and wife Sarah. Confirmation.	East Grinstead
1766 Jan. 3	Ruth MORLEY. [Delivered 4 Jan.]	Worth
1766 Jan. 3	William MORLEY.	Worth
1766 Jan. 3	William BROOKER, wife Ruth and children John 2y and Ruth 5m.	Worth
1767 Apr.30	John READ and wife Catherine. Confirmation.	Lindfield
1768 Feb. 8	James COBBY and wife Susan. [Delivered 12 Feb]	Burton
1768 Apr. 8	John BUDGEN, wife Elizabeth and children Elizabeth 10y, Mary 8y, Jane 6y and Ann 2y.	Bletchingley, Sry
1769 Aug. 5	Mary GIBB, singlewoman. [Delivered 12 August]	Gatton, Sry
1769 Aug. 5	John REEVES, wife Susanna and children Lydia 7y, Mary 5y and Phillis 2y. [Delivered 15 Aug]	Clayton
1769 Nov. 4	Thomas NEAL, and wife Mary. [Delivered 6 Nov.]	Chailey
1779 Feb. 4	Edward PAIN.	Lindfield
1781 Feb. 7	Jeremiah HIDER and wife Charlotte.	Fletching
1783 May 12	George MICHELL and wife Elizabeth. [Delivered 14 May]	Walkhampsted [Godstone]Sry
1792 Oct. 8	Benjamin BUDGEN, wife Mary and daughter Elizabeth 6m.	East Grinstead
1792 Sep.17	Mary ATTREE, the wife of Richard ATTREE.	Cowfold
1794 Jan. 3	William DAY and wife Sarah.	Maresfield

QUARTER SESSIONS REMOVAL ORDERS FROM WEST HOATHLY

		To
L 1649 Oct. 4	Edward WHEELER of Fletching and now residing in West Hoathly, is to be sent to Fletching, there to have a dwelling provided for him by the parish officers and to be set to work.	Fletching
L 1665 Oct. 5	George STACY and wife.	Horsted Keynes
L 1666 Jan.11	George STACY and wife; confirmed.	Horsted Keynes
L 1674 Jan.15	Thomas PAYNE, wife and children; confirmed.	Worth

L 1695 Jan.17	John STACEY; on appeal, to be settled at West Hoathly.	Fletching
L 1695 Jul.18	John STACEY, wife and family; confirmed.	Lindfield
L 1698 May 5	Elizabeth ELLYOTT, on appeal to be sent back to West Hoathly.	Willingham(sic) [?Ringmer]
L 1698 Oct. 6	Robert BUTCHER; confirmed, as he was an apprentice in East Grinstead.	East Grinstead
L 1704 Apr.27	Richard GARSTON; confirmed.	Albourne
L 1705 Jan.11	Thomas RIDGE; discharged.	East Grinstead
L 1709 May 5	Mathew TURNER; discharged.	Leatherhead, Sry
L 1711 Jul.12	Thomas RIDGE, wife Mary and son Thomas; confirmed.	Steyning
L 1712 May 1	Susan JENNINGS; discharged.	Brighton
C 1719 Apr. 6	John CLEAVE and wife Hannah; confirmed.	Buxted
L 1719 Oct. 8	Thomas PATTENDEN, wife and children; confirmed.	Petworth
L 1722 Jan.11	Henry STONE, wife Martha and daughter Mary; discharged.	Worth
L 1724 Jan.16	Thomas DAVEY and wife Mary; confirmed.	Lindfield
L 1725 Apr. 8	Daniel WARNETT and wife Ann Maria; discharged.	Horsted Keynes
L 1731 Jul.15	Philip POLLARD, wife Mary and son Thomas; confirmed.	Ardingly
L 1739 Oct. 4	Hester POTTER, wife of Joshua POTTER, and daughter Hallamsby 6-7y; respited.	East Grinstead
L 1740 Jan.17	Richard SMITH and wife Sarah; confirmed.	Uckfield
L 1740 Jan.17	Hester POTTER, wife of Joshua POTTER, and daughter Hallamsby 6-7y; confirmed.	East Grinstead
L 1744 Oct. 4	Francis ELLIS; confirmed.	East Grinstead
L 1749 Oct. 5	Thomas LEOPARD, wife Mary and children William 12y, Mary 11y, Sarah 8y, Elizabeth 4y and Thomas 6m; discharged.	Bletchingley, Sry
L 1751 Apr.18	Susan WELLER, singlewoman; respited.	Lindfield
L 1751 Jul.18	Susan WELLER, singlewoman; confirmed.	Lindfield
L 1751 Jul.18	John HILL and wife Elizabeth; confirmed.	Horsted Keynes
L 1752 Apr. 9	William HAYLER and wife Eleanor; respited.	Brighton
L 1754 Jul.18	John ALFREY, labourer; confirmed.	Cuckfield
L 1754 Jul.18	James BAXSHALL, wife Mary and children Ann, Benjamin and James; respited.	Ardingly
L 1754 Oct.10	James BAXSHALL, wife Mary and children Ann, Benjamin and James; discharged.	Ardingly
L 1757 Jan.13	Thomas HUMPHRY, wife Elizabeth and son John 1y; confirmed.	Horne, Sry
L 1757 Jan.13	Walter WALLER, wife Mary and son William 1y; confirmed.	Horsted Keynes
L 1761 Jul.16	Edward POST and wife Sarah; confirmed.	East Grinstead

L 1761 Jul.16	Nicholas PAYNE and wife Frances; confirmed.	East Grinstead
L 1767 Apr.30	John READ and wife Catherine; confirmed.	Lindfield
L 1808 Apr.29	William DAY, wife Sarah and sons William 3y and John 1y 9m; confirmed.	Pembury, Ken
L 1809 Jul.14	John BELTON; confirmed.	Burstow, Sry
L 1810 Jul.13	Mary BROOKER, (wife of William BROOKER, who has deserted her and left her), and son James 3m; respited.	Westmeston
L 1810 Jul.13	John LAMPON, wife Ann and children Ann 8y, Mary 6y, John 4y and William 1y; respited.	East Grinstead
L 1810 Oct. 5	John LAMPON, wife Ann and children Ann 8y, Mary 6y, John 4y and William 1y; confirmed.	East Grinstead
L 1810 Oct. 5	John COX, wife Jane and children Sophia 5y and William 2y; confirmed.	Fletching
L 1811 Jan.18	James SMITH, wife Ann and son James aged 13 weeks; confirmed.	Chailey
L 1812 Jul.17	Jonathan COOKE and wife Rebecca; confirmed.	East Grinstead
L 1813 Jan.15	Richard TESTER, wife Mary and an infant son not yet baptised; confirmed.	Cuckfield
L 1813 Apr.30	Cecilia COOKE, singlewoman; confirmed.	Fletching
L 1813 Jul.16	Sarah PEARCE 7y, illegitimate daughter of Jane PEARCE; confirmed.	Brighton
L 1814 Oct.21	John GOWER, wife Charlotte and children Charlotte 8y, Ann 4y and Elizabeth aged 10 weeks; respited.	Keymer
L 1815 Jul.14	Benjamin PEARCE 7y, illegitimate son of Jane PEARCE; confirmed.	Brighton
L 1816 Jan.12	Elizabeth MARCHANT, singlewoman; confirmed.	East Grinstead
L 1816 Apr.26	Richard TOWSE, wife Jane and daughter Harriet aged 9 weeks; confirmed.	East Grinstead
L 1816 Jul.19	Francis COMBER and wife Sarah; confirmed.	Lingfield, Sry
L 1816 Oct.18	John BENNETT; confirmed.	Steyning
L 1816 Oct.18	William TOWSE, wife Mary and children John 4y and Mary Ann 2y; confirmed.	Worth
L 1817 Jan.17	Elizabeth SIMMONDS, wife of William SIMMONDS and children James 4y, William 2y and Harriet 1y; confirmed.	East Grinstead
L 1817 Apr.18	John STANBRIDGE, wife Mary and children Amelia 2y and Moses 6m; quashed.	Newick
L 1817 Apr.18	Joseph COMBER, wife Sarah and children John 10y, Joseph 7y, Edward 4y and William 1y 6m; confirmed.	Ditchling
L 1817 Apr.18	William BAKER and wife Elizabeth; confirmed.	Horsted Keynes
L 1817 Apr.18	Thomas BONE and wife Harriet; confirmed.	Balcombe
L 1817 Jul.18	Thomas HOLDER and wife Sophia; confirmed.	Ifield

L 1817 Jul.18	William WHALEY otherwise RICE 7y, illegitimate child of Eleanor RICE, the wife of Mark RICE of West Hoathly, labourer; confirmed.	Worth
L 1817 Jul.18	George STEPHEN, glazier, wife Catherine and a child 4m, not yet baptised; confirmed.	Hawkhurst, Ken
L 1818 Jan.16	John BRISTER and wife Ann; respited.	Lingfield, Sry
L 1818 Apr. 3	John BRISTER and wife Ann; quashed.	Lingfield, Sry
L 1818 Jul.17	James HOLMAN, wife Elizabeth and son William 2y; confirmed.	Ardingly
L 1818 Jul.17	John BRISTER, wife Ann and son James 2m; confirmed.	Ifield
L 1818 Jul.17	William KING and wife Dorcas; confirmed.	Jevington
L 1818 Jul.17	James GOACHER and wife Mary; confirmed.	Cuckfield
L 1818 Oct.23	Richard TESTER, wife Ann and child Timothy 2y; confirmed.	Fletching
L 1819 Jan.15	Thomas Paine REED, wife Ann and son William; confirmed.	Lindfield
L 1819 Apr.23	Ann TAYLOR, singlewoman; confirmed.	Brighton
L 1819 Apr.23	Charles TAYLOR, wife Elizabeth and daughter Elizabeth aged 5 weeks; confirmed.	Horsted Keynes
L 1819 Jul.16	George LANGRIDGE and wife Mary; confirmed.	East Grinstead
L 1822 Jan.18	Thomas HUMPHREY and wife Mary; confirmed.	Wallington, Sry
L 1822 Apr.19	Thomas LONGHURST, wife Elizabeth and daughter Elizabeth 14y; respited.	Hartfield
L 1823 Apr.11	James ELLIOTT and wife Harriet; confirmed.	Lindfield
L 1829 Jul.16	William JONES and wife Sarah; respited.	Chailey
L 1829 Oct.22	William JONES and wife Sarah; confirmed.	Chailey
L 1829 Oct.22	Hannah CORK; confirmed.	St. Mary, Lambeth, Sry
L 1830 Apr.22	Richard PHILIPS; confirmed.	St. George, Southwark, Sry
L 1830 Apr.22	Thomas BACKSHELL, wife Philidelphia and daughter Sarah 1y 9m; confirmed.	Lindfield
L 1832 Jan. 5	Isaac AGATE and wife Elizabeth; confirmed.	West Hoathly
L 1832 Apr. 5	Edward CLARKE; confirmed.	Horsham

REMOVAL ORDERS TO WEST HOATHLY Par 379/32/3/1

		From
1698 Jul.14	William SAXBY. Order rescinded. [*Document damaged*]	Newick
1709 Jan.13	William BOTTING. Referred to next assizes for opinion as to settlement.	Slaugham

1715 Jul.20	John COMBER and wife Sarah. J.C. was last legally settled in West Hoathly as yearly servant to John BROWNING at Tickeredge.	East Grinstead
1719 Oct. --	Richard SHEPHEARD, wife Rebecca and children Thomas, John and Katherina.[*Document damaged*] *Catalogued under Par 379/32/2/1*	Harborough, Lei
1720 Jul.15	John WOOD, wife and children. On appeal, order discharged.	Ore
1722 Jul.10	Sarah DENNIS, widow and children Elizabeth 12y, Sarah 9y, Mary 7y, John 3y and William 1y. On appeal, order discharged. *Catalogued under Par 379/35/1/1*	Godstone, Sry
1725 Jun.14	William KITCHENHAM.	Bearsted, Ken
1729 Apr.17	Anne WHITE. On appeal, order discharged. *Catalogued under Par 379/35/1/1*	Fletching
1752 Oct. 5	Ann AWCOCK, singlewoman. On appeal, order discharged. *Catalogued under Par 379/35/1/1*	Ardingly
1769 Oct.18	Mary COLMAN, singlewoman.	Worth
1773 Aug.17	Sarah BLAND.	Fletching
1779 Feb.22	James FRIEND, wife Elizabeth and daughter Elizabeth 4y 6m.	Horsted Keynes
1784 Apr.19	Ann HORSEY, widow of William HORSEY deceased, and children Thomas 14y, Elizabeth 10y and William 8y.	Maresfield
1785 [torn] 6	Thomas TESTER and wife Mary. [*Document damaged*]	Maresfield
1790 Oct.11	Joseph JACKSON wife Ann and children Hannah 14y, Elizabeth 12y, Ann 10y, Isaac 8y, Mary 5y and Phillis 1y.	Hartfield
1792 Nov. 5	Sarah ISTED, singlewoman.	Fletching
1793 Jan. 7	William HENLEY. [*Document badly torn*]	Worth
1793 [torn] 8	John EDWARDS and wife Ann. [*Document damaged*]	East Grinstead
1793 Jan.11	Thomas OWDEN and wife Sarah.	Worth
1793 Feb. 4	Joseph PARKER, wife Cordelia and children Lucy 15y, Joseph 13y, Ann 10y, James 9y and Phoebe 5y.	East Grinstead
1793 Aug.21	Martha CHEESMAN, singlewoman.	East Grinstead
1794 Jan. 6	Joseph BALCOMB and wife Jemima.	Maresfield
1796 Jul. 4	John BROWN and wife Hannah. [Endorsed with letter to Mr.T.Pattenden. "... POUND tells me this pauper was two and a half years at the Denmans some years ago which is not a settlement and the pauper says the Fletching people except Lord	Fletching

	Sheffield, said he belonged to them. This order must be appealed against at the next sessions and we may give timely justice after next Assizes day unless we choose to have them. W.Gardner".]	
1799 Feb.23	Ann PECKHAM, singlewoman.	Hartfield
1806 Sep.10	James COMBER, wife Lydia and son James 15m.	Cuckfield

QUARTER SESSIONS REMOVAL ORDERS TO WEST HOATHLY

		From
L 1680 Jul.15	Nicholas HYDER.	Westmeston
L 1698 Jul.14	William SAXBY; discharged.	Newick
L 1720 Jul.15	John WOOD, wife and children; discharged.	Ore
L 1729 Apr.17	Anne WHITE; discharged.	Fletching
L 1740 Jul.17	Thomas THOMPSETT, wife Hester and children Hester 9y, Thomas 8y, Anne 5y, James 4y and Elizabeth under 3m; confirmed.	Maresfield
L 1741 Jan.15	Joseph LAMBERT and wife Jane; confirmed.	Streat
L 1761 Apr. 2	Elizabeth FAULKNER; confirmed.	Fletching
L 1763 Jan.13	William COOMBER and wife Lucy; confirmed	Framfield
L 1765 Jan.17	William TESTER, wife Elizabeth and children William, James, John, Elizabeth, Thomas and Ann; confirmed.	Fletching
L 1772 Jan.16	John PRUDENT and wife Sarah; confirmed.	Mayfield
L 1784 Oct. 7	Ann HORSEY, widow and relict of William HORSEY deceased, and children Thomas 14y, Elizabeth 10y and William 8y; confirmed.	Maresfield
L 1805 Apr.26	Richard BOTTING, wife Jane and daughter Elizabeth 3y 6m and son Friend 1y 9m; confirmed.	Chailey
L 1814 Apr.22	George SANDALLS, wife Hannah and children Ann, Elizabeth and George; confirmed.	East Hoathly
L 1817 Apr.18	James KILDER; respited.	Maresfield
L 1817 Jul.18	James KILDER; quashed.	Maresfield
L 1821 Jan.12	Celia PACKHAM, singlewoman; respited.	Chailey
L 1821 May 4	John GANDER, wife Eleanor and son John 2y 6m; respited.	Salehurst
L 1821 Jul.13	John GANDER, wife Eleanor and son John 2y 6m; quashed.	Salehurst
L 1822 Oct.14	Benjamin BUDGEN and wife Mary; respited.	Billingshurst
L 1823 Jan.13	Benjamin BUDGEN and wife Mary; confirmed as to Benjamin and quashed as to the said Mary, described in the order as his wife.	Billingshurst
L 1826 Oct.19	Elizabeth BOTLEY, singlewoman; confirmed.	Newick

WEST HOATHLY BASTARDY EXAMINATIONS Par 379/34/1/1.

1774 Aug.15 Ann GOURD, singlewoman, said that her father hired her to one Frances WING of West Hoathly, husbandman and broom maker, for a year from old Lady Day next and, a few days before her year expired, she hired herself again to him at wages of 20s 0d. That she lived with and served him until the middle of July last when, it appearing that she was with child, her master and dame turned her away, and paid her 6s 0d as part of her wages. [Mark of A.G.]

1780 Apr. 8 Charlot NORMAN of Hoadly [West Hoathly], singlewoman, said that she was delivered of a female child on 28 September last in Hoadly, christened Charlot, and that Jeremiah HIDER of Fletching, labourer, is the father. [Mark of C.N.]

1781 Mar.26 Ann BUDGEN of [West] Hoathly, singlewoman, said that she is with child and that Thomas TURNER of Hoathly, is the father of the child. [Mark of A.B.]

1799 Mar.11 Sarah ALLFREY of West Hoathly, singlewoman, has declared that she is with child and that Benjamin BUDGEN of East Grinstead, cordwainer, is the father of the child. [Signature of Sarah Alfrey (sic)]

WEST HOATHLY BASTARDY BONDS Par 379/34/3/1

1690 Oct. 8 Edward TAYLOR of West Hoathly, collier, and William VYNE of Barcombe, bound to the parish officers of West Hoathly in £40 in respect of Mary TAYLOR, daughter of the above E.T., who has lately been delivered of a male bastard child in West Hoathly. [*Part of document missing*]

1745 Sep.27 William THARP of Ardingly, husbandman, and Richard THARP of West Hoathly, husbandman, bound to the parish officers of West Hoathly in £80 in respect of Sarah JENNER of Ardingly, singlewoman, who has declared that she is great with child and that R.T. is the father. [*Part of document missing*]

1767 Mar. 6 Thomas COULES of Horsemountsucx [Hurstmonceaux], blacksmith, bound to the parish officers of West Hoathly in £40 in respect of Sarah PENFOLD of West Hoathly, who has lately been delivered of a male bastard child and has declared T.C. to be the father. [Signature of T.C.] [*Document damaged*]

1769 Sep. 6 The parish officers of Gatton, Surrey, bound to the parish officers of West Hoathly in £40 in respect of Mary GIBB, singlewoman, who is now with child. As her last legal place of settlement is Gatton, where there is no place convenient for her lying in, the parish officers of Gatton have requested the inhabitants of West Hoathly to permit M.G. to lie-in in the parish of West Hoathly, to which they have agreed, on being indemnified against all charges by Gatton parish.

1774 Dec.13 John COMBER, son of Turner COMBER of West Hoathly, yeoman, bound to the parish officers of West Hoathly in £40 in respect of Martha CHEESMAN of West Hoathly, singlewoman, who has declared that she is now with child and that J.C. is the father. J.C. to pay 2s 0d a week for so many weeks as she shall be in the workhouse before she shall be delivered of the child, also 40s 0d for a month's lying in and, when the month is expired, will indemnify the parish from further costs. [Signature of J.C.] [*Document damaged*]

1783 Jan.11 The parish officers of Lindfield agree that they will pay to the parish officers of West Hoathly any expenses on account of Jane BUDGEN and the child with which she is now pregnant, and acknowledge her to be legally settled in their parish.

1786 Sep.12 James FRIEND and William FRIEND, both of West Hoathly and labourers, bound to the parish officers of West Hoathly in £100 in respect of Ann BUDGEN of West Hoathly, singlewoman, who on 14 August last, declared herself to be with child, and that J.F. is the father. J.F. and W.F. agree to pay 40s 0d within one month for the expenses of lying in and, when the child is born, to pay 1s 0d a week as long as the child is chargeable. [Signatures of J.F. and W.F.]

WEST HOATHLY BASTARDY ORDERS Par 379/34/4/1

1784 Apr.26 Mary KILNER of West Hoathly, singlewoman, has declared that Thomas BROMLEY of Lingfield, Surrey, farmer, is the father of a female bastard child born to her on 18 January last, at the house of her father, Edward KILNER, in West Hoathly. T.B. to pay 40s 0d for cost of lying-in and 2s 0d a week; the mother to pay 6d a week.

1788 May 6 Ann BROWNE, singlewoman, has declared that James MURRELL is the father of a bastard child born to her [*where document has been torn in half any other information concerning the child is missing*] J.M. to pay £4.8s 0d for cost of lying- in and 2s 0d a week; the mother to pay 6d a week.

1788 May 6 Mary BROWNE, singlewoman, has declared that Francis ACTON is the father of a female bastard child born to her on 27 January last, at the house of [?Ann HOWARD - *torn*]. F.A. to pay £3.8s 0d for lying-in and 2s 0d a week; the mother to pay 6d a week. [*Document damaged*]

1793 May 20 Sarah ISTED, singlewoman, has declared that Nicholas WINTON the younger of Horsted Keynes, labourer, is the father of a female bastard child born to her on 25 February last, at the workhouse in West Hoathly. N.W. to pay £2.12s 0d for the lying-in and 1s 6d a week; the mother to pay 1s 0d a week.

1805 Aug. 9 Jane BROOKS, singlewoman, has declared that John DELVES, late of West Hoathly, labourer, is the father of a male bastard child born to her on 2 March 1803, at the workhouse in West Hoathly. J.D. to pay £18.15s 0d towards the lying-in and then 3s 0d a week; the mother to pay 6d a week. [*Document damaged*]

1805 Oct.18 Amelia BUDGEN, singlewoman, has declared that Lewellyn THOMAS, Sergeant in the Monmouth and Brecon Regiment of Militia, is the father of a female bastard child born to her on 18 July last, at her mother's house in West Hoathly. L.T. to pay £2.18s 0d for lying-in and 2s 0d a week; the mother to pay 6d a week.

WEST HOATHLY WARRANTS Par 379/34/2/1

1774 Aug.15 Ann GOURD of West Hoathly, singlewoman, has declared herself to be with child and that John WING, the younger, of West Hoathly, husbandman, is the father; and he is to be apprehended.

1787 Mar.27 James MERCHANT to be apprehended as [*first name not given*] BUDGEN has named him as the father of her unborn child. [*Document damaged*]

1791 Nov. 1 Mary GIBBS, of West Hoathly, singlewoman, has declared that she is with child and has named John GIBBS of East Grinstead, brickmaker, as the father; and he is to be apprehended.

1792 Nov. 7 Sarah ISTED, singlewoman, of West Hoathly has declared that she is with child and has named Nicholas WINTON of Horsted Keynes, husbandman as the father; and he is to be apprehended.

1795 Jul.27 Ann JACKSON, singlewoman, of West Hoathly, has declared that Philip WELCH, late of West Hoathly, is the father of a male bastard child born to her on 21 October last, at Stumblewood Common in West Hoathly; and he is to be apprehended.

1797 Feb.16 Ann PAINE, singlewoman, of West Hoathly, who has declared that she is with child, has named Thomas WALLER of West Hoathly, servant, as the father; and he is to be apprehended.

1806 Feb.21 Sarah BROWN, singlewoman, who has declared that she is with child, has named Isaac GATES, of East Grinstead, labourer, as the father; and he is to be apprehended.

WEST HOATHLY APPRENTICESHIP AGREEMENTS Par 379/33/1

1689 Sep.14 Bond. John LASHEMORE of Fletching bound in £50 to take as apprentice Alan COOKE until age of 2[?4] years. [Signature of John Lashmore (sic)] [*Quarter of document missing*]

1693 Nov. 6 Edward BROWN, apprenticed to William VELVICK of West Hoathly, until age of 24 years; husbandry. [Signature of Will Feldwicke (sic)]

1693 [torn] John MILLER, apprenticed to Richard DUGIN to age of 24 years; husbandry. [Mark of R.D.]

1693 Nov. 6 Richard VENALL, apprenticed to Thomas GIBB of West Hoathly, until age of 24 years; husbandry. [Mark of T.G.]

1697[torn]10 Mary MILLER, with consent of the parish officers, has put herself as apprentice to Richard HUNT, for seven years. [Signature of R.H.] [*Document in pieces*]

1708 Nov. 1 Sunak VINALL, of West Hoathly, has put himself as an apprentice to Benjamin BACKSHELL, husbandman of West Hoathly, for seven years; husbandry. [Signature of B.B.]

1715 Sep. 5 William PECKHAM, apprenticed to John DUFFEILD of Beddington, Surrey, sawyer, until the age of 24 years; trade of sawyer. [*Document in pieces*]

1724 Jun.27 Elizabeth BURTT, apprenticed to Peter AUSTIN of Maresfield, blacksmith, until age of 21 years or day of marriage. Consideration £1.10s 0d. [Mark of P.A.]

1748 Feb.10 Richard BRACKPOLE of West Hoathly, son of Thomas BRACKPOLE lately deceased, apprenticed to Joseph CHANDLER of Worth, blacksmith, for three years; trade of blacksmith. Consideration £10 paid to him by Constance SMITH. [Signature of Richard Brackpool (sic).] [Endorsed: 6d duty paid = 5s 0d on 29 March 1748.]

1781 Jan. 2 Ralph COATS, son of Ralph COATS of West Hoathly, husbandman, apprenticed to John CHAPMAN of East Grinstead, cordwainer, for seven years; trade of cordwainer. Consideration £12.12s.0d. [Signature of J.C.] [Endorsed: Duty paid at 6d = 6s 4d.]

1785 Mar.28 John POST, aged 13 years, apprenticed to David KNOX esq., of Worth, until age of 21 years. Consideration 30s 0d. [Signature of D.K.]

1807 Aug. 1 John GARTON, with the consent of his mother, Hannah GARTON, apprenticed to Thomas JONES of High Street, Lambeth, Surrey, shoemaker, for seven years; trade of shoemaker. Consideration of £10 paid by Hannah Garton. [Endorsed: Whereas the within written indenture is made for the term of seven years yet, at the time of the execution thereof, it was agreed that, in consequence of J.G. the apprentice being now near twenty years of age, that he shall be at liberty to quit the service of T.J. at the expiration of four years from the date thereof and T.J. does agree to discharge J.G. and also to deliver to him his indenture of apprenticeship safe and uncancelled (and of which the within written indenture is a counterpart) at the end of four years.] [Signature of T.J.]

WIVELSFIELD

Wivelsfield: 3,142 acres. Wealden parish N of Ditchling, 280ft in N, 200ft in E, 100ft in centre. Weald clay and mixed sand, with clay and sandstone subsoil; streams on W & E boundaries draining to rivers Adur and Ouse respectively. Arable and pasture. Two early settlements: near church and at Wivelsfield Green. Countess of Huntingdon Congregational Chapel as well as Baptist.

Population: 1676 123; 1724 311; 1801 442; 1811 468; 1821 537; 1831 559.

WIVELSFIELD SETTLEMENT CERTIFICATE — Par 252/32/1/1a

		To
1754 Dec.28	Thomas ATTREE, wife Mary and children Mary, Jesse, Elizabeth and Jane.	Newick

[Whilst no settlement documents have survived for the parish of Wivelsfield, a copy of the above settlement is among the Bolney Settlement Certificates endorsed: "Witness John TAYLOR overseer Bolney. This being a true copy of the certificate taken 27 March, 1796 by Mr. Edward VERRELL, overseer of parish of Newick". The copy would seem to have been applied for in connection with a settlement examination dated 1 April, 1796 made by Thomas ATREE (sic), now residing in Bolney, who said that he believed he was born in Newick, where his father resided under a certificate from Wivelsfield. Par 252/32/4/1]

QUARTER SESSIONS REMOVAL ORDERS FROM WIVELSFIELD

		To
L 1644 May 3	John FAIRFOOTE of Steyning has lately gone out of the country, leaving wife Anne and two children, which said Anne and children came to Wivelsfield to her own mother, a poor woman taking relief from that parish. As Anne and children are likely to become chargeable, they are to be sent back to Steyning.	Steyning
L 1660 Jan.12	William LASHMER of Clayton, with wife and child, hired a house in Wivelsfield, having been given money to depart from Clayton, which parish allege that W.L. never was a charge to them but, having begun to build a cottage there, they gave him money to help towards his materials; the family, now being chargeable to Wivelsfield, are to be returned to Clayton.	Clayton
L 1662 Jan.16	Widow CORKE came from Newington Butts to Hurstpierpoint and there died, leaving Daniel CORKE her son who has since come to Wivelsfield. Daniel to be returned to Newington Butts.	Newington Butts, Sry
L 1663 Oct. 8	John ASHFIELD, wife and family.	Lindfield

L 1673 Apr.10	Mary PEIRCE and Henry PEIRCE both under 7y, children of Judy PEIRCE, widow, are now at Wivelsfield but as Judy Peirce has, for two years, been an inhabitant of Hurstmonceaux, the children are to be sent to their mother at Hurstmonceaux.	Hurstmonceaux
L 1675 Jan.14	Abraham DUMBRELL and wife; confirmed.	West Hoathly
L 1684 Apr.10	William FAULKENER; discharged.	Lindfield
L 1685 Oct.19	Stephen PILBEAME, a poor child; to be sent to Lindfield to be with his father, Stephen PILBEAME.	Lindfield
L 1700 Oct.10	Henry HAMPER; confirmed.	Lindfield
L 1702 Jul.16	Gabriel WICKHAM; confirmed.	Cowden, Ken
L 1705 Apr.19	John GLASBROOKE; quashed and made void.	Chiltington
L 1705 Jul.12	John GLASBROOKE; discharged.	Chiltington
L 1708 Jan.15	Anne BENNETT; discharged.	Plumpton
L 1708 Jan.15	William PEIRCE; discharged.	Plumpton
L 1720 Apr.28	Elizabeth DANIELL, wife of John DANIELL, and two children; discharged.	Shipley
L 1724 Apr.16	Elizabeth HILLS; discharged.	Cuckfield
L 1724 Jul.16	Elizabeth HILLS; quashed for want of due service.	Lindfield
L 1725 Oct. 7	Thomas MOORE, wife Elizabeth and sons John and Thomas; discharged.	Newick
L 1732 Jul.13	Mary FILLERY; confirmed.	Tunbridge, Ken
L 1736 May 6	Richard TURNER and wife Mary; confirmed.	St. Michael, Lewes
L 1736 May 6	Thomas KING and wife Hannah; respited.	Bolney
L 1736 Jul.15	Thomas KING and wife Hannah; discharged.	Bolney
L 1736 Oct. 7	Thomas KING, wife Hannah and daughter Ann; confirmed.	Keymer
L 1739 Jan.11	Elizabeth IRELAND; confirmed.	Lindfield
L 1739 Oct. 4	Thomas MASON and wife Elizabeth; confirmed.	Lindfield
L 1740 Jul.17	Henry STONE, shipwright; confirmed.	Warblington, Ham
L 1741 Jul.16	Joseph PEIRCE; confirmed.	Clayton
L 1742 Apr.29	John RENVILLE and wife Anne; confirmed.	Patcham
L 1743 Jan.13	Thomas GEERE and wife Sarah; confirmed.	Albourne
L 1744 Oct. 4	John PIPER and wife Mary; confirmed.	Withyham
L 1746 Jan.16	Martha NORMAN; confirmed.	Beddingham
L 1746 Apr.10	Henry NEWMAN and wife Rachael; confirmed.	Buxted
L 1746 Jul.17	Elizabeth IRELAND, singlewoman; confirmed.	Lindfield
L 1753 May 3	Elizabeth WALTER, singlewoman; confirmed.	Plumpton
L 1756 Jul.15	William WOOD and wife Sarah; discharged.	Tunbridge, Ken
L 1757 Jul.14	Mary EDWARDS, singlewoman; respited.	Clayton
L 1757 Oct. 6	Mary EDWARDS, singlewoman; confirmed.	Clayton

L 1766 Jan.16	James EDWARDS; discharged.	Chiltington
L 1773 Jul.15	Thomas SHERWOOD; confirmed.	Horsmonden, Ken
L 1773 Jul.15	William SHERWOOD; confirmed.	Charing, Ken
L 1773 Jul.15	Joseph SHERWOOD and Rebecca SHERWOOD; confirmed.	Maidstone, Ken
L 1780 Jan.13	Mary THORP, singlewoman; respited.	Keymer
L 1780 Apr. 6	Mary THORPE, singlewoman; confirmed.	Keymer
L 1786 Jul.13	Thomas RAWLEY and wife Ann; confirmed.	Keymer
L 1791 Jul.14	Ann FARNCOMBE, widow, and son Joseph 5m; confirmed.	Cuckfield
L 1793 Jan.17	Thomas GEERING and wife Sarah; confirmed.	Keymer
L 1793 Jan.17	Joseph HUMPHREY, wife Ann and children Abigail 5y, Susannah 3y and Esther 2y; confirmed.	Brighton
L 1799 Apr. 4	Robert STIRRUP and wife Mary; confirmed.	Hadlow, Ken
L 1804 Apr.13	Mary PACKETT, wife of Edward PACKETT, and children Lydia 22m and Edward aged 11 weeks; quashed.	Ditchling
L 1805 Jul.19	William MILES, wife Ann and son Thomas aged 10 weeks; confirmed.	Lindfield
L 1805 Oct.11	William GOLDSMITH, wife Mary and children Jane and Sarah 11y, Harriet 9y, Thomas 7y and Henry 3y; confirmed.	Hurstmonceaux
L 1807 Jan.16	Elizabeth BLANCH, singlewoman; confirmed.	Chailey
L 1807 Jan.16	William WOOD, wife Elizabeth and children William 14y, Phille 3y and Nanny 2y; confirmed.	Uckfield
L 1811 Apr.26	Sarah WALLER, wife of George WALLER; confirmed.	Bolney
L 1811 Jul.19	Samuel QUINNELL and wife Elizabeth; confirmed.	Rotherfield
L 1812 Jan.17	William MILES, wife Sarah and children Mary 3y and William 2y; confirmed.	Keymer
L 1812 Jul.17	William BROWNE; confirmed.	Horsmonden, Ken
L 1813 Oct. 8	Ruth MAYNARD, singlewoman; confirmed.	Clayton
L 1815 Jan.13	Sarah COX, singlewoman; confirmed.	Lindfield
L 1815 Oct.20	Lydia COMBER, widow, and children James 11y, Elizabeth 9y and Thomas 7y; confirmed.	West Hoathly
L 1816 Oct.18	John DAVEY; confirmed.	Hurstpierpoint
L 1819 Apr.23	Luke BUDGEN, wife Charlotte and son Edward 10m, confirmed.	Ardingly
L 1819 Apr.23	Mary MAYNARD, singlewoman; respited.	Brighton
L 1820 Jul.14	Sophia MAY, singlewoman; quashed.	All Saints, Lewes
L 1827 Apr.26	Barbara NORTON, widow, and son William 1y; confirmed.	St. Mary, Lambeth, Sry

L 1827 Apr.26	James THORPE, wife Grace and son John 3y; confirmed.	Capel, Sry
L 1833 Jan. 3	George HEMSLEY, wife Lucy and a daughter aged 2m, not yet baptised; respited.	Brighton
L 1833 Apr.11	George HEMSLEY, wife Lucy and a daughter aged 2m, not yet baptised; confirmed.	Brighton

QUARTER SESSIONS REMOVAL ORDERS TO WIVELSFIELD

		From
L 1675 Jul.15	John BARTHOLOMEW; discharged as he has purchased an estate at Chailey, and to be returned there with his wife and children.	Chailey
L 1724 Apr.16	Elias SYMONDS, wife Ann and children Elias, Ann and Mary; discharged.	Fletching
L 1726 Jan.13	Thomas MOORE, wife Elizabeth and children John and Thomas both under 5y; court unable to decide whether to confirm or discharge this order, there being but four justices, two of one opinion and two of another.	Fletching
L 1733 Apr. 5	William LINFIELD and wife Ann; confirmed.	Plumpton
L 1736 Oct. 7	Joseph CORK, wife Margaret and sons John, Joseph and William; discharged as order is defective.	Chiltington
L 1754 Jan.17	Daniel FAULKONER otherwise CORK, wife Elizabeth and children Richard, Hannah, Daniel, James Arthur and Moses; confirmed.	Bexhill
L 1757 Apr.21	Elizabeth POMFREY, singlewoman; respited.	Hamsey
L 1757 Jul.14	Elizabeth POMFREY, singlewoman; discharged.	Hamsey
L 1773 Jan.14	Edward HAYLER, wife Ann and children Mary 11y, Ann 5y, Elizabeth 3y and Edward 13m; respited.	Sedlescombe
L 1773 Apr.22	Edward HAYLER, wife Ann and children Mary 11y, Ann 5y, Elizabeth 3y and Edward 13m; quashed.	Sedlescombe
L 1786 Apr.27	John HUGGETT and wife Mary; confirmed.	St. Thomas, Cliffe, Lewes
L 1806 Apr.18	Sophia LOWER 8y; confirmed.	Newhaven
L 1812 Apr.10	Sarah HEAVER, singlewoman; confirmed.	Plumpton
L 1814 Oct.21	Mary BRAZIER, wife of Thomas BRAZIER, and daughter Mary Ann; respited.	Wadhurst
L 1815 Apr. 7	Mary BRAZIER, wife of Thomas BRAZIER, and daughter Mary Ann; confirmed.	Wadhurst
L 1817 Apr.18	John CHATFIELD, wife Sarah and children Maria 6y and Sarah 4y; respited.	Brighton

L 1817 Jul.18	John CHATFIELD, wife Sarah and children Maria 6y and Sarah 4y; confirmed.	Brighton
L 1819 Apr.23	Mary Ann KNIGHT, singlewoman; confirmed.	Plumpton
L 1829 Apr.30	Mary KNIGHT, singlewoman, who is with child; confirmed.	Chailey
L 1834 Jan. 2	Mary TURNER, singlewoman; respited.	Westmeston
L 1834 Apr.11	Mary TURNER, singlewoman; quashed.	Westmeston

WOODMANCOTE

Woodmancote: 2,239 acres N of South Downs, SE of Henfield. Lower Greensand in centre and S, clay overlaid by alluvium in N. 2 streams, with sandstone rise of Blackstone between, drain to river Adur in NW corner, 160ft on southern ridge. Woodland and free warren. Early settlements at Bilsborough, Blackstone and Wick, with church and manor house near S boundary. Roman Greensand Way in S near Terry's Cross.

Population: 1676 120; 1724 142; 1801 231; 1811 247; 1821 294; 1831 342.

WOODMANCOTE SETTLEMENT CERTIFICATE — Par 214/32/1/1

		To
1762 May 17	John WORSELL and wife Hannah.	Charlwood, Sry

QUARTER SESSIONS REMOVAL ORDERS FROM WOODMANCOTE

		To
A 1665 Jan. 9	John PAYNE, wife and family; to be settled at Henfield.	Henfield
L 1665 Jul.13	John MACKRELL; confirmed.	Albourne
A 1675 Jan.20	Richard ANDREWS; respited.	West Grinstead
L 1679 Oct. 9	Alice BLUNDELL.	Kingston Buci
L 1693 Apr.27	William CHEYNEY, wife and family; confirmed.	Albourne
L 1702 Jan.15	Thomas RELFE; discharged.	Udimore
C 1710 Apr.17	Thomas WHITEING, wife and family; discharged.	Henfield
P 1733 Oct. 1	John HOLDER and wife Ann; confirmed.	Henfield
C 1744 Apr. 2	Henry BLABER, wife Elizabeth and daughter under 1y; confirmed.	Albourne
M 1753 Jan. 8	John COOK; confirmed.	Poynings
M 1774 Jan.10	Elizabeth MILLER, singlewoman; respited.	Penhurst
C 1774 Apr.11	Elizabeth MILLER, singlewoman; quashed.	Penhurst
H 1810 Jul.10	William GANDER, wife Hannah and children Sarah 4y, Henry 2y and Jane 7m; confirmed.	Albourne
P 1810 Oct. 2	William TIDEY and wife Hannah; respited.	Cowfold
C 1811 Jan.15	William TIDEY and wife Hannah; confirmed.	Cowfold
C 1811 Jan.15	William SLAUGHTER and wife Elizabeth; confirmed.	West Grinstead
H 1816 Jul.16	Elizabeth BOWRI, wife of Matthew BOWRI, and children Sarah 11y, Mary 8y, Matthew 6y, Henry 3y and Elizabeth 9m; respited.	Henfield
C 1816 Oct.15	Elizabeth BOWIE, wife of Matthew BOWIE, and children Sarah 11y, Mary 8y, Matthew 6y, Henry 3y and Elizabeth 9m; confirmed as to Elizabeth Bowie and quashed as to the five children .	Henfield

QUARTER SESSIONS REMOVAL ORDERS TO WOODMANCOTE

		From
L 1681 Oct. 6	Edmond HARDING; respited.	Brighton
M 1741 Jan.12	John VINSEN, wife Elizabeth and children Richard and Elizabeth; confirmed.	Horsham
L 1748 Apr.21	Mary HOBDEN; confirmed.	Falmer
L 1805 Apr.26	William TIDEY, wife Mary and children George, Henry, Thomas and Charles; respited.	Newtimber
L 1805 Jul.19	William TIDEY, wife Mary and children George, Henry, Thomas and Charles; quashed.	Newtimber
L 1809 Apr.14	John HOLMAN and wife Sarah; confirmed.	East Blatchington
H 1813 Jul.13	Ann HOLDEN, wife of Thomas HOLDEN, and children Ann 6y, Jane 4y and James 2y; respited.	Pulborough
P 1813 Oct. 5	Ann HOLDEN, wife of Thomas HOLDEN, and children Ann 6y, Jane 4y and James 2y; quashed as to above mentioned John (sic) and James and that the order of removal be amended as to the description of the first named Ann, that she be described as the wife of James GODDARD instead of the wife of Thomas Holden; and the order so amended be confirmed as to Ann and her daughter Ann.	Pulborough

WORTH

Worth: 13,331 acres E of Crawley; includes Turner's Hill, Copthorne and Crawley Down; 250ft in S to Worth Forest at 500ft. Soil sand on loam, sand and stone. 7 inns and 32 shopkeepers and tradesmen. Carrier to London.

Population: 1724 568; 1801 1501; 1811 1539; 1821 1725; 1831 1859.

WORTH SETTLEMENT EXAMINATIONS Par 516/32/4/1

1722 Dec.29 Thomas HUMPHERY said that he was born at Charlwood, Surrey, and there brought up in husbandry by his father till the age of ten years, at which time he went into service, and the last place he lived at was with John JEWELL of Nutfield, Surrey, where he lived two years and received for his wages £6 a year. That his master rented a farm in Tandridge, Surrey, at which farm he, this examinant, resided all the time of his service, and has not acquired any settlement since. [Signature of Thomas Humphrey (sic)]

1741 Dec. 4 John HUMPHRY of Worth, bricklayer, said that, in 1734, he bought a piece of ground in West Hoathly, whereon he built a house and resided there for four years, and was assessed and paid poor tax, and has not gained a settlement elsewhere. [Signature of John Humfery (sic)]

1742 Sep. 8 Mathew CRAWFORD said that, about 22 years ago, he hired himself as a manual servant to Thomas NEWNHAM of Lingfield, Surrey, for a year and that he lived with and served the said T.N. a whole year in Lingfield and, at the expiration thereof, received the wages due to him. That, from then until about six years ago, he lived at divers places about the country, sometimes working at his own hand and, at other times, under various contracts with different masters, none of which were for a year. That he married, at Withyham, Esther LAMB, and was thereupon, by an order, removed from Hartfield to Lingfield, and he has not gained any legal settlement since his service in Lingfield. [Signature of M.C.]

1769 Dec.29 Richard BILCLIFFE, now residing in the Foreign of Reigate, Surrey, said that he was born in Burstow, Surrey, and that, about ten years ago, he was hired by Thomas PENFOLD of Tinsley, Worth, for a year at wages of six pounds, that he served the year and received his wages and, afterwards, lived a year with Thomas FENNER of Horley, Surrey, under two hirings for half a year, and has not gained a settlement since. That, near eight years ago, he married Mary, his present wife, by whom he has one child named John, aged six years. [Mark of R.B.]

1780 Dec. 5 Mary BILCLIFFE, widow, now residing in the Foreign of Reigate, Surrey, said that she is the widow of Richard BILCLIFFE, late of the Foreign of Reigate, labourer, deceased, and that she has not, since his death, done any act to gain a settlement. That she has, now living with her, four children by her said husband, Jane 10y, Sarah 8y, Richard 5y and Benjamin 1y. [Mark of M.B.]

1787 Dec.26 Thomas BROOKER, now resident in Worth, husbandman, said that he was born in Worth, his parents being legally settled there, as he believes. That, four years ago, he hired himself to Mr. William WOODMAN in Horley, Surrey, farmer, by the year from old Ladytide to old Ladytide following, at wages of eight pounds, which he served and received his wages. That he then served a Mr. BROOKS in Nutfield, Surrey, for half a year, and then hired himself to Mr. Edward JENNER of East Grinstead, miller, bargaining with him from three weeks after old Michaelmas to old Ladytide following, at three shillings a week, which term he served and continued with his master to old Michaelmas day following, and then served his master until new Lady Day following, when he left by agreement and, since then, has not done any act to gain a settlement. [Signature of T.B.]

1788 Jan.14 Thomas PARKER, now resident in Worth, husbandman, said that he was born in Worth, his parents being legally settled there, as he has heard. That, 13 or 14 years ago at Ladytide, he hired himself to Mr. Thomas YOUNG of East Grinstead, surgeon, by the year at wages of £3, served this year and received his wages. That, since that time, he has lived in different parishes and has repeatedly been hired by the year but has never served his yearly time, nor has he done any act to gain a settlement otherwise than as above. [Signature of T.P.] [Endorsed: Sarah his wife, Henry and Sarah their children.]

1788 Feb.11 Thomas BROOKER - [*this examination is identical to the examination made on 26 Dec.1787 - see previous entry for that date*]

1788 Nov.13 John LUXFORD, residing in Worth, said that, five years ago Michaelmas last, he hired himself to Charles ORAM of Reigate, Surrey, farmer, for a year at wages of six pounds, which term he served and received full wages, and then hired himself to C.O. for another year at wages of seven pounds, which year he served and received his wages, and he has not since done any act to gain a settlement. [Mark of J.L.]

1789 Jan.12 James HILLS, now residing in Worth, said that he believes he was born in Horley, Surrey, where his father resided under a certificate from Nutfield, Surrey, and he has done no act to gain a legal settlement. [Mark of J.H.]

1798 Aug.29 James NEWMAN, late of the parish of Croydon, Surrey, but now of Worth, labourer, said that he was born in the parish or hamlet of Shingley Hill, Hertfordshire, but that his parents were legally settled in Ridge, Hertford, as he has heard and believes. That, about five or six years ago last Michaelmas day, he hired himself to Charles CHADDICK of South Mims, Hertfordshire (sic), farmer, for a year at wages of £2.12s 6d, and stayed till the Michaelmas day following and received his full wages, since which time he has done no act to gain a settlement. That he is married and his wife's name is Mary. [Mark of J.N.]

1804 Jan.30 George WRIGHT, late of Whitley [Witley], Surrey, but now of Worth, said that he believes he was born in Whitley, where his father was legally settled, and that he never lived a twelvemonth out of Whitley nor did any act whatever to gain a settlement elsewhere. [Signature of G.W.]

1805 Feb.22 Henry TINGLEY of Worth, labourer, said that he believes was born in Worth where his father was legally settled. That, seven or eight years ago, he hired himself to Mrs. Mary Budgen, of West Hoathly, to be her servant in husbandry at eight shillings a week, boarding and lodging himself, and worked for her about three months. That he then hired himself, at three shillings a week, to M.B. she finding him in board and lodging, under which contract he lived with her for three quarters of a year, when he was taken ill and went away, having first settled as to the amount of wages due but which was not then paid. That he was absent about a fortnight and then returned to M.B. where he continued in her service until Lady Day following, and he has not done any act since to gain a settlement. [Mark of H.T.]

1805 Feb.22 John RICE of Worth, miller, said that he believes he was born in Worth, where his parents were legally settled. That, when he was 14 or 15 years of age, he went into the service of his relation, John LOCK of Godstone, Surrey, miller, without making any bargain as to time or wages. That he did the business of a servant and lived with his said relation something more than 12 months, the said J.L. finding him in clothes and pocket money. That, at old Lady Day four and twenty years ago, he hired himself to Francis TULLEY of Worth for a year, at the wages of £3.10s 0d, which time he served and received his wages, and he has not gained a legal settlement since. [Mark of J.R.]

1805 Apr.19 Jane BALDWIN, now residing in Worth, said that her son, George BALDWIN, was born a bastard in the town of Sanderland (sic) sometime in December 1799, and that he is now residing with her in Worth. [Mark of J.B.]

1805 Apr.19 Jane BALDWIN said that her son, John BALDWIN, was born a bastard in Croydon, Surrey, on 7th or 8th August 1803 and baptised John King in Croydon parish church in the September following, and that he is now residing with her in Worth. [Mark of J.B.]

1809 Nov.17 John KNOWLES, now residing in Worth, said that he hired himself to John LACK of Horne, Surrey, yeoman, for a year at wages of ten guineas, which term he served and received his wages, since which he has done no act to gain a settlement. [Mark of J.K.]

1810 Aug.10 William JARVIS of Worth, said that, ten years ago last Christmas, he hired of Mr. William CARTER of Woodhatch, Surrey, a messuage, garden and six acres of land in Worth, at the rent of ten guineas per annum, on which he has resided for ten years, and that he is now actually chargeable to Worth, by which parish he has been relieved. [Mark of W.J.]

1818 Mar.24 Anne REED, wife of Thomas Payne REED, late of the parish of Worth, labourer, said that she was born at Findon, as she has been informed and believes. That, in April last, she was married by banns at Worth to the said T.P.R. and has since then, namely on 26 September last, been delivered of an infant son, named William, who is now living. That her said husband has since, namely about two months and three weeks ago, left and ever since deserted her and her child. That she has heard and believes that her husband was an illegitimate child, born in Lindfield, and is now settled there. That, being unable to support herself and child before her husband deserted her, she applied to the overseers of the last mentioned parish who, at first, placed her and her child in the poorhouse there and, since her husband deserted her, have allowed her three shillings a week but refuse to allow it any longer and insist upon taking her child from her, and tell her that she may go to service. [Mark of A.R.]

1820 Jun.16 William STEERE, now residing in Worth, said that he believes he was born in Burstow, Surrey, where his father was legally settled, and he has never, to the best of his knowledge, done any act to gain a settlement out of Burstow, and that he is married and has one son named John, aged five months. [Mark of W.S.]

1821 Jan.26 Ann STONE, residing in the parish of Ifield, said that she believes she was born in Charlwood, Surrey, but that her father, Ambrose STONE, was then and now is actually settled in Rusper. That, at Lady Day 1819, she went into the service of William BANNISTER of Worth, there being no particular agreement as to period of service but she was to have two and a half guineas for the year, if she stayed so long and that she continued there till Lady Day 1820 and received her wages, since which she has done no act to gain a settlement. [Mark of A.S.]

1832 Jan. 6 Charles POTTER, now residing in Romford, Essex, said that he is aged 36 and was born in Romford, at which time his parents belonged to Worth, as he has been informed by them, and his parents are now living in Romford and receive relief from Worth. That he has never lived anywhere as a yearly servant and was never bound apprentice or done any act to gain a settlement. That, about 17 years ago, he was married by banns in Romford parish church to Charlotte, his present wife, by whom he has five children living, all born in wedlock, Maria 16y, John 12y, Thomas 10y, Charles 7y and Louisa 3y. [Mark of C.P.]
Thomas POTTER, father of the above Charles Potter, now residing in Romford, Essex, was examined and said that his son is now aged 36 and was born in Romford, and that his son has never lived anywhere as a yearly servant, was never bound apprentice or done any act whatever to his knowledge to gain a settlement in his own right. That he, this examinant, at the time of the birth of his son, belonged to Worth parish where he was born, and that he is now relieved by that parish and acknowledged by the overseers thereof as legally settled there. [Mark of T.P.]

1833 May 10 William MORLEY now residing in Beckenham, Kent, labourer, said that that he had never done any act, by hiring and service for a year or otherwise to gain a settlement in his own right. That his father, John MORLEY, was legally settled in Worth, and was so considered by the parish officer there. To his knowledge his father received a weekly allowance from Worth for about two or three years, whilst residing in Westerham, Kent, and, to the best of his belief, his father, who has now been dead about 13 or 14 years, died in the poorhouse, Worth, and was buried at its expense. [Signature of W.M.]

WORTH SETTLEMENT CERTIFICATES Par 516/32/1

A settlement bond from Worth to another parish is listed separately following the main series.

		From
1700 Feb. 5	Edward JARLETT, wife Sarah and children Elias and Sarah.	Thursley, Sry
1700 Jun. 9	Solomon COOPER, wife and family.	Limpsfield, Sry
1700 Dec. --	Catherine FAIREHALL, widow of Richard FAIREHALL deceased, she being with child.	Burstow, Sry
1701 Apr. 6	Richard OLFREY, wife Mary and children.	West Hoathly
1702 Oct.19	Robert TYHURST, wife Mary and four children.	West Hoathly
1705 Mar. 2	Edward POTTER and wife.	Horne, Sry
1706 Jan.12	Richard JINNER, and wife Anne.	Burstow, Sry
1706 Jan.12	John KENT and wife Mary.	Burstow, Sry
1708 Mar.16	Henry BATCHELOR, husbandman, wife and family.	Horley, Sry
1708 Nov.15	William WOODMAN and wife.	Ifield
1709 Oct. 3	John BISHOP, wife and children.	Limpsfield, Sry
1710 Apr.10	Nicholas TOOTH, cordwainer, wife Anne and children.	East Grinstead
1710 Apr.17	William TITCHNER, wife and family.	Ifield
1711 Mar. 6	Thomas WILLETT, cordwainer, and his charge.	Reigate, Sry
1712 Jan.15	William ALLIN, wife Jane and children.	Lingfield, Sry
1713 Apr. 6	William POTTER and wife Catherine.	Burstow, Sry
1713 Jul.10	Richard DAVIS, wife Eamy and children.	Lingfield, Sry
1714 Feb. 4	Robert TYHURST, wife and family.	West Hoathly
1714 Feb. 5	John LUREY, wife and family.	Cuckfield
1714 Nov. 7	Richard GILLHAM junior, husbandman, wife Jane and family.	Horley, Sry
1717 Sep. 2	William NAISH, wife Sara and children.	Burstow, Sry
1718 Jan. 5	John DRIVER, weaver, wife and children.	Westerham, Ken
1719 Feb.19	Richard BANKS, wife and children.	Crawley
1720 Feb.27	John LEDGER, wife Mary and children Mary and Elizabeth.	Horne, Sry
1722 Nov. 3	Abraham BISHOP, wife Sarah and daughter Jane.	Horne, Sry
1723 Mar.14	Richard SKINNER, his wife and children.	Burstow, Sry
1723 Jun.17	Joseph PURDEY, cordwainer, and wife.	Brasted, Ken
1723 Dec. 2	William GLOVER, wife Katherine and children.	Reigate, Sry
1724 Apr. 3	George ELLIOTT, tailor, wife Mary and family.	Horley, Sry
1724 Dec.28	John JUPP, tailor, wife Mary and child.	Slaugham

1724 Dec.30	John MILLS, wife Judith and daughters Judith and Mary.	Horne, Sry
1725 Mar.16	Thomas FRANCES, wife Sarah and children Sarah, Thomas, Elizabeth and William.	Horne, Sry
1725 Jun. 5	Benjamin GARDNER, husbandman, wife and family.	Charlwood, Sry
1726 Jan.10	John SIVIER [SEIVER] and wife Joanna.	Cranbrook, Ken
1727 Apr. 3	John HAYLS, wife Elizabeth and daughter Elizabeth	Horne, Sry
1727 Dec. 6	Thomas BODLE, wife Mary and children.	East Grinstead
1728 Jul. 6	John SNELLING, husbandman, wife and children.	Horley, Sry
1728 Dec.29	Joel BORER, wife and family.	Betchworth, Sry
1731 Sep.29	Lephard HUMPHREY, wife and children.	Horley, Sry
1732 Jan.17	Thomas HANCOCK and wife Elizabeth.	Godstone, Sry
1734 Apr.30	Francis WHITBOURN, wife Dorothy and child aged 5 weeks.	Reigate, Sry
1736 Dec. 1	William BYSH, wife Hannah and children.	Burstow, Sry
1736 Dec. 1	Thomas RIGHT and wife Mary.	Burstow, Sry
1736 Dec. 1	John PREVAT, wife Susan and children.	Burstow, Sry
1737 Jan.29	John JENNER, wife Rebakah and children.	Burstow, Sry
1737 Mar.12	James ISGAT [ISGATE], wife and children.	Godstone, Sry
1737 Aug.27	Thomas GIBSON, wife Mary and child Mary.	Hurstmonceaux
1738 Mar. 5	Thomas SMITH, wife Mary and children Thomas, Robert, Sarah and Elizabeth.	Godstone, Sry
1738 Mar. 5	Richard KING, wife Ann and sons John and George.	Godstone, Sry
1739 Mar.24	Philip DENMAN, wife and children.	Crawley
1739 Apr.23	William SKINNER, wife Susannah ["with their children" crossed through.]	Burstow, Sry
1740 Jan. 5	Thomas POTTER, wife Susannah and children.	Horley, Sry
1740 Oct. 5	John HARDING, wife Debera and son William Henry.	Cowfold
1740 Oct.21	Richard MANTLE, butcher, wife Jane and children Richard, Edward, Joseph and William.	Reigate, Sry
1741 May 1	William DENCH, and wife Elizabeth.	Ifield
1741 Dec.20	William BISHOP, wife Sarah and children.	Ifield
1741 Dec.22	Daniel IZARD, wife Elizabeth and children Daniel, John, Elizabeth and William.	Chailey
1742 Jan. 8	John PAINE and wife Elizabeth.	Lingfield, Sry
1742 Feb. 4	Edward HARDS and wife Elizabeth.	Slaugham
1742 Mar.10	Charles SHIRLEY, husbandman, wife Mary and children Ann and Charles.	Reigate, Sry
1742 Mar.20	John WINN and Susan Winn	Balcombe
1742 Jun.24	John CLOWSER, wife Jane and son John.	Ifield
1742 Jul. 5	Thomas SALISBURY and wife Alice.	Hayes, Ken
1742 Oct.16	John BRYANT and wife Ann.	Oxted, Sry
1743 Apr.10	Anne WYNN, singlewoman.	Horley, Sry

1743 Jul.23	Thomas SYMONS, wife Mary and children Mary, Richard, Thomas, Elizabeth and Hugh.	Ardingly
1743 Nov.19	William PENDFOLD, husbandman, wife Sarah and children.	Horley, Sry
1744 Apr. 5	William WITHERS, wife Sarah and son James.	Burstow, Sry
1744 Aug. 2	Abraham BEADLE, blacksmith, wife Sarah and son John.	Reigate, Sry
1746 Apr.11	Henry UPTON and wife Elizabeth.	All Saints, Lewes
1746 Sep.28	John TASSKAR, wife Thomisin, and children John and William.	Balcombe
1746 Oct.17	Abraham WRIGHT, wife Mary and daughter Mary 14m.	Charlwood, Sry
1747 May 22	John COOK, wife Elizabeth and children William and Edward.	Beddington, Sry
1748 Nov.27	John PULLEN, husbandman, wife Sarah and children Thomas and Mary.	Godstone, Sry
1750 Jun.17	John BYSH, wife Sarah and children Mary, John, Elizabeth, William, Thomas and Edward.	Burstow, Sry
1750 Jun.24	John HERRIOTT, wife Ann and son James.	Edenbridge, Ken
1750 Oct.28	Isaac CHANDLER, wife Elizabeth and daughter Elizabeth.	Horne, Sry
1751 Mar. 8	John SANDERS, wife Katherine, and children Elizabeth 6y, Katherine 4y and Mary 5m.	Charlwood, Sry
1751 Apr. 8	John MILLS and wife Mary.	Steyning
1751 Sep.14	Edward WALKER, wife Catherine and daughter Sarah.	Dorking, Sry
[?1751]	Thomas GIBB, wife and child. Ack.	Horne, Sry
1751 Oct. 9	Thomas GIBB and Sarah his wife.	Horne, Sry
1752 Mar.22	John BASHFORD, wife Mary and children Thomas, James, Elizabeth and Jane.	Burstow, Sry
1752 Mar.26	Richard TULLETT, wife Mary and children.	Crawley
1753 Jul. 7	James THOMAS, wife Sarah and children John, James and Sarah.	Bletchingley, Sry
1753 Jul.15	Thomas SKINNER and wife Susanna.	Burstow, Sry
1753 Jul.23	George BURR and wife Catherine.	Burstow, Sry
1753 Oct.23	George APTED, wife Jane and daughters Elizabeth 6y and Jane 3y.	Horley, Sry
1754 Jul.28	Richard DENCH, wife Hannah and daughter Sarah 1y.	Balcombe
1755 Apr. 6	William JUPP, wife Sarah and children Mary 12y, Sarah 9y, William 5y and Benjamin 3y.	Horley, Sry
1755 Jul.13	John CAMPFIELD, wife Hannah and child or children. Ack.	Burstow, Sry
1755 Dec.26	John HUMPHREY, wife Mary and son George.	Horne, Sry
1757 Jan.29	Frances LANE, wife Ann and daughter Anne.	Nutfield, Sry

1758 Jul.31	Henry HEDGCOCK, wife Sarah and daughter Sarah 3y.	Warminghurst
1758 Dec.26	William NICHOLASS, wife Mary and children William 9y, Ann 8y, Bett 6y, John 2y and Harry 1y.	West Hoathly
1760 Jan.14	William PARKHURST and wife Elizabeth.	Ringmer
1760 Jun. 1	Michael BELLINGHAM and wife Ann.	Billingshurst
1760 Nov. 9	Stephen CLOWSER and wife Mary.	Speldhurst, Ken
1761 Feb.11	Thomas TOLLIS and wife. Ack.	San... [torn]
1761 Apr. 7	James KNIGHT and wife Sarah. [*Document damaged*]	Horley, Sry
1762 Sep.13	Edward GENNER, wife Elizabeth and daughter Sarah 9m.	Charlwood, Sry
1764 Jul. 1	Steaven BILCLIFF and wife Mary.	Burstow, Sry
1764 Sep. 8	Richard HUGGETT, wife Anne and daughter Jenny 2y 9m.	Heathfield
1766 Mar.15	Anthony HARLAND, wife Catherine and son John aged about 30 days.	Ifield
1766 Sep.28	John HARBOR, wife Esther and son John 1y 7m.	Edenbridge, Ken
1767 Apr. 5	James JENNER, wife Mary and child Mary.	Burstow, Sry
1767 May 6	John PEAT and wife Elizabeth.	Charlwood, Sry
1767 Nov.21	John ELLIOTT and wife Mary.	Charlwood, Sry
1768 Feb.21	Thomas PENEFOLD and wife Elisabeth.	Slaugham
1768 Apr.12	Ann STACEY, widow, and children Michael 7y, Mary 6y, Ann 4y, William 2y and Catherine 1y.	Horne, Sry
1768 Apr.30	John FINNES, wife Mary and daughter Ann 3m.	Nutfield, Sry
1773 Oct. 6	James GOWRING and wife Emy.	Godstone, Sry
1774 Oct. 7	William GREENFIELD, wife Elizabeth and children Sarah, Hannah, Elizabeth and William.	Balcombe
1775 Apr.23	William BISH and wife Elizabeth.	Burstow, Sry
1775 May 9	Thomas LIDBETTER, wife Mary and daughters Mary 3y and Elizabeth 9m.	Nuthurst
1776 Oct.30	William FAUKES, wife Elizabeth and son William 3m.	Mitcham, Sry
1776 Nov.17	John BENTLETT, wife Mary and sons William 8y and Nicholas 4y.	Fletching
1776 Nov.30	Richard BLAKER and wife Hannah.	West Hoathly
1776 Dec.26	Richard HOUNDSOM, wife Ann and children Philicia 4y and Mary 1y.	West Hoathly
1777 Dec. 9	Robert BURKIN.	Chaldon, Sry
1778 Dec.21	Richard APTED and wife Sarah.	Coulsdon, Sry
1779 Sep.25	Edward JENNER, wife Elizabeth and daughter Elizabeth 8m.	East Grinstead
1779 Dec.11	Thomas TYDY, and wife Susannah. [*Document torn*]	Oxted, Sry
1781 Jan.28	Henry BOTTING, wife Elizabeth and children Henry and John.	Balcombe

1782 Apr.19	John LANRIDGE and wife Elizabeth.	Burstow, Sry
1782 May 9	Thomas PATTENDEN, wife Sarah and sons Thomas 5y, Joseph 3y and William 1y.	Horsted Keynes
1786 Jul.29	Benjamin BYSH and wife Mary.	East Grinstead
1786 Oct.29	William TURREY and wife Susan.	Burstow, Sry
1787 Apr. 9	William LANGRIDGE, wife Sarah and children Richard 4y, Sarah 3y and William 1y	Bletchingley, Sry
1788 Mar.29	Thomas BROOKER and wife Mary.	East Grinstead
1788 Apr.14	Richard MARSDEN, wife Rachel and daughter Mary.	Dorking, Sry
1789 Mar.22	James HILL and wife Sarah.	Nutfield, Sry
1789 Oct.31	Thomas COOPER, wife Rachel and son James 6y.	East Grinstead
1790 Nov.29	Thomas DANIEL, wife and 2 children. Ack.	Lingfield, Sry
1791 Jan.11	Henry SHALLCROSS and sons James 4y and William 1y.	Bolney
1791 Sep.25	Francis HARDEN, tailor, and wife Hannah.	Newdigate, Sry
1792 Sep. 2	William BISHOPP, wife Ann and son Thomas.	Godstone, Sry
1793 Mar.30	Thomas COMBER and wife Amy.	Ardingly
Undated	Thomas STEERE and his wife. Ack.	Tandridge, Sry

CERTIFICATE OF SETTLEMENT IN WORTH Par 516/32/1

		To
1688 Mar.20	John WOOD, tailor, wife Elizabeth and children John and Stephen. children John and Stephen. Bond in £100, the parish officers of Worth being bound to the Parish Officers of Cuckfield.	Cuckfield

WORTH SETTLEMENT CERTIFICATES Par 516/31/9

At the beginning of the Overseers Account Book for the year 1764 there is a list of all the certificates that are stored in the parish chest in Worth church. The list contains 117 names with year of issue, 91 of which are included among the Settlement Certificates in Par 516/32/1. The remaining 26 are listed below in order of appearance:

2.	1731	William BONIFACE
3.	1762	Thomas BLAKER
5.	1743	John LOCK
15.	1747	James MILES
16.	1702	Thomas TYHURST
24.	1753	William SKINNER
30.	1758	Thomas WELLER
37.	1739	Jeremiah WELLS
40.	1750	Jonas HUMPHY
41.	1737	Richard BOURN

49.	1738	Abraham GADD
52.	1728	Thomas CHARLWOOD
53.	1739	Tobias SKUCE
66.	1756	Daniel SKINNER
69.	1750	John HIGHGATE
71.	1748	Henry BISHOP
73.	1741	John POTTER
83.	1760	Joseph WEDGBOUROUGH
84.	1760	William MILLS
89.	1713	John SIMONS
91.	1761	Abraham COLLINS
95.	1745	Elias EASTON
101.	1756	Thomas WALKER
108.	1764	Stephen BENTLY
--	1769	Joseph DANCY
--	1770	William CHEAL

REMOVAL ORDERS FROM WORTH Par 516/32/3/1

		To
1719 Jul.11	John CHANDLER, wife Mary and children John and Elizabeth. On examination J.C. said that he was bound apprentice to Jossua HOWARD of Horne, weaver.	Horne, Sry
1731 Nov.15	Richard NELSON, wife Susan and daughters Elizabeth 8y and Susan 6y.	Godstone, Sry
1736 May 6	John DRIVER, the son, wife Sarah and sons Thomas 3y and William 2y. On appeal, order confirmed.	Westerham, Ken
1739 Jan.11	Michael CARDEN and wife Corriner. Confirmation.	Lingfield, Sry
1740 Oct. 9	Henry PALMER, wife Mary and daughters Ann 14y, Christian 13y, and sons John 6y and William 3y. On appeal, order confirmed	St. Mary Magdalen, Old Fish St., Lnd
1741 Jan.15	Abraham EDWARDS and wife Elizabeth. On appeal, order confirmed.	Lingfield, Sry
1741 Nov.20	William BREWER. [Endorsed: 14 Dec.1741 carried W.B. to Coodham otherwise Cowden, Kent.] [*Document damaged*]	Cowden, Ken
1742 Jan.14	John VINALL and wife Mary. On appeal, order confirmed.	Lindfield
1742 Oct. 7	Mathew CRAWFORD. Confirmation.	Lingfield, Sry
1744 Apr. 9	Elizabeth WEEKS daughter of the late George WEEKS of Charlwood, Surrey. [Endorsed: Delivered 9 April.]	Charlwood, Sry
1745 Jan.17	John SAUNDERS and wife Mary. Confirmation.	Maresfield

1745 May 4	Thomas SALISBURY, living in Worth by reason of a certificate dated 5 July, 1742. [Endorsed: 6 May 1745. Be it remembered that the within named T.S. was this day conveyed from Worth to Hayes.]	Hayes, Ken
1745 May 20	Alice HACKETT. [Endorsed: Delivered on 29 May.]	St. Mary Magdalen, Bermondsey, Sry
1750 Oct. 4	Hannah PENFOLD, singlewoman. Confirmation.	Bletchingley, Sry
1752 Sep.14	Thomas SKINNER and wife Susan.	Burstow, Sry
1752 Oct. 3	Sara POTTER, singlewoman.	Burstow, Sry
1753 May 1	Mathew CRAWFORD, wife Hester and daughter 1y.	Lingfield, Sry
1753 Aug. 8	Elizabeth IZARD, singlewoman.	Chailey
1754 Jan.17	John GEALE, labourer, and wife Mary. Confirmation.	Benenden, Ken
1754 Jan.21	Ann LOCK, singlewoman.	Bletchingley, Sry
1754 Jun.10	John POTTER, wife Elizabeth and children Thomas 13y, Elizabeth 8y, John 5y and Ann 2y.	Betchworth, Sry
1754 Dec.27	Mary SYMONS and son William 10y.	Ardingly
1755 Jan.16	William BONY, wife Alice and 2 female children. On appeal, order confirmed as to William Bony and discharged as to Alice and the two children.	Chatham, Ken
1755 Jul. 5	John CANFEILD, wife Hannah and daughter Mary 1y.	Burstow, Sry
1756 Apr.29	John BARNS and wife Susannah. On appeal, order confirmed.	Goudhurst, Ken
1770 Jan.11	Jane WICKENDEN, singlewoman. On appeal, order confirmed	Burstow, Sry
1772 Jul.16	Rebecca CRIPS otherwise COBHAM. Confirmation.	Reigate, Sry
1775 Oct.17	Elizabeth KING.	East Grinstead
1776 Apr.18	Thomas BOLCHIN and wife Sarah. Confirmation.	Balcombe
1776 Oct.19	Richard BLAKER and wife Hannah. [Endorsed: Delivered 8 Nov.]	West Hoathly
1776 Oct.19	Richard HOUNSOME, wife Ann and daughters Felicea and Mary, both under 7y. [Endorsed: delivered 27 Nov.]	West Hoathly
1776 Oct.19	Robert WEBB, wife Mary and son Robert 10y. [Endorsed: Delivered 8 Nov.]	West Hoathly
1776 Oct.19	William FAUKES, wife Elizabeth and son William 3 months. [Endorsed: Delivered 25 Nov.]	Mitcham, Sry
1779 Oct.12	Richard TAMPLIN, wife Susannah and children Richard 2y and Hannah 1y 3m.	Charlwood, Sry
1780 Oct.11	Henry HEASMAN and wife Sarah.	Lingfield, Sry
1780 Oct.11	Lucy WOOD, singlewoman.	Crawley
1782 Apr.16	John LANGRIDGE and wife Elizabeth.	Burstow, Sry

1786 Nov. 7	William LANGRIDGE, wife Sarah and children Richard 4y, Sarah 3y and William 1y	Bletchingley, Sry
1787 Aug.28	Elizabeth EGINGTON, singlewoman.	Burstow, Sry
1787 Sep.14	Thomas PAGE, wife Elizabeth and children Thomas, John, Elizabeth and Mary.	Burstow, Sry
1788 Jan.14	Thomas PARKER, wife Sarah and children Henry and Sarah.	East Grinstead
1788 Feb.11	Thomas BROOKER, husbandman, and wife Mary.	East Grinstead
1788 Oct.18	Ann FENNER, widow, and children Ann 6y, John 4y, Richard 2y and Hannah 3m.	Horley, Sry
1788 Nov.13	John LUXFORD and wife Rachel.	Reigate, Sry
1789 Jan.12	James HILLS and wife Sarah.	Nutfield, Sry
1789 Feb. 9	Elizabeth FALKINER, singlewoman.	East Grinstead
1789 Apr.18	William LEGG otherwise ROSER, wife Elizabeth and son William 19m.	Lingfield, Sry
1791 Oct.14	Thomas WARREN and wife Sarah.	Reigate, Sry
1791 Oct.14	Josua LEGG, wife Sarah and children John 19y, Ann 16y and James 13y	Ripley, Sry
1792 Jan. 9	Elizabeth MONK, singlewoman.	Horley, Sry
1792 Apr.13	Joseph OLIVER.	Burstow, Sry
1792 Apr.13	William DENMAN, wife Elizabeth and infant son, unbaptised.	Charlwood, Sry
1797 Jul.22	Mary POLLARD, an unmarried woman who is with child.	Burstow, Sry
1797 Oct.13	Ann CONSTABLE, singlewoman. [Endorsed: Delivered 13 Oct.]	Ifield
1801 Jan.14	John CRAMP, wife Sarah and children Charlotte 13y, John 10y, Samuel 7y, Joseph 5y and William 18m.	Bexhill
1801 Aug.10	John LANGRIDGE, wife Elizabeth and children Sarah 12y and John 5y.	Burstow, Sry
1803 Apr. 9	Thomas REED.	Lindfield
1803 Jul.11	John CHART, wife Hannah and children James 6y and William 5y.	East Grinstead
1803 Jul.11	John Chart GREENFIELD, aged 10y illegitimate son of Hannah the wife of John CHART before her marriage, then Hannah GREENFIELD, single-woman.	Burstow, Sry
1805 Feb.25	Jane PARSONS, singlewoman.	Lingfield, Sry
1805 Aug. 9	Sarah King BALDWIN, 10y, the illegitimate daughter of Jane BALDWIN, singlewoman.	Folkestone, Ken
1808 Apr.25	Edward COLLIS and his children Patience 7y and. Mary 5y	West Hoathly
1809 Apr.14	John TASKER. Confirmation.	Richmond, Sry
1809 Apr.14	Thomas SIMMONDS and wife Mary. Confirmation.	Ardingly

1809 Apr.14	James BALDWIN, the illegitimate son of Jane BALDWIN, singlewoman. Confirmation.	St. Mary the Virgin, Dover, Ken
1809 Apr.14	John King BALDWIN, the illegitimate son of Jane BALDWIN, singlewoman. Confirmation.	Croydon, Sry
1809 Sep. 8	Phillis CHART and daughter Jane.	Horley, Sry
1810 Jul.13	Henry HUMPHREY, wife Annis and son Henry. Confirmation.	Horne, Sry
1810 Jul.13	Joseph STARLEY, wife Fanny and children Ann 3y, and Martha 1y. Confirmation.	Horne, Sry
1812 Jul.14	Jane WEST, singlewoman, who is with child. [Endorsed: Delivered to Rusper 14 July.]	Rusper
1812 Aug. 7	Thomas BISHOPP, wife Ann and son Thomas 5m.	Godstone, Sry
1812 Oct.12	Elizabeth WICKENS, wife of Samuel [George?] WICKENS who has left her, and son William 6y. On examination of said Elizabeth Wickens and Mary WICKENS, her place of settlement adjudged to be Rotherfield. [Delivered 17 October]	Rotherfield
1813 Apr.30	Susannah GRIGG, widow. Confirmation.	Ovington, Ham
1814 Jan.14	Mary STONE otherwise WOOD, singlewoman. Confirmation.	Charlwood, Sry
1814 Jan.14	Elizabeth LEADBEATER, widow, and children Henry 2y 6m and Mary 1y 3m. Respited.	Godstone, Sry
1814 Jan.14	Elizabeth FULLER, singlewoman. Confirmation.	Reigate, Sry
1814 Apr.22	Joseph PARKER, wife Mary and children Thomas 7y, Sarah 3y and George 1y. Confirmation.	West Hoathly
1814 Jul.15	Elizabeth LEADBEATER, widow, and her children Henry 2y 6m and Mary 1y 3m. Confirmation.	Godstone, Sry
1815 Jan.13	Elizabeth WARREN 16y, Mary 10y, Ann 8y, Thomas 5y and Sarah 4y, the children of Thomas WARREN and wife Mary who have absconded on a charge of felony. Confirmation.	Charlwood, Sry
1815 Jan.13	Elizabeth SMITH, the wife of William SMITH, and daughter Susan 2y. Confirmation. [*Catalogued under Par 516/32/2/1*]	Eythorne, Ken
1815 Jan.13	Henry CARPENTER. Confirmation.	Kingsley, Ham
1817 Apr.18	William TIDY the younger, wife Hannah and daughter Mary 18m. Confirmation.	Lingfield, Sry
1830 Feb.12	William WELLER.	Warlingham, Sry
1830 Feb.26	Henry CHEAL, wife Anna and children Henry 5y, William 3y and Sarah 7m. [Endorsed: Delivered 27 February.]	West Hoathly

QUARTER SESSIONS REMOVAL ORDERS FROM WORTH

		To
L 1645 Apr.17	Thomas GUR and wife, lately of West Hoathly, who came unduly into a cottage in Worth; to be returned to West Hoathly.	West Hoathly
L 1694 Jan.11	William DEUCK and wife; respited.	Horne, Sry
L 1708 Jan.15	Cornelius RUSSELL; confirmed.	East Grinstead
L 1721 Jan.12	Sarah SHERLOCKE; respited.	Abinger, Sry
L 1732 Jan.13	John DRIVER, wife Sarah and son Thomas; discharged as he was a certificate man and not actually chargeable.	Westerham, Ken
L 1736 Jan.15	John DRIVER, wife Sarah and sons Thomas 3y and William 2y; respited.	Westerham, Ken
L 1736 May 6	John DRIVER, wife Sarah and sons Thomas 3y and William 2y; confirmed.	Westerham, Ken
L 1739 Jan.11	Michael CARDEN and wife Corriner; confirmed.	Lingfield, Sry
L 1740 Jan.17	Henry PALMER, wife Mary, daughters Ann 14y and Christian 13y, sons John 6y and William 3y; respited.	St. Mary Magdalen, [Fish St], Lnd
L 1740 Oct. 9	Henry PALMER, wife Mary, daughters Ann 14y and Christian 13y, sons John 6y and William 3y; confirmed.	St. Mary Magdalen, [Fish St], Lnd
L 1741 Jan.15	Abraham EDWARDS and wife Elizabeth; confirmed.	Lingfield, Sry
L 1742 Jan.14	John VINALL and wife Mary; confirmed.	Lindfield
L 1742 Oct. 7	Mathew CRAWFORD; confirmed.	Lingfield, Sry
L 1745 Jan.17	John SANDERS and wife Mary; confirmed.	Maresfield
L 1745 Jan.17	Elias EASTON, wife Mary and children William 14y, Mary 8y, Elias 7y, Richard 5y and John 2y; confirmed.	Charlwood, Sry
L 1747 Jul.16	Anne LURY, widow, and children Sarah, Edmund, John and Jane; confirmed.	Beeding
L 1747 Jul.16	John FOWTRELL, wife Sarah and daughter Mary aged 16 weeks; confirmed.	Tenterden, Ken
L 1748 Apr.21	Hannah ILLMAN, singlewoman; confirmed.	East Grinstead
L 1750 Jul.12	Isaac CHAUNDLER, wife Elizabeth and daughter; respited.	Horne, Sry
L 1750 Oct. 4	Hannah PENFOLD, singlewoman; confirmed.	Bletchingley, Sry
L 1751 Jul.18	James POTTER, a bastard child; confirmed.	Abinger, Sry
L 1754 Jan.17	Richard DENCH, wife Hannah and daughter Sarah; discharged.	Crawley
L 1754 Jan.17	John GEALE, labourer, and wife Mary; confirmed.	Benenden, Ken
L 1754 Apr.25	Richard DENCH, wife Hannah and daughter Sarah; confirmed.	Balcombe

L 1754 Oct.10	William BONY, wife Alice and two female children; respited.	Chatham, Ken
L 1755 Jan.16	William BONY, wife Alice and two female children; confirmed as to William Bony and discharged as to wife Alice and the two children.	Chatham, Ken
L 1756 Jan.15	John BARNES, husbandman, and wife Susanna; discharged.	Ninfield
L 1756 Apr.29	John BARNES, husbandman, and wife Susanna; confirmed.	Goudhurst, Ken
L 1756 Jul.15	William WATKINS, wife Mary and four bastard children of the said Mary namely: Thomas 5y, Dianna 4y, Joseph 1y 10m and Richard aged 5 weeks; confirmed.	Old Church, Birmingham, War
L 1768 Apr.14	Ann STACEY, widow, and children Michael 7y, Mary 6y, Ann 5y, William 2y and Catherine 1y.	Horne, Sry
L 1769 Jan.12	Lazarus ROFFEY, wife Sarah and children Robert, Job, and Lazarus, all under 7y; discharged.	Horne, Sry
L 1770 Jan.11	Jane WICKENDEN, singlewoman; confirmed.	Burstow, Sry
L 1772 Jul.16	Rebecca CRIPS otherwise COBHAM; confirmed.	Reigate, Sry
L 1776 Apr.18	Thomas BOLCHIN and wife Sarah; confirmed.	Balcombe
L 1778 Jan.15	Philip FRANCIS, labourer; confirmed.	Burstow, Sry
L 1782 Jul.18	Sarah WEAVER, widow; quashed.	West Hoathly
L 1792 Jul.12	William REYNOLDS, wife Mary and children Sarah 16y, Ann 12y, Elizabeth 11y, Mary 9y, William 7y, Thomas 5y, Hannah 3y, and George 1y; confirmed as to William Reynolds, wife Mary and children, Thomas, Hannah and George, and quashed as to the other children, there being no adjudication of their settlement.	Llandogo, Mon
L 1795 Jan.15	Catherine COLLINS, widow of Edward COLLINS, and sons Abraham 7y, Edward 6y; respited.	Maresfield
L 1795 Apr.17	Catherine COLLINS, widow of Edward COLLINS, and sons Abraham 7y and Edward 6y. In 1761 Abraham COLLINS and his wife Mary, the father and mother of Edward Collins, the paupers late husband, came to Worth under a certificate from Maresfield. The said Edward Collins was born in Worth in 1762, married in 1786 and died without acquiring a settlement in his own right; order confirmed.	Maresfield
L 1802 Jan.14	Mary LEONARD, wife of John LEONARD; respited.	South Malling
L 1802 Apr.29	Mary LEONARD, wife of John LEONARD; confirmed.	South Malling

L 1803 Oct. 7	John CHART, wife Hannah and sons James 6y and William 5y; confirmed.	East Grinstead
L 1808 Apr.29	Thomas LANGRIDGE, wife Ann and children William 8y, Robert 5y, Mary 3y and Ann 9m; confirmed.	Horne, Sry
L 1809 Apr.14	John King BALDWIN, illegitimate son of Jane BALDWIN, singlewoman; confirmed.	Croydon, Sry
L 1809 Apr.14	James BALDWIN, illegitimate son of Jane BALDWIN, singlewoman; confirmed.	St. Mary, Dover, Ken
L 1809 Apr.14	John TASKER; confirmed.	Richmond, Sry
L 1809 Apr.14	Thomas SIMMONDS and wife Mary; confirmed.	Ardingly
L 1810 May 4	Joseph STARLEY, wife Fanny and children Ann 3y and Martha 1y; respited.	Horne, Sry
L 1810 Jul.13	Joseph STARLEY, wife Fanny and children Ann 3y and Martha 1y; confirmed.	Horne, Sry
L 1810 Jul.13	Henry HUMPHREY, wife Annis and son Henry; confirmed.	Horne, Sry
L 1811 Apr.26	Joseph VALLANCE, wife Ann and son Stephen 6m; quashed.	Lingfield, Sry
L 1811 Apr.26	William BARNES; confirmed.	Charlwood, Sry
L 1811 Apr.26	Milly RIDLEY, singlewoman; confirmed.	Charlwood, Sry
L 1813 Apr.30	Susannah GREGG, widow; confirmed.	Ovington, Ham
L 1814 Jan.14	Elizabeth LEADBEATER, widow, and children Henry 2y 6m and Mary 1y 3m; respited.	Godstone, Sry
L 1814 Jan.14	Mary STONE otherwise WOOD, singlewoman; confirmed.	Charlwood, Sry
L 1814 Jan.14	Elizabeth FULLER, singlewoman; confirmed.	Reigate, Sry
L 1814 Apr.22	Joseph PARKER, wife Mary and children Thomas 7y, Sarah 3y and George 1y; confirmed.	West Hoathly
L 1814 Jul.15	Elizabeth LEADBEATER, widow, and children Henry 2y 6m and Mary 1y 3m; confirmed.	Godstone, Sry
L 1815 Jan.13	Henry CARPENTER; confirmed.	Kingsley, Ham
L 1815 Jan.13	Elizabeth WARREN 16y, Mary WARREN 10y, Ann WARREN 8y, Thomas WARREN 5y and Sarah WARREN 4y, the five children of Thomas and Mary WARREN (who have absconded on a charge of felony); confirmed.	Charlwood, Sry
L 1815 Jan.13	Elizabeth SMITH, wife of William SMITH, and daughter Susan 2y; confirmed.	Eythorne, Ken
L 1817 Apr.18	William TIDY, the younger, and wife Hannah and daughter Mary 18m; confirmed.	Lingfield, Sry
L 1817 Apr.18	George BREWER, wife Mary and son James aged 10 weeks; confirmed.	Childrey (sic)
L 1817 Apr.18	Sarah LINN, singlewoman; confirmed.	East Grinstead
L 1817 Apr.18	Elizabeth MILES, wife of Thomas MILES; confirmed.	Cuckfield

L 1818 Jan.16	William SHURLOCK; confirmed.	Godstone, Sry
L 1818 Jan.16	James SHURLOCK; confirmed.	Burstow, Sry
L 1818 Jan.16	William BAKER and wife Mary; confirmed.	Podimore, Som.
L 1818 Apr. 3	Edward HEAVER; confirmed.	Wivelsfield
L 1818 Jul.17	John GIBBS and wife Joan; respited.	West Hoathly
L 1818 Oct.23	John GIBBS and wife Joan; respited.	West Hoathly
L 1820 Jul.14	William STEER, wife Amy and son John 5m; confirmed.	Burstow, Sry
L 1820 Jul.14	Jane WICKERSHAM, singlewoman; confirmed.	St. Paul, Covent Garden, Mdx
L 1821 Jan.12	Maria ROFFEY; singlewoman; confirmed.	Godstone, Sry
L 1821 Jan.12	George BENNETT, wife Martha and sons John 3y and William 2y; confirmed. *See Appendix.*	Steyning
L.1821 Jan.12	Elizabeth GEORGE, wife of William GEORGE, and children Amelia 3y, Louisa 2y 6m and John 1y; confirmed.	Sunbury, Mdx
L 1821 Jan.12	James GEORGE and wife Mary; confirmed.	Sunbury, Mdx
L 1821 Jan.12	Elizabeth RIDLEY, singlewoman; confirmed.	Fetcham, Sry
L 1822 Jan.18	Mary DANCY, singlewoman; confirmed.	Cuckfield
L 1822 Oct.18	John BALDWIN and wife Harriet; confirmed.	Burstow, Sry
L 1823 Jan.17	William EASTON, wife Alice and children William 18y, Jesse 15y, Daniel 10y, Esther 7y, Ephriam 2y, Jonathan 2y and Sidney 7m; quashed.	Tonbridge, Ken
L 1823 Apr. 7	William EASTON, wife Alice and children William 18y, Jesse 15y, Daniel 10y, Esther 7y, Ephriam 2y, Jonathan 2y and Sidney 12m; confirmed.	Capel, Sry
L 1824 Apr.30	Joseph BEARD and wife Mary; confirmed.	Maresfield
L 1824 Jul.15	Susannah NICHOLS; confirmed.	St. George, Bloomsbury, Mdx
L 1824 Oct.21	Maria ROFFEY, otherwise LIDBETTER; confirmed.	Godstone, Sry
L 1825 Jan.13	William MONK; confirmed.	Charlwood, Sry
L 1825 Jul.14	John STONE, wife Sarah and children Rebecca 2y 6m and Ambrose 8m; confirmed.	Rusper
L 1825 Oct.20	Edward TURNER, otherwise PETERS; confirmed.	Horley, Sry
L 1826 Apr. 6	James KILNER; confirmed.	Biddenden, Ken
L 1826 Jul.13	Susannah DENCH and children John 12y, Daniel 11y and Ann 8y; respited.	Brighton
L 1826 Jul.13	Sarah BOURNE, otherwise REEVES; confirmed.	Horne, Sry
L 1826 Jul.13	Phildelphia VIGAR; confirmed.	Burstow, Sry

L 1826 Oct.19	Susannah DENCH and children John 12y, Daniel 11y and Ann 8y; quashed.	Brighton
L 1827 Jan.11	Mary Ann WILSON, an unmarried woman who is with child; confirmed.	West Wickham, Ken
L 1827 Apr.26	William WORSELL, wife Sarah and children George 16y, Henry 15y, John 12y, Mary Ann 9y, Frederick 6y and Jane 9m; respited. *See Appendix*	Horne, Sry
L 1827 Jul.12	William WORSELL, wife Sarah and children George 16y, Henry 15y, John 12y, Mary Ann 9y, Frederick 6y and Jane 9m; quashed.	Horne, Sry
L 1828 Apr.17	Thomas ROVERY, wife Hannah and children Ann 11y, James 9y, Thomas 7y, Jane 5y, and Timothy 6m; confirmed.	Horne, Sry
L 1828 Apr.17	John ELLIS, wife Susannah and child Charity 13m; confirmed.	Lindfield
L 1828 Jul.17	Ann MARCHANT, an unmarried woman who is with child; confirmed.	Lindfield
L 1829 Jan.15	John VALLANCE and wife Lucy; confirmed.	East Grinstead
L 1829 Apr.30	Thomas SANFORD, wife Sarah and children William 12y, Sarah 9y, Thomas 7y, George 5y and Jane 2y; confirmed.	Wisborough Green
L 1829 Apr.30	Mary HOBDEN, (wife of John HOBDEN, who has deserted her), and children Harriet 7y, George 5y and Mary 2y; respited.	Hamsey
L 1829 Jul.16	Mary HOBDEN, (wife of John HOBDEN, who has deserted her), and children Harriet 7y, George 5y and Mary 2y; confirmed.	Hamsey
L 1830 Apr.22	William WELLER; quashed.	Warlingham, Sry
L 1830 Apr.22	Henry CHEAL, wife Anna and children Henry 5y, William 3y and Sarah 7m; respited.	West Hoathly
L 1830 Apr.22	Elizabeth CHART, an unmarried woman who is with child; confirmed.	St. Marylebone, Mdx
L 1830 Jul.15	Henry CHEAL, wife Anna and children Henry 5y, William 3y and Sarah 7m; quashed.	West Hoathly
L 1830 Jul.15	William WELLER; confirmed.	Burstow, Sry
L 1830 Jul.15	Thomas TAYLOR and wife Frances; confirmed.	Ifield
L 1830 Oct.21	Mary Ann SMITH, an unmarried woman who is with child; respited.	Rusper
L 1830 Oct.21	William SCOTT, wife Mary and son Richard 18m; confirmed.	Horsted Keynes
L 1830 Oct.21	Mary STEDMAN, an unmarried woman who is with child; confirmed.	Ifield
L 1831 Jan. 7	Thomas HILL otherwise TERRY 5y; confirmed.	Burstow, Sry
L 1831 Jan. 7	John BASHFORD, wife Mary and daughter Elizabeth 6y; confirmed.	Tandridge, Sry

L 1831 Jun.30	Hannah TINGLEY, an unmarried woman who is with child; respited.	Crawley
L 1831 Jun.30	Ann CONSTABLE, singlewoman; confirmed.	Charlwood, Sry
L 1831 Oct.20	Hannah TINGLEY, singlewoman, who is with child; quashed.	Crawley
P 1832 Apr. 2	Thomas HARDS, wife Elizabeth and children Sarah 11y, Charles 5y, Elizabeth 4y, Catherine 3y and Jane 1y; confirmed.	Shipley
L 1832 Apr. 5	Stephen HASTING; confirmed.	Tunbridge, Ken
L 1832 Apr. 5	John BENNETT; confirmed.	Steyning
L 1832 Apr. 5	Jane PAINE, widow, and her 3 children now living with her, Ellen 15y, Jane 12y, and Stephen 9y; confirmed.	East Grinstead
L 1832 Jul. 5	Charlotte BROOKER; confirmed.	Charlwood, Sry
L 1832 Oct.18	Mary ADES,(wife of Henry ADES who is now living apart from her), and children Alfred 10y and Mary Stanford 7y, both born in lawful wedlock; confirmed.	Otford, Ken
L 1833 Apr.11	Thomas BISHOPP and wife Amelia; confirmed.	Godstone, Sry
L 1833 Apr.11	Richard TURNER, wife Sophia and children James 3y and Richard aged 10 weeks; confirmed.	Fletching
L 1834 Jan. 2	William TINGLEY, wife Philadelphia, and children Ann 10y, Harriet 9y, John 7y, Edward 6y and Caroline 14m; quashed.	Penshurst, Ken
L 1834 Jan. 2	Mary HOBDEN, wife of John HOBDEN, and children Harriet 12y, George 10y, Mary Ann 6y, John 3y and William 1y; confirmed as to Mary Hobden and children Harriet, George, Mary Ann and John and quashed as to son William.	Hamsey
L 1834 Jan. 2	James FULLER, wife Rebecca and daughter Mary 6m; respited.	Nuthurst
P 1834 Apr.11	James FULLER, wife Rebecca and daughter Mary 6m; confirmed.	Nuthurst

REMOVAL ORDERS TO WORTH — Par 516/32/2/1

		From
1694 Jun.18	The female bastard child of Anne WHITEHEAD, now Anne DENCH, born in Worth long before Anne's marriage to Dench, was, by an order, removed from Horne to Worth but, through deceitful misinformation, Worth officers obtained an order so that the child was brought back to Horne, contrary to law. The child is now to be conveyed to Worth, the place of her birth.	Horne, Sry

1711 Apr.10	Edward WARD, wife Elizabeth and children Hannah, Anne, Nicholas, Benjamin and Joseph. On appeal, order quashed.	Deptford, Ken
1722 Jan.11	Henry STONE, wife Martha and daughter Mary. On appeal, order discharged.	West Hoathly
1763 Jul. 7	Sarah PARKER natural daughter of Elizabeth PARKER who declares Sarah to be of Worth.	Speldhurst, Ken
1764 May 3	George WILLIAMS, wife Mary and children George 7y, John 6y, Mary 3y and William 11m. On appeal, order discharged.	Ardingly
1772 Jul.16	Joseph TERRY and wife Catherine. On appeal, order quashed.	East Grinstead
1773 Apr. 3	Sarah [recte Martha] ROE aged ten years was apprehended in Horsham, wandering and begging. Sarah ROE, mother of the said Martha Roe said, on examination, that Martha was born a bastard in Worth and never gained a settlement in any place since her birth. [Mark of S.R.]	Horsham
1773 Apr.17	James KNIGHT.	Ifield
1775 Apr.27	Thomas WOOD, wife Mary and son Thomas 12m. On appeal, order quashed. East Grinstead to pay £2.2s 0d towards costs in attending this sessions.	East Grinstead
1777 Jan. 4	John WILLET and wife Philadelphia [and child].	Plumpton
1779 Jun. 8	John TAYLER and wife Mary.	East Grinstead
1780 May 16	George HARBOUR, wife Mary and children George 6y, Hannah 4y, Ann 2y 6m and Thomas 6m.	Burstow, Sry
1780 Aug.18	Thomas BROOKER.	St. Mary, Lambeth, Sry
1780 Dec. 5	Mary BILCLIFFE, widow of Richard BILCLIFFE deceased, and her children by the said Richard Bilcliffe, Jane 10y, Sarah 8y, Richard 5y and Benjamin 1y.	Reigate, Sry
1782 Jul.18	Thomas TERRY, wife Hannah, and daughters Sarah 1y and Mary aged seven days. On appeal, order quashed.	East Grinstead
1785 Nov.16	William FULLER, apprehended in Croydon as a rogue and vagabond, there wandering and lodging in the open air. On examination, William Fuller said that he is about 15 years old, born in Croydon where his father, John FULLER deceased, resided with a certificate from Worth. He has not gained a settlement himself. [Mark of W.F.]	Croydon, Sry
1786 --	William HOLDER and wife Ann. *Catalogued under Par 516/31/19 f130*	Dorking
1787 Apr.18	James SIMMONS, labourer, and wife Sarah.	Edenbridge, Ken

1787 Jul.24	Edward BALDWIN, aged 9y, bastard child of Jane BALDWIN, singlewoman, now the wife of Richard EDWARDS. On examination of Jane Edwards, Edward Baldwin is adjudged to be of parish of Worth.	Burstow, Sry
1787 Dec. 3	Bet STONER, singlewoman.	West Hoathly
1788 May 6	David GORING.	Balcombe
1788 May 6	William GORING, wife Mary and children James, Thomas, William, Mary, Elizabeth and Ann.	Balcombe
1798 Jan.19	Thomas HARBBER, wife Mary and children Hannah 1y 9m and Sarah 9m.	Shipley
1799 Nov.22	Hannah HILL, the wife of James HILL late a Private in the 3rd Regiment of Kent Militia but now a Private in the Coldstream Regiment of Guards, and her children Sarah 7y, John 5y, James 4y and Thomas 1y 8m.	Tunbridge, Ken
1801 Jan.10	Martha BROOKER, widow.	Horsham
1801 Apr. 4	William CONSTABLE and daughter Elizabeth 5y. [Endorsed: To the Governor of the workhouse, Worth. Admit William Constable and child.]	Rusper
1801 Jun. 3	John PALMER, wife Ann and children Ann, Henry and Maria, apprehended in Portslade as rogues and vagabonds lying in outbuildings, wandering abroad and lodging in the open air. On examination, John Palmer said that he believes he was born in Worth, where his father was an inhabitant, and that he has not gained a settlement in his own right. [Mark of J.P.]	Lewes
1801 Jun.16	Hannah EVEREST, widow, and children Elizabeth 4y 2m and John 2y 2m.	Burwash
1803 Jul.30	William TINGLEY and wife Ann.	Ifield
1803 Oct.25	Mary DENMAN, singlewoman.	Horley, Sry
1805 Jan. 8	Sarah MAYNARD, singlewoman.	Burstow, Sry
1805 Mar.23	Jane BALDWIN, singlewoman. Sick and unable to travel, fit to do so by 8 April.	St. John sub Castro, Lewes
1805 Jul. 6	Daniel CHART, wife Elizabeth and children John 2y and David and William (twins) aged 10 weeks.	Ifield
1808 Jun.11	Ann TURNER (late Ann BALCOMB, singlewoman) wife of John TURNER, a Private in the Royal Waggon Train who lately deserted therefrom and who is a native of Ireland and never gained a settlement in England, and her child by her said husband, named William aged seven weeks.	Horley, Sry
1808 Nov.16	George SIMMONS and his wife.	Ifield

Catalogued under Par 516/31/19 f130

1809 Feb.15	Elizabeth EASTON, singlewoman, who is now with child.	Pembury, Ken
1809 Nov.21	John ALLINGHAM.	Burstow, Sry
1810 Jan.22	Francis ARNOLD, aged 15y, the illegitimate child of Hannah KENT, formerly Hannah ARNOLD. On examination of H.K. the last legal settlement of Francis is adjudged to be Worth.	Edenbridge, Ken
1810 Apr. 5	Charlotte STEDMAN, singlewoman.	Balcombe
1810 Nov.12	Thomas RICE, wife Mary and children Elizabeth 6y, Mary 4y and Thomas 3m.	East Grinstead
1810 Dec. 1	Kenward POTTER.	Horsham
1810 Dec.15	Edward RIDLEY and wife Ann.	Bolney
1812 May 26	William CONSTABLE and wife Sarah.	Charlwood, Sry
1813 Mar.26	Charlotte HEASMAN, singlewoman, lately come into Bolney, being with child.	Bolney
1814 Oct.21	John CRAMP, wife Mary and children Mary 5y, John 3y and Samuel 1y. On appeal, order respited to next Sessions.	Bexhill
1814 Dec.28	John BAKER, labourer, wife Elizabeth and child Mary 11y.	Burstow, Sry
1815 Sep.12	Ann STANES. *Catalogued under Par 516/31/19 f130*	Lindfield
1815 Oct.17	Elizabeth HOMEWOOD, singlewoman. On appeal order quashed. Ifield to pay £2.4s 0d, paid by Worth for the maintenance of the pauper.	Ifield
1816 Jul. 1	Richard BRACKPOOL and wife Ann. *Catalogued under Par 516/31/19 f131*	Horsted Keynes
1816 Aug.16	William TOWES and family. *Catalogued under Par 516/31/19 f130*	West Hoathly
1816 Nov. 8	Jemima JOHNSON.	Bletchingley, Sry
1816 Dec.14	George HOLMAN and wife Ann. *Catalogued under Par 516/31/19 f130*	Chiddingstone, Ken
1817 May 13	William WALEY otherwise RICE.	West Hoathly
1817 Jul.15	Joseph VALLANCE, wife Ann and children Stephen 7y and Mary 1y 4m. On appeal, the family to be returned to Burstow, who are to pay 40s 0d and £2.10s 0d maintenance costs.	Burstow, Sry
1817 Jul.28	Sarah GLEESTON, a child aged 3y.	Brighton
1817 Oct.27	Thomas NORMAN.	East Grinstead
1817 Nov. 5	Stephen WILLET. *Catalogued under Par 516/31/19 f131*	Reigate, Sry
1817 Dec. 2	William PAYNE.	Burstow, Sry
1818 Aug.15	Mary CHARLWOOD, singlewoman.	Ifield
1818 Sep.19	Thomas STEDMAN, wife Phillis and children Mary 6y and Phillis 3y.	Ifield

1820 Jul.24	Sophia KNIGHT otherwise Sophia EASTON. *Catalogued under Par 516/31/19 f131*	Banstead, Sry
1820 Aug.21	William MAY, wife Charlotte and children Mary 3y and Joseph 10m. *See Appendix*	Brighton
1821 Feb. 3	Ann STONE, singlewoman.	Ifield
1821 Apr.21	Sarah ROFFEY, widow.	Woodmansterne, Sry
1821 May 12	John RICE and family. *Catalogued under Par 516/31/19 f131*	Nuthurst
1821 Dec. 3	Matilda MITCHELL, illegitimate daughter of Matilda the now wife of James MITCHELL of Mereworth. On examination of M.M., the mother, the last settlement of her daughter adjudged to be Worth.	Mereworth, Ken
1822 May 31	William ARNOLD alias STEADMAN. *Catalogued under Par 516/31/19 f 132*	Cuckfield
1823 Apr.15	Sarah BURBERRY. *Catalogued under Par 516/31/19 f 132*	Horsham
1823 Apr.28	John PARSONS. *Catalogued under Par 516/31/19 f 132*	Withyham
1823 Jul. 5	William WEBB. *Catalogued under Par 516/31/19 f 131*	Ifield
1823 Nov. 4	William PESCUD. *Catalogued under Par 516/31/19 f 132*	Horley, Sry
1824 Jan. 6	John PARSONS and wife Sarah. *Catalogued under Par 516/31/19 f 132*	Merstham, Sry
1824 Apr. 2	Ann SAYERS *Catalogued under Par 516/31/19 f 132*	Cuckfield
1825 Jan. 4	Elizabeth STRINGER. *Catalogued under Par 516/31/19 f 133*	Leigh [*County not given*]
1825 Aug.19	Amelia COLLINS. *Catalogued under Par 516/31/19 f 133*	Slaugham
1825 --	John PAYNE and wife Mary. *Catalogued under Par 516/31/19 f 133*	Lambeth, Sry
1826 Feb.20	Elizabeth ROGERS, widow.	Brighton
1826 Oct. 3	Sarah JUPP, widow *Catalogued under Par 516/31/19 f 133* *See Appendix*	Falmer
1827 Mar. 3	William BURT, wife Sarah and children Ann 2y and Caroline 6m. As W.B. unable to travel due to sickness order is suspended.	Croydon, Sry
1827 Mar.29	Sarah ROVERY, wife of Thomas ROVERY. *Catalogued under Par 516/31/19 f 133*	Slaugham
1827 Nov.23	Richard TAYLOR.	Ardingly

1829 Jul. 2	Tabitha HUMPHREYS, widow.	Minster, Isle of Sheppey, Ken
1829 Aug.25	James BOURNE, wife Elizabeth and children Mary 8y and James 2y, Mary not having gained a settlement in her own right. James Bourne sick and unable to travel but fit to do so by 11 September, and whole family can be removed. Worth to pay Balcombe £2.9s 6d maintenance, £2.2s 0d examination expenses, and 18s 0d charges for suspension of order.	Balcombe
1829 Nov.16	George TASKER, wife Hannah and children Elizabeth 5y and Phoebe nearly 3y. *See Appendix*	Bletchingley, Sry
1829 Dec.21	Martha PAYNE, widow.	Horne, Sry
1830 May 7	Thomas GARDNER, wife Jane and children William 13y, Henry 10y, Elizabeth 6y, Johanna 5y and Mary 3y.	Balcombe
1832 Dec.15	William SAYERS.	Ifield
1833 Jan.24	Thomas HILL, wife Mary and children Mary Eliza 8y, Thomas 4y, Caroline 2y and Henry 2m. Mary Hill sick and unable to travel but by 27 April fit to do so. Worth to pay costs of £7.3s 3d.	Streatham, Sry
1833 Apr. 3	Ambrose JENNER, wife Sara Bess and child Rosa 11m.	St. Giles, Camberwell, Sry

QUARTER SESSIONS REMOVAL ORDERS TO WORTH

		From
L 1690 Oct. 9	William HOLLIS and wife; order removing them from Southover to Worth is discharged as W.H. was last serving with John COLCOCKE of Ifield and, unless cause to the contrary is shown at the next sessions, W.H. and wife are to be sent to Ifield.	Southover
M 1723 Jan.14	William PARKER, wife and 4 children; confirmed.	Horsham
L 1743 Jul.14	Thomas CHAPMAN, wife Mary and son John 1y; discharged.	Hartfield
P 1743 Oct. 3	David CARTER, wife Mary and son David; confirmed.	Pulborough
H 1761 Jul.13	Henry WELLER, husbandman, and wife Rebecca; confirmed.	Rusper
L 1805 Apr.26	Jane BALDWIN, singlewoman; confirmed.	St. John sub Castro, Lewes
L 1813 Jan.15	John FRAZIER; confirmed.	Hailsham

L 1814 Oct.21	John CRAMP, wife Mary and children Mary 5y, John 3y and Samuel 1y; respited.	Bexhill
L 1818 Apr. 3	Isaac HARDY; respited.	Hartfield
H 1821 Jul.16	John PAYN and son William 13y; respited. *See Appendix*	Warnham
P 1822 Jan.14	Stephen HARBER, wife Elizabeth and children Elizabeth 16y, Stephen 11y, Harriet 9y, Mary 7y, Henry 5y, Ann 4y and William 2y; respited. *See Appendix*	Slindon
L 1823 Apr. 7	Richard SIPPETTS, wife Mary and children Richard 4y, Elizabeth 2y and Jane 3m; confirmed.	Hartfield
L 1827 Apr.26	Sarah PARKER 7y; respited. *See Appendix*	Brighton
L 1827 Oct.18	Sarah PARKER 7y; confirmed.	Brighton
P 1832 Jan. 2	Thomas HARDS, wife Elizabeth and children Sarah 11y, Charles 5y, Elizabeth 4y, Catherine 3y and Jane 1y; respited.	Shipley
P 1832 Apr. 2	Thomas HARDS, wife Elizabeth and children Sarah 11y, Charles 5y, Elizabeth 4y, Catherine 3y and Jane 1y; confirmed.	Shipley
P 1834 Apr. 7	Thomas HARBOUR, wife Eliza and children Sophia 6y, Hester 4y and Thomas 10m; confirmed.	Linchmere

WORTH BASTARDY EXAMINATIONS Par 516/34/2/1

1773 Mar.31 Mary BUCKLAND, widow now residing in Worth, said that she is with child which is likely to be born a bastard, and that George HARBER of Worth, husbandman, is the father. [Mark of M.B.]

1809 Dec.15 Elizabeth WORSELL, singlewoman residing in Worth, said that, in the spring of 1806, she hired herself to Mrs. WALLER, the wife of George WALLER of Horsham, for a year to commence on old May Day at the wages of £5.5s 0d, and entered her service the day before old May Day and served until old May Day 1807, and received her wages. That she continued in the service of Mrs. Waller by the month, a month's wages or a month's warning, until January last, when she quitted her service. That she is now with child and actually chargeable to Worth. [Mark of E.W.]
Catalogued under Par 516/32/4/1

1810 Apr. 5 Charlotte STEADMAN, singlewoman residing in Balcombe, said that, two years ago Ladyday last, she hired herself into the service of Richard DENCH of Worth, yeoman, for a year at wages of three pounds, which year she served and received her wages. That she has done no act to gain a settlement elsewhere and is now with child and actually chargeable to Balcombe. [Mark of C.S.]
Catalogued under Par 516/32/4/1

1819 Aug. 6 Mary CHARLWOOD of Worth, singlewoman, said that, at the beginning of March last, she was delivered of a male bastard child in the house of Mrs. TULLIT in Worth, and names the father as one KING of Singleton, gardener. [Mark of M.C.]

1820 Jun.16 Jane WICKERSHAM, now residing in Worth, said that she believes she was born in Worth, where her father was legally settled. That, in July 1818, she hired herself to James HOLLAND of St. Paul, Covent Garden, Middlesex, potato salesman, at wages of ten guineas a year, a month's wages or a month's warning. That she served him a year in that parish and received her wages, then hired herself again to J.H. at 11 guineas a year, and continued in such service for six months and a fortnight, since which she has done no act to gain a settlement, and is now with child which is likely to be born a bastard. [Signature of J.W.]

1827 Aug.25 Sarah TINGLEY, singlewoman, has declared that she is now with child, and that Isaac BARNES of Rotherfield is the father. [Mark of S.T.]

1828 May 23 Elizabeth VALLANCE of Copthorne, Worth, singlewoman, has declared that she is now with child, and that George WORSELL of Burstow, Surrey, is the father. [Mark of E.V.]

WORTH BASTARDY BONDS Par 516/34/1/1

1644 Oct. 5 Nicholas NETLINGAME of Worth, husbandman, bound to the parish officers of Worth in £14 in respect of his sister, Sara, who is now great with child, and he agrees to maintain and keep the child until the age of one and twenty years. [Mark of N.N.]

1699 Feb.13 William BOOKER of Horley, Surrey, husbandman, Thomas KENT of Worth, yeoman, and John BOOKER of Worth, yeoman, bound to the parish officers of Worth in £80 in respect of Susan HUMPHRY of Worth, widow, who has sworn against the said William Booker that she is with child by him. [Marks of W.B., J.B. and T.K.]

1714 Sep.16 Thomas SUDDS of Leigh, Surrey, farmer, and William SUDDS of Lingfield, Surrey, farmer, bound to the parish officers of Worth in £50 in respect of Sarah ERRIDGE, who now pretends herself the wife of the above Thomas Sudds, and who was lately delivered of a male child in Worth. The inhabitants of that parish are not satisfied of the legality of the pretended marriage and insist upon a security. [Mark of T.S., Signature of W.S.]

1714 Nov.15 Thomas HASLEDEN of Worth, husbandman, and wife Ann, bound to the parish officers of Worth in £50 in respect of a male child lately born in the house of Thomas Hasleden and Ann his wife, who will not disclose the father of the child but are willing to indemnify Worth for ten years. [Marks of T.H. and A.H.]

1738 Dec.23 Robert JUPP of Worth, yeoman, bound to the parish officers of Worth in £60 in respect of Mary EASTLAND, singlewoman, who has lately been delivered of a female bastard child in Worth. Robert Jupp, the reputed father, agrees to maintain, educate, clothe and bring up the female child until she is able to provide for and maintain herself. [Signature of R.J.]

1788 Mar.29 John BUTTS, the younger, and John BUTTS, the elder, of Chipstead, Surrey, yeomen, bound to the parish officers of Worth in £100 in respect of Catherine SAUNDERS of Worth, singlewoman, who has declared that she is with child and that John Butts the younger is the father. [Signatures of J.B. and J.B.] [*Document torn*]

1790 Aug.18 William DENCH the younger of Worth, servant, Richard DENCH and William DENCH of the same place, yeomen, are bound to the parish officers of Worth in £100 in respect of Charity STARLEY of Worth, widow, who has declared that she is with child likely to be born a bastard and that the above bounden William Dench [?the younger] is the father. [Signatures of W.D. Senior and Junior and R.D.]

1805 Aug.10 John BAKER of Pater Noster Row, in the City of London, carpet maker and Samuel BAKER of St. George, Southwark, Surrey, upholsterer, are bound to the parish officers of Worth in £50 in respect of Mary WEEKS of Turners Hill, Worth, singlewoman, who was, on 14 February last, delivered of a female bastard child, baptised Elizabeth Baker, and John Baker does acknowledge himself to be the father. [Endorsed: Paid to Easter 1811 - £7.5s 0d.] [Signatures of S.B. and J.B.]

1806 Nov.20 Edward ELLIS, of Fetcham, Surrey, miller, bound to the parish officers of Worth in £200 in respect of Mary HUMPHREY of Worth, singlewoman, who has declared that she is now with child and that Edward Ellis is the father. [Signature of E.E.]

1821 Dec. 6 William KING, the elder, of Worth, collier, and William KING, the younger, of Worth, carpenter, bound to the parish officers of Worth in £150 in respect of Mary WICKS of Worth, singlewoman, who was, on 12 February 1812, delivered of a male bastard child in Worth, baptised by the christian names of George King. Mary Wicks was also, in 1817, delivered of another male bastard child in Worth, baptised John, and on 2 July last, M.W. was delivered of a female bastard child in Worth, baptised Maria, which children are all living and likely to become chargeable to Worth. Mary Wicks has declared that William King the elder is the father of the said children, which he does admit and acknowledge to be true. William King, the elder, having requested William King, the younger, (his son) to join him in this bond, agrees to pay 3s 0d a week towards the maintenance of the children. [Signatures of W.K. Senior. and W.K. Junior]
See Appendix

WORTH BASTARDY ORDERS Par 516/34/4/1

1627 May 11 Jone ELLIS of Worth, widow, was delivered of a bastard child named John ELLIS, and John WEEKER of Worth, yeoman, the reputed father is ordered to pay sixteen pence a week towards the keeping of the child until he shall reach the age of 14 years. Also J.E., the mother, shall forthwith be conveyed to the House of Correction in the Cliffe, near Lewes.

1685 Jan.15 Ann WHITEHEAD was delivered of a female bastard child, and John SLATERFORD is the reputed father. As the inhabitants of Worth have expended the sum of £4 for the maintenance of the child since the birth, J.S. is ordered to pay the sum of £4 and 2s 0d a week.

1685 Jan.15 John SLATERFORD, committed to gaol for refusing to give security to perform the order of maintenance of a female bastard child born to Ann WHITEHEAD, is to remain in gaol till he shall give such security.
Catalogued under Par 516/34/5

1810 Aug.10 Charlotte STEADMAN, singlewoman, was delivered of a female bastard child on 27 June last, at the workhouse, Worth. John AVERY of Balcombe, servant, the father of the child, to pay £3.9s 0d toward the lying in and maintenance and 3s 0d a week; the mother to pay 1s 0d a week, in case she shall not take care of the child herself.

1811 Nov.15 Elizabeth WICKENS ["singlewoman" - crossed through] was delivered of a male bastard child on 6 February last, at her father's house in Worth. George STREET of Worth, labourer, the father of the child, to pay £5 8s 0d costs and 3s 0d a week; the mother to pay 1s 0d a week. [Endorsed: 468 weeks up to Lady Day 1821 at 3s 0d per week = £70.4s 0d.]

1813 Sep. 8 Charlotte STEDMAN, singlewoman, was delivered of a female bastard child on 16 May last, at the workhouse, Worth. William STENNING of Balcombe, servant, the father of the child, to pay £1.19s 0d costs, £2.10s 0d for expenses incident to the birth and 3s 0d a week; the mother to pay 1s 0d a week. [Endorsed: 104 weeks up to Lady Day 1821 at 3s 0d a week = £15.12.0d.]

1815 Jul. 7 Mary HUMPHREY, late Mary WALEY, singlewoman, was delivered of a female bastard child on 8 February 1806, at the workhouse in Worth. William POTTER of Balcombe, carrier, the father of the child, to pay £9.12s 0d costs and 3s 0d a week; the mother to pay 1s 0d a week.

1816 Jan.12 Ann STANES, singlewoman, was delivered of a male bastard child on 14 November 1815, at the workhouse, Worth. Thomas NICHALLS, late of Worth and now of Limpsfield, Surrey, servant, the father of the child, to pay £1.2s 0d costs, £2.10s 0d for charges relating to the birth, 10s 0d for cost of apprehending him,

10s 0d for cost of obtaining filiation order, and 2s 6d a week; the mother to pay 1s 0d a week. [Endorsed: 260 weeks up to Lady Day 1821 at 2s 6d a week = £32.10s 0d.]

1817 Aug. 1 Anna GARDNER, singlewoman, was delivered of a male bastard child on 19 May last, at her father's house in Worth. Thomas HUMPHREY of Worth, stonemason, the father of the child, to pay 16s 0d costs, 40s 0d towards the expenses of the birth, and 2s 6d a week; the mother to pay 6d a a week.

1818 Feb.13 Amelia CREASEY late Amelia STONE, singlewoman, was delivered of a male bastard child on 8 May 1811, at the house of John STONE in Worth. John RUTLEY of Petersfield, [Hampshire], mealman, the father of the child, to pay costs of £10.7s 6d, 50s 0d for cost of obtaining the order, and 2s 6d a week; the mother to pay 6d a week.

1818 Apr. 7 Sarah HILL, was delivered of a male bastard child on 10 February last. Isaac WHEATLEY of Leigh, Kent, servant, the father of the child, to pay 16s 0d and 2s 0d a week maintenance; the mother to pay 6d a week.
Catalogued under Par 516/31/19 f1

1821 Apr. 6 Hannah TINGLEY, singlewoman, was delivered of a male bastard child on 7 May 1819, at her mother's house in Worth. Richard DAVIS of Worth, labourer, the father of the child, to pay costs of £8.8s 0d, 40s 0d expenses incident to the birth, and 2s 0d a week; the mother to pay 6d a week.
See Appendix.

1821 May 3 Ann BROOKER, singlewoman, was delivered of a male bastard child on 12 January last, at the house of Thomas STONE in Worth. Jonathan RICE of East Grinstead, miller, the father of the child, to pay £1.19s 6d towards the expenses of birth, 13s 0d for cost of obtaining order, and 2s 6d a week ; the mother to pay 6d a week. [Endorsed, separate document: "Mr. Jonathan Rice. To the parish of Worth Dr. for the maintenance of his bastard child by Ann Brooker from 13 April 1825 to 25 March 1830, 257 weeks at 2s 6d = £32.2s 6d".]

1821 Sep.28 Sophia HAVELOCK, singlewoman, was delivered of a female bastard child on 24 August last, at the house of Mrs. BROOKER of Worth. Benjamin CHANDLER of Worth, mason, the father of the child, to pay 2s 6d costs, £2 for expenses at birth, 10s 0d for cost of apprehension, 18s 0d for costs of obtaining the filiation order, and 2s 6d a week; the mother to pay 6d a week.
See Appendix

1822 Apr. 4 Matilda GORING, singlewoman, was delivered of a male bastard child on 20 December last, at the workhouse, Worth. Henry BONES of Balcombe, labourer, the father of the child, to pay £1.2s 0d costs, 40s 0d charges relating to birth of child and 2s 0d a week; the mother to pay 6d a week.

1822 May 4 Mary Ann GIBBS, singlewoman, was delivered of a female bastard child on 26th December last in Worth. William FRANKS of Worth, labourer, the father of the child to pay £1.16s 0d costs, 10s 0d for cost of apprehending him and 2s 0d a week; the mother to pay 6d a week.
See Appendix

1822 Aug.23 Mary GORING, singlewoman, was delivered of a male bastard child on on 12 August last, in Worth. John CHART of Worth, labourer, the father of the child, to pay £5.14s 6d for expenses incident to the birth, 8s 0d for cost of apprehending him and 2s 0d a week; the mother to pay 6d a week. [Endorsed: Bill from 23 August 1822 to 12 July 1827 = £31.10s 6d.]

1824 Sep. 3 Sarah WALES, singlewoman, was delivered of a male bastard child on 27 June last, at her father's house in Worth. Richard LIDBETTER of Ifield, bricklayer's labourer, the father of the child, to pay £2 and £1.1s 6d for costs of order and 2s 6d a week maintenance; the mother to pay 6d a week.

1826 Sep.25 Mary Ann BROOKER, singlewoman, was delivered of a female bastard child on 25 March last, at the house of Mrs. BRACKPOOLE in Worth. John STRINGER of Worth, labourer, the father of the child, to pay 2s 6d a week maintenance and 13s 0d for cost of order; the mother to pay 6d a week.

1827 Feb.23 Amelia COLLINS, was delivered of a male child on 25 November 1825. Charles COOPER of Slaugham, broom maker, the father of the child, to pay £11.18s 0d and 2s 6d a week maintenance; the mother to pay 6d a week.
Catalogued under Par 516/31/19 f102

1827 Oct.26 Ann BRAZIER, singlewoman, was delivered of a female bastard child on 16 September last, at the house of her father in Worth. Robert DENCH of Worth, servant, father of the child, to pay 2s 0d expenses of birth, £1.3s 0d for cost of order and 2s 6d a week maintenance; the mother to pay 6d a week.

1828 Jul. 4 Matilda GORING, singlewoman, was delivered of a male bastard child on 8 May last, at the house of Richard EDWARDS in Worth. Edward SUMNER of Slaugham, labourer, the father of the child, to pay 2s 6d a week maintenance and 13s 0d for cost of order; the mother to pay 6d a week.

1828 Nov. 7 Mary Ann BROOKER, singlewoman, was delivered of a female bastard child on 28 August last, at her father's house in Worth. John STRINGER, the father of the child, to pay £2 for expenses of birth, 10s 0d costs of apprehending him, and 2s 6d a week; the mother to pay 6d a week.

1829 Jan. 6 Eleanor CHARLWOOD, wife of James CHARLWOOD of Charlwood, Surrey, late Eleanor CLIFTON, singlewoman, said that she was delivered of a female bastard child, baptised by the name of Esther on 19 March 1828, at the poorhouse, Worth. The parish officers of Worth to appear before a justice at the

Swan Inn in Reigate [Surrey] on 3 February to show cause why an order should not be made for payment of a weekly sum to the parish officers of Charlwood, for the maintenance of the child.

1829 Feb. 3 Eleanor CHARLWOOD, then Eleanor CLIFTON, singlewoman, on 19 March 1828, at the poorhouse in Worth was delivered of a female bastard child, baptised Esther, which child has become chargeable to Worth as a nurse child, and E.C. is not willing to part with her child until she has attained the age of seven years. As the churchwardens and overseers of Worth have not appeared before the Justices, they are ordered to pay £1 and, henceforth, 2s 6d a week.

1830 Jan. 1 Amelia GORRINGE, singlewoman, was delivered of a male bastard child on 8 November last in Worth. John PAIN of West Hoathly, labourer, the father of the child, to pay £2.7s 6d costs, 11s 0d for cost of obtaining this order, and 2s 6d a week; the mother to pay 6d a week. [Endorsed: The above are married.]

1831 Dec.23 Hannah TINGLEY, singlewoman, was delivered of a male bastard child on 23 June last, in Crawley. Robert LLOYD of Croydon, Surrey, mason, the father of the child, to pay £1.10s 0d for the lying-in, £2.2s 0d for costs of obtaining this order, and 2s 6d a week; the mother to pay 6d a week.

WORTH WARRANTS Par 516/34/3/1

1780 Jun. 2 Ann JUPP of Worth, singlewoman, has declared herself to be with child and that Richard ROFFE of Horne, Surrey, is the father; and he is to be apprehended.

1802 Jan. 7 Mary BARBER of Worth, singlewoman, has declared herself to be with child and that James HARMAN of Worth, labourer, is the father; and he is to be apprehended.

1804 Jan.12 Ann GIBB of Worth, singlewoman, has declared herself to be with child and that George WRIGHT, late of Croydon, Surrey, carter, is the father; and he is to be apprehended.

1804 Apr.17 Esther HOWARD of Worth, singlewoman, has declared that, on 28 March last, she was delivered of a male bastard child, and that Samuel REED of Burstow, Surrey, is the father of the child; and he is to be apprehended.

1809 Nov.17 Elizabeth GORING of Worth, singlewoman, declared that, on 13 October last, she was delivered of a male bastard child and that Isaac SUMNER late of Balcombe, servant, is the father of her child; and he is to be apprehended.

1813 Aug.11 John ROFFEY of Worth, labourer, to be apprehended as he has absconded and left his wife and family chargeable to the parish of Worth.
Catalogued under Par 516/37/8/1

1817 Oct.24 Thomas NICKALLS, late of Limpsfield, Surrey, servant, to be apprehended for refusing to perform an order of bastardy, made on him on 12 January 1816, in respect of a male bastard child born to Ann STANES of Worth, singlewoman; £10.5s 0d now being due.
Catalogued under Par 516/34/6

1819 Mar. 9 Sarah TINGLEY, singlewoman, has declared herself to be with child and that Richard KING of Worth, farmer, is the father; and he is to be apprehended.

1819 Aug. 6 Mary CHARLWOOD of Worth, singlewoman, has declared that, in the beginning of March last, she was delivered of a male bastard child at Worth and that James KING, late of Singleton, is the father of the child; and he is to be apprehended.

1824 Apr. 2 Ann SAYERS of Worth, singlewoman, has declared herself to be with child and that William Henry DAVIS of Worth, watchmaker, is the father of her child; and he is to be apprehended. [Endorsed: William Henry Davis recognaisance in £40 acknowledged 5 April 1824.]

1825 Mar. 4 Thomas GORING of Worth, labourer, adjudged to be the reputed father of a male bastard child lately born to Rebecca SAYERS, singlewoman, in Worth, is to pay maintenance of 2s 6d a week. As the sum of £11.14s 0d due has not been paid, T.G. is to be apprehended.
Catalogued under Par 516/34/4/1

WORTH APPRENTICESHIP AGREEMENTS Par 516/33/1/1

1614 Jun.25 Isbell SAYEAR, daughter of Thomas SAYEAR late of Worth deceased, apprenticed to William RENOWLS, tanner, of Worth, until age of 21 years. Consideration £3. [Signature of W.R.]

1616 Jul.20 William ROBERTS, "one of the poor friendless children of the parish of Worth", apprenticed to John BARTHOLOMEW alias POWNTEINE, ironworker of Tinchley and wife Mary, until age of 24 years. [Signature of J.B.]

1616 Jul.20 Bridget ROBERTS, apprenticed to John GYLLAM, blacksmith, and wife Margaret, of Turners Hill, Worth, until age of 21 years; "huswiffes work".

1616 Jul.20 William BROWNE apprenticed to Thomas KINGE of Worth, being one of the overseers of the poor, and wife Anna, until age of 24 years; husbandry. [Signature of T.King (sic)]

1617 Apr.22 Henry CLARKE, son of Henry CLARKE, apprenticed to John BILTON, yeoman of Worth, and wife Sara, until age of 24 years; husbandry. [Marks of J.B. and S.B.]

1617 Dec.26 Peter HARVY, the son of Thomsine HARVY of Worth, apprenticed to Rionald HARVY, "irnfinor", of Seale als Beeding, until age of 21 years; trade of ironworking.

1621 Apr.29 BOND. Agreed between the parish officers of Worth and John WEBB als CLARK of Godalming, Surrey, husbandman that, in consideration of £10, the first £5 to be paid at Michaelmas next and the other £5 at Christmas following, he will provide for the children of Thomas ROWLAND late deceased, called by the names John and Thomas ROWLAND, the £10 being allowed for the keeping of the children. [Mark of J.W.als C]
Catalogued under Par 516/37/7/1

1621 Dec.20 John ROWLAND and THOMAS ROWLAND apprenticed until they are aged 24 years to John WEBB als CLARKE of Godalming, Surrey, husbandman who is bound to the parish officers of Worth in £50. Consideration £10. [Mark of J.W.als C.]
Catalogued under Par 516/33/2/1

1625 Aug.20 BOND. John TULLY of Worth, husbandman, bound to the parish officers of Worth in £14, agrees to well and sufficiently foster, nourish, cherish, maintain and keep a certain child called Sara ELLIS (being put an apprentice unto the said John Tully and now in his custody) until she is aged 21 years. [Mark of J.T.]
Catalogued under Par 516/33/2/1

1625 Oct.29 John WELLENS, aged 10 years, apprenticed to John ALFREY, gent., of Worth, until age of 24 years.

1626 Jun.11 Elizabeth ELLIS, daughter of Christopher ELLIS, late of Worth, husbandman, deceased, apprenticed to John WINCHESTER, husbandman of Horley, Surrey, and Susan his wife, until age of 21 years; "to teach and instruct her in all manner of houswifes worke". Consideration £9.
[Mark of J.W.]

1626 Aug. 1 Nicholas ELLIS, son of Christopher ELLIS, husbandman, deceased, late of Worth, apprenticed to John JENNER, husbandman of Worth and wife Jonne, until age of 24 years; husbandry. Consideration: £3. [Mark of J.J.]

1627 Apr.15 William ROWLANDE, son of Thomas ROWLAND, (sic) husbandman, deceased and late of Worth, apprenticed to Andrewe FENNER, one of the churchwardens of the parish, and wife Judeth, for seven years, until age of 24 years; husbandry. [Signature of A.F.]

1627 Oct.13 John ELLIES, son of Jhone ELLIS (sic), widow, apprenticed to Thomas KINGE of Rudgwick, yeoman, and wife Hanah, until age of 24 years; husbandry. [Signature of T.King (sic)]

1628 Feb.25 BOND. Thomas WILLIAMS of Worth, labourer, bound to the parish officers, in £12, agrees that he will maintain and keep Richard FININS, son of Francis FININS now the wife of the said Thomas Williams of Worth, until R.F. is aged 18 years. [Mark of T.W.]
Catalogued under Par 516/33/2/1

1628 May 10 Anne GOMER, daughter of Hester GOMER, late of Worth, widow, grocer, apprenticed to John BURGES, husbandman, and wife Margaret, of Worth, until age of 21 years; housewifery. Consideration £5.

1630 Sep.11 John GRAME, apprenticed to William AUSTEN and wife Alice, of East Grinstead, until age of 24 years; husbandry. Consideration: £10. [Signature of W.A.]

1636 Oct.10 Sara MORGAN, daughter of Reze MORGAN, tanner, late of Worth, deceased, apprenticed to Benjamine HIDE and wife Gylian, until age of 21 years; housewifery. Consideration: £10.10s 0d. [Mark of B.H.]

1636 Oct.20 Katherine MORGAN, one of the daughters of Reze MORGAN, tanner, late of Worth, deceased, apprenticed to Nicholas WHISTON, Rector of Worth, and wife Katherine, until age of 21 years; housewifery. [Signatures of N.W. and K.W.]

1637 May 21 Edward DUFFELL, son of Margery DUFFELL, widow, late of Worth deceased, apprenticed to Richard BOWERER of Horley, Surrey, blacksmith, until age of 24 years. Consideration: £3. [Mark of R.B.]

1638 Nov.26 John DRIVER, son of John DRIVER of Burstow, [Surrey], husbandman, apprenticed to Tucky JANSON, mason, of Burstow and wife Jone, until age of 24 years; trade of mason. Consideration: 40s and clothes. [Mark of T.J.]

[?1638-9] John Kn... [torn] apprenticed to George BRIGSTOCK, gent., until age of 24 years. [Signature of G.B.] [*Document damaged*]

1640 Oct.12 BOND. Richard HARLING of Worth, husbandman, and Andrew VENN of Worth, yeoman, bound to the parish officers of Worth in £20, in

the keeping and bringing up of Edward HARLING, the son of John HARLING, late of Worth deceased. [Marks of R.H. and A.V.]
Catalogued under Par 516/37/7/1

1641 Nov. 8 Annis HARVIE, daughter of Edward HARVIE, husbandman, apprenticed to William SIMMONS, husbandman, until age of 21 years. [Mark of W.S.]

1642 Sep.26 Roger BOTTING, son of Roger BOTTING, late of Worth, husbandman, deceased, apprenticed to Elizabeth ELFECK, widow, until age of 24 years. [Mark of E.E.]

1644 Nov.13 Harbert [blank] the son of [blank] deceased, apprenticed to William RIDLEY, husbandman, until age of 24 years; husbandry. [Mark of W.R.]

1645 Feb.24 William ROBERDES, son of William ROBERDES, husbandman, deceased, apprenticed to John BARTHOLOMEW, hammerman, until age of 24 years; trade of hammerman. [Mark of J.B.]

1647 Jan.11 John TYE apprenticed to Alexander GARDINER, yeoman of Worth, until age 24 years; husbandry. [Signature of A.G.]

1648 Sep. 1 Richard KENT, son of Richard KENT, husbandman, apprenticed to John JEFFERY, thatcher, of Burstow, Surrey, until age of 24 years; trade of thatcher. [Mark of J.J.]

1651 Jun.24 Richard MASON, son of Richard MASON, husbandman, late of Worth, deceased, apprenticed to Richard CAMFIELD, a churchwarden of Worth, until age of 24 years; husbandry. [Mark of R.C.]

1655 May 31 John NICHOLAS, son of Mercey NICHOLAS (and John KNIGHT, he being the reputed father), apprenticed to Richard GARDINER, yeoman of Worth, until age of 24 years. [Signature of R.G.]

1655 May 31 John HUMPHREY apprenticed to Thomas CHILDERSTONE, warrener, until age of 24 years. [Signature of T.Chelderstone (sic)]

1660 Jan.28 Ralfe RUSSELL apprenticed to Roger BYSH esq., until age of 24 years.

1660 Jan.28 Richard BROAD apprenticed to George FRANCKE, yeoman, until age of 24 years.

1660 Jul. 9 BOND. Jonas STICKLAN of St. Thomas, Southwark, Surrey, silkweaver, and William WELFORD of Worth, yeoman, bound to the

parish officers of Worth in £40, Jonas Sticklan taking as an apprentice Mary TOOTH, until she is aged 21 years. [Mark of J.S. and signature of William Wilford (sic)]
Catalogued under Par 516/37/7/1

1660 Aug. 9 Mary TOOTH apprenticed to Jonas STICKLAN of St. Thomas, Southwark, Surrey, silkweaver, until she is aged 21 years. [Mark of J.S.]

1662 Apr. 4 Henry GOOD, aged 12 years, apprenticed to Walter ARNOLD until age of 24 years. [Signature of W.A.]

1662 May 10 Kathrien MIHILL (with the consent of Stephen COOPER of Worth, yeoman, executor of Richard MIHILL), apprenticed to George COOPER of Worth, husbandman, and wife Johne until age of 21 years. [Mark of G.C.]

1662 Jun. 2 John DAYNE apprenticed to Stephen COOPER of Worth, until age of 24 years. [Signature of S.C.]

1665 Nov.15 John MIHILL apprenticed to John PENFOLD, until age of 24 years. [Mark of J.P.]

1668 Feb. 5 Stephen COOPER has consented to be apprenticed to Henry WINTER, tailor, of St. Martin in the Fields, Middlesex, for eleven years. [Signature of H.W. and mark of S.C.]

1688 May 28 Nicholas RIDGE, son of Henry RIDGE of Worth, deceased, apprenticed to John LOCKE, thatcher, of the said parish, until age of 21 years; trade of thatcher. The parish officers paid £5 to John Locke but, if the said Nicholas Ridge should die within the space of one year, he shall pay back again the sum of 50s. [Mark of J.L.]

1688 May 28 Anne STRETER, daughter of Frances STRETER, late of Worth deceased, apprenticed to Elizabeth HOLAWAY, widow, and William HOLAWAIE (sic) her son, both of Worth, until the age of 21 years. Consideration: £6.10s 0d, 40s 0d of which to be paid back in the event of Ann Streter dying within one year. [Marks of E.H. and W.H.]

1688 Jul.19 Anne LONGLIE, daughter of Mary LONGLIE, late of Worth, deceased, apprenticed to Thomas RIDLY of Worth, husbandman, until the age of 21 years. [Signature of T.Ridley (sic)]

1689 Apr. 4 Ann STREETER, daughter of William STREETER, apprenticed to James RICE, yeoman, until the age of 21 years; housewifery. [Mark of J.R.]

1689 Jul.24 Richard BLAKE, son of Richard BLAKE, late of Worth, deceased, apprenticed to Nicholas BLAKE, porter, of St. Saviour's, Southwark, Surrey, until age of 21 years. [Signature of N.B.]

1689 Jul.24 Martha LONGLIE, daughter of Frances LONGLIE deceased, apprenticed to Richard GILLAM, yeoman, until the age of 24 years. [Signature of R.G.]

1689 Jul.24 Catheren BLAKE, daughter of Richard BLAKE of Worth, deceased, apprenticed to Edward WILLET, husbandman, of Worth, until the age of 21 years. [Signature of E.Willatt (sic)]

1689 Dec.18 Thomas BLAKE, son of Richard BLAKE of Worth, deceased, apprenticed to Edward CULPEPER, cordwainer of Worth, until age of 21 years; trade of shoemaker. [Mark of E.C.]

1691 Sep.28 Mary RIDGE, daughter of Henry RIDGE deceased, apprenticed to James RIDGE, husbandman, until the age of 21 years. [Mark of M.R.]

1691 Oct. 7 George HARLING, son of Richard HARLING of Worth, labourer, apprenticed to Thomas COLCOCK, husbandman of Worth, until age of 21 years. [Signature of T.C.]

1691 Oct. 7 BOND. George WHITE of Balcombe, butcher, bound to the parish officers of Worth in £10, to take as apprentice George VIRGOE until the age of 21 years. [Signature of G.W.]
Catalogued under Par 516/33/2/1

1691 Oct. 7 George VIRGOE, son of John VIRGOE, late of Worth, deceased, apprenticed to George WHITE, butcher of Balcombe, until age of 21 years. [Signature of G.W.]

1692 Mar.21 BOND. Thomas STEER of Horne, bound to the parish officers of Worth, in £20, to take Elizabeth CAMFEILD as an apprentice until the age of 21 years. Consideration: £10. [Mark of T.S.]
Catalogued under Par 516/37/7/1

1692 Mar.21 Elizabeth CAMFEILD, daughter of Robert CAMFILDE (sic) of Worth, apprenticed to Thomas STEER of Horne, Surrey, husbandman, until age of 21 years. [Mark of T.S.]

1692 Apr.13 Jane LONGLEY apprenticed to John PENFOLD (son of Henry PENFOLD) of Worth, for seven years; housewifery. [Signature of J.P.]

1694 May 21 William FASHEY, son of Jane TINGLY of Worth, apprentice to Thomas HASELDENE, of the said parish, blacksmith, until age of 21 years. [Mark of T.H.]

1697 Apr. 1 Humphry LONGLEY, son of Ann LONGLEY, late of Worth, spinster, apprenticed to Edward UNDERHILL, stonelayer of Worth, for nine years; trade of stonelayer. [Mark of E.U.]

1699 Apr. -- John RIDGE, apprenticed to Stephen AUSTEN, clocksmith, until age of 21 years. [Signature of S.A.] [Endorsed: Received £11 consideration money.]
[*Part of document missing*]

1700 Jul.25 Susanna SHERLY, apprenticed to Charity WORGER, widow of Tandridge, Surrey, until age of 21 years; housewifery. [Endorsed: 1 August, 1700: Paid to the Widow Worger at the sealing of this indenture, £6.5s 0d.] [Mark of C.W.]

1701 Apr.17 Henry HUMPHREY, apprenticed to Thomas TYLER, until age of 24 years; husbandry. [Mark of T.T.]

1701 Apr.17 Edward TINGLEE [TINGLY], apprenticed to William HALE, husbandman, of Worth, until age of 24 years; husbandry. [Signature of W.H.]

1701 Apr.17 John ERRIDGE, apprenticed to James RICE, husbandman, until age of 24 years; husbandry. [Mark of J.R.]

1701 May 5 Thomas LOCK apprenticed to John PENFOLD, carpenter of Worth, until age of 24 years; trade of carpenter. [Signature of J.P.]

1701 May 5 Nicholas CHANDLER, apprenticed to Thomas DAINSE, tailor of Worth, until age of 24 years; trade of tailor. [Signature of T.D.]

1701 May 5 Thomas HUMPHREY, apprenticed to Samuel GILBERT, weaver of Worth, until age of 24 years; trade of weaver. [Mark of S.G.]

1701 Oct.16 BOND. Samuel GILBERT and Robert BROMFIELD of Worth, husbandman, are bound to the parish officers of Worth in £10, to take as an apprentice Thomas HUMPHERY, during the term as by the Indentures expressed. [Marks of S.G. and R.B.]
Catalogued under Par 516/33/2/1.

1709 Nov.18 Thomas SHERLOCK, son of Walter SHERLOCK of Worth, collier, apprenticed to John FARRON, collier, of St. Martins, London, for seven years. [Signature of John Farren (sic)]

1712 Oct.10 Thomas STRETOR, apprenticed to Charles GOODWIN esq., of Worth, until age of 24 years; husbandry.

1712 Oct.30 Mary PENFOLD, apprenticed to John EWINS, warrener of Worth, until age of 21 years; housewifery. [Mark of J.E.]

1713 Jul. 1 John RUSSELL, apprenticed to Francis LEVETT of Worth, until age of 24 years; husbandry. [Signature of F.L.]

1713 Jul.15 Ann EDSLE, apprenticed to Richard HAWKES, wheelwright of Withyham, until age of 21 years or day of marriage; housewifery. [Signature of R.H.]

1713 Dec.19 John WICKENDEN, apprenticed to George VIRGOE, butcher of Worth, until age of 24 years; trade of butcher.

1715 Jun.13 Elizabeth DRAY apprenticed to Thomas JOHNSON, sawyer of Horne, Surrey, until age of 21 years or day of marriage, to be instructed "in all his or their lawful businesses". [Mark of T.J.]

1741 Sep.18 The parish officers of St. Mary Magdalene, Bermondsey, Surrey, put and place Elizabeth HACKETT, aged 13 years, as apprentice to Thomas SALSBURY of Worth, chapman, and wife Alice, until age of 21 years; housewifery. [Mark of E.H.]

1819 May 5 Joseph BEARD, the son of Edward BEARD, apprenticed to John LANGRIDGE shove maker, who is to instruct him in the trade of shove making for two years. Edward Beard has agreed to give J.L. £5 on this day of entering and the said E.B. is to find him clothes, washing and mending the whole time and J.L. is to find him lodging the whole time. [Signature of J.R.]
Catalogued under Par 516/33/2/1

APPENDIX

ADDITIONAL POOR LAW DOCUMENTS

The text of this volume has been deliberately confined to the formal records of the legal decisions by which questions of Settlement, Bastardy and Apprenticeship were dealt with. Occasionally these transactions are illuminated by more informal documents found among the parish record collections. In a few cases they may add factual information to the formal record; in others they will show some of the local practices and perceptions which guided the local officials. The following documents from the East Grinstead and the Worth parish records provide the most relevant examples. An asterisk indicates that reference to the pauper mentioned also appears in the main text. The Worth letters and account have been transcribed verbatim.

EAST GRINSTEAD PARISH RECORDS

Statement of case for appeal between the parish of East Grinstead and the parish of Cowden in Kent regarding Richard *Tailor. Par 348/37/5/4

The parish officers of Cowden procured an order of two Justices in Kent to remove Richard Tailor and his wife from Cowden to East Grinstead, the same being adjudged the place of his last legal settlement. The order, dated 29 August 1702, was not delivered to the officers of East Grinstead till Tuesday 6 October 1702, at which time the Sessions in Kent were begun. The officers of East Grinstead do appeal from this order and have given notice to the officers of Cowden 7 October, 1702, and to prove it:
THE CASE:
Richard Tailer, on 4 June 1700, bargained for a year with John Frye of Newpound in Cowden and served out his year there with his said master. After, in June 1701, he bargained with Mr. [?Gaynesford] of Hartfield in Sussex for a year and stayed three quarters and then his master turned him away. After the 20 March 1702 he bargained with Henry Lindley of East Grinstead for a year and served about a quarter and then, by consent of his master, went away and after worked in harvest last at Crowhurst in Surrey, and after that went to Cowden.
To prove whether he be removed legally upon the first day of the Sessions.

Letter relating to removal order of Ann *Munkton from Brentwood, Essex, to East Grinstead.1725. Par 348/37/3/1

To Mr. [Dudeney]
"Sir, Promised to lett you know where I was when I came to Towne but I could not do so untill I was setled, be pleased Sir to lett me know if you have heard any father then what you told me aboutt my husband for I have not heard any farther then what I have heard from you. Since I saw you by all the enquire I can possibly make I can hear nothing either of his being taken or of his surrender, except you will be pleased to lett me know the

Company exactly that he belongs to. It is not that I desier his company or his conversation `but I should be extreemly glad to hear of his wellfare. I have not bin att -Burnt Wood since I saw you, they say the buisness is not ended for they must have another triall yet and if they will have me there yea must oblige me to go and that is the reason am not the opertuneity of going to see my child, upon that account have sent several times and they will not lett me of it, which is all from your humble servant.
[Signature of Ann *Monkton (sic).]
October 5th from the Plough Ale House in Stocks Markett."

WORTH PARISH RECORDS

SETTLEMENT LETTERS Par 516/35

23 Feb. 1759 H. Burtenshaw of Lewes, [for overseers of Ringmer] to overseers of Worth.

"Gentlemen, I sent you my Bond a short time ago to indemnify your parish against all expences attending the lying in of one Mary Sharp and maintenance of her Child, since which I am told you are dissatisfied with her being in the parish - You will therefore please to deliver up my Bond to Cooper the Bearer of this Letter and he shall remove the woman, for this is a matter that the Father must not appear in nor give any security in his own person."
Par 516/35/5

Nov. 1813 Ann Batchelor of Betchworth, [Surrey], to Mr. Wells, overseer of Worth.

"Sir, I have a Paritioner of Your Parish of the Name of Jane Dedman living with Me. She would be much Oblige to You if You will... have the Kindness to let Her have a few Shillings to Get her a few Cloaths as She is Verry Short off - She is a Verry Willing person to Do the Best She Can."
Par 516/35/6

25 Apr. [1820]. Charlotte *MAY of No.5 Pimlico, Brighton to Mr. Hudson, overseer of Worth.

"Gentlemen, Mr. Mason has wrote to you Requesting an Answer. He has Still permited me to remain a few Dayes Longer for your Desion. I am Still Reman in this Deplorable Stat Extremely ill unable to do anything for Myself and famyly and that Wretched husband has not been near me to bring me one farthing Since last Saturday fortnight. I [would] not have trouble you if I had the means to have brought myself and famyly home have not any Other home. Please to Send means to come home or arange some plan you think Mos Advisable as it [is] Hard for me to go to prison for 7 Days under the vagrant Act as I have been moved home once before from Brighton parish, as I am Come to that

Unhapy Situwation, please to Scend or Come Immeadily as I Shall soon be without a house as well as Vituals from your Unfortunate parisoner Charlotte *May".
Par 516/35/23

17 Dec. 1821. James Staples of No. 6 Union Street, Borough Rode, [?Southwark] to Mr. Caffin of Worth, overseer.

"Sir, I took the uppertunity of Riteing To you to inform you that Stephen *Harber duse not be Long to Worth - He belongs To Cobham in Kent Near Gravesend by Renting a House and Stable at £14.16s 0d [a] year But you must Keep this as to yourself dont Tell Him Hoos Rote it."
Par 516/35/7

15 Apr. 1824. John Plummer of Brixton to overseers of Worth.

"Gentlemen, As it seems to be Ill convenient to you to Send the Widow Beals allowance monthly, I will take on myself to provide for her - If you will send her Allowance up once a Quarter it will answer all purposes - as she must have money to pay her shop goods and other necessaries every week."
Par 516/35/8

6 May 1824. Rev.J.H. Barber of 4 Regency Square, Brighton to overseers of Worth.

"Rev. J.H. Barber presents his Compliments to the overseers of the Parish of Worth and in consequence of not having heard from them in reply to his letter last week and the woman having been turned out of her lodging perfectly helpless and destitute - he is constrained to recommend her to find her way with her family to Worth - Mr.B. trusts that the husband who appears to be the chief author of her sufferings will not be suffered to escape due punishment."
Par 516/35/9

18 Jun. 1826. Rd. Woodman of Falmer [?overseer], to overseers of Worth.

"Sir, I am sorry to inform you that *Jupp continues in a very bad state, and that it is likely he will never be able to do any work, indeed it does not appear that he will live but a short time. It is the opinion of this Parish that he should go home to his Parish and think it will be best for you to send for them as soon as convenient."
Par 516/35/11

20 Apr.1827. S.Waller, [for overseers of Cuckfield], to overseers of Worth.

"Gentlemen, The next Quarter Sessions will be held at Lewes on the 27th instant when the Order for the Removal of Wm. *Worsell his Wife and Children to Horne should be recorded and if it is your Intention it should be so the person who delivered the Paupers to the Officers of that parish must attend with the Order."
Par 516/35/10

25 Apr.1827. S.Waller, [for overseers of Cuckfield], to ?S.Baker, the Workhouse, Worth.

"Sir, If it is the Intention of the Overseers to enter an Appeal against the Order for the Removal of the Child lately brought to your Parish from Brighton I will thank you to send me the Order of Removal by tomorrow Evening, or otherwise procure it to be delivered to me at Lewes on Friday.
Have the kindness to let Mr. Hudson know as soon as you get this, that I have so far come to an Understanding with Mr. Squire about the Road as to render it unnecessary for any of the Inhabitants to attend the Sessions on that Account.

Yourself als (sic) Paine. I have heard from the Plaintiffs Attorney, he says the Costs already incurred are £2.2. and he wishes to know if you are willing to settle the action by paying the Costs and delivering over the Goods. I have no hesitation in recommending a Settlement on Terms, as the only certain Mode of avoiding expence, and if I dont hear from you to the contrary I shall write to him by Friday's Post to inform him you are willing so to settle it."
Par 516/35/12

11 Mar.1828. James Thoburn, Police Officer of 67 Middle Street, Brighton to overseers of Worth.

"Sir, George *Tasker a person belonging to your parish and against whom I understand a Warrant has been issued for leaving his family chargeable to your Parish was apprehended by me on a charge of Vagrancy and Committed to the house of Correction at Lewes for one Calendar Month on the 18th Feby last. I thought it advisable to give you this Information so as to enable you to put the Warrant in force at the expiration of his sentence."
Par 516/35/14

3 Dec.1828. Robert Forster of Tottenham, near London, to overseers of Worth.

"Robert Forster respectfully informs the Churchwardens and Overseers of the parish of Worth, that the bearer James Abrams, has worked in the service of his father and himself for upwards of thirty five years and that he is an honest industrious man who has brought up a numerous family with much reputation, that his object in visiting Worth is in order

to obtain assistance for his daughter Ann Bonnett whose husband Edward Bonnett is said to have cruelly deserted her.
Robert Forster trusts the officers of the parish of Worth will kindly enter into the case and afford the poor woman and her father that attention which the case claims."
Par 516/35/13

28 Jan.1829. Thomas Finney, overseer of Tottenham, to Mr. Hudson, overseer of Worth.

"Gentlemen, The father of a poor woman who is now in your poorhouse with 2 children whose name is Ann Bonnet, has this day been with me and wished me to write to you in behalf of his daughter. He informs me you are about to allow her a Weekly Pension, for herself and Children, and for her to return to her fathers house here at Tottenham again. If so I should hope you will allow her something nearly to support herself and Children, or she may be likely to become chargeable again to our Parish. I should propose for the present time; as her whole time will be engaged with the care of her little ones, that you would allow her 7s 6d per week until she is able to Wean the Infant, after which time she might be able to do something herself and you might then Reduce the allowance to 6s 0d per week, should this meet your kind approbation we shall have no Objection to Pay her on your account and you can remitt us the Money Quarterly by Post or otherwise, and for the which purpose you will be kind enough to send us your Order so to do."
Par 516/35/15

17 Feb.1829. Ann Bonnett of Mr. Forsters Field, Tottenham High Cross to Mr. Hudson, overseer of Worth.

"Sir, I have taken the liberty of writing to you as it is Near a forghtnight since I came to my father's house with My two babies, the money you gave me being all gone therefore I applied to Mr. Finney, Overseer of Tottenham to know if he had Received a letter from you and he had not sir perhaps you have Forgotten to write therefore Mr. Finney wished me to write Immediately And would thank you if you would take the Trouble of writing by return of post."
Par 516/35/16

11 Apr.1829. S.Waller, [for overseers of Cuckfield], to overseers of Worth.

"Gentlemen, The order for the Removal of Henry Sarjent and family from Lingfield to Worth was some time since left in my Hands and I should be obliged by your informing me whether it is your Intention to appeal against it at the next Sessions."
Par 516/35/17

4 Jan.1831. Thomas Vincent, vestry clerk Holy Trinity, Guildford, [Surrey], to overseers of Worth.

"Gentlemen, I am instructed by the Vestry Assembled last evening to say a Man by the name of James Sheppard applied to them for Relief whose situation they are perfectly unacquainted with, should he on any future period require assistance they have refered him to you for that purpose to avoid any imposition on his part and to avoid any trouble and expence of removal on your part if you will on his Application communicate to them his situation and circumstances they will be most happy to attend to your suggestings."
Par 516/35/18

30 Jan.1831. James Burberry and Wm Brown overseers of Newdigate, [Surrey], to overseers of Worth.

"Gentlemen, We trust you will excuse the liberty we take in thus addressing you - and as it is on a subject in which both parishes are interested - we cannot doubt but you will see the propriety of our application.
Henry Hards - a pauper belonging to our Parish and residing in Crawley has applied to us for work - stating that he has been in the habit of finding employment in the parish of Worth but refused lately on the ground of his not being a Parishioner - in this parish resides William Webb a pauper belonging to you though hitherto employed among us - we therefore submit to your consideration - whether it would not be a benefit to both parishes were you to employ Hards as usual and Webb continue as he is at least during the remaining part of the Winter - or if you are determined on refusing work for every one not a parishioner of yours - we must adopt the same plan and remove Webb into his own proper parish in order to make room for our own paupers."
Par 516/35/19

14 Mar.1831. Elizabeth Dean of 10 Hanover Street, Brighton to Mr. Fuller, overseer of Worth.

"To Mr. Fuller and the gentlemun of Worth, I now Rite to inform that the intension of Elizabeth Harbour [?*Harber] is to Come Back to Worth this ladytide And I [know] not the reason of it ... But she is determin to go for She says That she will run away But She as a tutors a Aunt and Cousin and the Cousin is now coming back to Worth ... therefore Gentlemen I wish to Have My Money else she must come Home the same as she Came or pleas to rite wether you wish her stay as there is Mr. Smith - the gardner that Comes from Worth that noes she well Done for but her behaiver is very bad In Saying of Oaths and I Cannot break her of it ... if you wish me to keep her you must send word what you will do with [her] if she comes back to Worth ...I have no desire to keep [her] here".
Par 516/35/20

24 Nov.1831. Hugh Nash, overseer of Newdigate, [Surrey], to the overseers of Worth.

"Gentlemen, I should feel very much obliged to you, to employ the bearer Henry Hards for a few weeks at this dull season and we will in return continue to employ William Webb a parishioner of your[s] residing in our Parish through this critical season as I abhor the Idea of driving Men home to their own Parishes but necessity compels us at present to many disagreeable things and his employer told me the other day he certainly would not employ him any longer except you would employ one in return - in complying with this request you will much oblige."
Par 516/35/21

9 Dec.1831. W.J.Haddan, overseer, Bell Brewhouse, Tottenham, to overseers of Worth.

"Gentlemen, Will you have the goodness to send me per post a statement of the Account we have against you for payments made weekly to Ann Bonnet that is to say the Account of the last payment made by you and the time when up to and to whom sent. As there appears a long arrear due and we have Suspended the payment for three weeks past to her ... if convenient to state the payments you made last year shall feel obliged to you but particularly the last time you sent us money..."
Par 516/35/22

[undated] Peter Caffin [?to overseers of Worth].

"Gentlemen, The following information I received of a travelling man who says his name is Israel Lee, that John Chapman has a Wife now living whom he Married before he took up with the Woman he is now living with, he was Married at Marden in Kent, his Wife had three Children by him viz. Nathan, Phillip and a Daughter who Married Thomas Holden a Tinman at Maidstone in Kent. Her maiden name was Sarah Lee first Cousin to the above mentioned Israel Lee, she is now living with a man whose name is Barnabas Brown - Israel Lee will call on me again about Michaelmas."
Par 516/35/24

WORTH OVERSEERS ACCOUNTS. Par 516/31/22/6

Solicitor's bill: Worth parish D[ebto]r. to Barrow and Squire.

1821		£ s d
May 19	Swearing in 4 special constables for your parish.	4 0
	Summons to Richard Beal to shew cause why he refused to apprehend George *Bennett and family.	2 0
Jun. 1	Swearing Walter Stanbridge, special constable of your parish	1 0
Jun. 3	Attending you, consulting and advising as to George Bennett having returned into your parish without a certificate after having been removed therefrom by an order of removal when you desired us to procure copy order from clerk of the peace.	6 8
	Letter to clerk of the peace for copy order.	3 4
Jun. 7	Postage of letter from clerk of the peace inclosing copy order of sessions for confirming George Bennett's order to Steyning.	1 0
	Letter to him for copy original order of removal	3 4
Jun. 9	Postage of letter inclosing same.	1 0
	Paid clerk of the peace his fees for same.	15 6
Jun.16	Information on oath by Mr. F.A. Dowley against George Bennett for returning upon order of removal.	2 0
	Warrant to apprehend him.	1 0
	Information on oath of Mr. John Stanbridge.	2 0
	Examination of George Bennett in writing.	2 0
	Warrant of commitment 4 prisoners.	4 0
	Drawing and ingrossing conviction 25 folios.	17 6
	Fee paid clerk of the peace on filing.	1 0
Jun.21	Examination of Sophia *Havelock, bastardy.	2 0
	Warrant to apprehend reputed father.	1 0
Jul.16	You and Warnham. John *Payne having been removed upon you by Warnham. Instructions to enter appeal to give time to enquire as to settlement.	6 8
	Drawing brief to counsel to move.	6 8
	Fair copy.	3 4
	Fee to Mr. Courthope with same.	10 6
	His clerk and attendance.	4 4
	Attending him and Court. Appeal entered and respited.	13 4
	Paid clerk of peace for order and attendance.	11 8
Jul.21	George Bennett and family having returned from confinement in the House of Correction into your parish. Information against them on oath.	2 0
	Warrant to apprehend them.	1 0
	Informatiion of John Stanbridge and oath.	2 0
	Examination of George Bennett.	2 0
	Warrant of commitment 4 prisoners.	4 0
	Drawing and ingrossing conviction 25 folios.	17 6

	Fee paid clerk of peace on filing.	1 0
Aug.31	Allowance of Poors Rate	2 0
Sep.14	Order upon Framfield parish to reinburse you the expence of maintaining Thomas Brackpool a militia mans wife and family.	3 0
	Examination of Hannah *Tingley, bastardy.	2 0
	Warrant to apprehend Richard *Davis, reputed father.	1 0
Sep.28	Examination of Sophia Havelock; bastardy after birth.	3 0
	Warrant to apprehend Benjamin *Chander.	2 0
	Hearing oath, adjudication order of filiation and copy.	8 0
	Examination of Mary *Wicks, bastardy. A.B.	3 0
	Warrant to apprehend reputed father.	2 0
	Examination of Mary Wicks, another child. A.B.	3 0
	Warrant to apprehend reputed father.	2 0
	Examination of Mary *Dance to her settlement.	3 0
	Order of Removal to Cuckfield and duplicate.	4 0
	In Hannah Tingley's bastardy. Richard *Davis having been apprehended hearing Comp[lain]t when Davis refused to find sureties.	2 0
	Commitment.	1 0
Oct.19	Sussex Michaelmas Sessions at Lewes.	
	Instructions to confirm order of removal of Mary *Dancy [sic] from your parish to Cuckfield.	6 8
	Drawing Brief.	6 8
	Fair copy.	3 4
	Fee to Mr. Norton to move.	10 6
	His clerk and attendance.	4 4
	Attending him and Court when Court refused to confirm order, it having been executed on the commission day of the sessions.	13 4
	In Hannah Tingley's bastardy. Instructions to continue Davis in custody.	6 8
	Drawing brief.	6 8
	Fair copy.	3 4
	Fee to Mr. Norton to move.	10 6
	His clerk and attendance.	4 4
	Attending him and Court. Davis continued in custody.	13 4
Oct.29	Examination of Ann Holman, bastardy before birth.	2 0
	Warrant to apprehend reputed father.	1 0
	Mary Ann *Gibbs settlement. Summons to Mrs. Franks to give evidence hereon.	2 0
	Taking Mary Ann Gibbs examination and oath.	2 0
	Taking Mrs. Franks examination on oath.	2 0
	Instruction to see Mrs. Alfry of Lingfield and take her examination hereon.	3 4
	Information against Edward Arnold for leaving his wife and family chargeable to your parish.	2 0
	Warrant to apprehend him	1 0

	You and Henry Harbore hearing complaint against Henry Harbore for leaving his wife and family chargeable to your parish.	2 0
	Oath administered to witness.	1 0
	Warrant of commitment.	1 0
	Drawing and ingrossing conviction 18 folios.	10 6
	Fee to clerk of the peace on filing.	1 0
	Order for seisure of rents and goods for maintenance of wife and family and copy.	4 6
	Examination of Amelia Brooker. Bastardy before birth.	2 0
	Warrant.	1 0
Nov.20	Attending on Mrs. Alfrey of Lingfield. Examining her as to Mary Ann Gibbs settlement which it appeared was in your parish.	6 8
Nov.27	Summons against William Langridge for poor tax.	2 0
	In Amelia Brooker's bastardy. Recognizance of William Hills o[the]rwise Bell to appear at Sessions	2 6
	Recognizance of William Hills - his surety.	2 6
	In Mary Ann Gibbs. Bastardy examination before birth.	2 0
	Warrant to apprehend reputed father.	1 0
1822		
Jan.11	Epiphany Sessions at Lewes.	
	In Amelia Brooker's bastardy. Instructions to continue William Hills, o[the]rwise Bell, on his recognizance.	6 8
	Drawing brief.	6 8
	Fair copy.	3 4
	Fee to Mr. Norton with same.	10 6
	His clerk and attendance.	4 4
	Attending him and Court. Hills continued on his recognizance.	13 4
	In Hannah Tingley's bastardy. Instuctions to move to continue Richard Davis in custody	6 8
	Drawing brief.	6 8
	Fair copy.	3 4
	Fee to Mr. Norton with same.	10 6
	His clerk and attendance.	4 4
	Attending him and Court. Davis continued in custody.	13 4
	You and Henry Harbore. Instructions to record Harbore as a rogue and vagabond.	6 8
	Drawing brief.	6 8
	Fair copy.	3 4
	Fee to Mr. Norton to move.	1 1 0
	His clerk and attendance.	9 2
	Attending Court. Harbore recorded.	13 4
	Paid Clerk of peace recorded and attendance.	11 8

	You to Cuckfield. The Court having refused to confirm order at the last sessions attending Mr. Norton with brief to move.	3 4
	Attending him and Court order confirmed.	13 4
	Paid Clerk of the peace for order and attendance.	11 8
Feb.10	Summons against Thomas Stone for poor tax	2 0
Feb.15	Attending Mr. Downy, taking examination of Henry Ron Tester under peculiar circumstances and it was determined to remove him and obtain suspension of the order as to his wife.	6 8
	Taking deposition and oath.	3 0
	Order of removal.	3 0
	Two duplicates.	2 0
	Suspension.	2 0
	Two duplicates.	2 0
Mar. 6	Warrant to discharge Richard Davis out of custody.	2 0
	Information against Stephen Harbore for running away and leaving his wife and family chargeable to your parish.	2 0
	Warrant to apprehend him.	1 0
	Order of filiation on William *Franks and duplicate.	8 6
	Many attendances on you consulting and advising on various business during this year. Letters, postage of letters etc. etc.	13 4
		£29 10 10
	Deduct the 13s 4d [*different hand*]	13 4
		£28 17 6

INDEX OF PERSONAL NAMES

by Christine Leighton

This index includes all persons mentioned in the documents which make up the text, pages 41-388. No attempt has been made to distinguish between different individuals with the same name.

* An asterisk after a page number indicates that the name appears more than once on that page.

The original spelling of surnames has been retained, and obvious variants have been grouped together. Christian names in the text may occur in a variety of spellings, but in the index they have been given modern conventional form. Below is a list of the standardisations used and the variants encountered. Where it is obvious, Frances and Francis have been indexed under their normal feminine and masculine spellings.

Abigail (Abbigial)
Alan (Allen)
Alice (Allis)
Amy (Amey)
Andrew (Andrewe)
Anne (Ann)
Bannister (Bannester)
Barbara (Barbarah)
Bernard (Barnard)
Bet (Bett)
Carina (Corriner)
Cecily (Cecilia)
Charles (Chas)
Charlotte (Charlot)
Daniel (Daniell)
Deborah (Debera)
Diana (Dianah, Dianna, Dinah)
Drew (Drewe)
Edmund (Edmand)
Eleanor (Elenor, Ellenor)
Elizabeth (Elisabeth)
Emily (Emilia)
Esther (Hester, Hestor)
Faulkner (Faulkener)
Felicia (Felicea, Philicia)
Frances (Francis)
Francis (Frances)
Frederick (Fredricke)
George (Georg, Gorrg)
Gerard (Gerrard, Jerrard)
Gervaise (Gervase, Gervice)
Giles (Geyles)
Gillian (Gylian)
Hannah (Hanah, Hanna)
Harriet (Harriot, Harriott)
Herbert (Harbert)
Hettie (Hetty)
Honour (Honor)
Isabel (Isabella, Isbell)
Jemima (Jemmima)
Jeremiah (Jeremyah)
Jeremy (Jeremie)
Jethro (Jethrow)
Joan (Joahn, Joane, Johne, Jone)
Joanna (Joanah, Johanna)
Job (Jobe)
Joel (Jowel)
Joshua (Josua, Josuah)
Judith (Judeth)
Katherine (Catharine, Catheren, Catherine, Katharine, Katherin, Kathrien)
Kezia (Keziah)
Lydia (Lidia)
Margaret (Margarett)
Margery (Margerie)
Marian (Marrian)
Martin (Marten)
Matthew (Mathew)
Matthias (Mathias)
Mercy (Mercey)
Michael (Miccal, Michaell, Mychaell)
Naomi (Nahomi)
Nathaniel (Nathanial)
Ninian (Ninion, Nynnion)
Obediah (Obadiah)
Payne (Paine)
Philip (Phillip, Phillipe)
Phoebe (Phebe, Pheby)
Phyllis (Phillis)
Pierce (Piercy)
Practice (Praxed)
Priscilla (Pricilla, Prisilla)
Rachel (Rachael, Rachele, Rachell)
Ralph (Ralfe)
Rebecca (Rebaccah, Rebakah, Rebeccah)
Reuben (Ruben)
Reynald Rianald)
Robert (Robart)
Rosamund (Rosamond, Rosemond)
Rosanne (Rosanna)
Samson (Sampson)
Samuel (Samuell)
Sarah (Sara)
Stephen (Steaven)
Susanna (Susana, Susanah, Susannah)
Thomas (Tomas)
Thomasine (Thomasin, Thomisin)
Timothy (Thymothy)
William (Will, Wm)
Zechariah (Zachariah)
Zephaniah (Zephanah)

[*blank*], Herbert, and father, 373; Jeremy [female], 101

A

Abergavenny, Lady ... 316
Abott, Sarah, and daughter 237
Abrams, Anne, *later* Anne Bonnett 382; James 381
Ackerson, Robert 261
Ackney, Elizabeth 70*; William 70*
Acton, Francis 328
Adams, William 41
Adds, Robert 237
Ades, Alfred 357; Henry 357; Mary 357; Mary Stanford 357
Affield, Affielld *see* Field
Affield (Affielld), Thomas 269
Agate, Anne 86, 166, 173; Anne, and son 91; Elizabeth 166, 173, 324; Isaac 324; John 117, 166*, 173; Mary 166*, 173*; Philadelphia 166, 173; Sarah 117; Thomas 52, 54, 90; William 48
Agates, George 137; *see also* Gates
Agent, Elizabeth 157
Akehurst, Anne 216; William, and wife 59
Alcock (Allcock, Awcock, Awcocke), Abraham 200, 208, 218; Anne 44*, 318, 325; Elizabeth 163, 295; Elizabeth, and son 216; George 295*; John 163, 318*; Mary 163, 295, 318; Richard 163, 295; Richard, and father 155; Sarah 44, 295; Sarah, and son 214; Thomas 44, 210, 275, 295; William 243
Aldridge, Alan 288; Alfred 288; Anne 77, 144, 288; Elizabeth 288; Harriet 77; James 77; Mary 144; Robert 144*; Susanna 144; Thomas 288*
Alford, Mrs ... 260
Alfrey (Alfry, Allfrey), Mrs ... 386-387; Edward 237; Elizabeth 238; John 237*, 322; John, gent 371; Rebecca 70; Richard 217; Sarah 237, 327; Susan 237; Thomas 237; Zillah 236, 276
Allcock *see* Alcock
Allen (Allin), Mr ... 133; Elizabeth 244; Mr Francis 146; Jane 343; Mary 167, 176; Thomas 244; Thomas, and children 343; William 146, 303
Allfrey *see* Alfrey
Allin *see* Allen
Allingham, John 360
Amon, Samuel 44
Anderson, Matthias 211
Andrews, Frances 71; Margaret 169, 177; Richard 337; Robert 71; Thomas 71
Anscombe (Anscomb), Abigail 87; Alan 67; Anne 107; Hannah 285; John 66; John, and family 107; Mary 63*; Philip 92; Sarah 89; Sarah, and daughter 90; Susan, and daughter 93; Susan or Susannah, and daughter 97*; William 91, 285; William, and father 279
Anston, William 182
Ansty (Anstye) *alias* Holcombe, Dorothy 131; Katherine 131; Philip 131; Stephen 131; Walter 131
Anthony, Mary 101
Apps, Edward 122
Apted, Anne 233*; Elizabeth 345; George 345; Jane 345*; Richard 346; Sarah 346
Archer, Anne 189
Archpoole, Widow 106
Ares *see* Ayres
Aridge *see* Erredge
Arnold (Arnall, Arnolde), Anne, *later* Anne Steadman 119; Edward, and wife and family 386; Elizabeth 70; Francis 360; Hannah, *later* Hannah Kent 360; James 175, 218, 243; John 317; Mary 175; Mary, *alias* Mary Davis *formerly* Palmer 87; Walter 374; William 118; William, *alias* William Steadman 119, 361
Arston, John 128
Ascall, John 236
Ashby, James 166, 173; Sarah 166*, 173*; Thomas 166*, 173*; William 166, 173
Ashdown, Benjamin 144; Elizabeth, and daughter 211; John 144; Mary 144
Ashfield (Ashfeild), John 135; John, and wife and family 332
Ashfold, John 128, 131
Ashurst, Mary 271*; William 271*
Ather, Henry 246
Atherfold, Thomas 210
Atherill, John 294
Atree *see* Attree
Attersoll, Mary 318
Attfield, Mary 167; *see also* Field
Attree (Atree), Elizabeth 76, 86, 99, 332; Hannah 76, 86; James 76, 86*; Jane 332; Jesse 332; John 76, 86, 137; Mary 86, 99, 321, 332*; Richard 86, 321; Thomas 54-55; Thomas, and father 332; William 76, 86, 99; *see also* Tree
Attwood, Mr ... 152; Robert 161; *see also* Wood
Attwooll, George 188; Jane 188; John 188; *see also* Wooll
Aulcorne, Alexander 149
Austin (Austen), Alice 372; Anne 250; Elizabeth 250*, 320*; John 163; Katherine 250; Martha

250; Mary 320; Peter 250, 330; Richard 320; Sarah 163, 250; Stephen 376; William 221, 263, 372
Avery (Averie, Averye), Anne 130; Bridget 130; John 366
Aves, Frances 181; Robert 181
Avis, John 196; Susan 196; William 183
Awcock, Awcocke *see* Alcock
Aylmor, Robert 127
Aynscomb, Martha 86, 174, 180; William 86, 174, 180
Ayres (Ares), Anne 118; Charles 118; Francis 308; Henry 118; Isaac 303; Jane 308; John 118; Sarah, *alias* Sarah Plummer 284

B

Backshall (Backshell, Baxshall), Anne 322*; Benjamin 322*, 330; Elizabeth 319; James 189, 322*; John 319; Mary 189, 322*; Nicholas 245; Philadelphia 324; Sarah 324; Susanna 45; Thomas 324; William 319; William, and child 288; *see also* Boxshell
Badcock, Elizabeth 318; Thomas 318*
Bagnall, James 274*; Samson 69, 274*; Susanna 69, 274*
Bailey (Baily, Bally, Bayley), Elizabeth 159; Henry 130; Jane 193; John 203; Thomas 159, 203
Bakehurst, John 288; Mary 288
Baker, Anne 44, 290; Barbara 285, 288; Caroline 195-196; Charles 285, 288; Edward 150; Elizabeth 142, 323, 360, 365; Elizabeth, *alias* Elizabeth Coomber 310; Fances 160; James 202; Jane 290; John 207, 250*, 290, 360, 365; Joseph 77; Louisa 250; Lucy 250; Mary 195-196, 205, 208, 246, 355, 360; Richard 160, 290; S. 381; Samuel 365; Stephen 195-196; Thomas 241; William 142, 195-196, 246, 323, 355
Balcombe (Balcomb, Bawcom, Bawlcome), Anne, *later* Anne Turner 359; Edward 173; Elizabeth 318; Esther 47*; George 122, 129, 132; James 47*; Jemima 325; Joseph 325; Margaret 47*; Mary 173; Sarah 189; Thomas 189, 318; William 42, 71, 189, 242
Baldwin (Bauldyn), Edward 359; George 183, 341; Giles 243; Harriet 355; James 351, 354; Jane 341*, 350, 351*, 354*, 359, 362; Jane, *later* Jane Edwards 359; John 355; John King 341, 351, 354; Sarah King 350
Ball, Henry, *alias* Henry Heath 269; John 270; Mary, *alias* Mary Jupp 310
Ballard, John 204
Bally *see* Bailey
Banfield (Bamfield), George 73; James 238-239; John 73; Mary 89-90, 238; Sarah 256, 259; Thomas 256, 259; William 233
Banister *see* Bannister
Banks, ... 156; Richard 99; Richard, and wife and children 343
Bannister (Banister), Anne 168; Elizabeth 282; Jeremiah 267; Samuel 282; Sarah 282, 308*; Sarah, and son 125*; William 342; William, sen 138
Barber, Fanny 286, 296; Frances 258; John 246, 258; Mary 369; Rev J.H. 380; William 130, 246
Barden, Mary 65*; Thomas 106; William 209
Barham (Barram),Sarah 159; Sarah *formerly* Sarah Brown 222; William 147, 222; William, and children 159
Barnard *see* Bernard
Barnes (Barns), Isaac 364; John 349, 353*; Susanna 349, 353*; William 354
Barnett, Charity 257-258; John 247; Lucy 275; Martha 257-258; Sarah 275; Susanna 275; Thomas 275
Barnham, Amelia 100*; Mary Anne 100*; Richard 100*
Barns *see* Barnes
Barram *see* Barham
Barrett, Hugh 83; Jane 83; Richard 163, 171; Sarah 163, 171
Barrow, ... 385; John 243
Bartholomew (Bartholme, Bartlemew), Abraham 219; John 133, 219*, 335, 373; John, jun 219; John, *alias* John Pownteine 370; Sarah 124, 128; William 221
Bartlee *see* Bartley
Bartlemew *see* Bartholomew
Bartlett, Charles 286; John 127, 286; Richard 286; Temperance 286; William 286
Bartley (Bartlee), Barbara, and daughter 267, 269; Edward, and wife and children 61; James, jun 266; James, sen 266; Richard 134; Thomas 266
Barton, Anne 182; Mary 182*; Susanna 182; William 182*
Bashford, Celia 46; Eleanor

Bashford (*contd*) 190; Elizabeth 345, 356; James 345; Jane 345; John 345, 356; Lydia 44; Mary 345, 356; Thomas 345

Bassett (Basset), George 187; William 148, 187

Batchelor (Batcheler, Batcheller), Anne 196, 379; Edward 196, 288*; Elizabeth 41, 46*, 108, 205; Elizabeth, *alias* Elizabeth Borer 220; Elizabeth, *alias* Elizabeth Heasman 119; Henry 46; Henry, and wife and family 343; Henry, jun 288; James 41*; John 53, 61, 108*, 205; Mary 41, 79*-80, 196; Richard 96; Sarah 61*; Sarah, and daughter 300; Sarah, and son 204, 209; Sarah, *later* Sarah Whiting, and children 94*; Susanna 196; Thomas 92, 95*, 313; William 61, 79-80*, 94

Bateman, Henry, and wife and children 159; *see also* Batman

Bates (Battes), Anne 96; Anne, and son 92; Elizabeth 221; Katherine 309; Richard 221

Bateup (Baytop, Baytup), Edward 88*; Elizabeth, and daughter 92, 96; Henry 88*; James 88*; John 73, 80*; Martha 88*; Mary 80*; Thomas 73, 88*; William 88*

Batman (Battman), John 230; Joseph, and child 230; Sarah 230; *see also* Bateman

Battell *alias* Binion, Robert 99

Battes *see* Bates

Battman *see* Batman

Bawcomb, Bawlcome *see* Balcombe

Baxshall *see* Backshall

Bayley *see* Bailey

Baytop, Baytup *see* Bateup

Bazeley, John 220

Beachely, Beachley, Beachly *see* Betchley

Beadle (Bedle), Abraham 345; John 345; Sarah 345; William 120

Beal, Benjamin 47-48; Rebecca 285; Richard 385; Thomas 285; Widow 380

Beard, Charles 225; Edward 175*, 180*, 377; George 292; John 107, 159, 163, 175, 180, 257; Joseph 355, 377; Mary 107, 159*, 175, 180, 297, 355; Mary, and daughter 301; Philadelphia 163; Richard 290; Robert 292; Ruth 107, 159; Sarah 159, 292; Thomas 301; William 292

Beaver *or* ?Bevis, Anne 186; Mary 186

Bechely *see* Betchley

Beckett, John 240

Bedle *see* Beadle

Beech, John 159; William 206*

Belchamber (Bellchamber), Anne 166*; Francis 166*; George 303*; James 166; Jane 166; Mary 166; William 166

Belgrave, Edward, and wife and children 284*, 289

Bell *alias* Hills, William 387*

Bellchanber *see* Belchamber

Bellingham, Anne 346; Michael 346

Belton, John 323

Benlett, Robert 247*; Thomas 226, 247; *see also* Bentlett

Bennett (Bennet), Anne 161, 333; Edward 238; Eliza, *alias* Eliza Lish 237; Elizabeth 236; Fanny, *alias* Fanny Lish 237; Francis 154, 161; George 355; George, and family 385*; Henry 103; Jane 260; Jane, and son 268; John 81*, 161, 323, 355, 357; John, and wife and family 61; John, *or* John Burnett, 60; Martha 81, 355; Mary 161, 169; Mary, *alias* Mary Lish 237*; Noah 161; Richard 222; Robert 200; Thomas 72, 154, 236*; William 355; William, and family 56, 59; William, *alias* William Mitchell 261

Bentlett, John 346; Mary 346; Nicholas 346; William 346; *see also* Benlett

Bently, Mary 108; Stephen 348

Bernard (Barnard), Elizabeth, and son 264-265; William, and wife 58

Berrick, Edward 135

Berry (Burry, Bury), ... 316; Anne 70, 281, 301; Edward 139, 265; Henry 139, 265; John 281; Richard 305; William 70, 112, 139*

Berryman, Richard 99*

Best, Anne 162; Elizabeth 159, 169; Faulkner 48, 67; Isaac 162; John 147, 169, 299; John, and wife and children 320*; John, and wife and family 318; Mary 159*, 169*, 217, 219-220, 290; Richard 162, 290; Sarah 169; Susanna 169; Thomas, and wife and children 250; William 159, 169*

Betchley (Beachely, Beachley, Beachly, Bechely, Bethely), Elizabeth 320; John 128, 131; Jonathan 135, 137, 316, 320; Sarah 126

Bets, Cattern 80*; Job 80

Betsley, Mr ... 191

Bettie, Sarah 266

Bevis, Anne, *or* Anne Beaver 186; Mary, *or* Mary

Beaver 186; Thomas, and wife and family 166
Bewman, Henry 222
Bickley, Katherine 201; Katt 201
Bignall (Bignull), Anne 69; Benjamin 242; John 269; Robert 69; *see also* Picknell
Bilcliffe (Bilcliff), Benjamin 339, 358; Jane 339, 358; John 339; Mary 339*, 346, 358; Richard 339*, 358*; Sarah 339, 358; Stephen 346
Bilinghurst, Henry 231
Bilton, John 371; Sarah 371
Bing, Col ... 153
Binion *alias* Battell, Robert 99
Birch (Burch), ... 134; Richard, and family 159; Timothy [female] 134
Birchfell, James 57*; James, and child 59; Philadelphia 57, 59
Birchfield, Jane 283*; William 283*
Bird, Anne 254; Mary 254; Peter 254
Bish (Bysh, Byshe), Anne 166; Benjamin 347; Edward 133*, 345; Elizabeth 159, 166, 345-346; Francis 159, 166*, 168; Hannah 344; John 166, 175, 181, 345*; Lydia 175, 181; Mary 166, 345, 347; Philip 166; Roger, esq 373; Sarah 345; Thomas 345; William 345-346; William, and children 344; William, jun 205; William, sen 205
Bishop (Bishopp), Abraham 343; Amelia 357; Anne 347, 351; Elizabeth 109, 113, 281; Henry 348; James 109; Jane 343; John 109, 113; John, and wife and children 343; Sarah 343-344; Thomas 347, 351*, 357; Thomas, and children 281; William 347; William, and children 344
Blaber, Anne 42; Elizabeth 337; George 111, 114; Hannah 259; Henry, and daughter 337; John 42; Mary 111, 114; *see also* Blaker
Blackstone, Anne 164; Elizabeth 164; Hannah 164*; Henry 164; Mary 164; Thomas 164*
Blake, Mr Charles 147; Katherine 375; Nicholas 375; Richard 375*; Thomas 90, 375
Blaker, Elizabeth 134; Hannah 346, 349; Richard 130, 134, 346, 349; Richard, jun 130; Susanna 41; Thomas 134, 347; William 303; *see also* Blaber
Blanch, Anne 282, 286, 288; Anne, and son 300, 302; Anthony 292, 295; Elizabeth 334; James 282; James, jun 282; Sarah 292, 295
Bland, Judith 108*; Sarah 325; Thomas 108
Blanit, Thomas 245
Blank *alias* Wickham, Elizabeth 56; Mary 56; William 56, 59
Bleach, Hettie 189; John 189; William 204*
Blink (Blinck), Anne 254-255; Isaac 254-255
Bluet, James, and mother 133; John 133
Blundell, Alice 337
Board, J. 316; John, gent 303; William 106, 136; William, esq 135, 278
Boates (Boats), John 101, 293; Katherine 293
Bodle, John 221, 266; Mary 344; Thomas 146; Thomas, and children 344
Bokkom, Samuel 202
Bolchin, Sarah 349, 353; Thomas 349, 353
Bone, Harriet 323; Thomas 323
Bones, Henry 367
Boniface (Bonniface, Bonnyface), Anne 257; Anthony 243; Elizabeth 86, 257; Henry 86-87; John 86; Mary 267*; Thomas 244-245; William 243, 257, 347
Bonner, Jeremiah 245
Bonnett (Bonnet), Anne 384; Anne, *formerly* Anne Abrams 382*; Edward 382*
Bony, Alice 349, 353*; William, and daughters 349, 353*
Booker, Anne 109, 144; George 144; Jane 144; John 364; Maria 144; Mary 144; Richard 223; Sarah 144*; William 109, 204, 364
Boorn *see* Bourn
Borer (Borrer, Bowerer, Bowra), Anne 180; Anne, and son 218; Elizabeth, *alias* Elizabeth Batchelor 220; Jane 217; Joel, and wife 150; Joel, and wife and family 344; John 184; Reuben 195; Richard 372; William 200
Botley, Elizabeth 326
Botting (Botten), Amelia 291; Edward, and father 87; Edward, jun 84; Elizabeth 47*, 80*, 84, 326, 346; Friend 47*, 326; George 291, 299*; Hannah 86-87; Harry 50; Henry 50, 133, 346*; James 80*, 224, 280, 285*, 308; Jane 47*, 49*, 285, 326; John 87, 105, 310, 346; Mary 50, 285; Richard 47*, 49*, 80, 326; Roger 373*; Sarah 50, 213, 239; Susanna 50; William 86, 280, 288, 291, 308, 324

Bound, Amelia, and daughter 239; Anzilla, and daughter 241; Lydia, and child 230; William 247; William, and parents 76; William, *alias* William Boundy 94
Bourne (Boorn, Bourn), Benjamin 62; Cassandra 60; Elizabeth 50, 362; James 50*, 362; John 60, 63; Lydia 62, 173; Martha 60, 63; Mary 50*, 362; Matthew 173; Richard 60, 63, 347; Sarah, *alias* Sarah Reeves 355
Bowdidge, John 233-234; Patty 233-234; William 233-234
Bowell, Joan *alias* Sarah 233; John 44; May 44; Sarah 233; Sarah, and son 265; Sarah *alias* Joan 233
Bowie *or* Bowri, Elizabeth 337*; Henry 337*; Mary 337*; Matthew 337*; Sarah 337*
Bowra *see* Borer
Bowri *or* Bowie, Elizabeth 337*; Henry 337*; Mary 337*; Matthew 337*; Sarah 337*
Bowyer, Bennett 286; Edgar 168; John 105; Matthew 286
Box, Charity 44; John 42; Richard 44; William 44
Boxell, John 113
Boxshell, Deborah 100; Mary 100; William 100; *see also* Backshall
Boyland, James 300
Boyton, Sarah 289
Brackpool (Brackpole, Brackpoole), Mrs ... 368; Anne 360; Richard 330, 360; Thomas 330; Thomas, and wife and family 386
Bradford, Francis 243
Bran, Martha 168; Robert 168; Susanna 168
Brane, Martha 177; Robert 177; Susanna 177
Bransden, Edward 247
Brasted, Elizabeth 201; Frances 201; William 201
Bray, Ambrose 279; Edward, and wife and family 122*
Brazier, Anne, and father and daughter 368; Mary 335*; Mary Anne 335*; Thomas 335*
Bread, David 103; Elizabeth 243; Joan, and children 103
Breden, Charles 172; Craven 172; Cravey 173; Elizabeth 172*; Sarah 173; Thomas 172
Brethen, Bridget 243; Elizabeth 243
Brewer, William 348
Briant *see* Bryant
Bridger, Mary 158; Richard 246; William, and father 158
Bridgland, Mary 218*; Mary, and daughter 208
Brigden, Elizabeth 292; Tho. 304; Timothy 269; William 217
Briggs (Brigs), Mr ... 226; Elizabeth 181*; Hannah 60; Henry 181*; James 72, 81, 94; John 60; Sarah 181*; Thezia 81; William 181*
Bright, Elizabeth 315; John 315; Richard 315; Sarah 315
Brigs *see* Briggs
Brigstock, George, gent 372
Brinkhurst (Brinckhurst), Jane 158, 168; John 158, 168, 211
Brister, Anne 324*; James 324; John 324*; Susan 181
Bristow (Bristowe), Anne 115; Edward 133*; Elizabeth 115; Scipio 115; Turner 115, 125-126
Broad, Anne 79; Elizabeth 79*, 143; James 143; Jane 143; John 143; Mr John 280; Mary 79, 143, 254; Richard 79*, 373; Thomas 254, 278; William 79, 143*
Broadbridge, Benjamin 316; William 317
Bromfield *see* Broomfield
Bromhead, James 242
Bromley, Michael 210; Thomas 210, 328; Thomas, and wife 176
Brooker, Mrs ... 367; Amelia 387*; Anne 141, 165, 172, 190; Anne, and daughter 215; Anne, and son 367; Benjamin 165; Charlotte 357; Elizabeth 160, 165; Frances 108, 115, 308; George 108; Hannah 165*; James 108*, 143, 308, 323; James, and children 115; Jane 108; John 108, 160, 165, 220*, 321; Martha 359; Mary 160, 182, 190, 221, 323, 347, 350; Mary Anne, and daughter 368; Mary Anne, and father and daughter 368; Practice 160, 170, 177; Richard 151, 160*, 170*, 172, 177*; Ruth 321*; Sarah 160; Thomas 190, 347, 350, 358; Thomas, and parents 340*; William 151, 160, 165, 172, 192, 321, 323
Brookfield, Henry 109; John 232; Richard 232; Susanna 109
Brooks, ... 198; Mr ... 340*; Elizabeth 271, 287*; Jane, and son 328; John 271, 287*; Thomas 287; William 198, 287
Brooksbank, Mildred 174, 179; Thomas 174, 179
Broomfield (Bromfield), Anne 263*; Charles 263*; Henry 236; John 263*; Mary 263*; Robert 376; Stephen 263*; William 263*
Broughton, Richard 221
Brown (Browne), Abraham

154, 291; Anne 82, 84*; Anne, and child 328; Ansley 196; Barnabas 384; Charles 108; Edward 44, 162, 171, 330; Eliza Agnes 196; Elizabeth 64, 212, 222; Emma Harriet 196; Frances 291; Hannah 325; Hannah, and son 205; Henry 291; James 64, 84*, 265; James, and wife and children 96; John 64, 84*, 319, 325; John, and wife and family 160; Katherine 44, 64; Kezia 84*; Leah Ascuith 196; Maria 177; Martha 64*; Mary 162, 169, 171, 221, 313; Mary, and daughter 328; Mary, and son 65; Mary Annis 196; Nancy Caroline 196; Orson 213; Rhoda 294; Richard 279, 291*; Richard, and daughter 294; Sarah 84*, 172, 178, 189, 291, 319, 329; Sarah, and daughter 65; Sarah, *later* Sarah Barham 222; Stephen 259; Susanna 65, 259; Thomas 64, 84*, 259; Timothy 290; William 44, 158*, 169, 177, 189, 196, 219, 222, 319, 334, 371, 383

Browning, Anne 138, 236; John 168, 325; Susan 247; Susan, and father 226; Thomas 247; William 236, 247*

Brownings, Elizabeth 246; William 246

Broxham *alias* Broxcell, Anne 169, 177*; Esther 169, 177*; John 169, 177*; Mary 169, 177*; Nicholas 169, 177*; Sarah 169, 177*; William 169, 177*

Bryan, Francis 131*

Bryant (Briant), Alice 135; Anne 134, 344; Daniel 203; John 344; Margaret 127; Mary 151, 170, 177, 203

Bucher *see* Butcher

Buckland, Jane, and daughter 215; Mary 363

Buckman, Anne 283, 285; Edward 111, 283, 309; Elizabeth 111, 309-310; James 111*, 309*; John 283; Lydia 283; Mary 111*, 309*; Sarah 111, 309; Thomas 283; Thomas, and wife 59; Thomas, and wife and family 56; William 283, 285

Buckwell, Edmund, and father and children 252-253; George 122*, 309; Harriet 142; James 281; Jane 82, 309; John 142; Mary 283, 309*; Priscilla 122*; Sarah 142*, 252, 281; Stephen 309*; Walter 240

Budgen (Budgin, Budging), ... 329; Amelia, and mother and daughter 329; Anne 45, 185, 320-321, 327-328; Benjamin 320-321, 326*-327; Charlotte 46, 334; David 293; Edward 46, 334; Eliza 320; Elizabeth 45, 185*, 293, 320*-321*; George 300; James 217, 279, 285, 293*; Jane 321, 328; Jenny, and son 298; John 165*, 293, 321; Luke 46, 334; Mary 165*, 320-321, 326*; Mrs Mary 341; Richard 165*; Sarah 285; Thomas 45*; William 185, 217, 320

Bull, John 53-54, 247; William 279

Bunn, James, gent 55

Burberry, James 383; Sarah 361

Burch *see* Birch

Burchell (Burchele), Anne 56; Mary 56; William 56*; William, and family 59

Burchett (Burchet), Anne 254; Elizabeth 236, 259*; Jane 236; John 254, 259*; Mary 259*; Richard 254*; Sarah 259, 259*

Burgess (Burges, Burgis, Burgiss), Elizabeth 163, 193; George 74; Jane 74; John 117*, 372; Margaret 372; Mary 117*, 163, 222; Mary, and daughter 201; Michael 163; Robert, jun 202; Thomas 117

Burkin, Robert 346

Burley (Burleigh, Burly), Elizabeth 102; Jane 197; Jane, and daughter 200*, 209*; John 249; Mary 57; Mercy 160; Susanna 57*; Thomas 57, 160; William 57*; William, and wife and family 59

Burnell, William 112; William, and wife 107

Burnett (Burnet), Anthony 186; Elizabeth 161; Henry 161; John 62, 243; John, *or* John Bennett 60; Margaret 161; Thomas 243

Burnupp, Anthony 220

Burr, Anne 178*; Elizabeth 178; George 178, 345; Katherine 345; Lydia 213

Burredge, George 284

Burrell (Burrele), Counsellor ... 316; Anne 81; Edward 128, 245; Harriet 42*; Jane 134; John 42; Thomas 42, 128; Timothy, gent 138; Walter, esq 128, 132; William 42, 81

Burry *see* Berry

Burstow (Burstowe), Charles 117; Drew 133; John 177; Rose 158; William 134; William, and family 158

Bursty, William 141

Burt (Burtt), Anne 361; Benjamin 282; Caroline 361; Edward 124; Elizabeth 41, 330; Francis 128, 132, 162; Hannah 282; Henry 124; John 262; Mary 262; Nicholas 124; Richard 133, 135-136; Sarah 282, 361; Thomas 161, 282; Walter 132, 135, 136*; Walter, jun 128; Walter, sen 128; William 361
Burtenshaw (Burtenshawe), Anne 136, 203, 254; Bernard 254; Elizabeth 254, 256, 258; Francis 302; Harriet 262; Henry 137, 310; John 129; John, and wife and family 107; Louisa, and son 67; Mary, and daughter 127; Nicholas 238; Sarah 260, 310; Thomas 137, 226; William 127, 256, 258*, 260*, 310; *see also* Buttenshaw
Burton, Amy 86; Anne 173; Anne, *alias* Anne Etherington 262*; Elizabeth 86; John 220; Thomas, *alias* Thomas Etherington 262*; William 86
Burtt *see* Burt
Bury *see* Berry
Butcher (Bucher), Charles 301; Daniel, and wife 281; Edward 194; Elizabeth 187, 290; Elizabeth, and daughter 209; Elizabeth *later* Elizabeth Langridge 285; Francis 194; Frederick 194; Jemima 285; John 41*, 202, 234, 236; Margaret 202*; Mary 175, 180, 183; Robert 184, 320, 322; Robert, and wife and family 318; Sarah 285; Sophia 194; Susan 194; Susanna 281; Thomas 281, 290; William 187
Butching, John 228; Mary 149; Nathaniel 224
Butland, John 242
Butler, Anne 173; Elizabeth 130; Esther 160, 170; James 173, 177; Mary 151, 170; Mary, and daughter 198, 212*; Roger, gent 130; Sarah 177; Thomas 160, 170-171
Butten *see* Button
Buttenshaw, Sarah 121; *see also* Burtenshaw
Button (Butten), John 137; John, and wife and child 120; Sarah 122; Thomas 122*, 138; Thomas, and wife 114
Butts, John, jun 365; John, sen 365
Byne, Stephen 105
Byshe, Byshe *see* Bish

C

Caernarvon (Carnarvon), Rt Hon Marquis of 150, 169
Caffin (Caffyn), Mr ... 380; Anne 83-84; Eliza 83-84; James 83-84; Peter 384; Richard 83-84; Sarah 83-84; William 83-84
Cain, Hannah 231*; Thomas 231
Camfeild, Camfield, Camfilde *see* Campfield
Cammel, James 199; James, *alias* James Smith 217
Campbell, James 174, 179; Susanna 174, 179
Campfield (Camfeild, Camfield, Camfilde, Canfeild), Elizabeth 175, 180, 375*; Hannah 345, 349; John 349; John, and children 345; Mary 349; Richard 373; Robert 375
Campion *see* Champion
Candle, Adolphus 181-182; Beatrice 181-182; Edward 181-182; Frederick 181-182; John 181-182; Mary 181-182; Priscilla 181-182; Robert 181-182; Samuel 181-182; William 181*-182
Canfeild *see* Campfield
Capel (Capell), William 202
Capel (Capell), Andrew 202
Caplin, John 208
Capp, Richard 244
Card, Anne 256-257, 259*; Edee, and son 203; James 257; Katherine 162; Walter 162
Carden, Carina 348, 352; Michael 348, 352
Care, Frances 114; Simon 139; Thomas 114; William 240
Carew, Thomas, and wife and family 158
Carey, Anne 180*; Elizabeth 180*; Katherine 180*; Mary 180*; Penelope 196*; Thomas 180*
Cargill, Thomas 103
Carman, John, and wife and family 213
Carnarvon *see* Caernarvon
Carpenter, Anne 164; Elizabeth, and son 205, 210; Henry 351, 354; John 164*; Mary, and child 214; Mary, and son and daughter 214; Thomas, and wife and children 162
Carr, Charles 285, 287; George 285, 287; Hannah 45; Harriet 285, 287; James 46; Jane 285, 287; Mary 46; Phoebe 285, 287; Susanna 282; Thomas 46; William 45*-46, 282*
Carter, Anne 257; David 362*; Elizabeth, and child 241; Mary 362; Samuel 297; Sarah, *alias* Sarah Harland 119; Thomas, and wife and children 109; Mr William 341
Casleden, John, and family 107; Judith 107
Caught, John, and wife and children 159

Chaddick, Charles 340
Chalker, Thomas 138
Challen, J. 94; John, esq 228
Challoner (Challenor), Elizabeth 107, 112; Thomas 107, 112; Walter, and wife and family 289, 294
Chambers, Henry, and wife 141; Phoebe 145; Richard 145; Thomas 145; William, and children 144
Champion (Campion), Betty 108; Harriet 86; Jenny 86; Mary 108; Thomas 108; William 86*, 108*; William John 266
Chandler (Chander, Chantler, Chaundler), Anne 70, 205; Benjamin 367, 386; Elizabeth 345*, 348; Hannah 198; Isaac 345, 352; James 272; John 221, 348*; Joseph 330; Mary 272, 320, 348; Nicholas 376; Rebecca 168*, 211; Richard 320; Sarah 272; Thomas 272; William 272; William, and child 280
Channell, John 211
Chantler *see* Chandler
Chapman, Edward 186; Elizabeth 192, 195, 287; Elizabeth, and son 198; George 198; Hannah 178-179; Henry 217; James 178-179, 195, 267; James, and mother 198; Jane 99, 185*, 195; John 178-179, 198, 287, 330, 362; John, and daughter 384; Katherine 159, 178-179; Lucy 174, 178-180; Mary 163, 362; Milly 275; Nathan 384; Philip 384; Sarah (Lee) 384; Thomas 159, 163, 174, 178-180, 217, 362; Thomas, jun 218; William 41, 178-179
Charlwood, Amy 164; Eleanor, *formerly* Eleanor Clifton 368-369; Elizabeth 164; Isaac 164; James 368; Mary 360; Mary, and son 364, 370; Thomas 348
Charman, Elizabeth 312; Mary 272
Chart, Charlotte 310; Daniel 359; David 359; Elizabeth 187, 209, 356, 359; Elizabeth, and son 198, 212; Hannah 350, 354; Hannah, *formerly* Hannah Greenfield 350; James 310, 350, 354; Jane 351; John 209, 350, 354, 359, 368; Phyllis 351; William 182, 350, 354, 359
Chasemore (Chasemere, Chasmore), Anne 257*; Elizabeth 61; James 60; John 61, 257*; Sarah 60-61*
Chate, Abraham 283; Charles 283; John 73, 283*; Martha 283
Chatfield (Chatfeild), ... 167, 176; Anna, Maria 121; Anne 121*, 306; Benjamin 108, 306; Edward 121; Eliza 260; Elizabeth 56, 108; George 292; Henry 56; John 56*, 139, 204, 260, 272, 335-336; John, and wife and family 59; Maria 335-336; Martha 121; Mary 56*, 121; Robert 136; Sarah 274, 335*-336; Stephen Browne 117; William 108, 143, 204, 209, 212, 274; William, and daughters 56; William, and wife and family 59
Chaundler *see* Chandler
Cheal (Cheale, Cheall), Anna 351, 356*; Benjamin 168; Henry 211, 356*; Henry, and children 351*; Henry, and wife and family 167; John 168, 177; Richard 168; Sarah 351, 356*; William 348, 351, 356*
Cheesman (Chesman), Anne 311; Henry 197, 200, 209*, 311; John 74, 200, 206; John, and family 232; Joseph, wife and family 236; Joseph, and wife and children 305; Martha 325, 328
Chelsam, Robert 128
Cheriholme, John 167
Cherriman (Cherryman), Elizabeth 45*; George 49*; John 45*, 49; Martha 49*; Mildred 45; Rachel 49; Richard 60, 63; Sarah 60, 63; William 280
Chesman *see* Cheesman
Cheyney, William, and wife and family 337
Child, Anne 80; Charity, and daughter 300; David 80; Hannah 80; John 45, 297; Mary 45, 80; Mary, and daughter 301; Robert 80
Childerstone (Chelderstone), Thomas 373
Children, Arabella 161; Barbara 161; George 161*; Isabel 161; Sarah 161; Thomas 161
Childs, Elizabeth 292; Mary 47; Sarah 292; Thomas 292
Chipping, Robert 154
Christian, Mary, and daughter 297-298
Christopher, Anne 253; Elizabeth 253; Richard, 253*; Ruth 253; Susan 253
Churcher, Grace 164; James, and infant 164; Mary 229; William 229, 237, 241
Clare, Daniel 153
Clark (Clarke), Anne 102, 163, 309*; Diana 309; Edward 195, 324; Elizabeth 195, 237; George 237; Henry 237, 371*; John 309; John,

Clark (*contd*)
alias John Webb 371*; Margaret 102; Mary 163, 195; Phil. 102; Sarah 163*, 195, 309*; Thomas 163, 309; Thomas, and infant 195; Thomas, and wife and children 141; William 102, 163, 237*, 309, 309*
Clarkson, Mrs ... 194
Cleave, Hannah 322; John 322
Clifton *later* Charlwood, Eleanor 368-369; Esther 368-369
Clowser, Jane 344; John 344*; Mary 346; Stephen 346
Club, Frances 296; James 296; Kitty 296*
Coale, Anne 245; *see also* Coles
Coaly, John, and wife 59
Coape, Col John 147
Coates (Coats), Anne 80; Edward 80; George 196*; James 80; John 118; Katherine 56, 58; Mary 196; Ralph 330*; Robert 272; Thomas 253
Cob, Henry 167
Cobby, Edmund 73; James 321; Susan 321; Thomas 316; William 226; William, *alias* William Stillaway 231
Cobham *alias* Cripps, Rebecca 349, 353
Cockerell (Cockrell), Clements 186; Henry 186; Mary 177; Simon 171, 177
Cockett, Katherine 221
Cockrell *see* Cockerell
Coffin, Anne 242
Colchin, Alice 107; Thomas 107
Colcock (Colcocke), John 362; Thomas 375
Colden, Sarah 249; Thomas 249
Coleman (Colman), Charles 199; Mary 325; Richard 114
Coles, John 85, 88; Mary 85, 88; *see also* Coale
Coley, Anne 310; John 310; Mary 281, 284; William 281, 284
Collens *see* Collins
Colleyer, Daniel 286; Elizabeth 286
Collins (Collens, Collings), Abraham 348, 353*; Amelia 361; Anne 144; Anne, and son 368; Edward 144, 281*, 353*; Jane 147, 281; John 129, 133; Katherine 353*; Mary 281*, 353; Richard 131*, 281; William 147, 239, 241
Collis, Edward 350; Mary 350; Patience 350
Colman *see* Coleman
Colstock *see* Coulstock
Colven, Susanna 292, 296
Comber *see* Coomber
Combridge, John 65; Mary 186, 320; Robert 186, 320
Comfort, Mary 176
Compber *see* Coomber
Comper, Anne 231; Charles 231; Edward 231; James 231; *see also* Coomber
Conner, David 213; Elizabeth 168
Constable, Anne 350, 357; Edward 293; Elizabeth 359; Harriet 311; James 311; Jane 310; John 310*; John, and wife and children 107; Mary 293; Matthias 293; Sarah 360; Sophia 298; William 359-360
Coo, Mary 102
Cook (Coock, Cooke), Alan 330; Anne 56*, 165*, 171-172*, 204, 212, 287; Anne, and son 209; Cecily 323; Charlotte 80; Edward 345; Elizabeth 56, 64*, 115, 345; Francis 221; Hannah 165, 172; Hannah, *or* Hannah Coombs 229; Hannah, *alias* Hannah Jackson 231; Harriet 43; Henry 64, 229; Jane 162, 291; Jeremiah, *alias* Jeremiah Jackson 231; John 43, 80, 109, 165, 172, 287, 337, 345; Jonathan 193, 323; Mary 80, 109; Nathaniel 165*, 172*; Rebecca 193, 323; Richard 43, 57*; Richard, and wife and family 59; Sarah 43, 57, 109; Susan 162; Thomas 56*; Thomas, and family 59; William, 57, 64, 80, 204, 212, 242* 345; William, and daughter 291; William *or* William Coombs 229
Cooksey, Daniel 234*; Elizabeth 234*; Jane 234*; Penelope 234*
Coomber (Comber, Compber, Coumber, Cumber), Amy 347; Anne 41, 75, 79, 81; Barbara 60, 62; Easter 151, 170; Edward 323; Elizabeth 79, 334; Elizabeth, *alias* Elizabeth Baker 310; Francis 323; James 326*, 334; Jane 79, 81, 284, 288; John 79*, 81*, 168, 169, 212, 272, 281, 287, 297-298, 323, 325, 328; John, and wife 159, 320; Joseph 323*; Joseph, *alias* Joseph Powell 183; Lucy 326; Lydia 326, 334; Martha 191; Mary 84, 141, 169, 237, 272, 281*, 287*; Richard 79, 81; Richard, and son 237; Samuel 249; Samuel, and wife and children 176; Sarah 41, 62, 168, 237, 323*, 325; Stephen 136; Thomas 75, 281*, 287*, 334, 347; Turner 328; William 62, 75, 323, 326; William, jun 282; William, sen 281; *see also* Comper

Coombs *or* Cook, Hannah 229; William 229
Cooper, ... 250*, 379; A. 184; Anne 188, 255; Anne, and child 175, 194-195; Charles 368; Cooper 166, 173; Daniel 188; Edward 166, 173, 188, 243*; Edward, and wife 165; George 374; Hannah 166, 173; Henry 221; James 255, 347; Jane 168; John 166, 173; Joseph 188; Mary 188, 319; Rachel 347; Richard 136; Solomon, and wife and family 343; Stephen 374*; Thomas 227, 243, 319, 347
Coppard, Charlotte 237; Nathaniel 44; Sarah, and son 44; Thomas 238; William 127
Cork (Corke), Anne 46; Daniel 332; Daniel, *alias* Daniel Faulkner 335*; Elizabeth, *alias* Elizabeth Faulkner 335; Hannah 324; Hannah, *alias* Hannah Faulkner 335; James Arthur, *alias* James Arthur Faulkner 335; John 335; Joseph 335*; Margaret 335; Moses, *alias* Moses Faulkner 335; Richard, *alias* Richard Faulkner 335; Widow, 332; William 335
Cornish, Robert 220
Cosens, Thomas 138
Cosham, Elizabeth 149; Thomas 149
Cossum, Henry 268; Thomas 268
Coster, Jane, *alias* Jane Gendre 126; John 220
Coules, Thomas 327
Coulstock (Colstock, Coulestock, Coulstocke, Cowlstock), Edward 295*; John 129; Joseph 264
Coumber *see* Coomber
Courthope (Courthop), Mr ... 385; George 149
Cowdrey (Cowdery), John 154, 198
Cowlstock *see* Coulstock
Cox, Anne 231; Arthur 224; Daniel 227, 231, 240; Elizabeth 291; Henry, and children 271-272; James 135, 291*; Jane 323; Jeremiah 227; John 105*, 113*, 224, 291, 323; John Burtenshaw 298; Mary 105, 113, 318; Richard 114; Richard Burtenshaw 298; Sarah 334; Sophia 323; Stephen 318; Walter 224; Widow 300, 302; William 323
Cramp, Charlotte 350; John 350*, 360*, 363*; Joseph 350; Mary 360*, 363*; Samuel 350, 360, 363; Sarah 350; William 350
Crawford, Esther 349; Esther, *formerly* Esther Lamb 339; Matthew 339, 348, 352; Matthew, and daughter 349
Crayford, Matthew 250
Creasey (Creasie, Creasy), Amelia, *formerly* Amelia Stone, and son 367; Elizabeth 278, 285; George 170; John 170; Mary 170-171; Ninian 223; Ninian, and wife and children 159; Richard 278; Sarah 223; Susanna 217; Thomas, jun 65
Crew, Anne 174, 179; Nathaniel 174, 179
Cripps (Crips), Anne 308*; Edward 272; Elizabeth 272, 308; John 162, 249, 308; Mary 162, 249, 308; Rebecca, *alias* Rebecca Cobham 349, 353; Robert 159; Sarah 308; Susanna 308; William 272*
Crittenden, Sarah 193; Sarah, and son 218*
Crocker, Margaret, *formerly* Margaret Figless 86; Richard 86
Cross, Bartholomew 150
Crosskey, Mr ... 255
Croucher, Charles 127; John 127
Crundwell, Edward 200
Cufftree, John 154
Culpeper, Edward 375
Cumber *see* Coomber
Curtis (Curtes, Curthoys), Anne 108, 116, 160; Barbara 283; Elizabeth 283; George 160; Griffith 160; Jane 112, 115; John 108, 116; Michael 283; Richard 112, 115; Richard, and wife 108; Samuel, and wife and family 107; Sarah 283; William 214
Cuthbert, Robert 153

D

Dadswell, Edward 182*; James 182; John 182; Martha 182
Dainse, Thomas 376
Dale, Elizabeth 161, 172, 178; Henry 254*; John 117*, 172, 178; Mary 117; Michael 172, 178; Sarah 161, 172, 178, 254; Thomas 254; William 161*
Dalton, John 246
Dancy (Dance), Anne 175*; Anne, *or* Anne Davey 181; Joseph 175*, 348; Joseph, *or* Joseph Davey 181; Mary 355, 386*
Dane, Jane 221; Robert 205; Thomas 316; Walter 316; *see also* Dann
Daniel, Anne 100; Elizabeth 100*, 333; John, and children 333; Joseph 185; Thomas, and wife and children 347
Dann, Henry 183; *see also* Dane
Davey (Davie, Davy, Davye), Abraham 282; Alan 230, 282; Anne 107, 283, 289; Anne, and children 79;

Davey (*contd*)
Anne, *or* Anne Dancy 181; Edmund 110, 282; Elizabeth 164, 245, 275, 306*; George 107; Henry 124, 306*; James 107*, 245; Jane 282; Joan 107; John 79, 107, 124, 306*, 334; John, and child 234; Joseph 164, 282-283; Joseph, *or* Joseph Dancy 181; Lucy 110; Martha 282; Mary 107, 249, 274*, 289*, 320, 322; Sarah 113, 234, 282; Stephen 274*; Stephen, and children 79; Susanna 68, 282, 283*, 306*; Thomas 107, 320, 322; Thomas, and wife and children 281*; Walter 249, 289; William 289, 306*
David, Elizabeth 295; James 295
Davie *see* Davey
Davis (Davys), Anne 164; David 164; Eamy 343; Elizabeth 103, 164; Francis 164*; Joan 103; Mary, *alias* Mary Arnold *formerly* Palmer 87; Richard 367, 386*, 388; Richard, and children 343; Thom. 103; William Henry 370
Davy, Davye *see* Davey
Davys *see* Davis
Daw, Alan, and family 122; Mary 196; William 196
Dawes (Daws, Dawse), Anne 46*; Edward 64; Elizabeth 64; John 46; L. 188; Mildred 48; Richard 124; Sarah 274; Thomasine 124
Dawson, James 174, 180; Jane 174, 180; Mary 174, 180; Sarah 44, 174, 180; Thomas 44, 174, 180; Thomas, and wife and family 217
Day, Benjamin 193; Charlotte 144; David 159; Elizabeth 159, 193; Goody, and husband and child 123; James 159; Jane 123; John 159, 309*, 323; Mary 159, 309*; Richard 159, 201, 209; Sarah 144, 192, 321, 323; Susanna 159; William 144, 297, 301, 309*, 321, 323*
Dayne, John 374
Deadman (Dedman), Elizabeth 59, 60*, 109*; Jane 379; John 57, 59; Mary 60, 109; Sarah 57, 59-60, 109; Thomas 60, 109; William 109
Dean (Deane), Elizabeth 383; Isaac 109, 250; John 109*, 250*; Mary 252; Mary, and daughter 267; Sarah 109*, 250*; Thomas 109, 250, 252; William, and wife 159
Dearling, Amelia 184; Eliza 184; Katherine 184*; Mary 183; Thomas 184; William 184
Dedman *see* Deadman
Delves, John 328
Dench, Anne 355-356; Anne, *formerly* Anne Whitehead, and daughter 357; Daniel 79, 355-356; Elizabeth 79, 344; Hannah 345, 352*; Harriet 315; James 315; John 79, 355-356; Mary 79*; Richard 345, 352*, 363, 365; Richard, and wife and child 308; Robert 368; Sarah 79, 315, 345, 352*; Susanna 355-356; Thomas 79*; William 315*, 344, 365; William, jun 365
Denman, Amy 99*; Anne 61, 116, 305-306; Anne, *later* Anne Smith 305; Christopher 116; David 276; Eleanor 143, 263; Elizabeth 116*, 143, 350; Isaac 61, 305; John 61, 305; Joseph 143; Mary 359; Philip, and wife and children 344; Samuel, and son 143; Sarah, and daughter 267; William, and son 350
Denness *see* Dinnis
Dennett, Alfred George 63; Arthur 63; Charles 63; Charlotte 63; Emma 63; Henry 63; John 63; Mary 63; Robert 276; Sarah 276
Dennis, Capt ... 103; Amy 169; Elizabeth 325; John 325; Mary 325; Robert 169*; Sarah 325*; William 169, 325; *see also* Dinniss
Denton, Richard 220; Thomas 202; William 202
Denyer, John 171; Mary 171
Deuck, William, and wife 352
Devall, Margaret 321; Mary 162; Mary, and daughter 204; Richard 162, 204; Sarah 162*; William 222
Devayne, Francis 241
Dew (Dewe), George 160, 169; Mary 160, 169
Dewdney (Dudeney), Mr ... 378; Anne 86; Mary 86; Samuel 86; Sarah 86; William 66*, 86
Dewe *see* Dew
Dewney, William 245*
Dicker, Anne 195*; Edward 195*; Joseph 230; Mary 230
Dier *see* Dyer
Dinnis (Denness, Dinness), Amy 160; Robert, and children 160; Robert, and wife and children 160; *see also* Dennis
Diplock, John 199
Dismore, John 206
Divall (Diveall, Divole), Anne 233*; George 70; John 70, 171*, 188*, 219; Mary 70; Richard 233*; Richard, and infant 70; Sarah 188; Sarah

formerly Sarah Farnes 171; Thomas 54-55, 70, 220
Dix, Anne 285; Jacob 285; Philadelphia 287
Dixon, Mary 101
Doble (Dobell, Doubell), Daniel 207; Edward 111*, 114; Jane 111, 122
Dodd (Dod), Henry 246*; John 207; Richard 207; Thomas 53; William, gent 273
Dodswell *alias* Lambton, Edward 184
Dorridge, William 271
Dorrington, Sarah, and daughter 242
Doubell *see* Doble
Douch, Mordecai 169
Dowlen, Edward, sen 53
Dowley, Mr F.A. 385
Downard (Downward), Edward 254; James 215
Downer, Henry 72; John 43-44; Mary 43-44; Thomas 72
Downing, Mary Anne 183; Sarah 183
Downward *see* Downard
Downy, Mr ... 388
Draper, Ambrose 183; Elizabeth 310
Dray, Elizabeth 377
Drewett, Richard 54
Drinkwater, Richard 106
Driver, John 352*, 372*; John, and wife and children 343; John, jun 348; Sarah 348, 352*; Thomas 348, 352*; William 348, 352*
Dudden, William 144
Dudeney *see* Dewdney
Dudley, Daved 149; Edward 144*; Jane 144*, 287; Samuel 144*; Sarah 287; Thomas 287
Duffeild *see* Duffield
Duffell, Edward 372; Margery 372; Richard, *alias* Richard Duffield 96
Duffield (Duffeild), James 289, 295; John 330; Richard, *alias* Richard Duffell 96
Dugin, Richard 330
Duglas, Elizabeth 186; William 186*
Duke, Jane 243; John 244
Dumbrell (Dumberell, Dumbrel), Abraham 298; Abraham, and wife 333; Elizabeth, and daughter 126; Elizabeth, and son 125; John 135; Mary 113, 115*; William 128, 132
Dumsday, Jane 161, 170*, 177; John 153*, 161, 170*, 177
Dungate, Elizabeth 192
Dunn, John 179; Mary 179*; Philadelphia 179; William 179
Dunstall, John 129, 247
Dunthon, John 315
Dunton, Anne 254, 257; Elizabeth 262; Henry 257; Joan 106; John 257, 270*; John, and wife 111; John, and wife and children 106; Richard 257; Thomas 257*, 262
Durham, John 236; Mary 236; Thomas 236
Durrant, Anne 320; Benjamin 291, 295; Elizabeth 163*; Isaac 163; James 163; John 238; Lydia 291, 295; Mary 163; Richard 163; Sarah 163; Sarah Anne 291, 295
Durtnall, Henry 70*; Sarah 70*
Dwite, Sarah 141
Dyer (Dier), Agnes 102; Elizabeth 141

E

Eade, Elizabeth 109*; George 109; Sarah 109
Eager, Anne 64*; Elizabeth 142*; James 144; Lucy 144; Richard 269; Sarah 144; Thomas 64, 142*; William 142-143
Eareland, John 244*
Earle, George 262; John 161; Mary 262
Eastland, Mary, and daughter 365
Easton, Alice 355*; Daniel 355*; Elias 348, 352*; Elizabeth 360; Ephraim (Ephriam) 355*; Esther 355*; Henry 243; Jesse 355*; John 83, 352; Jonathan 355*; Mary 352*; Richard 352; Sidney 355*; Sophia, *alias* Sophia Knight 361; William 352, 355*
Eastwood, Deborah, and daughter 210
Ede (Eede), Anne 271, 276; Charlotte 271; Edward 271; George 208; Henry 235*; Jane 60; John, and wife and family 230; Martha 235; Mary, and son 298; Mary, *later* Mary Leppard 74; Sarah 271; William 271
Edee, John 43
Edmunds, William 277
Edsle, Anne 377
Edwards, Abraham 348, 352; Anne 188, 253, 258, 325; Edward 171; Elizabeth 113, 115, 170, 348, 352; Elizabeth, and daughter 268; Esther 175, 181; Hannah 178, 207; Harriet 175, 181; Henry 53, 178; James 108*, 113*, 334; Jane 175, 181; Jane, *formerly* Jane Baldwin 359; John 111, 173, 175, 181, 207, 325; John Bleach 204; Joseph 175, 181; Katherine 111; Martha 193; Mary 152, 170*, 175, 181, 189, 198, 204, 207, 213, 295*, 333*; R. 188; Richard 155, 189*, 204, 213, 225, 359, 368; Samuel 295*; Sarah 108*, 113*, 173, 199, 218, 263; Sarah, and son 198; Thomas 108, 113, 115, 150, 152, 170, 193, 253; Thomas, and

Edwards (*contd*)
mother and sisters 155*; Thomas, and wife and children 160; Thomas Wood 225; William 111
Eede *see* Ede
Eginton, Elizabeth 350
Ekins, William 315
Eldridge, Anne 258; Barbara 258; Elizabeth Lloyd 258, 261; Harriet 258; John Lloyd 258; Mary 258
Elfeck *see* Elphick
Elles *see* Ellis
Ellgate, Dighton 139
Elliass, Ellies *see* Ellis
Elliker, Anne 290; Henry 290; Mary 290*; Prudence 290; Robert 290
Elliott (Ellyott), Elizabeth 322; George, and family 343; George, and father 280*; Hannah 288; Harriet 293, 324; James 293, 324; John 346; Louis 288; Mary 280, 343, 346; Sarah 280; William, and infant 288
Ellis (Elles, Elliass, Ellies), Anthony 173, 178, 202; Charity 356; Charlotte 181, 295; Charlotte, and father 291; Christopher 371; Edward 365; Elizabeth 119, 121, 181, 218, 371; Elizabeth, and father 291; Francis 321-322; George 119, 121, 173*, 178*, 181*; Henry 139, 181; James 119; Joan 366, 372; John 72, 220, 248, 356, 366, 372; John, gent 245; Joseph 70*; Katherine 119; Martin 173, 178, 181; Mary 119, 181, 282; Mary Anne 119; Nicholas 371; Sarah 173, 178, 371; Susanna 356; Thomas 173, 178, 225, 227, 238, 282*; William 241
Ellsey *see* Elsey
Ellyot *see* Elliott
Elms, Richard 227
Elphick (Elfeck, Elphicke), Eleanor 308; Elizabeth 373; Hannah 80-81; James 81; James, and wife 80; Philadelphia 296*; Sarah 80-81*
Elsey (Ellsey), Charity 288; Eliza 288; Elizabeth 44, 76; George 44; John, and parents 76; William 288
Elvey, John 185, 225
Emery (Emray), Mary 254; Peter 254; Peter, and family 59; Sarah 254
Engerfield, Elizabeth 167; Thomas 167*
English, Anne 165; Harriet 165; Joseph 165*; Mary 108, 250; Moses 108; William 165
Erridge (Aridge, Eridge, Erridg), Betty *alias* Elizabeth 189; Cornelius 222; Elizabeth 195; John 197, 209, 376; Sarah 364; *see also* Uridge
Esgate (Esgate), Philip 222
Eson, Richard, and wife 271
Etherington *alias* Burton, Anne 262*; Thomas 262*
Etherton, Anne 310; Hannah 310; James 62; Jesse 310; John 62; Parkhurst 310; Richard 310*; Sarah 62
Evans, Anne 234; George 63; Sarah 45
Evarist *see* Everest
Evelyn, Edward, esq 152
Evenden, Mary 122-123
Everest (Evarist, Everist), Anne 163; Edward 152, 166, 225; Elizabeth 163, 359; Hannah 359; John 163, 166, 290*, 359; Mary 190; Sarah 166, 290; Thomas 160, 163, 169; William 163
Evershed, Elizabeth 173; Mary, and father 191; Philadelphia 173; Richard 173*; Richard, and wife and infant 166
Ewins (Uwins), Anne 57; Charlotte 296; Elizabeth 63, 143; George 63; Harriet 143; James 143*; Jane 296; John 63, 143, 296, 377; Lucy 143; Mary 57, 59, 143, 296; Reuben 143; Richard 143; Robert 76; Ruth 143; Sarah 57; Thomas 57*, 137, 143, 296*; Thomas, and children 59
Eyre, Elizabeth, and son 299

F

Fairall *see* Fairhall
Faircloth, Elizabeth 165; Joseph 165*; Sarah 165; William 165
Fairehall *see* Fairhall
Faires *see* Fairs
Fairfoote, Anne 332; John, and children 332
Fairhall (Fairall, Fairehall), Henry 109; Henry, and family 301; James 53; Jane 109; Katherine 343; Richard 343; Sarah 63, 87
Fairs (Faires), Francis 235; John 89, 91
Falconer, Falkener, Falkiner, Falkner *see* Faulkner
Fanges, ... 147
Farley, Anne 310; Elizabeth 161*, 310; Henry 161*, 310; Mary 310; Richard, and son 310*; Stephen 235
Farley Elizabeth 235
Farmer, Adam 102; John 160, 212; Mary 116, 160*; Robert 176; Thomas 207; William 205
Farncombe (Farncomb), Anne 334; Joseph 334; William 300
Farnes (Farne, Farns), James 186; John 186; Mary 186-187; Philadelphia, *alias* Philadelphia Standing 172; Sarah, *later* Sarah Divall 171
Farrant, Elizabeth 161; Mary

161; Philadelphia 161; Sarah 161; Thomas 161; William 161
Farrell, Anne 275
Farren (Farron), John 376
Fashey, William 376
Fassell, William 167, 176, 184
Faukes, Elizabeth 346, 349; William 346*, 349*
Faulkner (Falconer, Falkener, Falkiner, Falkner, Faulconer, Faulkoner), Anne 57, 163, 278, 285; Anne, and husband 147; Charles 123; Daniel, *alias* Daniel Cork 335*; Elizabeth 190, 264, 266*, 326, 350; Elizabeth, *alias* Elizabeth Cork 335; George 123; Hannah, *alias* Hannah Cork 335; Henry 123; James 264, 266*; James Arthur, *alias* James Arthur Cork 335; John 49, 57*, 123, 163*; John, and wife and family 59; Lydia 123*; Martha 123; Mary 45, 57*, 249; Mary, *later* Mary Knight 264, 266*; Moses, *alias* Moses Cork 335; Richard, *alias* Richard Cork 335; Thomas 123; William 123*, 208, 218, 264, 266*, 333; William, jun 208
Feast (Feist, Fieast, Fiest, Fist), Anne 83-84*; Elizabeth 83-84, 86; Fanny 80; Francis 86; James 86; Jane 81; John 83-84, 86; Joseph 65; Mary 83-84, 187; Nicholas, and wife and children 308; Nicholas, and wife and family 79; Thomas 83; Thomas, and children 80; Thomas, and infant 84; William 187
Feild *see* Field
Feilder, Anne 171; Richard 171
Feist *see* Feast
Feldwick (Feldwicke, Velvick), Anne 141; Elizabeth 126, 141*; James 126, 141*; Jane 141*; William 126, 330
Fenall, Richard 245; *see also* Vinall
Fenner, Andrew 372; Anne 350*; Elizabeth 144; Hannah 350; James 144; John 350; Judith 372; Richard 350; Thomas 304
Fewson, Benjamin 281
Fieast *see* Feast
Field (Affield, Affielld, Feild), George, and child 308; Mary 112, 308; Michael 126; Michael, and infant 117*; Robert 104, 112; Robert, and wife and family 107; Sarah 117; Thomas 269; *see also* Attfield
Fielders, Anne 119*; Eliza 119*; James 119*; John 119*; Martha 119*; Mary 119*; Sophia 119*; William 119*
Fiest *see* Feast
Figless, Joseph 86; Margaret, *later* Margaret Crocker 86
Fillery (Fillare, Phillary, Phillery), Elizabeth 120, 141; James 57, 92, 97, 247; Jesse 104, 112; John 52, 57, 247; John, and wife and family 59; Lydia 57; Mary 57, 104, 112, 333; Richard 128; William 104*, 112*; William, and wife and children 106-107
Fin *alias* Finch, Ruth 146
Finch, Daniel 189, 194; Elizabeth 121, 194*; Henry 124; John 207; Mary 189, 207, 306*; Robert 189; Ruth, *alias* Ruth Fin 146; Thomas 121; Thomas, and wife and children 282; William 207
Fine, James 103
Finnes *see* Finnis
Finney, Thomas 382*
Finnis (Finnes), Anne 346; Frances, *later* Frances Williams 372; John 346; Mary 346; Richard 372
Fish, Mr ... 147
Fisher, Thomas 74*
Fist *see* Feast
Fitness, Elizabeth 249; James 249
Fletcher, John 198, 209, 212
Flint, Abigail 80; Addah 262; Anne 80; Anne, *alias* Anne Tidy 256, 260; Elizabeth 80; Francis 80; James, *alias* James Tidy 256, 260; John 80; Mary 80; Richard, *alias* Richard Tidy 256, 260
Float, Elizabeth 233; Henry 233; John 233; Lydia 233
Florance, James 165; Richard 165; Sarah 165
Floyd, Ensign ... 150; Elizabeth 151; Samuel 151, 203
Foice *see* Foyce
Ford, Harriet 197; John 89-90; Lydia 272; Robert 272
Foreman (Forman), Arthur 90; Elizabeth 81; Thomas, and wife and family 272
Forster, Mary 144; Robert, and father 381-382; William 144; *see also* Foster
Forwood (Forwoode), Mercy 129; Thomas 129
Foster, Mr ... 226; Anne 229, 235; Elizabeth 190; James 235; James, and father 229; John 190, 257; *see also* Forster
Fowle, Thomas 125, 164
Fowler, Charlotte 119; Elizabeth 119; Elizabeth, and child 306; George 119; Henry 119*; John 152, 289; Louisa 119; Mary 119*, 289; Sarah 83; William 83

Fowtrell, John 352; Mary 352; Sarah 352
Fox, Elizabeth 81; George, *alias* George Reynolds 219; Margaret 81; Thomas 81, 90; William, *alias* William Reynolds 220
Foyce (Foice), James 227*; John 227
Frampton, Anne 100; Eliz. 147; George, and child 100; Mary 147; William 147
Francis (Frances, Franncis), Anne 84; Elizabeth 344; James 92, 96; John 205; Mary 102; Nicholas 210; Nicholas, jun 205; Philip 353; Sarah 344*; Thomas 344*; William 84, 129, 132, 344
Francke, George 373
Franks, Mrs ... 386*; Hannah 237; John 280; Jonathan 237; Matilda 237; William 190, 368, 388
Franncis *see* Francis
Frazier, John 362
Freeman, Richard 87; William 96, 220; William, and father 78
Freind *see* Friend
French (Frenche), Charles 120, 305*; Elizabeth 112, 136; Francis 131; Frederick 111, 138; James 216; Joan 130*; John 108; Margaret 186; Mary 108, 120*; Mary, and daughter 125; Mary, jun, and son 123, 127; Mary, *later* Mary Lutman 305*; Richard 128, 132; Sarah 62, 120, 305*; Silvester 254; Thomas 186; William 112
Friend (Freind), Amy 162*; Elizabeth 162, 325*; James 162*, 325, 328; Willard 238; William 162, 328
Frogley *later* Hedgcock, Mary 74
Frould, John 302*
Fry (Frye), John 378; Rebecca 207; Thomas, and family 274
Fryer, John 123; Mary 123
Fuller, Mr ... 383; Caleb 302; Caleb, and father 300; Charity 70*; Edward 184*; Elizabeth 241, 286, 351, 354; James 285, 357*; John 70*, 260, 358; Mary 357*; Michael 124; Rebecca 357*; Sarah 70*, 260; Thomas 286; William 260, 358
Funnell, Anne 296*; Elizabeth 285; John 285; Thomas 285, 296; William 285, 296
Furlonger, Martha 69
Furminger, Andrew 151
Furner, Kezia 45; Mary 250*; Robert 250*
Fuson, Joseph, and children 281; Mary 281

G
Gadd, Abraham 348
Gale, Elizabeth, *alias* Elizabeth Hulat 148; L. 104, 146
Gallard, Anne 121-122; Edward 121; Elizabeth 121; Henry 121-122; Sarah 121; Susanna 121
Galyon, John 105
Gander, Anne 221; Eleanor 326*; Hannah 337; Henry 163, 337; Jane 275, 337; John 326*; Mary 254, 282; Sarah 254, 337; William 254, 282, 337; William, jun 254
Gandy, Edward 151, 161, 169, 177; Elizabeth 151, 161, 170, 177; Jane 151, 161, 169, 177; Thomas 151, 161, 170, 177
Gardner (Gardener, Gardiner, Gardyner), Alexander 373; Anna, and father and son 367; Anne 175*, 181*; Benjamin, and wife and family 344; Edmund, and wife and family 79; Elizabeth 50*, 114, 362; Henry 50*, 362; Jane 50*, 175*, 181*, 362; Joanna 50*, 165, 362; John 175*, 181*, 245; Katherine 104; Lodwicke 104; Mary 49-50*, 362; Nathaniel 303; Richard 373; Thomas 50*, 362; Thomas, and family 166; W. 326; William 50*, 165, 175*, 181*, 362
Garrett, James 156; Thomas 156
Garston, Richard 318, 322
Garton, Hannah 331; John 132, 272, 331; Sarah 272
Gasson, John 135; Mary 282; Miriam 282; Moses 282; Sarah 175*, 181; Thomas 135, 175*, 181; William 282
Gasston (Gastone), John 272; Lucy Anne 286; Sarah 272; Thomas 286*; William 286
Gates, Caroline 309*; Edward 311; Eliza 311; Elizabeth 200; Elizabeth, and son 208, 218-219; George 215; Henry 138; Isaac 329; Jane 315; Philadelphia 184; Richard 311; Thomas 136*; William 311; *see also* Agates
Gatford, John 63, 80; Lucy 63; Mary 79-80; Rebecca 63; Sarah 63; Susan 80; Susanna 80; William 63, 80
Gatland, Anne 134; Edward 135; Fanny 173; Henry 111, 134; John 41; John, and wife and family 107; Mary 173; Phoebe 41; Sarah 173; Thomas 173
Gatton (Gatten), Charles 181, 195; Charles, jun 192, 196*; Elizabeth 181*, 195; John 130, 181, 272; Lydia 218; Mary 192, 196*; William 130

Gaynesford, Mr ... 378

Geale (Gealle, Jeale), Elizabeth 169*; John 130*, 169, 349, 352; Mary 349, 352

Gearing (Gearen, Gearin, Geering, Geeringe), Anne 56, 70*; Caroline 276; Eliza 259; Elizabeth 244; Emily 276; Henry 56*, 66, 68, 112, 139, 299; Henry, and wife 58; Henry, and wife and children 274; Jane 70*; John 274*; Mary 70*; Priscilla 259; Rebecca 306; Richard 56, 306; Richard, and wife 58; Sarah 56*, 70*, 276, 306, 334; Sophia 276; Susanna 56, 124, 128; Thomas 56, 140, 259, 306*, 334; William 276*

Geere (Geer), Edward 142; Elizabeth 289; Ellis 137; Eve 134; Frances 262-263, 281, 287; George 281, 287; Henry 262-263; John 188, 195; John, and father and wife and children 253; Lydia 259; Mary 134, 188, 195, 262-263; Sarah 142, 333; Thomas 128, 333; William 262-263

Geeres, Elizabeth 98; Thomas 98

Geering, Geeringe *see* Gearing

Gell, Francis 241; Mr Francis 237

Gendre, Jane, *alias* Jane Coster 126; Peter 126

Genner *see* Jenner

George, Amelia 355; Elizabeth 355; James 355; John 355; Louisa 355; Mary 355; William 355

Gibb (Gib), Anne 171, 178, 274*, 369; Charles 190; Elizabeth 165; George 89, 95*, 184*; James 184*; Jane 184*; Joan 318; John 165, 184*, 225, 274; Joseph 190; Lydia 190; Mary 171-172, 183, 274, 321, 327; Mary Anne 184*; Rachel 184*; Richard 171*, 184*; Richard, and family 161; Sarah 171, 345; Sarah, and daughter 213-214; Sarah, and son 210; Storer 181; Susanna 181; Thomas 165*, 184*, 330; Thomas, and wife and child 345; William 184*, 318

Gibbs, George 84*; Jane 84*; Joan 355*; John 52, 84*, 329, 355*; Mary 329; Mary Anne 386-387*; Mary Anne, and daughter 368; Sarah 84*; William 84*

Gibson, Abraham 49; Edward 200; Elizabeth 56; John 56; Mary 344*; Sarah 49; Thomas 49, 344; William 56*; William, and wife and family 59

Gilbert (Gilbart), Arthur 177; John, and wife and child 159; John, and wife and family 176*; Samuel 376*; Thomas 194

Giles, Anne 258, 261; Edward 173, 179; George 255*, 261*; James 258; Mary 261; Phoebe 255*; Richard 209; Sarah 173, 179; Thomas 258; William 261

Gilham (Gillam, Gillham, Gilliam, Gyllam), Edward 289; Jane 343; John 49, 54, 370; Katherine 116; Margaret 370; Mary, and son 123; Richard 375; Richard, jun, and family 343; Thomas 116

Ginner *see* Jenner

Glasbrook, Glasbrooke *see* Glazebrook

Glass, Thomas 139

Glazebrook (Glasbrook, Glasbrooke), Ambrose 142*; Anne 107, 142*; Benjamin 142*; Charity 142*; Elizabeth 142*; Esther 142*; Henry 54; James 260-261, 306*; Jane 260; John 142*, 333*; Mary 306*; Sarah 142*, 261; Thomas 107, 142*

Gleeston, Sarah 360

Glover, Betty 170; James 150, 170; Katherine 343; William, and children 343

Goacher, Daniel 240; James 324; Mary 324

Goble, Thomas 247

Goddard, Anne, *alias* Anne Holden 338*; Edward 143; James 338; John 143; Kitty 231; Lydia 143; Philip 231

Godley (Godlee, Godly), Anne 287; Edward 287; Jane 258; Mary 303; Sarah 217; Sarah, and daughter 267

Godman, Hannah 57; Hannah, *formerly* Hannah Martin 59; Isabel 235, 259; Margaret 235, 259; Mary 60, 64; Thomas 57*, 59*-60, 235, 259; William 235, 259

Godsmark (Godsmarke), Henry 259; James 259; John 318; Mary, and daughter 66; Michael 55, 66, 139; Sarah 259; William 66

Goffe, Edward 244; John 245

Gold, Jacob 244

Golds (Goldes), Frances 260, 263; George 260, 263

Goldsmith, Anne 231; Frances 99; Harriet 334; Henry 334; Jane 334; John 56*; John, and wife 59; John, jun 99; Mary 56, 334; Philadelphia 178; Sarah 334; Thomas 334; William 56, 334

Gomer, Anne 372; Esther

Gomer (*contd*) 372
Good, Henry 374
Goodwin, Charles, esq 377; Mary 258*; Robert 203; Robert, and wife and family 159
Goose (Gouse), George 319; Mary 319
Goring (Goringe, Gorrenge, Gorringe), Amelia, and son 369; Anne 199, 359; David 359; Elizabeth 174, 179, 359; Elizabeth, and son 369; George 119; James 174, 179, 206, 359; John 153; Katherine 275; Mary 359*; Mary, and son 368; Matilda, and son 367-368; Sarah 119; Thomas 359, 370; William 99, 174*, 179*, 359*
Gourd (Goord), Anne 164, 329; Anne, and father 327; Frances 219; John 164; Thomas 164; William 164
Goure, Thomas 221
Gouse *see* Goose
Gower (Goware), Anne 119, 323; Charlotte 119*, 323*; Elizabeth 119, 286-287, 323; Harriet 119; Jeremiah 277; John 119, 323; Mary 176; Rosamund, and son 91, 95*; Thomas 243; William 176
Gowring, Emy 346; James 346
Grame, John 372
Grant, Elizabeth 233*; Richard 233*; Thomas 233*
Gratwick (Gratwicke), Elizabeth 313; John 244*, 313; Joseph 313; Mary 44, 313; Owen 243; William 72, 94
Graveley (Gravely, Greavely), Anne 55; Anne, and child 83, 313*; John 55; Thomas 55*
Grayling, Charity 163, 172; Elizabeth 163, 172; Richard 163, 172
Greavely *see* Graveley
Green (Greene), Anne 230; Edward 108; Elizabeth 274; George 270; John 57, 109; Katherine 57; Mary 109*; Matthew 109; Sarah 108-109, 274; Stephen 274; Susanna 117; Thomas 108, 114; William 117, 230; William, and wife 107
Greenfield, Anne 110*; Elizabeth 82*, 346*; Hannah 346; Hannah, *later* Hannah Chart 350; John 82, 110; John Chart 350; Rebecca 172*; Richard 172; Sarah 82, 346; Thomas 110, 236; William 346*; Zechariah, and father 228
Greenway, Elizabeth 172; *see also* Grinaway
Greenwood, Michael 149
Gregg *see* Grigg
Grevatt (Grevate), Hannah 69; Richard, and daughter 69; William 230, 236, 271
Grigg (Gregg), Susanna 351, 354
Grimes, Anne 283; Elizabeth 103*; Francis 103; Mary 283; Prudence 283; Sarah 283; William 103, 283
Grinaway, William 246; *see also* Greenway
Grinham, Adam 183; Anne 183; Charlotte 183; William 183
Grove, Benjamin 193, 196; Frances 193, 196; George 193, 196; Katherine 212; Obediah 193, 196; Oliver 197; Rachel 185; Richard 221; Robert 193, 196; William 185, 193, 196, 222
Grover, William 253
Groves, Anne 319; Benjamin 158; Caroline 191; Ernest 191; George 191; Henry 191; Jeremiah 319; Lucy 191; Martha 41; Mary 258; Philadelphia 191; Philip 41; Thomas 198, 212; William 319
Guess, Joan 103
Gulston, Fran. 188
Gunner, Elizabeth 162; George 162*; Hannah 164; Jane 162, 164; Sarah 164; William 162, 164
Gunter, John 132; Judith 128
Gurr (Gur), Charles 277; Thomas 130; Thomas, and wife 352
Gyinner *see* Jenner
Gyllam *see* Gilham
Gynner *see* Jenner

H

Hackett, Alice 349; Elizabeth 377
Hackman, Caleb 297
Haddan, W.J. 384
Hailor *see* Hayler
Haines *see* Haynes
Hair, ... [boy] 42
Halcomb *see* Holcombe
Hale, William 376
Hall, Anne 108, 110, 297*; Elizabeth 295; Jane 110, 316; John 108, 110; Mary 108, 110; Richard 93, 278, 295; Robert, and children 110; Sarah 295*; Thomas 278, 284
Hallaway, James 206
Hallett, Anne 143; Lucy 141; Lucy, and daughter 264
Hambleden, Hambledon, Hamblin, Hambline *see* Hamlin
Hamlett, James 261; Mary Anne 261
Hamlin (Hambleden, Hambledon, Hamblin, Hambline, Hamlyn, Frances 136; Francis 223-224; Joseph 104, 146; Thomas 137
Hammond (Hammonds, Hamond), Richard 131, 135; William 232*

Hamms, Sarah 320
Hamond *see* Hammond
Hamper, Henry 108*, 333; Jane 108*, 127; John 108; Mary 143; Phoebe 127; Sarah 108
Hampton, Mary 289-290; Robert 290; Sarah 289-290
Hamshar, Mr ... 157; Edward 315*; Elizabeth 315; Mary 315
Hancock, Elizabeth 344; Thomas 344
Hand, Anne 233; John 233*; William 233
Hanshet, George 75; Sarah, *formerly* Sarah Matthews 75; Thomas 75
Harbour (Harbber, Harber, Harbor, Harbore), Ambrose 50; Anne 358, 363; Eliza 363; Elizabeth 363*; Elizabeth, and aunt and cousin 383; Esther 50, 346, 363; George 358*, 363; Hannah 358-359; Harriet 363; Henry 363; Henry, and wife and family 387*; Jane 50; John 346*; Mary 358-359, 363; Sophia 363; Stephen 363*, 380; Stephen, and wife and family 388; Thomas 358-359, 363*; William 50, 363
Harden, Francis 347; Hannah 347
Hardham Mary, and daughter 126
Harding, Anne 81, 259*, 312; Anthony 164; Charles 81, 259*; Deborah 344; Edmond 338; Emina 117; Francis 110; Frank 164; James, and wife and child 249; Jane 164; Jenny 164; John 88, 312, 344; Mary 135, 259*; Sarah 81, 110, 164, 312; Susanna 110, 312*; William 299; William Henry 344
Hards, Charles 357, 363*; Edward 344; Elizabeth 258, 344, 357*, 363*; George 258*; Hannah 235, 241; Henry 383-384; Jane 357, 363*; Katherine 357, 363*; Martha, and son 242; Mary 117; Mary, and son 299; Mary Anne 119; Patience 258; Robert 152, 161; Sarah 357, 363*; Susanna 152, 161, 170; Thomas 357, 363; William 117, 126
Hardy, Isaac 363
Harfie *see* Harvey
Harland, Anthony 346; Daniel 262-263, 276; Elizabeth 133; James 276; John 346; Katherine 346; Martha 276; Mary 262-263, 276, 313*; Richard 137; Sarah 276; Sarah, *alias* Sarah Carter 119; Thomas 124, 128, 133; William 313*
Harling, Edward 373; George 375; John 373; Richard 372, 375; Richard, jun 172
Harman, Anne 172, 230; Benjamin, and children 230; Elizabeth 107, 112; Harriet 46; Isaac 107, 112; James 369
Harmes, Mary 261; Michael 68; Michael, jun 125; Michael, sen 125
Harper, Edward 146*
Harriott, Thomas 302
Harris, Anne 161, 171, 177, 187, 191, 208; Benjamin 190; Edward 161, 171, 177; Elizabeth 190-191; Jane 254; John 154, 161, 171, 177, 254; Mary 191*; Sarah 191; Thomas 191; William 187*, 191*
Hart (Harte), Jane 131; John 109*, 243*; Mary 109*; Richard 131; William 253
Hartfield, Mary 182, 196*
Hartop, Caleb 152; Timothy, *alias* Timothy Prudden [female] 152
Harvey (Harfie, Harvie), Annis 373; Edward 128, 132, 373; Peter 371; Reynold 371; Thomasine 371
Harwood, Edmund 67; Edward, jun 54; Edward, sen 67; John 227; Susanna 185; Thomas 185*, 195
Haselden (Haseldene, Hasleden), Anne 201-202, 223, 364; Edward 223; Thomas 376; Thomas, and male child 364
Haselgrove, Haslegrove *see* Hazelgrove
Hasleden *see* Haselden
Hasting, Stephen 357
Hatten, Jane 104; John 104; Mary 104
Havelock, Sophia 385-386; Sophia, and daughter 367
Hawkes, Richard 377
Haybittle, Barbara 78*; Mary 78; Thomas, and parents 78
Hayler (Hailor, Haylor), Anne 60, 123, 254, 335*; Edward 335*; Eleanor 322; Elizabeth 254, 335*; Elizabeth, and son 238; Henry 123; Jane, *alias* Jane Hayley 144; John 254*; John, *alias* John Hayley 144; Mary 335*; Richard 60; Richard, and wife 59; Sarah 236, 306; Thomas 217; William 322
Hayley *alias* Hayler, Jane 144; John 144
Haylor *see* Hayler
Hayls, Elizabeth 344*; John 344
Haynes (Haines, Hayne, Heaine), Anne, and mother and daughter 300; Harriet, and father 293; John 245; Mary 147;

Haynes (*contd*)
Richard 244, 265; Thomas 247
Hayward, Anne 166; Edward 182*; Elizabeth 182*; John 166, 182*; Mary 166, 182*; Robert 182*; Sarah 182*; Thomas, gent 207; William 182*
Hazelgrove (Haselgrove, Haslegrove, Hazlegrove, Heaslegrove), Alice 244; Elizabeth 259, 283, 285; John 283, 285; Leonard 103, 269; Leonard, and wife 111; Mary 69*, 274; Richard 244; Sarah 117; Thomas 67, 224, 274
Head, Mr ... 158, 199; Anne 193, 309; Elizabeth 162; Humphrey, and infant 179; Jane 162*, 179*; John 179; Mary 162, 179; Richard 162; Susanna 179; William 193, 281, 309; William, and wife and family 158
Heaine *see* Haynes
Heaslegrove *see* Hazelgrove
Heasman (Hesman), Anne 110, 126; Anne, and daughter 215; Anne, *alias* Anne Peters 63; Bernard 52; Bet 62*; Bet, and children 86*; Bet, and daughter 92, 95*; Charlotte 60, 62, 360; Elizabeth 60, 62, 116*; Elizabeth, and son 93; Elizabeth, *alias* Elizabeth Batchelor 87, 119; Frances 110*; Francis 263; George 116*; Henry 52, 116*, 349; Henry, and family 107; James 116*; Jane, and daughter 66; John 62, 110, 275; Mary 60, 116*, 281; Sarah 182; Thomas 110*, 223; Wat (Watt) 60; William 125, 223, 281
Heath, Henry 135; Henry, *alias* Henry Ball 269; James 138; Jane 131; Robert 157; Thomas 303*; William 210
Heathfield (Hethfield), Edmund 200
Heaver (Hever), Edward 355; Mary 200, 219; Sarah 335; William 76, 272
Hedgcock 92; Elizabeth 74; Henry 346; James 74; Mary, *formerly* Mary Frogley 74; Sarah 346*; William 74
Hemsley, Agnes 183; Charles William 183; Eliza 183*; Emma 237; Fanny 183; Frances 237; George, and daughter 335*; Henry 183; James 117; John 144, 237; Louisa 237; Lucy 335*; Mary 117, 141, 237; Philadelphia 117; Sarah 117, 144; Susanna 237; Tirzah 183; Tirzah Fanny 183; William 237; William, jun 183
Henley (Hendley), Caroline 44; Harriet 44; Jane 46; John 57, 59; Mary 44; Phoebe 44; Sarah 57, 59, 262; Stephen 262; Susanna 262-263; Thomas 44, 46; William 262, 325
Henty, Edward 204, 213; Elizabeth 306*
Heriott *see* Herriott
Herring, John 138
Herriott (Heriott, Herriot, Heryet), Anne 345; James 345; John 345; Mary 127, 264; Richard 128; Thomas 128, 132
Hervy, Lord ... 218
Heryet *see* Herriott
Hesketh *alias* May, Sarah 46
Hesman *see* Heasman
Hethfield *see* Heathfield
Hever *see* Heaver
Hewett, John 166; Margaret 166
Hewits, Mr ... 147
Hibben, Andrew 158; Anne 158*; Elizabeth 158; George 158; John 158
Hide *see* Hyde
Hider *see* Hyder
Highgate, Joan 348
Hill, Caroline 362; Edward 309; Elizabeth 309*, 322; Hannah 318*, 359; Henry 362; James 318, 347, 359*; Jasper 309; John 237, 309, 318*, 322, 359; Mary 362; Mary Eliza 362; Peter 42; Peter, jun 125; Richard 318; Sarah 318, 347, 359; Sarah, and son 367; Thomas 359, 362*; Thomas, *alias* Thomas Terry 356; William 309, 318; *see also* Hills
Hillman, Edward, and family 110, 121; Henry, *alias* Henry Illman 170; James 258; John, *alias* John Illman 170; Sarah 258; Susan 258; Susanna, *alias* Susanna Illman 170; Thomas 268
Hills, Anne 281; Anne, and child 83; Anne, and son 93; Elizabeth 109, 333*; Elizabeth, and son 112; George 240; James 350; James, and father 340; Jane 46; John 249, 281*; Mary 281, 306; Sarah 350; Sarah Anne 249; William 109; William, *alias* William Bell 387*; *see also* Hill
Hillyar, James 235; Philadelphia 235
Hilton, Christopher 137
Histed *see* Isted
Hoad, Thomas 240; *see also* Hood
Hoader, Thomas 277
Hoadley (Hoadly), Anne 234; Elizabeth 172, 289; Henry 234; James 234*; John 172, 289; Louisa 234; Mary 234, 290, 313; Richard 113*, 115*; Sarah 113*, 115*, 234; Thomas 172, 290, 313;

Thomas, and wife and child 79*
Hoath, Elizabeth 182; John, and family 161; Mary Anne 182; Thomas 182
Hobbs, William 253
Hobden, George 356*-357; Harriet 356*-357; John 44-45, 315, 356*-357*; Mary 44-45, 338, 356*-357; Mary Anne 357; William 357
Hobley, Francis 161
Hoborn, Anne 107*; Daniel 107; Walter 107
Hockham *see* Holcombe
Hoder, Sarah 284, 287; Thomas 284, 287
Hodges (Hodge), Emily 191, 216-217; Emily, and son 208; Maria 237; Mary, and daughter 240; Thomas 240
Hodgkins, Jonathan 81; Mary 81
Hodson, Mr ... 157; Mr Thomas 157
Hogsflesh, Benjamin 235, 247; Elizabeth 262; Jane 235
Holaway, Holawaie *see* Holloway
Holcombe (Halcomb, Hockham, Holcom, Holcomb), Dorothy, *alias* Dorothy Ansty 131; Francis 264; George 128; John 264; Katherine, *alias* Katherine Ansty 131; Philip, *alias* Philip Ansty 131; Richard 128; Stephen, *alias* Stephen Ansty 131; Susan 129, 132; Thomas 137; Walter 128-129, 133; Walter, *alias* Walter Ansty 131
Holden, Anne 113, 115; Anne, *alias* Anne Goddard 338*; Charles 234; Elizabeth 117*, 234; James 109, 115, 117, 240, 338*; James, and family 232; James, jun 117; James, *or* James Holding, and wife and child 230; Jane 117, 234-235, 237, 338*; Jane, and daughter 242; Jane, and son 242; John 234, 338; Joseph 113; Louisa 235; Mary 117, 254; Robert 245; Susan 281; Thomas 234, 244, 338*, 384; William 234, 254, 281
Holder, Anne 337, 358; Caroline 231-232; Edward 235; Hannah 296; Henry 165, 178*; John 165, 178*, 295, 337; John Peckham 296; Mary 165, 178*; Sophia 323; Thomas 323; William 165, 178*, 358
Holding *or* Holden, James, and wife and child 230
Hole, Anthony 258; Anthony, and wife and child 255; Elizabeth 258*; Mary 258
Holford, ..., and family 61
Holibone *see* Hollibone
Holland, James 364
Hollands, Edward, and children 160; Elizabeth 164; Mary 160; William 164*
Hollibone (Holibone, Hollybone), Elizabeth 110, 253, 257; Mary 110*, 253*, 257*; Thomas 110, 137, 253, 257
Hollingdale, Charlotte 143; Edward 69, 262; James 143*; Mary 69*, 234; Mary Anne 256; Philadelphia 256; Thomas 256; William 256
Hollingham, John 74*, 110; Sarah 110
Hollis, William 271, 362
Holloway (Holaway, Holawaie), Anne 306-307; Celia 45; Elizabeth 374; Frances 306-307; James 61, 306-307; Jane 61, 63; John 63, 306-307*; Joseph 272; Mary 272; Moses 61, 63; Rachel 61, 63, 306-307; Richard 272; Sarah 306*; Thomas 306-307; William 45, 61, 63, 374
Hollybone *see* Hollibone
Holman, Amelia 182; Anne 360, 386; Elizabeth 50, 324; George 360; James 165, 182, 324; John 46, 182, 338; Joseph 50, 90; Mary 165, 174; Phobe 46; Richard 46*; Robert 149; Sarah 182, 338; Thomas 174, 180, 182*, 265; William 324
Holmas, Mary 179; Thomas 179
Holmes (Holms), Mr ... 228; Alexander 190, 215; Anne 106; Edmund Eabs 189; Elizabeth 178, 186*; George 221; Jeptha 125; Joseph 149, 159, 178; Philadelphia 189; Robert 106; Ruth 159; Sarah 190; Sarah, and child 215; Sarah, and daughter 210; Susan, and son 123; Susanna 125; William 197; William, and child 186*
Holt, John, and father and wife 226
Homewood (Homwood), Anne, and parents and siblings 279; Elizabeth 272, 295, 360; Francis 279; Harriet 295; Henry 295; John 222, 295; Phoebe 295; Richard 295; Ruth 271*; William 294
Honour (Honor), William 245
Hood, Anne 262; *see also* Hoad
Hook, Robert 149, 169
Hooker, Mary 175, 180, 217
Hordlee, Richard 108*; Sarah 108*; Thomas 108
Horsey, Anne 317*, 325-326;

Horsey (*contd*)
Elizabeth 325-326; Thomas 325-326; William 325-326*
Horten, Elizabeth 166; Joseph 166
Hoskins, William, esq 151
Hounsome (Houndsom), Anne 346, 349; Felicia 346, 349; Mary 346, 349; Richard 210, 346, 349
Hovenden, John, and children 176; Mary 176
Hover, Henry 130
How *see* Howe
Howard, ... 153; Anne 128, 328; Esther, and son 369; John 253, 259; Joseph 259; Joshua 221, 348; Mary 159, 259*; Timothy 159
Howe (How), Barbara 142; Sarah 119, 309*; Thomas 119, 309*; William 142*
Howell, Mr ... 104; Elizabeth 250*; John 109, 313; Sarah 109
Hoyden, William, and wife and son 158
Hubbard, Alice 297; John 298
Hubbart, Edward 42; Thomas 42
Huber, ... [girl] 42
Hudson, Mr ... 379, 381-382*; Richard 253*; Sarah 253
Hues *see* Hughes
Huggett (Hugget), Abraham 197; Anne 346; Anthony 137; Benjamin 214; Elizabeth 206; George 151, 258; George, and wife and family 268; Hannah 258; Jenny 346; John 335; Mary 258, 335; Richard 346; William 216
Hughes (Hues), Elizabeth 83; George 191; James, and infant 83; Mr James 158; Mr John 78; Katherine 191; Lucy 118; Robert 191; Thomas 73; William 118
Hulat, Elizabeth 148; Elizabeth, *alias* Elizabeth Gale 148; Mary 148; William 147-148
Hull, Alan 78
Humfery, Humfry, Humpherey, Humphery *see* Humphrey
Humphres *see* Humphreys
Humphrey (Humfery, Humfry, Humpherey, Humphery, Humphry, Umphrie), Abigail 334; Anne 160, 334; Annis 351, 354; Elizabeth 73, 163, 172, 319, 321-322; Esther 334; George 163, 345; Henry 172*, 351*, 354*, 376; John 129, 136, 160, 172*, 319, 321-322, 339, 345, 373; John, and wife 160; John, and wife and family 168, 176; Joseph 73, 334; Lephard, and wife and children 344; Luke 255; Margaret 255; Martha 99; Mary 324, 345, 365; Mary, *formerly* Mary Whaley 366; Richard 136; Susan 364; Susanna 163, 169, 334; Thomas 319, 321-322, 324, 367, 376*; Thomas, and father 339; William 255, 318
Humphreys (Humphres, Humphrys), John, and wife and family 108; Tabitha 362; Timothy 114
Humphry *see* Humphrey
Humphrys *see* Humphreys
Humphy, Jonas 347
Hunt, Henry 193; Jemima 193; Mary 193; Richard 330; Robert 193
Huntingdon, Countess of 53
Huntley, Sarah 182
Hurst, Thomas 128
Hussee, Nathaniel 131
Hutchinson, Jane 188, 195; Thomas 188, 195
Hyde (Hide), Benjamin 372; Edward 49; Gillian 372
Hyder (Hider), Charlotte 321; Henry 41, 315*; James 315*; Jeremiah 321, 327; John 268; Mary 41, 294; Nicholas 326; Samuel 138; Sarah 315*; William 41
Hysted *see* Isted

I

Ifeild, Jane 318; Mary 318*; William 318
Ifold, Elizabeth 69; William 69*
Illman (Ilman), Alexander 275; Edward 143; Elizabeth 232; Hannah 188, 352; Henry, *alias* Henry Hillman 170; John 275*; John, *alias* John Hillman 170; Mary 275*; Rebecca 275; Richard 128, 132; Susanna, *alias* Susanna Hillman 170; William 159, 275
Ingram, Elizabeth 115; Gamaliel 149; Joseph 115
Ings, Katherine 67
Ireland, Eden 285; Elizabeth 297, 333
Isard *see* Izzard
Isgate (Isgat), James, and wife and children 344
Isted (Histed, Hysted), Anne 160, 169; Edward 282, 317; Elizabeth 161; Fanny 165; Henry 203, 208; James 165; John 160*-161, 169*; Mary 172; Mary, and son 211; Michael 161; Philadelphia 165; Sarah 161, 282, 325; Sarah, and daughter 328-329; Thomas 161, 316; William, and parents 157*
Izzard (Isard, Izard), Anne 309*; Daniel 344*; Elizabeth 344*, 349; John 319, 344; Matilda 311; Sarah 319; Susan 319; William 225, 344

J
Jackson, ... 212; Anne 182*, 325*; Anne, and son 329; Eliza 182*; Elizabeth 44, 121, 325; Hannah 325; Hannah, *alias* Hannah Cook 231; Isaac 325; Jeremiah, *alias* Jeremiah Cook 231; John 182*; Joseph 325; Kitty 182*; Mary 182*, 325; Phyllis 325; Thomas 182*
Jaervis *see* Jarvis
Janson, Joan 372; Tucky 372
Jarlett, Edward 343; Elias 343; Sarah 343*
Jarrett (Jarratt), Anne 286; Elizabeth 150, 170; James, and child 185; Jane 56*; Marian 136; Mary 185, 287; Sarah, and son 205; Thomas 56, 287; Winifred 172
Jarvis (Jaervis, Jervice, Jervis), Edward 233, 246-247*, 260*; John 232; Richard 246; Sarah 254; Thomas 254; William 341
Jay, Hannah, and grandparents 252
Jeale *see* Geale
Jeffery (Jeffrey), Edward 204; John 373; Thomas 125
Jencks, John, and family 79
Jenden, Frances 231; Henry 231; James 93, 97*; John 88*; Lucy 87; Lucy, *alias* Lucy Mitchell 88*; Richard 88*; Steele 88*; Thomas 87
Jener *see* Jenner
Jenings *see* Jennings
Jenkins, George 128
Jenner (Genner, Ginner, Gyinner, Gynner, Jener, Jinner), ... 257; Agnes 129, 133; Ambrose 362; Amy 217; Anne 178, 190, 310, 343; Daniel 260; David 213; Edward, 114, 128, 137, 205, 346*; Mr Edward 340*; Elizabeth 49*, 60*, 189, 193, 346*; Fortune 186; Fortune, and son 212; Frances 112, 114, 260; Francis 105, 109, 113, 133, 135; Grace 134; Isaac 205; James 189-191, 195, 260, 296, 346; James, *alias* James Martin 89, 93, 97*; Jane 193; Joan 3712; John 43, 48, 112, 114, 130, 135, 138, 178, 371; John, and children 344; Maria 193; Mary 49, 105, 107, 109, 113, 164*, 190, 346*; Mary Anne 296*; Nicholas 128; Rebecca 344; Richard 49*, 107, 164, 193, 343; Rosa 362; Samuel 193; Sarah 179, 190-191, 327, 346; Sarah Bess 362; Stephen 133; Susanna 199, 218; Thomas 60, 128, 131, 220; Thomas, and wife and child 107; Thomasine 137; William 49, 136, 190, 193, 310
Jennings (Jenings), George 135; John 311*; Sarah 311; Susan 322; William 43
Jervice, Jervis *see* Jarvis
Jessop (Jesap, Jessup), Anne 165, 172; John 165*, 172*, 206; Robert 206; Robert, jun 207; Thomas, and wife 163
Jested, William, and wife and children 71, 81
Jewell (Jewele), John 339; Richard, jun 165
Jinner *see* Jenner
Johnson, ... 302; Anne 183; Charles, and father 193; Charles *alias* Nathaniel 183; Edward 302; Elizabeth 166*; Henry 183, 189; Jemima 360; John 77, 82, 166; John Boghurst 183; Joseph 66; Mary 77, 82; Nathaniel *alias* Charles 183; Sophia 183; Susanna 183; Thomas 377; W. 280
Jones, Jo. 101; Sarah 324*; Thomas 331; William 324*
Jordan, Anne 214; Edward 190; Henry 216; John 225; Sarah, and son 216
Judgen, John 236; Mary 236; Stephen 236
Judin, Mary 254; Thomas, and family 254
Juniper, Frances 234; Francis 121; James 234
Jupp (Jup, Juppe), ... 380; Anne 310, 369; Barbara 108; Benjamin 345; Edward 135; Eleanor 305; Elizabeth 261, 276*, 311; Elizabeth, and daughter 265; Frederick 310; Henry 261; James 310; Jenny 57; John 47*, 57, 105, 108, 114, 276*, 310; John, and child 343; Joseph 57; Joseph, and children 59; Mary 47, 57*, 59, 105*, 114*, 172, 343, 345; Mary, *alias* Mary Ball 310; Mary Anne 310; Robert 286, 289, 294, 365; Sarah 345*, 361; William 57, 105, 114, 128, 132, 136, 172, 208, 310, 345*; William, and wife and family 59

K
Kayne, ... 141
Keale, Elizabeth 137; John 139
Kearrie, Frances 129; Joan 129
Keene, George 227
Kelsey, John 53
Kember, William 207
Kemp (Kempe), Elizabeth 60, 159; George 159; James 60; John 213; Lucy 60; Lydia 60; Thomas 160; William 60
Kempshall, William 128
Kempton, Hannah 301

Kennard 285
Kent, Elizabeth 99; Hannah, *formerly* Hannah Arnold 360; John 279, 343; Martha 279; Mary 99*, 343; Philip 99; Richard 373*; Thomas 364
Kentfick, Robert 102
Key, Richard 253
Kidman, John 223
Kildare, Sarah, and father 191
Kilder, James 326*
Killick (Killicke), Anne 175, 181; Elizabeth 244; James, and daughter 175; James, and infant 181; Jane 244; Mary 160; Ralph 160; Sarah 175, 181
Killingbeck (Killingbank), Humphrey 67
Kilner (Killner), Anson 249*; Caroline 2498; Edward 164, 328; Elizabeth 162, 173, 177; Fanny 249*; Frederick 249*; James 355; Jenny 164; John 177, 249*-250; Lydia 249*; Mary 164; Mary, and daughter 328; Richard 162; William 164
King (Kinge), ... 364; Anna 371; Anne 269, 310*, 333, 344; Anne, and daughter 66; David 81, 310*; Dorcas 324; Edmund 137; Edward 107, 268; Elizabeth 56, 62, 83, 156, 189, 349; Elizabeth, *alias* Elizabeth Tidy 64, 256*, 259-260; George 344; Hannah 264, 333*, 372; Henry 119, 261; Henry, and wife and family 318; James 216, 370; Jane 261; Jane, and father 260; Jenny 81; John 56, 83, 228, 300, 344; John, and wife 58; John, and wife and children 107; Joseph, and children 294; Mary 119, 135, 261, 264, 314; Mary, *alias* Mary Tidy 256*, 259-260; Peter 267, 269; Richard 54-55, 164, 266, 344, 370; Robert 310; Rosanne 164; Sarah 89, 95*, 119, 255, 261, 294; Thomas 68, 314, 333*, 371-372; William 56, 68, 119, 255, 261, 297, 314, 324; William, and family 214; William, and wife 59; William, jun 365; William, sen 365;
Kinsett, Elizabeth 235; Mary Anne 235; William 235
Kitchenham, William 325
Kn..., John 372
Knapp, William 241
Knight, Abraham 295; Anne 44; Avis 87; Barbara 63; Caleb 295; Edward 231; Eleanor 74; Eliza 63; Elizabeth 74, 164, 231*, 295; Elizabeth, and son 91, 95*; George 119, 204, 293; Henry 308; James 63, 74, 119, 293, 295, 315, 346, 358; John 74, 87, 119*, 221, 231, 264, 272, 295, 315, 373; John, and wife 308; Katherine 63; Lucy 295; Martha 74; Mary 44, 56, 87, 119, 119*, 272, 293, 336; Mary, *formerly* Mary Faulkner, 264, 266*; Mary Anne 336; Richard 52, 56, 74, 121, 140, 163*, 222, 267; Richard, and wife 58; Robert 163, 198; Sarah 44*, 119, 125, 156, 231, 293, 315, 346; Sophia, *alias* Sophia Easton 361; Susan 230, 233; Susan, and son 239; Susanna, and son 315; Thomas 63, 231*; Timothy 231; Timothy [female] 163; William 44*, 119, 164, 293
Knowles (Knolls, Knowls), Anne 61; Elizabeth 79-80; Fanny 61; James 79-80, 265; Jane 80; John 77, 283, 341; Philip 61, 265; Richard 265; Sarah 283*; Thomas 80*, 91; William 61
Knox, David, esq 330

L

Lack, John 341
Ladbury, John 112
Lagg, Robert 61*
Laker, Anne 173, 178, 286; James 286; John 173, 178; Louisa 231; Richard 231
Lamb, Esther, *later* Esther Crawford 339; William 53
Lambert, Jane 326; Joseph 326; Mary, *later* Mary Merritt 156
Lambton *alias* Dodswell, Edward 184
Lampon, Anne 323*; John 323*; Mary 323*; William 323*
Lanaway, Mary Anne 234; Thomas 234
Lander, Elizabeth 82; George 82
Lane, Anne 345; Anthony, and wife and children 289; Francis 163, 345; Hannah 163; Margery 129
Langden, Anne 165; Thomas 165
Langford, Elizabeth 85; Harriet 231; James 87*; John 71; Maria Anne 87; Mary 71; Sarah 83-84, 87; Sarah, and son 93, 98; Stephen 87; Thomas 83-84, 93
Langley, Anne 234; Susanna 166; William 240
Langridge (Lanridge), Anne 354*; Elizabeth 347, 349-350; Elizabeth, *formerly* Elizabeth Butcher 285; George 324; Henry 285; John 106, 347, 349-350*, 377;

Mary 324, 354; Richard 347, 350; Robert 354; Sarah 347*, 350*; Thomas 354; William 347, 350*, 354, 387
Lanham, Amy 251; Anne 251; Eliza Clare 251; Frances 251; Henry 251; Katherine Katharine, Katherin, Kathrien) Amy 251; Sophia 251; Susan Sarah 251
Lankaster, John 244
Lanridge *see* Langridge
Lasford, Frederick 50; John 50; Mary 50; Richard 110; William 50
Lashmar (Lashmer, Lashemore, Lashmore, Lasmer), Anne 186, 189, 195, 320-321; Edward 131; John 128, 330; Mary 113, 115; Richard 113, 115; Thomas 113, 115; William 133, 189; William, and wife and child 332
Latham, James 246
Latter, Edward 174, 202
Launders, Elizabeth 77; William, and parents 77
Lawrence, William 202
Leadbeater, Elizabeth 351*, 354*; Henry 351*, 354*; Mary 351*, 354*
Ledger, Andrew 221; Elizabeth 343; John 343; Mary 343*
Ledward, Hope 45; John 45*
Lee, Alice 147; Frances 147, 168, 176; Israel 384; Jane 291; John 72; Mary 147, 168*, 176*, 185; Philadelphia, and daughter 268; Phyllis 119; Richard 291; Sarah (Chapman) 384; Susanna 95*; Thomas 147*, 168*, 176*; *see also* Leigh
Leffan (Leffen), Elizabeth, and children 230; John 230; Mary, and son 239
Legate, Anne, and child 70
Legg, Anne 350; Elizabeth, *alias* Elizabeth Roser 350; James 350; John 238, 350; Joshua 350; Sarah 350; William, *alias* William Roser 350*
Leigh, Richard 102; *see also* Lee
Lelliott (Lelliot, Lilliot, Lilliott, Lylliott), Abraham 88; Anne 254; James 88; John 254, 305; Peter 240; Rebecca 85; Susan 88*; Susanna 85; Susanna, and Rebecca (Muzzale) her daughter 81; Thomas 242; William 85
Leney, Francis 266; James 116; Maria Grace 116; Phoebe 258*, 262
Leoford, Richard, and wife 159
Leonard, John 353*; Mary 353*
Leppard (Leopard), Anne 110; Anne, and son 302; Elizabeth 110, 322; Elizabeth, and daughter 266; Esther 175; James 110; Jenny 110; John 91, 95*, 110, 175; Mary 110, 294, 319, 322*; Mary, *formerly* Mary Ede 74; Richard 47; Sarah 110, 322; Thomas 74, 110*, 302, 322*; Thomas, and children 319; William 46, 322
Leury *see* Lency
Levens, Richard 216
Levett (Levet, Levitt), Anne 220; Francis 377; James 222; John 220; Richard 220; Thomas 219-220
Levis, Thomas 249
Levitt *see* Levett
Lewer, Matthew 281; Susanna 281; *see also* Lower
Lewery *see* Lewry
Lewis (Lewes, Lewice), Mr ... 157; Jane 160; Mary 160; Robert 160; Thomas 128
Lewry (Lewery, Lurey, Lury), Anne 352; David 263-264; Edmund 352; Elizabeth 262-263*; George 263; Henry 262*-263; Jane 57, 352; John 57, 352; John, and wife 59; John, and wife and family 343; Maria 263; Mary 262*; Richard 282, 287*, 301; Sarah 282, 287, 352; William 182, 263
Lidbetter, Elizabeth 346; Maria, *alias* Maria Roffey 355; Mary 346*; Richard 227*, 368; Thomas 346
Likeman, Harriet 144; Jesse 144; Susan 144
Lilliot, Lilliott *see* Lelliott
Lincoln, Anne 175, 181-182; James 175, 181-182
Lindfield (Lindfeild, Linfield), Anne 75, 335; Betty 201; Elizabeth 117*; Fanny 275; Frances 143; Henry 75*; James 63, 202; James, jun, gent 203; Joan 121; John 117, 143, 254*; Mary 63; Mary, *later* Mary Price 201; Samuel 117; Sarah 117, 201, 254, 270; Sophia 143; Thomas 143; William 252, 335
Lindley, Henry 378; Maria, and son 210
Linfield *see* Lindfield
Linken, James 183; Sarah 183
Linn *see* Lynn
Linney, Anne, and child 293
Lintott (Lintot), William 67
Lish, Anne 233; Eliza, *alias* Eliza Bennett 237; Elizabeth 237; Fanny, *alias* Fanny Bennett 237; Mary, *alias* Mary Bennett 237*; William 237
Lloyd, Lydia 285; Robert 369
Lock (Locke), Anne 159, 161*, 349; Elizabeth 162; John 65*, 161, 341, 347,

Lock (*contd*)
374; Robert 162; Thomas 65, 376; William, and children 159
Lockyer, Jane 207; Sarah 207
Long (Longe), Anne 233; David 233; Edward 233; Gervaise 150, 152; Henry 111*; John 252*, 255, 257; Mary 111, 255, 257
Longhurst, Anne 113, 116; Edward 88*; Elizabeth 324*; Lydia 191; Margaret 103; Thomas 324; William 113*, 116
Longley (Longlie, Longly), Anne 116, 374, 376; Edward 250; Elizabeth 250, 311; Frances 250, 375; Humphrey 376; James 242; James, and son 116; Jane 375; Martha 375; Mary 250*, 374; Richard 55, 236; Robert 250; Sarah 113, 115, 250; William 224, 250, 311
Lovelidge, Elizabeth 148, 169; Thomas 148, 169
Lovewell, Anne 286; Moses 286
Lower, Sophia 335; *see also* Lewer
Lucas, Edward 180*; Elizabeth 180*; John 317; Martha 180*; Mary, and child 216; Thomas 244; William 172, 192
Lucken (Luckin), Hannah 285; Richard, gent 124; Robert 285; Robert, *alias* Robert Luckins 301
Lulham, Benjamin 144; Charlotte 234; Eliza 234; Elizabeth, and son 207; Isaac 234*; John 171, 177, 205; Lucy 144
Lunn, William 188
Lurey, Lury *see* Lewry
Lusher, Robert 222
Lusted, Anne 192; Hannah 192; Jane 192; John 195; Lucy 192; Mary 192, 195; Rebecca 192, 195; Samuel 195; Sarah 192; Susanna 192, 195; William 195
Lutman (Luteman), Mary 56, 113*, 115; Mary, *formerly* Mary French 305; Thomas 56, 113*, 115, 120, 305; Thomas, and wife 58
Luxford, Charles 202; Charles, gent 203; John 139, 340, 350; Katherine, and son 240; Mary 250; Rachel 350
Lyewood, William 200, 219
Lylliott *see* Lelliott
Lynn (Linn), Edward 186; James 210; Sarah 354

M

Mabb, William 144
Mabsby, Sarah 122
Mackrell (Mackarrall), John 337; Richard 257
Malyan, Mary 188; Robert 188
Manfield, Mary 257
Manners, Henry 260, 263*
Mannywell, Anne 291
Mansbey *see* Mansby
Mansbridge, Elizabeth 87; Henry 63; James 63, 87; Mary, and son 90; Sarah 63; Thomas 63; Thomas Blake 87; William 63*, 87
Mansby (Mansbey), Anne 231, 233; Elizabeth 231*, 233*; Jane 231, 233; John 231*, 233*; Sarah 231, 233; Thomas 231, 233
Mansell, Anne, and daughter 241
Manson, Mary 102
Mantle, Edward 344; Jane 344; Joseph 344; Richard 344*; William 344
Manvell, Anne 234
Marchant (Marchent, Merchannt, Merchant), Anne 110, 118, 293-294, 356; Anne, and daughter 301; Betty 257; Edmund, jun, and father, wife and children 279; Edward 162; Elizabeth 44*, 110, 162, 164, 175, 294, 323; Henry 50, 110, 136; James 50*, 110, 329; John 44*-45, 62, 110; John, and wife and family 159; John, gent 126*; Martha 46, 50; Mary 50, 62*, 292; Michael 164; Sarah 45, 50; Susanna 110; Thomas 103-104, 164, 257; Thomas, sen 265; William 62, 292
Marden, Elizabeth 164; Henry 164; James 164; John 164*; John, jun 207; John, sen 207; Joseph 164; Mary 164; William 164
Marlett, John 308
Marner, James 163, 188; Sarah 163
Marsden, Mary 347; Rachel 347; Richard 347
Marshall, James 259; John 267; John, and wife and family 106
Martin (Martain, Marten), ... 161-162; Anne 41, 88*, 162, 178, 257, 272, 274; Anne, *formerly* Anne Pilbeam 86; Christopher 206; Edward 162, 164; Elizabeth 56-58, 106, 111, 162; Elizabeth, and son 268; Hannah, *later* Hannah Godman 59; Henry 41, 57; James 88*, 178; James, *alias* James Jenner 89, 93, 97*; Jane 287; John 57*, 179, 198, 250*, 274; John, and child 106; John, and children 59, 318; John, and wife and family 186; Joseph 225; Mary 57, 83-84, 121, 151, 170, 173, 177, 179, 192, 206, 213, 218, 250*, 318; Mary (Webb) 162; Michael 135, 277; Richard 136, 155;

Richard, and wife and family 159; Sarah 164; Susanna 164; Tho 161; Thomas 76, 155, 222, 250*, 287; W. 255; Widow 161; William 83*-84, 88*, 121, 156, 164, 179, 228, 250*; William, and infant 83-84, 121

Mascall (Maskall), Alice, and child 294; Benjamin 121; Charles 42; Edward, and wife 294; George 42; John 142, 188; Louisa 42; Richard 142; Sarah 42, 121, 142*; Thomas 142; William 42*, 142, 188

Mascoe, John 174; Katherine 174

Maskall *see* Mascall

Mason, Mr ... 379; Anne 76, 109*, 261; Elizabeth 333; Francis 76; Henry 283-284; Richard 373*; Sarah 76, 283-284; Susan 118; Susanna (Preston), and son 148; Thomas 283-284*, 333; William 76, 109, 207

Masters *alias* Roberson, Joseph 293

Mate, Matthew [female] 319; Richard 319

Mather, Gibbon 104, 112

Mathews *see* Matthews

Matthew, Elizabeth 75, 114, 116; George 268; Thomas 75, 114, 116

Matthews (Mathews), Elizabeth, and father and daughter 91; Jane 176; John 87; Lydia 82; Mary, and father and son 93; Nanny 82; Richard 176; Sarah 87; Sarah, *later* Sarah Hanshet 75

May, Charlotte 250, 361; Charlotte, and husband and family 379-380; Edward 270; Elizabeth 189; John, gent 168; Mr John 147; Joseph 361; Margaret 270; Mary 265, 361; Sarah, *alias* Sarah Hesketh 46; Sophia 334; William 270, 361

Maynard, Harber 164; James 164; John 164, 189; Mary 164, 334; Ruth 334; Sarah 164, 359

Mead, Mary 174, 180; Nicholas 318; Sarah 318*

Meads, James 192; William 192

Mears (Meeres), Anne 170; Elizabeth 144, 170; Joseph 150; Joseph, and daughter 170*; Mary 170; Thomas 144

Medhurst *see* Midhurst

Melleish, Thomas 155

Mepham, John 161; Susanna 161

Mercer, John 244; Sarah 255*; Thomas 255*

Merchannt, Merchant *see* Marchant

Merifields, Anne 102

Merritt, Mary, *formerly* Mary Lambert 156; Thomas 155

Messer, Anne 82; Peter 82, 89, 94

Mew (Mewe), John 277, 285; Margery 130; Mary 46; Mary Anne 143; Philadelphia 285; Sarah 143; William 130, 143

Miall, Amy 118*; John 118*; Joseph 191; Mary 191; Richard 191; Richard, *alias* Richard Mighell 124, 128

Michel, Michell *see* Mitchell

Middleton, Christopher Arthur 206, 224; John 206

Midhurst (Medhurst), Abigail 163; Anne 152; Edward 158, 168; Elizabeth 172; George 154, 163*; John 244; Margaret 163; Sarah 163; Susan 158; Thomas 245

Mighell *alias* Miall, Richard 124, 128

Mihill, John 374; Judith 109, 282; Katherine 374; Richard 109, 282, 374; Sarah 109, 282; Susanna 109, 282

Miles (Myles), Amy, *formerly* Amy Peckham 157; Anne 157, 191, 195, 306*, 334; Barbara, 70*, 258*; Betty 306; Edward, *or* Edward Mills 125; Elizabeth 131, 161, 354; Emy 191, 195; Esau 258; Harriet 191, 195; Henry 191, 195; James 46, 80, 161*, 191, 195, 258, 286, 347; James, and father 157; Jane 163; John 41, 46, 80, 161, 258, 261, 263, 282, 286, 306; Lydia 282; Maria 70; Mary 41, 46, 123, 128-129, 132, 183, 261, 263, 286, 334; Mildred 46, 286; Richard 128*, 131-132, 161; Sarah 80, 161*, 282, 334; Thomas 128, 161, 334, 354; Thomas, and wife 56, 59; William 70*, 154, 161, 163, 191, 195, 258, 282, 303, 334*

Mill, Susanna 178; *see also* Mills

Millams, Henry 146, 168

Miller, Anne 122*; Charles, *alias* Charles Sergeant 218; Elizabeth 337*; Esther 143; John 122*, 164, 330; Mary 122*, 164, 330; Thomas 122*; William 143, 164

Mills, Anne 189; Charity 276; Christian 142; Edward, *or* Edward Miles 125; Elizabeth 142; Elizabeth, and child 298; Elizabeth, and son 272; Frances 276; Frederick 276; Henry 142, 276; James 189; John 125*, 142, 223, 274, 344-345; Judith 344*; Katherine, and daughter 66; Mary 142*, 167*, 189, 344-345; Pierce 142;

Mills (*contd*)
Richard 75, 167, 223; Thomas 129, 205; Thomas, gent 204; Thomas, jun 205; William 129, 276, 348; *see also* Mill
Mirgen, Elizabeth 212
Mitchell (Michel, Michell, Mitchel), Alan 80; Anne 61, 80*, 89, 94, 142*, 165, 292; Anne, and daughter 210; Barbara 306; Charity 287; Charlotte 307; Edmund 99, 142*; Edward 292; Eliza 87; Elizabeth 41, 62, 87, 123*, 142*, 161, 170, 177, 205, 263, 321; Fanny 117; Fanny, and son 263; Frances 142*; George 126, 135, 321; Hannah 56, 80, 206, 262*; Harriet 306; Henry 123, 125, 128, 132, 292, 295; Isaac 80, 92; James 152, 161, 170, 177, 268, 306, 361; Jane 62, 123*, 296*; John 43, 75, 123*, 138-139, 161, 170, 177, 190, 254, 292, 307; John Awcocke 296; Katherine 62*; Katherine, and daughter 66; Lucy 80, 165; Lucy, and husband 275; Lucy, *alias* Lucy Jenden 88*; Lydia 76; Mary 82, 99, 117, 123*, 134, 142*, 161*, 170*, 177*, 190, 216, 254, 295, 306; Mary Anne 307; Matilda 361*; Philadelphia 99, 142*; Philip 56, 61; Philip, and wife 58; Rebecca 63; Richard 62, 134, 142*, 239; Richard, *alias* Richard Taylor 138; Sarah 61-62, 75, 118, 123*, 142*, 161, 165, 170, 177, 230, 290, 292, 295; Sarah, and son 94; Sarah, *later* Sarah Stringer 91; Stephen 62, 80; Thomas 68, 75, 78, 87, 114, 123*, 295, 297, 303; Thomas, and wife 99; William 62, 76, 88, 165, 230, 275, 307*; William, and children 75; William, and wife and family 165; William, *alias* William Bennett 261
Mitchellborne, John 215; John, jun 215; John, sen 215
Mitten, Henry 130
Moatt, Mary 159; Philip 159
Mobsby, Henry 89
Mobsly, Lucy, and daughter 93
Mockford, George 113
Molesworth, Col ... 150
Monk (Moncke, Monke), Elizabeth 350; John 222; Sarah, and son 200; William 355
Monkton (Munkton), Anne 186; Anne, and husband 378-379; Anne, and son 197; John 186, 197
Montague, Lucy 174, 179
Moon, William 156, 190; William, and family 214
Moore (Moor, More), Mr ... 215; Anne 61, 297*; Anne, and child 97*; Anne, and father 89; Anne, and father and son 92*; Mrs Anne 128; Charles 314; Christian 84; Edward 256; Edward, and family 284, 286; Edward, and wife 41; Elizabeth 84, 333, 335; Elizabeth, and daughter 92, 96; George 238, 243, 255; Hannah 255; Henry 133*; John 84, 333, 335; Lydia 83-84*; Lydia, and son 96; Mary 314; Ralph, and wife 232*; Richard 84*; Richard, and infant 84; Stephen 84; Thomas 333*, 335*
Moreton *see* Morton
Morgan (Morgen), Elizabeth 221; Henry 242; James 91, 94; John 200, 235; Katherine 372; Nicholas 176; Reze 372*; Richard 235; Sarah 372; Susanna 221
Morley, Anne 192-193; Edwin 143; Elizabeth 69, 82, 143, 199, 254; George 69; George, and family 254; Henry 82, 143*; James 82; Jane 82; Joan 129; Jo[?hn], 129*; John 129, 244, 342; Katherine 82; Louisa 143; Mary 269; Richard 82; Ruth 321; Sarah 82, 143; Sarah Anne 143; William 82*, 192, 321, 342
Morphew, William 224
Morrell, Mary, and mother 294; William, and mother 294
Morris (Morrice), Mr ... 268; Anne 57*; Benjamin 277; Humphrey 113, 115; James 225; Jane 192, 265; John 57, 192*, 284; Mary 113, 115, 125, 284; Sarah 57; Susanna 57; Thomas 57; Thomas, and wife and family 59; *see also* Norris
Morton (Moreton, Mortten), Anne 295; Anthony 130; James, esq 52; Jane 116
Mose (Mosse), James 81; Mary 81; William, and wife 56, 58
Moth, Eliza 310; Esther 310; George 310; Harriet 310; Jane 310; Jemima 310; Phoebe 310; Samuel 310; William 310
Mott, Mr ... 157
Mougridge *see* Mugridge
Mountjoy, Lord ... 150
Mowgridge *see* Mugridge
Muddle, Charles 294; Edmund 181; Elizabeth 181; Mary 181; Phoebe 181; Stephen, and infant 181; Susanna 170*, 177*;

William 170; William, and wife and child 161; William, and wife and children 159; William, jun 177
Mugridge (Mougridge, Mowgridge, Muggridge), Anne 272; Edward 272; Elizabeth 272; James 272; John 272*; John, and wife and family 272; Mary 272*; Richard 282, 287; Sarah 282, 287; Thomas 272
Munery, Anne 311; Edward 311; John 311; Mary 311; Michael 311
Munkton *see* Monkton
Murrell (Murrall), Edward 274, 276; Eleanor 274; Eleanor, *formerly* Eleanor Riddles 276*; James 328; John and wife and child, 281; John, jun 65; John, sen 65
Mutton, James, gent 264; Thomas 264; William 257
Muzzell (Muzzale, Muzzall), Abel (Abell) 254; Abraham 254; Elizabeth 235, 254; Hannah 236; Henry 254; John 235; Mary 254; Rebecca, and Susanna (Lelliott) her mother 81; Thomas 236; William 254
Myles *see* Miles

N

Nailard, Mrs ... 89; Elizabeth 65*; Jane 65*
Naish *see* Nash
Napper, Elizabeth 113, 115; Henry 113, 115; Phyllis 113, 115; Robert 108, 113, 115; Sarah 113, 115; Sarah, *formerly* Sarah Parrott 108
Nash (Naish), Anne 159; Hugh 384; James 172; John 164; Mary 164, 172; Sarah 343; William 159; William, and children 343; William, and wife 254
Naylor, Elizabeth 106, 114
Neal (Neale), Elizabeth 194; James 194; John 194; Mary 194, 321; Thomas 321
Nelson (Nellson), Elizabeth 316, 348; Jane 316; Richard 348; Richard, and wife and family 159; Susan 348*
Netlingame, Nicholas 364; Sarah 364
Newick, Hannah 110; John 110
Newland, ... 103; John 269
Newman, Anne 79; Henry 333; James 78*; James, and parents 340; James, *or* James Newnham 82*; Mary 78*, 340; Mary, *or* Mary Newnham 82*; Rachel 333; William 78-79; William, *or* William Newnham 82
Newnham (Newnam), Anne 231; Elizabeth 160, 169; James, *or* James Newman, 82*; John 71; John Watson 193; Mary 231*; Mary, *or* Mary Newman, 82*; Peter, and parents 74; Thomas 149, 160, 169, 231*, 339; William, *or* William Newman, 82*; *see also* Nunham
Newton, George, gent 303
Nichalls *see* Nicholls
Nicholas (Nicholass), Anne 346; Bet 346; Elizabeth 46; Harry 346; John 346, 373; Mary 257, 346; Mercy 373; William 212, 346*
Nicholl (Nycoll), Edward, jun 220; Edward, sen 220
Nicholls (Nichalls, Nichols, Nickalls), Lydia 292*; Susanna 355; Thomas 292*, 366, 370; Walter 292; William 267, 269
Nightingale, Robert 111, 114
Nixon, John 90
Noble, Ambrose 120; Charles 120; Charlotte 120; Horace 120; Julia 120; Sarah 120; Susan 120; Walter 120; William 120
Nolan, Mr ... 78
Norman, Anne 233*; Barbara 251*; Charlotte 327*; Elizabeth 130, 251*; James 275; Jane 275; Joan 130; John 251*; Martha 333; Richard 130; Robert 170, 177; Sarah 251*; Sophia 251*; Susanna 251*; Thomas 175, 181, 260, 360; William, and children 160
Norris, Edward 287; Elizabeth 287; Faith 287; Hannah 294; John 294*; Sally 287; Sarah 287; Thomas 106, 287*; *see also* Morris
Northampton, Rt Hon the Countess Dowager of 150
Norton, Mr ... 386-387*, 388; Barbara 334; John 245, 247; William 334
Noys, Anne 179; Elizabeth 179; John 179*; Mary 179
Nunham, Thomas 212; *see also* Newnham
Nutley (Nuttley), Esther 319; Henry 128, 132; John, and wife and family 141*; Richard 319; William 131
Nycoll *see* Nicholl
Nye, Anne 82*, 84*; Benjamin 61, 118, 234; Frances 234-235, 260; George 113, 115, 118, 234; Hannah 56, 109; Henry 111; James 56, 254; Jane 56, 109, 254, 256; John 56-57, 82, 84, 109, 297; John, and wife 59; John, jun 82, 84; Martha 118; Mary 56-57, 67, 254; Richard 56, 254, 266, 297; Richard, and

Nye (*contd*)
wife and children 58; Sarah 56, 234*, 266; Susanna 118; Thomas 66, 136; Thomas, and infant 234; Thomas, jun 264; Thomas, sen 264

O

Ockenden (Ockendean), Edward 62; Henry 62*; James 52; John 52-53; John, and wife and family 59; Mary 62*; Samuel 62; Sarah, 127Marten, Thomas 127
Older, Benjamin 292; John 292; Mary, and mother and son 299; Richard 108; Sarah 108, 265, 292; Thomas 245, 292
Olfrey, Mary 343; Richard, and children 343
Oliver, Joseph 350; Ruth 139
Ollive, Anne 193, 196; Caley 193, 196; Eliza 193, 196; Elizabeth 193*, 196*; John 193, 196; Mary 193, 196; William 193, 196
Olly, Thomas 141
Oram (Oreham), Anne 70; Charles 340; Daniel 66; Henry 63, 69*-70; John 63; Lucy 69; Lydia 69; Philadelphia 276*; Sarah 70; Stephen 70; Susannh 63
O'Reyly, Roger 103
Orgles, John 160, 212; Sarah 160
Osborne (Osborn, Osbourne), Abraham 204; Anne 161; Anne, and daughter 199; Charles 281; Edward 114; John 161; Thomas, and wife 176, 286
Ottaway, Hannah 163; John 163; Mary 163
Ottive, Anne 41
Ousley, Edward 134; Frances 134
Outridge, ... 317
Ovell (Oval, Ovel), Elizabeth 161; John 104, 146, 154, 156, 161*, 249; John, and wife and children 168; Sarah 161*; Winifred 187, 198; Winifred, *later* Winifred Smith 171; Winifred, *later* Winifred Smith, and father and son 155; Winny 156, 172
Overton, Anne 310*; Eliza 310; Harriet 310; James 310; John 310; Mary 310; Obed 310*; Thomas 310; William 310
Owden, Hannah 121; John 121; Robert 121; Sarah 325; Susan 121; Thomas 325
Owen, John 108; Susan 108

P

Packett (Packet), Edward 334*; Frances 143; Lydia 334; Mary 334
Packham, Anne 275; Celia 326; Elizabeth, 275, Elizabeth, *later* Elizabeth Simmons 314; Fanny 117; Henry 275; Henry, *alias* Henry Simmons 314; John, *alias* John Packham Stoner 270; Judith 319; Mary 117, 275; Mary, and daughter 216; Peter, jun 117; Thomas 117, 319; William, jun 275; *see also* Peckham
Packham Stoner, John, *alias* John Packham, 270
Pagden, Anne 287; John 287
Page (Paige), Anne Bradford 88; Edward 270; Eliza 191, 285, 287; Elizabeth 282, 350*; George 246; Hannah 191, 285, 287, 291, 312; James 86; John 88, 166, 173, 185, 191, 274*, 285, 287, 303, 350; John, and family 282; John, and wife and children 107; Joseph 57; Lydia 57; Mary 166, 173, 189, 236*, 350; Richard 219, 303; Richard, and wife and family 281; Robert 236*; Ruth 236*; Thomas 128-129, 350*
Paice, John 222
Paige *see* Page
Pain, Paine *see* Payne
Painter, John 175*, 180*; Mary 175, 180; Sarah 175*, 180*
Paley, Thomas 208
Palmer, Alice 160; Anne 348, 352*, 359*; Charlotte 87; Christian 348, 352*; Henry 348, 352*, 359; John 348, 352*, 359; Maria 359; Mary 348, 352*; Mary, *later* Mary Arnold *alias* Davis 87; Nicholas 160; William 160, 348, 352*
Pamplin, William Solomon 260*
Panfold, Harding 142; Lucy 142
Pannell *or* Powell, Edward 83, 85; Mary 83*, 85*; Rebecca 83, 85; William 83, 85
Pannett, John 256; Sarah 256
Paris (Parris), Amy 177; Elizabeth 170, 177; John 170*, 177*, 279; Susanna 279
Parke *see* Parks
Parker, Mrs ... 93; Amos 117; Anne 117, 229, 325; Caroline 196*; Cordelia 325; Edward 69; Eliza Anne 196*; Elizabeth 117*, 358; Frances 277; George 351, 354; Harriet 196*; Harriet, and son 210; Henry 190, 196*, 212, 228, 241, 340, 350; Isaac 238; James 238, 325; John 286, 288; Joseph 317, 325*, 351, 354; Lucy 325; Martha 122; Mary 117, 277, 351, 354; Mary, *alias* Mary Sayer 277; Phoebe 325; Sarah 190*, 196*, 286, 288, 340*, 350*, 351, 354, 358, 363*; Susanna

196*; Thomas 190, 350-351, 354; Thomas, and parents 340; William 117, 200; William, and wife and children 362
Parkes *see* Parks
Parkhurst, Elizabeth 346; William 346
Parks (Parke, Parkes), Christopher 234, 284; Richard 130*
Parris *see* Paris
Parrott *later* Napper, Sarah 108
Parry, Edward 231, 234; Elizabeth 231; Jane 231, 234; John 231, 234; Mary 231*, 234*; William 231*, 234*
Parrym, Elizabeth 234
Parsons (Parson), Alan 114; Alan *or* James 115; Anne 121, 253, 264, 284, 286; Caroline 60, 63; Charles 93; Dorothy 121; Edmund 253; Edward 60, 63, 243; Eliza 260, 263; Elizabeth 109, 121, 264; Elizabeth, and son 239; Francis 303; George 109, 260, 263, 295*; Henry 303; Isaac 142, 283*, 285*; James 93, 98, 142*; James *or* Alan 115; Jane 60, 260*, 263*, 350; Jenny 67; John 66-67, 108, 121, 135, 244, 260, 263, 361*; John, and wife 253*; Joseph 257; Katherine 253; Mary 108*, 115*, 202, 232, 271; Nicholas 60, 63, 67; Philip 115*; Richard 135, 303; Samuel 271; Sarah 65, 108, 232, 255*, 257, 271*, 295*, 361; Susanna 257, 283, 285; Thomas 139, 253, 255*, 257; William 108, 215, 232*, 295*
Passell, John, and wife and family 114; Martin 135
Patching, Christian 231; Elizabeth 235; James 192; Peter 228; Susan 230; Thomas 230
Paterson, John 49
Pattenden, Charlotte, and father and daughter 47-48; Edward 249; Frances 249; Hannah 119, 195, 236; Harriett 48; Jeremiah 195, 204, 209, 223; John 249; Joseph 347; Mary 223; Sarah 319, 347; Mr T. 325; Thomas 204, 249, 319, 347*; Thomas, and wife and children 322; William 347
Payne (Pain, Paine, Payn, Peine), ... 381; Anne 62*-63, 184, 194*, 199*, 329; Bet 118; Mr Charles 149; Charles Newnham 183; Cornelius 118; Daniel 63; Edward 216, 220-221, 290, 321; Elizabeth 160, 344; Ellen 357; Frances 188*, 321, 323; Hannah 144, 183; Hannah, and son 210; Harriet 118; Harrington 223; Henry 201; James 52, 62*, 213; James, and daughter 314; Jane 159, 192, 357*; Jane, and son 217; Jeremiah 139*; John 139, 159, 175, 181, 199*, 203-204, 224, 259*, 344, 361, 363, 369, 385; John, and wife and child 230; John, and wife and family 337; Katherine 314*; Lucy 178, 213; Martha 166, 320, 362; Mary 166, 225, 233*, 259, 285, 361; Mary Anne 118, 175, 181; Matilda 118; Nicholas 188*, 321-322; Rebecca 175, 181; Rhoda 118; Richard 159, 199, 218, 225, 237; Robert 118, 178, 188, 213; Samuel 118; Sarah 170, 320; Sarah, and daughter 240; Sophia 320; Stephen 357; Susanna 62*, 177; Thomas 144, 166, 192, 201*, 217, 285; Thomas, and wife and children 321; Walter 62*, 101; William 118, 160, 175, 181, 183, 194*, 199, 211*, 320*, 360, 363
Peacock (Peacocke), John 306; Katherine 306; Peter 306; Thomas 313*, 315*; William 306
Peacy, Sarah 206
Pearce (Peirce, Perce, Pierce), Benjamin 323; Elizabeth 54, 64, 308; Frances 281; Godfrey 101; Harriet 98; Henry 56, 333; Henry, and wife 58; Jane 120, 122, 323; John 54*, 64, 308; Joseph 281, 333; Judy 333; Mary 54, 86, 294, 333; Richard 73; Sarah 56, 309*, 323; Thomas 86; Thomas, and father 74; William 309*, 333
Pearsen, John 149
Peat, Elizabeth 346; John 346
Peckham, Amy, *later* Amy Miles 157; Anne 143, 202-203, 326; Edward 287; Elizabeth 134, 287; James 206, 287; Jane 123; John 252, 299; M 287; Mary 109, 206; Richard 123; Thomas 109; William 330; *see also* Packham
Peeters *see* Peters
Peine *see* Payne
Peirce *see* Pearce
Peircey (Peircy), John 138
Pelham, Abraham 131; Frances 41; James 96
Peling, Richard 132
Pell, John 236
Pellatt *see* Pellett
Pellen, Jerimy 248
Pellett (Pellatt), Richard 245; Thomas 156
Pelling, Agnes 129; Richard 129; Thomas 128, 133
Penfold (Pendfold, Penefold, Pennifold), Anne 285,

Penfold (*contd*) 311*; Edward 311*; Elizabeth 311*, 346; Elizabeth, and daughter 238; Frank 116; Hannah 349, 352; James 255*, 269; Jane 311*; John 110, 116, 374-376; Martha 311*; Mary 311*, 377; Phyllis 311*; Richard, and father 72; Mr Richard 229; Sarah 116; Sarah, and children 345; Sarah, and son 327; Susanna 255; Thomas 66, 270, 339, 346; William 255, 285, 345

Pentecost (Penticourst), Edward 196; Elizabeth 108; Henry 196; Isaac 196; John 108; Martha 196; Mary 287; Philadelphia 118*; Priscilla 287, 295*; Ruth 108; Sarah 196; Thomas 108, 196; William 196*

Pepper (Peper), Edward 134; John 130; Katherine 137-138; Richard 130; Thomas 130, 149

Perce *see* Pearce

Periman, Walter 102

Perrier (Perryer), George 182; Mary 272*; Thomas 272

Perrin, Anne 282; Mary 282; Richard 282; Susan 309; Susanna 282; Thomas 282*, 309

Perry, Henry 223; John 223; Thomas 67; William 116

Pescud, William 361

Peskett (Pesket, Peskitt), Anne 86; James 86; Rebecca 86; Sarah 310; William 86, 227-228*

Peter, Anne 69; Elizabeth 69*; Henry 69*; John, and wife and family 230; Mary 69; Thomas 69; William 69

Peters (Peeters), Alexander 199, 216; Anne, *alias* Anne Heasman 63; Charles 57; Edward 57; Edward, and wife and family, 59; Edward, *alias* Edward Turner 355; Hannah 90, 94; Henry 57; James 57, 65; Jane 256; Mary 57, 64, 113, 115; Mary, and son 91; Richard 256; Samuel 57; Sarah 57; Stephen 108; Thomas 137; William 113*, 115*

Pettit (Pettet), Elizabeth 113; Robert 159

Philcox, John 45

Philips *see* Phillips

Phillary, Phillery *see* Fillery

Phillips (Philips, Phillipps), John 107; Richard 245, 324; Thomas 103; Mr William 78

Phillpott *see* Philpott

Philp, Emily 100*; Esther 100*; Henry 100*; John 100*; Joseph 100*; Richard 100*; William 100

Philpott (Phillpott), Elizabeth 102; Mary 306

Pickard, George Gerrard 314; Mary, *later* Mary Stenning 314

Picke, Elizabeth 112; Henry 222; James 112

Pickett, Anne 258; Benjamin 183; Eliza 183; Ellen 183; Esther 183; Frederick 183; Henry 258; Jane 258; John 258; Martha 183; Nathaniel 258; Sarah 183, 258; Thomas 183; William 258

Picknell (Picknall, Picknold), John 104, 278; Samuel 119; Sarah 64; Thomas 64; Thomas, jun 238; Thomas, sen 238; *see also* Bignall

Pierce *see* Pearce

Pierciefield, Richard 102

Pigott, John 150, 170

Pilbeam (Pilbeame), Anne 107; Anne, *later* Anne Martin 86; George 107; Henry 139; John 89, 265; John, jun 125; John, sen 125; Katherine 107; Mary, *later* Mary Titkell 107; Mary Anne 86, 91; Sarah 86; Sophia, and son 48; Stephen 333*; William 86, 265; William, and wife and child 250

Pilfold, Mr Thomas 245

Pillven, Sarah 87

Pim, Anne 285; John 285

Pinion, John 297; Mary, *formerly* Mary Vinall, and son 297

Piper, Daniel, jun 203; Daniel, sen 203; John 203, 265, 333; John, and wife and children 281; Mary 333

Pitman, Katherine, *formerly* Katherine Wimark 159; Robert 159*

Plummer, John 380; Katherine 85; Sarah, *alias* Sarah Ayres 284

Pobgee, William 109, 163, 214

Pocknell, Barbara 160; Francis 220; Thomas 160, 219-220

Pocock, Sarah (Puplett) 148; Thomas 67

Pointing, Sarah 276

Pollard, Anne 80; Frances 82; James 82; John 80, 220; Joseph 118*; Mary 82, 320, 322, 350; Philip 320, 322; Ruth 118*; Sarah 80, 82; Thomas 80*, 320, 322; William 118*

Pomfrey, Elizabeth 335*

Pooley, Anne, and son 93, 97; Barbara 95

Pope, Betty 172*; Charles 172; John 171, 177; Thomas 172

Popey, James 91

Port, Elizabeth 143; John 143; Mary 270; Mary, and daughter 268-269; Thomas 270

Porter, John 241*, 294
Post, Anne 213; Charles 171; Edward 188, 213, 321-322; John 275, 330; Lucy 275; Sarah 188, 321-322
Potlett, Mercy, *alias* Mercy Potter, and daughter 299*
Potter, Anne 349; Charles, and parents 342*; Charlotte 342; Edward 343; Elizabeth 349*; Esther 187, 321-322*; Francis 173; Hallamsby 187, 321-322*; James 352; John 214, 342, 348-349*; Joshua 187*, 321-322*; Katherine 173, 343; Kenward 360; Leonard, and wife 110; Louisa 342; Maria 342; Mary 64; Mary, and daughter 66; Mary, and son 67; Mercy, *alias* Mercy Potlett, and daughter 299*; Sarah 349; Stephen 275; Susanna 344; Thomas 342*, 349; Thomas, and children 344; William 298, 343, 366
Poulter, Gerrard 61
Pound, ... 325
Powell (Powel), Mr ... 153; Anne 282; Edward, *or* Edward Pannell 83, 85; Joseph, *alias* Joseph Coomber 183; Mary, *or* Mary Pannell 83*, 85*; Rebecca, *or* Rebecca Pannell 83, 85; Richard 282; Samuel 287; William, *or* William Pannell 83, 85
Pownteine *alias* Bartholomew, John 370
Preston, Henry 148; Susanna (Mason) 148
Prevat, John, and children 344; Susan 344
Price (Pryce), Edward 101, 147; Edward, gent 201; John 194; Maria 194; Mary, *formerly* Mary Lindfield 201; Richard 240
Prince, William 146, 168
Pring, Elizabeth 160; Isaac 112*, 123, 128, 159; Isaac, and wife 148; Jacob 160; Jane 160; John 159, 189; Mary 112; Temperance (Tooth) 159
Prior (Pryer), Elizabeth 116; James 116; Samson 190; Susanna 157*, 190*; Thomas 156, 190
Pritchard, Edward 143*; Elizabeth 143
Pritchett, Thomas 164
Proctor, John 123
Pronger, Edmund 69*; James 240; Peter 69*; Richard, and wife and children 83; Robert 256; Sarah 69*, 256; Susanna 69*
Provet, Samuel 259*; Susan 259*
Prudden, John 153*, 170; Timothy, *alias* Timothy Hartop [female] 152, 170
Prudent, John 326; Sarah 326
Pryce *see* Price
Pryer *see* Prior
Pullen, John 345; Mary 345; Sarah 345; Thomas 345
Puplett, John 148, 169; Sarah (Pocock) 148, 169; Thomas 169
Purdey, Joseph, and wife 343
Purser, Anne 57; Diana 57; Edward 57; Edward, and wife and family 59; Thomas 57; Thomas, and wife 107
Purvey, Joan 82; Richard, and wife and family 79; Sarah 82
Puryour, Thomas 303
Putham, Dame ... 156
Putland, Anne 185, 195; John 185, 195; Lydia 185, 195; Thomas 185, 195; William 185, 195, 197
Puttock, Anne 41; Elizabeth 119*; Mary Anne 119; Phoebe 310; Thomas 41; William 310

Q

Quaife, Henrietta 122; Mary 122
Quinnell (Quennell, Quinel, Quinell), Diana, *alias* Diana Styleing 197; Elizabeth 334; Jane 202; Richard 197-198; Richard, *alias* Richard Styleing 198; Samuel 334; Thomas 202

R

Rabson, Thomas 289
Raby, Mr ... 317
Radford, Anne 47; Thomas 47
Railton, Joseph, and wife and child 96
Ramsdon, Rev Mr ... 43
Ramsey, Martha 272
Ramton, Mary 221; Richard 200
Randall (Randal, Rendall, Randoll), ..., and wife and family 114; Edmund 128; Joan 128, 131; John, and wife and family 110
Randalls (Randals), Elizabeth 282; Jane 282; John, *alias* John Randolph 304; William 282
Randoll *see* Randall
Randolph *alias* Randalls, John 304
Rapley, Anne 109, 113, 116; James 109, 113, 116, 135; Moses 116
Rastrigg, John 203
Rawley (Rawlie), Anne 334; Elizabeth 245; Thomas 334
Read, Reade *see* Reed
Reads, John 73
Ready *see* Reddy
Reason, Philip 104
Reddy (Ready), Bet 156; Elizabeth 165-166, 175, 180; James, and father 156; Jenny 156, 165; John 156, 165; Katherine 151; Lewis (Lewes) 151, 175, 180; William 166
Redman, Edward 227

Reed (Read, Reade), Anne 292, 324, 342; George 257; John 321, 323; Katherine 321, 323; Mary 41; Philadelphia, and son 302*; Samuel 369; Sarah 301; Thomas 350; Thomas Payne 292, 324, 342; William 292, 301, 324, 342

Reeding, Sarah 249

Reeve, Anne 257*; James 254; John 79; Mary 257; Samuel 257; Samuel, and wife 58; Sarah 254*; Simon 257; Stephen 254, 257*; Thomas 254; Zephaniah 257

Reeves, Edward 313-314*; Elizabeth 313-314*; Harriet 313-314*; James 313-314*; John 70, 313-314*, 321; Katherine 313-314*; Louisa 310; Lucy 313-314*; Lydia 321; Mary 69, 321; Matthew 160; Peter 313-314*; Phyllis 321; Richard 313-314*; Sarah, *alias* Sarah Bourne 355; Stephen 313, 314*; Susan 160; Susanna 321; William 313-314*

Relfe, Thomas 337; Thomas, jun 148; Thomas, sen 148

Rendall *see* Randall

Renfield (Renfeild), Hannah 238; Hannah, and daughter 239; Pierce 57, 59, 108; Thomas 57, 59, 108, 236, 278

Rennolds, Renolds, Renowls *see* Reynolds

Renville (Renvell), Anne 333; John 333; Sarah, and son 264

Revet, William 253

Reynolds (Rennolds, Renolds, Renowls), Anne 353; Elizabeth 353; George 353; George, *alias* George Fox 219; Hannah 353; John 220; Mary 353*; Sarah 284, 286, 353; Thomas 353; William 284, 286, 353*, 370; William, *alias* William Fox 220

Rice, Eleanor, *alias* Eleanor Whaley 324; Elizabeth 110, 174, 179, 360; James 374, 376; John 110*; John, and family 361; John, and parents 341; Jonathan 367; Mary 174*, 179*, 360*; Sarah 110; Susanna 110; Thomas 174*, 179*, 360*; William *alias* William Whaley 324, 360

Rich, Mary 169; Sarah 169; Thomas 169*; William 169

Richardson, Adam 152; Anne 180, 255, 313; Elizabeth 180, 315*; Fanny 250; Francis 57*, 250; Hannah 180; Henry 57, 73, 123, 250, 283; James 180; James, and daughter 261, 263; Jenny 57, 59; John 57, 250, 255, 283, 313*; Lydia 261, 263; Mary 123, 180, 250, 255*, 283; Matilda 250; Riah 283; Richard 123; Susan 57; Thomas 138, 313; William 57, 73, 123, 149, 250, 255

Richbill, Elizabeth 318; John 318

Rickwood, Thomas 284

Riddles (Riddalls), Eleanor, *later* Eleanor Murrell 276*; James 276*

Rideout, Rev W. 229

Ridge, Henry 374-375; James 375; John 376; Mary 322, 375; Nicholas 374; Thomas 322*

Ridgway, Edward 221; Mary 222

Ridley (Ridly), Anne 62, 249*, 360; Edward 62, 278, 360; Elizabeth 191, 199, 216, 355; Elizabeth, and daughter 299; Henry 293, 296; Mary 293, 296; Milly 354; Richard 243; Sarah 293, 296; Sarah, and son 300, 302; Thomas 243, 374; William 249*, 373

Rigglesford (Rigglesfoord), William 289*, 294

Right *see* Wright

Ringfield, Anne 241

Risbridger, Robert 109; Sarah 109

Rist, John, and wife and children 109

Rivers, Elizabeth 109*; Elizabeth Tamar 160; Guy 109; Henry 160; Jane 160; Samuel 160

Roach, Jenny 164; Mary 164; Philley 164; Rachel 164; Sall 164; Thomas 164; William 164, 253

Roads, Mary 54; William 54

Roaks (Rokes), Felix 224; John 149

Roberdes *see* Roberts

Roberson, John 165; Joseph, *alias* Joseph Masters 293

Roberts (Roberdes), Anne 253*; Bridget 370; Elizabeth 163; John 104; Stephen 211, 253; William 101, 163*, 370, 373*

Robins, Thomas 141; Tobias 103

Robinson, Elizabeth 42; James 42*; Lydia 42; Mary 42; Rudgwick 42

Roborow, Henry 44

Roddell, Amy 192; John 192

Roe, Martha 358; Sarah 358; Sarah [*recte* Martha] 358

Roffey (Rofe, Rofey, Roffe, Roffee), Edward 182; Henry 174, 180; James 284; Job 353; John 174, 180; John, and wife and family 370; Lazarus 198, 353*; Maria 174, 180, 355; Maria, *alias* Maria Lidbetter 355; Richard 245, 369; Robert 353; Sarah 173-174, 180, 182, 353, 361; William 174,

180
Rogers, Charles 284; Charles, and parents 277; Elizabeth 361; James 246; John 116; Mary 284; Sarah 116
Roker, John 244
Rokes *see* Roaks
Roode, Anne, *alias* Anne Sibley 186; Elizabeth, *alias* Elizabeth Sibley 186; Rebecca 186; Rebecca, *alias* Rebecca Sibley 186-187; Richard, *alias* Richard Sibley 186; Susanna, *alias* Susanna Sibley 186
Rook, John 257*; Sarah 257; Thomas 257
Rosar *see* Roser
Rose, Elizabeth 186*, 195*; Richard 186*, 195*, 222; Sarah 186*, 195*
Roser (Rosar), Anne 319; Barbara 319; Elizabeth 44, 319; Elizabeth, *alias* Elizabeth Legg 350; John 44, 319; Margery 284; Maria, and daughter 296, 299; Mary 319; Richard 299; Susan 319; William, *alias* William Legg 350*
Rovery, Anne 356; Hannah 356; James 356; Jane 356; Sarah 311, 361; Thomas 311, 356*, 361; Timothy 356; William 311
Rowland (Rowlande), Charity 116; George, jun 116; Henry 62; James 61-62, 85, 315; John 315, 371*; Nathaniel 61, 85; Rebecca 315*; Sarah 62, 256; Thomas 61, 85, 256, 371*-372; Thomas, and wife and daughters 61, 85; William 315, 372
Ruddock, Charles 45; Hannah 45; Maria 45; Robert 45*; William 45
Russell (Russel), Anne 178*; Anne, and son 197, 209; Anthony 195, 201; Charles 173; Cornelius 352; Edward, and infant 185; Elizabeth 185, 195; John 155-156, 178*, 377; John, sen 201; Mary 173; Ralph 373; Richard, and wife and family 56, 58; Sarah 187, 195; William 128, 296, 299-300
Rutley, John 367
Rye, Edward 193

S

Sackville, Lord John 105
Sadler, William 143
Salcombe, Mary 296*; Samuel 296; Sarah 296
Salisbury, Alice 344; Thomas 344, 349
Salter, Nicholas 128, 132
Sammes (Samms), Samuel 303
Sandal, Peter 292
Sandells (Sandalls), Anne 326; Bet 250; Elizabeth 250, 292, 295, 326; Esther 250; George 326*; Hannah 326; John 250; Mary 250; Samuel 292*, 295*; Stephen 292, 295; Susanna 290; Thomas 290*
Sanders, Abraham 53; Barbara 51*; Daniel 165; Elizabeth 144, 205, 233*, 345; Henry 61; James 144*; John 51*, 233*, 345, 352; Katherine 345*; Mary 345, 352; Richard 189; Sarah 61, 165, 189; Thomas 51*; *see also* Saunders
Sandford (Sanford), George 356; Jane 356; Mary 118; Sarah 118, 356*; Thomas 118, 356*; William 356
Sarjent *see* Sergeant
Saunders, Charles, and parents 77; Charlotte 122; Elizabeth 122, 255*; James 122*; Jenny 122; John 78, 255*, 348; Katherine 365; Margaret 122; Mary 78*, 348; Richard 138; Sarah 122; Thomas 255; William 122, 138; *see also* Sanders
Savage (Savadg, Savadge), ... 78; Alan 129, 132, 134*; Anne 197; Charles 136; Dorothy 124; John 64; Samuel 137; Sarah 64; Thomas, and father 112
Sawyer, Ann Baker 165; Elizabeth 165; George 174; John 91, 95*, 203; Richard 165; Stephen 206
Sawyers, John, and father 317
Saxby (Saxbye), Robert 151; William 324, 326
Sayer (Sayear, Sayears, Sayers, Seare, Seeres), Aaron, and infant 83, 85; Abraham 286; Abraham, and wife and children 69; Anne 84, 118, 361, 370; Edmund 264; Edward 85; Elizabeth 60, 62, 100; Frances 85, 306; Harriet 118; Isaac 118; Isabel 370; James 100; Jane 83, 85; John 76, 83, 85, 118; John, and parents 76; Joseph 100; Mary 83, 85, 100, 116*, 118*; Mary, *alias* Mary Parker 277; Nanny 76; Philip 268-269; Ralph 277; Rebecca, and son 370; Richard 84, 235; Robert 201; Samuel 78, 83-85; Samuel, and father 79; Sarah 85, 100*; Stephen, and son 84; Thomas 85, 118, 370; William 49, 118, 264, 362; William, and infant 116*
Scott, James 171; Mary 171, 356; Richard 356; Sophia 196; Thomas 171; William 356
Scragg, John 52
Scrase (Scrace), Brie 47; Dorcas 108; Edward 172; Francis 128; John 108, 139; Mary 64, 283;

Scrase (*contd*)
Stephen 108, 283; Thomas 139; William, and child 64
Scriven, Anne 120
Scrivens, Elizabeth 70
Scutt, Elizabeth 56; John, and family 56; John, and wife 58; Mary 67; Richard 244; Richard, and wife 58; Richard, and wife and family 56; William 58
Seagrove (Seagrave), Anne 282; Charity 81, 83, 88; Elizabeth 282; John 282; Mary 282
Sealy, Joseph 213
Seare *see* Sayers
Searle, Charles 311; Eliza 311; George 311; Henry 311*; Rev Henry 50; James 311; Mary Anne 311*; William 311; *see also* Serles
Seeres *see* Sayers
Seiver *see* Sivier
Selcomb, Mary 263*; Samuel 263; Sarah 263
Selsby, Joseph 226
Sergeant (Sarjent, Sergent, Serjeant), Charles, *alias* Charles Miller 218; Henry, and family 382; John 230, 276*; Mary 230; Stephen 193; Susanna 193
Sergison, Charles 123
Serjeant *see* Sergeant
Serles, Mary 162*; William 162; *see also* Searle
Setford, Anne 175*, 181, 215; Elizabeth 215; James 175*, 181
Sevenoak (Sevenok), Jeremiah or Jeremy 223
Sewbridge, John 242; John, and mother 242
Sewell, Mr ... 317
Sewer, Edward 242
Seymour, Col ... 103
Shallcross, Henry 347; James 347; William 347
Sharp (Sharpe), Anne 197, 306; Edward 195; Edward, and family 176; Edward, and wife and family 184*; Elizabeth 118; Fanny 118; Harriet 118; Henry 135; John 118; Mary, and child 379; Mary Anne 42; Richard 306; Sophia 118
Shaw, Abraham 312*; Aesop 312*; Anne 179; Charlotte 80; Ebenezer 312*; Elizabeth 179, 258; Issac 312*; Jabez 312*; James, and father 72; James, jun 80; Kezia 312*; Mary 179, 312*; Sarah 80, 179, 312*; Susanna 179, 291; Thomas 80, 179, 258*; William 83, 93, 258, 270*
Shearlock *see* Sherlock
Sheffield, Lord ... 325-326
Shelley, Anne 288; Elizabeth 288; Frances 288; James, and daughter 288*; Mary 236, 288*
Shepherd (Shepheard, Sheppard, Sheppeard), Elizabeth 69*; Isaac, and wife 163; James 383; John 246-247, 325; Katherina 325; Mary 113, 124; Rebecca 325; Richard 325; Thomas 246, 325; William 227, 311
Sherlock (Shearlock, Sherlocke, Shurlock), Anne 235; Elizabeth 90, 174*, 180*, 230; Elizabeth, and daughter 90; George 80, 246; James 355; Martha 174, 180; Mary 80-81, 174, 180; Richard, and children 230; Richard, and wife and child 236; Sarah 80, 174, 180, 352; Thomas 376; Walter 376; William 80-81, 107, 174, 180, 355; William, and wife and daughter 107; William, jun 183
Sherly *see* Shirley
Sherman, Anne 185; Edward 129, 132; Thomas 185
Sherwood, Joseph 334; Rebecca 334; Thomas 334; William 334
Shipley, Charles 188
Shirley (Sherly, Shurley), Anne 64, 113, 115, 344; Charles 113, 115, 344*; Elizabeth 282; Hannah 60-61*, 108, 113; John 113, 116, 282*; Martha, and daughter 66; Mary 113, 115, 282, 344; Richard 113; Sarah 313; Susan 108; Susanna 376; Thomas 113, 136, 313; William 60-61*, 64, 108*, 113
Shoebridge (Shooebridge, Shoubridge), Ann *or* Jane 77; Jane 188, 206; Jane *or* Anne 77; William 77
Sholders *see* Shoulders
Shoosmith, Jane 190; Jane, and son 210
Short, James 291; John 291; Thomas 291
Shorter, Francis 83; Mary 83
Shoubridge *see* Shoebridge
Shoulders (Sholders, Shoulder), Anne 109, 113; David 231; Edward 235; John 109, 113, 128, 132, 246; Joseph 229; Mary 231; Thomas 231
Shove, Eizabeth 163; Jane 163; John 163; Mary 163
Shurley *see* Shirley
Shurlock *see* Sherlock
Sibley, Anne, *alias* Anne Roode 186; Elizabeth, *alias* Elizabeth Roode 186; Rebecca, *alias* Rebecca Roode 186-187; Richard, *alias* Richard Roode 186; Susanna, *alias* Susanna Roode 186; William 149
Sidford, Anne 116; John 116
Sidwell, Joseph 167
Silsby, Mary 261; William 261, 314

Simmons (Simmans, Simmins, Simmonds, Simons, Symmonds, Symmons, Symond, Symonds, Symons), Amelia 261; Anne 144, 183, 254, 335*; Anne, and son 213, 266; Caroline 117*; Edward 162; Elias 335; Elizabeth 165, 323, 345; Elizabeth, *formerly* Elizabeth Packham 314; Francis 261; Frederick 292; George 183; George, and wife 359; Hannah 183*; Harriet 323; Henrietta 157; Henry 249, 257, 272, 313; Henry, *alias* Henry Packham 314; Hugh 208, 345; James 261, 292, 323, 358; Jane 271; John 44, 55, 108, 183, 205, 254, 261*, 313-314, 348; John, and father 157; Joseph 63, 224; Kitty 63*; Mary 117*, 183, 254, 272, 296, 335, 345*, 349-350, 354; Naomi 292; Richard 47, 117*, 345; Rose 162, 172; Sarah 108, 165, 358; Susanna 109, 254; Thomas 44, 109, 162, 165, 183, 213, 254*, 345*, 350, 354; William 213, 225, 292*, 323*, 349, 373; William, and child 271

Sinden, Anne 260; John 260

Sippetts (Sippets), Elizabeth 162, 363; Jane 363; Mary 363; Richard 162, 363*

Sisly, John 140

Sivier (Seiver), Jane 344; John 344

Skeffington, Mr John 128

Skelton, Gen ... 154

Skinner, Anne 174, 180*; Daniel 348; Elizabeth 165, 172, 287; George 186; Jane 186; John 129, 165, 172, 174, 180*; Mary 180, 287*; Philip 287*, 302; Richard, and wife and children 343; Robert 165, 172; Susan 349; Susanna 344-345; Thomas 345, 349; William 215, 347; William, and children 344

Skuce, Tobias 348

Slater, Anne 143; Henry 143; Henry, jun 143

Slaterford, John 366*

Slaughter, Elizabeth 337; Sarah 241; William 337

Sleech, Richard 138

Small, Mary 187, 224; William 187

Smith (Smyth), Mr ... 383; Ambrose 263; Anne 253, 323; Anne, *formerly* Anne Denman 305; Charles 56-61*; Charles, and wife 58; Constance 330; Dedimier 272; Edward 171, 223; Elizabeth 62*, 134, 160, 172, 202, 253, 344, 351, 354; Frances 62*; Henry 62*, 116; James 57, 72, 138, 281, 323*; James, and wife and family 59; James, *alias* James Cammel 217; Jane 172; John 41*, 102, 105, 112, 114, 180, 236, 245, 249, 252, 281; John, and wife and children 160; John, esq 224; John Peter *or* Johannes Petrus 62*; Joseph, jun 144; Katherine 57; Lucy 57; Mary 56, 60, 61-62*, 113, 116, 129, 144, 203, 253*, 272, 281*, 344; Mary Anne 356; Nathaniel 272; Richard 272, 321-322; Robert 129, 344; Samuel 155, 160, 171*; Sarah 69, 116, 122, 180, 253, 321-322, 344; Stephen 62; Susan 351, 354; Thomas 62, 344*; Thomas, and wife and family 232; William 122*, 134, 223, 245, 253, 263, 272, 305, 351, 354; Winifred, *formerly* Winifred Ovell, 171*; Winifred, *formerly* Winifred Ovell, and father and son 155

Smithers, Charles 310; Elizabeth 310; Mary 310; Seth 310; Thomas 310; William 310

Smyth *see* Smith

Snashall (Snashell), James 174, 179; John 43, 174, 179, 279; Mary 312*; Reuben 174, 179; Sarah 174, 179

Snashfold, Susanna 309; William 309

Snatt (Snat), Anne 117; James 117; Kezia 117; Mary 117; Sarah 117; Susanna 117; Thomas 246

Snell, Anne 126; Elizabeth 282; Susan 282

Snelling, John, and wife and children 344

Snook (Snooke), Thomas 246

Snow, James 175, 181*; Luke 225; Mary 79; Susanna 175, 181*; Thomas 79

Soane, James 224; William 205

Souter, James 144; Sarah 144

Sparkes, Elizabeth 147, 168; George 147*, 168

Spencer, Louisa 175, 180; Sarah 179

Sprag, Elizabeth 102; Gaman 102

Squire, ... 385; Mr ... 381; Richard 284, 286

Stacey (Stacy), Ann 353*; Anne 346*; Elizabeth 162; George 211; George, and wife 321*; John, and son in law William 162; John, and wife and family 322*; Katherine 346, 353; Mary 346, 353; Michael 346, 353; William 346, 353

Staines (Stanes), Anne 285, 360; Anne, and son 366, 370; Mary, and daughter 300
Staley, Thomas 136
Stammer, Hannah 50*; Joan 135
Stanbridge (Standbridge), Mrs ... 278; Amelia 323; John 323, 385*; Mary 323; Moses 323; Robert 128, 133, 308; Walter 385
Standing (Standen), Anne 116, 261; Edmund 116*; Hannah 249; Henry 116; John 73, 91, 261; John Richardson, and parents 77; Joseph 72, 116; Mary 113, 115, 249; Mary Anne 77; Mary, and son 300; Naomi 269; Naomi, and daughter 267; Philadelphia 116; Philadelphia, *alias* Philadelphia Farnes 172; Richard 73; Sarah 172; Thomas 248-249; William 113, 115, 248
Standley, Mary 135
Stanes *see* Staines
Stanford, Mr ... 253; Anne 80, 179; Anne, and son 216; George 281; John 73, 80*, 179; John, jun 75; John, sen 75; Mary 80, 177-178, 281; Sarah 80; William 80, 181
Stanning, Thomas 112, 114
Staple, William 161-162
Staples, James 380
Stapley, Anne 120, 124; Elizabeth 169; Joseph 169; Richard, get 65; William 169
Starley, Anne 351, 354*; Charity 365; Fanny 351, 354*; Henry 55, 60, 63, 87; Joseph 351, 354*; Martha 351, 354*; Thomas 55
Stayley, Thomas 74
Steadman (Stedman, Steedman), Anne 61*, 119; Anne, *formerly* Anne Arnold 119; Charles 360; Charlotte 363; Charlotte, and daughter 366*; James 292; John 45; Lucy 99*; Mary 99, 292, 356, 360; Oby 292; Phyllis 360*; Richard 61*, 110; Sarah 99, 292; Thomas 61, 360; William 99*, 133; William, jun 126; William, sen 126; William, *alias* William Arnold 119, 361
Steapley (Steaply), Anne 125; Anne, and child 125
Stedman, Steedman *see* Steadman
Steele (Steell), Edward 128, 134-135; Joan 131, 134; John 131; Thomas 53, 92, 96
Steer (Steere), Amy 355; Frances 231; James 231; John 342, 355; Sarah 231; Thomas 375*; Thomas, and wife 347; William 184, 355; William, and father and wife 342
Steerly, James 64; John 64*; Sarah 64; Stephen 64
Stemp, Henry 244
Stenning (Stening), Anne 307; Edward 239, 307-308; Edward, jun 239; Eliza 231; Elizabeth 61*; James 231*; Jane 61*; John 219, 307; John, and wife and children 106; John, and wife and family 111; Mary 231; Mary, *formerly* Mary Pickard 314; Rebecca 231*; Sarah 240; William 61, 366
Stent, John 163; Mary 163; Richard 247
Stephen, George, and child 324; Katherine 324; *see also* Stevens
Stephens *see* Stevens
Stepney, Anne 142; George 142; Katherine 196*; Rachel 120*; William 120*, 196*
Stevens (Stephens), Anne 194; Edward 49; Elizabeth 49; Elizabeth, and son 201; James 90; Joan 121-122; John 127, 176, 194; Mary 188; Mary Anne 119; Sarah 207; Stephen 49; Thomas 129, 131, 275*; William 275; *see also* Stephen
Stevenson, George 223
Stickland (Sticklan), Anne 287-288*; Emma 287-288*; John 287-288*; Jonas 373-374*; Joseph 287-288*
Stiler *see* Stiller
Still, Elizabeth 254; George 57; George, and wife and family 59; Jasper 53, 254; John 230, 312; Mary 57, 230*, 312; Robert 219; Sarah 57; William 57, 312
Stillaway, Caroline, and son 242; William, *alias* William Cobby 231
Stiller (Stiler), George 155; Susanna 173
Stilwell (Stillwell), Sarah 163; William 155, 163
Stirley, Henry 87; Sarah 87
Stirrup, Mary 334; Robert 334
Stoffell (Stoffall, Stoffeld), Richard 85; Stephen 54; William 311
Stokes, Elizabeth 244*; William 244
Stone, Ambrose 342, 355; Amelia, *later* Amelia Creasey, and son 367; Anne 342, 361; George 162; Henry 322, 333, 358; John 64, 295, 355, 367; Kezia 311; Maria 295; Martha 322, 358; Mary 55, 290, 295, 322, 358; Mary, *alias* Mary Wood 351, 354;

Philadelphia 295; Rebecca 355; Rose 162; Samuel 99; Sarah 355; Thomas 367, 388; William 131
Stoneham (Stonham), Dennis 245; James 199, 218; Mary 260; William 260
Stoner, Anne 65, 80-81, 83; Bet 359; Elizabeth 77, 81; Hannah 81; Henry 81; James 91, 158; Jane 63; John 63, 77, 87; John, and wife 97; Martha 83; Mary 309; Philip 80-81; Philip, and parents 77; Phoebe 109*; Sarah 80, 87, 89; Sarah, and daughter 91; Sophia 83; Thezia 94; Thomas 81, 83*, 109; William 81, 83; *see also* Stonyer
Stonestreet (Stonestreete, Stonstreat, Stonstreet, Stonstreete), Anne 220; Anne, and daughter 200*; Elizabeth, and mother 185; John 219; Mary 284; Philip 219
Stonham *see* Stoneham
Stonstreat, Stonstreet, Stonstreete *see* Stonestreet
Stonyer, Anne 57, 59; Philip 57, 59; *see also* Stoner
Stopford, Henry 95
Storer (Storrer), Elizabeth 223; James 139
Streater *see* Streeter
Streatfield (Streatfeild), Mary 159; Robert 152, 161; Robert, and family 159; Susanna 161
Stredwick, John 255*, 258*; Mary 255, 258
Street, Ebenezer 306; Elizabeth 313; George 366; Henry 313; Mary 249
Streeter (Streater, Streter, Stretor), ... 319; Anne 318*, 319, 320*, 374*; Charity 318, 320; Frances 374; John 318, 320; Mary 318-320; Richard 320; Sarah 318, 320; Thomas 377; William 374
Streeton, Barbara 259; Gany 259; Henry 259
Streter, Stretor *see* Streeter
Stringer, Col ... 150; Amy 80, 86; Benjamin 52, 80, 86; Edward 80, 86*; Elizabeth 361; Hannah 89; Hannah, and daughter 125; John 368*; Mary 80; Sarah 76; Sarah, *formerly* Sarah Mitchell, and son 91; Stephen 86; William 76, 91; William, and parents 76
Stuckey, George 298
Sturt, Hannah 84; John 41; Mary 306; Robert 61, 64; Thomas 84
Styleing, Diana, *alias* Diana Quinnell 197; Honour 197-198; Richard, *alias* Richard Quinnell 198
Sudds, Thomas, and son 364; William 364
Sumner, Edward 368; Isaac 369; James 110; John 276; Mary 110; Sarah 110, 116; William 110, 116
Surgeon (Surgion), Elizabeth 262; Mary 262; Mary, and daughter 264; Richard 262
Sutford, William 183
Sutton, Lawrence 154
Swan, George, and wives 146; Jane 146
Sylliban, Alexander 101; Jane 101
Symmonds, Symmons, Symond, Symonds, Symons *see* Simmons

T

Tabb, Anne 284, 301; Francis 289; Margaret 289*
Tailor *see* Taylor
Talmy, Anne 268
Tamplin, Hannah 349; Richard 349*; Susanna 349
Tanner, Elizabeth 247; Sarah 232
Tapsell, Edward 160; Edward, and children 160; Hannah 160; Mr Henry 148; John Glasington, *alias* John Glasington Vinall, and wife 281
Tasker (Tasskar), Elizabeth 362; Sir George 381; George 362; Hannah 362; John 345*, 350, 354; Phoebe 362; Thomasine 345; William 345
Taster, James, and wife and family 106
Tate, Edward, and child 49; Mary 49; Naomi 143-144
Taylor (Tailor, Tayler), Anne 150, 169, 276, 324; Charles 324; Edward 182, 327; Elizabeth 174, 179, 324*; Frances 356; George 160, 283, 289; Grace 160; Hannah 160; Harriet 182; James 174, 179; Jemima 182; John 54, 66, 97, 172, 174*, 180*, 218, 332, 358; Mary 108, 172, 174*, 180, 320*, 327, 358; Mary Anne 174, 179, 182; Naomi 174*, 180; Richard 45, 174, 179, 185, 272, 361, 378*; Richard, *alias* Richard Mitchell 138; Sarah 234, 283, 289*; Thomas 198, 234, 356; William 108, 160, 174*, 180, 234, 320
Teage, William 249
Tebbott, Martha 288
Teeling, Elizabeth 295; Richard 295
Teewes *see* Towse
Teidey *see* Tidy
Terrell (Terell), Anne 81; Elizabeth 87-88*; John 88*; Joseph, and wife 58; Mary 86; Richard, and father 72; Sarah 88*
Terry (Terrey), Benjamin, and parents 74; Elizabeth

Terry (*contd*) 74, 108; George 218*; Hannah 178*, 251, 358; James 68; Joseph 178, 358; Joseph, and wife and child 79; Katherine 178, 358; Mary 108*, 178*, 358; Sarah 178*, 313, 358; Susan 129, 132; Susanna 199, 217; Thomas 178*, 358; Thomas, *alias* Thomas Hill 356; William 108, 251*

Tester, Anne 87*, 324, 326; Edward 288; Elizabeth 45, 50, 288, 319, 326*; Elizabeth, and daughter 211; George 45; George, jun 45; Henry 45; Henry Ron, and wife 388; James 326; Jane 134; Jenny 50*; John 128, 134, 326; Lucy 87; Maria Louisa 45; Mary 43, 50*, 323, 325; Matthew 87*; Richard 319, 324; Richard, and son 323; Sarah 45; Thomas 325-326; Thomas, and former wife 50*; Timothy 324; William 50, 222, 326*

Tharp (Tharpp), John 104; John, and daughter 278; Lucy 278; Richard 327; Sarah 282; Thomas 282; William 327

Theobald, James 187; Rebecca 187; William 187*

Thoburn, James 381

Thomas, Elizabeth 143*; George, and daughter 143*; George, jun 127; George, sen 127; James 345*; John 345; Llewellyn 329; Mark 305; Sarah 345*; William 219-220

Thompset, Thompsett *see* Tomsett

Thorpe (Thorp), Elizabeth 318; Frances 318; Grace 335; Henry 196; James 56, 143, 318, 335; James, and wife 58; Jane 196; John 335; Katherine 56; Lucy 196; Martha 143; Mary 196, 318, 334*; Thomas 240

Tidy (Teidey, Tidey, Tyday, Tydey, Tydy), Amy 86; Anne, and daughter 93, 97*; Anne, *alias* Anne Flint 256, 260; Charles 82, 87, 338*; Elizabeth 56, 112*, 114*; Elizabeth, *alias* Elizabeth King 64, 256*, 259-260; George 338*; Hannah 337*, 351, 354; Henry 338*; James 87; James, *alias* James Flint 256, 260; Jane 87; John 87; Lucy 86-87, 88*, 307; Mary 87-88*, 112, 114, 307, 338*, 351, 354; Mary, *alias* Mary King 256*, 259-260; Mary, *later* Mary Wood 314; Richard 86, 239; Richard, *alias* Richard Flint 256, 260; Ruth, *alias* Ruth Wood 314; Sarah 82, 86*, 256, 259*; Sephen 87; Stephen 86*, 88*, 256, 259*, 307; Susanna 346; Thomas 123, 127, 338*, 346; William 337-338*; William, and family 56; William, and wife 58; William, jun 351, 354

Tilley, Hannah 271; John 68, 188

Tilt, Elizabeth 160; James 136; Robert 152, 160

Tiltman, Edward 134; Thomas 134

Tinet *see* Tynnett

Tingley (Tinglee, Tingly), Anne 357, 359; Caroline 357; Edward 357, 376; Elizabeth 44; Hannah 357*, 386*-387; Hannah, and mother and son 367; Hannah, and son 369; Harriet 357; Henry, and father 341; Jane 199, 376; Jane, *later* Jane White 158; John 357; Philadelphia 357; Sarah 364, 370; Thomas 296, 300, 302; William 44, 357, 359

Tinker, William 219

Tipping, Dorothy 141; Edward 108

Titchner, William, wife and family 343

Titkell, John 107; Mary, *formerly* Mary Pilbeam 107

Title, Anne 124, 286; Anne, and son 114; Elizabeth 110; Mary 110*; Thomas 110

Tobutt, Elizabeth 272

Todman, Elizabeth 309*; Henry 213; Mary, and child 214; Richard 309

Tollhurst, Elizabeth 110, 116; John 110, 116; Mary 110, 116

Tollis, Thomas, and wife 346

Tompsett *see* Tomsett

Tompson *see* Tomson

Tomsett (Thompset, Thompsett, Tompsett, Tomset), ... 286; Anne 326; Elizabeth 85, 109, 235, 326; Esther 290, 326*; James 326; Jane 69, 195, 286; John 195*, 235; Joseph 85; Margaret, and son 299; Mary, and daughter 269; Sarah 69; Thomas 69, 109, 326*; Thomas, *or* Thomas Tomson 132

Tomson (Tompson), John 116; Mary 116; Thomas 129; Thomas, *or* Thomas Tomsett 132

Tooth, Anne 343; Edward 171, 224; Hannah 213; John 44*, 139*; Mary 44, 171, 177-178, 374*; Nicholas 200; Nicholas, and children 343; Sarah 44, 171; Temperance

(Pring) 148; Thomas 224; William 44*, 171*, 178, 224*
Tourle (Tourl), Edward 118; Elizabeth 206; Hannah 118; John 118; Mary, and daughter 299; Peter 98
Towes *see* Towse
Townshend (Townesend), John 32; Samuel 144
Towse (Teewes, Towes), Elizabeth 156, 172; Harriet 193, 323; James 156, 172; Jane 193, 323; John 323; Joseph 228, 235*; Joseph, and father 227; Mary 235*, 237, 241, 323; Mary Anne 323; Richard 193, 323; William 323; William, and family 360
Trainfield, Joseph 210
Transome (Transum), Francis 297-298
Tree, Anne 160; Valentine 160; *see also* Attree
Trennell, John 243
Tribe, James 228; William 241
Triggs, Anne 109, 114; John 109, 114; Mary 109, 114
Trower, Edward, and child 235; Eliza 235
Trulock (Truelock), Bannister 173; Bannister, and wife 157-158, 224*
Tuarts, Mr Thomas 105
Tucker, John 92, 96
Tugwell, Susanna 86; Susanna, and daughter 90, 94
Tullett (Tulet, Tullet, Tullit, Tulott), Mrs ... 364; Anne 271*; Edward 249; Hannah 249; James 85, 98, 262; Jemima 82; John 271*; Katherine, and daughter 92, 96; Mary 345; Richard, and children 345; Sarah 89, 96; Susanna 85, 262; William 72*, 271*
Tulley *see* Tully
Tullit *see* Tullett
Tully (Tulley), Benjamin 43-44; Charles 118; Edwin 293; Frances 293*; Francis 341; Hannah 43-44; Henry 256; James 293; John 47-48, 293, 371; John, and infant 43-44; Mary 203; Richard 256; Robert 293; Sarah 60, 256*, 260
Tulott *see* Tullett
Tuppen, Capt William 246
Turl (Turle, Turrle), Elizabeth 57, 171; Mary 57; Richard 213; William 57, 171; William, and wife and family 59
Turley, John 75
Turner, Mr ... 192; Anne 166, 182; Anne, *formerly* Anne Balcombe 359; Caroline 193; Charles 182; Edward 81, 90, 94; Edward, and wife and children 164; Edward, *alias* Edward Peters 355; Eliza 182; George 197; Henry 81; James 123, 357; Jethro 214*-215; Joanna 107; John 202, 222, 359; John, and children 107; John, and family 211; Luke 197; Margaret 98; Martha 197*; Mary, 182, 259*, 333, 336*; Mary Elizabeth 81; Matthew 322; Peter 182; Philip 158; Richard 333, 357*; Sarah 79, 166, 182, 190; Sophia 357; Thomas 201, 327; Thomas, and child 79; Thomas, and family 281; Thomasine 98; William 53, 157, 166, 182; William, and daughter 259
Turnis, Edward 230; Mary 230
Turrey, Susan 347; William 347
Turrle *see* Turl
Tyday, Tydey, Tydy *see* Tidy
Tye, Elizabeth 282; Fanny 285; Henry 282; John 373
Tyhurst, Mary 343; Robert, and children 343; Robert, and wife and family 343; Thomas 347
Tyler, Andrew 233; Edward 110*; John 110; Mary 110; Sarah 110; Thomas 376
Tyne, Anne 120; Henry Finch 120
Tynnett (Tinet), George 219

U
Unday, John 149, 212
Underhill, Abraham 206; Edward 376; George 211; George, and wife and family 167; John 222; Mary 286; Susanna 206
Underwood, Anne 166, 178; James 166*, 178; Mary 166*, 178; William 166*, 178*, 188
Unicum, Creasy 183
Unwins, Robert, and wife 124
Upton, Anne 250; Elizabeth 345; Henry 345; Jane 81; John 81, 114, 250; Susanna 114, 250; Thomas, and wife and family 106
Uridge, Richard 169; *see also* Erridge
Uwins *see* Ewins

V
Vallance, Anne 257, 354, 360; David 257; Elizabeth 257*, 364; James 57, 59, 257; John 356; Joseph 354, 360; Lucy 356; Margaret 257; Mary 257, 360; Mary, and daughter 267; Sarah 57, 59; Stephen 354, 360; Thomas 257*; William 257
Vandyke (Van Dyke), Elizabeth 282; George 282; Henry 282; John 282*; Mary 282; Thomas

Vandyke (*contd*) 282
Varge, William 159
Varnam (Varnham), Anne 292, 296; Elizabeth 292*, 296*; Harriet 296; James 296; Mary 292, 296; Mary, and son 300, 302; Sarah 292, 296; William 292, 296
Varnes *alias* Vaughans, William 111
Varnham *see* Varnam
Vaughan, John 126, 159; Jude 159; Sarah 126*
Vaughans *alias* Varnes, William 111
Velvick *see* Feldwick
Venall *see* Vinall
Venn (Venne), Andrew 372; Henry 129, 133
Vennall *see* Vinall
Venne *see* Venn
Venner, John 281; Sarah 281
Venterman (Ventiman), Anne 162, 171; Thomas 162, 171
Verrall (Verall, Verrell), Mr Edward 332; Henry 267; Joseph 312; Mary 267, 312*; Richard 128; Richard, and wife 271; Richard, *or* Richard Vinall, 49; Richard *or* Richard Vinall, and wife and child 120; Richard Knight 267;
Vigar, Phildelphia 355
Vilders, Agnes 128; Richard 128, 132, 137
Vinall (Venall, Vennall, Vynall), Anne 79; Elizabeth 109*, 254, 281; George 239, 248; Harriet 96; John 79*, 93, 281*, 348, 352; John, and parents 73; John Glasington *alias* John Glasington Tapsell, and wife 281; Mary 254, 348, 352; Mary, and son 298; Mary, *later* Mary Pinion, and son 297; Nicholas 109*, 281; Richard 109, 281, 330; Richard, *or* Richard Verrall 49; Richard, *or* Richard Verrall, and wife and child 120*; Sarah 281, 330; William 239*, 254*; William, *alias* William Tapsell 281; *see also* Fenall
Vincent, James 255, 258*; John 217; Mary 255, 258*; Richard 65, 90; Richard Weeks 89; Thomas 129, 133, 255, 258*, 383
Vine (Vyne), Edward 60, 62; John 188; Susanna 188; William 327
Vines, Sarah 175, 180
Vinor, William, jun 247
Vinson (Vinsen), Elizabeth 290, 338*; John 338; Richard 338
Virgo (Virgoe), David 313; Edward 301; Fanny Elizabeth 231; Frances 315*; George 231, 375*; George, and daughter 313*; John 375; Lydia 313; Martha 231; Mary 313; Thomas 258, 315*; William 213, 231
Vynall *see* Vinall
Vyne *see* Vine

W

Wadey (Wady), Elizabeth 82; Martha 262
Wakeford, Robert 214
Wakelin, Grace 222; Thomas 222
Wakham, Gabriel 286
Walch, Edmund 287; Sarah 287; Thomas 287; *see also* Welch
Walder, Elizabeth, and son 90; Martha 117; Michael 117*
Wales, Anne 301; Elizabeth 137; Richard 75; Sarah 45; Sarah, and father and son 368; *see also* Walles
Waley *see* Whaley
Walker, Edward 345; Elizabeth 165; Hannah 165; James 165; Katherine 345; Margeret 165*; Martha 165; Nancy 165; Sarah 345; Susanna 165; Thomas 348
Walkett, ... 262
Waller, Mrs ... 363; Anne 289; Charles 256; Elizabeth 239, 260; George 334, 363; Henry 189, 195; James 247; Lydia 82; Mary 322; S. 381*, 382; Sarah 189, 334; Thomas 289, 329; Thomas, and wife 58; Thomas, and wife and children 56; Walter 321-322; William 216, 322
Walles, Sarah, and daughter 214; *see also* Wales, Wallice, Walls
Wallia, William 221
Wallice, William, and family 211; *see also* Walles
Wallpole, Capt ... 104
Walls, Anne 163, 188; Elizabeth 118; John 188; Martin 163; Sarah 207*; Thomas 163; William 118
Walter, Elizabeth 284, 286, 333; John 121; Joseph 140; Thomas 219, 284, 286*; Thomas, jun 284; William 303
Ward (Wards), Anne 142, 358; Benjamin 358; Charles 228*; Edward 235, 358; Elizabeth 358; George 134; Hannah 358; James 235; John, and mother 233*; Joseph 358; Martha 235, 241*; Mary 128, 131, 235; Mr Michael 241; Nicholas 358; Philip 238; Richard 72, 73; William 142, 238
Warden, John 129-130, 133
Wards *see* Ward
Wariner *see* Warrener
Warnett, Ann Maria 320, 322; Anne Maria

318-319; Daniel 318-320, 322; Edward 138, 318; Elizabeth 284; George 319; Hannah 318-319; James 284; John 284, 318-319; Mary 137; Thomas 318; William 318
Warnham (Wornham), ... 385; Elizabeth 311; Harriet 311; James, jun, and son 311; John 149*, 160; Mary 311
Warren, Mr ... 54-55; Anne 351, 354; Elizabeth 351, 354; Mary 351*, 354*; Sarah 350-351, 354; Thomas 350-351*, 354*
Warrener (Wariner), Mr ... 279; John, and wife and children 109; Sarah, and son 47
Warton *see* Wharton
Wase (Was), Mary 79; Thomas 79; Thomas, and wife and children 229
Washer, John 79
Waterman, Henry 106, 137; Henry, and family 106; Joan 106
Waters (Wattlers), John 184, 195; Robert 183; William 205
Wates *see* Watts
Watford, Anne 275; Charles 275*; James 275; Lucy 275; Richard 281; Sarah 281; Sealy 275; Teriah 275; Thomas 281; *see also* Watsford
Watkins, Diana 353; Joseph 353; Mary 353; Richard 353; Thomas 353; William 353
Watsford, Anne 234, 236; John 234, 236; *see also* Watford
Watson, Elizabeth 49*; George 49*, 215; James 99; Jane *alias* Jenny 278, 285; Martha 99; Simon 283; Thomas 99*; William 278, 285*; William, and parents 278*
Wattlers *see* Waters
Watts (Wates), Samuel 167; Stephen 138-139
Weaire *see* Weare
Weakling, Thomas 187
Weare (Weaire, Wiear), Thomas 163, 199, 225; William 225
Weaver, Charlotte 234; Fanny 320; John 234; Sarah 234, 320, 353; William 234*
Webb, Anne 105, 121-122*, 172; Henry, and wife 144; Jane 122, 162; John 162, 172; John, *alias* John Clark 371*; Joseph 136; Martha 172; Mary 122*, 349; Mary (Martin) 162; Robert 349*; Thomas 122*; William 361, 383-384; William, and children 257
Webber, Mary, and children 48; Mary, and father and son 47
Webster, John, esq 148
Wedgborough, Joseph 348
Weeden, Thomas 240
Weeding, Giles 56; Giles, and wife 58; Mary 56; Richard 316
Weeker, John 366
Weeks (Weekes, Wikes), Elizabeth 60, 63, 348; George 200, 348; James 125; John 60, 63, 236; Mary 236, 365
Welch (Weltch), Amelia 308*; Charles 308*; Elizabeth 308*; John 54, 150, 308*; Philip 329; Sarah 311; *see also* Walch
Welfare (Wellfare), Edward 166*, 173*; Henry 292; John 142; Philadelphia 166, 173; Richard, and father, wife and children 279; Thomas, and wife 111, 114; William 166, 173
Welford (Wilford), William 373
Wellens, John 371
Weller, Anne 117; Edward, and wife and children 305*; Eliza 309; Elizabeth 164-165, 178; Henry 208, 362; James, and infant 309*; Jane 208; Joan 309; John 129, 132, 164, 298; Judith 188; Mary 70; Michael, and daughter 249; Rebecca 362; Sarah 178, 249; Susan 322*; Susanna 309; Thomas 128, 132, 165, 188, 317, 347; William 81, 129, 351, 356*; William, and son 178
Wellfare *see* Welfare
Welling, Abigail 254; Anne 254; Benjamin 99; George 254; Henry 99; Susanna 99*; Wheeler 99
Wells, Anne 311; Benjamin 311; Daniel 55; Elizabeth 110, 163, 311; George 110, 319; Henry 319; James 50; Jeremiah 347; Job 311; John 319; Lydia 311; Mary 185, 195, 319*; Nicholas 185, 195; Richard 163; Simeon 185, 195; Sophia 50; Stephen 311; Thomas 163, 311; Mr Thomas 216
Weltch *see* Welch
Wenborne, Thomas 220
Wentus, Edward 310
West, Anne 113, 116, 138, 237; Anne, *formerly* Anne Wickersham 203; Bernard 237; Daniel 265; Dorcas 56, 58; Edward 246; Elijah, and parents 157*; Elizabeth 166, 173, 203, 237; Henry 113, 237*; Jane 351; John 206, 237; Mary 237; Mary Anne 237; Sarah 113, 237; Stephen 137; Thomas 56, 58, 129, 131-132, 134, 166, 173,

West (*contd*)
203, 206; Thomas, and wife and family 106; Widow 79; William 237; Zelpha 157*
Weston, Henry 253; James 201; James, and wife 167*, 176; Mr Richard 156; Ruth, and son 204, 209; William 198
Whaley (Waley), Eleanor, *alias* Eleanor Rice 324; Mary, *later* Mary Humphrey 366; William, *alias* William Rice 324, 360
Wharton (Warton), John 49*-50; Ruth 50; Ruth, *formerly* Ruth Wheeler 49*
Wheatland, Mary 231*; Richard 231; Thomas 231
Wheatley (Wheatly), Edward 203; Elizabeth 204; Isaac 367; John 203
Wheeler, Charles 288*; Diana 309; Edward 321; Elizabeth 203, 249; Jasper 249; John 284; John, jun 286; Mary 218; Ruth, *later* Ruth Wharton 49*; Samuel 49; Sarah 288*, 309*; William 49
Whiskey (Wiskey), Anne 281; Edward 236*, 281; Frances 281
Whiston, Katherine 372; Nicholas 372
Whitbourn, Dorothy 344; Francis, and child 344
White, Mr ... 78-79; Anne 179, 255-256, 265, 325-326; David 82, 261; Edward 202; Elizabeth 118*, 254, 255*-256*; Frances 60, 314*; George 375; Henry 255-256; Hugh 240; James 255-256; Jane 174, 179; Jane, *formerly* Jane Tingley 158; Joan 243; John 60*, 82, 118*, 179, 255-256, 314*; John, and wife and children 232*; Kate 255-256; Martha 261; Martha, and parents 81; Mary 60, 118*, 254-256, 261, 314; Mary, and son 240; Nicholas 176; Peter 261; Rebecca 82; Richard 125; Richard, and family 274; Richard, and infant 82; Richard, and wife 262; Robert 179; Sarah 266; Simon 158, 199; Simon, jun 174, 179; Thomas 85, 124, 255-256; Thomas, and family 254; Widow 176; William 243, 254*, 255-256, 265; William, and father 72; William, and wife and family 80
Whitebread, Thomas 217
Whitehead, Anne, and daughter 366*; Anne, *later* Anne Dench, and daughter 357
Whiteing *see* Whiting
Whiteman, Richard 93, 97
Whiting (Whiteing, Wighting), Anne 311; Charlotte 75; Elizabeth 81; Hannah 311; James 81, 311; James, and parents 75; John 53, 60, 63; John, jun 60, 63; Mary 60*, 63*; Richard 80-81, 94; Richard, and child 84*; Sarah 60, 63, 80-81, 84*; Sarah, *formerly* Sarah Batchelor, and children 94*; Thomas 81; Thomas, and wife and family 234, 337; William 115, 311*
Whitpaine, Richard, gent 269
Whitten (Witten), Elizabeth 85, 305; James 85, 305; John, and family 236; Thomas 85*, 305*
Whittington, Mary, and child 176*; Thomas 176*
Wiatt *see* Wyat
Wickenden, Jane 349, 353; John 377
Wickens (Wickins), Anne, and daughter 297; Elizabeth 296, 351; Elizabeth, and father and son 366; George 280; George *or* Samuel 351; James 191; John, *or* John Wiggens 270; Martha 275; Mary 351; Samuel *or* George 351; William 297, 351
Wickersham, Anne 202*; Anne, *later* Anne West 203; Jane 355; Jane, and father 364; Thomas 203
Wickes *see* Wicks
Wickham, Mr ... 253; Anne 283; Edward 129, 134; Elizabeth, *alias* Elizabeth Blank 56; Gabriel 333; Isaac 295; Jethro 295; Mary 62*; Mary, *alias* Mary Blank 56; Richard 136; Sarah 295; Stephen 129; William 283; William, *alias* William Blank 56; William, *alias* William Blank, and wife and family 59
Wicking, John 299; Mary, and son 207; William 198
Wicks (Wickes, Wix), Elizabeth 255; George King 365; Hannah 115; James 255; John 265*, 365; Maria 365; Mary 365, 386*; Richard 115; Sarah 194
Wiear *see* Weare
Wiggens, Alice 276*; John, *or* John Wickens 270; William 276*
Wighting *see* Whiting
Wikes *see* Weeks
Wildish, Alice, and daughter 215
Wilds, Susan 118; William 118
Wilford *see* Welford
Wilkins, Elizabeth 159, 168; George, jun 225; George, sen 225
Willard, Elizabeth 159; James 159
Willatt *see* Willett
Wille, Elizabeth 291;

Nathaniel 291; Sarah 291; William 291
Willett (Willatt, Willet), Anne 81, 83, 94; Edward 375; Elizabeth 89-90; John 81-83; John, and child 358; Penelope 60; Philadelphia 358; Rebecca 82; Sarah 82; Stephen 360; Thomas 245; Thomas, and charge 343
Williams, Elizabeth 103; Frances, *formerly* Frances Finnis 372; George 44*, 358*; Henry 46, 175, 181; James 300, 302; Jane 46, 175, 181; Joh. 103; John 44, 358; Mary 44*, 358*; Thomas 372; William 44, 302, 358
Willington, Anne 186; Henry 186; Mary, and daughter 201, 209; Sarah 186
Willis, Rebecca 122*
Willix, Elizabeth 187; James 187; Mary 187
Willson *see* Wilson
Wilmore, Elizabeth 64
Wilson (Willson), Edward 273*; Henry 243; James 153; Mary 165, 172; Mary, and children 153; Mary, and son 167; Mary Anne 356; William 153, 165, 172, 177
Wimark, Anne 159; Elizabeth 159; Katherine, *later* Katherine Pitman 159
Wimsett (Wimset), Mary 212; Mary, and son 197
Win *see* Winn
Winchester, Barbara 103; John 371; Richard 191; Susan 371
Wing, Francis 317, 327; John, jun 329
Winn (Win, Wynn), Anne 344; Joan 106; John 344; Susan 344
Winter, Henry 374; Mary 136
Winton, Frank, jun 239; Gerrard 129; Nicholas 328-329; William, sen 201
Wisdom, Anne 203
Wise, Daniel 161-162; Edward 301; Susanna 265
Wiseman, Sir Thomas, bart 201-202
Wiskey *see* Whiskey
Withers, James 345; Sarah 345; William 345
Witten *see* Whitten
Wix *see* Wicks
Woldridge, Thomas 132
Wood, Anne 61, 179, 250, 262, 291; Anthony 56; Anthony, and wife 58; Edward 291; Eleanor 304; Elias 179; Eliza 236; Elizabeth 56, 106, 255, 262, 334, 347; Fanny 314; Frederick 236; George 210, 213-214, 236; Harriet 288; Henry 236, 315; Henry, and wife 158; Henry, gent 240; James 65, 97, 255*, 314; Joanna 115*; John 106*, 115*, 179, 279, 285, 287, 291, 315-316, 318, 347*; John, and wife and children 325-326; John, gent 65; John, jun 65; Joseph 250, 304; Katherine 250; Lucy 179, 349; Lucy, and child 214; Mary 84, 178-179, 193, 196, 358; Mary, *alias* Mary Stone 351, 354; Mary, *formerly* Mary Tidy 314; Nanny 334; Peter 236; Phille 334; Randolph 304; Richard 68, 262; Richard, and wife and child 313; Robert 282; Ruth, *alias* Ruth Tidy 314; Sarah 236*, 288, 333; Sophia 236; Stephen 106, 347; Susanna 285, 287; Thomas 92, 96, 178*, 205, 291, 358*; Thomas, jun 203; William 84, 136, 225, 288*, 333, 334*; *see also* Attwood; Woods
Woodgate, Charity 295; Edward 146, 296; George 296; Jane 295-296; John 295-296; Joseph 296*; Mary 188, 296; Richard 296; Susanna 295*; Walter 168
Woodin, Sarah, and daughter 239
Woodley, Elizabeth, and daughter 240
Woodman, Mr ... 380; Elizabeth 43; John 43; Mary 43; Sarah 43; William 148; William, and wife 343; Mr William 340*
Woods, Joan 130; Richard 130; *see also* Wood
Wooldred, Thomas 129
Woolgar (Woolger, Woollger), Anne 192; Elizabeth 195; Isaac 254; James 192; Jane 230, 233*, 255; John 230, 255; Margaret 254; Mary 274; Sarah 274; Stephen 244; William 192*, 195, 233*
Wooll, John 281; Mary 281; *see also* Attwooll
Woollger *see* Woolgar
Woolven (Woollven, Woollvin), Edward 82; Elizabeth 78, 87, 97; Henry 78; James 77; John 80; Mary 65, 77, 80*, 82; Mary, and daughter 92; Mildred 80, 86; Richard 82, 238; Thomas 82
Wooster, Sarah 315*
Worger, Charity 376; John 223; John, and family 167; William 223
Wornham *see* Warnham
Wornut, James 129
Worsell, Elizabeth 256, 363; Frederick 356*; George 256, 356*, 364; Hannah 337; Henry 356*; Jane 356*; John 337, 3568; Mary Anne 356*; Sarah 356*; William 356*; William, and wife and

Worsell (*contd*)
children 381
Worsley, John, and wife and family 217
Wren, John 232; William 208
Wright (Right), Abraham 345; Anne 154, 188; George 369; George, and father 340; James 115; Jane 287; Mary 344, 345*; Richard 272; Thomas 118, 344; William 154
Wyat (Wiatt), Mr ... 229; William 245
Wynn *see* Winn

Y

Yateman, Sarah 183; William 183
Yeomans, Frances 170; John 154, 170; Sarah 170
Yockhorst, Richard 229
Young, Amy 193; Elizabeth 275; Henry 94; James, and daughter 193; John 275*, 281; Lucy 193; Mary 162, 176, 193; Richard 176; Robert 133*; Sarah 176, 275; Thomas 105, 162*, 303; Mr Thomas 340

INDEX OF PLACE NAMES

by Rosie Ritchie

Names in this index are normally those of parishes, since the parish was the unit on which the Poor Law machinery was based. However, townships and hamlets are usually indexed separately but identified by the parish in which they lay.

Minor place names, such as streets and farms, are listed under their parish.

Where no county name is given Sussex is to be understood.

Counties other than Sussex are identified by three letters (the Chapman Code):

Bdf	Bedfordshire	Lin	Lincolnshire
Bkm	Buckinghamshire	Lnd	London
Brk	Berkshire	Mdx	Middlesex
Cam	Cambridgeshire	Mon	Monmouthshire
Chs	Cheshire	Nfk	Norfolk
Con	Cornwall	Nth	Northamptonshire
Dby	Derbyshire	Oxf	Oxfordshire
Dev	Devon	Sal	Shropshire (Salop)
Dor	Dorset	Sct	Scotland
Ess	Essex	Som	Somerset
Gls	Gloucestershire	Sry	Surrey
Ham	Hampshire	War	Warwickshire
Hrt	Hertfordshire	Wil	Wiltshire
Iow	Isle of Wight	Wor	Worcestershire
Ken	Kent	Yks	Yorkshire
Lei	Leicestershire		

For the central London area the information given in the documents is often imprecise and identifications are often difficult. The following arrangement has therefore been adopted.

> Parish, street and minor place names within the City of London have been put under "London, City".
>
> Other parishes have been included separately and identified by their counties e.g. Middlesex (Mdx) or Surrey (Sry).
>
> Townships and hamlets have been included separately, and normally linked with their parish.
>
> Other street names and minor place names have normally been placed under their parish; but where no parish has been given in the text they have been indexed under "London, Streets".

The following terms have also been included;

> Almshouses; County Hall, Lewes; Excise; Houses of Correction; inns, taverns and brewhouses; naval vessels; posting houses; prisons; regiments and other military units; ships; transportation [of convicts]; workhouse.

A
Abinger, Sry, 76, 352
Addington, Sry, 151, 170, 171, 174, 177, 179, 203
Adversane, Billingshurst, 76
ALBOURNE, 2, 7, 10, 11, 19, 28, 30, 32, **41, 42**, 63, 71, 73, 77, 81, 85, 113, 116, 125, 161, 169, 170, 177, 236, 249, 254, 257-259, 265, 297, 305, 306, 314, 318, 322, 333, 337; Green, 41; Place, 41; Street, 41; Bishops Place, 41
Alcester, War, 161
Alciston, 147
Aldgate, Mdx, 153
Alfold, Sry, 49, 127, 227, 310
Alfriston, 176, 196, 253, 270, 276
Almshouses, 3, 5
Alton, Ham, 106
Altrincham, Chs, 179
Alverstoke [Stoke], Ham, 189 190, 192
Amberley, 52, 81, 83, 306
Amersham, Bkm, 271
Angmering, 102, 122, 236, 252, 253, 281
Ansty, Cuckfield, 101
Appledore, Ken, 185
ARDINGLY, 2, 7, 12, 19, 28, 30, 32, **43-48**, 49, 50, 61, 76, 114, 117, 121, 125, 139, 155, 159, 163, 175, 178, 181, 249, 278, 279, 281-286, 288, 289, 291, 299, 313, 318-320, 322, 324, 325, 327, 334, 345, 347, 349, 350, 354, 358, 361; Wakehurst Place, 43
Arlington, 188, 194, 195, 275, 281, 287
Army *see* Regiments
Arundel, 34, 164, 166, 195, 196, 232, 255, 258, 289, 295
Ashburnham, 101, 164, 172
Ashford, Ken, 163, 171, 281
Ashington, 54, 76, 110, 230, 272, 319
Ashurst, 78, 80, 83, 84, 86, 172, 229, 231, 232, 234, 236, 245, 281, 282
Astley, Sal, 160
Awfold, 227
Axminster, Dev, 150
Aylesford, Ken, 23, 222, 316

B
BALCOMBE, 2, 7, 11, 19, 28, 30, 32, 43-46, **49-51**, 60-63, 106, 107, 109, 110, 114, 120-121, 124-126, 130, 172, 175, 180, 191, 243, 259, 265, 277, 281, 288, 306, 309, 323, 344-346, 349, 352, 353, 359, 360, 362, 363, 366, 367, 369, 375
Banstead, Sry, 99, 239, 241, 361
Barbados, West Indies, 293
Barcombe, 121-123, 144, 161, 243, 249, 250, 279, 285, 287, 296, 315, 327
Barking, Ess, 70
Barming, Ken, 87
Basingstoke, Ham, 183
Battersea, Sry, 116, 174
Battle, 34, 167, 179, 183, 282, 294
Bearsted, Ken, 281, 325
Beckenham, Ken, 277, 342
Beckley, 262
Beddingham, 86, 107, 181, 287, 333
Beddington, Sry, 330, 345
Beeding, 41, 58, 59, 60, 79, 81, 82, 83, 84, 85, 88, 99, 110, 111, 122, 126, 133, 170, 176, 177, 181, 196, 230, 231, 232, 234, 235, 236, 237, 242, 275, 305, 306, 308, 309, 310, 312, 316, 320, 352, 371; *see also* Lower Beeding
Benenden, Ken, 349, 352
Berkshire, 32, 167
Bermondsey, Sry, St Mary Magdalen, 181, 349, 377
Berwick, 87, 144
Betchworth, Sry, 107, 150, 183, 219, 344, 349, 379
Bexhill, 144, 216, 335, 350, 360, 363
Bicester, Oxf, 159
Biddenden, Ken, 298
Billingshurst, 79, 108, 116, 172, 227, 228, 236, 246, 272, 281, 286, 306, 308, 326, 346
Bilsborough, Woodmancote, 337
Birmingham, War, 75; Old Church, 353
Bishops Tree, Lei, 290
Bishopstone, 196, 295
Blackstone, Woodmancote, 337
Bletchingley, Sry, 154, 156, 159, 213, 267, 272, 321, 322, 345, 347, 349, 350, 352, 360, 362
Bloomsbury, Mdx, St George, 82, 150, 170, 177, 355; St George, Great George Street, 153
Bobbing, Ken, 86
BOLNEY, 2, 7, 12, 19, 28, 30, 32, **52-68**, 72-74, 80, 81, 83-87, 92, 93, 95, 97, 98, 106-109, 112, 114, 116, 125, 129, 162, 172, 178, 238, 246, 252, 255-260, 265, 270, 271, 283, 305, 308-310, 313, 314, 319, 332-334, 347, 360
Boroughbridge, Yks, 154, 188
Botolphs, 310
Bozeat, Nth, 189
Bramber, 19, 233, 236, 254
Bramfield, Hrt, 45
Brasted, Ken, 166, 343
Brentwood, Ess, 186, 378
Bridewell, Ldn, 190
Bridgwater, Som, 147
Brighthelmston *see* Brighton
Brighton, 19, 45, 46, 50, 57, 59, 61-65, 67, 70, 82, 83, 86-88, 99-101, 103, 108-111, 115, 117-120, 122, 123, 138, 139, 141-144, 159, 160, 191, 225, 226, 229-232, 234-237, 241, 242 246, 247, 250-253, 256, 258-263, 267, 269, 270 272, 274-277, 281, 288, 291, 293, 294, 296, 303, 306, 310, 315, 322-324, 334-336, 338, 355, 356, 360, 361, 363, 379, 381; Hanover Street, 383; Middle Street, 381; Regency Square, Brighton, 380
Brixton, Sry, 380
Broadwater, 70, 142, 231, 232, 242, 276, 311
Bromley, Ken, 148, 174
Buckland, Sry, 83, 85
Budleigh, Dev, 286
Burgess Hill, 69, 274
Burpham, 69, 272, 306
Burstow, Sry, 133, 158, 162, 164, 190, 205, 249, 308, 323, 339, 342-347, 349, 350, 353, 355, 356, 358-360, 364, 369, 372, 373
Burton, 246, 316, 317, 321

Burwash, 49, 144, 186, 192, 193, 201, 295, 359
Bury, 271
Buttinghill Hundred Courts, Clayton, 69
Buxted, 148, 169, 182, 196, 272, 277, 287, 291, 322, 333
Byfleet, Sry, 150, 170

C
Camberwell, Sry, 105, 121, 166, 183, 193, 292; St Giles, 292, 362
Canterbury, Ken, 104, 112; St Dunstans, 148
Capel *see* Capel, Ken; Capel, Sry
Capel, Ken, 193; *see also* Capel, Sry
Capel, Sry, 79, 106, 111, 335, 355; *see also* Capel, Ken
Carshalton, Sry, 49, 156, 190
Cartagena, Colombia [Carthergina, West Indies], 153
Catsfield, 122, 183, 206
Chailey, 41, 47, 53, 72, 103, 107, 111, 116, 117, 119, 122, 143, 158, 164, 168, 176, 182, 234-236, 249, 250, 263, 269, 279-282, 286, 288, 291, 292, 294-296, 299, 312, 321, 323, 324, 326, 334-336, 344, 349
Chaldon, Sry, 346
Chalvington, 194, 295
Charing, Ken, 334
Charlton, Ken, 103, 194
Charlwood, Sry, 44, 63, 80, 99, 119, 126, 173, 249, 256, 337, 339, 342, 344-346, 348-352, 354, 355, 357, 360, 368
Charmouth, Dor, 234
Chart Sutton, Ken, 178
Chatham, Ken, 71, 117, 146, 150, 152, 155, 160, 168, 170, 349, 353
Chealy *see* Chailey
Cheam, Sry, 54
Chelsea, Mdx, St Luke, 121, 278, 285
Chesham, Bkm, 154
Chevening, Ken, 171, 175, 177, 181
Chichester, 34, 102, 122, 316; City of, 64; St Olave, 234; St Pancras, 254, 316; St Peter the Great, 309
Chiddingfold, Sry, 253
Chiddingly, 47, 194, 296
Chiddingstone, Ken, 50, 117, 152, 161, 163, 171, 177, 179, 183, 283, 284, 360
Chidham, 87
Childrey, Oxf, 354
Chiltington, 64, 107, 275, 293, 296, 306, 333-335; *see also* West Chiltington
Chingford, Ess, 165
Chipstead, Sry, 157, 365
Chislehurst, Ken, 46
Clapham, 116, 228, 255
CLAYTON, 2, 7, 11, 19, 28, 30, 32, 56, 58, 63, 68, **69, 70**, 107, 110, 117, 119, 121, 140, 141, 168, 210, 233, 253-256, 258-260, 270, 274, 275, 277, 286, 287, 313, 321, 332-334
Clerkenwell, Mdx, St James, 114
Cliffe, Lewes, 146, 148, 271, 305; St Thomas, 177
Cobham, Sry, 76, 86, 380
Colchester, Ess, 160
Compton, 11, 33, 61, 71, 178
Coombes, 237, 241
Copthorne, Worth 339, 364
Cornwall, 32, 101, 103
Correction, House of *see* House of Correction
Corscombe, Dor, 169
Coulsdon, Sry, 162, 165, 180, 346
County Hall, Lewes *see* Lewes, County Hall, 268
Covent Garden, Mdx, St Paul, 355, 364
Cowden, Ken, 159, 163, 164, 166, 167, 171, 173, 178, 183-185, 187, 193, 219, 222, 283, 318, 320, 333, 348, 378
COWFOLD, 2, 7, 19, 28, 30, 32, 52, 53, 54, 55, 56, 57, 58, 59, 60, 61, 62, 63, 69, **71-98**, 104, 107-110, 113, 114, 116, 119, 121, 124, 125, 129, 158, 164, 171, 174, 180, 231, 232, 256, 257, 259, 262, 274, 305, 306, 309, 313, 314, 321, 337, 344
Cranbrook, Ken, 161, 176, 226, 344
Cranleigh, Sry, 53, 255
CRAWLEY, 2, 7, 11, 19, 28, 30, 32, 57, 59, 60, 66, **99, 100**, 109, 121, 165, 271-273, 308, 309, 339, 343-345, 349, 352, 357, 369, 383
Crawley Down, 339
Crayford, Ken, 185
Crowhurst, Sry, 65, 154-157, 160, 161, 163, 170-172, 175, 177, 180, 181, 194, 198, 202, 378
Croydon, Sry, 46, 90, 108, 116, 117, 149, 159, 173, 187, 194, 202, 203, 207, 216, 249, 289, 340, 341, 351, 354, 358, 361, 369
CUCKFIELD, 2, 7, 28, 30, 32, 43, 44, 48-50, 53, 54-64, 67, 69, 74, 76, 80, 82-84, 87, **101-140**, 141, 143, 161, 163, 166, 175, 181, 186, 203, 217, 224, 233, 234, 249, 253-255, 257, 258, 260, 261, 264, 271, 272, 274, 281-288, 290, 293, 302, 303, 305, 308, 309-311, 314, 315, 319, 320, 322-324, 326, 333, 334, 343, 347, 354, 355, 361, 381, 382, 386, 388

D
Dallington, 163, 172
Dartford, Ken, 192, 256
Denmans, [?Cuckfield] 325
Denton, Ken, 258, 276
Deptford, Ken, 294, 358
Ditchingham, Nfk, 175, 181, 182, 183
DITCHLING, 2, 7, 11, 28, 30, 32, 41, 53, 60, 62, 69, 99, 107, 113-115, 117, 120, 141, 142, 144, 254, 255, 258, 260, 263, 268, 269, 271, 275, 281, 284, 286, 289, 290, 313, 323, 332, 334; Lodge Hill, 141
Dorking, Sry, 60, 74, 116, 118, 152, 155, 160, 161, 188, 189, 235, 287, 289, 310, 311, 345, 347, 358
Dorney, Bkm, 160
Dover, Ken, 74, 189; St Mary, 351, 354
Duncton, 317
Dunsfold, Sry, 155, 163
Duxford, Cam, 148, 169

E
Easebourne, 50, 86, 310
East Blatchington, 338

East Dean, 249
EAST GRINSTEAD, 2, 7, 13, 17-19, 23, 28, 30, 32, 38, 41, 43-46, 50, 65, 84, 86, 104, 107, 110, 112-114, 142, **146-225,** 257, 260, 274, 282, 285, 287, 288, 293, 306, 309, 310, 313, 317, 318, 320-325, 327, 329, 330, 340, 343, 344, 346, 347, 349, 350, 352, 354, 356, 357, 358, 360, 367, 378
East Hoathly, 158, 193, 196, 320, 326
East Peckham, Ken, 192, 281, 290
Eastbourne, 44, 118, 144, 146, 193, 196, 287
Eastchurch, Ken, 191
Eckington, Dby, 81
Edburton, 52, 232, 235, 237, 254, 256, 258, 259, 262, 274, 294, 313
Edenbridge, Ken, 87, 115, 126, 146, 160, 172, 178, 179, 182, 185-187, 189, 200, 218, 220, 259, 290, 345, 346, 358, 360
Effingham, Sry, 229
Elizabeth & Mary see ships
Eltham, Ken, 127
Epsom, Sry, 81, 82, 86, 192, 284, 289
Etchingham, 188, 207, 283
Ewell, Sry, 158, 192, 193
Ewhurst, 82, 99, 104
Excise, Officer of, 100
Eythorne, Ken, 351, 354

F
Falmer, 10, 28, 115, 260, 263, 295, 338, 361, 380
Faringdon, Brk, 148
Farnham, Sry, 192, 290
Faversham, Ken, 160, 183
Felkirk?, Yks, 167
Fernhurst, 288
Ferring, 50
Fetcham, Sry, 355, 365
Findon, 159, 228, 281, 283, 288, 342
Fittleworth, 197
Flanders, 150
Fletching, 45, 46, 47, 70, 120, 122, 130, 161, 163-165, 172, 175, 180, 186, 188, 189, 195-198, 200, 226, 247, 250, 252, 253, 278, 282, 284, 285, 289, 290, 292, 294-297, 300, 302, 316, 321-327, 330, 335, 346, 357
Folkestone, Ken, 350
Folkington, 83
Fordingbridge, Ham, 147, 148
Foreign of, Reigate, 339; *see also* Reigate
Forest Ridge, 146
Forest Row, East Grinstead 198, 208, 213, 217
Framfield, 121, 144, 250, 289, 294, 309, 326, 386
Frampton, Gls, 172
Frant, 88, 183
Friern Barnet, Mdx, 117
Frindsbury, Ken, 102
Frinsted, Ken, 84
Friston, 250
Fulham, Mdx, 121
Fulking, 258

G
Gatton, Sry, 110, 321, 327
Gillingham, Ken, 117
Glynde, 108
Godalming, Sry, 179, 297, 371
Godstone, Sry, 45, 60, 107, 109, 148, 152, 155, 157-173, 175-178, 181-184, 187, 193, 198, 202, 205, 216, 222, 292, 303, 310, 314, 317, 321, 325, 341, 344-348, 351, 354, 355, 357; *see also* Walkhamstead
Good Pinck *see* Ships
Goudhurst, Ken, 43, 44, 46, 113, 116, 226, 349, 353
Graffham, 284
Great Brickhill, Bkm, 293
Great Stanmore, Mdx, 148
Guildford, Sry, 158, 168, 383; St Mary, 168

H
Hackney, Mdx, 44
Hadlow, Ken, 118, 234, 255, 334
Hailsham, 47, 123, 195, 211, 236, 254, 256, 362
Halden, Ken, 142
Halse, Taunton, Som, 147
Ham Street, Romney Marsh, Ken, 280
Hambledon, Ham, 108, 118, 175, 180
Hammersmith, Mdx, 174, 179
Hampshire, 102
Hamsey, 44, 45, 108, 189, 190, 195, 210, 215, 256, 262, 291, 300, 335, 356, 357
Handcross, Slaugham, 91, 92, 94, 308
Hangleton, 228
Hapstead, Ardingly, 43
Harborough, Lei, 325
Hardingstone, Nth, 101
Hartfield, 65, 114, 151, 152, 154, 158-166, 170-173, 175, 177-181, 183-188, 190, 195, 196, 201, 202, 206, 211, 212, 224, 230, 249, 274, 282, 324-326, 339, 362, 363, 378
Haslemere, Sry, 74, 102, 107
Hastings, 199, 249, 287; All Saints, 292
Hawkhurst, Ken, 113, 183, 288, 289, 324
Hayes, Ken, 344, 349
Haywards Heath, 277
Headley, Ham, 285
Heathfield, 119, 122, 183, 192, 195, 346
Hellingly, 144, 147
HENFIELD, 2, 7, 19, 28, 30, 32, 41, 45, 56, 58-60, 63, 75-77, 79-81, 83, 87, 91-93, 97, 108, 115, 118, 119, 142, **226-248**, 254, 255, 258-260, 282, 284, 297, 305, 308, 313, 314, 337; Mock Bridge, 305
Herstmonceux, 259, 327, 333, 334, 344
Hever, Ken, 160, 164, 166, 169, 185, 217, 221
Hickstead, Twineham, 65, 313
High Cross, Mdx, 147, 168, 176, 185
High Easter, Ess, 199
Highbrook, 316
Holborn, Ldn, 274
Holborn, Mdx, St Andrew, 69, 183
Hollington, 290
Holybourne, Ham, 44
Hoo, Ken, 125
Hooe, 144
Horley, Sry, 49, 61, 113, 115, 118, 134, 154, 163, 164, 170, 177, 180, 186, 188, 199, 216, 271, 339, 340, 343-346, 350, 351, 355, 359, 361, 364, 371, 372
Horne, Sry, 16, 50, 159-163, 166, 168, 171, 173, 176,

188, 189, 203, 220, 221, 281, 319, 321, 322, 341, 343-346, 348, 351-357, 362, 369, 375, 377, 381
Horsgate, Cuckfield, 135
Horsham, 34, 49, 51, 52, 64, 71-73, 77-79, 81, 86-88, 90, 91, 94, 96, 98-100, 104, 108, 109, 113-118, 120, 122, 124, 142, 144, 154, 157, 159-161, 163, 181, 197, 200, 209, 223, 231, 236, 243, 250, 251, 255, 256, 261, 262, 271, 272, 289, 294, 295, 306, 308, 309, 311, 324, 338, 358-362, 363; Horsham gaol *see* Prisons
Horsmonden, Ken, 179, 334
HORSTED KEYNES, 2, 5, 7, 11, 19, 28, 30, 32, 44-46, 49, 60, 61, 81, 104, 106, 109, 146, 151, 156, 160, 162-166, 168-170, 173, 174, 177-180, 182, 183, 187-189, 193, 224, **249-251**, 275, 277, 281, 282, 284-294, 301, 308, 317-325, 328, 329, 347, 356, 360; Horsted Green, 106
Horton, Sry, 284, 289
Houghton, 231
House of Correction, 5, 20, 25, 45, 46, 96, 112, 168, 190-193, 194, 211, 215, 218, 232, 241, 261, 291, 293, 310, 366, 385; Cliffe, Lewes, 366; Lewes, 46, 193, 291, 293, 310; Winchester, Ham, 192
Hove, 230, 296
Hucking, Ken, 161, 162
Hurst, Wivelsfield, 280
HURSTPIERPOINT, 2, 7, 10, 15, 19, 28, 30, 32, 38, 41, 52, 57, 59, 63, 64, 66, 67, 69, 70, 77, 81, 82, 85, 98, 99, 103, 105-107, 109-119, 139, 141, 143, 164, 230, 231, 233, 235, 238-240, **252-270**, 272, 274-276, 281, 286, 310, 313, 314, 332, 334; Danny Park, 252
Hythe, Ken, 280

I

IFIELD, 2, 7, 11, 19, 28, 30, 32, 56, 58, 59, 65, 75, 79, 80, 81, 84, 99, 118, 119, 120, 124, 142, 143, 227, 230, **271-273**, 311, 323, 324, 342-344, 346, 350, 356, 358-362, 368
Iford, 106, 234, 285
Ightham, Ken, 277, 284, 311
Ilchester, Som, 172
Inns, Taverns & Brewhouses: *Bell Brewhouse*, Tottenham, 384; *Bull*, East Grinstead, 186; *Kings Head Inn*, Horsham, 96, 97; *Kings Head, Horsham*, 95; Sheffield Arms, Fletching, 214, 215; *Sloop Inn*, Lindfield, 277; *Swan*, East Grinstead, 217; *Swan*, Forest Row, 215, 216; *The Talbot Inn*, Cuckfield, 48; *White Horse Inn*, Steyning, 242
Ireland, 101, 103, 359
Isfield, 63, 87, 167, 173, 176, 206, 249, 312
Isle of Oxney, Ken, 139
Isle of Wight, Ham, 32, 293
Islington, Mdx, 173
Itchingfield, 47, 106, 107, 112, 117

J

Jevington, 196, 324

K

Kemsing, Ken, 159
KEYMER, 2, 7, 11, 19, 28, 30, 32, 46, 52, 61, 63, 67, 69, 70, 103, 112, 119, 121, 123, 127, 139-144, 162, 185, 234, 238, 247, 253, 255, 257, 258, 261, 262, **274-276**, 277, 282, 284, 287, 291, 323, 333, 334
Kidderminster, Wor, 279
Kings Lynn, Nfk, 104
Kingsley, Ham, 351, 354
Kirdford, 83, 113, 115, 227, 236, 255, 258, 310

L

Lamberhurst, 166, 172, 173, 178, 285, 290
Lambeth, Sry, 50, 191, 259, 309, 361; High Street, 331; St Mary, 189, 290, 324, 334, 358; Washways, 215
Lancing, 41, 74, 89, 90, 110, 232, 234, 236
Laughton, 196, 268
Leadenham, Lin, 99
Leatherhead, Sry, 234, 322
Leeds, Ken, 93, 97
Leicester, Lei, 112; St Martin, 112
Leigh, 466
Leigh, Ken, 57, 174, 177, 179, 182, 190, 199, 208, 217, 282, 361, 364, 367; *see also* Leigh; Leigh, Sry
Leigh, Sry, 57, 282; *see also* Leigh; Leigh, Ken,
Lewes, All Saints, 64, 123, 143, 144, 149, 160, 168, 260, 262, 263, 281, 295, 310, 312, 334, 345; County Hall, 268; SS Peter & Mary, 84, 295; SS Peter & Mary Westout, 292; St John, 242; St John Castro, 237; St John sub Castro, 262, 263, 359, 362; St Michael, 107, 109, 111, 112, 114, 118, 142, 193, 260, 270, 285, 288, 333; St Thomas at Cliffe, 178, 181, 182, 229, 235, 335
Lewisham, Ken, 49, 174, 294
Lewknor, Oxf, 259
Limpsfield, Sry, 154, 161, 163, 172, 205, 231, 309, 343, 366, 370
Linchmere, 262, 363
LINDFIELD, 2, 7, 13, 19, 21, 28, 30, 32, 38, 45, 46, 60-62, 74, 108-114, 116-119, 123, 128, 135, 141-142, 148, 159-161, 164, 166, 175, 177, 181, 183, 191, 198, 234, 249, 250, 259, 268, 269, 274, **277-304**, 316, 318, 319, 320, 321, 322, 323, 324, 328, 332, 333, 334, 342, 348, 350, 352, 356, 360
Lingfield, Sry, 44, 105, 108, 109, 116, 139, 143, 147, 149, 150, 152, 153, 156, 159-170, 172-187, 191, 202, 203, 208, 212, 217, 218, 220, 222, 265, 281, 284, 286, 323, 324, 328, 339, 343, 344, 347, 348, 349, 350, 351, 352, 354, 364, 382, 386, 387
Lingwell [Lindfield?], 303
Linworth [Lindfield?], 280

Little Bowden, Nth, 290
Little Dean, Gls, 103
Little Horsted, 264, 266, 317
Llandogo, Mon, 353
Llangefni, Anglesey, Wls, 101
Llanwnog, Mon, 147
London (unspecified): 22, 32, 35, 99, 101, 141, 146, 152, 153, 226, 277, 303, 339, 365
London, City of: St Dunstan, 189; St Katherine, 104; St Lawrence Pountney, 159, 168; St Martin, 376; St Mary Magdalen, Old Fish St, 348, 352; St Mary Somerset, 104; St Mary Woolchurch, 190; St Sepulchre, 152, 153
London, Streets: Grub Street, 157; Old Bond Street, 213; Pater Noster Row, 365; Portland Place, 218
Lower Beeding, 46, 78, 311, 312; *see also* Beeding
Lower Mitton, Wor, 291
Lurgashall, 113

M

Maidstone, Ken, 176, 186, 188, 334, 384
Maresfield, 45, 49, 56, 70, 119, 121, 122, 141, 165, 180, 184-187, 193, 195, 196, 203, 204, 224, 230, 249, 250, 276, 281, 286, 291, 292, 296, 316, 319, 321, 325, 326, 330, 348, 352, 353, 355
Marylebone, Mdx *see* St Marylebone, Mdx
Mayfield, 149, 159, 169, 173, 179, 193, 196, 204, 250, 303, 312, 326
Mereworth, Ken, 233, 361
Merstham, Sry, 174, 180, 240, 249, 308, 361
Mickleham, Sry, 229
Midhurst, 34, 109, 148, 169, 213, 263
Milton, Ken, 102
Minster in Sheppey, Ken, 102, 362
Mitcham, Sry, 146, 346, 349
Montgomeryshire, Wls, 147
Morden, Sry, 81, 90
Mortlake, Sry, 60
Mountfield, 87
Much Wenlock, Sal, 101

N

Navy, Vessels: HMS Southampton, 52
Nep Town, Henfield, 226
New Fishbourne, 159
New Shoreham, 122, 143, 226, 235, 237, 246, 276, 281, 307, 310; *see also* Shoreham
Newbury, Brk, 178
Newdigate, Sry, 64, 309, 311, 347, 383, 384
Newhaven, 216, 335
Newick, 55, 61, 107, 110, 111, 114, 116, 122, 172, 258, 276, 279, 285, 286, 296, 300, 302, 323, 324, 326, 332, 333
Newington Butts, Sry, 177, 332
Newington, Sry, St Mary, 192
Newport, Isle of Wight, Ham, 153, 293
Newtimber, 53, 82, 253-257, 259, 260, 262, 338
Ninfield, 353
North Cray, Ken, 158
North Stoke, 230
Northchapel, 227, 231
Norwich, Nfk, St Giles, 149
Norwood, Sry, 217
Nottingham, 188
Nutfield, Sry, 159, 177, 193, 339, 340, 345-347, 350
Nuthurst, 50, 53, 57, 59, 61, 62, 72, 74, 75, 77, 79-82, 86-88, 91, 100, 110, 133, 157, 227, 260, 287, 295, 306, 307, 310, 311, 315, 346, 357, 361
Nutknowle, Woodmancote, 237

O

Ockley, Sry, 107, 228, 235, 272
Old Shoreham, 86, 236, 257, 258; *see also* Shoreham
Olney, Bkm, 189
Ore, 191, 316, 318, 325, 326
Oreham Common, Henfield, 226
Orsett, Ess, 156
Otford, Ken, 357
Otham, Ken, 191
Ovingdean, 69, 145, 258
Ovington, Ham, 351, 354
Oxted, Sry, 151, 159, 160, 162, 172, 249, 263, 344, 346

P

Paddington, Mdx, 118
Parkminster, Cowfold, 71
Patcham, 42, 65, 69, 144, 237, 261, 263, 266, 315, 333
Pease Pottage, Crawley, 99, 308
Pembury, Ken, 153, 285, 287, 323, 360
Penge, Battersea, Sry, 180
Penhurst, 337
Penn, Bkm, 159
Penshurst, Ken, 45, 84, 121, 164, 166, 190, 207, 282, 357
Penton Mewsey, Ham, 163
Pentonville, Islington, Mdx, Nowells Row, 157
Penzance, Con, 101
Peper Harow, Sry, 60, 61, 108, 113
Petersfield, Ham, 287, 367
Petworth, 34, 96, 201, 241, 322
Pevensey, 176
Piddinghoe, 144
Pimlico, Brighton, 379
Plumpton, 60, 107, 141, 142, 144, 234, 254, 257, 265, 279, 281, 284-287, 295, 296, 302, 315, 333, 335, 336, 358
Podimore, Som, 355
Poling, 79, 109
Poole, Dor, 102
Poorhouses *see* Workhouses
Portslade, 49, 56, 58, 115, 262, 292, 359
Portsmouth, Ham, 74, 133, 293; Portsmouth harbour, 74
posting house, 99
Poynings, 144, 175, 194, 195, 234, 237, 256-258, 337
Preston, 61, 69, 175, 181, 230, 253, 257, 262, 263, 276, 285
Prinkham, Lingfield, Sry, 151
Prisons: H.M. Prison, Horsham, 94; Horsham gaol, 117
Pulborough, 67, 86, 113, 116, 159, 227, 231, 235, 252, 282, 297, 338, 362
Pyecombe, 57, 59, 70, 108, 144, 236, 238, 256, 257, 262, 272, 276, 312

R
Rackham, 237
Ratcliff, Stepney, Mdx, St.Dunstan, 120
Reading, Brk, St Lawrence, 102
Reformation Pink see Ships
Regiments and army units: 1st Battalion Royal Artillery, 235, 259; 2nd Regiment of Foot, 105, 234; 2nd Regiment of Foot Guards, 147; 3rd Regiment of Kent Militia, 359; 23rd Regiment of Foot Guards, 188; 35th Regiment, 60, 293; 38th Regiment of Foot, 70; 39th Regiment of Foot, 118; 51st Regiment of Foot, 241; 95th Regiment of Foot, 192; Col. Bing's Company of Foot Guards, 153; Col. Molesworth's Regiment, 150; Col. Seymour's Regiment at Steyning, 103; Col. Stringer's Regiment of Foot, 150; Coldstream Regiment of Guards, 359; Corps of Royal Artillery Drivers, 291, 295, 305; Corps of Sappers and Miners, 260, 263; East Middlesex Militia, 75; Gen. Skelton's Regiment of Foot, 154; H.M.'s Regiment of Foot, 192; His Majesty's Regiments in North America, 266; Kent Regiment of Militia, 279; Lord Montjoy's Regiment, 150; militia man, 386; Monmouth and Brecon Regiment of Militia, 329; Royal Artillery, 180, 235; Royal Staff Corps, 280; Royal Waggon Train, 359; South Gloucester Militia, 241; Surrey Militia, 46; Sussex Militia, 54, 218; Sussex Regiment of Militia, 117, 157, 199, 314; Waggon Train, 193; West Essex Regiment of Militia, 51
Reigate, Sry, 43, 57, 59, 106, 109, 113, 115, 139, 142, 159, 179, 191, 200, 208, 281, 287, 294, 311, 339, 340, 343-345, 349-351, 353, 354, 358, 360, 369; *see also* Foreign of Reigate, Sry
Richmond, Sry, 350, 354; Kew Gardens, 43
Ridge, Hrt, 71, 340, 374
Ringmer, 64, 108, 144, 149, 183, 189, 192, 194, 195, 196, 268, 272, 280, 292, 295, 322, 346, 379
Ripley, Sry, 350
Rochester, Ken, 112; St Margaret, 112
Rochford, Ess, 102
Rodmell, 142, 285, 288
Rogate, 109, 114, 198
Rolvenden, Ken, 60, 63
Romford, Ess, 342
Romney Marsh, Ken, 280
Romsey, Ham, 101, 116
Rotherfield, 64, 122, 158, 159, 160, 165, 168, 169, 171, 172, 174, 176-179, 182, 184, 194, 198, 204, 209, 212, 215, 223, 279, 334, 351, 364
Rottingdean, 143, 173, 262
Rudgwick, 42, 52, 62, 85, 88, 157, 166, 173, 182, 282, 287, 310, 372
Rusper, 108, 174, 180, 191, 195, 264, 272, 342, 351, 355, 356, 359, 362
Ryarsh, Ken, 148, 159
Rye, 70, 86

S
St Katherine, Mdx, 289
St Marylebone, Mdx, 45, 182, 286, 356
St Osyth, Ess, 169, 177
St Pancras, Mdx, 192
St Sepulchre, Mdx, 113, 115
Salehurst, 100, 161, 183, 283, 289, 326
Salisbury, Wil, 46, 171
Sanderland *see* Sunderland
Sanderstead, Sry, 152
Seaford, 83, 84, 96
Seal, Ken, 187
Sedlescombe, 141, 189, 335
Selsfield Common, West Hoathly, 316
Send, Sry, 235, 379, 380
Sevenoaks, Ken, 46, 62, 149, 160, 178, 188, 189, 207, 294
Shere, Sry, 310
Sherfield [?], Ham, 147, 168
SHERMANBURY, 2, 7, 11, 19, 28, 30, 32, 44, 54, 56-59, 61, 62, 73, 76-79, 82-86, 94, 97, 113, 115, 116, 120, 226, 231-235, 254, **305-307**, 313, 314
Shervill [Sherfield?], Ham, 147, 168
Shipbourne, Ken, 249
Shipley, 54, 56, 58, 80, 81, 85, 108, 113, 115, 117, 153, 161, 170, 177, 231, 233, 236, 244, 280, 281, 285, 286, 289, 294, 295, 333, 357, 359, 363
Ships: *Elizabeth & Mary*, 110, 138, 159, 169, 170, 320, 350; *Good Pinck* or *Reformation Pink*, 138
Shoreditch, Mdx, St Leonard, 87
Shoreham, 101, 226, 245; *see also* New Shoreham, Old Shoreham
Shoreham, Ken, 193
Sidlesham, 233
Singleton, 364, 370
Sittingbourne, Ken, 102
SLAUGHAM, 2, 7, 11, 19, 28, 30, 32, 41, 49, 52-59, 61, 64, 66, 73, 75, 76, 86, 94, 105-108, 110-119, 125, 129, 131, 157, 193, 254, 271, 280, 282, 284, 291, 306, **308-312**, 324, 343, 344, 346, 361, 368
Slindon, 233, 262, 363
Slinfold, 72, 73, 78, 158, 173, 174, 179, 230, 236
Snodland, Ken, 159, 169
Sompting, 41, 231, 239, 283, 285
South Malling, 60, 235, 238, 253, 353
South Mimms, Hrt, 340
South Weald, Ess, 197
Southampton, Ham, 103, 148
Southease, 124, 276, 302
Southover, Lewes, 130, 141, 190, 201, 233, 250, 290, 362
Southwark, Sry, 78, 147, 168, 183, 190, 211, 222, 284, 373, 374, 380; St George, 148, 173, 178, 303, 324, 365; St Olave, 168; St Saviour, 186, 375; Union Street, Borough Road,, 380
Southwick, 82, 260, 263, 296
Speldhurst, Ken, 60, 81, 87, 159, 162, 171, 173, 183, 250, 292, 319, 346, 358
Stalisfield, Ken, 287
Stamford, Lin, 188

Stanmer, 148, 196, 237, 275
Stansted, Ess, 118
Staplefield, Cuckfield, 101
Stepney, Mdx, 120
Steyning, 34, 41, 42, 60, 62, 70, 76, 80, 81, 87, 102, 105, 107, 108, 110, 112, 114, 121, 122, 141, 143, 216, 229-231, 233-236, 241, 242, 253, 255-257, 258, 264, 271, 272, 281, 282, 322, 323, 332, 345, 355, 357, 385
Stoke, Gosport, Ham, 189
Stokenchurch, Bkm, 83
Stone, Ken, 69, 71, 191
Stonecross, 268
Stony Stratford, Bkm, 91
Stopham, 244
Storrington, 44, 232, 233, 236
Stratford, Ess, 116
Strathmiglo, Fife, Sct, 103
Streat, 56, 58, 69, 70, 83, 101, 126, 143, 144, 147, 157, 237, 261, 263, 285, 326
Streatham, Sry, 183, 362
Sullington, 56, 59, 72, 81, 84, 228, 309, 314, 315
Sunbury, Mdx, 355
Sunderland, 341
Sundridge, Ken, 104, 107, 112, 121, 163
Switzerland, 62

T

Tandridge, Sry, 152, 166, 167, 171, 182, 207, 314, 339, 347, 356, 376
Tarring Neville, 233
Tatsfield, Sry, 169
Telscombe, 108, 171, 178, 228
Tenterden, Ken, 203, 352
Thakeham, 231, 261, 272
Thornbury, Gls, 160
Thursley, Sry, 343
Ticehurst, 149, 186, 191, 255, 286, 296
Tickeredge, West Hoathly?, 168, 325
Tillington, 62
Tinsley, Worth, 339, 370
Tonbridge, Ken, 110, 121, 158, 165, 173, 178, 190, 192, 289, 333, 355, 357, 359
Tottenham, Mdx, 147, 168, 176, 185, 381, 382; High Cross, 382
transportation [of convict], 88, 180
Tring, Hrt, 119
Trotton, 233, 252, 255, 257
Tudely, Ken, 249
Tunbridge Wells, Ken, 71
Turners Hill, Worth, 365, 370
TWINEHAM, 2, 7, 10, 11, 19, 28, 30, 32, 41, 53, 55, 56, 58-63, 65, 66, 69, 77, 83-85, 89, 91, 95, 97, 06, 107, 111, 112, 114, 159, 230, 241, 254-256, 260, 261, 263, 285, 306, 308, **313-315**

U

Uckfield, 21, 45, 56, 58, 61, 164, 166, 173, 185, 195, 254, 255, 259, 282, 283, 287, 288, 291, 295, 300, 317, 321, 322, 334
Udimore, 337
Upper Beeding, *see* Beeding; Lower Beeding

W

Wadhurst, 116, 165, 176, 220, 287-289, 335
Waldron, 176, 188, 294, 309
Walkhamstead *otherwise* Godstone, Sry, 155; *see also* Godstone, Sry
Wallington, Sry, 324
Wandsworth, Sry, 183, 184
Wapping, Mdx, St John, 246
Warbleton, 147, 190
Warblington, Ham, 261, 333
Warborough, Oxf, 44
Warlingham, Sry, 183, 351, 356
Warminghurst, 117, 346
Warnham, 46, 56, 59, 60, 108, 110, 174, 175, 180, 181, 251, 272, 363, 385
Warninglid, Slaugham, 308
Washington, 50, 72, 78, 228, 236, 241, 258, 311
Wateringbury, Ken, 249
Wellingham, Ringmer, 322
Wells, Som, 146, 379; St Cuthbert, 142
Werrington, Dev, 183
West Chiltington, 94; *see also* Chiltington
West Dean, 71, 286
West Firle, 276, 290, 305
West Grinstead, 56-59, 62, 65, 72-75, 77-80, 82-84, 86-88, 92, 96, 98, 116, 124, 164, 230, 231, 233, 235, 236, 238, 241, 253, 258, 259, 283, 306, 307, 315, 337; Ivorys, 73; Westlands, 73, 89
West Ham, Ess, 189
WEST HOATHLY, 2, 7, 19, 30, 32, 43-45, 47, 86, 107, 108, 113, 115, 118, 155, 156, 158-162, 165, 167-169, 172, 174-176, 180-189, 191-193, 195, 201, 204, 215, 217, 222, 249, 258, 272, 278, 284, 285, 290, 292, 293, 297, 302, 308, 315, **316-331**, 333, 334, 339, 341, 343, 346, 349-356, 358-360, 369
West Indies, 153
West Tarring, 254
West Wickham, Ken, 356
West Wittering, 83, 84
Westerham, Ken, 113, 162, 176, 343, 348, 352
Westham, 276
Westmeston, 41, 42, 82, 107, 111, 118, 122, 123, 141, 144, 157, 191, 195, 275, 276, 286, 293, 296, 302, 323, 326, 336
Westminster, Mdx, 75, 153, 169, 174, 189, 223, 289; St George Hanover Square, 115, 179; St James, 115, 150, 169, 189, 289; St James Street, 153; St Margaret, 179, 182, 261; St Martin in the Fields, 189, 374; Strand, 198
Whatlington, 292
Whippingham, Iow, 143
Wick, Woodmancote, 337
Wiggonholt, 171
Wilcot, Oxf, 148
Willingdon, 116, 259, 313
Wilmington, 164, 166, 173, 199, 271
Winchester, Ham, 192
Wisborough Green, 80, 118, 173, 227, 233, 308, 356
Wiston, 49, 71, 76, 116, 229
Withyham, 41, 50, 83, 84, 86, 107, 149, 160, 162-164, 167, 170, 171, 173, 182, 185, 189, 190, 193-197, 200, 203-205, 210, 218, 221, 272, 275, 289, 312, 333, 339, 361, 377
Wittersham, Ken, 139
WIVELSFIELD, 2, 6, 7, 11, 28, 30, 32, 41, 46, 55, 56,

58, 59, 77, 82, 107-109, 112, 113, 118, 141-143, 151, 170, 177, 259, 274, 275, 278-280, 283, 285, 286, 300, 318, **332**-336, 355
Woking, Sry, 174, 180
Woodhatch, Sry, 341
WOODMANCOTE, 2, 7, 11, 19, 28, 30, 32, 41, 62, 63, 71, 73, 74, 82, 83, 109, 113, 117, 160, 227, 228, 229, 230, 231, 233, 234, 235, 237, 238, 239, 240, 255, 257, 260, 261, 265, 267, 274, 306, **337, 338**
Woodmansterne, Sry, 361
Woolwich, Ken, 206, 235, 259, 279
Wootton Bassett, Wil, 193
Workhouses, 2, 4-6, 26, 46, 48, 67, 71, 91-95, 97, 125, 155, 215, 218, 239, 240, 242, 268, 269, 286, 210, 290, 296, 299, 300, 302, 328, 329, 342, 343, 359, 366, 367, 368, 369, 381, 382; Bolney, 67; Cowfold, 91-95, 97; Cuckfield, 125; East Grinstead, 215, 218; Henfield, 239, 240; Hurstpierpoint, 268, 269; Lindfield, 290, 296, 299, 300, 302; Marylebone, Mdx, 286; Steyning, 216; West Hoathly, 328, 329; Worth, 343, 359, 366, 367, 368, 381
WORTH, 2, 7, 12, 13, 14, 16, 18, 19, 22, 26, 28, 30, 32, 35, 38, 43, 44, 45, 49, 50, 55, 60-62, 65, 93, 99, 106, 108, 113, 116, 119, 147, 160, 162, 164, 165, 169, 170-172, 174-176, 178-181, 184, 185, 188-190, 197, 198, 200, 205, 208, 209, 217-219, 222, 271, 272, 280, 283, 285, 288, 294, 300, 302, 308, 311, 318, 319, 321-325, 330, **339-377**, 378-385; Worth Forest, 339
Worthing, 97, 241
Wrotham, Ken, 121, 192